A TEXTBOOK OF CHRISTIA

A TEXTBOOK OF CHRISTIAN ETHICS
Second Edition

ROBIN GILL

T&T CLARK
EDINBURGH

T&T CLARK LTD
59 GEORGE STREET
EDINBURGH EH2 2LQ
SCOTLAND

First edition 1985
Second edition 1995

ISBN 0 567 29280 0

British Library Cataloguing-in-Publication Data
A catalogue record for this book is available from the British Library

Typeset by Trinity Typesetting
Printed and bound in Great Britain by Page Bros, Norwich

CONTENTS

Section 2 POLITICS, ECONOMICS AND JUSTICE

Section 3 WAR AND PEACE

Section 4 THE ENVIRONMENT

Section 5 HUMAN LIFE AND INTERPERSONAL RELATIONSHIPS

ALAN MORTON GILL
1909-1985

paternus adjutor et doctus lector

ACKNOWLEDGEMENTS

Thanks are due to the following for permission to use copyright passages:

Penguin Books Ltd (*City of God* and Copleston: *Aquinas*)

Prior Provincial, O.P., St Dominic's Priory, London (*Summa Theologica*)

Fortress Press (*Luther's Works* and Bonino: *Doing Theology in a Revolutionary Situation*)

Basil Blackwell (*Aquinas: Selected Political Writings*)

William B. Eerdmans (*Nicene and Post Nicene Fathers*)

Doubleday (*Summa Contra Gentiles*)

Macmillan and SCM Press (Bonhoeffer: *Ethics*)

Oxford University Press (Barth: *The Epistle to the Romans*)

Geoffrey Bles Ltd (Berdyaev: *Freedom and the Spirit*)

Charles Scribner's Sons (Niebuhr: *Moral Man and Immoral Society*)

Shepheard-Walwyn & SPCK (Temple: *Christianity and Social Order*)

Catholic Truth Society (*Veritatis Splendor, Pacem in Terris* and *Humanae Vitae*)

Orbis Books and SCM Press (Miranda: *Marx and the Bible*)

Orbis Books (Ruether's *Faith and the Intifada*). Rosemary Radford Ruether, 'Western Christianity and Zionism', Naim S. Ateek, Marc H. Ellis and R.R. Reuther (eds.), *Faith and the Intifada*, 1992, pp.147–157.

Verlag Herder (Welty: *A Handbook of Christian Social Ethics*)

Princeton University (Fletcher: *Morals and Medicine*)

The Westminster and SCM Press (Fletcher: *Situation Ethics*)

Abingdon Press and Marcia Wood (Ramsey: *Who Speaks for the Church?*)

US National Conference of Catholic Bishops (*The Challenge of Peace*). Excerpts are taken from *The Challenge of Peace: A*

PREFACE TO THE REVISED EDITION

It is now ten years since this Textbook was first published. In the meantime Christian ethics has continued to change and to flourish. There has been a strong emphasis upon ecology and the natural environment. There have been a number of sharp critiques of Christianity on moral grounds – sometimes for despoiling the environment, sometimes for being racist and anti-Semitic, and sometimes for being 'inescapably' patriarchal. Feminist theology has become even more important than it was a decade ago, and quite a number of feminist theologians are now firmly established in the front rank of modern theology. Hermeneutics and biblical interpretation have also begun to overturn exegesis, source and form criticism as the dominant scholarly ways of approaching the Bible. And the challenges of relativism and postmodernism have been reflected even within papal encyclicals.

As a result a new section has been added to the Textbook on the environment and about half of the extracts have been chosen afresh. The system of analysis remains – but this had already been well tested over generations of students at Edinburgh University, at Newcastle University and now at Canterbury (and by colleagues in several other academic centres). In my original Preface I mentioned that writing begun on the Textbook whilst I was on sabbatical in Zambia in 1980, continued whilst teaching at Dartmouth College, New Hampshire, and effectively finished whilst teaching at the United Theological College, Bangalore in 1984. Extensive travel since then, as a result of my present job, has also helped to open up new vistas in Christian ethics for me which I have tried to incorporate into the Textbook. It has been increasingly difficult to keep track of all the students and faculty members around the world who have helped to shape the contents. However I would particularly like to thank my own students who have acted as guinea-pigs on the various Texts and Extracts. Without them I would never have known which to discard and which to include. And my former colleagues at Edinburgh – Duncan Forrester, Ian McDonald and Michael Northcott, as well as Simon Robinson – all gave most generously of their time in helping to make these revisions. I am sure that errors must remain and I have no doubt that future generations of students will still point them out to me with great glee! Before they mention it, the spellings in the Texts and Extracts follow the conventions of the books from which they have been drawn – sometimes British and sometimes American. But then the Textbook is intended for both audiences.

Readers will soon be aware of the fact that Christian ethics is a highly pluralistic discipline. Fundamental differences are apparent in the presuppositions, methods, and conclusions of the various writers represented here. It might have been possible to produce a book on moral issues which ignored this pluralism and diversity – but not a serious Textbook of Christian Ethics. A mature understanding of the discipline cannot bypass diversity. In his recent *Christian Ethics: A Historical Introduction* (Westminster/John Knox, 1993, and SPCK, 1994) Philip Wogaman argues helpfully that this diversity 'would be scandalous if one thought of the tradition as a deposit of truth "once for all delivered to the saints". But if one thinks rather of the tradition as a witness to the transcendent reality of the living God, then is there not room for growth and new insight?'

If diversity is admitted, where is the unity in Christian ethics to be found? A superficial reading might conclude that it is wholly absent – the diversity appears overwhelming. But that would, I believe, be a superficial reading. At certain key points a unity is suggested mainly in certain *biblically consonant values held in tension*. Whilst remaining critical of simplistic attempts to derive individual values from the Bible, it is a feature of most of the exponents of Christian ethics represented in this Textbook that they seek to hold in creative tension values that are consonant with distinctively Christian, and particularly biblical, resources (recognising that these resources themselves represent a variety of tensions). So 'love' (*agape*) as an isolated value is not usually seen as a sufficient Christian resource, but 'love' in tension with 'justice' is. Differing exponents of Christian ethics emphasise this particular tension in varying ways, but for most it is an essential, irreducible and creative tension – and, indeed, a crucial point of unity in an otherwise diverse discipline.

At various points a number of these tensions will be noted – between 'peace' and justice', between 'compassion' and 'moral indignation', and finally between what is termed in the final pages the adeodatic axiom and the agapistic axiom. That these tensions are essential and irreducible derives from the nature of Christianity itself. As theologians such as Augustine (with his notion of the two cities) and Luther (with his notion of the two kingdoms) were well aware, Christianity is always a mixture of the 'now' and the 'not yet'. Indeed, the Synoptic concept of the Kingdom of God seems to contain both present and future elements. To reflect this, a degree of creative tension will always be a crucial feature of an adequate understanding of Christian ethics. Precisely because it is structured around essential, but elusive, tensions Christian ethics will always be subject to popular misrepresentation and reduction. It is only too easy to present 'Christian values' simplistically and with scant regard to their role-in-tension within Christianity. I will be content if this Textbook is able to contribute even a little to a more mature understanding of Christian ethics.

Finally I would like to thank my family and especially my wife and best friend, Jenny. I remain relieved that most of my family never read my books. However my father, who died in May 1985 just months before the Textbook was originally published, not only read my books but meticulously corrected their spelling (before the days of spell-checks), grammar and sometimes logic. To him I continue to owe a special debt.

INTRODUCTION

STRUCTURE

The structure of this Textbook is built around a systematic comparison of texts with extracts. These two terms are used simply for convenience to distinguish between classical excerpts from Augustine, Aquinas and Luther and present-day (i.e. within the last 70 years) excerpts – the first being termed texts and the second extracts. This structure differs significantly from the historical approach of Waldo Beach and H.Richard Niebuhr's *Christian Ethics* and of Arthur F. Holmes' *War and Christian Ethics* in a number of ways: (a) it does not attempt to present a selection of historical writings in Christian ethics – an important undertaking successfully achieved in these and other books, but one that does lead to the reproduction of repetitive material; (b) it stresses the value of the comparative approach as an important means of learning; (c) it provides a systematic means of analysis for each text and extract, which in turn makes comparative study more possible; (d) it places an emphasis upon the relevance of the discipline today. This last point is certainly a feature of a number of readers in Christian social ethics, including my own *Readings in Modern Theology*, but from the perspective of the theological teacher they often lack historical and analytical dimensions and are in any case readers and not textbooks.

This book is designed to be a Textbook and, at the end of this introduction, a method of using it as such is suggested. The fact that it is a Textbook and not simply a Reader has determined the choice of Texts and Extracts. After many experiments it was decided to limit the Texts to three key theologians in the belief that this gives more coherence to the five Sections and brings out better the main options and variables within Christian ethics. Naturally, at times, references are made to Church Fathers earlier

1

than Augustine (particularly Tertullian, Origen and Ambrose), to Scholastics other than Aquinas and to Reformers other than Luther (notably Calvin) and it was tempting to include texts from them all. But that would seriously have distorted the aims of this as a Textbook and might have turned it instead into a historical Reader. By confining the Texts to these three key theologians, it is hoped that the student will be encouraged to focus clearly upon the differences between them and to distinguish their differing effects upon present-day Christian ethics. Not only do they represent three of the most powerful post-New Testament influences on Christian theology, but they also represent the three distinct phases of Western Christianity – the Undivided Catholic Church, the Medieval Roman Church and the Protestant/Reformed Church.

The Extracts, too, have been chosen with the needs of a Textbook and not simply of a reader in mind. They are not necessarily 'the best' from recent Christian ethics. Some are intended simply to represent positions that have influenced the contemporary churches. It has been our experience in teaching the subject that students can learn from weaker Extracts as well as from those which are more intellectually sophisticated, although the balance is intended to be in favour of the latter. As will be explained presently, the Extracts have been chosen to represent a wide range within and between differing Christian traditions.

The book is divided into five Sections with the three Texts and at least five Extracts in each. The first Section is concerned with methodological issues and the subsequent Sections with substantive issues in Christian ethics. Sections 2-4 are mainly concerned with issues in social ethics and Section 5 with personal ethics, although these divisions sometimes become somewhat arbitrary (e.g. marital issues are clearly personal issues, but, at least within the Judaeo-Christian tradition, they also have a relationship with society at large). The Sections are self-contained and contain many cross-references to other Sections and therefore can be studied in any order. Each Section is introduced by an introduction to the main issues raised within it as they relate to Christian ethics. Each Text and group of Extracts is introduced by a sixfold system of analysis and at the end of each a critique is given.

SYSTEM OF ANALYSIS

The six-fold system of analysis introducing each Text and group of Extracts consists of (1) Background (2) Key Issues (3) Ethical Arguments (4) Bases of Christian Ethics (5) Social Determinants and (6) Social Significance. The critique at the end of each forms a seventh part. In more detail they are as follows:

1. *BACKGROUND*

This part of the analysis suggests relevant biographical details and identifies the document from which the Text or Extract has been taken. Since part of the present introduction is concerned with comparing Augustine, Aquinas and Luther, it will not be necessary to repeat these biographical details every time a Text is introduced. Until the central differences between the three theologians become clearer, a student would be well advised to keep referring back to this part of the introduction. In this Textbook a strong assumption is that biographical details are, at times, directly relevant to an understanding of the thought of a particular theologian. Thus some knowledge of Berdyaev's life is considered to be essential for an adequate understanding of Extract 7.

2. *KEY ISSUES*

The overall introduction to each Section seeks to provide a summary of the main issues arising from the Texts and Extracts within it. But here secondary issues will also be raised and it will be indicated how the specific Text or Extract in question relates to the main issues. The aim of this part of the analysis is to help students to isolate specific issues from the Text or Extract so that they can relate them to the other Texts or Extracts. One of the surprising features of examining, in detail, even quite a short excerpt from a given author, is to discover how many of his or her characteristic ideas occur within it. Thus, if examined thoroughly, even a short Text from a theologian as complex as Aquinas contains quite a number of his assumptions and ideas. Again from experience of teaching Christian ethics, Texts or Extracts need not be lengthy to be instructive, they must merely be studied with care and attention.

3. ETHICAL ARGUMENTS

A vital feature of analysis in Christian ethics involves the identification of differing types of ethical argument. An important distinction must be made between moral decision-making and ethical analysis. In so far as it is an academic discipline, ethics, and with it Christian ethics, is usually considered to be concerned more with the second than with the first. It is concerned with examining the nature of prescriptive language, the grounds on which moral beliefs are held, the types of argument which those who hold them use to promote them, and the consequences that they involve. If decision-making is involved, this is usually achieved on the basis of a systematic or developed theory. Ethics, or moral philosophy, understood in this way is clearly related to intelligent moral decision-making, but is not identical with it. Similarly, Christian theology is not usually considered to be identical with Christian belief: it is an intellectual, theoretical and second-order discipline. So, whereas all Christians may make moral decisions and hold certain religious beliefs, only some are exponents of Christian ethics and of Christian theology. It is in this sense that the terms will be used here, even though elsewhere the terms 'theology' and 'ethics' are often used in a broader and less academic sense.

It would be inappropriate to attempt an outline of general ethics or moral philosophy. Instead good introductions can be found in the following:

Phillippa Foot (ed), *Theories of Ethics*; A. MacIntyre, *A Short History of Ethics*; P.H. Nowell-Smith, *Ethics*; G.J. Warnock, *Contemporary Moral Philosophy*; Mary Warnock, *Ethics Since 1900*.

In addition, A.V. Campbell's *Moral Dilemmas in Medicine* provides a clear and readable account of the classical approaches to ethics using medical issues as case-studies. Ian C.M. Fairweather & J.I.H. McDonald's, *The Quest for Christian Ethics*, gives a more detailed account of the approaches.

For the purpose of this Textbook three basic types of ethical argument should be clearly identified – deontological, consequential, and personalist:

(a) *Deontological ethical arguments*
It is a feature of deontological arguments – derived from the Greek for 'necessary' or 'imperative' – that by nature they are absolutist. One cannot argue beyond them. So, if one maintains that murder is wrong and is asked to give a reason, a deontological response would be: 'Because it is against the law of nature', or 'Because it is against God's will', or 'Because it breaks the Sixth Commandment', or even 'Because it is simply wrong'. Such responses merely refer the other person to some norm or absolute beyond which there can be no further argument. There is no attempt here to argue that it is the consequences of murder that make it wrong; indeed, murder is seen as wrong regardless of its consequences. Of course, there may be situations in which two or more norms conflict (as in euthanasia – see Extract 22) and further argument is then required in order to determine moral priorities (sometimes termed 'casuistry'), but values, as such, cannot be justified other than by reference to the norm from which they are derived. Immanuel Kant's (1724-1803) concept of the categorical imperative is a clear example of deontological ethics, whereby morality is regarded as autonomous, categorical (in the sense that it is a 'given' of the human mind – it is not a human invention and requires no proof), imperative (it is to be obeyed, not argued with) and universal. For Kant the categorical imperative of morality commands that we act only on the maxim that we would wish our behaviour to become a universal law: morality is an end in itself and not a means to something else. As will be seen, it is quite different from utilitarianism which is essentially conditional and a means to a further end (e.g. pleasure or happiness). A more recent example of deontological ethics is some uses of the concept of 'rights' – as in the 'right to

life' or 'the right of the woman to choose' positions often used on opposite sides of the abortion debate.

Again, one can argue about whether or not a given situation really constitutes a clear-cut moral case. So, although murder might be considered always to be wrong, one might still argue about whether a particular situation does or does not involve murder. Thus, many of those who believe that murder is wrong, but that killing in war can be justified, argue that the latter does not involve the former (e.g. since war does not involve privately motivated killing – see Aquinas' Text VIII). Others, using a conflict theory, might argue that although killing in war is wrong, it is overridden by the greater wrong of not defending one's country when called to do so. In both instances a deontological stance is still taken on the issue of murder.

It will be seen in the various Sections that both Augustine's and Luther's biblical arguments are predominantly deontological. Indeed deontology is also a feature of Aquinas' moral arguments, even though his commitment to Aristotle's maxim that 'happiness is the chief good' tends him also to consequentialism. Many would argue that, in some form, deontology is an essential feature of all Christian ethics. However, this is an issue which will be debated at length throughout this Textbook.

(b) *Consequential ethical arguments*
It is a feature of consequential arguments – sometimes termed teleological arguments although the two can be distinct – that they treat morality, not as autonomous or as an end in itself, but as a means to something else. At its simplest, one is enjoined to be good so that one may receive some reward – either in the form of some present or near future state, such as 'pleasure' or 'happiness', or in the more distant form of an earthly utopia or of a transcendent eternal life. To return to reasons for believing that murder is wrong, consequential responses typically might be: 'Because murder, if allowed, would destroy society', or 'Because murder does not contribute to general happiness'. In each response murder is thought to be wrong, not because it is wrong in itself, but because it leads to something else which is

thought to be wrong or perhaps just undesirable – e.g. the break-down of society, the absence of general happiness, or the reception of eternal punishment. If this 'something else' is itself thought to be wrong, then clearly consequential arguments eventually do have a deontological basis. On the other hand, if this 'something else' is thought to be no more than undesirable, it may have no such basis (and for this reason some maintain that therefore it is not a moral argument at all). In addition to the object varying, in consequential arguments, the recipient envisaged also varies. In some forms of the argument, it is the agent whose ends are considered, whereas in others it is those of society as a whole. However, in all, moral conduct is judged in terms of its goals or consequences (teleological arguments stress more the first and consequential arguments more the second).

Various types of ethical utilitarianism and pragmatism constitute forms of consequential argument. For Jeremy Bentham (1748-1832) morality was concerned with attempting to increase the total pleasure of humankind and the avoidance of pain – an explicit form of hedonism, albeit not calculated on an individualistic basis (i.e. it concerns, not the specific pleasure of the agent, but the greatest amount of pleasure for the greatest number of people). For John Stuart Mill (1806-73) morality should be empirically based, ascertaining first what people really find 'desirable' and then arranging society so that as much as possible (quantitatively as well as qualitatively) of what people desire can be obtained, by as many as possible, in an orderly and co-operative way.

In some forms of the Christian tradition consequential arguments have assumed a strongly eschatological character. For example, in the 6th-century Rule of Benedict, monks were told: 'If we wish to escape the pains of hell and attain to eternal life we must hasten to do such things only as may profit us for eternity, now, while there is time for this and we are in this body and there is time to fulfil all these precepts by means of this light' (*The Rule of Benedict*, Prologue, trans. W.K. Lowther Clarke, 1931).

A more immediate form of consequentialism, rooted clearly in deontology, is evident in the following paragraph from the *Didache*:

> My son, flee from all wickedness and from everything like it. Do not become angry, for anger leads to murder. Do not become jealous, or quarrelsome, or irritable, for it leads to fornication. And do not use obscene language, or let your eye wander, for from all these come adulteries.... My child, do not be a liar, because a lie leads to theft; be not greedy of money or empty glory, for from all this come thefts. My child, do not be a grumbler, because it leads to blasphemy, do not be proud or malicious, for from all these arise blasphemies (*Didache*, v, from Ludwig Schopp (ed), *The Apostolic Fathers*, vol 1, *The Fathers of the Church*).

Whatever is thought of the logic of the links in this very early (possibly early 2nd century) document – anger leads to murder, jealousy leads to fornication, grumbling leads to blasphemies, and so forth – their consequential nature is evident. One thing is considered wrong because it leads to (or it might even derive from) something else which is already known to be wrong – in this instance because murder, adultery, stealing and blasphemy are known to be wrong from the Decalogue (i.e. the Ten Commandments).

Consequential arguments will be seen alongside deontological arguments in a number of the Texts and Extracts. Utilitarianism in the more formal, philosophical sense will be seen to be present in Fletcher's Extract 2.

(c) *Personalist ethical arguments*

It is a feature of personalist arguments that they view morality, not as obedience to autonomous, absolute principles or as a means to something else, but as an expression of individual feeling, conscience or love. It is frequently argued by exponents of personalist ethics that moral dilemmas cannot be resolved in advance of particular situations. Thus, it makes no sense to argue, as an abstract principle, about whether or not murder is wrong. Only in particular situations when the individual is confronted with the possibility of murder, can that individual determine whether or not it is wrong. Confronted with the prospect of murdering one's sister now, the personalist can reply that this murder is wrong: 'Because I feel that it is wrong', or 'Because my conscience tells me that it is wrong', or 'Because it would contradict my love for her or my respect for her as a person'. In these responses it can be seen that there are elements of both deontology and consequentialism. Feelings, conscience, love and respect for persons are all treated as normative and only in relation to them are actions considered to be right or wrong. Nonetheless, the emphasis is individualistic and situational. It is conceivable that, given a change in the situation or in the persons involved, an individual might reach the verdict that to murder one's sister would be right. It might be war-time and the sister might be discovered to be working for the Gestapo. The deontologist could feel impelled to murder the sister in these circumstances, but would tend to argue, either that it was not really murder in this instance, or, that it was murder and was therefore wrong, but that it would be a greater wrong to allow one's country to be betrayed. The consequentialist, on the other hand, might argue that the happiness or well-being of society determines that the murder of all traitors is right. In contrast to the deontologist, the personalist may argue that this actual murder is right, even if it is still thought to be murder. In contrast to the consequentialist, the personalist argues that general pronouncements about traitors being murdered should not be made in advance of particular situations. This does not mean that society should not make laws on issues like this (in order to discourage traitors in war-time it may feel obliged to do so), but such laws should not be confused with moral laws. By definition, the latter cannot be codified. The positions of the deontologist and the consequentialist can be and frequently have been codified (both Bentham and Mill sought to influence law-making as well as moral philosophy). But the most that the personalist can offer are general moral guidelines, which can be overridden in particular situations.

Personalism, in one form or another, has proved to be very attractive to a number of recent moral philosophers and theologians. There has been a widespread loss of confidence in natural law theories and the more sophisticated forms of utilitarianism seem to many to involve tortuous and unrealistic moral calculations. Within moral philosophy emotive theories of ethics (criticised in Copleston's Extract 3) have been popular. It is interesting that even a critic of these theories like R.M. Hare bases his own theory on the Golden Rule (do-as-you-would-be-done-by or, in more explicitly Christian terms, 'Love your neighbour as yourself'). Theologians have additional reasons for finding personalist theories attractive: (i) the anti-legalism of Paul (and possibly Jesus) seems to conflict with some forms of deontology; (ii) personalism fits in well with the Dominical Commands to Love; (iii) the aims of some forms of utilitarianism seem distinctly unChristian (e.g. the sole pursuit of 'pleasure', as distinct from 'happiness' in Aquinas' sense).

In the Extracts, Fletcher's theory of Situations Ethics in Extract 2, and implicit in Extract 22, seeks to combine a general personalist ethical theory with a specifically Christian position around the concept of *agape*. Although Bonhoeffer's Extract 1 explicitly rejects secular ethics, his own approach based solely on the 'Call of Christ' does have similarities to Fletcher (see *below* p.61).

Fletcher's position has been the subject of considerable debate in recent Christian ethics. Arguments about its strengths and weaknesses will occur at several points in this Textbook. However, it is important to note here that, although Augustine's overall position was undoubtedly deontological, there was also a strong stress upon love in his writings. To claim that he was actually a situationist would be to claim far too much. Nonetheless, his celebrated saying 'Love God, and do what you want' sums up at least a part of what be believed. His sermons also reveal a repeated stress upon love:

If deeds deny him, without doubt deeds also declare him. No man, therefore, says, 'Jesus is Lord', whether with mind, word, deed, heart, mouth, or work, no man says, 'Jesus is Lord', but in the Holy Spirit; and no man says so but he who loves him... What therefore we have now to learn is that he who loves already has the Holy Spirit, and that his present possession entitles him to a larger possession and the larger possession to a larger love (*Joh.Ev. Tractatus* 74.1-2).

It will be evident that these three approaches to ethics – deontological, consequential, and personalist – are not entirely separable. It might be more accurate to describe them as emphases rather than as discrete theories. But, however interrelated, an ability to distinguish their differing characteristics is important for the analysis necessary in Christian ethics.

4. BASES OF CHRISTIAN ETHICS

The question 'In what way is Christian ethics different from general ethics?' is one that is central to Christian ethics and, as a result, recurs frequently in this Textbook. Apart from the Extracts cited a number of books will be found useful in this context:

Peter Baelz, *Ethics and Belief*; Kieran Cronin, *Rights and Christian Ethics*; George W. Forell, *History of Christian Ethics*; James M. Gustafson, *Can Ethics be Christian?* and *Theology and Ethics*; Michael Keeling, *The Foundations of Christian Ethics*; Enda McDonagh, *Invitation and Response* and *Gift and Call*; John Mahoney, *The Making of Moral Theology: A Study of the Roman Catholic Tradition*; Jean Porter, *The Moral Act and Christian Ethics*; Keith Ward, *Ethics and Christianity* and *The Divine Image*; J. Philip Wogaman, *Christian Ethics: A Historical Introduction*.

In addition, an extremely useful resource for students is provided by James Childress & John Macquarrie (ed), *A New Dictionary of Christian Ethics*.

If the question of Christian distinctiveness is asked at an empirical level, the answer to the above question may be that in the West Christian and non-Christian ethics differ hardly at all. In all five Sections a considerable amount of disagreement between Christians is evident – seemingly almost as much as disagreements between non-Christians. This point can be exaggerated (Sections 2-5 will each conclude with points that unite Christians), but, granted a transposition theory, it may have some basis. According to this theory, Western values are still largely the product of a Christian past. Even though they may no longer be formally nourished by the churches, values in society at large have been mainly transposed from Christianity. Not surprisingly then, it is argued, the results of Christian ethics and moral philosophy in the West often still coincide. Certainly, Miranda's Extract 11 and Bonino's Extract 16 see an affinity between Christian and explicitly Marxist values, an affinity that some see as related to the indirect influence of Christian values on Marx himself.

However, if the question 'In what way is Christian ethics different from general ethics?' is asked at a more theoretical level a number of answers are possible. These range from the near identification of the two in Fletcher's Extract 2 to the denial of any similarity between them in Bonhoeffer's Extract 1. However, Bonhoeffer's position is difficult to maintain and it will be seen that there are reasons for doubting whether, in fact, he did maintain it consistently. At the very least, it is evident that the three ethical approaches outlined above occur in both disciplines.

One way of approaching the question is to isolate the specifically Christian appeals that are characteristically made within Christian ethics. Of these, four in particular can be isolated (although, in practice, they are often made together): appeals to the Bible, to Christian tradition, to Christian experience, and to Christian belief:

(a) *Appeals to the Bible*
Of all the specifically Christian appeals, within Christian ethics, this has become the most complex. Whilst all Christians afford the Bible an important role, the combined disputes generated, first in the 16th century by the Reformation and then in the 19th century by the advent of Biblical Criticism, have ensured that the relationship between Christianity and the Bible is now considerably more varied than, for example, the relationship

between Islam and the Koran. Biblical hermeneutics – examining different and sometimes contradictory ways in which the Bible has been interpreted from one culture to another and from one age to another – have also increased this complexity. At several points in this Textbook this hermeneutical complexity will be noted.

Appeals to the Bible, within Christian ethics, now face a number of serious problems – of which the following have been suggested in the literature referred to at the end of this sub-section:

(i) It has always been evident that many passages in the Bible can be interpreted in more than one way. It will be seen presently that Augustine varied in his interpretation of Genesis 3, his earlier allegorical interpretations giving way to literalistic ones. Section 3 will show that Tertullian gave a thoroughgoing pacifist interpretation of Matthew 5.39 ('turn the other cheek'), whereas Augustine repudiated this interpretation with the claim that 'what is here required is not a bodily action, but an inward disposition' (see Text VII.8). Biblical Criticism increased this problem enormously. Redaction Criticism, for example, requires one to recognise that the Gospel is a multi-layered phenomenon and is considerably more pluralistic than was generally realised in the past (e.g. see James D.G. Dunn's *Unity and Diversity in the New Testament*).

(ii) Debates about the authority of the Bible are amongst the most vexed in Christian theology. The problems raised by the Reformation have proved particularly serious. Whilst before Luther most Christians would have assumed the infallibility of the Bible, particular tension was caused by his stress on the Bible as the sole source of authority for Christian ethics and belief. This tension is still evident in the Extracts that follow, as is also the issue of whether or not Christian tradition and/or experience should be allowed in Christian ethics as separate sources of authority in addition to the Bible. For most Roman Catholic theologians, and for many Anglican theologians (following in the tradition of Hooker, who insisted that God's law is operative, not only in the Bible, but also in human reason and conscience), Luther's *sola Scriptura* stress, however understandable in the context of 16th-century Europe, is too theologically restrictive. Again, Biblical Criticism has further aggravated this situation. Once the literal infallibility of every verse in the Bible is rejected, and contradictions and factual and moral errors, anachronisms and inconsistencies are claimed, the exponent of Christian ethics can no longer adequately base moral claims on particular proof-texts in the manner of Augustine, Luther and, even at times, Aquinas. As a result, differing concepts of the authority of the Bible will be evident in the various Extracts. It would, of course, be ridiculous to criticise Augustine, Aquinas or Luther themselves for treating the Bible in a pre-critical manner. But, once the changed social context brought about by the advent of Biblical Criticism is taken into account, the exponent of Christian ethics is confronted with formidable problems. It is not the aim of this introduction to resolve these problems, but rather to point to the various ways they have changed the present-day discipline.

(iii) It is difficult for even the most literalistic biblicist not to be operating *de facto* a 'canon within the Canon'. That is, it is difficult to treat all parts of the Bible with equal seriousness and attention and not to be biblically selective. It will be seen later that, in this sense, Luther was selective. An overview of the history of Christian theology might suggest that each age 'rediscovers' some aspect of the Gospel and forgets others. In the 20th century, through the stimulus of Weiss and Schweitzer, theologians 'rediscovered' the concept of the Kingdom of God and the eschatological notions associated with it, and rejected the 'lives of Jesus' of the previous century. Doubtless future centuries will judge our own as guilty of neglecting other aspects of the Gospel. Again, when the diversity of the Bible generally and of the Gospels, in particular, is accepted, some degree of selectivity seems inevitable – if only the sort of selectivity involved in isolating 'the central message of Jesus' or 'the Gospel'. Yet this clearly creates problems, since many forms of selectivity, themselves based on extra-biblical criteria, are possible. The index at the end of this Textbook clearly shows a stress on Matthew and Romans in many of the Texts and Extracts.

(iv) A major difficulty for Christian ethics has always been determining the degree to which the Jewish Bible – or 'the Old Testament' as Christians term it – should be taken as seriously as the New Testament. Tensions between Old Testament moral precepts and Christian teaching are already present in the New Testament (e.g. on the issues of fasting or retribution) and continue today. In Section 3 it will be seen that attitudes to the issue of war are affected by the relative weight given to the Old or New Testaments, since pacifism is clearly not envisaged in the former whereas, in the latter, arguably it is. Nowhere is this issue more crucial than in the role given in Christian ethics to the Decalogue. Differences of attitude to the Ten Commandments will be noted in the Texts between Aquinas and Luther. And today, despite their continued use in many liturgies and their place in Western folk religion, some theologians would maintain that they are largely irrelevant to present-day Christian ethics. For them the discipline cannot be based upon a series of largely negative moral injunctions, which do not envisage many of the most important modern moral dilemmas (such as war in a nuclear age or the problems created by technology and biotechnology), which are too closely related to a traditional Jewish culture (e.g. not pronouncing the name of God and keeping the Jewish sabbath). Again this is an issue which will recur in this Textbook.

(v) Related to this, is the problem of how much weight should be afforded to the words of Jesus himself. Most Christians might agree, in principle, that the words and ideas of Jesus, once established, should be given a central place in Christian ethics. So, there has been considerable discussion over the centuries on whether Matthew 5.32 permits divorce – with the Roman Catholic, Orthodox and Anglican Churches reaching a wide variety of conclusions (see Ware's Extract 23). However, Biblical Criticism again greatly complicates the issue. The so-called quest for the historical Jesus, even after more than one hundred years, shows few signs of ending, and the construction of an account of Jesus', as distinct from the early church's, thought has become one of the most difficult and risky undertakings in New Testament studies. Thus, whilst there is now a good deal of agreement about Jesus' use of the concept of the Kingdom of God, there is little agreement about his use of the equally crucial concept of the Son of Man. The depth of research necessary and the tentativeness of the eventual conclusions, is well illustrated by a study of attitudes to wealth and poverty in the Gospels, David Mealand's *Poverty and Expectation in the Gospels*. Mealand outlines four layers – redaction, sources, oral tradition and Jesus' own teaching and action – in the Synoptic Gospels, each with a different attitude towards wealth and poverty and each related to a different socio-political context. Alongside such research, the biblical claims of the Texts and some of the Extracts may appear highly simplistic. In addition, the christological assumptions of the exponent of Christian ethics will affect the relative weight that is afforded to Jesus' own words and ideas. The more importance that some of the Extracts attach to the humanity of Christ, the more inclined they may be to see him as an example for other human beings: on the other hand, a relatively 'high' christology may be more inclined to see Christ as the law-giver (the position more of the Texts).

(vi) The 19th and 20th centuries initiated considerable debate amongst New Testament theologians about how far the teaching of Paul can be reconciled with what can be known about the teaching of Jesus. Since Paul, as will be seen, played such an important role in the writings of both Augustine and Luther, this question cannot be ignored. This issue was particularly important for a theologian such as Schweitzer. His detailed studies, first of the eschatological teaching of Jesus and then of the mystical world of Paul's concept of being 'in Christ', led him to conclude that they were difficult to reconcile, both with each other and with the modern world. Some of the present differences between Reformed and Catholic theologians may be due to the relative importance the former give to Paul.

(vii) Finally, a number of the most crucial present-day moral dilemmas – particularly in the areas of technology, biotechnology and medicine, as will be seen in Sections 4 and 5 – were never envisaged in biblical times. Of course, we can make inferences from injunctions that do exist in the Bible, but such inferences are notoriously hazardous. Further, if, as is widely accepted by New Testament scholars, it is believed that Jesus and his most immediate followers confidently expected the *parousia* to arrive very soon, it is hardly surprising that they apparently showed little interest in social ethics. As a result, Augustine, faced with a radical change in the socio-political status of Christianity, was confronted with a new moral situation for which the New Testament provided few clear answers. The problem here is a double one: in the New Testament some issues are treated, but only ambiguously and fleetingly, as befits those living in a soon-to-be-destroyed world, whereas others are ignored or simply not envisaged. Together they present serious difficulties for a form of ethics based upon the Bible alone.

Stated so baldly this may appear excessively negative. There have in fact been a number of important attempts to face these various problems in Christian ethics. J.I.H. McDonald's *Biblical Interpretation and Christian Ethics* gives a very useful overview of the differing ways the Bible has been used in the history of Christian ethics. These seven sets of problems should be studied carefully in relation to each of the Texts and Extracts. Whilst an overview of the latter demonstrates that the Bible still plays a vital role in most traditions of Christian ethics, this role is now extremely complex and varied. A study of the ethics of the New Testament itself reveals some of this complexity, as the following suggest:

J.L. Houlden, *Ethics and the New Testament*; John Knox, *The Ethics of Jesus in the Teaching of the Church*; Barnabas Lindars, 'The Bible and Christian Ethics', *Theology*, 76, 1973; T.W. Manson, *Ethics and the Gospel*; Jack T. Sanders, *Ethics in the New Testament*.

It is compounded further by a study of the way in which the Bible is used by Christians; for this see:

James Barr, *The Bible in the Modern World*; C.H. Dodd, *The Authority of the Bible*; D.E. Nineham, *The Use and Abuse of the Bible*.

(b)   *Appeals to Christian Tradition*

The ways in which Churches appeal to Christian tradition reveal some of the most important historical differences between them. In very broad terms, Orthodox appeal only to the decisions of the historical Ecumenical Councils, Roman Catholics include appeals even to the most recent Papal Encyclicals, Anglicans make only a general appeal to Christian tradition, and Lutherans subordinate all such appeals to the principle of *sola Scriptura*. However, today these generalisations can be made with less accuracy. Internal opposition to a strict interpretation of papal infallibility in present-day Roman Catholicism, Anglican divisions between Liberals, Anglo-Catholics and Evangelicals, and an increased catholicity amongst many Reformed theologians, have made traditional divisions less clear-cut than they might once have appeared. A study of the Texts and Extracts reveals many of these differences and areas of overlap.

In the Texts, Aquinas' Text VIII shows his use of Augustine as an authority. The latter also had a profound influence on Luther. But Text III shows the extent of Luther's acceptance of the notion of justification by faith alone and his radical rejection of papal authority, papal councils and long-accepted traditions of Catholic piety.

In the Extracts, Welty's Extract 12 shows a traditional approach of Roman Catholics to papal authority. In contrast, Miranda's Extract 11, Fiorenza's Extract 5 and Ruether's Extract 26 show far more radical Roman Catholic approaches. The issue of papal authority has been most seriously tested for many Roman Catholics today by Paul VI's Extract 24 and has been an abiding issue for John Paul II (see his Extract 4). The traditional Orthodox appeal to Christian tradition is seen in Ware's Extract 23, whereas a more independent voice is raised in Berdyaev's Extract 7. A comparison of Fletcher's Extract 22 with Temple's Extract 9 and Clark's Extract 20 reveals very different Anglican assumptions about the authority of tradition. Finally, a comparison of Bonhoeffer's Extract 1 with Niebuhr's Extract 8 and then McFague's Extract 21 also reveals very different assumptions within the Reformed tradition.

A number of questions can be isolated under this heading: what constitutes Christian tradition?; is Christian tradition self-authenticating?; what happens if Christian tradition conflicts with itself or with biblical evidence?; is Christian tradition still in formation today? The Extracts show that, on all of these questions, there is disagreement amongst Christians. In addition, the following books show something of the range of this disagreement:

G.R. Dunstan, *The Artifice of Ethics* and *Duty and Discernment*; James M. Gustafson, *Protestant and Roman Catholic Ethics*; V.T. Istavridis, *Orthodoxy and Anglicanism*; Hans Küng, *Infallible?*; Paul Lehmann, *Ethics in a Christian Context*; Edward LeRoy Long, Jr, *A Survey of Christian Ethics*; James P. Mackey, *Power and Christian Ethics*; Ian S. Markham, *Plurality and Christian Ethics*.

(c) *Appeals to Christian Experience*
An appeal to conscience, in some form, constitutes an element in many types of Christian ethics, including those of Luther (see Texts VI and IX) and Aquinas (see Copleston's Extract 3). At least four attitudes towards conscience are evident in the discipline:

(i) An appeal to the conscience of all people, whether Christian or not. At times, this seems to be the position of the Quakers – i.e. if only they will listen carefully to the voice of conscience, all people have the truth already in their hearts.

(ii) An appeal to specifically Christian conscience. This appears to have been the position of George Fox himself. His *Journal* suggests that he believed in a literal understanding of Genesis 3 and therefore, apart from Christ, in inescapable human sinfulness. To the jury at Lancaster Assizes in 1664 he said: 'I was a man of tender conscience, and if they had any sense of a tender conscience, they would consider that it was in obedience to Christ's commands that I could not swear' (p.231). Yet there was also a universal element in his christology and, with it, in a radical appeal to conscience. In 1653 he wrote: 'To that God in your consciences I speak; declare or write your dissatisfactions to any one of them whom you call Quakers, that Truth may be exalted, and all may come to the light, with which Christ has enlightened every one that cometh into the world' (p.90). This seems nearer to position (i).

(iii) A belief that conscience is but one important element of the moral life of the individual, provided that this conscience is instructed by other elements, such as the Bible or Christian tradition. This is the position of Copleston's Extract 3, of Roman Catholicism generally, and of those sections of Anglicanism which follow in the Hooker tradition (see, for example, Kenneth E. Kirk's *Some Principles of Moral Theology*). Exponents of this position often insist that, for a number of reasons, individual conscience cannot be treated as the sole source of authority for Christian ethics: (a) conscience is affected by sin and thus it is often distorted; (b) it is influenced by psychological and sociological factors and therefore cannot be regarded as fully independent; (c) it can too easily be confused with prejudice or convention, so that individuals can have consciences about trivial matters, such as the length of their hair; (d) consciences are often ambivalent and, on that account, unable adequately to judge what is right in particular situations. On the other hand, these exponents usually insist that without individual free-will and conscience the moral life would not be moral. In short, it is a *sine qua non* of morality in Christianity, but it is not its sole base.

(iv) A radical rejection of conscience. This is apparently the position of Bonhoeffer's Extract 1. Conscience is seen as an element of secular ethics which is rejected by the radical 'Call of Christ' to the individual. The Christian moral life is seen, not as an attempt to distinguish right from wrong and then to follow right, but rather as a life obedient to the 'Call of Christ'. Again, it will be argued later that Bonhoeffer's position was not fully consistent. It is even possible that his understanding of life in Christ was similar to position (ii).

Appeals to Christian experience may also appear in other forms. For example, some forms of agapeism may be generated by an initial experience in Christ of *agape*; mystical experience may be linked with morality in Christianity (see Berdyaev's Extract 7); and, in religious ethics generally, numinous experience, involving as it does a mixture of attraction, awe and fear, has obvious relevance (see Rudolf Otto's *The Idea of the Holy*). In addition, most understandings of Christian ethics today would regard existential commitment, on the part of the individual, as an essential element of the moral life: that is, an individual is regarded as moral, not simply because of acting morally, but also because of intending to act morally.

One concept that is particularly relevant in this context is that of 'vision'. Under the influence of writers such as Iris Murdoch (see her *The Sovereignty of the Good* and also articles by her and Ronald Hepburn in I.T. Ramsey (ed), *Christian Ethics and Contemporary Philosophy*) morality is seen primarily in terms of vision: the individual is invited to 'see' or 'perceive' the world and social relationships in a particular way. This idea has been imaginatively employed in Christian ethics by Stanley Hauerwas (see his Extract 15). The following books are useful:

James Gustafson & J.T. Lamey (ed), *On Being Responsible*; David B. Harned, *Grace and Common Life* and *Faith and Virtue*; Stanley Hauerwas, *Vision and Virtue* and *Character and the Christian Life*; C.A. Pierce, *Conscience in the New Testament*.

In addition, the difficulties faced by classical theories of conscience are usefully discussed in H.D. Lewis' article in *Christian Ethics and Contemporary Philosophy*.

(d) *Appeals to Christian Belief*
There is a real danger in a Textbook of Christian ethics of giving the impression that it is a thoroughly pluralistic discipline, with disagreements evident in all its aspects. Indeed, an important feature of analysis in any academic discipline should involve an appreciation of the range of disagreements within it. Appeals to Christian tradition and to individual conscience tend to divide, rather than unite, Christians. However, appeals to the Bible and to Christian beliefs in principle should unite them, even if in practice different understandings of the Bible and of Christian

belief abound within Christianity. Nonetheless, a number of exponents of Christian ethics have argued that, however internally varied, these latter appeals do differentiate Christians from non-Christians. So, Keith Ward has argued, in his *The Divine Image*, that the doctrine of creation gives Christians grounds for taking ethics more seriously than non-believers, since they are given grounds for believing that the moral life and the life of the world generally are not fortuitous, but the products of a loving God. For the theist, morality and cosmology are necessarily related to each other.

Sometimes this contention has been used as the basis for Christian apologetics, as it is in the following passage from A.E. Taylor's 1926 Gifford Lectures, *The Faith of a Moralist*:

> I should infer that... the moral life itself, at its best, points to something which, because it transcends the separation of 'ought' from 'is', must be called definitely religion and not morality, as the source and inspiration of what is best in morality itself, and that the connection between practical good living and belief in God is much more direct than Kant was willing to allow. I cannot doubt that morality may exist without religion. An atheist who has been taught not to steal or lie or fornicate or the like is, probably, no more nor less likely, in average situations, to earn his living honestly, to speak the truth and to live cleanly, than a believer in God. But if the atheist is logical and in earnest in his professed view of the world, and the believer equally so with his, I think I know which of the two is more likely to make irreparable and 'unmerited' grievous calamity a means to the purification and enrichment of personality (Vol.1, pp.155-6).

In different ways, John Paul II's Extract 4, Temple's Extract 9, Gregorios' Extract 18, and Clark's Extract 20, illustrate this approach. The method of deriving Christian ethics systematically from the Christian doctrine of creation, which is a feature, to some extent, of all these Extracts, raises important possibilities which go well beyond their own premises. After all, a doctrine of

Creation unites Christians, Jews and Muslims, and a system of ethics derived from it can be highly relevant to inter-religious dialogue and co-operation. However, a central difficulty is raised by Temple: the particularisation of general ethical principles, themselves derived from general Christian beliefs, notoriously divides, rather than unites Christians. In order to overcome this problem, Temple developed the notion of 'middle axioms' used in the Life and Work Movement. The difficulties confronting this notion will be discussed in relation to Temple's Extract 9.

Clearly, Christian beliefs cannot be regarded as the only source of Christian ethics, since they themselves are dependent on other sources – such as the Bible, Christian tradition and even Christian experience. Yet, it is possible that they form the parameters of the discipline, parameters that give it a degree of unity – a unity of general attitude rather than specific content (although, occasionally, even a specific content can be isolated). The term 'moral theology', frequently used in the past by Roman Catholic and by Anglican theologians, served to emphasise this, but is little used here, since its scope was often regarded as including, in addition to ethics, pastoral theology and ecclesiastical practice.

However, this approach to Christian ethics must face an important criticism. If ethical prescriptions are derived, even in part, from Christian doctrines, it might seem that an 'ought' is being derived from an 'is'. This criticism can be raised in relation to specific Extracts, even if it is initially conceded that the 'ought' and the 'is' are not always wholly separable (see Helen Oppenheimer, 'Ought and Is', *Theology*, 76, 1973).

5. *SOCIAL DETERMINANTS*

It has already been claimed that biographical details are relevant to an understanding of the thought of a particular theologian. However, an analysis of the social determinants of theological positions (and a subsequent analysis of their social significance), goes beyond this claim. It assumes that ideas can be related to social structures – an assumption which is central to the sociology of knowledge. That is, that theological and ethical ideas may be influenced by society (i.e. socially determined) and may, in their

turn, have an influence upon society (i.e. socially significant).
Within highly cognitive approaches to theology and philosophy,
it is often assumed that ideas from one social or historical context
can straightforwardly be compared with those from another. So,
ideas from the Texts can be compared directly with ideas from
the Extracts. But, for a more sociologically-minded approach,
such direct comparisons ignore the degree to which specific ideas
are related to specific social contexts. According to this approach,
comparisons should be made only after social analysis. It is this
approach which this Textbook aims to encourage by including
in the system of analysis an examination, first of social
determinants and, then, of social significance.

A number of theologians have attempted to apply social analysis
to ideas in theology and Christian ethics. Ernst Troeltsch's *The
Social Teaching of the Christian Churches* and H.R. Niebuhr's
The Social Sources of Denominationalism have proved to be of
abiding interest, not only to theologians, but also to sociologists
of religion. Dietrich Bonhoeffer's very early work, *Sanctorum
Communio,* also demonstrated an interest in sociology. Amongst
sociologists, Max Weber, particularly in his seminal *The
Protestant Ethic and the 'Spirit' of Capitalism,* showed a
considerable interest in and knowledge of, theology, as do
present-day sociologists such as Peter Berger and David Martin.
Recent examinations of the methodological problems facing
attempts to analyse theology sociologically can be found in the
following:

Gregory Baum, *Religion and Alienation: A Theological Reading of
Sociology;* Robin Gill, *The Social Context of Theology,Theology and
Social Structure,* and (ed) *Theology and Sociology;* D. Martin, J.
Orme-Mills, & W.S.F. Pickering (ed), *Sociology and Theology:
Alliance and Conflict.*

A number of points must be made:

(a) An analysis of social determinants too easily gives rise to a
suspicion of an overall social determinism. It would be false to
assume that all those who attempt to uncover the social

determinants of something are committed to a position of thoroughgoing and mechanistic determinism. However, it will be argued in Section 1 that the latter would probably be disastrous to all but the most strictly 'Lutheran' understandings of Christian ethics. If free-will in some form is essential to Christian ethics (see especially Augustine's Text I), a thoroughgoing sociological, psychological or biological determinism would appear particularly destructive. Indeed, it will be seen that theological determinism, based, for example, on a rigid predestinarianism, faces the same problem. Some of the serious logical difficulties involved in thoroughgoing theories of social determinism are amusingly isolated in Peter Berger's *A Rumor of Angels*. Most obviously, there is the status of the theories themselves – presumably they are themselves socially determined – and on this account Berger suggests the task of 'relativising the relativisers'. It should emphatically be stressed that in this Textbook social determinism is not consciously assumed.

(b) Social scientists are nonetheless committed to providing as total explanations of social phenomena as possible. Just as 'god of the gaps' arguments are discouraged in the physical sciences, so social scientists, in so far as they are acting as social scientists, should not be expected to account for religious phenomena in anything other than social terms. After all, it is their task to do so, even if they happen to be religious people in their private life. Berger, in his *The Social Reality of Religion (The Sacred Canopy)*, has termed this attitude methodological atheism. This should not be confused with actual or ontological atheism or with sociological imperialism. Rather, it assumes that separate and seemingly self-contained accounts of human behaviour can be built up from a variety of perspectives – sociological, psychological, physiological, biochemical, theological, etc. Whereas it might be difficult to form any overall picture of particular moments of interpersonal behaviour using all the perspectives simultaneously, it would be wrong to assume that only one of the perspectives may provide a 'legitimate' explanation. In the past it was the theologian who tended to be imperialistic in this way, but today it is more likely to be the physical or social scientist. Again, it should be underlined that this Textbook does not intentionally subscribe to any such imperialism.

(c) Related to this point, a confusion is sometimes made between 'explaining something' and 'explaining something away'. The fact that Marx, Durkheim or Freud explained religious phenomena in social terms does not necessarily mean that they were 'explaining away' these phenomena. Durkheim and Freud, at least, were usually aware of this distinction. An exposure of the origins of particular ideas tells us nothing logically about their validity (the genetic fallacy), although, of course, they may be psychologically distressing to believers. Thus, even if it is agreed that religious belief may be the product of a neurotic perpetuation of childhood fantasies, it is still open to the believer to claim that God acts through these fantasies. However, if one always sees religious claims as linked to these fantasies, psychologically one might find it difficult to remain convinced of their truth. Such a Freudian explanation may well appear as a threat to the believer, but it is not strictly a logical threat. Indeed, an element in Christian theology has always stressed the 'oddness' or even absurdity of Christian belief. It is important that this point should be kept in mind, especially when examining the social determinants of the ideas of people as psychologically interesting as Augustine or Luther.

(d) Behind the attempt in this Textbook to isolate the social determinants of particular ideas and positions, is the belief that such analysis produces a sharper critical understanding of the Texts and Extracts. Thus, it will be maintained that it is important to know that Augustine's theological understanding of the relation between Church and State was developed at a time of very considerable political upheaval, or that his concept of the 'just war' coincided with a newly established political status for Christianity. Again, it should be stressed that such analysis does not thereby invalidate Augustine's ideas, or render them anachronistic for present-day Christian ethics. But it does entail that they should be compared point-for-point with the latter only with considerable caution.

(e) A full appreciation of the social determinants of any of the Texts and Extracts would be beyond the scope of this Textbook, but it is hoped that the student will be encouraged to develop them further. Considerable selectivity is inevitable. In relation to the Texts, different points will be raised in the context of the various contributions from each of the three authors. Further, it is usually easier to suggest the social determinants of much-studied classical authors than it is of the Extracts of recent authors. A complete understanding of their social determinants would involve a consideration, at one end of the spectrum, of the psychological peculiarities of particular authors, their family, early training, socialisation and later development and, at the other end of the spectrum, of the overall political structure and culture of the age in which they lived. In addition, the various levels of influence of these differing factors would have to be recorded in terms ranging, from the loosest coincidence, to the tightest causal relationship. Even if such an ideal version of the sociology of knowledge could be achieved, it is clearly not appropriate here. However, as the following demonstrate, this task has already begun in ethics generally:

John H. Barnsley, *The Social Reality of Ethics*; J. Habermas, *Knowledge and Human Interests*; Alasdair MacIntyre, *A Short History of Ethics*, *Against the Self-images of the Age*, and especially *After Virtue*; Maria Ossowska, *Social Determinants of Moral Ideas*;

and accounts of the sociology of knowledge are summarised in my *Theology and Social Structure* and can be studied in:

J.E. Curtis & J.W. Petras (ed), *The Sociology of Knowledge: A Reader*; Peter Hamilton, *Knowledge and Social Structure*; and Peter Berger and Thomas Luckmann's *The Social Construction of Reality*.

6. *SOCIAL SIGNIFICANCE*

An interactionist account of knowledge requires an examination, not just of the social determinants of particular ideas, but also of their social significance. It maintains that ideas may act, both as dependent and as independent variables, within society – both being shaped by society and, in turn, helping to shape society. The fact that a particular idea or position has been structured by society does not prevent it from having a subsequent influence upon that society, or indeed upon a quite different society. One has only to think of the influence of the Nicene Creed, in order to realise this. Church historians have no difficulty in showing that some of the central terms used in this Creed owe their existence to a particular social context and to the polemics of the fourth-century church. However, once accepted by the Church, the Creed soon had, and, indeed, still has, a very considerable influence upon the way in which christological issues have been debated.

A two-way process is thus presupposed. Ideas, influenced by a number of social factors, may also be seen to have their own influence in a variety of ways. Clearly, this is the case with the Texts. Whatever social determinants may be identified, the ideas of Augustine, Aquinas and Luther have obviously had a profound effect upon theologians, upon the churches and upon Western ideas in general. By systematically comparing the Texts with the Extracts, some of this profound influence should become evident. Naturally, it will often be more difficult to assess the social significance of the Extracts, but even here some immediate points are possible.

A number of qualifications must be made:

(a) The interactionist analysis required will sometimes be extraordinarily complex. Thus, whilst Luther's influence upon the Reformation may be relatively clear, his relationship to the Renaissance is not. It has proved extremely difficult to assess to what extent the Reformation was influenced by the Renaissance and what was the relative influence of each upon subsequent Western culture. It is even difficult to determine their relative influence upon the churches.

(b) A full analysis of the social significance of particular Texts or Extracts would also be a very lengthy undertaking, requiring several levels of analysis and a range of causal terms. At least four levels of analysis can be isolated: the influence of particular ideas and positions upon theologians in an academic context; their influence upon those who preach or teach in a more popular context; their influence upon lay Christians who listen directly to the preachers or teachers; and their influence upon society at large. It is too easy to assume that these levels of influence will always be broadly similar (in *Theology and Social Structure*, for example, I argued that different levels of influence can be detected in the differing responses to *Honest to God* in the early 1960s). Considerable selection is again inevitable.

(c) It is important to stress that an analysis of the social significance of ideas in Christian ethics is not an attempt to belittle the theological importance of these ideas. For example, if Weber's contentions are accepted – that Luther's concepts of election and predestination and his attack on monastic asceticism had a profound influence upon the rise of the spirit necessary for the development of Western Capitalism – it does not follow that Luther's theology is thereby belittled. It could still be maintained, that the theological significance of these ideas was even greater than their socio-economic significance. The former is not, of necessity, enhanced or belittled by the latter. However, Weber's analysis might give a theologian like Bonino, in Extract 16, additional reason for distrusting traditional Lutheranism – but this would stem from his own prior political and theological commitments.

7. *CRITIQUE*

At the end of each Text and group of Extracts a brief critique is appended. This position is deliberate, not because critique is considered unimportant, but rather because analysis must be as full and informed as possible before a serious critique is made. Of course, students should be encouraged to make their own critique. It is an essential part of learning. In each case an attempt is made to suggest some of the strengths and weaknesses of the particular excerpt, not only in relation to the internal ideas of the work from which it is taken, but also in relation to the ideas and theories of other exponents of Christian ethics.

FURTHER READING

Books suggested as further reading, in relation to each Text and set of Extracts, are intended to provide a stimulus to the student. Although a fairly full biography (which includes the publishing details of books cited earlier) is supplied as an Appendix, no attempt has been made to supply an exhaustive reading list. Since repetition of suggested reading would have been tedious, especially in relation to the Texts, reference should constantly be made back to this Introduction. Naturally, the Texts and Extracts should never be regarded as substitutes for referring back to the original books, but, ideally, they should provoke enough interest in students to do this for themselves. The further reading suggested consists, first, of relevant books by the author himself or herself and, then, of bibliographical or theological books about the author or about the issue in question.

THE TEXTS: AUGUSTINE, AQUINAS AND LUTHER

In any understanding of Christian theology or ethics, Augustine, Aquinas and Luther are three of the most important figures. Each stood at a pivotal moment in Christian history and each has had an abiding influence upon Christian thought. Together, they cover a very broad spectrum of possibilities within Christian ethics. An analysis of the differences between them reveals many of the central differences that are still evident today.

Of course, there is a real danger in comparing the ideas of these theologians, especially in the light of the type of social analysis already discussed. Each stood within a radically different social context, each presupposed a different political situation, and each has influenced different sections of the churches – although it will be seen that, in a more ecumenical age, their separate influences are now less clear-cut than they were in the past. Since it has already been insisted that socio-political differences should never be ignored, it would obviously be odd to compare these three theologians' ideas point-for-point, as if they were always writing about the same things, albeit from different perspectives. Nonetheless, the very fact that their primary writings are still widely used in contemporary ethical decision-making by Christians makes some comparison inevitable, if only to reveal differences between their situations and our own. Most obviously, as seen in Sections 2 and 3, the political and economic views of Augustine, Aquinas and Luther have had a major influence upon Christian thought and continue to shape attitudes today. At the same time, it is soon realised that their thoughts were developed in political and economic contexts which bear little relation to present-day, Western, post-industrial society. In this situation, the task of distinguishing between perennial and ephemeral problems in Christian ethics, can be seen to be highly important.

AUGUSTINE (c. 354-430) was born at Thagaste, a small inland town in Proconsular Numidia in North Africa (the modern Tunisia and eastern Algeria). His mother was a devout and somewhat ascetic 'Catholic' Christian, but his father, a relatively impoverished citizen of curial rank, remained a 'pagan' for most of his life. Augustine was a catechumen in his youth, but was not baptised until he was 33. He became a student at Carthage at 16 and a follower of Manichaeism at 19. He remained a follower for nine years, wrestling for much of this time with the problem of evil, which the radical dualism of Manichaeism seemed to solve. He finally abandoned this form of religion when the celebrated Manichaean bishop, Faustus, failed to answer his questions to his satisfaction. Subsequently, he became increasingly impressed with the sermons and arguments of the Catholic bishop of Milan, Ambrose. He had a son, Adeodatus, but despite a long-standing relationship with the boy's mother, he never married her. Brilliant at debate, rhetoric and logic he became a professor of rhetoric, founding his own school at Rome in 383. After his break with Manichaeism and a period of contact with Ambrose, he finally became a 'Catholic' Christian after a conversion experience at Milan. He was profoundly influenced by neo-Platonism and was baptised by Ambrose in 387. He returned, with a small group of family and friends, to lead a monastic life in Africa, but, with great reluctance, was soon ordained priest and then elected a bishop of Hippo in 396. He remained there as bishop for 34 years, living in community and writing extensively. He died as the Vandals were laying siege to Hippo. Indeed, he lived at a crucial stage in the breakup of the Roman Empire, albeit in the relative isolation of North Africa. He wrote *The City of God* in order to rebuff the charge, that the official adoption of Christianity by Constantine was the reason for this break-up. He was forced to work out afresh the implications of this adoption for Christianity and felt impelled, at various stages, to defend 'Catholic' Christianity against Manichaeans, Donatists and Pelagians – even enlisting the help of the civil authorities to suppress the latter. Through his many writings he gave Christianity a new intellectual depth and status and had a profound influence upon both Aquinas and Luther.

AQUINAS (c.1225-74) was born at the castle of Roccasecca at Aquino, between Naples and Rome. The son of a count, he was sent to the abbey of Monte Cassino for his elementary schooling and in 1239 went to university at Naples. There, much against the wishes of his father, he entered the Dominican Order. He studied under the Dominican, Albert the Great, at Paris and then at Cologne and, in 1252, returned to Paris as a lecturer, becoming a regular professor of theology in 1256. From 1259 to 1269 he taught successively at Amagni, Orvieto, Rome and Viterbo, before again returning to Paris. In 1272 he went to Naples and in 1274 he was summoned by Pope Gregory X to take part in the Council of Lyons, but on the way there he died. Towards the end of his life he had a number of mystical experiences and, four months before his death, after an experience whilst saying Mass, he stopped work on his *Summa Theologica*, saying that 'all I have written seems to me like so much straw compared with what I have seen and with what has been revealed to me'. He wrote this monumental work as a systematic exposition of theology for 'novices'. His other most important work, *Summa Contra Gentiles*, was written earlier, in order to combat the 'naturalistic' thinking of Graeco-Islamic philosophy. In both works he was concerned to show that the Christian faith rests upon a rational foundation and that philosophy (largely in the form of newly rediscovered Aristotelianism) and theology are not mutually exclusive types of activity. Aquinas lived at the time of the greatest power and influence of the Catholic Church in the West. At this stage of medieval history, the Catholic Church came nearest to being a Universal Church – a phenomenon that can be traced back to the age of Augustine. Aquinas has continued to have a profound effect upon Roman Catholic moral and systematic theology, re-enforced by Pope Leo XIII's encyclical letter of 1879, *Aeterni Patris*, declaring his to be the 'perennial philosophy'.

LUTHER (1483-1546) was born at Eisleben in Saxony. A miner's son, he went to school at Mansfeld, Magdeberg and Eisenach and entered university at Erfurt in 1501 to study law. However, after a profound experience during a thunderstorm, he abandoned his legal studies at the age of 21 and, despite parental disapproval, entered an Augustinian monastery at Erfurt. There he led an extremely ascetic life. He was sent to the University of Wittenberg and eventually became professor of biblical studies there. Convinced of the necessity of seeking his own salvation by keeping the biblical commandments, he became gradually persuaded of his own inability to do this. In 1507 he underwent a conversion experience, reputedly whilst climbing the Scala Santa at Rome and, in 1517, posted his celebrated 95 Theses against the abuses created by the Church's sale of indulgences (authorised by Pope Leo X, in part to pay for the building of St Peter's in Rome) on the door of the Castle Church in Wittenberg. He refused to retract to the papal legate, Cardinal Cajetan, and appealed directly to the Pope and then in 1519 to the new Emperor, Charles V, who was himself of German extraction. Excommunicated by Leo X in 1520 and tried by Charles V at Worms, Luther was placed under imperial ban by the Edict of Worms of 1521. His break with Rome was now complete and he spent the rest of his life (albeit with the vital support of a number of German princes) translating the Bible, revising the liturgy, writing hymns, preaching and writing books on many aspects of the Christian life, and reorganising churches in defiance of Rome. Luther lived in an age of very considerable social and political change, which saw the breakup of medieval Christendom and the rise of early capitalism and of new forms of nationalism in Europe. He witnessed a major rebellion of the

German peasants in 1525 and died in the year in which war broke out between Reformers and Catholics – a war that ended only with the Treaty of Augsburg, 1555, which allowed the German princes to choose to follow Catholicism or Lutheranism and to coerce their subjects accordingly. Himself a highly influential figure in all these changes, he has continued to be one of the most significant theologians within Reformed or Protestant forms of Christianity.

From these brief biographies a number of key points of contrast can be drawn. Each theologian represented widely different cultures – North African, Italian and German – in radically different ages. And, even though both Aquinas and Luther were deeply influenced by Augustine, temperamentally they were very different from each other and tended to emphasise different elements in his writings. It is sometimes held that, whereas Aquinas was heir more to the ecclesiastical side of Augustine's writings, Luther, with his rejection of Augustinian monasticism, was heir more to Augustine's Pauline theology. Nonetheless, it is possible to make some comparisons between them, finding similarities, now between Augustine and Aquinas, now between Augustine and Luther, and sometimes between Aquinas and Luther – provided, of course, that their radically different social, political and cultural contexts are kept in mind:

(1) Both Augustine and Luther lived in ages of revolution. Augustine witnessed the gradual breakup of the Roman Empire, dying as Hippo itself was under siege. Luther witnessed the break-up of medieval Catholic Europe and also died surrounded by war. Yet neither man was himself a revolutionary. Augustine wrote to defend Christians against the charge that they were responsible for Rome's collapse and he remained a Roman in much of his thinking. He even enunciated a just-war theory, in contrast with the pacifism of previous generations of Christians (see Text VII). And Luther, to their amazement, bitterly rejected the cause of the revolutionary peasants (see Text IX). Aquinas lived at what might, at first, appear to have been one of the most settled ages in European history. But the seeds of the Renaissance were already present in the 13th century, with the art of Giotto

(c.1266-1337), celebrating the life of Francis of Assissi, and the poetry of Dante (1265-1321), reflecting parts of Aquinas' *Summa Theologica*, soon to change cultural understandings in a manner relevant eventually to the Reformation. By looking forward to the Renaissance and even to the Reformation and backwards to the newly established relationship between the Church and State in the 4th and 5th centuries, Aquinas stands as a pivot between the two.

(2) In terms of class or social stratification, the origins of the three men were quite distinct. Aquinas' origins were clearly the most aristocratic, Augustine's were those of a relatively impoverished middle class in an age of rapid inflation, and Luther's, although by no means totally impoverished, were unmistakably lower class. Viewed from a more dynamic perspective, only Luther's family was upwardly socially mobile, moving from a situation of working as miners, actually to owning mines and then being in a position to be able to send their son to university to study law. Whilst all three belonged to the minority of university-educated writers and thinkers, Luther's socially mobile background made him the most suitable to be an agent of radical social change, while Aquinas' comparatively static social background made him the least suitable. Amongst the upwardly socially mobile it is also not uncommon to find an antipathy towards those belonging to the class of their origins: a tendency to radical innovation can be combined with a dismissiveness of those of a lower social class. It is possible that Luther's rejection of the writings and actions of the revolutionary peasants may have owed something to this factor. His tendency to side, at times, with the rulers over-and-against the ruled, is seen particularly in the way he, like Augustine before him, enlisted the help of the rulers to suppress dissension and even 'heresy'. However, the fact that all three men went to university and became monastic Catholic priests means that there is also a strong similarity of socialisation between them.

(3) All three experienced celibacy and some form of ascetic monasticism. Nonetheless, their experiences here were distinct. Aquinas, highly cerebral and evidently rather corpulent, became

a Dominican as a young man and remained one until his death. Augustine, having rejected Christianity for so long, became extremely ascetic only after his conversion – although there can be little doubt that he was always serious-minded and intense and by no means the sensual youth he is sometimes thought to have been. Even his celebrated relationship was long-standing, apparently faithful, loving and in accord with contemporary Roman moral practice. In contrast, Luther was fiercely ascetic only before his radical break with monasticism and Rome. Both Augustine and Luther were fathers, but only Luther married – Augustine painfully broke off his relationship, whilst Luther married a former nun, seemingly out of duty, though he soon discovered great happiness in marriage.

(4) In terms of religious psychology, both Augustine and Luther had what is sometimes called a 'twice-born' and Aquinas a 'once-born' type of religious temperament. Augustine and Luther had almost classic Pauline conversion experiences and, not surprisingly, thereafter showed a particular affinity for the Pauline epistles. Like Paul, Luther was 'converted' from a life of legalistic pietism to one of entire dependence upon grace. Augustine, on the other hand, was 'converted' from a relatively free-thinking attachment to Manichaeism to ascetic 'Catholic' Christianity. Before their 'conversions', both men experienced a considerable period of emotional and psychological turmoil – displaying what some psychologists would undoubtedly identify as obsessive religious personalities, and, after these conversions, comparative calm. A number of psychological and sociological studies of conversion would suggest that this comparative calm hid a good deal of continuing doubt, uncertainty and marginality/ liminality – and this may be another point of contrast between these two men and Aquinas. Certainly, whilst Aquinas was concerned to defend 'orthodoxy' against 'heresy' (as, for example, in the *Summa Contra Gentiles*, see *below*, p.174), there is little in his writings to equal the polemics, scorn and, sometimes, vitriol, particularly of the later Augustine and Luther (see Text XV). Of the three, Aquinas was by far the most conciliatory in style, appealing more consistently to reason than to emotion, although, as has been seen, his life was not without mystical experience.

Indeed, the very rationality of Aquinas has given offence to some. In contrast, Book VIII of Augustine's *Confessions*, written twelve years after the event, gives his classic, and highly influential, account of conversion, containing many of the key empirical features of a conversion experience: extreme anxiety, voices, a sense of the 'numinous', a random opening of the Bible, an instrumental text (in this case Rom. 13.13-14), sexual remorse, catharsis and withdrawal.

These four sets of psychological and sociological variables – political context, social stratification, marital status and religious psychology – are all vital to an adequate understanding of the differences between the three theologians and should be examined carefully in relation to the Texts. Again it needs to be stressed that a preparedness to take them seriously does not necessarily reduce the significance given to internal theological factors determining their thought. In addition, three other points of contrast can be made from the biographical sketches:

(5) It is often pointed out that whereas Augustine did much to relate Platonic or neo-Platonic ideas (books were so scarce in his day that he only knew of Plato's ideas through the work of Plotinus) to 'Catholic' orthodoxy and thereby rendered Christianity more intellectually respectable to his contemporaries, Aquinas achieved a similar correlation with the newly rediscovered Aristotelian ideas of his time. Luther, on the other hand, might have regarded any such undertaking with strong suspicion: for him it was the Scriptures which must form the main axiom for theology. But, as so often in his writings, Augustine was ambivalent in this correlation, simultaneously being attracted by some Platonic notions and repelled by others such as polytheism (e.g. see *The City of God* VIII.9f). It will be seen from the Texts, that Aquinas' understanding of the relationship between philosophy and theology is more consistent than that of Augustine and it was his thought which was instrumental in the eventual triumph, in Roman Catholic theology, of Aristotelianism over Platonism. The more naturalistic Aristotelianism seems to have provided him with a more congruous rational/natural basis, than transcendental

Platonism for the supernatural overlay of Christian belief. Precisely because Platonism locates the 'really real' in a transcendent realm, outside everyday experience and the everyday world, it presents those following Aquinas with a potentially more damaging challenge than Aristotelianism. If Platonic transcendentalism and biblical revelation conflict, any real correlation between them breaks down, since the conflict appears as a conflict between two supernatural views of the world. In contrast, a correlation between Aristotelian naturalism and Christian supernaturalism considerably reduces this risk of conflict.

(6) Both Augustine and Luther were church leaders of very considerable contemporary influence. As a bishop of Hippo for 34 years, Augustine's pastoral, as well as his theological, influence extended far beyond the provincial confines of North Africa. And Luther's contemporary fame and influence were even greater. Apart from his key role in sparking the Reformation, for over 25 years he was engaged in an astonishing range of activities aimed at reforming the German churches. It is difficult to find another church leader with a comparable range of gifts and versatility. Only Aquinas remained the academic that the other two had once been and took very little part in ecclesiastical politics. Ironically, he died on his way to a church council. Regarded as a dangerous theological innovator by some of his contemporaries, his work gradually became established in the Roman Catholic Church, receiving its final endorsement in 1879. However, as the 'perennial philosopher' of his church, his work has had, until .ery recently, a position of primacy afforded to few in other churches.

(7) All three were voluminous writers and even present-day collections of their work require multi-volume editions. For Augustine alone there are extant 113 books and over 200 letters and 500 sermons. Amongst present-day theologians only Barth is comparable. But, perhaps inevitably, volume fits uneasily with consistency. Of the three, Aquinas was by far the most consistent and systematic, but even in some of his ideas changes can be traced. Generalisations about their ideas must be carefully

qualified and, with Augustine and Luther, it is often important to relate their ideas to the particular point in their lives in which they were expressed. As writers, however, their overall tasks were distinct. Augustine wrote extensively to defend the Catholic Christianity to which he returned against attacks from 'pagans' and from 'heretical' Christians. Aquinas wrote his *Summa Theologica* as a systematic exposition of Christianity for 'novices' within Catholicism. Luther wrote many of his books to restate the Gospel in contrast to what he regarded as the corruptions of contemporary Catholicism. Of course, in other respects there are similarities between their writings. Aquinas wrote his *Summa Contra Gentiles* as well as his *Summa Theologica* and, in this respect, appears like Augustine. And, both Augustine and Luther have bequeathed to us volumes of sermons. Yet their overall distinctiveness as writers remains.

With these seven points of contrast in mind, a number of key theological comparisons between their respective theological notions can be made. Others will emerge from a detailed study of the Texts, but, in view of their importance for Christian ethics, the following deserve special attention:

8. *THEIR USES OF THE BIBLE*

In comparison to many of the Extracts, Augustine, Aquinas and Luther have much in common with each other, since: (a) their ethical prescriptions are regularly related to biblical texts; (b) the Bible is regarded by them as normative in Christian ethics and theology; (c) the Bible is used in a pre-critical and literalistic manner. All three, for example, might have understood Genesis 3 to be literal history (even though Augustine, in his early writings, attempted an allegorical interpretation of this passage – see *De Genesi ad Manichaeos* 2.15). In contrast to Fletcher's Extract 2, they would all have stressed the normative role of the Bible in Christian ethics. The contrast, in this respect, between present-day Christian ethics and that of the Texts, is well illustrated by the attitude of Augustine and of Luther to polygamy (see *below*, pp.461f.). In parts of the Old Testament, polygamy is clearly accepted, so Augustine could not bring himself to say that it was ethically wrong and even Luther, at one point, concluded that it would be better for Philip of Hesse to take a second wife, like the Old Testament patriarchs, rather than go against the Matthean prohibition of divorce. In this respect Augustine's arguments are particularly interesting. In seeking to defend the Bible against Faustus' attacks he wrote:

Jacob the son of Isaac is charged with having committed a great crime because he had four wives. But here there is no ground for a criminal accusation: for a plurality of wives was no crime when it was the custom; and it is a crime now, because it is no longer the custom. There are sins against nature, and sins against custom, and sins against the law. In which, then of these senses did Jacob sin in having a plurality of wives? As regards nature, he used women not for sensual gratification, but for the procreation of children. For custom, this was the common practice at that time in those countries. And for the laws, no prohibition existed. The only reason of its being a crime now to do this, is because custom and the laws forbid it. (*Reply to Faustus the Manichean*, XXII.47).

Aquinas would not have seen polygamy as consonant with nature (see Text XIV), but, in spite of its offence to their contemporary sensitivities, the fact that it is condoned in parts of the Old Testament, led both Augustine and Luther to view it as ethically neutral.

Despite this overall agreement, Augustine, Aquinas and Luther might have disagreed with each other about the extent to which the Bible is to be used as the sole arbiter within Christian ethics. Luther might have been the more emphatic: the Bible is the only arbiter of Christian faith (his stress on *sola Scriptura*, which was to act as one of the guiding principles of the Reformation). The importance he gave to translating and expounding the Bible naturally follows from this emphasis. Even though it will be noted that, at times, there are appeals to conscience and natural law evident in his Texts, his intended *sola Scriptura* stress remains. It is important to emphasise the word 'intended'. Occasions will be noted when Luther's position goes clearly beyond the biblical evidence. Nevertheless, in his mind, he was always attempting to be faithful to the Bible – in contrast to the Roman Catholic Church which had, in his view, constructed an entirely extra-biblical, and therefore illegitimate, structure. Augustine, too, was emphatic about the key role of the Bible in the Christian life, as his sermons clearly demonstrate. Nonetheless, he made frequent appeals to church tradition, saw convergencies, at times, between neo-Platonic and Christian values and even sometimes (as will be seen in Section 3) borrowed from pagan philosophy when the Bible failed positively to resolve moral dilemmas.

A *sola Scriptura* stress might perhaps have made least sense to Aquinas. Given his understanding of natural law (see Text II), reason is able to ascertain moral truths which can also be known through biblical revelation. Aquinas' method of using the Bible is seen very clearly in Text XIV: his argument is based upon natural law and logical reasoning and biblical evidence is only quoted once that argument is completed. Thus, the Bible is seen to confirm what can already be known through a proper use of reason. As a result of this method and understanding, he was able to borrow freely from Aristotle, Augustine, and church tradition generally, provided, of course that such borrowings did not seem to conflict with the Bible. In overall, and perhaps too schematic terms, whereas Luther intended normally to start from the Bible and use other evidence only if it was congruent with it, Aquinas tended to start from natural reason and demonstrate that it was in accord with, or, at least, did not conflict with, the Bible. It will be seen that these different methods were linked to their different understandings of grace.

It is possible that there is another tendency which Augustine and Luther had in common. Both had a strong disposition towards the Pauline Epistles. In the light of what has already been suggested concerning their 'twice-born' religious temperaments, this disposition is very understandable. Further, the early Luther was suspicious of the theology implicit in James and Revelation. As a result, some have claimed that their use of the Bible was unwittingly determined by some 'canon within the canon' – a permanent difficulty facing all emphatically biblical approaches to Christian ethics. The same difficulty will be raised in the context of some of the present-day Extracts, such as Miranda's Extract 11. The more pluralistic the Bible is thought to be in the light of modern critical scholarship, the more this difficulty is increased.

9.   THEIR THEOLOGICAL ANTHROPOLOGIES

Augustine, Aquinas and Luther might have agreed on several points that differentiate them from a number of the Extracts: (a) they assumed that the Fall was (to use an anachronism for the moment) an 'historical event'; (b) as a result, apart from Christ, humans are in a state of original sin; (c) original sin is not simply a propensity towards sin, but involves concupiscence which itself involves actual guilt; (d) as a result, apart from Christ, none can be saved. However, their theological anthropologies can be differentiated from each other by the way in which these points were interpreted by them. In Augustine, there is a stress upon the 'original righteousness' of Adam: he is sometimes portrayed, before the Fall, as an ideal athlete, philosopher and saint (see Text X). But, in Aquinas, Adam's original righteousness consists, quite explicitly, in supernatural qualities (*donum supernaturale* or sometimes *donum superadditum*), so the Fall represents a fall from a supernatural to a natural level: Adam, and through him humanity subsequently, is still human and not a beast, still rational and possessing the properties belonging properly to human nature (*pura naturalia*). For him, then, the Fall is a privation rather than a deprivation.

There is considerable debate about how far these scholastic notions of Aquinas can be applied to Augustine, whose theological anthropology often appears somewhat ambivalent, but they certainly cannot be attributed to Luther. Luther rejected the notion of *donum supernaturale* and tended to see the Fall rather as a fall from the human to the sub-human. Not surprisingly, he tended to mistrust human independent rational abilities, a capacity to know God apart from revelation, and even free-will in moral decision-making – three human characteristics that Aquinas would have considered essential.

The ambivalence of Augustine is demonstrated by his belief that humankind constitutes a single 'lump of sin' (*massa peccati* or *massa perditionis*) lacking freedom (*libertas*) but still possessing free-will (*liberum arbitrium*) – an extraordinarily difficult distinction that he sometimes made. In Text I it will be seen that he combined a strong stress upon the prescience of God with a belief that sinful humanity does have genuine free-will. However, he does little to resolve the tension between these two positions – but perhaps some degree of tension here is inevitable in all serious theological discussion.

There is a growing recognition today that assumptions about theological anthropology have a profound effect upon the rest of theology. If this is so in theology, it must be the case *par excellence* in Christian ethics. The differences here between Augustine, Aquinas and Luther are still of considerable relevance to the Extracts and help to explain some of the crucial differences between such Extracts as Hauerwas' Extract 15 and Welty's Extract 12 and between Barth's Extract 6, Berdyaev's Extract 7 and Niebuhr's Extract 8.

10. *THEIR SOTERIOLOGIES*

All three might have agreed that: (a) God's revelation in Jesus Christ is essential to salvation; (b) God's laws can be known, in part at least, from an inspection of the natural world, but that knowledge of these laws does not of itself lead to salvation; (c) those who reject Jesus Christ are damned. Yet, when these points are elaborated, differences between them immediately arise, and again, some of the Extracts would dissent even from these general points. So, Bonhoeffer's Extract 1 seems to deny the initial assumption in (b) that the natural world can reveal anything about God and many might feel uneasy about taking (c) as literally as do the Texts. Even on (a) there is an evident difference between the exclusive christologies of Barth and Bonhoeffer and the more inclusive christologies of Temple, Abraham and McFague.

Aquinas and Luther present the clearest and most sharply differentiated accounts of the relations between nature and grace and between reason and revelation. If, for the former, these relations were continuous, for the latter they were discontinuous. For Aquinas, 'natural' religion and morality were crowned by revelation: natural reason could establish the existence and some of the attributes of God, but only revelation could establish the triune nature of God: in short, grace completes or crowns nature and revelation adds to what can be known through reason and makes us fit for salvation. Thus, faith is not a contradiction of reason, as it appears to be, at times, in a theologian like Kierkegaard, but rather is a stage beyond reason, albeit a necessary stage for salvation. However, for Luther, what can be established through reason or natural law can, at best, simply show us the impossibility of achieving moral perfection through our own efforts. Humanity is so embedded in original sin and through this concupiscence is such a powerful force in the world, that, at worst, the apparent 'good deeds' of nonChristians are really sins. Even the Ten Commandments can do little more on their own than convict us of our sinfulness:

We have in the Ten Commandments a summary of divine teaching. They tell us what we are to do to make our lives pleasing to God. They show us the true fountain from which, and the true channel in which, all good works must flow. No deed, no conduct can be good and pleasing to God, however worthy or precious it be in the eyes of the world, unless it accord with the Ten Commandments. Now let us see what our noted saints find to boast in their holy orders and the great and difficult tasks they have invented for themselves, at the same time neglecting the commandments as if they were too trivial or had long ago been fulfilled. My opinion is that we shall have our hands full in keeping these commandments – in practising gentleness, patience, love towards our enemies, chastity, kindness, and whatever other virtues they may include... Poor, blind people! They do not see that no one can perfectly observe even so much as one of the Ten Commandments; but the Creed and the Lord's Prayer must help us. Through them we must seek and beseech the grace of obedience, and receive it continually. (from *The Large Catechism*, conclusion to the Ten Commandments, trans. John Nicholas Lenker, *Luther On Christian Education: Luther's Catechetical Writings*).

For Luther, then, salvation is achieved emphatically not through human efforts, but solely through God's action. The notions of election and justification by faith were central to this position and, indeed, to the Reformation as a whole. God alone chooses whom to save and people in turn are saved, not through any works of their own, but solely by faith, that is, by faith itself given to people by God. For Luther, God 'foresees, determines and actually does all things, by his unchangeable, eternal and infallible will. By this thunderbolt the whole idea of free-will is smitten down and ground to powder' (*De Servo Arbitrio* 1.10). He would have flatly denied the advice of *The Rule of Benedict* that: 'If our wish be to have a dwelling place in his Kingdom, let us remember it can by no means be attained unless one run thither by good deeds' (from the Prologue, trans. W.K. Lowther Clarke, 1931). Yet Luther refrained from the, more strictly logical, Calvinist doctrine of double predestination, according to which the lot of both the saved and those to be eternally damned are predestined by God.

In Augustine, many of these ideas sat together uneasily. He held a doctrine of predestination, but it was relatively uninfluential compared with Luther's doctrine, being known mainly, not to ordinary churchgoers, but to scholars. He frequently emphasised grace and maintained that his own efforts to find God through the gnosis of Manichaeism had been disastrous. He knew and used Paul's notion of justification by faith and, like Luther, was convinced that all those who were not justified, even unbaptised infants who died, were damned. In contrast, Aquinas argued that unbaptised infants go to Limbo, where they certainly would not be punished. On the other hand, it has already been seen that Augustine did not reject free-will or rational/philosophical argument and that he used natural law positively, although not as systematically as Aquinas. Further, he did write, at times, about the Christian seeking moral perfection – but then, even Paul, despite his stress on grace, could also say that God 'will render to every man according to his works' (Rom. 2.6). If the bias of Augustine's soteriology is in Luther's direction, it is not a consistent bias.

Most complicated of all is Augustine's concept of 'grace'. For him, grace was essential, both to enable people to act rightly in the first place, and to allow them to continue to act rightly (cf. the scholastic distinction between prevenient and co-operant grace). Grace appears to be irresistible but, at the same time, it does not destroy free-will. Further, through its operations some, who are still damned, are enabled to do certain good works (i.e. Jews, 'heretics' and schismatics, but not complete 'pagans'), some are foreordained to become Christians through baptism, but backslide and are also damned, and others are elected, not just to be Christians, but also to receive the gift of final perseverance and, eventually, that of eternal life in heaven (cf. the scholastic distinction between sufficient and efficacious grace).

The issues raised here go to the very heart of some of the present-day differences within Christian ethics and constitute some of the most intractable problems facing the discipline. They also have strong resemblances to some of the key problems facing moral philosophy generally, notably those concerned with the issue of free-will versus biological or social determinism, that of reason versus emotion, and that of subjectivism versus objectivism within ethical analysis (see John Paul II's Extract 4).

11. *THEIR DOCTRINES OF CHURCH AND STATE*
It is often held that their doctrines of Church and State are readily distinguishable since: Augustine regarded Church and State as entirely separate realms, with the Church, as a temporary and, somewhat uneasy, resident in the State; Aquinas regarded them simply as different spheres of a single society, with the Church having primacy of authority; while Luther regarded the Church as always subordinate to the authority of the State. These positions are then frequently compared with Calvin's concept of theocracy and the Anabaptists' radical rejection of the State. But these superficial contrasts (which are well in evidence in Texts IV-VI) disguise more subtle differences and similarities between their positions. In relation to their socio-political contexts, Aquinas and Luther were closer to each other than to

Augustine. Augustine was writing at the beginning of the attempt by Christians to come to terms with the State and to make sense of the moral problems confronting, not just the individual within the State, but the State itself. Constantine's adoption of Christianity – for whatever personal motives – presented Christians with new problems, or problems from a new perspective which Ambrose almost alone, before Augustine, had begun seriously to tackle. It is hardly surprising that Augustine did not present a thoroughly consistent theory of the State, or of the relation between Church and State. Nor is it surprising that, in view of the State's pagan and sometimes anti-Christian past, he remained wary of identifying the Church too closely with the State. Yet, despite his sometimes vivid contrasts between the earthly and heavenly cities, Text IV shows that Augustine did see a relationship between earthly and heavenly peace, while Text VII shows how, at the risk of contradicting centuries of Christian pacifism, he adapted to the moral perspective created by the changed Church/State relations.

The socio-political contexts of Aquinas and Luther were quite different from that of Augustine. The 13th century witnessed the climax of the close relationship between the State and the Catholic Church, and Aquinas never appeared to regard the overall relationship as problematic. The boundaries between the two were boundaries of power and authority, not of opposing aims, values and social orders, and even Luther's challenge was concerned primarily with the former, rather than the latter. Neither Aquinas nor Luther conceived of anything resembling the 19th and 20th century notions of the 'secular State'. From this latter perspective, Calvin's Geneva and Rome in Aquinas' time appear remarkably similar. It is significant too that Luther, in Text VI, is still basically a medieval in his underlying economic assumptions – despite the possibility that he may have been instrumental in undermining these assumptions.

If these socio-political factors are taken seriously – and in this area of Christian ethics, at least, they surely must be taken seriously – it is dangerous to assume that when Barth appealed to Romans 13, as in Extract 6, his presuppositions, ideas and language were the same as those of Luther or Augustine when they appealed to the same passage. And none of them may have had much in common with the eschatalogically fragile world of Paul himself. The task of distinguishing between these various socio-political factors and the underlying Christian principles essential to an adequate theological understanding of Church-State relationships today, is one of the most difficult, but important, facing exponents of Christian ethics. It is also a task that directly affects one's understanding of the problems raised in the Extracts in Sections 2-5. In this sense, these are, indeed, perennial problems.

Students of Augustine, Aquinas and Luther are well served by these readable and authoritative studies:

Peter Brown, *Augustine of Hippo: A Biography* (his *Religion and Society in the Age of Saint Augustine* is also very useful); F.C. Copleston, *Aquinas* (see also his *History of Philosophy*); Roland H. Bainton, *Here I Stand: A Life of Martin Luther*.

Although there is no substitute for going back to their primary writings, other books will be recommended in relation to particular Texts. In attempting to make comparisons between their theological concepts of grace and original sin, it is worth recalling the important works of Williams:

N.P. Williams, *The Ideas of the Fall and of Original Sin*, the 1924 Bampton Lectures, and *The Grace of God*, a much slighter, but still readable, book.

THE EXTRACTS

The Extracts have been chosen to represent a wide spectrum of approaches within recent Christian ethics. So each Section attempts to offer a range of Extracts from Roman Catholic, Orthodox, Anglican and Reformed traditions. In addition, the Extracts from each of these traditions have been chosen to represent differing internal emphases (themselves sometimes as great as differences between traditions).

Thus, the Roman Catholic Extracts contain parts of three papal encyclicals, John XXIII's *Pacem in Terris*, Paul VI's *Humanae Vitae*, and John Paul II's *Veritatis Splendor*, Extracts 10, 24 and 4 (themselves of very different emphasis), traditionalist positions in Copleston's Extract 3 and Welty's Extract 12, a reformist position in the US Roman Catholic Bishops' Extract 14, and radical positions in Fiorenza's Extract 5, Miranda's Extract 11, and Ruether's Extract 26. Miranda is evidently influenced by the Reformed tradition and, possibly, has more in common with non-Roman Catholic Liberation theology than with traditional Roman Catholic Moral theology. Certainly he compares interestingly with the Methodist Bonino's Extract 16. Ruether now sits only ambiguously within the Roman Catholic tradition at all.

The Anglican Extracts vary from the modified natural law position of Temple in Extract 9, through the philosophically and theologically oriented approach of Clark's Extract 20, to the iconoclasm of Fletcher's Extracts 2 and 22. Anglican 'comprehensiveness' is well in evidence in these Extracts.

However, the Reformed Extracts show, perhaps, the greatest variety and the greatest internal divisions. Niebuhr's Extract 8 has similarities in style to the modified natural law approach of Temple. At the other end of the spectrum, is the radical rejection of secular ethics of Bonhoeffer's Extract 1, Barth's Extract 6 and Hauerwas' Extract 15. A combination of Reformed Christian ethics and radicalism can be found in both Bonino's Extract 16 and McFague's Extract 21.

The Orthodox tradition is represented in Berdyaev's Extract 7, Gregorios' Extract 18 and Ware's Extract 23. Ware represents a traditionalist approach to marriage and divorce, whereas Gregorios' offers a unique Indian/Orthodox approach to technology and the environment. Berdyaev was clearly influenced by his Russian Orthodoxy, but he was always too independent a philosopher to rest firmly in any single tradition. His mystical individualism was most evident in his understanding of sexuality. For him, the sexual act 'shackles man to that decadent order of nature, where reigns the endless relay of birth and death'; true love is 'a tormenting search for the androgynous image, for cosmic harmony', with male and female natures mystically fused into the androgynous image of God (*The Meaning of the Creative Act*, p.193). Overall, the strong Orthodox stress upon the Spirit and the spiritual is apparent in all three Extracts.

The internal variations apparent within these traditions, make inappropriate any simplistic identification of particular ethical approaches or stances with particular Churches. Naturally, there always have been internal differences within the Roman Catholic, Orthodox, Anglican or Reformed Churches. However, ecumenism and, with it, the growing tendency of professional theologians to read widely in traditions other than their own, make these differences considerably more complicated to analyse. At the same time, they make comparative analysis all the more interesting. Aquinas and Luther can no longer be described as the property of particular churches.

METHOD OF STUDY

The fact that this is a Textbook and not simply a Reader, requires that it should be used systematically. The System of Analysis, already outlined, requires particular attention and the description of it should be re-read as study of the Texts and Extracts progresses. There are three vital phases of a systematic study of these Texts and Extracts – comprehension, comparison, and critique – which should always be undertaken in that order:

1. *COMPREHENSION*
A student should read each Text and Extract several times carefully, first, to understand the general argument and, then, to be able to comprehend it in terms of the System of Analysis. At this stage, there is often a danger of becoming too involved in

the substantive issues in question, or of making premature comparisons or criticisms. Comprehension must take priority.

2. *COMPARISON*

The main comparison, around which this Textbook has been constructed, is that between Texts and Extracts. The System of Analysis is designed to make this comparison easier. In addition, the introduction to each section makes a number of overall comparisons between the Texts and the Extracts within it. It has already been thoroughly emphasised that comparisons between documents coming from very different ages and socio-political contexts should only be made with caution. Further, it should be stressed, that the thoughts of one theologian should only be compared with those of another *in all their complexity*. It is precisely this that has caused some of the greatest difficulties already in comparing the ideas of Augustine, Aquinas and Luther. Their views on a given issue were not always consistent throughout their writings. For example, Augustine's views on sexuality were, at some stages, more Manichaean and dualist than at other stages and Luther may have become more anti-Semitic as he grew older. Comparisons between Texts and Extracts, should keep in mind comparisons between the Texts or Extracts of a single author, represented elsewhere in this Textbook.

A third type of comparison can also be made, i.e. that between the various Extracts. This can be done in three separate ways; by comparing differing views on the substantive issue in question, by comparing the approaches of different traditions, or by comparing approaches from the same tradition but from different Sections of the book. All these comparisons will be made, at times, in the System of Analysis accompanying the various Texts and Extracts.

3. *CRITIQUE*

This is the most important phase, but it should be the last. An attempt should be made to assess the strengths and weaknesses of particular Texts and Extracts. Reference should be made, both to the method used and to the substantive issues raised and should be concerned both with the internal consistency of an author's arguments and with their external consistency with the arguments of other authors. It will also be important, sometimes, to raise questions about the social effects of a particular author's ideas.

As already mentioned, the five Sections of this Textbook can be studied in any order. Nonetheless, these three phases of study and their relative order should always be used in whichever Section is to be studied.

SECTION 1

METHODOLOGY

SECTION 1

METHODOLOGY

Fundamental differences are evident amongst exponents of
Christian ethics on both external and internal questions about
the nature of their discipline. And the following Texts and
Extracts have been chosen to illustrate some of these differences.
They are evident on *the external question* of the distinctiveness of
Christian ethics vis-à-vis secular forms of ethics. They are also
evident on *the internal question* of the relative importance to be
given, within the discipline, to the distinctively Christian appeals
to the Bible, to Christian tradition, to Christian experience and/
or to Christian belief. Yet answers to these questions have a
crucial effect upon the way the discipline of Christian ethics is
conceived and practised. It will be the object of this introduction
to focus upon these two questions.

The external question about the distinctiveness of Christian ethics
vis-à-vis moral philosophy is, in part, a modern problem. It was
Kant, after all, who insisted so emphatically that ethics is an
autonomous discipline (even though he subsequently advanced
a moral argument for the existence of God). And the separate
attacks of Kant and Hume on an assumed bond between
Christian ethics and Christian dogma did more than anything
else to produce the present-day gulf between Christian ethics
and moral philosophy. Our 20th-century assumption that moral
philosophy can, in principle, be conducted without reference to

55

God, is a clear product of 18th-century rationalism and a sharp departure from the medieval assumptions of Aquinas or from those of Luther (and one that is increasingly questioned today in Christian ethics – see Extracts 15 and 20). Even Augustine was primarily concerned with contrasting Christian ethics with 'heresy' and 'paganism' rather than with atheism (although see Text I.8).

Nonetheless, the fact that Aquinas was so concerned to explore correlations between Aristotelian ethics and Christian ethics makes his work highly relevant to a discussion of the external question. It does, at least, provide a clear answer to the problem of the relationship between Christian ethics and moral philosophy (as presented in Copleston's Extract 3). For Aquinas, there was no inherent conflict between Aristotelianism and Christianity, since the first was primarily concerned with what could be known through natural reason, whereas the second relied, in addition, upon supernatural revelation. As it was the same God who created the natural world, who established its laws, and was then revealed in Jesus Christ, there could be no inherent conflict between reason and revelation and thus, surely, no inherent conflict between Christian ethics and moral philosophy. Of course, particular moral philosophers might make mistakes in their reasoning, or they might even be wilfully perverse in their reasoning, and this, in turn, might lead to a conflict between the two disciplines. But, inherently, on Aquinas' assumptions, there need be no conflict.

In terms of the presuppositions derived from Luther, conflict appears distinctly more likely. Bonhoeffer's sharp contrast between ethics and Christian ethics, whilst owing something, as will be argued, to his particular social context, is consistent with his Lutheranism. Any individual quest for moral perfection, especially one guaranteed by the ministrations of the clergy or of the papacy, was rejected by Luther in favour of the doctrine of justification by faith. Morality is essentially a product of faith, not a means to faith, and certainly not an autonomous entity apart from faith. Whilst Luther clearly recognised the need for society to make laws in moral areas, and, indeed, continued to make appeals to natural law and to conscience when it suited his argument, his overall position was quite different from that of

Aquinas, (see *above*, pp.43f.). Human nature is far too corrupted by sin for it to be a reliable source of ethical judgments. By somewhat extending Luther's position, Bonhoeffer maintains that even evidence of human conscience, is, in fact, evidence of human disunion with God. When someone aspires to be a moral person, whilst ignoring Christ, that person is actually sinful. However, for Niebuhr, such a conclusion would be quite untenable. Although his Extract 8, in the next Section, shows a frequent stress upon sin and an attack on what Niebuhr regarded as unrealistic Christian utopianism, nonetheless he argued later in life that each person does have, naturally, some knowledge of the good and, indeed, that without this, 'faith in Christ could find no lodging place in the human soul' (*The Nature and Destiny of Man*, vol 1, p.281).

In relation to the external question, both of these overall positions can find echoes in Augustine's writings. In Text I he emphasises the reality of human free-will, despite its evident conflict with God's prescience. But, elsewhere he was not so consistent. For example, when expositing Romans 9.10, he wrote that, 'in this enquiry we laboured indeed on behalf of human free-will: but the grace of God won the day' (*Retractions* 2.1). More illuminatingly, elsewhere he could write that, 'to will or not to will is in the power of the man who wills or wills not, only in such a way that it does not impede God's will or vanquish his power' (*De Corr. et grat.* 14.43). But, even here, he could disconcertingly add that, 'God has men's wills more in his power than they themselves have their wills in their own power' (14.45). Since the reality of human free-will is a prerequisite of Aquinas' understanding of moral decision-making, but seems irrelevant to that of Luther, this ambivalence is highly significant. It is also an ambivalence which still affects present-day exponents of Christian ethics.

Serious doubts about the reality of human free-will stem from three distinct, although frequently interrelated, considerations. The first is a belief in the omniscience and omnipotence of God. This was one of Augustine's main problems: if God knows everything in advance and indeed created everything that exists, how is it that people can be said to choose anything on the basis of human volition, since even the will to choose has been created by God and all its contents are known to God at the moment of creation? The second concerns the corruption of humans and it was this which was one of the central focuses of Luther's thinking. If humans, through Adam, live in a constant state of sin, so that even the 'best' aspirations are corrupted by sin, it is difficult to see how, in any real sense, the human will remains 'free'. Indeed, from this perspective (viewing the Fall as a deprivation and not simply as a privation – see *above*, p.42), an insistence upon free-will raises suspicions of Pelagianism.

The third consideration involves social and physical determinism. If full account is taken of the sociological, psychological, biological and genetic factors determining human behaviour, it becomes notoriously difficult to maintain nonetheless that humans do possess free-will. The present-day explosion of knowledge about the human genome adds considerably to this problem. Once such determining factors are related to an individual's act of moral decision-making in a concrete situation, little room may have been left for free-will. In fact, even those philosophers who still claim that humans do possess free-will tend to admit that it is considerably more restricted than is popularly imagined (e.g. H.D. Lewis in *Philosophy of Religion*). In most situations one acts in one way, rather than another, because one is genetically shaped to do so, because one has been brought up to do so, because one is expected to do so by others and etc. – not because one consciously and freely chooses to do so. Although, naturally, he knew nothing of Freudian, Weberian, or genetic analysis, Augustine's critique of astrology shows that he knew something of these various factors (see *The City of God* V.2).

There are obvious connections here with other highly intractable problems in theology and philosophy. The problem of evil, in the context of Christianity, is intensified by an insistence upon the omnipotence and omniscience of God. And one of the 'solutions' offered by Christian theodicy is precisely that, if God were to give humans free-will, then God must also have allowed humans the possibility of moral evil as well as moral good – since the second makes no sense without the first. In this respect 'the problem of evil' and 'the problem of good' are inter-connected, though equally intractable. Again, if a Lutheran, such as Bonhoeffer, is tempted to distinguish 'better' secular regimes from others (as he appears to do elsewhere in *Ethics*) he may be in danger of reintroducing those secular ethical categories that he has methodologically rejected.

If a tension is often felt in theology between God's omnipotence and omniscience and human free-will and moral evil, the tension in philosophy between free-will, self-determination and physical and social determinism is just as severe. Recently, a number of philosophers, sometimes termed Compatibilists, have argued that free-will and thoroughgoing determinism are compatible. In various ways, they maintain that, the fact that people can reason and then act morally is sufficient evidence of free-will, even if their moral decisions are entirely predictable. So an ability to predict accurately the moral behaviour of particular individuals, or an ability to identify the antecedent causes of their moral reasoning, do not belittle the reality of their moral decision-making. Indeed, there is a clear difference, between an individual such as a psychopath who is incapable of moral reasoning, and an individual who is so capable, even if it is entirely predictable how both will behave.

An adapted version of Compatibilism could also be used to resolve some of the tension between God's omnipotence and omniscience and human free-will. So, it could be maintained that, the fact that God has created individuals whose actions are already known before their birth, does not of itself invalidate their moral reasoning. The key difference, here, between this version of Compatibilism and philosophical Compatibilism, is that the determinant (God) is already aware of what is determined. But this, in itself is a very crucial difference and is considerably complicated by the fact that terms like 'know' and even 'create' are used of God only analogically. If people could understand, in any literal sense, what it means for God to 'know' everything in advance, they would, of course, be God and not people.

Both versions of Compatibilism will seem unsatisfactory to some. The notion of free-will offered by Compatibilists is, clearly, not strong, particularly if the act of moral reasoning itself is thought to be determined. And in philosophical Compatibilism it might seem that an ontological, rather than simply methodological, determinism is too often assumed (see *above*, pp.24–5). In most recent understandings of Christian ethics, a rather stronger notion of free-will would seem to be required. It might even be possible for the Christian apologist to argue that, it is the fact that one believes in a created, rather than fortuitous, world and in people, within that world, who are created in the image of a loving God – a God possessing free-will – that one is given grounds for belief that people do have real free-will. Thus, without this creationist belief one might find it difficult to escape the conclusion that human actions are wholly determined by an ultimately fortuitous world. It is not necessary to draw from this argument the additional conclusion that secular ethics is a worthless undertaking, as Bonhoeffer might. The theist can still maintain that free-will, which is thought to be necessary by some secular moralists, is made possible by a loving God – whether or not the non-theist knows this.

The internal question concerning the relative importance to be given to the distinctively Christian appeals to the Bible, Christian tradition, Christian experience and Christian belief, reveal just as many differences between the Texts and the Extracts in this Section. The single-minded focus upon the Bible in Luther is apparent in all his Texts. In contrast, there are more appeals to tradition and to Aristotle than to the Bible in Aquinas' Text II. Interestingly, though, Luther's Text III opens with the criterion that if one finds one's 'heart confident that it pleases God, then the work is good' (III.1). Augustine, in Text I, is more philosophical than exegetical. However, their differing approaches to the Bible have already been discussed (see *above*, pp.39–42).

Within the Extracts, one of the most important differences is caused by the claims of situation ethics. Fletcher's book *Situation Ethics*, coinciding with the radical writings and utterances of Bishop John Robinson in Britain and of Bishop Pike and others in the States, proved remarkably influential in the 1960s and early 1970s. Its somewhat anecdotal and superficial style reads oddly in comparison with the other Extracts, but its position cannot be ignored. Indeed, few works in Christian ethics have been written, since its publication, without making some reference to it. Its iconoclasm has irritated many and soon it will be observed that its criticisms of 'legalism' fail to take fully into account Aquinas' complex theory of exceptions. Further, many have argued that Fletcher's characteristic method of arguing from irregular paradigms (see 2.18f) distorts Christian ethics – just as, at the secular level, no nation can construct a legal system on the basis of exceptions. Fletcher tends to write as if no one had ever thought seriously about exceptions before him. However, when all these points have been made, his thoroughgoing stress upon *agape* and his overall personalist approach to Christian ethics, have undoubtedly found important sympathisers. For them, personalism and agapism accord more fully with present-day consciousness than Aquinas' theory of natural law.

There are also obvious similarities between Fletcher's and Bonhoeffer's accounts of Christian ethics. For Bonhoeffer, too, the discipline is predominantly personalist (see 1.13f) and it is based upon a single criterion, the 'Call of Christ'. Further, both men justify their positions in relation to what they take to be the central thrust of the New Testament (see 2.9-10). But, in relation to the external question, mentioned earlier, they are quite different. Bonhoeffer sees a sharp divide between ethics and Christian ethics, whereas, for Fletcher, Christian and non-Christian situation ethics differ only in the *summum bonum* (highest good) regarded as their standard (see 2.11) and, in practice, he moves almost imperceptibly from one discipline to the other (see Extract 22). Fletcher's approving quotation from Bonhoeffer (2.5) ignores this crucial difference between them.

Fletcher's differences with other Anglicans also emerge in Extract 2. He specifically rejects the notion of 'middle axioms' that Temple and others within the Life and Work Movement in the 1930s believed to be so important. In part, his rejection is based upon a semantic quibble (2.13), but, in part, it may be based upon a correct realisation that the notion of 'middle axioms' assumes a modified natural law theory – itself, of course, assumed by Temple. The Church of Scotland's war-time 'Baillie Commission' accurately described this notion:

It is... the duty of the Church in our day and place to guide the individual, within... limits of its competence... what to do with his vote and in what directions to exercise his influence. The requisite principles for the implementing of this duty are fully available to us in the New Testament. No new principles are necessary or are permissible, but only the application of the dominical and apostolic teaching to a situation different from that in which our Lord and His first disciples were ever called upon to stand... It is clear, however, that the carrying out of such a task will involve the formulation, in each case, of certain secondary and more specialised principles to the particular field of action in which guidance is needed. 'Middle axioms' they have been called... They are not such as to be appropriate to every time and place and situation, but they are offered as legitimate and necessary applications of the Christian rule of faith and life to the special circumstances in which we now stand (*God's Will for Church and Nation*, pp.445).

This understanding of Christian ethics adheres, more strictly, to a use only of those principles that can be derived from the Bible, than do traditional understandings of natural law theory. It clearly wishes to avoid the sort of casuistry and complex theory of exceptions also associated with the latter. Nonetheless, it seeks to take both general principles and the exigencies of particular situations seriously by developing, admittedly fallible, secondary principles for these exigencies. It is in this sense that it can be identified as a modified natural law theory and it is probably in this aspect that it is most sharply differentiated from Fletcher's situation ethics.

Finally, Fletcher's case-study on abortion can be compared with Paul VI's Extract 24 (and the latter, in turn, with Fiorenza's Extract 5). The substantive issues will be discussed in Section 5, but, for the moment, it is worth comparing Fletcher's suppositions about 'legalist' positions with those of Paul VI. Again, it appears that Fletcher has blurred distinctions and oversimplified positions. Nonetheless, it is perhaps, his position on abortion which more nearly represents the position of many Christians today. In contrast, his position on euthanasia in Extract 22 may be more radical than that of many Christians. Taken together, the two Fletcher Extracts point to the pluralism that has increasing appeared to characterise Christian ethics at the turn of the millennium. It will be noted in the critique at the end of this Section that even when positions in Christian ethics are asserted stridently – as they are in John Paul II's Extract 4 and Fiorenza's Extract 5 – when set side by side they ironically become examples of moral pluralism within Christianity (and, in this instance, of pluralism within Catholicism).

TEXT I
AUGUSTINE
God's foreknowledge and human free-will

1. BACKGROUND

This Text comes from *The City of God* V.9-11 (Pelican Classics, trans. Henry Bettenson and David Knowles (ed), Penguin, 1972, pp.190-6). Consisting altogether of 22 books, *The City of God* was Augustine's most substantial work and a vital source for his mature theology. It was inspired by Alaric's sacking of Rome in 410 and in it he set out to demonstrate that this event was a punishment for Rome's paganism and not the result (as 'pagans' claimed) of the Emperor's adoption of Christianity. To achieve this demonstration he attempted to expose a number of key 'pagan' notions (e.g. 'fate') and to ridicule the whole idea that the 'pagan gods' had, in any way, protected Rome from her enemies. In contrast to this, Augustine elaborated the concept of the heavenly city, founded and ruled alone by God revealed in Jesus Christ (see further, Text IV). He started the work in 413, but did not finish it until 426, writing Book V in about 416. He later described it as follows: 'The first five books refute those who attribute prosperity and adversity to the cult of the gods or to the prohibition of this cult. The next five are against those who hold that ills are never wanting to men, but that worship of the gods helps towards the future life after death. The second part of the work contains twelve books. The first four describe the birth of the two cities, one of God, the other of this world. The second four continue their story, and the third four depict their final destiny' (*Retractions* 2,43,2). In relation to the following Text, it is important to realise that the Pelagian controversy was taking place then, but, despite its obvious relevance to the theme of free-will, it is seldom mentioned in the work. Cicero's *On the Nature of the Gods*, which had been an important influence on Augustine in his Manichaean phase, however, is explicitly attacked here.

2. KEY ISSUES

Augustine is concerned in this Text to defend both God's prescience and human free-will. He is fully aware of a potential conflict between the two, but rejects Cicero's resolution of this conflict in terms of denying God's prescience (I.2-3). For Augustine, God 'knows all things before they happen', but this does not imply either a notion of 'fate' or a denial of human free-will (I.4). Distinguishing between 'natural' and 'voluntary' causes, he regards God as the author of the first, but insists that God still allows humans the second (I.6-8). So human will has 'only as much power as God has willed and foreknown' (I.9). Augustine also seeks to refute the Stoic understanding of 'necessity' as a limitation which abolishes freedom for God or humans (I.10-11). Free-will is not invalidated by God's foreknowledge, but rather, the very fact that God does foreknow human free-will, demonstrates its genuine existence – since otherwise there would be nothing to foreknow (I.12-13). God has indeed created humans free (I.14).

3. ETHICAL ARGUMENTS

There is a strong deontological emphasis throughout his refutation of Cicero and the Stoics. Augustine treats both God's prescience and human free-will as given and simply accuses his opponents of 'profanity' and 'impudence'(I.4), potential atheism (I.8) and 'blasphemy' (I.12). For him, their position is manifestly wrong and it is sufficient to demonstrate that they deny either prescience or free-will. Natural law assumptions are also apparent in the Text, notably in his claim that 'evil wills do not proceed from him because they are contrary to the nature which proceeds from him': the natural, for natural law theory, in itself is always good (I.7). A more consequential argument is introduced in I.12-13: the reality of human free-will, prayer, exhortations and sin can be derived from the fact that God foresees them, since, if they did not exist, God could not foresee them.

4. BASES OF CHRISTIAN ETHICS

Augustine's two uses of the Psalms in this Text illustrate two different uses of the Bible. In I.4 the Psalms play a central role in his argument, but in I.8 they merely provide a flourish at the end of the argument. However, it is the doctrine of creation which provides the central basis of Augustine's position (especially in I.14). He is particularly offended by Cicero, since he believes that his contentions undermine the very basis of God as creator (I.8). In his defence of the latter, he is convinced that 'pagan' notions, such as fate, must be refuted by the Christian as 'profane and irreverent impudence' (I.4).

5. *SOCIAL DETERMINANTS*

Various facets of Augustine's pre-Christian life have influenced the argument in this Text. Cicero's notions are singled out for particular attack and Augustine's own previous interest in, and subsequent rejection of, astrology is evident. Free-will is defended, but, above all, he stresses the power of God: his own rejection of Pelagianism is evident, as is the strong conviction of the convert that it is God who is triumphant. Augustine, the former rhetorician, is also strongly in evidence (although this is even more the case in his much earlier *On the Free Choice of the Will*). It might even be claimed that a defence of free-will comes more naturally to one from the middle classes than one, like Luther, who has known, at first hand, the social constraints upon the agrarian working classes. In addition, in his arguments about the very notions of 'prescience' and 'free-will', Augustine shows that he was heir, more to the Graeco-Roman world, than to the Hebraic world: even his declaration of faith (in I.14) uses the non-biblical notions of 'omnipotence' and 'soul' (see further, p.268 *below*).

6. *SOCIAL SIGNIFICANCE*

Augustine's twin stresses upon the prescience/omnipotence of God and the free-will of humans had a very considerable effect upon subsequent theology and upon Western thought. His correlation between neo-Platonic and biblical notions proved enormously influential and served to give Christianity a new intellectual credibility. He also bequeathed a, sometimes puzzling, combination of Graeco-Roman and Hebraic notions, particularly in the areas of Christian anthropology and eschatology.

FURTHER READING

In addition to the primary reading from *On the Free Choice of the Will* and from *The City of God* and the secondary reading suggested in the Introduction on Augustine, N.P. Williams' *The Ideas of the Fall and of Original Sin* is particularly important.

TEXT I

AUGUSTINE

God's foreknowledge and human free-will

I.1

For our part, whatever may be the twists and turns of philosophical dispute and debate, we recognise a God who is supreme and true and therefore we confess his supreme power and foreknowledge. We are not afraid that what we do by an act of will may not be a voluntary act, because God, with his infallible prescience, knew that we should do it. This was the fear that led Cicero to oppose foreknowledge and the Stoics to deny that everything happens by necessity, although they maintained that everything happens according to fate.

I.2

Now what was it that Cicero so dreaded in prescience of the future, that he struggled to demolish the idea by so execrable a line of argument? He reasoned that if all events are foreknown, they will happen in the precise order of that foreknowledge; if so, the order is determined in the prescience of God. If the order of events is determined, so is the causal order; for nothing can happen unless preceded by an efficient cause. If the causal order is fixed, determining all events, then all events, he concluded, are ordered by destiny. If this is true, nothing depends on us and there is no such thing as free will. 'Once we allow this,' he says, 'all human life is overthrown. There is no point in making laws, no purpose in expressing reprimand or approbation, censure or encouragement; there is no justice in establishing rewards for the good and penalties for the evil.'

I.3

It is to avoid those consequences, discreditable and absurd as they are, and perilous to human life, that Cicero refuses to allow any foreknowledge. And he constrains the religious soul to this dilemma, forcing it to choose between those propositions: either there is some scope for our will, or there is foreknowledge. He thinks that both cannot be true; to affirm one is to deny the other. If we choose foreknowledge, free-will is annihilated; if we choose free-will, prescience is abolished. And so, being a man of eminent learning, a counsellor of wide experience and practised skill in matters affecting human life, Cicero chooses free-will. To support this, he denies foreknowledge and thus, in seeking to make men free, he makes them irreverent. For the religious mind chooses both, foreknowledge as well as liberty; it acknowledges both, and supports both in pious faith. 'How?' asks Cicero. If there is prescience of the future, the logical consequences entailed lead to the conclusion that nothing depends on our free-will. And further, if anything does so depend, then, by the converse logical process, we reach the position that there is no foreknowledge. The argument proceeds thus: if there is free-will, everything does not happen by fate; if everything does not happen by fate, there is not a fixed order of all causes; if there is not a fixed order of all causes, there is not a fixed order of events for the divine prescience, for these events cannot take place unless preceded by efficient causes; if there is not a fixed order for God's prescience, everything does not happen as he has foreknown them as due to happen. Thus, he concludes, if everything does not happen as foreknown by God, then there is in him no foreknowledge of all the future.

I.4

Against such profane and irreverent impudence we assert both that God knows all things before they happen and that we do by our free-will everything that we feel and know would not happen without our volition. We do not say that everything is fated; in fact we deny that anything happens by destiny. For we have shown that the notion of destiny, in the accepted sense, referring to conjunction of stars at the time of conception or birth, has no validity, since it asserts something which has no reality. It is not that we deny a causal order where the will of God prevails; but we do not describe it by the word 'fate', unless perhaps if we understand fate to be derived from *fari* (speak), that is from the act of speaking. We cannot in fact deny that it is written in Scripture, 'God has spoken once, and I have heard those two things: that the power belongs to God; and that mercy belongs to you, Lord, and you render to each in accordance with his works' [Ps. 61.11f]. The words 'has spoken *once*' mean 'he has spoken *immovably*', that is, unalterably, just as he knows unalterably all that is to happen and what he himself is going to do. For this reason we should be able to use the work 'fate', deriving it from *fari*, except that this word is generally used in a different sense, a sense to which we should not wish men's hearts to be directed.

I.5

Now if there is for God a fixed order of all causes, it does not follow that nothing depends on our free choice. Our wills themselves are in the order of causes, which is, for God, fixed, and is contained in his foreknowledge, since human acts of will are the causes of human activities. Therefore he who had prescience of the causes of all events certainly could not be ignorant of our decisions, which he foreknows as the causes of our actions.

I.6

Cicero's own concession that nothing happens unless preceded by an efficient cause is enough to refute him in the present question. It does not help his case to assert that while no event is causeless, not every cause is the work of destiny, since there are fortuitous causes, natural, and voluntary causes. It is enough that he admits that every event must be preceded by a cause. For our part, we do not deny the existence of causes called 'fortuitous' (from the same root as the word 'fortune'); only we say that they are hidden causes and attribute them to the will, either of the true God, or of spirits of some kind. The 'natural' causes we do not detach from the will of God, the author and creator of all nature. The 'voluntary' causes come from God, or from angels, or men, or animals – if indeed one can apply the notion of will to the movements of beings devoid of reason, which carry out actions in accordance with their nature, to achieve some desire or to avoid some danger. By the wills of angels I mean both the wills of the good angels of God, as we call them, and of the evil 'angels of the devil', or even 'demons'. The same applies to the wills of men; there are those of good men, and those of evil.

I.7
This implies that the only efficient causes of events are voluntary causes, that is, they proceed from that nature which is the 'breath of life'. ('Breath' also refers to the air or the wind; but since that is corporeal, it is not the 'breath of life'.) The breath of life, which gives life to everything, and is the creator of every body and every created Spirit (breath), is God himself, the uncreated spirit. In his will rests the supreme power, which assists the good wills of created spirits, sits in judgment on the evil wills, orders all wills, granting the power of achievement to some and denying it to others. Just as he is the creator of all natures, so he is the giver of all power of achievement, but not of all acts of will. Evil wills do not proceed from him because they are contrary to the nature which proceeds from him. Bodies are mostly subject to wills, some to our wills – that is to the wills of mortal beings, the wills of men rather than of animals – the others to the wills of angels. But all bodies are subject above all to the will of God, and to him all wills also are subject, because the only power they have is the power that God allows them.

I.8
Thus the cause which is cause only, and not effect, is God. But other causes are also effects, as are all created spirits and in particular the rational spirits. Corporeal causes, which are more acted upon than active, are not be counted among efficient causes, since all they can achieve is what is achieved through them by the wills of spirits. How then does the order of causes, which is fixed in the prescience of God, result in the withdrawal of everything from dependence on our will, when our acts of will play an important part in that causal order? Let Cicero dispute with those who assert that this causal order is decided

by destiny, or rather who give that order the name of destiny, or fate – a position which shocks us particularly because of that word 'fate', which is generally understood in a way which corresponds to nothing in the real world. But when Cicero denies that the order of all causes is completely fixed and perfectly known to God's foreknowledge we execrate his opinion even more than do the Stoics. For either he denies the existence of God, which indeed he has been at pains to do, in the person of a disputant in his treatise *On the Nature of the Gods*; or else, if he acknowledges God's existence while denying his foreknowledge, he is even so saying, in effect, exactly what 'the fool has said in his heart'; for he is saying, 'God does not exist' [Ps. 14.1]. For a being who does not know all the future is certainly not God.

I.9

Thus our wills have only as much power as God has willed and foreknown; God, whose foreknowledge is infallible, has foreknown the strength of our wills and their achievements, and it is for that reason that their future strength is completely determined and their future achievements utterly assured. That is why, if I had decided to apply the term 'destiny' at all, I should be more ready to say that the destiny of the weak is the will of the stronger, who has the weak in his power, than to admit that destiny, in the Stoic sense of 'the causal order' (a use peculiar to Stoics, in conflict with the generally accepted one) does away with the free decision of our will.

I.10

There is no need, then, to dread that 'necessity', through fear of which the Stoics took such pains to distinguish between the causes of things, withdrawing some of them from the sway of necessity, subjecting others to it, and classing our wills among the causes they wished to emancipate from necessity, for fear, I suppose, that they would not be free if subject to it. Now if, in our case, 'necessity' is to be used of what is not in our control, of what achieves its purpose whether we will or no – the 'necessity' of death, for example – then it is obvious that our wills, by the exercise of which we lead a good life or a bad, are not subject to a necessity of this kind. We do a great many things which we should not have done if we had not wished to. In the first place, our willing belongs to this class of acts. If we so wish, it exists; if we do not so wish, it does not; for we should not will, if we did not so wish.

I.11

If, on the other hand, we define 'necessity' in the sense implied when we say that it is necessary a thing should be thus, or should happen thus, I see no reason to fear that this would rob us of free will. We do not subject the life and the foreknowledge of God to necessity, if we say that it is 'necessary' for God to be eternal and to have complete foreknowledge; nor is his power diminished by saying that he cannot die or make a mistake. The reason why he cannot is that, if he could, his power would certainly be less; and he is rightly called 'all-powerful', although he has not the power to die, or to be mistaken. 'All-powerful' means that he does what he wills, and does not suffer what he does not will; otherwise he would be by no means all-powerful. It is just because he is all-powerful that there are some things he cannot do. The same applies when we say that it is 'necessary' that when we will, we will by free choice. That statement is undisputable; and it does not mean that we are subjecting our free-will to a necessity which abolishes freedom. Our wills are ours and it is our wills that affect all that we do by willing, and which would not have happened if we had not willed. But when anyone has something done to him against his will, here, again, the effective power is will, not his own will, but another's. But the power of achievement comes from God. For if there was only the will without the power of realisation, that will would have been thwarted by a more powerful will. Even so, that will would have been a will, and the will not of another, but of him who willed, although it was incapable of realisation. Hence, whatever happens to man against his will is to be attributed not to the wills of men, or angels, or any created spirits, but to the will of him who gives the power of realisation.

I.12

It does not follow, then, that there is nothing in our will because God foreknew what was going to be in our will; for if he foreknew this, it was not nothing that he foreknew. Further, if in foreknowing what would be in our will, he foreknew something, and not nonentity, it follows immediately that there is something in our will, even if God foreknows it. Hence we are in no way compelled either to preserve God's prescience by abolishing our free-will, or to safeguard our free-will by denying (blasphemously) the divine foreknowledge. We embrace both truths, and acknowledge them in faith and sincerity, the one for a right belief, the other for a right life. And yet a man's life cannot be right without a right belief about God. Therefore, let us never dream of denying his foreknowledge in the interests of our freedom; for it is with his help that we are, or shall be, free.

I.13

By the same token, it is not true that reprimands, exhortations, praise and blame are useless, because God has knowledge of them before; they are of the greatest efficacy in so far as he has foreknown that they would be effective. And prayers are effectual in obtaining all that God foreknew that he would grant in answer to them; and it is with justice that rewards are appointed for good actions and punishments for sins. The fact that God foreknew that a man would sin does not make a man sin; on the contrary, it cannot be doubted that it is the man himself who sins just because he whose prescience cannot be mistaken has foreseen that the man himself would sin. A man does not sin unless he wills to sin; and if he had willed not to sin, then God would have foreseen that refusal.

I.14

Thus God is the supreme reality, with his Word and the Holy Spirit – three who are one. He is the God omnipotent, Creator and maker of every soul and every body; participation in him brings happiness to all who are happy in truth and not in illusion; he has made man a rational animal, consisting of soul and body; and when man sins he does not let him go unpunished, nor does he abandon him without pity. He has given, to good men and bad alike, the existence they share with the stones; he has given man reproductive life which he shares with the plants, the life of the senses, which he shares with the animals, and the life of the intellect, shared only the with the angels. From him derives every mode of being, every species, every order, all measure, number, and weight. He is the source of all that exists in nature, whatever its kind, whatsoever its value, and of the seeds of forms, and the forms of seeds, and the motions of seeds and forms. He has given to flesh its origin, beauty, health, fertility in propagation, the arrangement of the bodily organs, and the health that comes from their harmony. He has endowed even the soul of irrational creatures with memory, sense, and appetite, but above all this, he has given to the rational soul thought, intelligence, and will. He has not abandoned even the inner parts of the smallest and lowliest creature, or the bird's feather (to say nothing of the heavens and the earth, the angels and mankind) – he has not left them without a harmony of their constituent parts, a kind of peace. It is beyond anything incredible that he should have willed the kingdoms of men, their dominations and their servitudes, to be outside the range of the laws of his providence.

CRITIQUE

It has already been seen that the tension between ascribing prescience/omnipotence to God and free-will to humans is a serious one – in Christianity, Judaism and Islam. If God is seen as all-powerful, all-knowing and all-loving, then it is difficult to see why there is evil in the world and how humans are really able to have free-will. Augustine solved neither problem.

At one level, his argument in I.12-13 appears to work. If George is able to foretell what Stephen is going to will in a particular situation, this fact does not diminish Stephen's free-will. It might imply a notion of 'fate' apparently incompatible with real free-will, but his own foreknowledge as such does not do so. But the difference between George and God is that one is creature and the other creator. If it is the creator, who has given existence to all that is, including Stephen's very will, who is the one to know, in advance, what Stephen is to will, his free-will appears considerably more problematic. The greater the stress on the power of God, the more people appear as automata created by God. Further, Augustine only vaguely considers the possibility that, whilst God may know of all the millions of human potential choices at the moment of creation, nevertheless, God's loving condescension might allow humans to make the actual choices.

Naturally, it is no criticism of Augustine to say that he did not fully resolve all of these major problems. Many exponents of ethics, whether Christian or not, would insist that free-will is a prerequisite of moral behaviour and, as a result, they are forced into the tensions mentioned earlier. Indeed, there is something curiously circular and nonsensical about thoroughgoing theories of social, biological or even theological, determinism: for, if they are true, then we cannot properly know them to be true, since presumably, both they and our perceptions of them, are themselves completely determined and possibly thereby distorted (see further, Extract 4).

TEXT II
AQUINAS
Natural law

1. BACKGROUND

This Text comes from *Summa Theologica*, 1a2ae, 94, 4-6 (vol XXVIII of the English Dominican translation, Blackfriars with Eyre & Spottiswoode, London, and McGraw-Hill, New York, 1966). Aquinas wrote this, his major but unfinished work, from 1265 until his mystical experience of December 1273, shortly before his death. It is designed as a textbook for 'theological novices' – hence its style of starting with a question, raising objections and counter-objections and then giving a reply and conclusions. As befits a textbook, *Summa Theologica* is liberally sprinkled with quotations, from Aristotle (e.g. *Ethics* in II.1.2), the Bible, Cicero, the early Fathers, Augustine (see particularly Text VIII), Isidore (of Seville, d.636, whose *Etymologies* was the main encyclopedia of classical learning for the Middle Ages, in II.1 & 8.3) and more recent authorities like Gratian (whose *Decretum* of 1141, reviewing existing legislation in the Western Church, was regarded as seminal in the Middle Ages, along with Lombard's *Sentences* in theology, in II.1.1, 7.1 & 8). The text comes from the major section in *Summa Theologica*, *Prima Secundae*, which, together with *Secunda Secundae*, deals with Christian ethics. The initial section, *Prima Pars* (cited in II.11.2), is mainly concerned with the existence and attributes of God, while the last section, *Tertia Pars*, deals with christology and ecclesiology. Aquinas has distinguished four types of law – eternal, natural, human and divine. For him 'law is nothing but a dictate of practical reason issued by a sovereign who governs a complete community'. God is indeed a sovereign and it can be held that 'the whole community of the universe is governed by God's mind'. This governance is eternal law. However, this law can be known properly only to God and those who have seen

God. As intelligent creatures, humans can join in and make this eternal law their own and, in so far as they do, this is natural law: 'natural law is nothing other than the sharing in the eternal law by intelligent creatures'. Human laws, themselves derived from natural law, are also necessary, because of the limitations of human reason. And finally, divine law is essential for salvation: humans have been designed for 'an eternal happiness out of proportion to their natural resources... and therefore must need be directed by a divinely given law above natural and human law... Although through natural law the eternal law is shared in according to the capacity of human nature, nevertheless in order to be directed to their ultimate supernatural end men have to be lifted up' (*S. T.*, 1a2ae 91). Hence the need for revelation. Thus, grace can be seen to crown nature and faith can be seen to crown reason (see *above*, pp.43–5).

2. *KEY ISSUES*

In this Text, Aquinas focuses specifically upon natural law and responds to three questions:

(a) Is natural law the same for all? Despite empirical indications to the contrary (see further Copleston's Extract 3), Aquinas is convinced that natural law is ubiquitous in humans. Following Aristotle, he believes that humans have a natural tendency towards happiness or well-being (*eudaimonia*), leading ultimately, for the Christian, to a beatific vision of God. This is the 'end' of humans (in both senses) and is the main spur for morality in all people. Morality is to be discerned through the use of 'practical reason' whereas 'science' is to be discerned through theoretic reason. But, of course, humans are fallible in their use of practical reason – even more fallible than in their use of theoretic reason (II.4). But the general principles of both types of reason remain the same for all people, whether they actually recognise them or not. Secondary principles, derived from the general principles of morality, are also the same for most people. But here, error, sin or bad customs may distort these secondary principles (II.6).

(b) Can natural law be changed? General principles are unalterable, but secondary principles may occasionally be altered.

Like Augustine, (see *above*, p.39), Aquinas believed, on the basis of the Old Testament, that God can sometimes go against natural law (II.11.2). In addition, although humans cannot contradict natural law, they can sometimes add to it (II.11.3).

(c) Can natural law be abolished from the human heart? Again, general principles cannot be destroyed in any person, although, in particular situations, 'lust and passion can over ride them, (II.13). Secondary principles, in contrast, can be effectively destroyed by error, sin and bad customs.

3. ETHICAL ARGUMENTS

The Aristotelian framework to Aquinas' theory of ethics tends to give it a consequential bias. The *telos*, *finis* or 'end' of humans provides the spur for morality and, as will be seen in the substantive Texts, ultimately directs his ethical analysis of particular issues. Thus, for him, 'the objects to which men have a natural tendency are the concern of natural law, and among, such tendencies it is proper to man to act according to reason' (II.2). But, as can also be seen from this quotation, there is a strong deontological assumption underlying it: an understanding of human nature reveals human moral obligations. An identification is made between description and prescription: people 'are' created thus and also 'ought' to behave thus. Further, the precepts of natural law are also contained (prescriptively) in divine law (II.7.1).

4. BASES OF CHRISTIAN ETHICS

The Bible is seen to be in keeping with natural law, although, of course, it adds to it (II.7.1) and, sometimes, produces exceptions to it (II.11.2). Significantly and, perhaps erroneously, he views Romans 2 in the light of natural law theory (II.12.1). As already noted, he characteristically refers to a large body of Christian and pre-Christian tradition and, through Aristotle, to the natural rational 'experience' of humans. Further, just as humans perceive the general principles of theoretic reason through *intellectus*, they perceive the general principles of practical reason through *synderesis* (not quite 'conscience', but still an innate human faculty).

5. SOCIAL DETERMINANTS

Aquinas derived this theory of natural law from a number of classical and Christian sources (see P.M. Farrell, 'Sources of St.Thomas' Concept of Natural Law', *The Thomist*, 20, 3, 1957). Aristotle distinguished between natural justice and conventional, or written, law, and Aquinas extensively used and adapted his theory of knowledge. In addition, Aquinas used Roman legal thinking, often mediated through Cicero, and Augustine's concept of eternal law. The whole balance that he achieved between the four types of law may well reflect the confidence and feltbalance of medieval Christendom. Certainly, it is far removed from the radical discontinuities of Augustine and of Luther, in their ages of revolutionary change. In addition, the 'once born' religious personality of Aquinas might possibly be compared with the liminality of Augustine's and Luther's convert personalities. Correlation and inclusiveness characterised both his theoretical position and his personality.

6. SOCIAL SIGNIFICANCE

Through modern Thomism and neo-Thomism, Aquinas' theory of natural law has continued to have a considerable effect upon theology. Even Reformed theologians, such as Niebuhr in his later writings, have been significantly influenced by it. There are signs, too, that Aquinas' work continues to be of interest among some moral philosophers. Although he borrowed extensively from previous sources, his achievement in producing a system of moral, theological and metaphysical concepts is unique. In this respect, he both reflected and surpassed the ambitions of 13th-century Catholicism.

FURTHER READING

S.T. 1a2ae 90-7 is the basic primary source for Aquinas' natural law theory. Copleston's *Aquinas* (Extract 3) offers a sympathetic guide to his theory and D.J. O'Connor's *Aquinas and Natural Law* provides a critical account of it in the light of present-day moral philosophy. N.D. O'Donoghue's article 'Towards a Theory of Exceptions', *Irish Theological Quarterly*, Sept, 1968, provides a clear account of Aquinas' theory of exceptions in the light of the situation ethics debate – there will be further discussion of this in relation to Extract 3, Text VIII and Text XIV. For an analysis of the wider legal, political and ethical aspects of natural law theory, see A.P. D'Entrèves' *Natural Law: An Introduction to Legal Philosophy*. For a recent sympathetic, but more radical, approach to Aquinas, see Jean Porter's *The Recovery of Virtue: The Relevance of Aquinas for Christian Ethics* and *Moral Action and Christian Ethics*.

TEXT II
AQUINAS
Natural law

Is natural law the same for all?

II.I.
OBJECTIONS:
   i. Apparently natural law is not the same for everybody. It is stated in the *Decretum* that 'the natural law is that contained in the Law and the Gospel'. Taken so it is not common to everybody; it is said in Romans, 'All do not obey the Gospel' [Rom. 10.16]. Therefore natural law is not the same for everybody.

   ii. According to the Ethics, 'All lawful acts are said to be just acts'. Yet in the same work it is remarked that nothing is so just for all as not to vary for some. Natural law, then, is not identical for all.

   iii. Or put the matter like this, it has been said that objectives sought because of man's very constitution belong to natural law. These are different in different men, for by their constitution some are moved by desire for pleasure, others by ambition for honour, and others by other incentives. Therefore there is not one natural law for all.

ON THE OTHER HAND Isidore says, Natural right is common to all nations.

II.2
REPLY: As we have shown, the objects to which men have a natural tendency are the concern of natural law, and among

suchtendencies it is proper to man to act according to reason. Now a characteristic of reason is to proceed from common principles to particular conclusions: this is remarked in the *Physics*. However the theoretic reason and the practical reason set about this somewhat differently. The business of the theoretic reason is with natural truths that cannot be otherwise, and so without mistake it finds truth in the particular conclusions it draws as in the premises it starts from. Whereas the business of the practical reason is with contingent matters which are the domain of human acts, and although there is some necessity in general principles the more we get down to particular cases the more we can be mistaken.

II.3
So then in questions of theory, truth is the same for everybody, both as to principles and to conclusions, though admittedly all do not recognise truth in the conclusions, but only in those principles which are called 'common conceptions'. In questions of action, however, practical truth and goodwill are not the same for everybody with respect to particular decisions, but only with respect to common principles; and even those who are equally in the right on some particular course of action are not equally aware of how right they are.

II.4
So then it is evident that with respect to general principles of both theory and practice what is true or right is the same for all and is equally recognised. With respect to specific conclusions of theory the truth is the same for all, though all do not equally recognise it, for instance some are not aware that the angles of a triangle together equal two right angles. With respect to particular conclusions come to by the practical reason there is no general unanimity about what is true or right, and even when there is agreement there is not the same degree of recognition.

II.5
All hold that it is true and right that we should act intelligently. From this starting point it is possible to advance the specific conclusion, that goods held in trust are to be restored to their

owners. This is true in the majority of cases, yet a case can crop up when to return the deposit would be injurious, and consequently unreasonable, as for instance were it to be required in order to attack one's country. The more you descend into the detail the more it appears how the general rule admits of exceptions, so that you have to hedge it with cautions and qualifications. The greater the number of conditions accumulated the greater the number of ways in which the principle is seen to fall short, so that all by itself it cannot tell you whether it be right to return a deposit or not.

II.6

TO SUM UP: as for its first common principles, here natural law is the same for all in requiring a right attitude towards it as well as recognition. As for particular specific points, which are like conclusions drawn from common principles, here also natural law is the same for most people in their feeling for and awareness of what is right. Nevertheless in fewer cases either the desire or the information may be wanting. The desire to do right may be blocked by particular factors – so also with physical things that come to be and die away there are occasional anomalies and failures due to some obstruction – and the knowledge also of what is right may be distorted by passion or bad custom or even by racial proclivity; for instance, as Julius Caesar narrates, the Germans did not consider robbery wicked, though it is expressly against natural law.

II.7

HENCE:

    i. The text should not be taken to mean that everything in the Old and New Laws is of natural law, since many things there imparted are above our nature. It means that natural law precepts are there fully covered. So when Gratian says that 'natural right is what is contained in the Old and New Laws' he explains himself at once, and adds: 'By which everyone is commanded to do to others what he would have done to himself, and forbidden to do to others what he would not have done to himself'.

    ii. Aristotle's statement should be understood to refer to things which are naturally just, not merely according to general principles, but also according to certain conclusions drawn from them. In most cases these are rightful, yet in a few cases they fail to meet the situation.

iii. Since mind in man dominates and rules his other powers, so their natural urges should be subordinated to mind. Hence it is generally held that it is right for all human tendencies to be directed according to intelligence.

Can natural law be changed?

II.8
OBJECTIONS:

i. It seems that natural law can be changed. For on the text of Ecclesiasticus, 'He gave instructions and the law of life' [17.9], the Gloss comments, 'He willed the document of the Law to be written in order to correct natural law'. Now what is corrected is changed. Therefore natural law can be changed.

ii. Moreover, the killing of the innocent is against natural law, and so is adultery and theft. Yet you find God changing these rules, as when he commanded Abraham to put his son to death, the people of Israel to spoil the Egyptians, and Hosea to take a wife of harlotry. Natural law, then, can be altered.

iii. Furthermore, Isidore says that 'common ownership of property and the same liberty for all are of natural law'. Human law seems to change all this, and therefore natural law can be changed.

ON THE OTHER HAND it is said in the *Decretum*, 'Natural law dates from the rise of rational creation, and does not vary according to period, but remains unchangeable'.

II.9
REPLY: A change can be understood to mean either addition or subtraction. As for the first, there is nothing against natural law being changed, for many things over and above natural law have been added, by divine law as well as by human laws, which are beneficial to social life.

II.10
As for change by subtraction, meaning that something that once was of natural law later ceases to be so, here there is room for a

distinction. The first principles of natural law are altogether unalterable. But its secondary precepts, which we have described as being like particular conclusions close to first principles, though not alterable in the majority of cases where they are right as they stand, can nevertheless be changed on some particular and rare occasions, as we have mentioned in the preceding article, because of some special cause preventing their unqualified observance.

II.11
HENCE:

i. The written Law is said to have been for the correction of natural law because it supplied what was wanting there, or because parts of natural law were decayed in the hearts of those who reckoned that some things were good which by nature are evil. This called for correction.

ii. All men without exception, guilty and innocent alike, have to suffer the sentence of natural death from divine power because of original sin, according to the words, 'The Lord kills and brings to life' [1 Sam. 2.6]. Consequently without injustice God's command can inflict death on anybody whether he be guilty or innocent. Adultery is intercourse with a woman to whom you are not married in accordance with divinely given law; nevertheless to go unto any woman by divine command is neither adultery nor fornication. The same applies to theft, the taking of what belongs to another, for what is taken by God's command, who is the owner of the universe, is not against the owner's will, and this is of the essence of theft. Nor is it only in human affairs that whatever God commands is just, but also in the world of nature, for as stated in the *Prima Pars*, whatever God does there in effect is natural.

iii. You speak of something being according to natural right in two ways. The first is because nature is set that way; thus the command that no harm should be done to another. The second is because nature does not bid the contrary; thus we might say that it is of natural law for man to be naked, for nature does not give him clothes; these he has to make by art. In this way common ownership and universal liberty are said to be of natural law, because private property and slavery exist by human contrivance for the convenience of social life, and not by natural law. This does not change the law of nature except by addition.

Can natural law be abolished from the human heart?

II.12
OBJECTIONS:

i. It would seem that natural law can be abolished from the human heart, for a text in Romans speaks of the Gentiles 'who have not the law' [2.14]. The Gloss comments, 'The law of justice blotted out by fault, is engraved on man's heart when he is restored by grace'. The law of justice is natural law, and this, therefore, can be abolished.

ii. Again, the law of grace is more powerful than the law of nature. Yet it can be wiped away by sin, and this therefore, and with all the more reason, can happen to natural law.

iii. Besides, what is established by law is set forth as being just. Now many human statutes have been enacted against natural law. Therefore natural law can be destroyed in men's hearts.

ON THE OTHER HAND Augustine says, 'Thy law is written in men's hearts, and no wickedness can efface it'. This is natural law, and it cannot be effaced.

II.13.
REPLY: As we noticed when speaking of what belongs to natural law, to begin with there are certain most general precepts known to all; and next, certain secondary and more specific precepts which are like conclusions lying close to the premises. As for these first common principles in their universal meaning, natural law cannot be cancelled in the human heart, nevertheless it can be missing from a particular course of action when the reason is stopped from applying the general principle there, because of lust or some other passion, as we have pointed out.

II.14
As for its other and secondary precepts, natural law can be effaced, either by wrong persuasions – thus also errors occur in theoretical matters concerning demonstrable conclusions – or by perverse customs and corrupt habits; for instance robbery

was not reputed to be wrong among some people, nor even, as
the Apostle mentions, some unnatural sins [i.e. Rom. 1.24].

II.15
HENCE:
i. Sin cancels natural law on some specific point, not as to its
general principles, unless perhaps with regard to secondary
precepts in the manner we have touched on.

ii. Though grace is more powerful than nature, nevertheless
nature is more essential to man, and therefore more permanent.

iii. This argument is true of secondary precepts of natural
law, against which human legislators have sometimes passed
wrongful enactments.

CRITIQUE

In view of the historical and modern importance of Aquinas'
natural law theory, it is not surprising that it has generated
extensive analyses and critiques (see further on Text XIV, which
provides a striking illustration of the theory). Serious criticisms
can be made of each of the replies he gives to the three questions
in the Text:

(a) *Is natural law the same for all?* Both the existence of a
ubiquitous natural law and the moral use to which Aquinas puts
it have been questioned. In view of the extraordinary moral
differences between groups of humans revealed by social
anthropology, it may be more difficult today to maintain that
these differences are simply due to the distortions caused by
error, sin or bad custom (though see Extract 3). Further, as
D.J. O'Connor asks, 'what is there in common between a human
being of the capacity of Newton or Shakespeare and the brief
sub-animal existence of a monstrous birth?' (*Aquinas and Natural
Law*, p.30). But, even if such a natural law is accepted, can one
derive, as Aquinas does, human moral ends legitimately from
human natural tendencies? For many, this seems a pre-Humean
confusion of the 'ought' with the 'is': description is conflated
with prescription. This is still a particularly contentious area in
moral philosophy, but it raises important issues in Christian ethics
(see *above*, p.21). For, example, if ethical precepts are derived

from the theory of evolution, as they are in some forms of evolutionary ethics, this criticism clearly applies: evolutionary 'development' is not simplistically to be identified with moral 'progress', unless a category error is to be made (see A.G.N. Flew, *Evolutionary Ethics*). But, if such an undertaking were to be made from the explicit perspective of a world created by God, it is not so clear that a category error would be involved. Granted a belief in the Christian God, it might well be assumed that natural human tendencies accord with the way God wishes people to behave – unless, of course, one accepts Luther's (and especially Calvin's) position that these tendencies have become thoroughly distorted by sin (see further, *below* p.166).

(b) *Can natural law be changed?* Aquinas' distinction between general and secondary principles raises many problems. The relationship between them is by no means always clearly specified and many have found the general principles to be so general as to be vacuous (e.g. the principle that good ought to be done and evil avoided). The question of whether general principles can be usefully specified will recur in Section 3 in relation to just-war theory. Furthermore, the notion that humans can sometimes add to natural law (II.11.3), now seems particularly dangerous in view of the way Aquinas used it to justify the existence of slavery. Again, as O'Connor asks, 'if slavery can be excused in this way, why not contraception or abortion or euthanasia?' (p.64).

(c) *Can natural law be abolished from the human heart?* For Aquinas, it is *synderesis* which enables humans to apprehend general principles, it is reason that humans must use to derive secondary principles from these general principles, and it is conscience (*conscientia*) that prompts humans to act on them. The nature and existence of this innate disposition, *synderesis*, able infallibly to apprehend general principles, has been the subject of debate amongst Thomist scholars and moral philosophers. Clearly, this has similarities to the wider debate about conscience in Christian ethics (see *above*, pp.19–21). Further, Luther (and again especially Calvin) might have responded that sin and the Fall have radically reduced the significance of natural law and that, in any case, the whole attempt to build a system of morality from it distorts the doctrine of justification by faith. This point leads naturally to the next Text.

TEXT III
LUTHER
Treatise on good works

1. *BACKGROUND*

This Text comes from the *Treatise on Good Works* of 1520 (from *Luther's Works*, vol 44, Fortress Press, Philadelphia, 1966, trans. W.A. Lambert and rev. James Atkinson, sections 4-6, 8, 12, 13-14 & 16). This year was crucial for Luther, coming between the Leipzig Disputation of 1519 (when he debated his new radical position in public with John Eck, appealing in the same year unsuccessfully to the Pope and then, later, to the Emperor) and the Diet of Worms of 1521. The latter finally placed Luther under the Imperial ban and forbade the publication of his works, or the proclamation, or defence, of his opinions. Luther spent the respite (between Leipzig and the arrival of Pope Leo X's Bull excommunicating him, in the October of 1520) writing in great haste. Believing himself to be a doomed man, he was determined to write as much as possible. Both the *Treatise on Good Works* and *The Appeal to the German Nobility* come from this period, as do *The Papacy at Rome, The Babylonian Captivity* and *The Freedom of the Christian Man*. Together, they sealed Luther's decisive break with Rome. Begun as sermon material for his congregation, *Treatise on Good Works* soon grew into a small book. In it, Luther was particularly concerned to refute the criticism that a stress upon justification by faith alone leads to a neglect of good works and to general antinomianism. He elaborated his argument in the context of a discussion of the Decalogue – this Text comes from the opening sections on the first Commandment. In the work as a whole, the medieval distinction between 'religious' good works (fasting, prayer recitations, attendance at mass, almsgiving etc.) and 'secular' good works, is challenged. For Luther it was just as important that an individual should be a good father, in faith, as that he should do 'religious' works, in faith. However trivial it might seem to others, whatever is done in faith is pleasing to God. It is faith alone that is vital.

2. *KEY ISSUES*

Luther's central argument, the very touchstone of the Reformation, comes out clearly in this Text. It is faith alone that matters: 'good' works, without faith, are worse than worthless, they are actually sin. Monasteries, and the church generally, are deeply implicated in this sin. Paul's notion of justification by faith is seen to refute conventional understandings of morality and piety. In the sequence presented here, the argument is as follows: Work without faith is sin (III.1). Faith has been turned into just another virtue and even a work (III.2). But in faith all works become equal (III.3). Faith needs no instruction (III.4), but is rather like the spontaneity of love in marriage, which is destroyed by efforts to win favour (III.5). The Christian does things that need to be done, not to gather merit, but simply to please God (III.6). So no amount of fasting, confession, intercessions, monasteries or churches can function without faith in God (III.7). Outward works, without faith, lead only to idolatry and hypocrisy (III.8) and of such are the papal bulls, seals, flags and indulgences (III.9). Of course, faith does not forbid good works: the vital thing is that faith should always come first (III.10). Indeed, if everyone lived by faith, there would be no need for laws or ceremonies (III.11 – see further Text VI). Faith can eliminate all sins – even the most deadly (III.12).

3. *ETHICAL ARGUMENTS*

In one sense, Luther's position is strongly anti-ethical. The moral calculations of his contemporaries are condemned as the following of 'blind reason and heathen ways of thinking' (III.2). An unequivocally theological stance is taken against ethical argument. But, in another sense, there is an evident personalism involved in his position, both in his initial appeal to the inspection of an individual's feelings (III.1) and in the analogy of married love (III.5). Indeed, the claim that 'a Christian man living in this faith has no need of a teacher of good works, but he does whatever the occasion calls for' (III.4) is characteristically personalist. It is even possible that natural law has influenced his analogy in III.5 (cf. VI.5). The example of married love (he did not marry himself for another five years) gains greater strength if there is actually an *analogia entis* – that is, if the affinity between husband-and-wife love and God-and-humans love actually results from the way the world is created by God.

4. BASES OF CHRISTIAN ETHICS

The principle of *sola Scriptura* is well in evidence: all but four of the paragraphs contain direct biblical quotations. Not surprisingly, a strong affinity for Paul is apparent, but there are also several quotations from the Old Testament and from the Gospels. In contrast to Aquinas, no reference is made to Christian tradition, other than to disparage contemporary papal practices. Luther's appeal to the feelings of the individual Christian have already been noted and the whole Text is clearly dominated by a theological concern for faith.

5. SOCIAL DETERMINANTS

At the psychological level, Luther's debt to Paul (possibly through Augustine – see *above*, p.45) is apparent in his central notion of justification by faith. But, as with Paul, it is important to see his stress upon this in the context of his personal experience of the failure of 'legalism'. He came to identify his own struggles as a monk with Paul's life as a Pharisee: increased 'works' served only to precipitate their crises of faith. And, as with Augustine, the converted Luther characteristically despised his pre-conversion life. At the more social level, the undoubted excesses of the 16th-century Catholic Church, with its sometimes astonishingly corrupt papacy, both provoked and confirmed Luther's rejection of contemporary practices and beliefs. As his personal rift with Rome deepened, so his animosity towards it and his identification of the Pope with the 'anti-Christ' increased. At the political level, it is often argued that a growing German nationalism was also relevant to this rift.

6. SOCIAL SIGNIFICANCE

Luther's writings of 1520 were crucial to the subsequent development of the Reformation. In attacking papal indulgences and insisting so forcefully on individual faith, Luther was instrumental in effecting a radical change in church structure and in Western consciousness. Few theologians can even approximate to the vast influence he has had upon both the Western Church and Western society. The challenge to papal authority, evident in this Text, caused lasting repercussions in the West. The already ailing power of Rome would never again be able to dominate Europe. And the 'new' understanding of Christian living, vocation and faith would encourage a new consciousness which Weber saw as related to the rise of Western Capitalism (see *above*, p.28). The consequences of Luther's understanding of faith are that 'all works become equal' (III.3) and that the person of faith 'has no need of a teacher' (III.4), of ecclesiastical intermediaries, or even 'of the laws of the church and of the state' (III.11). In short, the new European must work out his or her own individual relationship to God and to each other. The individualistic, business entrepreneur is but one product of this radical shift of consciousness.

FURTHER READING
In addition to this primary source and to the secondary sources referred to in the Introduction, a number of books will be found useful. Max Weber's theory is found in *The Protestant Ethic and the 'Spirit' of Capitalism* and in his *The Sociology of Religion*. Criticisms of this theory are numerous, but see, especially, Michael Hill's *A Sociology of Religion* for a review of some of the sociological discussion of it. For interpretations of Luther's theological notions here, see George W. Forell's *Faith Active in Love* and *History of Christian Ethics* and Gustav Wingreen's *Luther on Vocation* and *The Christian's Calling*.

TEXT III
LUTHER
Treatise on good works

III. 1
Now everyone can notice and feel for himself when he does what is good and what is not good. If he finds his heart confident that

it pleases God, then the work is good, even if it were so small a thing as picking up a straw. If the confidence is not there, or if he has any doubt about it, then the work is not good, even if the work were to raise all the dead and if the man were to give his body to be burned. This is the teaching of St Paul in Romans 14 [.23], 'Whatsoever is not done of faith or in faith is sin.' It is from faith as the chief work and from no other work that we are called believers in Christ. A heathen, a Jew, a Turk, a sinner may also do all other works; but to trust firmly that he pleases God is possible only for a Christian who is enlightened and strengthened by grace.

III.2

That these words seem strange, and that some people call me a heretic because of them, is due to the fact that they have followed blind reason and heathen ways of thinking. They have set faith not above but beside other virtues. They have made faith into a kind of work of its own, separated from all works of the other virtues, although faith alone makes all other works good, acceptable, and worthy because it trusts God and never doubts that everything a man does in faith is well done in God's sight. In fact, they have not let faith remain a work but have made it a *habitus*, as they call it, although the whole of Scripture gives the name good, divine work to no work except to faith alone. Therefore, it is no wonder that they have become blind and leaders of the blind. And this faith soon brings along with it love, peace, joy, and hope. For God gives his spirit immediately to him who trusts him, as St Paul says to the Galatians, 'You have received the spirit not from your good works but because you have believed the work of God' [Gal. 3.2].

III.3

In this faith all works become equal, and one work is like the other; all distinctions between works fall away, whether they be great, small, short, long, many, or few. For the works are acceptable not for their own sake but because of faith, which is always the same and lives and works in each and every work without distinction, however numerous and varied these works always are, just as all the members of the body live, work, and take their name from the head, and without the head no member can live, work, or have a name.

III.4

It further follows from this that a Christian man living in this faith has no need of a teacher of good works, but he does whatever the occasion calls for, and all is well done. As Samuel said to Saul, 'You shall become another man when the spirit enters you; do whatever your hand finds to do, for God is with you' [1 Sam. 10.6-7]. So also we read of St Anna, Samuel's mother. When she believed the priest Eli, who promised her God's grace, she went home in joy and peace [1 Sam. 1.17-18], and from that time paced the floor no longer: this means that whatever happened to her was all the same to her. St Paul also says, 'Where the Spirit of Christ is, there all is free' [Rom. 8.2]. For faith does not permit itself to be bound to any work or to refuse any work, but, as the first Psalm says, 'it yields its fruit in its season' [Ps. 1.3], that is, in the normal course of events.

III.5

We may see this in an everyday example. When a husband and wife really love one another, have pleasure in each other, and thoroughly believe in their love, who teaches them how they are to behave one to another, what they are to do or not to do, say or not to say, what they are to think? Confidence alone teaches them all this, and even more than is necessary. For such a man there is no distinction in works. He does the great and the important as gladly as the small and the unimportant, and vice versa. Moreover, he does them all in a glad, peaceful, and confident heart, and is an absolutely willing companion to the woman. But where there is any doubt, he searches within himself for the best thing to do; then a distinction of works arises by which he imagines he may win favour. And yet he goes about it with a heavy heart and great disinclination. He is like a prisoner, more than half in despair, and often makes a fool of himself.

III.6

Thus a Christian man who lives in this confidence toward God knows all things, can do all things, ventures everything that needs to be done, and does everything gladly and willingly, not that he may gather merits and good works, but because it is a pleasure for him to please God in doing these things. He simply serves God with no thought of reward, content that his service pleases God. On the other hand, he who is not at one with God, or is in a state of doubt, worries and starts looking about for ways and means to do enough and to influence God with his many good works. He runs off to St James, to Rome, to Jerusalem, hither and thither; he prays St Bridget's prayer, this prayer and that prayer; he fasts on this day and that day; he makes confession here and makes confession there; he questions this man and that man, and yet he finds no peace. He does all this with great effort and with a doubting and unwilling heart, so that the Scriptures rightly call such works in Hebrew *aven amal*, that is, labour and sorrow. And even then they are not good works and are in vain. Many people have gone quite crazy with them and their anxiety has brought them into all kinds of misery. Of these it is written in Wisdom (of Solomon) 5 [.6]. 'We have wearied ourselves in the wrong way and have followed a hard and bitter road; but God's way we have not acknowledged and the sun of righteousness has not risen upon us'...

III.7
As I have already said, I have always praised faith and rejected all works which are done without such faith in this way in order to lead men from the false, pretentious, pharisaic good works done without faith, with which all monasteries, churches, homes, and the upper and lower classes are overfilled, and to lead them to the right, true, genuine, real works of faith. Nobody strives against me in this except the unclean beasts who do not part the hoof (as the law of Moses decrees) and who will tolerate no distinction of any kind between good works, but go lumbering along. If only they pray, fast, establish endowments, go to confession, and do enough, everything is supposed to be all right, although in all this they have had no faith in the grace of God and no certainty of his approval. In fact, they regard these works most highly when they have done a great many major ones for a long time, without any such confidence, and they look for good only after the works have

been performed. And so they build their confidence not on God's favour, but on the works they have done. That is building on sand and water, and in the end they must fall, as Christ said in Matthew 7 [.26-27]. This good will and favour, on which our confidence rests, was proclaimed by the angels from heaven when they sang on Christmas morn, 'Glory be to God on high, peace on earth, good will to men' [Luke 2.14]...

III.8

See for yourself what a difference there is between the fulfilment of the first commandment with outward works and fulfilment with inward trust. For it is the latter which makes true, living children of God; the former makes for a wretched idolatry and the most pernicious hypocrites on earth, who with their great show of righteousness lead countless folk into their way, yet they leave them without faith. So these folk are led astray pitiably and bogged down in external wailing and show. Christ speaks of their kind when he said in Matthew 24 [.23], 'Beware then if any one says to you, "Lo, here is the Christ!" or "There he is!"' Or again, John 4 [.21-3], 'I say to you, the time will come when you shall not worship God either on this mountain or in Jerusalem, for the Father seeks spiritual worshippers.'

III.9

These and passages like them have moved me (and ought to move everybody else) to repudiate the ostentatious display of bulls, seals, flags, and indulgences, by which the poor people are led to build churches, to give, endow, and pray. Even then faith is not mentioned at all and is even suppressed, for since faith makes not distinction among works, then where faith is present such trumpeting and urging of one kind of work above another cannot exist. Faith desires to be the only way of serving God, and will allow this name and honour to no other work, except in so far as faith imparts it, as it does when the work is done in and by faith. This perversion is indicated in the Old Testament when the Jews left the Temple and sacrificed at other places, in gardens and on the mountains [Isa. 65.3, 66.17]. These men do exactly the same. They are zealous to do all works, but this chief work of faith they never have any regard for at all...

III.10

Therefore, when some people say, as they do, that when we preach faith alone good works are forbidden, it is as if I were to say to a sick man, 'If you had health you would have the full use of all your limbs, but without health the works of all your limbs are nothing', and from this he wanted to infer that I had forbidden the works of his limbs. Whereas on the contrary I meant that the health must first be there to work all the works of all his limbs. In the same way faith must be the master-workman and captain in all the works, or they are nothing at all.

III.11

You might ask, if faith does everything through the first commandment, why then do we have so many laws of the church and of the state, and so many ceremonies of churches, monasteries, and holy places, which urge and tempt men to do good works through them? The answer: simply because we do not all have or heed faith. If every man had faith we would need no more laws. Everyone would of himself do good works all the time, as his faith shows him...

III.12

But you say, how can I be absolutely sure that all my works are pleasing to God, when at times I fall, talk, eat, drink, and sleep too much, or otherwise transgress in ways I cannot avoid? Answer: This question shows that you still regard faith as a work among other works and do not set it above all works. It is the highest work because it blots out these everyday sins and still stands fast by never doubting that God is so favourably disposed toward you that he overlooks such everyday failures and offences. Yes, even if a deadly sin should arise (which, however, never or rarely happens to those who live in faith and trust in God), nonetheless faith always rises again and does not doubt that its sin is already gone. As it is written in 1 John 2 [.1-2], 'My dear children, I am writing this to you so that you may not sin; but if any one does sin, we have an advocate before God, Jesus Christ, who is the forgiveness for our sins'. And Wisdom [of Solomon] 15[.2], 'And though we have already sinned, we are still thine, and know that thou are great'. And Proverbs 24 [.16], 'A righteous man may fall seven times, but he always rises up as many times'. Yes, this confidence and faith must be so high and strong that a man knows that all his life and works are nothing but damnable sins in the judgment of God, as it says in Psalm 143 [.2], 'For no man living is found righteous before thee'. He must despair entirely of his works, and believe that they cannot be good except through this faith which expects no judgment but only pure grace, favour, kindness, and mercy.

CRITIQUE

There are elements in Luther's understanding of the doctrine of justification by faith which almost all Christians today might accept. Most would agree that the Christian life is primarily about pleasing God and not seeking to gather merit (III.6) and that, for the Christian, faith should be regarded as primary and works as secondary (III.10). They might even agree that if everyone lived by faith there would be no need for laws (III.11 – see further, *below*, pp.178–9).

However, it is important to recognise that Aquinas would also have accepted these propositions. So, just because Luther's contemporaries appeared to reject them and were, in a number of cases, highly corrupt, an acceptance of them does not commit one to a rejection of Catholicism as such. Arguments against a corrupt papacy and a corrupt church are not necessarily arguments against papacy and Catholicism as such – a point that Luther sometimes appeared to forget, particularly as, in later life, his writings became more irascible. Aquinas would have insisted that good works do not on their own achieve salvation – grace being essential for that – but, nonetheless, they are still important prerequisites for salvation: works are necessary, but not sufficient, for salvation. Whatever merits are achieved by works, salvation, as such, most certainly is not. Nor would Augustine have accepted such a Pelagian position: for him, grace was essential, both to enable people to act rightly in the first place and to allow them to continue to act rightly (see *above*, p.44).

Further, many have argued that there is a dangerous antinomianism inherent in Luther's arguments. At first, Augustine's dictum 'love God, and do what you want' might seem to have similarities to Luther's position, particularly when it is used in conjunction with Paul's notion of justification by faith. But Augustine's position was less single-minded than that of Luther: like Paul himself, he could still talk about 'merit' (see *above*, p.45). It is possible that the sort of single-minded stress of Luther, of Bonhoeffer in Extract 1, or of Fletcher in Extract 2, does less than justice to Christian ethics. In the case of all three, it will be seen later that they may bring more presuppositions to moral decision-making than they realise (for Luther, see the analysis of Text IX).

Finally, there may be a dangerous exclusivism inherent in Luther's position. For him, all good works without faith in Christ are nothing but sin. The shocking attitude he adopted towards the Jews in Text XV, in later life, was consistent with this position. Indeed, there always may be a danger in drawing negative conclusions from a positive position on faith. So, to claim that, for the Christian, faith is primary and works only secondary, or even that works only flow from faith, it is not necessary to claim, at the same time, that the good works of those who do not share this faith are entirely without virtue. Augustine shrank from this negative conclusion, in at least some of his works (see Text IV). And, clearly, it would not accord with Aquinas' theory of natural law. Whereas the notions of 'empty works' and hypocrisy are obviously important for Christians today (thanks in part to Luther), the complete denigration of the moral actions of all but explicit Christians might be accepted by comparatively few.

EXTRACTS 1-5
BONHOEFFER, FLETCHER, COPLESTON, JOHN PAUL II AND FIORENZA

1. *BACKGROUND*

Dietrich Bonhoeffer's Extract 1 comes from *Ethics* (SCM, 1978, pp.3-6 & 9-13), Joseph Fletcher's Extract 2 from his *Situation Ethics*, (SCM, 1966, pp.26-30, 30-3 & 37-9). F.C. Copleston's Extract 3 from his *Aquinas* (Harper & Row and Search, 1976, pp.22-35), Pope John Paul II's Extract 4 comes from his Encyclical *Veritatis Splendor* (Catholic Truth Society, 1993, sections 31-7, pp.51-60), and Elisabeth Schüssler Fiorenza's Extract 5 comes from 'Women: Invisible in Church and Theology', *Concilium* (T&T Clark, 1985, No.182, pp.6-12).

The chapter in *Ethics* from which the Bonhoeffer Extract comes, 'The Love of God and the Decay of the World', can be dated to the period 1939-40 and is thus almost contemporary with his *The Cost of Discipleship* of 1937 and Reinhold Niebuhr's *The Nature and Destiny of Man*. Obviously, this was an extremely turbulent period for both theologians. Niebuhr wrote in his preface that 'these lectures were given in April and May of 1939 when the clouds of war were already hovering ominously over Europe'. Bonhoeffer had already joined the Confessing Church and had returned in 1935 from America to Hitler's Germany. Whilst in America, Bonhoeffer (1906-45) studied at the Union Theological Seminary, where Niebuhr had been Professor of Christian Ethics since 1928. Niebuhr later recollected that Bonhoeffer had said at this critical stage in his life, 'I shall have no right to participate in the reconstruction of Christian life in Germany after the war if I do not share the trials of this time with my people' (quoted in the preface to *The Cost of Discipleship*, SCM, 1978, p.11). At the time of writing this Extract, Bonhoeffer was still head of the College of the Confessing Church at Finkenwalde.

Joseph Fletcher (1905-92) was, like Bonhoeffer, a pastor before he became an academic. He was appointed as Professor of Social

Ethics at the Episcopal Theological School, Cambridge, Massachusetts, in 1944 (from where he wrote *Situation Ethics*) and taught finally in the University of Virginia. By 1955, when he first published *Aquinas*, Copleston, a Jesuit and Oxford trained philosopher, was Professor of Metaphysics in the doctorate course at the Gregorian University in Rome. He was appointed Professor of the History of Philosophy at Heythrop College, in 1939 at the age of 28, retired in 1974 from a chair in London University and was author before his death of the multi-volume *History of Philosophy*. Cardinal Karol Wojtyla of Poland was elected Pope, John Paul II, in October 1978. His Encyclical Letter *Veritatis Splendor* was first published in 1993, expressing the title in his opening words (reflecting Gen. 1.26): 'The Splendor of Truth shines forth in all the works of the Creator and, in a special way, in man, created in the image and likeness of God'. Elisabeth Schüssler Fiorenza is also a Roman Catholic, albeit one considerably more radical and feminist than Pope John Paul II. She has worked as both a New Testament scholar and as a modern theologian and is currently Krister Stendahl Professor of Divinity at the Harvard Divinity School. Her best known books are *In Memory of Her: A Feminist Theological Reconstruction of Christian Origins* (1983) and *Discipleship of Equals: A Critical Feminist Ekklesialogy of Liberation* (1993). She has also edited several volumes of *Concilium* (from which this Extract is taken).

2. KEY ISSUES

Bonhoeffer highlights the difference between ethics and Christian ethics: unaided ethical deliberations and conscience merely reflect a disunion with God. Humanity was originally created in the image of God, with a knowledge of an origin in God, but, through the Fall, this knowledge has been reversed, so that people are now thought to be their own creators and originators of good and evil (1.1-4). Human conscience (1.10) and quest for self-knowledge (1.11) both illustrate this reversal, since they falsely try to reach God through interpersonal relationships: in contrast, Jesus' ethics start from his unity with God (1.15).

Fletcher has criticised legalist and antinomian approaches to

Christian ethics earlier in his book and now, in Extract 2, seeks to defend a third approach, that of situation ethics. In this, ethical maxims are treated as illuminators (but not as rules or laws) in particular situations: if love is better served, they can be compromised or set aside (2.1 & 12). Like natural law, situation ethics accepts reason in moral decision-making (2.2) and even involves rational calculation (2.12f: elsewhere in *Situation Ethics* he accepts the term 'utilitarianism' to describe this function). But it rejects the 'objectivity' of natural law (2.2) and accepts only one *summum bonum* – or 'highest good' – as law (2.10-11). For the Christian situationist, this *summum bonum* is *agape* (2.10): only the commandment to love, for the Christian, is categorically good: and only general 'principles', not rules or laws, can be derived from this *summum bonum* (2.3-9).

Copleston's concerns in Extract 3 are more philosophical than theological. He is concerned to clarify Aquinas' natural law theory in the light of modern relativist and emotive theories of ethics (3.13). In contrast to relativist objections to a theory of unalterable moral precepts, he points out that empirical differences on moral issues between people, do not, of themselves, disprove Aquinas' theory (3.3-5). With emotivists, he agrees that Aquinas' theory is not simply rationalistic – moral decision-making involves rational and prudential reflection on human nature *as known in experience* (3.8: an important point to compare with Fletcher's criticisms of 'legalism'). Against emotivists, however, he points out that Aquinas' position assumes an objective moral relationship: whilst feelings are important in moral decision-making, they are too subjective to form the basis of morality (3.12).

John Paul II's Extract 4 is concerned with the tension between secular conceptions of personal freedom and autonomy and traditional natural law theology. He notes that there is a heightened sense of freedom and autonomy in the modern world (4.1-3), yet he believes that this is sometimes exalted to an absolute status – individual conscience becoming the supreme tribunal of moral judgment (4.4). In the process any notion of a universal moral truth is lost: individuals possess only their own relative truths (4.5). Ironically, some of the behavioural sciences question the reality of individual human freedom, rendering morality highly relativistic (4.7-8). In contrast, for Catholic theology morality is objective and rights and obligations are related to each other (4.9). Some Catholic moral theologians have themselves been wrongly influenced by secular subjectivism (4.10-11). Vatican II insisted that human freedom is not unlimited since people are called to accept the moral law given by God which both protects and promotes that freedom (4.12-14). Catholic moral theology which forgets this is misleading (4.15-20).

Fiorenza's Extract 5 sets out the challenge of feminist theology. She admits that this theology is influenced by the women's liberation movement, as well as by church and theological institutions (5.1). Feminist theology seeks to change the patriarchal state and church and, indeed, all intellectual institutions (5.2-3). Like other forms of liberation theology, it seeks to recover and reconstruct theological symbols and expressions for a discipleship of equals (5.5). A variety of approaches are evident within feminist theology (5.6-7), but together they offer a challenge to androcentrism (5.8). This does constitute a distinctive theological method, based upon dialogue, participation and non-hierarchy (5.10-11). Sexism, racism and militaristic colonialism all have roots in patriarchy, which feminist theology seeks to oppose (5.13-17).

3.   *ETHICAL ARGUMENTS*

It has already been argued that there are obvious similarities and differences between the personalism of Bonhoeffer and the situationism of Fletcher (see *above*, p.61). Bonhoeffer's personalism is evident also in his earlier writings. As an assistant minister in Barcelona, he wrote in 1929 that, 'there are not and cannot be Christian norms and principles of a moral nature; the concepts of "good" and "evil" exist only in the performance of an action, i.e. at any specific present, and hence any attempt to lay down principles is like trying to draw a bird in flight' (*No Rusty Swords*, Fontana, 1970, p.36). And again, 'there are no actions which are bad in themselves – even murder can be justified – there is only faithfulness to God's will or deviation from it' (p.41). Thus, 'we can give no generally valid decisions which we might then hold out to be the only Christian one, because in so doing we are only setting out new principles and coming into conflict with the law of freedom. Rather can we only seek to be brought into the concrete situation of the decision and to show one of the possibilities of decision which present themselves at that point' (p.42). Affinities with situation ethics are evident here. But, in the same lecture, there is also evident his radical division between ethics and Christian ethics. In addition, unlike Fletcher, it is the 'will of God', rather than *agape*, that he regards as central in Christian ethics: for him 'there is no other law than the law of freedom' (p.40): *agape* cannot be treated as law: 'the new commandments of Jesus can never be regarded merely as ethical principles' (p.41). Clearly this position is different from that of Fletcher in 2.10.

The Extracts of Copleston, John Paul II and Fiorenza differ from those of Bonhoeffer and Fletcher in that they all postulate a strong form of deontology. Interestingly, Copleston concluded a critical review of *Situation Ethics*, by insisting that 'belief that in Christian ethics love is the supreme value seems to me unquestionably valid' (quoted in the third impression of *Situation Ethics*). Nonetheless both Extract 3 and Extract 4 offer clear defences of natural law theory. For John Paul II, particularly, natural law offers a form of moral objectivism which has been considerably eroded in secular morality. Extract 5, although not so obviously based upon natural law, is still highly deontological. Fiorenza simply assumes that feminist theology is rightly concerned with the 'transformation of the patriarchal state and church' (5.2) and that 'academic institutions need to be redefined and transformed' (5.3). She also regards sexism, racism and militaristic colonialism as self-evidently wrong.

4. *BASES OF CHRISTIAN ETHICS*

This point leads naturally to the next part of analysis. Only in Bonhoeffer's Extract 1 and John Paul II's Extract 4 is the Bible used as the basic resource of Christian ethics. Fletcher also makes (rather uncharacteristic – see Extract 22) use of the New Testament in 2.9, yet his discussion is mainly dictated by appeals to Christian tradition. In Copleston's Extract 3 the discussion is rather dictated by philosophy. Indeed, Copleston wrote his *Aquinas* primarily, 'to make it easier for the reader to consider sympathetically his style of philosophising and his interpretation of the world' (p.17), not to defend his theology as such, and Fiorenza starts Extract 5 by acknowledging her debt to the secular women's movement. Despite his early interest in sociology and psychology (e.g. in *Sanctorum Communio*), it is doubtful whether Bonhoeffer would have considered such philosophical or secular concerns to be worthwhile undertakings in Christian ethics. They belong more to the tradition of Augustine and Aquinas than to that of Luther.

Appeals to Christian experience are made, at times, by all five theologians. In Extract 1 Bonhoeffer appears to reject conscience, but later in *Ethics*, he claims that 'it can never be advisable to act against one's own conscience' (p.211). This, it would seem, is conscience which has already been informed by Christian faith, rather than an innate human faculty. Even Fletcher has a puzzling reference to 'problems of conscience' in 2.8. However, Bonhoeffer's rejection of secular conscience is complicated by the fact that, as the German Church became increasingly divided in the war and a number of secular liberals started to stand out against Hitler, he began to note an affinity of 'consciousness' of values between their position and that of his own. It became clear to him that 'it was not the Church that was seeking the protection and alliance of these concepts; but, on the contrary, it was the concepts that had somehow become homeless and now sought refuge in the Christian sphere... The children of the Church, who had become independent and gone their own ways, now in the hour of danger returned to their mother' (*Ethics* pp.38-9). However, this 'consciousness' may still not be an innate human faculty or tendency: it may, instead, be better understood in terms of a transposition theory (see *above*, p.12).

5. *SOCIAL DETERMINANTS*

These Extracts represent four distinct phrases of Western theology: the late-1930s, the mid-1950s, the mid-1960s, and the 1990s. The first phase was dominated by the neo-orthodox reaction of Barth and others against theological liberalism and by impending world war. The second was a period of some optimism and attempts at theological construction. The third was characterised by theological ferment and radical self-criticism. And the fourth seems to be characterised by increasing pluralism – with sharp divisions emerging between radicals and neo-conservatives.

Both Niebuhr and Bonhoeffer were heirs to the Barthian theological revolution. The early Niebuhr, evident in Extract 8, rejected theological liberalism and he always remained critical of 'Christian utopianism'. Yet his mature theological writings showed a considerable hostility towards a rigidly neo-orthodox approach to Christian ethics. Bonhoeffer, in contrast, remained firmly attached to this approach and shows the considerable influence of Barth in Extract 1. In some respects, both he and Barth are more Lutheran than Luther: for instance, residual elements of natural law theory (present in Luther's own writings) are consciously denied by them. Their negative understanding of humanity apart from Christ may owe much to their experience of political collapse and chaos in the 1920s and 1930s. Indeed, their suspicion of natural law may owe something to their observations of its misuse in Nazi Germany.

This contrasts with the tentative attempt at reconstruction offered by Copleston in the 1950s. His tentativeness is, doubtless, a response to the severe strictures of English philosophy in the 1930s and 1940s against theology and metaphysics and, characteristically, he seeks to 'clarify' rather than defend. In contrast again, the radical innovations of the 1960s are strongly reflected in Fletcher's iconoclasm (see further Extract 22). Some have suggested that there is a strong middle-class, Western intellectual assumption in *Situation Ethics* (as in Harvey Cox's *Secular City*), that the individual is capable of making unstructured moral decisions from one situation to the next. In part, Paul VI's Extract 24 was a reaction against this assumption.

The fourth phase is evident in the contrast between Pope John Paul II's Extract 4 and Fiorenza's Extract 5. Extract 4 offers a forceful Christian apologetic against the characteristic assumptions of secularism and Extract 5 a feminist critique of assumptions within both Christianity and the world at large.

Despite the evident conviction of both Extracts, set side by side they serve to reinforce the considerable pluralism that is characteristic of both theology and intellectual life generally in the 1990s. Many depict this as the postmodern context of present-day theology (see further my *Readings in Modern Theology*).

6. SOCIAL SIGNIFICANCE

All five theologians have had a profound influence upon Christian ethics. Interest in Bonhoeffer's writings was inevitably sharpened by his martyrdom, but in their own right his books remain important for theology. Copleston, until his death in 1992, established himself, through his *History of Philosophy*, as the most influential Roman Catholic philosopher in England. His *Aquinas* successfully presented his subject as one to be taken seriously by present-day philosophers, who might otherwise deny his theological and biblical presuppositions. Fletcher's *Situation Ethics*, as already noted, has had a major effect upon Christian ethics and few within the discipline fail to take it into account (if only to deny its premises). Pope John Paul II has already proved himself to be one of the most forceful and remarkable Popes of the 20th century. His considerable use of power within the Roman Catholic Church has been a significant feature of his ministry and is evident here (e.g. 4.15-20) in his attempt to constrain Catholic moral theologians. Fiorenza remains a Catholic, albeit with the freedom to teach outside Catholic structures, and is now one of the most significant feminist theologians. Her book *In Memory of Her* has been extremely influential.

FURTHER READING

Bonhoeffer has been the subject of many studies, but, amongst these, Eberhard Bethge's *Dietrich Bonhoeffer* and John D. Godsey's *The Theology of Dietrich Bonhoeffer* are still amongst the most important. Comparisons of Niebuhr's and Bonhoeffer's ethical methods are contained in Edward LeRoy Long, Jr's *A Survey of Christian Ethics*. Suggested reading on natural law theory has already been given in relation to Aquinas' Text II. Fletcher's *Situation Ethics* has been subjected to considerable criticism, including J.C. Bennett (ed), *Storm Over Ethics*, G.R. Dunstan, *The Artifice of Ethics*, and Stanley Hauerwas, *Vision and Virtue*. Fletcher responded to some of the early criticism in his *Moral Responsibility*.

EXTRACT 1
BONHOEFFER
Ethics and Christian ethics

1.1
The knowledge of good and evil seems to be the aim of all ethical reflection. The first task of Christian ethics is to invalidate this knowledge. In launching this attack on the underlying assumptions of all other ethics, Christian ethics stands so completely alone that it becomes questionable whether there is any purpose in speaking of Christian ethics at all. But if one does so notwithstanding, that can only mean that Christian ethics claims to discuss the origin of the whole problem of ethics, and thus professes to be a critique of all ethics simply as ethics.

1.2
Already in the possibility of the knowledge of good and evil Christian ethics discerns a falling away from the origin. Man at his origin knows only one thing: God. It is only in the unity of his knowledge of God that he knows of other men, of things, and of himself. He knows all things only in God, and God in all things. The knowledge of good and evil shows that he is no longer at one with this origin.

1.3
In the knowledge of good and evil man does not understand himself in the reality of the destiny appointed in his origin, but rather in his own possibilities, his possibility of being good or evil. He knows himself now as something apart from God, outside God, and this means that he now knows only himself and no longer knows God at all; for he can know God only if he knows only God. The knowledge of good and evil is therefore separation from God. Only against God can men know good and evil.

1.4
But man cannot be rid of his origin. Instead of knowing himself in the origin of God, he must now know himself as an origin. He interprets himself according to his possibilities, his possibilities of being good or evil, and he

therefore conceives himself to be the origin of good and evil. *Eritis sicut deus*. 'The man is become as one of us, to know good and evil', says God (Gen. 3.22).

1.5

Originally man was made in the image of God, but now his likeness to God is a stolen one. As the image of God man draws his life entirely from his origin in God, but the man who has become like God has forgotten how he was at his origin and has made himself his own creator and judge. What God had given man to be, man now desired to be through himself. But God's gift is essentially *God's* gift. It is the origin that constitutes this gift. If the origin changes, the gift changes. Indeed the gift consists solely in its origin. Man as the image of God draws his life from the origin of God, but the man who has become like God draws his life from his own origin. In appropriating the origin to himself man took to himself a secret of God which proved his undoing. The Bible describes this event with the eating of the forbidden fruits. Man now knows good and evil. This does not mean that he has acquired new knowledge in addition to what he knew before, but the knowledge of good and evil signifies the complete reversal of man's knowledge, which hitherto had been solely knowledge of God as his origin. In knowing good and evil he knows what only the origin, God Himself, can know and ought to know. It is only with extreme reserve that even the Bible indicates to us that God is the One who knows of good and evil. It is the first indication of the mystery of predestination, the mystery of an eternal dichotomy which has its origin in the eternally One, the mystery of an eternal choice and election by Him in whom there is no darkness but only light. To know good and evil is to know oneself as the origin of good and evil, as the origin of an eternal choice and election. How this is possible remains the secret of Him in whom there is no disunion because He is Himself the one and eternal origin and the overcoming of all disunion. This secret has been stolen from God by man in his desire to be an origin on his own account. Instead of knowing only the God who is good to him and instead of knowing all things in Him, he now knows himself as the origin of good and evil. Instead of accepting the choice and election of God, man himself desires to choose, to be the origin of the election. And so, in a certain sense, he bears within himself the secret of predestination. Instead of knowing himself solely in the reality of being chosen and loved by God, he must now know himself in the possibility of choosing and of being the origin of good and evil. He has become like God, but against God. Herein lies the serpent's deceit. Man knows good and evil, but because he is not the origin, because he acquires this knowledge only at the price of estrangement from the origin, the good and evil that he knows are not the good and evil of God but good and evil against God. They are good and evil of man's own choosing, in opposition to the eternal election of God. In becoming like God man has become a god against God.

1.6

This finds its expression in the fact that man, knowing of good and evil, has finally torn himself loose from life, that is to say from the eternal life which proceeds from the choice of God. 'And now, lest he put forth his hand, and take also of the tree of life, and eat, and live for ever... he drove out the man; and he placed at the east of the garden of Eden Cherubims, and a flaming sword which turned every way, to keep the way of the tree of life' (Gen. 3.22 & 24). Man knows good and evil, against God, against his origin, godlessly and of his own choice, understanding himself according to his own contrary possibilities; and he is cut off from the unifying, reconciling life in God, and is delivered over to death. The secret which man has stolen from God is bringing about man's downfall.

1.7

Man's life is now disunion with God, with men, with things, and with himself.

1.8

Instead of seeing God man sees himself. 'Their eyes were opened' (Gen. 3.7). Man perceives himself in his disunion with God and with men. He perceives that he is naked. Lacking the protection, the covering, which God and his fellow-man afforded him, he finds himself laid bare. Hence there arises shame. Shame is man's ineffaceable recollection of his estrangement from the origin; it is grief for this estrangement, and the powerless longing to return to unity with the origin. Man is ashamed because he has lost something which is essential to his original character, to himself as a whole; he is ashamed of his nakedness. Just as in the fairy-story the tree is ashamed of its lack of adornment, so, too, man is ashamed of the loss of his unity with God and with other men. Shame and remorse are generally mistaken for one another. Man feels remorse when he has been at fault; and he feels shame because he lacks something. Shame is more original than remorse. The peculiar fact that we lower our eyes when a stranger's eye meets our gaze is not a sign of remorse for a fault, but a sign of that shame which, when it knows that it is seen, is reminded of something that it lacks, namely, the lost wholeness of life, its own nakedness. To meet a stranger s gaze directly, as is required, for example, in making a declaration of personal loyalty, is a kind of act of violence, and in love, when the gaze of the other is sought, it is a kind of yearning. In both cases it is the painful endeavour to recover the lost unity by either a conscious and resolute or else a passionate and devoted inward overcoming of shame as the sign of disunion...

1.9

In shame man is reminded of his disunion with God and with other men; conscience is the sign of man's disunion with himself. Conscience is farther from the origin than shame, it presupposes disunion with God and with man and marks only the disunion with himself of the man who is already disunited from the origin. It is the voice of apostate life which desires at least to remain one with itself. It is the call to the unity of man with himself. This is evident already from the fact that the call of conscience is always a prohibition 'Thou shalt not'. 'You ought not to have'. Conscience is satisfied when the prohibition is not disobeyed. Whatever is not forbidden is permitted. For conscience life falls into two parts: what is permitted and what is forbidden. There is no positive commandment. For conscience permitted is identical with good, and conscience does not register the fact, that even in this, man is in a state of disunion with his origin. It follows from this also that conscience does not, like shame, embrace the whole of life; it reacts only to certain definite actions. In one sense it is inexorable; in forbidden actions it sees a peril to life as a whole, that is to say, disunion with oneself; it recalls what is long past and represents this disunion as something which is already accomplished and irreparable, but the final criterion remains precisely that unity with oneself which is imperilled only in the particular instances in which the prohibition is disobeyed. The range of experience of conscience does not extend to the fact that this unity itself presupposes disunion with God and with men and that consequently, beyond the disobedience to the prohibition, the prohibition itself, as the call of conscience, arises from disunion with the origin. This means that conscience is concerned not with man's relation to God and to other men but with man's relation to himself. But a relation of man to himself, in detachment from his relation to God and to other men, can arise only through man's becoming like God in the disunion.

1.10

Conscience itself reverses this relation. It derives the relation to God and to men from the relation of man to himself. Conscience pretends to be the voice of God and the standard for the relation to other men. It is therefore from his right relation to himself that man is to recover the right relation to God and to other men. This reversal is the claim of the man who has become like God in his knowledge of good and evil. Man has become the origin of good and evil. He does not deny his evil; but in conscience man summons himself, who has become evil, back to his proper, better self, to good. This good, which consists in the unity of man with himself, is now to be the origin of all good. It is the good of God, and it is the good for one's neighbour. Bearing within himself the knowledge of good and evil, man has become judge over God and men, just as he is judge over himself.

1.11
Knowing of good and evil in disunion with the origin, man begins to reflect upon himself. His life is now his understanding of himself, whereas at the origin it was his knowledge of God. Self-knowledge is now the measure and the goal of life. This holds true even when man presses out beyond the bounds of his own self. Self-knowledge is man's interminable striving to overcome his disunion with himself by thought; by unceasingly distinguishing himself from himself he endeavours to achieve unity with himself.

1.12
All knowledge is now based upon self-knowledge. Instead of the original comprehension of God and of men and of things there is now a taking in vain of God and of men and of things. Everything now is drawn in into the process of disunion. Knowledge now means the establishment of the relationship to oneself; it means the recognition in all things of oneself and of oneself in all things. And thus, for man who is in disunion with God, all things are in disunion, what is and what should be, life and law, knowledge and action, idea and reality, reason and instinct, duty and inclination, conviction and advantage, necessity and freedom, exertion and genius, universal and concrete, individual and collective; even truth, justice, beauty and love come into opposition with one another, just as do pleasure and displeasure, happiness and sorrow. One could prolong the list still further and the course of human history adds to it constantly. All these disunions are varieties of the disunion in the knowledge of good and evil. 'The point of decision of the specifically ethical experience is always conflict.' But in conflict the judge is invoked; and the judge is the knowledge of good and evil; he is man.

1.13
Now anyone who reads the New Testament even superficially cannot but notice the complete absence of this world of disunion, conflict and ethical problems. Not man's falling apart from God, from men, from things and from himself, but rather the rediscovered unity, reconciliation, is now the basis of the discussion and the 'point of decision of the specifically ethical

experience'. The life and activity of men is not at all problematic or tormented or dark: it is self-evident, joyful, sure and clear.

1.14

It is in Jesus's meeting with the Pharisee that the old and the new are most clearly contrasted. The correct understanding of this meeting is of the greatest significance for the understanding of the gospel as a whole. The Pharisee is not an adventitious historical phenomenon of a particular time. He is the man to whom only the knowledge of good and evil has come to be of importance in his entire life; in other words, he is simply the man of disunion. Any distorted picture of the Pharisees robs Jesus's argument with them of its gravity and its importance. The Pharisee is that extremely admirable man who subordinates his entire life to his knowledge of good and evil and is as severe a judge of himself as of his neighbour to the honour of God, whom he humbly thanks for this knowledge. For the Pharisee every moment of life becomes a situation of conflict in which he has to choose between good and evil. For the sake of avoiding any lapse his entire thought is strenuously devoted night and day to the anticipation of the whole immense range of possible conflicts, to the reaching of a decision in these conflicts, and to the determination of his own choice. There are innumerable factors to be observed, guarded against and distinguished. The finer the distinctions the surer will be the correct decision. This observation extends to the whole of life in all its manifold aspects. The Pharisee is not opinionated; special situations and emergencies receive special consideration; forbearance and generosity are not excluded by the gravity of the knowledge of good and evil; they are rather an expression of this gravity. And there is no rash presumption here, or arrogance or unverified self-esteem. The Pharisee is fully conscious of his own faults and of his duty of humility and thankfulness towards God. But, of course, there are differences, which for God's sake must not be disregarded, between the sinner and the man who strives towards good, between the man who becomes a breaker of the law out of a situation of wickedness and the man who does so out of necessity. If anyone disregards these differences, if he fails to take every factor into account in each of the innumerable cases of conflict, he sins against the knowledge of good and evil.

1.15

These men with the incorruptibly impartial and distrustful vision cannot confront any man in any other way than by examining him with regard to his decisions in the conflicts of life. And so, even when they come face to face with Jesus, they cannot do otherwise than attempt to force Him, too, into conflicts and into decisions in order to see how He will conduct Himself in them. It is this that constitutes their temptation of Jesus. One need only read the twenty-second chapter of St Matthew, with the questions about the tribute money, the resurrection of the dead and the first and great commandment, and then the story of the good Samaritan (Luke 10.25) and the discussions about the keeping of the Sabbath (Matt. 12.11), and one will be most intensely impressed by this fact. The crucial point about all these arguments is that Jesus does not allow Himself to be drawn in into a single one of these conflicts and decisions. With each of His answers He simply leaves the case of conflict beneath Him. When it is a matter of conscious malice on the part of the Pharisees Jesus's answer is the still cleverer avoidance of a cleverly laid trap, and as such it may well have caused the Pharisees to smile. But that is not essential. Just as the Pharisees cannot do otherwise than confront Jesus with situations of conflict, so, too, Jesus cannot do otherwise than refuse to accept these situations. Just as the Pharisees' question and temptation arises from the disunion of the knowledge of good and evil, so, too, Jesus's answer arises from unity with God, with the origin, and from the overcoming of the disunion of man with God. The Pharisees and Jesus are speaking on totally different levels. That is why their words so strikingly fail to make contact, and that is why Jesus's answers do not appear to be answers at all, but rather attacks of His own against the Pharisees, which is what they, in fact, are.

EXTRACT 2
FLETCHER
Situation Ethics

2.1
A third approach, in between legalism and antinomian unprincipledness, is situation ethics. (To jump from one polarity to the other would be only to go from the frying pan to the fire). The situationist enters into every decision-making situation fully armed with the ethical maxims of his community and its heritage, and he treats them with respect as illuminators of his problems. Just the same he is prepared in any situation to compromise them or set them aside *in the situation* if love seems better served by doing so.

2.2
Situation ethics goes part of the way with natural law, by accepting reason as the instrument of moral judgment, while rejecting the notion that the good is 'given' in the nature of things, objectively. It goes part of the way

with Scriptural law by accepting revelation as the source of the norm while rejecting all 'revealed' norms or laws but the one command – to love God in the neighbour. The situationist follows a moral law or violates it according to love's need. For example, 'Almsgiving is a good thing *if...*' The situationist never says, 'Almsgiving is a good thing. Period!' His decisions are hypothetical, not categorical. Only the commandment to love is categorically good. 'Owe no one anything, except to love one another.' (Rom. 13.8). If help to an indigent only pauperises and degrades him, the situationist refuses a handout and finds some other way. He makes no law out of Jesus' 'Give to every one who begs from you.' It is only one step from that kind of Biblicist literalism to the kind that causes women in certain sects to refuse blood transfusions even if death results – even if they are carrying a quickened fetus that will be lost too. The legalist says that even if he tells a man escaped from an asylum where his intended victim is, if he finds and murders him, at least only one sin has been committed (murder), not two (lying as well)!

2.3

As Brunner puts it, 'The basis of the Divine Command is always the same, but its content varies with varying circumstances.' Therefore, the 'error of casuistry does not lie in the fact that it indicates the infinite variety of forms which the Command of love may assume; its error consists in deducing particular laws from a universal law... as though all could be arranged beforehand... Love, however, is free from all this predefinition' (*The Divine Imperative*, pp.132f). We might say, from the situationist's perspective, that it is possible to derive general 'principles' from whatever is the one and only universal law (*agape* for Christians, something else for others), but not laws or rules. We cannot milk universals from a universal!

2.4

William Temple put it this way: 'Universal obligation attaches not to particular judgments of conscience but to conscientiousness. What acts are right may depend on circumstances... but there is an absolute obligation to will whatever may on each occasion be right' (*Nature, Man and God*, p.405). Our obligation is relative *to* the situation, but obligation *in* the situation is absolute. We are only 'obliged' to tell the truth, for example, if the situation calls for it; if a murderer asks us his victim's whereabouts, our duty might be to lie. There is in situation ethics an absolute element and an element of calculation, as Alexander Miller once pointed out. But it would be better to say it has an absolute *norm* and a calculating method. There is weight in the old saying that what is needed is 'faith, hope and charity'. We have to find out what is 'fitting' to be truly ethical, to use H.R. Niebuhr's word for it in his *The Responsible Self*. Situation ethics aims at a contextual appropriateness – not the 'good' or the 'right' but the *fitting*.

2.5

A cartoon in a fundamentalist magazine once showed Moses scowling, holding his stone tablet with its graven laws, all ten, and an eager stonecutter saying to him, 'Aaron said perhaps you'd let us reduce them to "Act responsibly in love"'. This was meant as a dig at the situationists and the new morality, but the legalistic humour in it merely states exactly what situation ethics calls for! With Dietrich Bonhoeffer we say, 'Principles are only tools in God's hands, soon to be thrown away as unserviceable'. (*Ethics*, p.51).

2.6

One competent situationist, speaking to students, explained the position this way. Rules are 'like "Punt on fourth down," or "Take a pitch when the count is three balls." These rules are part of the wise player's know-how, and distinguish him from the novice. But they are not unbreakable. The best players are those who know when to ignore them. In the game of bridge, for example, there is a useful rule which says "Second hand low". But have you ever played with anyone who followed the rule slavishly? You say to him (in exasperation), "Partner, why didn't you play your ace? We could have set the hand." And he replies, unperturbed, "Second hand low!" What is wrong? The same thing that was wrong when Kant gave information to the murderer. He forgot the purpose of the game... He no longer thought of winning the hand, but of being able to justify himself by invoking the rule.'

2.7

This practical temper of the activist or *verb-minded* decision maker, versus contemplative *noun-mindedness*, is a major Biblical rather than Hellenistic trait. In Abraham Heschel's view, 'The insistence upon generalisation at the price of a total disregard of the particular and concrete is something which would be alien to prophetic thinking. Prophetic words are never detached from the concrete, historic situation. Theirs is not a timeless, abstract message; it always refers to an actual situation. The general is given in the particular and the verification of the abstract is in the concrete.' (*God in Search of Man: A Philosophy of Judaism*, p.204). A 'leap of faith' is an action decision rather than a leap of thought, for a man's faith is a hypothesis that he takes seriously enough to act on and live by.

2.8

There are various names for this approach: situationism, contextualism, occasionalism, circumstantialism, even actualism. These labels indicate, of course, that the core of the ethic they describe is a healthy and primary awareness that 'circumstances alter cases' – i.e., that in actual problems of conscience the situational variables are to be weighed as heavily as the normative or 'general' constants.

2.9

The situational factors are so primary that we may even say 'circumstances alter rules and principles'. It is said that when Gertrude Stein lay dying she declared, 'It is better to ask questions than to give answers, even good answers.' This is the temper of situation ethics. It is empirical, fact-minded, data conscious, inquiring. It is antimoralistic as well as antilegalistic, for it is sensitive to variety and complexity. It is neither simplistic nor perfectionist. It is casuistry (case-based) in a constructive and nonpejorative sense of the word. We should perhaps call it 'neocasuistry'. Like classical casuistry, it is case-focused and concrete, concerned to bring Christian imperatives into practical operation. But unlike classical casuistry, this neocasuistry repudiates any attempt to anticipate or prescribe real-life decisions in their existential particularity. It works with two guidelines from Paul: 'The written code kills, but the Spirit gives life' (2 Cor. 3.6), and 'For the whole law is fulfilled in one word, "You shall love your neighbour as yourself"' (Gal. 5.14)...

2.10

Christian situation ethics has only one norm or principle or law (call it what you will) that is binding and unexceptionable, always good and right regardless of the circumstances. That is 'love' – the *agape* of the summary commandment to love God and the neighbour. Everything else without exception, all laws and rules and principles and ideals and norms, are only *contingent*, only valid *if they happen* to serve love in any situation. Christian situation ethics is not a system or program of living according to a code, but an effort to relate love to a world of relativities through a casuistry obedient to love. It is the strategy of love. This strategy denies that there are, as Sophocles thought, any unwritten immutable laws of heaven, agreeing with Bultmann that all such notions are idolatrous and a demonic pretension.

2.11

In non-Christian situation ethics some other highest good or *summum bonum* will, of course, take love's place as the one and only standard – such as self-realisation in the ethics of Aristotle. But the *Christian* is neighbour-centred first and last. Love is for people, not for principles; i.e. it is personal – and therefore when the impersonal universal conflicts with the personal particular, the latter prevails in situation ethics. Because of its mediating position, prepared to act on moral laws or in spite of them, the antinomians will call situationists soft legalists, and legalists will call them cryptoantinomians.

2.12

It is necessary to insist that situation ethics is willing to make full and respectful use of principles, to be treated as maxims but not as laws or precepts. We might call it 'principled relativism'. To repeat the term used above, principles or maxims or general rules are *illuminators*. But they are not *directors*. The classic rule of moral theology has been to follow laws but to do it *as much as possible* according to love and according to reason (*secundum caritatem et secundum rationem*). Situation ethics, on the other hand, calls upon us to keep law in a subservient place, so that *only* love and reason really count when the chips are down!

2.13

Situationists have no invariable obligation to what are sometimes called 'middle axioms', logically derived as normative propositions based on love. An example of what is meant is the proposition that love of the neighbour in practice *usually* means putting human rights before property rights. The term 'middle axiom', first used by J.H. Oldham and William Temple, and notably by John C. Bennett in America, is well-meant but unfortunate, since an axiom is a self-validating, nonderivative proposition and it cannot stand in the 'middle' between something logically prior to it and a subsequent derivative. Middle-axiom theorists must beware lest they, too, slip into the error of deriving universals from universals.

2.14

There are usually two rules of reason used in moral inquiry. One is 'internal consistency', and nobody has any quarrel with it – a proposition ought not to contradict itself. The other is 'external consistence' (analogy), the principle that what applies in one case should apply in all similar cases. It is around this second canon that the differences arise. Antinomians reject analogy altogether, with their doctrine of radical particularity. Situationists ask, very seriously, if there ever are enough cases enough alike to validate a law or to support anything more than a cautious generalisation. In Edmond Cahn's puckish phrase, 'Every case is like every other case, and no two cases are alike.'

2.15
There is no real quarrel here between situationism and an ethic of principles, unless the principles are hardened into laws. Bishop Robinson says: 'Such an ethic [situationism] cannot but rely, in deep humility, upon guiding rules, upon the cumulative experience of one's own and other people's obedience. It is this bank of experience which gives us our working rules of "right" and "wrong", and without them we could not but flounder.' (*Honest to God*, pp.119-20). Nevertheless, in situation ethics even the most revered principles may be thrown aside if they conflict in any concrete case with love. Even Karl Barth, who writes vehemently of 'absolutely wrong' actions, allows for what he calls the *ultima ratio*, the outside chance that love in a particular situation might override the absolute. The instance he gives is abortion.

2.16
Using terms made popular by Tillich and others, we may say that Christian situationism is a method that proceeds, so to speak, from (1) its one and only law, *agape* (love), to (2) the *sophia* (wisdom) of the church and culture, containing many 'general rules' of more or less reliability, to (3) the *kairos* (moment of decision, the fullness of time) in which *the responsible self in the situation* decides whether the *sophia* can serve love there, or not. This is the situational strategy in capsule form. To legalists it will seem to treat the *sophia* without enough reverence and obedience; to antinomians it will appear befuddled and 'inhibited' by the *sophia*.

2.17
Legalists make an idol of the *sophia*, antinomians repudiate it, situationists *use* it. They cannot give to any principle less than love more than tentative consideration, for they know, with Dietrich Bonhoeffer, 'The question of the good is posed and is decided in the midst of each definite, yet unconcluded, unique and transient situation of our lives, in the midst of our living relationships with men, things, institutions and powers, in other words in their midst of our historical existence.' (*Ethics*, p.185) And Bonhoeffer, of course, is a modern Christian ethicist who was himself executed for trying to kill, even *murder*, Adolf Hitler – so far did he go as a situationist...

Abortion – a situation
2.18
In 1962 a patient in a state mental hospital raped a fellow patient, an unmarried girl ill with a radical schizophrenic psychosis. The victim's father, learning what had happened, charged the hospital with culpable negligence and requested that an abortion to end the unwanted pregnancy

be performed at once, in an early stage of the embryo. The staff and administrators of the hospital refused to do so, on the ground that the criminal law forbids all abortion except 'therapeutic' ones when the mother's life is at stake – because the *moral* law, it is supposed, holds that any interference with an embryo after fertilisation is murder, i.e. the taking of an innocent human being's life.

2.19

Let's relate the three ethical approaches to this situation.

The rape has occurred and the decisional question is: May we rightly (licitly) terminate this pregnancy, begun in act of force and violence by a mentally unbalanced rapist upon a frightened, mentally sick girl? Mother and embryo are apparently healthy on all the usual counts.

2.20

The legalists would say NO. Their position is that killing is absolutely wrong, inherently evil. It is permissible only as self-defence and in military service, which is held to be presumptive self-defence or justifiable homicide. If the mother's life is threatened, abortion is therefore justified, but for no other reasons. (Many doctors take an elastic view of 'life' and thereby justify abortions to save a patients *mental* life as well as physical.) Even in cases where they justify it, it is only *excused* – it is still held to be inherently evil. Many Protestants hold this view, and some humanists.

2.21

Catholic moral theology goes far beyond even the rigid legalism of the criminal law, absolutizing their prohibition of abortion *absolutely*, by denying all exceptions and calling even therapeutic abortion wrong. (They allow killing in self-defence against malicious, i.e. deliberate, aggressors but not in self-defence against innocent, i.e. unintentional, aggressors.) Thus, if it is a tragic choice of the mother's life or the baby's, as can happen in rare cases, neither can be saved.

2.22

To this ethical nightmare legalism replies: 'It is here that the Church appears merciless, but she is not. It is her logic which is merciless; and she promises that if the logic is followed the woman will receive a reward far greater than a number of years of life.' Inexplicably, shockingly, Dietrich Bonhoeffer says the same thing: 'The life of the mother is in the hand of God, but the life of the child is arbitrarily extinguished. The question whether the life of the mother or the life of the child is of greater value can hardly be a matter for human decision.' (*Ethics*, p.150).

2.23

The antinomians – but who can predict what *they* would say? Their ethic is by its nature and definition outside the reach of even generalities. We can only guess, not unreasonably, that if the antinomian lives by a love norm, he will be apt to favour abortion in this case.

2.24

The situationists, if their norm is the Christian commandment to love the neighbour, would almost certainly *in this case*, favour abortion and support the girl's father's request. (Many purely humanistic decision makers are of the same mind about abortion following rape, and after incest too.) They would in all likelihood favour abortion for the sake of the patient's physical and mental health, not only if it were needed to save her life. It is even likely they would favour abortion for the sake of the victim's self-respect or reputation or happiness or simply on the ground that no *unwanted* and *unintended* baby should ever be born.

2.25

They would, one hopes, reason that it is not killing because there is no person or human life in an embryo at an early stage of pregnancy (Aristotle and St Thomas held that opinion), or even if it *were* killing, it would not be murder because it is self-defence against, in this case, not one but *two* aggressors. First there is the rapist, who being insane was morally and legally innocent, and then there is the 'innocent' embryo which is continuing the ravisher's original aggression! Even self-defence legalism would have allowed the girl to kill her attacker, no matter that he was innocent in the forum of conscience because of his madness. The embryo is no more innocent, no less an aggressor or unwelcome invader! Is not the most loving thing possible (the right thing) in this case a responsible decision to terminate the pregnancy?

2.26   What think ye?

EXTRACT 3
COPLESTON
Objections to natural law

3.1

Aquinas' theory of the natural moral law gives rise to a number of questions. I can comment, however, only very briefly on a few selected questions.

And I begin with the one which is perhaps most likely to present itself to the reader's mind.

3.2

Aquinas believed that actions which are contrary to the natural moral law are not wrong simply because God prohibits them; they are prohibited by God because they are wrong. Suicide is wrong and eating meat on Friday when one is bound by the ecclesiastical law of abstinence is also wrong. But while there is nothing wrong in itself in eating meat on Friday, so that to do so is wrong only when and because it is forbidden, suicide is contrary to the natural moral law and so is wrong in itself. Ecclesiastical precepts like the law of abstinence on Fridays can be suspended or changed, but the natural moral law in unalterable. It is true that Aquinas distinguishes between primary and secondary precepts, derived from the first, and says that the last can be 'changed' for special reasons in a few particular cases. But what he means is that in some particular cases the circumstances of an act may be such that it no longer falls under the class of actions prohibited by the precept. For instance, we can say in general that if someone entrusts his property to us for safe keeping and asks for it back we ought to return it. But no sensible man would say that if someone entrusts us with a knife or a revolver and asks for it back when he is in a state of homicidal mania we are obliged to return it. In its general form, however, the precept remains valid. And we can say with truth that Aquinas believed in a set of unalterable moral precepts.

3.3

The question arises, however, whether this theory is compatible with the empirical fact that different people and different social groups have held divergent moral convictions. Do not the empirical facts suggest that the moral law is not unalterable but changeable? Or, to use the value-language, do not the empirical facts suggest that values are historically relative and that there are no universal and absolute values? Believing in a human nature which is constant Aquinas was led to postulate an unchangeable moral law; but some of the precepts which he regarded as forming part of its content have not been regarded by many people in the past and are not now regarded by many people as moral precepts at all. Is it not reasonable to conclude that Aquinas simply canonized, as it were, the moral convictions and standards of his time or at least of the society to which he belonged?

3.4

This is a far-reaching problem, and I must content myself with making the following relevant point, namely that differences in moral convictions do not by themselves constitute a disproof of the theory that there is an unchangeable moral law. For there might be an unchangeable moral law and at the same time varying degrees of insight into the content of this law, these differences being explicable in terms of the influence of a variety of empirical factors. To use the value-language, there might be objective and absolute values and at the same time different degrees of insight into these values. I do not mean to imply either that the existence of an unchanging moral law was for Aquinas an uncertain hypothesis or that the explicability of differences in moral conviction on the theory that there is such a law proves of itself that the theory is true. My point is that differences of opinion about moral precepts and moral values do not constitute a proof of the relativist position. And this point is one that should be taken into consideration in any discussion of the problem.

3.5

Aquinas himself was not ignorant of the fact that different groups have held different moral convictions. According to him all men are aware of the most fundamental principles in their most general form. All men would agree that in some sense good is to be pursued and evil avoided. If a man denies this principle he is probably denying not the principle itself but that what another man or a given society calls good is good. But when we come to less general and more particular conclusions, derived from the fundamental principles, ignorance is certainly possible. 'In the case of some the reason is blinded by passion or by bad habits or by physical conditions. For example, according the Julius Caesar robbery used not to be considered wrong among the Germans, although it is expressly against the natural law' [i.e. II.6 *above*]. *A fortiori* there can be differences of opinion about the application of precepts to particular cases. Conscience may be erroneous, whether through our own fault or through some cause for which we are not responsible. And if our conscience tells us that we ought to perform a particular act, it is our moral duty to perform it. 'Every conscience, whether it is right or wrong, whether it concerns things evil in themselves or things morally indifferent, obliges us to act in such a way that he who acts against his conscience sins' (*Quodlibetum*, 3, 27). This does not mean that there is no such thing as right reason and no such thing as an objectively correct moral conscience; but ignorance and mistakes are possible in moral matters, and the nearer we come to particulars the greater is the field for error.

3.6

But though the reader may be prepared to admit that differences in moral convictions do not by themselves alone constitute a disproof of Aquinas' theory of an unalterable moral law, he may easily feel that the latter's whole approach to the subject of moral precepts is extremely artificial and excessively rationalistic. For Aquinas talks as though people derive or deduce less general from more general moral precepts and then proceed to apply these precepts to particular actions. But surely, it may be said, this picture does not represent the facts. Moral precepts seem to be ultimately reducible to the expression of feelings of approval or disapproval of certain actions or of certain types of action. True, we do enunciate general moral precepts; and moral philosophers have not unnaturally tried to rationalize their own moral convictions or those of the group or society to which they belonged. But feeling comes first: it is the whole basis of ethics. It may indeed appear that ethical disputes can be settled by rational argument, and in a certain sense they can sometimes be so settled. For example, if two men can agree on a definition of murder they can discuss in a rational manner whether the action of killing someone who is dying from a painful and incurable disease falls under the definition or not. Each man points out to the other features of the action in question which he thinks that the other has overlooked, and it is at any rate possible that in the end one will succeed in convincing the other. But rational argument is possible only when there is already a certain measure of moral agreement. Is it not a notorious fact that if two people disagree about fundamental moral issues or defend sharply opposed sets of values, neither can be convinced simply by the arguments advanced by the other? They will either agree to differ or they will end in anger and even abuse. Moreover, the function of any arguments which may be advanced by one of them seems to be that of facilitating a change of feeling or of emotional attitude. And perhaps the same can be said of discussions concerning the moral quality of particular actions or types of action when these discussions cannot be reduced to a quasi-logical problem of classification. If two men discuss the question whether so-called 'mercy killing' is right or wrong, the one maintaining that it is right, the other that it is wrong, the function of drawing attention to aspects of the action which the one man believes to have been overlooked by the other seems to be that of facilitating a change of emotive reaction in the other. The one man desires to substitute in the other man a feeling of approval for a feeling of disapproval or *vice versa*, as the case may be; and the arguments and appeals to reason which are employed are techniques used to facilitate this change of emotive response. *In fine*, morality is 'more properly felt than judged of', to use Hume's words (*Treatise*, 3,1,2).

3.7

It can hardly be denied that Aquinas' language sometimes seems to imply an extremely rationalistic interpretation of the way in which people form their moral judgments. But we have to look at what he means by the statements which he makes. He compares, for example, the precept that good is to be pursued and evil avoided with the proposition that the whole is greater than any one of its parts. And while he thought that this proposition is known to all human beings once they have had experience of material things he did not mean to say that every human being explicitly enunciates it to himself in so many words, even though he would certainly assent to it if it were proposed to him. 'In the cognitive powers there can be inchoate habits... And the understanding of [first] principles is termed a natural habit. For it is owing to the very nature of the intellectual soul that once a man knows what is a whole and what is a part he knows that every whole is greater than any one of its parts, though he cannot know what is a whole and what is a part except through ideas derived from images' (*S.T.*, Ia, IIae, 51,1). Directly a human being has experience of material wholes he recognizes immediately the relation between whole and part, and that he knows this can be seen by the fact that he never assumes that any part is greater than the whole of which it is a part. But it does not necessarily follow that he ever says to himself in so many words that a whole is greater than any one of its parts. Similarly, a human being obtains the idea of good, of a thing considered as perfecting or as satisfying his nature in some way, only through experience of actual objects of desire and sources of satisfaction. But because of his innate inclinations to the good in this sense he immediately apprehends it as something to be pursued, while he apprehends evil, considered as that which is opposed to his nature and natural inclinations, as something to be avoided. The fact that he does apprehend the good or the perfection as something to be pursued and the evil, that which is opposed to or thwarts his natural inclinations, as something to be shunned and avoided is shown by the whole of his conduct. For every human being naturally shuns whatever appears to him as opposed to his nature. But it does not necessarily follow that he ever explicitly enunciates to himself the proposition that good is to be pursued and evil avoided. One may be tempted to say that all this belongs to the instinctive level and the level of feeling rather than the level of rational apprehension. But Aquinas would doubtless comment that a man does not shun death, for example, simply in the same way that an animal can be said to do so. For he shuns it not only instinctively but because and in so far as he apprehends it with his reason as destructive of his nature. And since he shuns it and avoids it as evil, knowledge that evil is to be shunned and avoided is implicitly presupposed. Though we could have no idea of evil except through experience of things opposed to our natural inclinations, apprehension of the principle that evil is to be avoided is logically presupposed by recognition of the fact that this particular thing is to be avoided because it is evil.

3.8

As regards deduction, Aquinas did not think that we can deduce the proposition that to have sexual intercourse with someone else's wife is wrong from the precept that good is to be pursued and evil avoided simply by contemplating, as it were, this latter precept. We can no more do this than we can deduce from the principle of non-contradiction the proposition that a thing which is white all over cannot at the same time be red all over. We obtain our ideas of whiteness and redness from other sources than an analysis of the principle of non-contradiction. At the same time we reject the proposition that a thing can be simultaneously white all over and red all over precisely because it involves a contradiction. Similarly, we do not obtain our ideas of other people and of wives and of sexual intercourse simply by analysing the precept that good is to be pursued and evil avoided. But once we have obtained those ideas we reject, if we do reject, the proposition that it is right to have sexual intercourse with someone else's wife because we apprehend actions of this sort as being evil. The word 'deduction', therefore, can be very misleading; and what Aquinas actually says is that other precepts of the natural law are 'founded on' or 'based on' the precept that good is to be done and evil avoided. The concrete good for man can be known only by reflection on human nature as known in experience.

3.9

It has been said above that we reject, 'if we do reject', the proposition that it is right to have sexual intercourse with someone else's wife because we apprehend actions of this sort as being evil. As we have seen, Aquinas thought that the nearer we come to particulars the more possible becomes ignorance or error concerning the objective good for man, and so concerning the particular precepts of the natural moral law. But some particular types of action are practically always apprehended as evil, as opposed in some way or other to human nature. For example, even at the lowest level of civilization some acts will be immediately 'felt' to be destructive of social cohesion in the group and so opposed to human nature considered under its social aspect. And they will awaken disapprobation in a quasi-instinctive manner. I have put the word 'felt' in inverted commas and I have spoken of a 'quasi-instinctive' manner because I think that while Aquinas might agree that the term 'feel' has a use in drawing attention to the difference between, say, a primitive man's apprehension of an act as evil and a moral philosopher's reflective appreciation of its moral quality he would still maintain that the primitive man mentally apprehends the act as evil and that the term 'feel' is inappropriate in so far as it suggests the absence of any mental activity.

3.10

One can put the matter in this way perhaps. Aquinas thought that all men share some very vague ideas about the good for man, precisely because they are men and possess certain natural tendencies and inclinations in common. For instance, men see that knowledge of the truths required for life should be sought for. And if one wishes to draw attention to the immediacy of the perception one might perhaps say that they 'feel' this. But Aquinas would doubtless insist that mental activity is involved and that some word like 'apprehend' or 'understand' is more appropriate.

3.11

But when it comes to apprehending what are the truths necessary for life and, in general, to determining in a concrete way what is the good for man and to forming moral judgments which are less general than what Aquinas calls the primary principles of the natural law in their widest form, there is room for prolonged reflection and discussion. There is room also for the intervention of a variety of factors other than rational reflection, which can exercise an important influence in the formation of man's moral outlook and set of determinate values. And these factors can be internal, physiological and psychological, as well as external, like upbringing and social environment.

3.12

Finally, when there is the question of applying principles to individual cases, of deciding whether a given action belongs to this class or that class, and is right or wrong, Aquinas recognizes (cf. his commentary on *Ethics*, 2, c.2, *lectio* 2) that though the moral philosopher can provide some help, by drawing attention, for example, to different features of the action, he cannot settle a person's perplexity by a process of sheer logical deduction. Ultimately a man has to make his own decision. And Aquinas observes that a man's actual decision may be perfectly correct even though the abstract problem has not been satisfactorily settled. Perhaps we might say that in such cases the man 'feels' that the action is right or wrong, as the case may be, in order to emphasize the difference between the immediacy of the judgment and a piece of logical or mathematical deduction. But Aquinas would doubtless say that the virtue of 'prudence' often enables a man to discern the objective moral quality of an action even when he is unable to give adequate reasons, which would satisfy a moral philosopher, for saying that the action is right or wrong. An action is right or wrong for Aquinas in virtue of its relation to the good for man, and this relation is discerned by the mind, even though the immediacy of the discerning may be such as to incline one to use the word 'feeling'. And the (or at least a) fundamental difference between Aquinas' theory and a purely emotive moral theory is that the former asserts an objective and determinable relationship in virtue of which actions are good or bad, right or wrong, whereas the latter does not.

3.13

In this section I have mentioned ideas suggested by the relativist and emotive theories of ethics. My purpose in doing so, however, was clarificatory rather than polemical, and to avoid misunderstanding I want to explain this point. It was not my intention to 'expound' these theories; and therefore I have carefully avoided mentioning the name of any philosopher save that of Hume, who was mentioned as the author of a proposition which it is usual to quote on these occasions. Nor was it my intention to refute the theories by means of Aquinas' philosophy. My purpose was simply that of using some ideas suggested by these theories to clarify the latter's position. The chief plank on which the relativistic theory of morals rests is probably the empirical fact that different people have held divergent views about moral matters. And as facts are facts whatever conclusions may be drawn from them, it is important to ask whether Aquinas had any idea of these facts and whether his ethical theory is capable of accounting for them or of allowing for them. Similarly, in the moral life of ordinary people deduction, as this is understood in logic and mathematics, does not seem to play any very conspicuous role, whereas something that might plausibly be described as 'feeling' appears to be an important factor. It is therefore a pertinent question to ask whether Aquinas thought that everyone forms his or her moral convictions by a process of logical deduction and whether his theory can account for the factor of immediacy in our moral and valuational judgments. In other words, my purpose was simply that of making a brief contribution to the clarification of Aquinas' position with the aid of ideas suggested by later ethical theories.

EXTRACT 4

JOHN PAUL II

The crisis of moral truth

> *'You will know the truth, and the truth will make you free'*
> (Jn. 8.32)

4.1

The human issues most frequently debated and differently resolved in contemporary moral reflection are all closely related, albeit in various ways, to a crucial issue: *human freedom*.

4.2
Certainly people today have a particularly strong sense of freedom. As the [Vatican II] Council's Declaration on Religious Freedom *Dignitatis Humanae* had already observed, 'the dignity of the human person is a concern of which people of our time are becoming increasingly more aware'. Hence the insistent demand that people be permitted to 'enjoy the use of their own responsible judgment and freedom, and decide on their actions on grounds of duty and conscience, without external pressure or coercion'. In particular, the right to religious freedom and to respect for conscience on its journey towards the truth is increasingly perceived as the foundation of the cumulative rights of the person.

4.3
This heightened sense of the dignity of the human person and of his or her uniqueness, and of the respect due to the journey of conscience, certainly represents one of the positive achievements of modern culture. This perception, authentic as it is, has been expressed in a number of more or less adequate ways, some of which however diverge from the truth about man as a creature and the image of God, and thus need to be corrected and purified in the light of faith.

4.4
Certain currents of modern thought have gone so far as to exalt freedom to such an extent that it becomes an absolute, which would then be the source of values. This is the direction taken by doctrines which have lost the sense of the transcendent or which are explicitly atheist. The individual conscience is accorded the status of a supreme tribunal of moral judgment which hands down categorical and infallible decisions about good and evil. To the affirmation that one has a duty to follow one's conscience is unduly added the affirmation that one's moral judgment is true merely by the fact that it has its origin in the conscience. But in this way the inescapable claims of truth disappear, yielding their place to a criterion of sincerity, authenticity and 'being at peace with oneself', so much so that some have come to adopt a radically subjectivistic conception of moral judgment.

4.5
As is immediately evident, the crisis of truth is not unconnected with this development. Once the idea of a universal truth about the good, knowable by human reason, is lost, inevitably the notion of conscience also changes.

Conscience is no longer considered in its primordial reality as an act of a person's intelligence, the function of which is to apply the universal knowledge of the good in a specific situation and thus to express a judgment about the right conduct to be chosen here and now. Instead, there is a tendency to grant to the individual conscience the prerogative of independently determining the criteria of good and evil and then acting accordingly. Such an outlook is quite congenial to an individualist ethic, wherein each individual is faced with his own truth, different from the truth of others. Taken to its extreme consequences, this individualism leads to a denial of the very idea of human nature.

4.6
These different notions are at the origin of currents of thought which posit a radical opposition between moral law and conscience, and between nature and freedom.

4.7
Side by side with its exaltation of freedom, yet oddly in contrast with it, modern culture radically questions the very existence of this freedom. A number of disciplines, grouped under the name of the 'behavioural sciences', have rightly drawn attention to the many kinds of psychological and social conditioning which influence the exercise of human freedom. Knowledge of these conditionings and the study they have received represent important achievements which have found application in various areas, for example in pedagogy or the administration of justice. But some people, going beyond the conclusions which can be legitimately drawn from these observations, have come to question or even deny the very reality of human freedom.

4.8
Mention should also be made here of theories which misuse scientific research about the human person. Arguing from the great variety of customs, behaviour patterns and institutions present in humanity, these theories end up, if not with an outright denial of universal human values, at least with a relativistic conception of morality.

4.9
'Teacher, what good must I do to have eternal life?' The question of morality, to which Christ provides the answer, cannot prescind from the issue of freedom. Indeed, it considers that issue central, for there can be no morality without freedom: 'It is only in freedom that man can turn to what is good'. But what sort of freedom? The Council, considering our contemporaries who 'highly regard' freedom and 'assiduously pursue' it, but who 'often

cultivate it in wrong ways as a licence to do anything they please, even evil', speaks of 'genuine' freedom: 'Genuine freedom is an outstanding manifestation of the divine image in man. For God willed to leave man "in the power of his own counsel", so that he would seek his Creator of his own accord and would freely arrive at full and blessed perfection by cleaving to God' (*Dignitatis Humanae*). Although each individual has a right to be respected in his own journey in search of the truth, there exists a prior moral obligation, and a grave one at that, to seek the truth and to adhere to it once it is known. As Cardinal John Henry Newman, that outstanding defender of the rights of conscience, forcefully put it: 'Conscience has rights because it has duties'.

4.10
Certain tendencies in contemporary moral theology, under the influence of the currents of subjectivism and individualism just mentioned, involve novel interpretations of the relationship of freedom to the moral law, human nature and conscience, and propose novel criteria for the moral evaluation of acts. Despite their variety, these tendencies are at one in lessening or even denying the dependence of freedom on truth.

4.11
If we wish to undertake a critical discernment of these tendencies – discernment capable of acknowledging what is legitimate, useful and of value in them, while at the same time pointing out their ambiguities, dangers and errors – we must examine them in the light of the fundamental dependence of freedom upon truth, a dependence which has found its clearest and most authoritative expression in the words of Christ: 'You will know the truth, and the truth will set you free' (Jn. 8.32).

Freedom and law

'Of the tree of the knowledge of good and evil you shall not eat'
(Gen. 2.17)

4.12
In the Book of Genesis we read: 'The Lord God commanded the man, saying, "You may eat freely of every tree of the garden; but of the tree of the knowledge of good and evil you shall not eat, for in the day that you eat of it you shall die"' (Gen. 2.16-17).

4.13
With this imagery, Revelation teaches that the power to decide what is good and what is evil does not belong to man, but to God alone. The man

is certainly free, inasmuch as he can understand and accept God's commands. And he possesses an extremely far-reaching freedom, since he can eat 'of every tree of the garden'. But his freedom is not unlimited: it must halt before the 'tree of the knowledge of good and evil', for it is called to accept the moral law given by God. In fact, human freedom finds its authentic and complete fulfilment precisely in the acceptance of that law. God, who alone is good, knows perfectly what is good for man, and by virtue of his very love proposes this good to man in the commandments.

4.14

God's law does not reduce, much less do away with human freedom; rather, it protects and promotes that freedom. In contrast, however, some present-day cultural tendencies have given rise to several currents of thought in ethics which centre upon an alleged conflict between freedom and law. These doctrines would grant to individuals or social groups the right to determine what is good or evil. Human freedom would thus be able to 'create values' and would enjoy a primacy over truth, to the point that truth itself would be considered a creation of freedom. Freedom would thus lay claim to a moral autonomy which would actually amount to an absolute sovereignty.

4.15

The modern concern for the claims of autonomy has not failed to exercise an influence also in the sphere of Catholic moral theology. While the latter has certainly never attempted to set human freedom against the divine law or to question the existence of an ultimate religious foundation for moral norms, it has, nonetheless, been led to undertake a profound rethinking about the role of reason and of faith in identifying moral norms with reference to specific 'innerworldly' kinds of behaviour involving oneself, others and the material world.

4.16

It must be acknowledged that underlying this work of rethinking there are certain positive concerns which to a great extent belong to the best tradition of Catholic thought. In response to the encouragement of the Second Vatican Council, there has been a desire to foster dialogue with modern culture, emphasising the rational – and thus universally understandable and communicable – character of moral norms belonging to the sphere of the natural moral law. There has also been an attempt to reaffirm the interior character of the ethical requirements deriving from that law, requirements which create an obligation for the will only because such an obligation was previously acknowledged by human reason and, concretely, by personal conscience.

4.17
Some people, however, disregarding the dependence of human reason on Divine Wisdom and the need, given the present state of fallen nature, for Divine Revelation as an effective means for knowing moral truths, even those of the natural order, have actually posited a complete sovereignty of reason in the domain of moral norms regarding the right ordering of life in this world. Such norms would constitute the boundaries for a merely 'human' morality; they would be the expression of a law which man in an autonomous manner lays down for himself and which has its source exclusively in human reason. In no way could God be considered the Author of this law, except in the sense that human reason exercises its autonomy in setting down laws by virtue of a primordial and total mandate given to man by God. These trends of thought have led to a denial, in opposition to Sacred Scripture (cf. Mt 15:3-6) and the Church's constant teaching, of the fact that the natural moral law has God as its author, and that man, by the use of reason, participates in the eternal law, which it is not for him to establish.

4.18
In their desire, however, to keep the moral life in a Christian context, certain moral theologians have introduced a sharp distinction, contrary to Catholic doctrine, between an ethical order, which would be human in origin and of value for this world alone, and an order of salvation, for which only certain intentions and interior attitudes regarding God and neighbour would be significant. This has then led to an actual denial that there exists, in Divine Revelation, a specific and determined moral content, universally valid and permanent. The word of God would be limited to proposing an exhortation, a generic *paraenesis*, which the autonomous reason alone would then have the task of completing with normative directives which are truly 'objective', that is, adapted to the concrete historical situation. Naturally, an autonomy conceived in this way also involves the denial of a specific doctrinal competence on the part of the Church and her *Magisterium* with regard to particular moral norms which deal with the so-called 'human good'. Such norms would not be part of the proper content of Revelation, and would not in themselves be relevant for salvation.

4.19
No one can fail to see that such an interpretation of the autonomy of human reason involves positions incompatible with Catholic teaching.

4.20

In such a context it is absolutely necessary to clarify, in the light of the word of God and the living Tradition of the Church, the fundamental notions of human freedom and of the moral law, as well as their profound and intimate relationship. Only thus will it be possible to respond to the rightful claims of human reason in a way which accepts the valid elements present in certain currents of contemporary moral theology without compromising the Church's heritage of moral teaching with ideas derived from an erroneous concept of autonomy.

EXTRACT 5
FIORENZA
Ethics and feminist theology

5.1

Feminist theology seeks to unmask the oppressive function [of] patriarchal theology. It explores women's experience of oppression and discrimination in society and religion as well as our experiences of hope, love, and faith in the struggle for liberation and well-being. Feminist theology has a dual parentage: the women's liberation movement in society and church as well as the academy and theological institutions.

5.2

Feminist studies and theology are proud to be the daughters of the women's movement and at the same time ambivalent about their origin and setting in the academy. Whereas in the last century the women's movement sought access for women to the academy and the ministry by pointing to women's special 'feminine' contributions, in this century it did so by claiming women's full personhood and 'equal rights.' However, women began to realize that it does not suffice to argue for a special sphere or domain for women or to integrate women into male-dominated society and church. What is necessary is the transformation of the patriarchal state and church into institutions that allow for the full participation of women as well as men in society and church.

5.3

In the last century women gained access to academic work and theological studies at first through special courses or seminaries for women. Then women were admitted to full academic and theological studies if they could prove that they were as good as, if not better than, their male colleagues.

Although women scholars have fulfilled all the standards of academic excellence, only a very few have achieved faculty status or scholarly influence. Today feminist theologians no longer seek merely to become incorporated into the androcentric academy and theological institutions. Rather, women scholars have come to realize more and more that all intellectual institutions and academic disciplines need to be redefined and transformed if they are to allow women to participate fully as subjects of academic research and theological scholarship. Feminist studies, therefore, seek to engender, in the words of Thomas Kuhn, a paradigm shift from the male-centered scholarship that is produced by the patriarchal academy and church to a feminist comprehension of the world, human life, and Christian faith.

5.4

Just as feminist studies in general have affected all areas of academic inquiry, so also feminist theology has worked for the transformation of theology. It seeks to integrate the emancipatory struggles for ending societal and ecclesial patriarchy with religious vision, Christian faith, and theological reflection. If theology is 'faith seeking understanding' [Anselm] then feminist theology is best understood as the reflection on Christian faith-experiences in the struggle against patriarchal oppression. If theology, as Karl Rahner puts it, has the vocation to engage the whole church in self-criticism, then feminist theology has the task to engender ecclesial self-criticism, not just of the church's androcentrism but also of its historical patriarchal structures.

5.5

Feminist theology thus begins with the experience of women struggling against patriarchal exclusion and for liberation and human dignity. Just as other liberation theologies so a critical feminist theology of liberation understands itself as a systemic exploration and 'second order' reflection on this experience. Its methods are therefore critical analysis, constructive exploration, and conceptual transformation. As a critical theology feminist theology identifies not only the androcentric dynamics and misogynist elements of Christian Scriptures, traditions, and theologies but also those structures of the church that perpetuate patriarchal sexism as well as racism, classism, and colonialism in and outside the church. As a constructive theology feminist theological studies seek both to recover and reconstruct all those theological symbols and expressions that reflect the liberative faith experiences of the church as the discipleship community of equals, the experiences of the people of God who are women.

5.6

However, it must be noted that feminist studies articulate emancipatory struggles and liberatory perspectives in different ways and with the help of varying philosophical or sociological-political analyses. While liberal feminisms, for example, emphasize the autonomy and equal rights of the individual, socialist or Marxist feminisms see the relationship between social class and gender within Western capitalism as determinative of women's societal oppression. Third World feminisms in turn insist that the interactions of racism, colonialism, and sexism are defining women's oppression and struggle for liberation. Such a variety of analyses and theoretical perspectives results in different conceptions of feminism, of women's liberation, and of being human in the world.

5.7
A diversity in approach and polyphony in feminist intellectual articulations are also found in feminist theology and in feminist studies in religion. It is therefore misleading to speak of feminist theology in the singular or of *the* feminist theology without recognizing many different articulations and analyses of feminist theologies. These articulations not only share in the diverse presuppositions and theoretical analyses of women's experience but also work within diverse theological frameworks, e.g. neo-orthodoxy, liberal theology, process theology, evangelical theology, or liberation theology. As theological articulations they are rooted in diverse ecclesial visions and pluriform political-religious contexts. I have defined my own approach as a critical theology of liberation that is indebted to historical-critical, critical-political, and liberation-theological analyses and is rooted in experience and engagement as a Catholic Christian woman.

5.8
Insofar as feminist theology does not begin with doctrines about God and revelation but with the experience of women struggling for liberation from patriarchal oppression, its pluriform vision is articulated by the voices of women from different races, classes, cultures, and nations. These theological voices challenge androcentric forms of liberation theology to articulate the preferential 'option' for the poor and oppressed as the option for poor and oppressed *women*, because the majority of the poor and exploited today are women and children dependent on women for survival. As the African theologian Mercy Amba Oduyoye has pointed out:

> [Feminist theology] is not simply a challenge to the dominant theology of the capitalist West. It is a challenge to the maleness of Christian theology worldwide, together with the patriarchal presuppositions that govern all our relationships as well as the tradition; a situation in

which men (male human beings) reflected upon the whole of life on behalf of the whole community of women and men, young and old.

5.9

If the primary theological question for liberation theology is not 'How can we believe in God?' but 'How can the poor achieve dignity?' then a critical feminist theology of liberation must articulate the quest for women's dignity and liberation ultimately as the quest for God. The hermeneutical privilege of the poor must be articulated as the hermeneutical privilege of poor women. Liberation theologies of all colors must address the patriarchal domination and sexual exploitation of women.

5.10

In short, feminist theologians do not limit themselves either to studies about women or to the academy. They do not seek to articulate a theology of woman nor restrict their questions to women. Rather, they understand themselves as charting a different method and an alternative perspective for doing theology. Therefore, a critical feminist theology of liberation constructs theology neither in terms of the traditional taxonomies and dogmatic *topoi* of theology such as God, Christ, creation, church, sacraments, or eschatology, nor in terms of an academic religious studies approach. Both approaches are valuable and necessary; but they attempt to chart new visions and roads with the help of the old maps of doctrinal or academic theology.

5.11

Instead, a critical feminist liberation theology seeks to adopt an interdisciplinary approach and framework that does not reinscribe professional divisions among the various theological disciplines but uses their methods as tools for investigating women's theological questions. It does not envision theology as a doctrinal system but as an active theological reflection on liberation struggles, as an emancipatory way of 'doing' theology. Hence feminist theological studies seek dialogic, participatory, non-hierarchical processes of doing research and teaching that cultivate the gifts and talents of everyone. In short, feminist studies demand not just the admittance of women to the academy and the recognition of women's intellectual contributions in the past and the present. They also require a reconceptualization and revision of accepted theoretical assumptions and frameworks that until very recently have been based entirely on the experiences and studies of 'educated' men.

5.12

A critical theology of liberation calls for a paradigm shift in theological and ecclesial self-understanding. It insists that the androcentric-clerical theology produced in Western universities and seminaries no longer can claim to be a Catholic Christian theology if it does not seek to become a theology inclusive of the experiences of all members of the church, women and men, lay and clergy. Dominant theology cannot even claim to be a Christian theology proclaiming the 'good news' of salvation if it does not take seriously its call to be a theology subversive of every form of sexist-racist-capitalist patriarchy.

5.13

As a critical theology of liberation feminist theology conceives of feminism not just as a theoretical worldview and analysis but as a women's liberation movement for societal and ecclesial change. Patriarchy in this view is not just a 'dualistic ideology' or androcentric world-construction in language, not just the domination of all men over all women, but a sociocultural political system of graded subjugations and dominations. Sexism, racism, and militaristic colonialism are the roots and pillars of patriarchy. Since the silence and invisibility of Catholic women are generated by patriarchal laws and structures of the church and maintained by androcentric, i.e., male-defined, theology, a critical feminist liberation theology seeks to investigate in what ways androcentric language, theoretical frameworks, and theological scholarship sustain and perpetuate patriarchal structures in society and church.

5.14

The term 'patriarchy' is often used interchangeably with 'sexism' and 'androcentrism.' However, these feminist analytical categories must be distinguished. Androcentrism or androcentric dualism is to be understood as a world-construction in language. It indicates a framework, mindset, or ideology that legitimates patriarchy. Patriarchy in turn is a societal system of domination and exploitation that is structured by heterosexism, racism, nationalism, and classism.

5.15

Patriarchal sexism is enforced by female 'sexual slavery' that cuts across all lines of race, class, and culture. Whereas patriarchal racism defines certain people as subhuman in order to exploit their labor, patriarchal sexism seeks to control women's procreative powers and labor. Violence against women and children is increasing at a time when women claim the full human rights and dignity accorded to male citizens. The political Right's attack on feminism, its battle for the recriminalization of women and their doctors, and its rhetoric for the 'protection of the Christian family' seek to reinforce women's economic dependency; to strengthen the patriarchal controls of women's procreative powers, and to maintain the patriarchal family as the mainstay of the patriarchal state. Sexual violence against women and children in and outside the home sustains the patriarchal order of male dominance:

> Anonymous verbal and bodily assault: rape – rape in general, racial rape, marital rape, wartime rape, gang rape, child rape – wife and women battering; abortion and birth control laws; involuntary sterilizations; unnecessary hysterectomies; clitoridectomies and genital mutilations; prostitution and female slavery; sexual harassment in employment; aggressive pornography [Ruth Bleier's *Science and Gender*].

5.16
All these and more are forms of sanctioned violence against women. Whereas sociobiologists view rape as a natural, biological tendency in males, as a *biological* imperative, feminist studies have documented that rape and other forms of institutionalized violence against women are a *social* imperative necessary to uphold patriarchy by force.

5.17
The struggle against the violence and dehumanization of societal and religious patriarchy in Western societies is at the heart of all liberation struggles against racism, colonialism, militarism, and poverty. Feminist theology does not just reflect on these struggles; it is also shaped by them and in turn inspires them. Androcentric legitimations of patriarchal domination and victimization become more pronounced and forceful whenever claims to equality and self-determination gain public recognition and broad acceptance. Feminist thought is labelled extremist, subversive, irrational, or abnormal because it seeks to put forward an alternative to patriarchy as the basis of Euro-American society or church. It demystifies and rejects cultural or religious values of male domination and subordination, which are the very standard of reasonableness, veracity, and knowledge.

CRITIQUE

An internal comparison of the Extracts will generate a number of important criticisms – e.g. by comparing Copleston's and

Fletcher's theories of exceptions (the last sentence in 2.2 is clearly an oversimplification). In addition, a number of specific criticisms can be isolated:

Bonhoeffer's Extract must face crucial questions: (1) If we have no prior knowledge of God or of morality, how do we accept the truth of Christianity in the first place? (2) Does Bonhoeffer altogether avoid general ethical categories? At various points in his life he appeared to hold deontological views on such issues as pacifism and abortion. Further he shared these views with some nonChristians over-and-against other Christians (see, particularly, *Ethics*, ch. 3). (3) In their stand against Hitler, does he sometimes allow secular moralists some relative value? A parallel point will arise in relation to Augustine's Text IV and all these questions must be addressed to Barth's Extract 6.

Most exponents of Christian ethics might agree that *agape* is a central concept, but few might agree with Fletcher that it is a sufficient concept (see *below*, pp.564–6). Empirically, it can be asked whether many of us are sufficiently free or strong to make continuous moral decisions, without knowing, in advance, any of the requirements of *agape*. And, at the theoretical level, it would seem that Fletcher himself does, at times, assume criteria other than *agape* in his examples of moral decision-making. For example, in 2.24 he suggests the ground that 'no unwanted and unintended baby should ever be born': but, clearly, many 'unwanted and unintended' babies are still loved, so some other factor seems to be contributing to this ground. And, in 2.25, the force of his argument depends upon the prior belief that 'murder' is wrong and that 'insanity' relieves the individual of moral responsibility.

Copleston's Extract does not answer some of the most serious problems already raised in relation to Aquinas' Text II. So, even allowing for human error, custom or sin, he does not specify the positive evidence needed to suggest that there are moral precepts common to all human beings. Whilst evidence of empirical differences on moral issues between people may not actually disprove Aquinas' theory, unless there is also some positive evidence in its favour it must undermine our confidence in it.

It has already been observed that, despite their strong deontological claims, John Paul II and Fiorenza, perhaps unwittingly, provide striking examples of the pluralism of present-day theology. There are hints in Fiorenza that there are divisions within feminist theology itself (5.6-7) and the polemical tone of parts of *Veritatis Splendor* indicates that there are evident divisions within present-day Catholic theology (4.10-11 and 15-18). However, the characteristic mode of both theologians in dealing with such divisions tends to be that simply of assertion.

In contrast, Catholic moral theologians such as John Mahoney argue for a much franker admission of diversity within Catholicism. He maintains that 'there cannot be any doubt... that the Roman Catholic Church's teaching over the centuries and in recent decades has changed markedly in many respects – as in the field of biblical studies; in the possibility of salvation for unbelievers outside the Catholic Church; in ecumenism; in the matter and form of the Sacrament of Orders; in recognizing the moral possibility in marriage of birth-control through periodic abstinence from intercourse' (*The Making of Moral Theology*, pp.325-6).

SECTION 2

POLITICS, ECONOMICS AND JUSTICE

SECTION 2

POLITICS, ECONOMICS AND JUSTICE

Within recent Christian ethics the cluster of issues surrounding the overall themes of politics, economics and justice have proved particularly important. The rise of Liberation theology, especially, has made apparent some of the differences within the discipline, just as the inter-war political crisis revealed crucial theological differences for a previous generation. The problem of the relationship of Christianity to the political order and to the issues of social and economic justice, is not simply of theoretical interest, but of considerable practical importance. At the individual level, the Christian attempts to arrive at an understanding of the implications of his or her faith for involvement in political realities. At the corporate level, ecclesiastical institutions attempt to decide how far they are to be involved in specifically political institutions and in detailed political decision-making. The focus of this Section will sometimes be on the individual level and sometimes on the corporate one. In some of the Texts and Extracts attention is given to overall political structures, whereas in others it is the specific issues of economic or social justice which are of primary concern. However, it must be stressed firmly at the outset, that each of the Texts or Extracts must be set in its own socio-political context before it is (anachronistically) related to others within the Section. It must not be assumed, too readily, that the various authors all attach the same meaning to their social or political terms.

One way of demonstrating the variety of positions in Christian ethics in this area is to compare possible answers to the following questions:

(1) Can specific political structures, ideals or programmes be derived unambiguously from the Gospel?
(2) How far can the Church be identified with specific political regimes, ideals or programmes?
(3) Should the individual Christian be totally obedient to specific political regimes, ideals or programmes?

If a positive response is given to (1), the two other questions may appear relatively unproblematic: the Church can identify fully with such political regimes, ideals or programmes and, likewise, the individual Christian clearly should be obedient to them. But, of course, even for those who would accept (1), most might acknowledge that actual politicians or political regimes seldom adopt unsullied Christian ideals or programmes. Even if they disagree with the dichotomy that Niebuhr advanced, between individual Christian ethics and political moral practice, they might still agree that Christian ethics makes demands upon politicians and political regimes which are frequently ignored. If, however, a negative response is given to (1), either because the Gospel is thought to be too ambiguous on many political issues, or because it is thought to be uninterested in them, any close identification of the Church with specific political regimes, ideals or programmes would seem to be precluded. For many, total obedience of the individual Christian to specific political regimes, ideals or programmes would also be thereby precluded. But to some, as will be seen, it would still be required, on the grounds that political regimes are always divinely appointed, even when they conflict with Christian ideals and principles.

Within this broad framework it is possible to locate the overall positions of the authors of the Texts and Extracts in this Section. A very broad acceptance of (1) is evident in Aquinas and John XXIII. In very different ways, it is also evident in Miranda. A rejection of (1), on the grounds of the lack of interest of the Gospel in specific political matters, is evident at times in Augustine and Berdyaev. And an extreme wariness of (1), combined with a rejection of (2), but an insistence on (3), is evident in Luther and Barth. These three clusters of possibilities must each be examined separately: like all such clusters, they may reveal similarities, but blur real differences.

Aquinas' use of natural law is very evident here: 'it would seem best to deduce the duties of a king from the examples of government in nature' (V.I). He believed that from nature he could both justify and understand monarchical, hierarchical government. But, as always, the Bible was thought to accord with this justification and understanding; the latter could be derived from direct analogical argument from Genesis 1.3. If this position is accepted, it might seem to follow that the Church can be identified with specific political regimes, ideals and programmes, and that the individual Christian does have a general duty to be obedient to them. Naturally, this position is further reinforced by the peculiarities of the Church/State relationship in 13th-century Europe. It has already been noted (see *above*, p.46) that this consisted of boundaries of power and authority, not of opposing aims, values and social orders. Indeed, only in the Extracts is the concept of the secular State assumed.

Aquinas' derivation of political monarchy from natural law and from biblical bases compares interestingly with Calvin's justification of democracy (albeit in the changed context of 16th-century middle Europe). Calvin's *Institutes* declared emphatically, that some form of government was essential and he was sharply critical of any form of Christian anarchism: 'some fanatics who are pleased with nothing but liberty, or rather licentiousness without any restraint, do indeed boast and vociferate, that since we are dead with Christ to the elements of this world and, being translated into the kingdom of God, sit among the celestials, it is a degradation to us and far beneath our dignity to be occupied with those secular and pure cares which relate to things altogether uninteresting to a Christian man' (*Institutes* III.2). In contrast, he maintained that political government and the reign of Christ 'are in no respect at variance with each other'. He even admitted that, if one compares differing types of government – monarchy, aristocracy or democracy – 'their advantages are so nearly equal that it will not be easy to discover of which the utility preponderates'. Nonetheless, once he had analysed them in terms of their dysfunctions, he did decide for democracy:

> It is true that the transition is easy from monarchy to despotism; it is not much more difficult from aristocracy to oligarchy, or the faction of a few; but it is most easy of all from democracy to sedition. Indeed, if these three forms of government which are stated by philosophers be considered in themselves, I shall by no means deny that either aristocracy or a mixture of aristocracy and democracy far excels all others; and that indeed not of itself but because it very rarely happens that kings regulate themselves so that their will is never at variance with justice and rectitude... The vice or imperfection of men therefore renders it safer and more tolerable for the government to be in the hands of many, that they may afford each other mutual assistance and admonition, and that if anyone arrogate to himself more than is right, the many may act as censors and masters to restrain his ambition. This has always been proved by experience, and the Lord confirmed it by his authority when he established a government of this kind among the people of Israel, with a view to preserve them in the most desirable condition till he exhibited in David a type of Christ (*Institutes* III.8).

The differences between Calvin and Aquinas (separated by differing cultures and centuries) are instructive. On face value, Aquinas might have agreed with the opening sentence of this quotation, but from it he would have derived the conviction that monarchy accords most closely with natural law. He might also have agreed with the last sentence: natural experience accords with biblical revelation. However, the central section of the quotation clearly differentiates their positions. Calvin's support for democracy appears here as a negative support: it is the least dysfunctional form of government and offers the greatest hope of checking sin. Nonetheless, from this position he did then go on to insist that a properly functioning government does require the obedient support of the individual Christian.

Variants of Aquinas' position can be seen in John XXIII's Extract 10 and Temple's Extract 9. Both are written from the 20th-century perspective of the secular State and, in this sense, differ radically from Aquinas. Yet, both also contain a mixture of natural law and biblically based arguments; both believe that the Gospel does imply specific political structures, ideals and programmes and that, as a result, the Church should be identified with them; and both believe that this confronts the individual Christian with specific duties. Pope John's *Pacem in Terris* is a detailed exposition of the rights and duties (both of the individual and of the State) on the major issues threatening the peace of the world. Unlike Niebuhr, he apparently sees no difficulty in moving from the individual to the social level on ethical issues. The fascinating and important challenge of John XXIII's Extract is that it enlarges categories usually used in theological debate, in order to justify the right of individual nations to survival and self-determination and in order to argue for the necessity of some form of world government. Temple's canvas is smaller and less directly dependent on Aquinas, seeking to distinguish between general political principles, which can and ought to be adopted, both by the Church and by the individual Christian, and particular political policies, which will be more divisive and are more subject to specialist judgment.

The positions of Luther and Barth, in relation to these central political questions, differ sharply from those already mentioned. Luther's *To The Christian Nobility* of 1520 was a passionate attack on the medieval concept of the relationship between Church and State and specifically on the control of the former over the latter. In advancing his positive theory of the relative autonomy of the political order (though not, of course, the concept of the secular State), he frequently insisted that it is the individual Christian who should be obedient to the State and not the State that should be obedient to the individual Christian or to the Church. In the next Section it will be seen that, for Luther, obedience to the appointed ruler was crucial, even if the latter was a tyrant and thoroughly unChristian (see IX.11f). Luther was resigned to the belief that there would sometimes be a very considerable gap between the moral behaviour of the Christian and that either of the ruler or of the majority of people in society (see VI.23f). His notion of the Two Kingdoms – the spiritual and the temporal Kingdoms of God – sometimes accentuated this gap still further. Nonetheless, the obedience of the individual Christian was always required – as indeed it seems to be in Barth's early writings.

Here again there is a crucial difference from Calvin. The latter's overall position was similar to that of Luther and Barth's Extract 6: government is essential to society, is appointed by God, and should be obeyed by the individual. So, in his exegesis of Romans 13, Calvin argued: 'The reason why we ought to be subject to magistrates is because they are constituted by God's ordination. For since it pleases God thus to govern the world, he who attempts to invert the order of God, and thus to resist God himself, despises his power; since to despise the providence of him who is the founder of civil power is to carry on war with him' (*Commentary on the Epistle to the Romans* 13.1). This differs from Barth's analysis of the same passage only in its reference to 16th-century magistrates. But, crucially, Calvin believed that there were circumstances when authorities should be resisted, particularly when what they were doing was inimical to the Gospel. For example, in commenting on Daniel's civil disobedience, he wrote:

We must remember that passage of Peter, 'Fear God, honour the king' [1 Peter 2.17]. The two commands are connected together, and cannot be separated from one another. The fear of God ought to precede, that kings may obtain their authority. For if anyone begins his reverence of an earthly prince by rejecting that of God, he will act preposterously, since this is a complete perversion of the order of nature... For earthly princes lay aside all their power when they rise up against God, and are unworthy of being reckoned in the number of mankind. We ought rather utterly to defy than to obey them whenever they are so restive and wish to spoil God of his rights, and, as it were, to seize upon his throne and draw him down from heaven (*Commentary on Daniel*, Lecture 30).

In the *Institutes* the emphasis is somewhat different: private individuals must be obedient and suffer unjust rulers, but magistrates have a positive duty to oppose them. Indeed, there, Calvin insisted that, if magistrates 'connive at kings in their oppression of their people, such forbearance involves the most nefarious perfidy because they fraudulently betray the liberty of the people, of which they know that they have been appointed protectors by the ordination of God' (*Institutes* III.31).

Ironically, despite this crucial difference between Calvin and Luther, the latter was not particularly obedient, in practice, to civil authorities. Luther spent a life of constant strife with a number of civil and ecclesiastical authorities: his civil obedience was at best selective. Interestingly, too, the growth of Nazism presented Barth with both a personal and a theological crisis: the sharp contrasts of *Romans* became more ambivalent as the 1930s proceeded. Here, *par excellence*, the influence of socio-political realities upon theological positions is evident.

Many of these issues and positions can be found in the very varied writings of Augustine. More than most other theologians Augustine was forced, in an age of immense transition in the social status of Christianity, to agonise over the position of Christianity in relation to political realities. Confronted by the confusion created by Christianity, on the one hand having been adopted in the previous century as the state religion and, on the other, by it being attacked as the cause of the State's present demise, Augustine's views were highly ambivalent. On the issue of war, he came to accept (albeit reluctantly) a defence of the state's position (see Text VII): on that of sexuality, his views usually diverged sharply from the dominant ethos of Roman culture (see Section 5). Within *The City of God*, his understanding of the relationship between the two cities – the earthly and the heavenly – often appears strained. He was always emphatic that the heavenly city is by far and away the most important, but he appears to oscillate between regarding the earthly city as a source of relative good and seeing it simply as a painful necessity. Neo-Platonic and Manichaean tendencies were never entirely eliminated from his writings.

An emphatic stress upon the primacy of the spiritual and the consequent relative unimportance of the political, is also found (in a somewhat different form) in Berdyaev's Extract 7. Despite living through momentous political upheavals, first in revolutionary Russia and then in German occupied Paris, his writings were often remarkably apolitical. Even when he considered explicitly Marxist themes (which had been particularly important to him as a young man), this generally remained the case. Describing himself as a 'Christian theosophist' and even as a gnostic, the spiritual always takes considerable precedence over the temporal and, in this respect, he appears even more Platonic than Augustine.

Quite apart from differences in socio-political context (which, obviously, must be given especial attention in this Section), a number of theological factors appear to affect the response of particular theologians to political issues. The relative balance given to the spiritual and the temporal (or however this is to be expressed in less Hellenistic terms) is clearly crucial. The acceptance or rejection of some notion of 'natural law' or 'natural order' is also crucial. The extent to which political realities are seen as inherently sinful is also a factor. Biblical exegesis is also very important and has become considerably more complex in the light of recent critical scholarship. For many it has become increasingly difficult to derive detailed and unambiguous structures, ideals or programmes from the New Testament. Later Sections should serve to reinforce this point. However, it is perhaps in Liberation theology, and in recent responses to Liberation theology, that these differences have now become most crucial. As an approach to theology it is unified in its attempt to adopt a position alongside all those who are deemed to be oppressed, but it is less unified in the actual methods or policies that it adopts. In addition, it is an approach which interestingly cuts across divisions between churches, as Extract 16 from the Methodist Bonino, in the next Section, and Extract 11 from the Roman Catholic Miranda, in this Section, demonstrate.

TEXT IV
AUGUSTINE
The earthly and heavenly cities

1. BACKGROUND
This Text comes from *The City of God* XIX.14-17 (Pelican Classics, trans. Henry Bettenson and ed. David Knowles, Penguin, 1972, pp.872-9). Book XIX opens the fifth and final section of *The City of God* and was thus written in the period, of CE 420-6 (see *above*, p.64) – well over 20 years after Text VII. At last Augustine could set out what he saw as the destinies of the earthly and heavenly cities. Against 'pagan' critics of Christianity, such as Porphyry, Augustine insisted that his was not a narrow, parochial religion which was incapable of making sense of world history. To the cultured Roman 'pagan', Christianity appeared to be just that: it lacked any serious historical and cultural roots and, since its adoption a century before by Constantine, had demonstrably contributed to the demise of Rome. However, Augustine saw the concept of the two cities as one which could not only make sense of history, but also give clarity to the extraordinarily difficult relationship of Church to State. For both personal and intellectual reasons, he could neither totally identify Church with State nor totally separate them. The concept of the two cities was used to clarify this relationship, but it was not identical with it – it was much broader and more far-reaching:

> Although there are many great peoples throughout the world, living under different customs in religion and morality and distinguished by a complex variety of languages, arms, and dress, it is still true that there have come into being only two main divisions, as we may call them, in human society: and we are justified in following the lead of our Scriptures and calling them two cities. There is, in fact, one city of men who choose to live by the standard

of the flesh, another of those who choose to live by the standard of the spirit. The citizens of each of these desire their own kind of peace, and when they achieve their aim, that is the kind of peace in which they live (*City of God* XIV.1).

Here the concept of the 'cities' (*civitates*) represents, not particular institutions or locations, but rather basic human divisions and differentiating loyalties. Whatever points of contact undoubtedly exist between the two cities, their ultimate aims and aspirations are thoroughly distinct: the one concerned with the temporal and even demonic and the other with the divine.

2. KEY ISSUES
This passage expresses very clearly the quite different aspirations and aims of the two cities. The end of the earthly city is earthly peace, consisting of concord between body and soul and an ordered life and health, whereas that of the heavenly city is eternal peace (IV.1). Insofar as they have rational souls, mortal humans are in need of divine direction and assistance (IV.2). The latter is evident in the two chief precepts, love of God and love of neighbour. Specifically, earthly peace and ordered harmony involve obeying the rules of not harming anyone and helping everyone whenever possible (IV.3). Ordered harmony at the domestic level, however, is not to be confused with domination. Human dominion applies to a dominion over the natural world and not over fellow humans: slavery, for example, results mainly from sin or is a punishment for sin (IV.4 & 5). Domestic harmony or peace – between members of a family and between master and slave – ought to contribute to the peace of the city (IV.7). Yet all these versions of peace, domestic or social, appear in the context of faith as relative to heavenly peace. The person of faith is like a pilgrim in a foreign land: earthly peace has some use, but is still a temporary and passing phenomenon (IV.8). Indeed, there are polytheistic and pagan elements in the earthly city which are antithetical to the heavenly city, so that the laws of religion, particularly, cannot be the same in the two cities (IV. 9). The heavenly city does not annul earthly laws, but follows them insofar

as they do not hinder the Christian religion. The pilgrim of the heavenly city makes use of earthly peace and laws, but regards heavenly peace as the only form of peace that really deserves the name of peace (IV.10).

3. ETHICAL ARGUMENTS

Augustine's understanding of the value of earthly peace seems to oscillate between consequentialism and deontology. Consequentialism is particularly evident in IV.8. Here Augustine maintains that the heavenly city 'must needs make use of' earthly peace 'until this mortal state, for which this kind of peace is essential, passes away', not only because it provides for an ordered society, but also because it provides for a 'harmony' between the two cities. On this understanding, earthly peace is not accorded any merit in itself, but only in its usefulness to the heavenly city. Other paragraphs, however, seem to imply a more deontological or natural law understanding of earthly peace – particularly IV.1 & 2 and explicitly in the first sentence of IV.4. And there does appear to be a relationship between the dominical commands or precepts at the beginning of IV.3 and the two rules for social order given in the middle of the same paragraph. Set against this, there is a typical Augustinian stress upon sin in his understanding of slavery in IV.4 & 5. This stress always makes it difficult simply to interpret Augustine in terms of a natural law theory: the more wholly corrupt people are thought to be, the less one can identify their natural propensities or ends.

4. BASES OF CHRISTIAN ETHICS

The Bible is used here more frequently and pivotally than in Text I, with two direct Old Testament quotations, three direct New Testament quotations and several indirect allusions. Further, the use of the Bible in IV.3, 4 & 5 is prescriptive and crucial to the argument. The issue of slavery, particularly, presents Augustine with a dilemma and his uneasiness with it is apparent in his discussion in IV.4 & 5. His derivation of *servus* is in fact mistaken – although it was widely accepted by his contemporaries. And he avoids the obvious point that nowhere in the Bible is slavery actually condemned. However, his overall aim, of attempting to show that his understanding of the two cities accords with the Bible and makes sense of human history, is clear.

5. SOCIAL DETERMINANTS

The influence of the transition of Christianity from a sectarian to a more church-type position in society is evident (see further, on Text VII). Given the radically changed socio-political status of Christianity since Constantine, and given the criticisms from traditionalist non-Christians, Augustine felt constrained to articulate an understanding of the relationship between Church and State. However, as a result of both his neo-Platonic modes of thought and his indebtedness to the Bible (see *above*, p.66) he made his articulation in the somewhat ethereal terms of the concept of the two cities. So, the earthly city cannot be identified with 'secular' society or with the State and the heavenly city certainly cannot be equated with the extant institutional Church. The overall concept of the two cities also reflects Augustine's background in African Christianity. In that context, it was already so commonplace that he could refer to it at one point as that 'which everyone brought up in the traditions of the holy church should know' (*Enarr. in Ps.* 136.1).

6. SOCIAL SIGNIFICANCE

It would be difficult to exaggerate the importance of Augustine's position here. His *The City of God*, written in old age, represented a major achievement and presented the late classical world with its most sustained and cultured Christian apologetic. In view of the precarious position of Christianity in the early 5th-century Roman world, the social significance of such an apologetic is evident. Even if his particular understanding of political realities (it cannot be claimed that he actually advanced a political theory) proved to be too firmly located in the social context of the late Roman Empire, his overall conception of the tension between the Christian vision and political actualities has remained important in much contemporary theology. The ways he resolved this tension varied considerably in his writings, but it is always apparent.

FURTHER READING

Important discussions of *The City of God* will be found in David Knowles' Introduction to the Pelican translation of *The City of God*, in Peter Brown's *Augustine of Hippo* and in R.W. Barrow's *Introduction to St Augustine: 'The City of God'*. Augustine's discussions of the concept of the two cities occur particularly in Books XIV-XV and XVIII-XIX of *The City of God*.

TEXT IV

AUGUSTINE

The earthly and heavenly cities

IV.1

We see, then, that all man's use of temporal things is related to the enjoyment of earthly peace in the earthly city; whereas in the Heavenly City it is related to the enjoyment of eternal peace. Thus, if we were irrational animals, our only aim would be the adjustment of the parts of the body in due proportion, and the quieting of appetites – only, that is, the repose of the flesh, and an adequate supply of pleasures, so that bodily peace might promote the peace of the soul. For if bodily peace is lacking, the peace of the irrational soul is also hindered, because it cannot achieve the quieting of its appetites. But the two together promote that peace which is a mutual concord between soul and body, the peace of an ordered life and of health. For living creatures show their love of bodily peace by their avoidance of pain, and by their pursuit of pleasure to satisfy the demands of their appetites they demonstrate their love of peace and soul. In just the same way, by shunning death they indicate quite clearly how great is their love of the peace in which soul and body are harmoniously united.

IV.2

But because there is in man a rational soul, he subordinates to the peace of the rational soul all that part of his nature which he shares with the beasts, so that he may engage in deliberate thought and act in accordance with this thought, so that he may thus exhibit that ordered agreement of cognition and action which we called the peace of the rational soul. For with this end in view he ought to wish to be spared the distress of pain and grief, the disturbances of desire, the dissolution of death, so that he may come to some profitable knowledge and may order his life and his moral standards in accordance with this knowledge. But he needs divine direction, which he may obey with resolution, and divine assistance that he may obey it freely, to prevent him from falling, in his enthusiasm for knowledge, a victim to some fatal error, through the weakness of the human mind. And so long as he is in this mortal body, he is a pilgrim in a foreign land, away from God; therefore he walks by faith, not by sight. That is why he views all peace, of body or of soul, or of both, in relation to that peace which exists between mortal man and immortal God, so that he may exhibit an ordered obedience in faith in subjection to the everlasting God.

IV.3

Now God, our master, teaches two chief precepts, love of God and love of neighbour; and in them man finds three objects for his love: God, himself, and his neighbour; and a man who loves God is not wrong in loving himself. It follows, therefore, that he should be concerned also that his neighbour should love God, since he is told to love his neighbour as himself; and the same is true of his concern for his wife, his children, for the members of his household, and for all other men, so far as is possible. And, for the same end, he will wish his neighbour to be concerned for him, if he happens to need that concern. For this reason he will be at peace, as far as lies in him, with all men, in that peace among men, that ordered harmony; and the basis of this order is the observance of two rules: first, to do no harm to anyone, and, secondly, to help everyone whenever possible. To begin with, therefore, a man has a responsibility for his own household – obviously, both in the order of nature and in the framework of human society, he has easier and more immediate contact with them; he can exercise his concern for them. That is why the Apostle says, 'Anyone who does not take care of his own people, especially those in his own household, is worse than an unbeliever – he is a renegade' [1 Tim. 5.8]. This is where domestic peace starts, the ordered harmony about giving and obeying orders among those who live in the same house. For the orders are given by those who are concerned for the interests of others; thus the husband gives orders to the wife, parents to children, masters to servants. While those who are the objects of this concern obey orders; for example, wives obey husbands, the children obey their parents, the servants their masters. But in the household of the just man who 'lives on the basis of faith' and who is still on pilgrimage, far from that Heavenly City, even those who give orders are the servants of those whom they appear to command. For they do not give orders because of a lust for domination but from a dutiful concern for the interests of others, not with pride in taking precedence over others, but with compassion in taking care of others.

Man's natural freedom; and the slavery caused by sin
IV.4

This relationship is prescribed by the order of nature, and it is in this situation that God created man. For he says, 'Let him have lordship over the fish of the sea, the birds of the sky... and all the reptiles that crawl on the earth' [Gen. 1.26]. He did not wish the rational being, made in his own image, to have dominion over any but irrational creatures, not man over man, but man over the beasts. Hence the first just men were set up as shepherds of flocks, rather than as kings of men, so that in this way also God might convey the message of what was required by the order of nature, and what was demanded by the deserts of sinners – for it is understood, of course, that the condition of slavery is justly imposed on the sinner. That is why we do not hear of a slave anywhere in the Scriptures until Noah, the just man, punished his son's sin with this word; and so that son deserved this name because of his misdeed, not because of his nature. The origin of the Latin word for slave, *servus*, is believed to be derived from the fact that those who by the laws of war could rightly be put to death by the conquerors, became *servi*, slaves, when they were preserved, receiving this name from their preservation. But even this enslavement could not have happened, if it were not for the deserts of sin. For even when a just war is fought it is in defence of his sin that the other side is contending;

and victory, even when the victory falls to the wicked, is a humiliation visited on the conquered by divine judgment, either to correct or to punish their sins. We have a witness to this in Daniel, a man of God, who in captivity confesses to God his own sins and the sins of his people, and in devout grief testifies that they are the cause of that captivity. The first cause of slavery, then, is sin, whereby man was subjected to man in the condition of bondage; and this can only happen by the judgment of God, with whom there is no injustice, and who knows how to allot different punishments according to the deserts of the offenders.

IV.5

Now, as our Lord above says, 'Everyone who commits sin is sin's slave', [Jn. 8.34], and that is why, though many devout men are slaves to unrighteous masters, yet the masters they serve are not themselves free men; 'for when a man is conquered by another he is also bound as a slave to his conqueror' [2 Pet. 2.19]. And obviously it is a happier lot to be slave to a human being than to a lust; and, in fact, the most pitiless domination that devastates the hearts of men, is that exercised by this very lust for domination, to mention no others. However, in that order of peace in which men are subordinate to other men, humility is as salutary for the servants as pride is harmful to the masters. And yet by nature, in the condition in which God created man, no man is the slave either of man or of sin. But it remains true that slavery as a punishment is also ordained by that law which enjoins the preservation of the order of nature, and forbids its disturbance; in fact, if nothing had been done to contravene that law, there would have been nothing to require the discipline of slavery as a punishment. That explains also the Apostle's admonition to slaves, that they should be subject to their masters, and serve them loyally and willingly [cf. Eph. 6.5]. What he means is that if they cannot be set free by their masters, they themselves may thus make their slavery, in a sense, free, by serving not with the slyness of fear, but with the fidelity of affection, until all injustice disappears and all human lordship and power is annihilated, and God is all in all.

Equity in the relation of master and slave

IV.6

This being so, even though our righteous fathers had slaves, they so managed the peace of their households as to make a distinction between the situation of children and the condition of slaves in respect of the temporal goods of this life; and yet in the matter of the worship of God – in whom we must place our hope of everlasting goods – they were concerned, with equal affection, for all the members of their household. This is what the order of nature prescribes, so that this is the source of the name *paterfamilias*, a name that has become so generally used that even those who exercise unjust rule rejoice to be called by this title. On the other hand, those who are genuine 'fathers of their household' are concerned for the welfare of all in their households in respect of the worship and service of God, as if they were all their children, longing and praying that they may come to the heavenly home, where it will not be a necessary duty to give order to men, because it will no longer be a necessary duty to be concerned for the welfare of those who are already in the felicity of that immortal state. But until that home is reached, the fathers have an obligation to exercise the authority of masters greater than the duty of slaves to put up with their condition as servants.

IV.7

However, if anyone in the household is, through his disobedience, an enemy to the domestic peace, he is reproved by a word, or by a blow, or any other kind of punishment that is just and legitimate, to the extent allowed by human society; but this is for the benefit of the offender, intended to readjust him to the domestic peace from which he had broken away. For just as it is not an act of kindness to help a man, when the effect of the help is to make him lose a greater good, so it is not a blameless act to spare a man, when by so doing you let him fall into a greater sin. Hence the duty of anyone who would be blameless includes not only doing no harm to anyone but also restraining a man from sin or punishing his sin, so that either the man who is chastised may be corrected by his experience, or others may be deterred by his example. Now a man's house ought to be the beginning, or rather a small component part of the city, and every beginning is directed to some end of its own kind, and every component part contributes to the completeness of the whole of which it forms a part. The implication is quite apparent, that domestic peace contributes to the peace of the city – that is, the ordered harmony of those who live together in a house in the matter of giving and obeying orders, contributes to the ordered harmony concerning authority and obedience obtaining among the citizens. Consequently it is fitting that the father of a household should take his rules from the law of the city, and govern his household in such a way that it fits in with the peace of the city.

The origin of peace between the heavenly society and the earthly city, and of discord between them

IV.8

But a household of human beings whose life is not based on faith is in pursuit of an earthly peace based on the things belonging to this temporal life, and on its advantages, whereas a household of human beings whose life is based on faith looks forward to the blessings which are promised as eternal in the future, making use of earthly and temporal things like a pilgrim in a foreign land, who does not let himself be taken in by them or distracted from his course towards God, but rather treats them as supports which help him more easily to bear the burdens of 'the corruptible body which weighs heavy on the soul' [Wisd. 9.15], they must on no account be allowed to increase the load. Thus both kinds of men and both kinds of households alike make use of the things essential for this mortal life; but each has its own very different end in making use of them. So also the earthly city, whose life is not based on faith, aims at an earthly peace, and it limits the harmonious agreement of citizens concerning the giving and obeying of orders to the establishment of a kind of compromise between human wills about the things relevant to mortal life. In contrast, the Heavenly City – or rather that part of it which is on pilgrimage in this condition of mortality, and which lives on the basis of faith – must needs make use of this peace also, until this mortal state, for which this kind of peace is essential, passes away. And therefore, it leads what we may call a life of captivity in this earthly city as in a foreign land, although it has already received the promise of redemption, and the gift of the Spirit as a kind of pledge of it; and yet it does not hesitate to obey the laws of the earthly city by which those things which are designed for the support of this mortal life are regulated; and the purpose of this obedience is that, since this mortal condition is shared by both cities, a harmony may be preserved between them in things that are relevant to this condition.

IV.9

But this earthly city has had some philosophers belonging to it whose theories are rejected by the teaching inspired by God. Either led astray by their own speculation or deluded by demons, these thinkers reached the belief that there are many gods who must be won over to serve human ends, and also that they have, as it were, different departments with different responsibilities attached. Thus the body is the department of one god, the mind that of another; and within the body itself, one god is in charge of the head, another of the neck and so on with each of the separate members. Similarly, within the mind, one is responsible for natural ability, another for learning, another for anger, another for lust; and in the accessories of life there are separate gods over the departments of flocks, grain, wine, oil, forests, coinage, navigation, war and victory, marriage, birth, fertility, and so on. The Heavenly City, in contrast, knows only one God as the object of worship, and decrees, with faithful devotion, that he only is to be served with that service which the Greeks call *latreia*, which is due to God alone. And the result of this difference has been that the Heavenly City could not have laws of religion common with the earthly city, and in defence of her religious laws she was bound to dissent from those who thought differently and to prove a burdensome nuisance to them. Thus she had to endure their anger and hatred, and the assaults of persecution; until at length that City shattered the morale of her adversaries by the terror inspired by her numbers, and by the help she continually received from God.

IV.10

While this Heavenly City, therefore, is on pilgrimage in this world, she calls out citizens from all nations and so collects a society of aliens, speaking all languages. She takes no account of any difference in customs, laws, and institutions, by which earthly peace is achieved and preserved – not that she annuls or abolishes any of those, rather, she maintains them and follows them (for whatever divergences there are among the diverse nations, those institutions have one single aim – earthly peace), provided that no hindrance is presented thereby to the religion which teaches that the one supreme and true God is to be worshipped. Thus even the Heavenly City in her pilgrimage here on earth makes use of the earthly peace and defends and seeks the compromise between human wills in respect of the provisions relevant to the mortal nature of man, so far as may be permitted without detriment to true religion and piety. In fact, that City relates the earthly peace to the heavenly peace, which is so truly peaceful that it should be regarded as the only peace deserving the name, at least in respect of the rational creation; for this peace is the perfectly ordered and completely harmonious fellowship in the enjoyment of God, and of each other in God. When we arrive at that state of peace, there will be no longer a life that ends in death, but a life that is life in sure and sober truth; there will be no animal body to 'weigh down the soul' in its process of corruption; there will be a spiritual body with no cravings, a body subdued in every part to the will. This peace the Heavenly City possesses in faith while on its pilgrimage, and it lives a life of righteousness, based on this faith, having the attainment of that peace in view in every good action it performs in relation to God, and in relation to a neighbour, since the life of a city is inevitably a social life.

CRITIQUE

One of the great strengths of this Text and of *The City of God* generally is that it takes seriously the tension that Christians should always feel between a vision of the transcendent and the expectations of the world. Whereas the modern New Testament scholar would tend to express this tension in terms of the Synoptic concept of the Kingdom of God – with its relevance to, but distance from, the temporal and its present and future references – most might maintain that some degree of tension is essential. On this understanding, it would be equally as wrong to identify the Kingdom of God wholly with some particular political programme, as to assert that it is totally without political relevance. Within these parameters, there are many variant positions, each subject to particular weaknesses.

The weakness of Augustine's position in this Text is that the heavenly city is so marginally related to the earthly city that it appears little interested in effecting changes within it. The pilgrim status of Christians effectively means that they may simply have to endure injustice rather than attempt to change it. So, finally, his advice to slaves is that, 'if they cannot be set free by their masters, they themselves may thus make their slavery, in a sense, free, by serving not with the slyness of fear, but with the fidelity of affection, until all injustice disappears and all human lordship and power is annihilated, and God is all in all' (IV.5 – see also Text X). The individual Christian is not encouraged to oppose slavery or actively to combat injustice, but rather to endure it and wait for the time when 'God is all in all'. A radically different Christian interpretation is evident in Miranda's Extract 11 and Bonino's Extract 16. In Augustine, the martyr understanding of Christianity is still apparent (see the last sentences of IV.9 and VII.8) and, indeed, in his battles with the Donatists in North Africa he sometimes expected to be martyred himself (whilst, at the same time, rejecting the Donatist's own martyr-seeking attitude: cf. Text XIII). Augustine was always more keen to combat what he regarded as Christian 'heresy' than to uphold social justice.

TEXT V
AQUINAS
On princely government

1. BACKGROUND

This Text comes from *De Regimine Principum*, XII-XIV (On Princely Government, from A.P. D'Entrèves (ed), *Aquinas: Selected Political Writings*, Blackwell, Oxford, 1948, trans. J.G. Dawson, pp.67-77). The authentic parts of *De Regimine Principum* (mainly Book I from which this Text is taken) were written during Aquinas' time of teaching in Italy (1259-69) as specific advice to the King of Cyprus. Aquinas was not, of course, primarily a political theorist and his writings on political matters are thoroughly medieval, hierarchical and theocratic. He followed Aristotle in arguing that a human is by nature a social and political animal and that natural law requires rule by kings. Accordingly, he opened *De Regimine Principum* as follows:

> Our first task must be to explain how the term king is to be understood. Now whenever a certain end has been decided upon, but the means for arriving thereat are still open to choice, some one must provide direction if that end is to be expeditiously attained. A ship, for instance, will sail first on one course and then on another, according to the winds it encounters, and it would never reach its destination but for the skill of the helmsman who steers it to port. In the same way man, who acts by intelligence, has a destiny to which all life and activities are directed; for it is clearly the nature of intelligent beings to act with some end in view. Yet the diversity of human interests and pursuits makes it equally clear that there are many courses open to men when seeking the end they desire. Man, then, needs guidance for attaining his ends (D'Entrèves, p.3).

On this basis, princely government rightly (according to natural law) directs individual lives, but it, in turn, is subordinate to divine law and to the ecclesiastical ministers of this law. The latter crowns the former as grace crowns nature (see *above*, pp.43f.). In contrast to Luther's Text IX, Aquinas maintained that the tyrant need not always be obeyed:

> Tyrannical law, not being according to reason, is not law at all in the true and strict sense, but is rather a perversion of law. It does, however, assume the nature of law to the extent that it provides for the well-being of the citizens. Thus it bears some relationship to law in so far as it is the dictate to his subjects of some one in authority; and to the extent that its object is the full obedience of those subjects to the law. For them such obedience is good, not unconditionally, but with respect to the particular regime under which they live (D'Entrèves, p.119, from *Summa Theologica* 1/11.92).

In so far as princely government promotes the well-being of individuals, it accords with natural law and provides the basis on which grace can then act.

2. KEY ISSUES

Having attempted to establish that monarchy accords with nature and offers the best form of government, Aquinas now considers the duties of a king. He suggests a strong analogy between, on the one hand, God's control over the universe, and, on the other, reason's control over the individual and a king's control over society. If he is faithful to this analogy, a king should be guided by reason, justice, mildness and clemency (V.I). Whereas God is both creator and governor of the universe, usually a king is only governor of a city or kingdom. Yet, in governing, he ought to be aware of the purposes for which the city or kingdom was founded (V.2). Unlike God, the founder of a city or kingdom does not create from nothing, but chooses, from an existing place, a suitable site for his city or kingdom, plans the positions for his buildings, orders the people and provides for their needs – all functions which resemble the work of God as creator (V.3). The king, as governor – again analogous with God's work – must seek to guide his people to their appointed end and not simply to preserve the status quo (V.4). The end of humans is that final blessedness and enjoyment of God to be known after death (V.5) and not merely some human perfection which already exists (V.6). Since this end cannot be attained alone by natural human virtue, but only through divine grace, it can only be divine rule, rather than a human government, which can lead humans to it (V.7). This divine rule is entrusted to the Papacy and to the Church – to which all subordinate, temporal rulers must be subject (V.8).

3. ETHICAL ARGUMENTS

Analogical arguments, based upon natural law, are apparent throughout this Text. Natural law provides the deontological basis for the discussion (see Text II). The world of nature reveals how human society should be ordered and how the king should behave. Yet the work of God himself can be used as the basic analogy for human moral and social behaviour. For Aquinas, the concept of an analogy of being (*analogia entis*) between creator and created was crucial: indeed, precisely because the creature was the direct product of the creator, the former could be used to infer the existence and certain attributes of the latter, and the latter could be used to discover how the former should live. In much Reformed theology, sin is thought to have so distorted the creator/created relationship, that such analogical argument is impossible. But, for Aquinas, it is the key to his argument. The Aristotelian stress upon the end or *telos* of humans – seen here, though, in terms of the beatific vision (V.5) – gives the argument an eventual consequentialist or teleological bias.

4. BASES OF CHRISTIAN ETHICS

The quotation from Genesis (in V.3) plays an important role in this Text. Aquinas derives the principles for founding a city or kingdom analogically from it. This kind of analogical interpretation is obviously dependent on his overall understanding of theology and exegesis. The quotations from Paul, however, (in V.5 and V.7) are not used analogically, but rather to substantiate specifically theological points. Aquinas' assumption of ecclesiastical tradition and papal primacy is apparent in V.8: this tradition is simply presented prescriptively.

5. SOCIAL DETERMINANTS

Aquinas' discussion of political realities is, perhaps inevitably, deeply coloured by the social context of 13th-century Italy. Most obviously is this seen in his frequent mention of a king of 'a city or a kingdom': it reflects the world of relatively autonomous cities, or autocratic local leaders and of small-scale dynasties. It is also apparent in his assumptions about ecclesiastical tradition (cf. Text VIII.7-12) and about the structural unity of Church and State (see *above*, p.46). Indeed, this particular Text is so evidently dependent on a specific social context that it may appear today as one of the most anachronistic of the Aquinas Texts.

6. SOCIAL SIGNIFICANCE

It is difficult to know whether or not *De Regimine Principum* had any serious influence upon politics. At the most, it provided a legitimation for the status quo of 13th-century Italy. Nonetheless, the specific way in which Aquinas attempted to derive the duties of political leaders, both from natural law and from the concept of creation, has had a continuing influence upon Catholic political thought. This influence is clearly present in John XXIII's Extract 10, in John Paul II's Extract 4, and even in Temple's Extract 9.

FURTHER READING

The introduction by A.P. D'Entrèves to his *Aquinas: Selected Political Writing* and his *The Notion of the State* are both useful. However, reference should also be made to books concerned with Aquinas' understanding of war (see Section 3) and to those concerned with his notion of natural law (see *above*, p.79). For a recent Catholic perspective see James P. Mackey's *Power and Christian Ethics*.

TEXT V

AQUINAS

On princely government

The duties of a king; the similarity between royal power and the power of the soul over the body and of God over the universe

V.1

To complete what we have so far said it remains only to consider what is the duty of a king and how he should comport himself. And since art is but an imitation of nature, from which we come to learn how to act according to reason, it would seem best to deduce the duties of a king from the examples of government in nature. Now in nature there is to be found both a universal and a particular form of government. The universal is that by which all things find their place under the direction of God, who, by His providence, governs the universe. The particular is very similar to this divine control, and is found within man himself, who, for this reason, is called a microcosm, because he provides an example of universal government. Just as the divine control is exercised over all created bodies and over all spiritual powers, so does the control of reason extend over the members of the body and the other faculties of the soul: so, in a certain sense, reason is to man what God is to the universe. But because, as we have shown above, man is by nature a social animal living in community, this similarity with divine rule is found among men, not only in the sense that a man is directed by his reason, but also in the fact that a community is ruled by one man's intelligence; for this is essentially the king's duty. A similar example of such control is to be found among certain animals which live in community, such as bees, which are said to have a king. But in their case, of course, the control has no rational foundation, but springs from an instinct of their nature, given them by the supreme ruler who is the author of nature. A king, then, should realise that he has assumed the duty of being to his kingdom what the soul is to the body and what God is to the universe. If he thinks attentively upon this point he will, on the one hand, be fired with zeal for justice, seeing himself appointed to administer justice throughout his realm in the name of God, and, on the other hand, he will grow in mildness and clemency, looking upon the persons subject to his government, as the members of his own body.

Further development of this analogy and of the conclusions to be drawn from it

V.2

We must now consider what God does in the universe, and thus we shall see what a king should do. There are, in general, two aspects of the work of God in the world. The first is the act of creation; the second His governance of it once He has created it. Similarly, the action of the soul upon the body presents two aspects. In the first place it is the soul which gives form to the body and secondly it is by the soul that the body is controlled and moved. It is the second of these two operations which pertains more particularly to the king's office; for all kings are bound to govern, and it is from this process of directing the government that the term king (*rex*) is derived. The former task, however, does not fall to all kings; for not every king founds the city or kingdom over which he rules; many fulfil their duties in cities or kingdoms which are already flourishing. It must not, however, be forgotten that if there had been no one in the first place to establish a city or a kingdom, there would be nothing to govern: so that the kingly office must also cover the founding of a city or a kingdom. Some kings have, in fact, founded the cities over which they afterwards ruled, as Ninus founded Nineveh, and Romulus Rome. It is furthermore the ruler's duty to protect what he governs and to make use of it for the ends for which it was intended: but he cannot be fully aware of the duties of his office if he fails to acquaint himself with the reasons for government. Now the reason for the foundation of a kingdom is to be found in the example provided by the creation of the world: in this we must first consider the creation of things themselves, and then their orderly distribution throughout the universe. Then we see how things are distributed in the various parts of the universe according to their different species; the stars in the heavens, birds in the air, fishes in the sea and animals upon the earth. Finally we note how abundantly divine providence furnishes each species with all that is necessary to it. Moses has described this orderliness shown in creation with great care and subtlety.

V.3

He first considers the creation of things by the words: 'In the beginning God created heaven and earth' [Gen. 1.1]; then he notes that all things became, by divine command, distinct according to their appropriate order, as day from night, the heights from the depths, and the waters from dry land. Then he tells how the heavens were adorned with stars, the air with birds, the sea with fishes, and the earth with animals. Finally, he tells how dominion was given to men over the whole earth and the animals thereon. As for plant life, he says that it was given by providence for the use of both animals and men. Now the founder of a city or of a kingdom cannot create out of nothing the men or the dwelling places or all the other things necessary to life; he must use instead what nature has already provided. Just as all other arts find their materials from natural sources; the smiths working with iron and the builder with wood and stone. So one who is about to establish a city or a realm must, in the first place, choose a suitable site; healthy, to ensure the health of the inhabitants; fertile, to provide for their sustenance; one which will delight the eye with its loveliness and give natural security against hostile attack. Where any of these advantages are lacking, the site chosen will be the more suitable to the extent that such conditions, or at least the more indispensable of them, are fulfilled. Having chosen the site, the next task which confronts the founder of a city or of a kingdom is to plan the area to meet all the requirements of a civic life. When founding a kingdom, for example, one must decide where to build the towns and where to leave the countryside open, or to construct fortifications: centres of study, open places for military training, and markets, all have to be taken into consideration: and similarly for every other activity which goes to make up the life of a kingdom. If it is a city which is to be established, sites must be assigned to churches, to administrative offices, and to the workshops of various trades. The citizens then have to be grouped in various quarters of the city according to their calling. Finally, provision must be made so that no person goes in want, according to his condition and calling: otherwise neither city nor kingdom would long endure. Such, very briefly, are the points a king must consider when establishing a city or a kingdom, and they can all be arrived at by analogy with the creation of the world.

Comparison between the priestly power and that of a king
V.4
Just as the creation of the world serves as a convenient model for the establishment of a city or a kingdom, so does its government allow us to deduce the principle of civil government. We must first have in mind that to govern is to guide what is governed to its appointed end. So we say that a ship is under control when it is sailed on its right course to port by the skill of a sailor. Now when something is ordered to an end which lies outside itself, as a ship is to harbour, it is the ruler's duty not only to preserve its integrity, but also to see that it reaches its appointed destination. If there were anything with no end beyond itself, then the ruler's sole task would be to preserve it unharmed in all its perfection. But though there is no such example to be found in creation, apart from God who is the end of all things, care for higher aims is beset with many and varied difficulties. For it is very clear that there may be one person employed about the preservation of a thing in its present state, and another concerned with bringing it to higher perfection; as we see in the case of a ship, which we have used as an example of government. Just as it is the carpenter's task to repair any damage which may occur and the sailor's task to steer the ship to port, so also in man himself the same processes are at work. The doctor sets himself to preserve man's life and bodily health; the economist's task is to see that there is no lack of material goods; the learned see to it that he knows the truth; and the moralist that he should live according to reason. Thus, if man were not destined to some higher end, these attentions would suffice.

V.5
But there is a further destiny for man after this mortal life; that final blessedness and enjoyment of God which he awaits after death. For, as the Apostle says [2 Corinthians 5.6]: 'While we are in the body we are absent from God.' So it is that the

Christian, for whom that blessedness was obtained by the blood of Christ, and who is led to it through the gift of the Holy Ghost, has need of another, spiritual, guide to lead him to the harbour of eternal salvation; such guidance is provided for the faithful by the ministers of the Church of Christ.

V.6

Our conclusion must be the same, whether we consider the destiny of one person or of a whole community. Consequently, if the end of man were to be found in any perfection existing in man himself, the final object of government in a community would lie in the acquisition of such perfection and in its preservation once acquired. So that if such an end, whether of an individual or of a community, were life and bodily health, doctors would govern. If, on the other hand, it were abundance of riches, the government of the community could safely be left in the hands of the economist. If it were knowledge of truth, the king, whose task it is to guide the community, would have the duties of a professor. But the object for which a community is gathered together is to live a virtuous life. For men consort together that they may thus attain a fullness of life which would not be possible to each living singly: and the full life is one which is lived according to virtue. Thus the object of human society is a virtuous life.

V.7

A proof of this lies in the fact that only those members may be considered part of the community who contribute jointly to the fullness of social life. If men consorted together for bare existence, both animals and slaves would have a part in civil society. If for the multiplication of riches, all who had common commercial ties would belong to one city. But it is those who obey the same laws, and are guided by a single government to the fullness of life, who can be said to constitute a social unit. Now the man who lives virtuously is destined to a higher end, which consists, as we have already said, in the enjoyment of God: and the final object of human association can be no different from that of the individual man. Thus the final aim of social life will be, not merely to live in virtue, but rather through virtuous life to attain to the enjoyment of God. If, indeed, it were possible to attain this object by natural human virtue, it would, in consequence, be the duty of kings to guide men to this end. We believe, however, that it is the supreme power in temporal affairs which is the business of a king. Now government is of a higher order according to the importance of the ends it serves. For it is always the one who has the final ordering of affairs who directs those who carry out what pertains to the attainment of the final aim: just as the sailor who must navigate the ship advises the shipwright as to the type of ship which will suit his purpose; and the citizen who is to bear arms tells the smith what weapons to forge. But the enjoyment of God is an aim which cannot be attained by human virtue alone, but only through divine grace, as the Apostle tells us [Romans 6.23]: 'The race of God is eternal life'. Only a divine rule, then, and not human government, can lead us to this end. Such government belongs only to that King who is both man, and also God: that is to Jesus Christ, our Lord, Who, making men to be Sons of God has led them to the glory of heaven.

V.8

This, then, is the government entrusted to Him: a dominion which shall never pass away, and in virtue of which He is called in the Holy Scriptures, not only a priest but a king; as *Jeremias* says [23.5]: 'A king shall reign and shall be wise'. It is from Him that the royal priesthood derives; and, what is more, all the Faithful of Christ, being members of Him, become thus, priests and kings. The ministry of this kingdom is entrusted not to the rulers of this earth but to priests, so that temporal affairs may remain distinct from those spiritual: and, in particular, it is delegated to the High Priest, the successor of Peter and Vicar of Christ, the Roman Pontiff, to whom all kings in Christendom should be subjects, as to the Lord Jesus Christ Himself. For those who are concerned with the subordinate ends of life must be subject to him who is concerned with the supreme end and be directed by his command. And because the pagan priesthood and everything connected with the cult of pagan gods was directed to the attainment of temporal benefits, which form part of the common weal of the community, and which lie within the king's competence, it was right that pagan priests should be subject to their kings. Similarly in the Old Testament, temporal benefits were promised to the people in reward for their faith, though these promises were made by the true God and not by demons; so that under the Old Law we read that the priesthood was subject to kings. But under the New Law there is a higher priesthood through which men are led to a heavenly reward: and under Christ's Law, kings must be subject to priests.

V.9

For this reason it came about by the admirable dispensation of divine providence, that in the city of Rome which God chose to be the main centre of Christendom, it gradually became the custom for the rulers of the city to be subject to the pontiffs.

CRITIQUE

The negative and dysfunctional side of Aquinas' understanding (and indeed medieval understanding generally) of government appears elsewhere in his writings. It was theocratic and thoroughly intolerant of any form of religious opposition. A.P. D'Entrèves pointed out:

> The theory of St. Thomas is the theory of the orthodox State. We are apt to forget it. We have grown so accustomed to the threat which comes from the State [D'Entrèves was writing in 1948], that we are only too ready to hail the Church as the champion of freedom. Medieval intolerance had at least one great advantage over modern totalitarianism. It subtracted entirely the definition of orthodoxy from the hands of the politician. It put a bar on Erastianism. It would never have allowed that 'the General Will is always right'. It was an intolerance of a different and more noble brand. But it was intolerance all right, and a thorough, totalitarian intolerance (from his Introduction to *Aquinas: Selected Political Writings*, p.xxii).

As evidence of Aquinas' intolerance he cited his advice in *De Regimine Judaeorum* that Jews must not be harmed but must nevertheless remain outcasts in the Christian community and should be forced to earn their living in non-usurious ways: 'Jews of both sexes and in all Christian lands should on all occasions be distinguished from other people by some particular dress' (D'Entrèves, p.95: see further on Luther's XV). But, most of all, for Aquinas and his contemporaries, it was the Christian apostate who was to be treated harshly: 'if it be just that forgers and other malefactors are put to death without mercy by the secular authority, with how much greater reason may heretics not only be excommunicated, but also put to death, when once they are convicted of heresy (*S.T.* II.11. Q.11. Art.3). This link, between theocratic and religiously intolerant attitudes, is particularly striking in someone, like Aquinas, who otherwise appears to have been a gentle and equable person (see further, *below*, pp.464f.).

More positively, his stress upon the duties of kings and his admission that tyrants need not always be obeyed, contrast favourably with Luther. Even his ironic observation, that if the main aim of society is really thought to be the acquisition of an 'abundance of riches, the government of the community could safely be left in the hands of the economist'(V.6), provides an interesting commentary on modern nation states!

TEXT VI
LUTHER
Trade and usury

1. *BACKGROUND*

This Text comes from *Trade and Usury* (from *Luther's Works*, Vol. 45, Fortress Press, Philadelphia, 1966, trans. Charles M. Jacobs and rev. Walther I. Brandt, pp.245-6, 247-54 & 255-60). Luther published this treatise in 1524 together with a re print of his *Long Sermon on Usury* written earlier in 1520 (see *above*, p.89). Both works demonstrate his dislike of what he regarded as commercial greed (he was himself always disinterested in personal wealth) and his basic ignorance of economic realities. Luther accepted many of the medieval presuppositions about financial matters, notably Aristotle's notion that money does not produce money and the medieval ecclesiastical condemnation of usury. But he argued that contemporary practice failed to live up to these notions and, indeed, failed to live up to biblical norms on wealth. In addition, he was unhappy about the failure of the diets of Nürnberg in 1522 and 1524 to deal effectively with the monopolistic practices of the trading companies. Luther was also reacting, in 1524, against the rigorist positions of the evangelical preachers Jacob Strauss and Wolfgang Stein, who maintained that a debtor is not even obliged to repay his debt to a usurer, for otherwise he would share in the usurer's guilt. The notion of surety or property insurance (VI.14) was first developed in the 14th century and was held to be non-usurious, except when it was used to guarantee a loan. Despite the general advice to traders at the beginning of this treatise, it becomes clear (e.g. in VI.19) that Luther's primary concern here is with Christians in their relation to wealth and commercial activity. At this level, the treatise is arguably still relevant to Christian ethics.

2. KEY ISSUES

Even though he is pessimistic about his advice being heeded, Luther sets out what he considers to be the proper position of the Christian merchant (VI.1-2). The trade of essential commodities is necessary in the world (VI.3). But there are abuses – two of which are outlined in this Text. Firstly, merchants can become greedy and try to sell their goods as expensively as possible (VI.5-6). Instead, they should sell them only at a price that is just and in a way that does no injury to others (VI.7). Differing circumstances render it difficult to make rules about just prices, but temporal authorities could appoint wise and honest men to do this or it could be left to market forces (VI.8-9). In this Christians must act according to their conscience (VI.10-11) and be prepared to confess any inadvertent sins resulting from trading (VI.12-13). The second abuse arises from merchants standing surety for individuals (VI.14). This practice is against Scripture (VI.14-15) and it puts a false trust in humans rather than in God (VI.16-18). In contrast, there are four specifically Christian ways of exchanging goods. First, Christians can simply let others steal their property (VI.19). Secondly, they can give to anyone in need (VI.20). Thirdly, they can lend expecting nothing in return (VI.21). But, if followed in a sinful world, these three ways would lead to the break down of trade: in such a world, laws for nonChristians are essential (VI.23-4). Fourthly, Christians can buy and sell in cash alone, not relying upon credit or upon surety (VI.26).

3. ETHICAL ARGUMENTS

In contrast to Text III, this Text contains a variety of explicit forms of ethical argument. There is an appeal to natural law (VI.5) and several to individual conscience (VI.7 and 10-11). Consequentialism is evident in VI.7 and the arguments in VI.13 are distinctly pragmatic. But there is an overall deontological basis to the positions maintained in the Text: 'avarice', 'greed', 'robbing' and, indeed, 'injustice' (VI.5) are all assumed to be self-evidently wrong. Standing surety is also believed to be wrong primarily because it offends against Scripture (VI.14). Even popular German proverbs are used deontologically to reinforce his argument (VI.9 & 15). This Text is particularly important in illustrating the clear dichotomy that Luther often felt between the standards appropriate for the Christian and those to be required of the non-Christian.

4. *BASES OF CHRISTIAN ETHICS*

Both Old and New Testaments are used throughout this Extract. Indeed, Scripture characteristically forms the basis and constant point of reference for Luther's contentions (cf. Text III). This is particularly evident in his use of Proverbs (VI.14), Genesis (VI.18) and Matthew (VI.19). But there is also a strong doctrinal basis to his argument in VI.16-17 and the concept of the counsel of perfection for the clergy (VI.19) is heavily dependent upon Christian tradition rather than the Bible. There is also an important reference to 'Christian love' in VI.6. It might even be possible to argue that Luther was a situationist as far as Christians were concerned: laws were considered necessary only because most people were not Christian: if the world consisted only of Christians, Christian love would be a sufficient guide for proper action. This position is most evident in the treatise of the previous year, *Temporal Authority: To What Extent It Should Be Obeyed*, that he refers to in VI.23, as the following excerpt demonstrates:

If all the world were composed of real Christians, that is, true believers, there would be no need for or benefits from prince, king, lord, sword, or law. They would serve no purpose, since Christians have in their heart the Holy Spirit, who both teaches and makes them to do injustice to no one, to love everyone, and to suffer injustice and even death willingly and cheerfully at the hands of anyone. Where there is nothing but the unadulterated doing of right and bearing of wrong, there is not need for any suit, litigation, court, judge, penalty, law or sword... because the righteous man of his own accord does all and more than the law demands. But the unrighteous do nothing that the law demands; therefore, they need the law to instruct, constrain, and compel them to do good... All who are not Christians belong to the kingdom of the world and are under the law. There are few true believers, and still fewer who live a Christian life, who do not resist evil and indeed themselves do no evil. For this reason God has provided for them a different government beyond the Christian estate and kingdom of God. He has subjected them to the sword so that, even though they would like to, they are unable to practice their wickedness, and if they do practice it they cannot do so without fear or with success and impunity... If this were not so, men would devour one another, seeing that the whole world is evil and that among thousands there is scarcely a single true Christian. No one could support wife and child, feed himself, and serve God. The world would be reduced to chaos. For this reason God has ordained two governments: the spiritual, by which the Holy Spirit produces Christians and righteous people under Christ; and the temporal, which restrains the un-Christian and wicked so that – no thanks to them – they are obliged to keep still and to maintain an outward peace (*Luther's Works*, vol 45, pp.89-90).

This is one of Luther's clearest expressions of the notion of 'the two kingdoms'.

5. SOCIAL DETERMINANTS
The extent to which Luther was dependent upon medieval notions of finance has already been indicated and is particularly evident in his unworkable solution in VI.26. In addition, it might be argued that the sharp dichotomy that he made between the ethical requirements for Christians and those for non-Christians was exacerbated by his own particular social context. An accompaniment of the empirical phenomenon of conversion (see *above*, pp.35–7) can be a subsequent tendency to exaggerate the depravity of the pre-conversion state and those associated with it. Certainly, in this Text Luther's estimate of 'non-evangelical Christians' appears very low. Doubtless, the excesses of parts of the 16th-century Catholic Church also contributed to the dichotomy that Luther drew (see *above*, p.91). Luther attempted to maintain a position mid-way between the Anabaptists' rejection of Christians participating in political and economic matters and the Church of Rome's assumption of all earthly authority within itself.

6. *SOCIAL SIGNIFICANCE*

It is ironic that, whilst Luther upheld the central convictions of medieval Christendom about the evils of usury, of unrestrained trade based upon maximum profit, and of unjust and unjustifiable prices, he may have contributed indirectly to their propagation. Returning to Weber's thesis of *The Protestant Ethic and the 'Spirit' of Capitalism* (see *above*, p.91), the very success of Luther's challenge to the Church of Rome's authority, may have helped to remove the sanctions enforced by this authority. Thus, on the issue of usury, Luther clearly despised it and tragically associated the Jew with it (see Text XV). Yet one of the social effects of his theological challenge may have been to promote a new individualism in Europe and the structural demise of effective sanctions against usury. It would be false to claim either that this was the sole factor in effecting economic change in Europe or that Luther himself (or Calvin) was directly and consciously responsible for the rise of the spirit of rational capitalism (the so-called 'work ethic'). Weber's thesis depends on neither claim. But it is possible to see Luther's challenge contributing significantly to changes already present in European society.

FURTHER READING

Luther's writings of the 1520s have been the subject of a considerable amount of books. Some of these have already been mentioned in relation to Text III. They can be compared fruitfully with Calvin's political writings in John T. McNeill (ed), *Calvin: On God and Political Duty*. 'On the issue of usury', J.T. Noonan, Jr, *The Scholastic Analysis of Usury* is useful.

TEXT VI

LUTHER

Trade and usury

VI.1

The holy gospel, now that it has come to light, rebukes and reveals all the 'works of darkness', as St Paul calls them in Romans 13 [.12]. For it is a brilliant light, which illumines the whole world and teaches how evil are the works of the world, and shows the true works we ought to do for God and our neighbour. As a result even some of the merchants have been awakened and become aware that in their trading many a wicked trick and hurtful financial practice is in use. It is to be feared that the words of Ecclesiasticus apply here, namely, that merchants can hardly be without sin [Ecclus. 26.29]. Indeed, I think St Paul's saying in the last chapter of the first epistle to Timothy fits the case, 'The love of money is the root of all evils' [1 Tim. 6.10], and again, 'Those who desire to be rich fall into the devil's snare and into many useless and hurtful desires that plunge men into ruin and perdition' [1 Tim. 6.9].

VI.2

I suppose that my writing will be quite in vain, because the mischief has gone so far and has completely gotten the upper hand in all lands; and because those who understand the gospel are probably able in such easy, external things to judge for themselves what is fair and what is not, on the basis of their own consciences. Nevertheless, I have been asked and urged to touch upon these financial evils and expose some of them so that, even though the majority may not wish to do right, at least some people – however few they are – may be delivered from the gaping jaws of avarice. For it must be that among the merchants, as among other people, there are some who belong to Christ and would rather be poor with God than rich with the devil, as Psalm 37 [.16] says, 'It is better for the righteous to have a little than to have the great possessions of the wicked.' For their sake, then, we must speak out.

VI.3

It cannot be denied that buying and selling are necessary. They cannot be dispensed with, and can be practised in a Christian manner, especially when the commodities serve a necessary and honourable purpose. For even the patriarchs bought and sold cattle, wool, grain, butter, milk and other goods in this way. These are gifts of God, which he bestows out of the earth and distributes among mankind. But foreign trade, which brings from Calcutta and India and such places wares like costly silks, articles of gold, and spices – which minister only to ostentation but serve no useful purpose, and which drain away the money of land and people – would not be permitted if we had [proper] government and princes. But of this it is not my present purpose to write, for I expect that, like overdressing and overeating, it will have to stop of itself when we have no more money. Until then, neither writing nor teaching will do any good. We must first feel the pinch of want and poverty...

VI.4

It is our purpose here to speak of the abuses and sins of trade, insofar as they concern the conscience. The matter of their detrimental effect on the purse we leave to the princes and lords, that they may do their duty in this regard.

VI.5

First. Among themselves the merchants have a common rule which is their chief maxim and the basis of all their sharp practices, where they say: 'I may sell my goods as dear as I can.' They think this is their right. Thus occasion is given for avarice, and every window and door to hell is opened. What else does it mean but this: I care nothing about my neighbour; so long as I have my profit and satisfy my greed, of what concern is it to me if it injures my neighbour in ten ways at once? There you see how shamelessly this maxim flies squarely in the face not only of Christian love but also of natural law. How can there be anything good then in trade? How can it be without sin when such injustice is the chief maxim and rule of the whole business? On such a basis trade can be nothing but robbing and stealing the property of others.

VI.6

When once the rogue's eye and greedy belly of a merchant find that people must have his wares, or that the buyer is poor and needs them, he takes advantage of him and raises the price. He considers not the value of the goods, or what his own efforts and risk have deserved, but only the other man's want and need. He notes it not that he may relieve it but that he may use it to his own advantage by raising the price of his goods, which he would not have raised had it not been for his neighbour's need. Because of his avarice, therefore, the goods must be priced as much higher as the greater need of the other fellow will allow, so that the neighbour's need becomes as it were the measure of the goods' worth and value. Tell me, isn't that an un-Christian and inhuman thing to do? Isn't that equivalent to selling a poor man his own need in the same transaction? When he has to buy his wares at a higher price because of his need, that is the same as having to buy his own need; for what is sold to him is not simply the wares as they are, but the wares plus the fact that he must have them. Observe that this and like abominations are the inevitable consequence when the rule is that I may sell my goods as dear as I can.

VI.7

The rule ought to be, not, 'I may sell my wares as dear as I can or will,' but, 'I may sell my wares as dear as I ought, or as is right and fair.' For your selling ought not to be an act that is entirely within your own power and discretion, without law or limit, as though you were a god and beholden to no one. Because your selling is an act performed toward your neighbour, it should rather be so governed by law and conscience that you do it without harm and injury to him, your concern being directed more toward doing him no injury than toward gaining profit for yourself. But where are there such merchants? How few merchants there would be, and how trade would decline, if they were to amend this evil rule and put things on a fair and Christian basis!

VI.8

You ask, then, 'How dear may I sell? How am I to arrive at what is fair and right so I do not take increase from neighbour or overcharge him?' Answer: That is something that will never be governed either by writing or speaking; nor has anyone ever undertaken to fix the value of every commodity, and to raise or lower prices accordingly. The reason is this: wares are not all alike; one is transported a greater distance than another and one involves greater outlay than another. In this respect, therefore, everything is and must remain uncertain, and no fixed determination can be made, any more than one can designate a certain city as the place from which all wares are to be brought, or establish a definite cost price for them. It may happen that the same wares, brought from the same city by the same road, cost vastly more in one year than they did the year before because the weather may be worse, or the road, or because something else happens that increases the expense at one time above that at another time. Now it is fair and right that a merchant take as much profit on his wares as will reimburse him for their cost and compensate him for his trouble, his labour, and his risk. Even a farmhand must have food and pay for his labour. Who can serve or labour for nothing? The gospel says, 'The labourer deserves his wages' [Luke 10.7].

VI.9

But in order not to leave the question entirely unanswered, the best and safest way would be to have the temporal authorities appoint in this matter wise and honest men to compute the costs of all sorts of wares and accordingly set prices which would enable the merchant to get along and provide for him an adequate living, as is being done at certain places with respect to wine, fish, bread, and the like. But we Germans have too many other things to do; we are too busy drinking and dancing to provide for rules and regulations of this sort. Since this kind of ordinance therefore is not to be expected, the next best thing is to let goods be valued at the price for which they are bought and sold in the common market, or in the land generally. In this matter we can accept the proverb, 'Follow the crowd and you won't get lost.' Any profit made in this way I consider honest and proper, because here there is always the risk involved of having to suffer loss in wares and outlay, and excessive profits are scarcely possible.

VI.10

Where the price of goods is not fixed either by law or custom, and you must fix it yourself, here one can truly give you no instructions but only lay it on your conscience to be careful not to overcharge your neighbour, and to seek a modest living, not the goals of greed. Some have wished to place a ceiling on profits, with a limit of one-half on all wares; some say one-third; others something else. None of these measures is certain and safe unless it be so decreed by the temporal authorities and common law. What they determine in these matters would be safe. Therefore, you must make up your mind to seek in your trading only an adequate living. Accordingly, you should compute and count your cost, trouble, labour, and risk, and on that basis raise or lower the prices of your wares so that you set them where you will be repaid for your trouble and labour.

VI.11

I would not have anyone's conscience be so overly scrupulous or so closely bound in this matter that he feels he must strike exactly the right measure of profit to the very *heller*. It is impossible for you to arrive at the exact amount that you have earned with your trouble and labour. It is enough that with a good conscience you make the effort to arrive at what is right, though the very nature of trade makes it impossible to determine this exactly. The saying of the Wise Man will hold good in your case too: 'A merchant can hardly act without sin, and a tradesman will hardly keep his lips from evil' [Ecclus. 26.29]. If you take a trifle too much profit unwittingly and unintentionally, dismiss the matter in the Lord's Prayer where we pray, 'Forgive us our trespasses' [Matt. 6.12]. After all, no man's life is without sin; besides, the time will come in turn when you get too little for your trouble. Just throw the excess in the scale to counterbalance the losses you must similarly expect to take.

VI.12

For example, if you had a business amounting to a hundred *gulden* a year, and you were to take – over and above all the cost and reasonable profit you had for your trouble, labour, and risk – an excessive profit of perhaps one or two or three *gulden*, that I would call a business error which could not well be avoided, especially in the course of a whole year's trading. Therefore, you should not burden your conscience with it, but bring it to God in the Lord's Prayer as another of those inevitable sins (which cling to all of us) and leave the matter to him. For it is not wickedness or greed, but the very nature and necessity of your occupation which forces you into this mistake. I am speaking now of goodhearted and Godfearing men, who would not willingly do wrong. It is like the marital obligation, which cannot be performed without sin; yet because of its necessity, God winks at it, for it cannot be otherwise.

VI.13

In determining how much profit you ought to take on your business and your labour, there is no better way to reckon it than by computing the amount of time and labour you have put into it, and comparing that with the effort of a day labourer who works at some other occupation and seeing how much he earns in a day. On that basis figure how many days you have spent in getting your wares and bringing them to your place of business, and how much labour and risk was involved; for a great amount of labour and time ought to have a correspondingly greater return. That is the most accurate, the best, and the most definite advice and direction that can be given in this matter. Let him who dislikes it, better it himself. I base my case (as I have said) on the gospel that the labourer deserves his wages [Luke 10.7]; and Paul also says in 1 Corinthians 9 [.7], 'He who tends the flock should get some of the milk. Who can go to war at his own expense?' If you have a better ground than that, you are welcome to it.

VI.14

Second. A common error, which has become a widespread custom not only among the merchants but throughout the world, is the practice of one person becoming surety for another. Although this practice seems to be without sin, and looks like a virtue stemming from love, nevertheless it generally ruins a good many people and does them irreparable harm. King Solomon often forbade it, and condemned it in his proverbs. In Proverbs 6 [.1-5] he says, 'My son, if you have become surety for your neighbour, you have given your hand on it; you are snared in the utterance of your lips, and caught in the words of your mouth. Then do this, my son, and save yourself, for you have come into your neighbour's power: Go, hasten and importune your neighbour. Give your eyes no sleep, and your eyelids no slumber. Save yourself like a gazelle from the hand, and like a bird from the hand of the fowler.' Again... 'Take a man's garment when he has given surety for another, and take a pledge from him for the stranger's sake' [Prov. 27.13].

VI.15
See how strictly and vehemently the wise king in Holy Scripture forbids one's becoming surety for another. The German proverb agrees with him, 'Guarantors to the gallows'; as much as to say: It serves the surety right when he is seized and has to pay, for he is acting rashly and foolishly in becoming surety. Hence, it is decreed according to Scripture that no one shall become surety for another, unless he is able and entirely willing to assume the debt and pay it himself. Now it does seem strange that this practice should be wrong and be condemned, although a good many have learned by experience that it is a foolish thing to do, and have had subsequent misgivings about it. Why, then, is it condemned? Let us see.

VI.16
Standing surety is a work that is too lofty for a man; it is unseemly, for it is a presumptuous encroachment upon the work of God. In the first place, Scripture commands us not to put our trust and reliance in any man, but in God alone. For human nature is false, vain, deceitful, and unreliable, as Scripture says and experience daily teaches. He who becomes surety, however, is putting his trust in a man, and risking life and property on a false and insecure foundation. It serves him right when he fails, falls, and is ruined.

VI.17
In the second place, the surety is trusting in himself and making himself God (for whatever a man trusts in and relies upon is his god). But his own life and property are never for a single moment any more secure or certain than those of the man for whom he becomes surety. Everything is in the hand of God alone. God will not allow us a hair's breadth of power or right over the future, nor will he let us for a single moment be sure or certain of it. Therefore, he who becomes surety acts in an un-Christian way; he deserves what he gets, because he pledges and promises what is not his and not in his power, but solely in God's hands.

VI.18

Thus we read in Genesis 43 and 44, how the patriarch Judah became surety to his father Jacob for his brother Benjamin, promising to bring him home again or bear the blame forever [Gen. 43.8-9]. God nicely punished this presumption, and caused him to flounder and fail so that he could not bring Benjamin back until he gave himself up for him [Gen. 44.14-34] and then was barely freed by grace. The punishment served him right, for these sureties act as though they didn't even have to consult God on the matter or give thought to whether they are even sure of a tomorrow for their own life and property. They act without fear of God, as though they were themselves the source of life and property, and these were in their own power as long as they themselves willed it. This is nothing but a fruit of unbelief...

VI.19

Perhaps you will say, 'How then are people to trade with one another if surety is improper? That way many would be left behind who might otherwise get ahead.'

Answer: *There are four Christian ways* of exchanging external goods with others, as I have said elsewhere.

The first way is to let them rob or steal our property, as Christ says in Matthew 5 [.40], 'If anyone takes away your cloak, let him have your coat as well, and do not ask it of him again.' This way of dealing counts for nothing among the merchants; besides, it has not been held or preached as common teaching for all Christians, but merely as a counsel or a good idea for the clergy and the perfect, though they observe it even less than do the merchants. But true Christians observe it, for they know that their Father in heaven has assuredly promised in Matthew 6 [.11] to give them this day their daily bread. If men were to act accordingly, not only would countless abuses in all kinds of business be avoided, but a great many people would not become merchants, because reason and human nature flee and shun to the uttermost risks and damages of this sort.

VI.20

The second way is to give freely to anyone who needs it, as Christ also teaches in the same passage [Matt. 5.42; Luke 6.30]. This too is a lofty Christian work, which is why it counts for little among the people. There would be fewer merchants and less trade if this were put into practice. For he who does this must truly hold fast to heaven and look always to the hands of God, and not to his own resources or wealth, knowing that God will support him even though every cupboard were bare, because he knows to be true what God said to Joshua, 'I will not forsake you or withdraw my hand from you' [Josh. 1.5]; as the proverb has it, 'God still has more than what he ever gave away.' But that takes a true Christian, and he is a rare animal on earth, to whom the world and nature pay no heed.

VI.21

The third way is lending. That is, I give away my property, and take it back again if it is returned to me; but I must do without it if it is not returned. Christ himself defines this kind of transaction in what he says in Luke 6 [.35], 'Lend, expecting nothing in return.' That is, you should lend freely, and take your chances on getting it back or not. If it comes back, take it; if it does not, it is a gift. According to the gospel there is thus only one distinction between giving and lending, namely, a gift is not taken back, while a loan is taken back – if it is returned – but involves the risk that it may become a gift. He who lends expecting to get back something more and something better than he has loaned is nothing but an open and condemned usurer, since even those who in lending demand or expect to get back exactly what they lend, and take no chances on whether they get it back or not, are not acting in a Christian way. This third way too (in my opinion) is a lofty Christian work; and a rare one, judging by the way things are going in the world. If it were to be practised generally, trade of all sorts would greatly diminish and virtually cease.

VI.22

These three ways of exchanging goods, then, observe in masterful fashion this matter of not presuming upon the future, and not trusting in any man or in oneself but clinging to God alone.

Here all transactions are in cash, and are accompanied by the word which James teaches, 'If God wills, so be it' [Jas. 4.15]. For here we deal with people as with those who are unreliable and might fail; we give our money freely, or take our chances on losing what we lend.

VI.23

Now someone will say 'Who can then be saved? And where shall we find these Christians? Why, in this way there would be no trade left in the world; everyone would have his property taken or borrowed away, and the door would be thrown open for the wicked and idle gluttons – of whom the world is full – to take everything with their lying and cheating.' Answer: I have already said that Christians are rare people on earth. That is why the world needs a strict, harsh temporal government which will compel and constrain the wicked to refrain from theft and robbery, and to return what they borrow (although a Christian ought neither to demand nor expect it). This is necessary in order that the world may not become a desert, peace vanish, and men's trade and society be utterly destroyed; all of which would happen if we were to rule the world according to the gospel, rather than driving and compelling the wicked by laws and the use of force to do and allow what is right. For this reason we must keep the roads safe, preserve peace in the towns, enforce law in the land, and let the sword hew briskly and boldly against transgressors, as St Paul teaches in Romans 13 [.4]. For it is God's will that people who are not Christian be held in check and kept from doing wrong, at least from doing it with impunity. Let no one think that the world can be ruled without bloodshed; the temporal sword must and shall be red and bloody, for the world will and must be evil, and the sword is God's rod and vengeance upon it. But of this I have said enough in my little book on *Temporal Authority*.

VI.24

Borrowing would be a fine thing if it were practised between Christians, for every borrower would then willingly return what had been lent him, and the lender would willingly forego repayment if the borrower were unable to pay. Christians are brothers, and one does not forsake another; neither is any of them so lazy and shameless that he would not work but depend simply on another's wealth and labour, or consume in idleness another's goods. But where men are not Christians, the temporal authorities ought to compel them to repay what they have borrowed. If the temporal authorities are negligent and do not compel repayment, the Christian ought to tolerate the robbery, as Paul says in 1 Corinthians 6 [.7], 'Why not rather suffer wrong?' But you may exhort, insist, and do what you will to the man who is not a Christian; he pays no attention because he is not a Christian and has no regard for Christ's doctrine.

VI.25

You still have a grain of comfort too in the fact that you are not obligated to make a loan except out of your surplus and what you can spare from your own needs, as Christ says of alms, 'What you have left over, that give in alms, and everything is clean for you'. Now if someone wishes to borrow from you an amount so large that you would be ruined if it were not repaid, and you could not spare it from your own needs, then you are not bound to make the loan. Your first and greatest obligation is to provide for the needs of your wife and children and servants; you must not divert from them what you owe them. The best rule to follow is this: If the amount asked as a loan is too great, just go ahead and give something outright, or else lend as much as you would be willing to give, and take the risk of having to lose it. John the Baptist did not say, 'He who has one coat, let him give it away,' but, 'He who has two coats, let him give one to him who has none; and he who has food, let him do likewise' [Luke 3.11].

VI.26

The fourth way of exchanging goods is through buying or selling, but for hard cash or payment in kind. He who would use this method must make up his mind to rely not on something in the future but on God alone; also, that he will have to be dealing with men, men who will certainly fail and lie. Therefore, the best advice is this: whoever sells should not give credit or accept any security, but sell only for cash. If he wishes to lend, let him lend to Christians, or else take the risk of loss, and lend no more than he would be willing to give outright or can spare from his own needs. If the temporal government and regulations will not help him to recover his loan, let him lose it. Let him beware of becoming security for anyone; let him much rather give what he can. Such a man would be a true Christian merchant; God would not forsake him because he trusts properly in Him and cheerfully takes a chance in dealing with his untrustworthy neighbours.

VI.27

If there was no such thing in this world as becoming surety, if the free lending portrayed in the gospel were the general practice, and if only hard cash or wares on hand were exchanged in trade, then the greatest and most harmful dangers and faults and failings of trade and commerce would be well out of the way. It would then be easy to engage in all sorts of business enterprises, and the other sinful faults of trade could the more readily be prevented. If there were none of this becoming surety and this lending without risk, many a man would have to maintain his humble status and be content with a modest living who now aspires day and night to reach an exalted position, relying on borrowing and standing surety. That is why everyone now wants to be a merchant and get rich. From this stem the countless dangerous, and wicked devices and dirty tricks that have today become a joke among the merchants. There are so many of them that I have given up the hope that trade can be entirely corrected; it is so overburdened with all sorts of wickedness and deception that in the long run it will not be able to sustain itself, but will have to collapse inwardly of its own weight.

VI. 28

In what has been said I wished to give a bit of warning and instruction to everyone about this great, filthy, widespread business of trade and commerce.

CRITIQUE

The limitations of some of Luther's medieval economic concepts have already been noted. Nonetheless, the central thrust of his treatise still has undoubted force. At a time, in the West, when the division between Christians and non-Christians, and between the churches and society at large, is often felt to be increasing, his argument assumes fresh relevance. Religious people, generally, may feel a requirement to distinguish more carefully than in a number of previous ages and societies, between what sort of behaviour is appropriate for them and what sort is to be enforced within society. In a number of areas of social ethics this problem may not be acute, but in the areas of personal ethics it often is. So, injunctions against murder and stealing, once they are socially defined, are expected to apply to all. But in areas of sexual morality any attempt at public enforcement has become increasingly more controversial. It will be seen later in Section 5 that even this distinction (i.e. between social and personal ethics) is difficult to maintain consistently and that there are many issues that might claim to be both (e.g. marriage and abortion). Nonetheless, Luther's dilemma remains a real one. There is, indeed, a sense in which there would be no need of laws, courts, prisons etc., if everyone lived consistently by the rule of *agape*: all would tell the truth, respect the property and persons of others, and would be self-less and self-giving. Further, Luther is obviously and sadly correct in asserting that society is just not constituted by such agapeistic people – so laws, courts, prisons are essential if social chaos is to be avoided. He would have made an excellent critic of Fletcher's attempts in Extract 2 to work out a system of ethics for all based solely upon *agape*. The dilemma for Christian businesspeople remains broadly as Luther depicted: they are not working in a society composed solely of sincere Christians and, if they were to follow the injunctions of the Sermon on the Mount literally, their business would probably collapse (as it would if they followed Luther's advice literally). Some present-day theologians, such as Miranda in Extract 11, would see this as good reason for the Christian businesspeople abandoning Western capitalism altogether. But for those who cannot accept this, tension seems inescapable. It is a tension evident in several of the Extracts in this Section.

Even if it is accepted that some dichotomy between Christian ethics and the ethical standards to be required of society is inevitable, Luther's depiction of this can still be criticised. His view of his contemporaries was bleak and he seemed to believe that if people could not be converted to Christianity they could only be restrained like beasts (see especially VI.23). Not only does this present a highly exclusive understanding of Christianity (see *above*, p.98), but it makes no allowance for transposed Christian values having an effect upon society at large (see *above*, pp.11–12).

EXTRACTS 6-11
BARTH, BERDYAEV, NIEBUHR, TEMPLE, JOHN XXIII, AND MIRANDA

1. BACKGROUND

Karl Barth's Extract 6 comes from his commentary *The Epistle to the Romans* (OUP, 1929 edition, on Rom. 12.21 & 13.1), Nicolas Berdyaev's Extract 7 from his *Freedom and the Spirit* (Geoffrey Bles Centenary Press, London, 1935, pp.x-xiv and xvi-xviii), Reinhold Niebuhr's Extract 8 from his *Moral Man and Immoral Society* (Scribner's, New York, 1960 re-issue, pp.257-9 & 268-75), William Temple's Extract 9 from his *Christianity and Social Order* (Shepheard-Walwyn & SPCK, London, 1976 re-issue, pp.58-9, 60-2, 67-8, 69-71, 72-4, 75 & 77), Pope John XXIII's Extract 10 from his Encyclical Letter *Pacem in Terris* (Catholic Truth Society, London, trans. Henry Waterhouse SJ, 1980, paras. 80-96, 130-46 & 161-71) and José Porfirio Miranda's Extract 11 from his *Marx and the Bible* (SCM, London, and Orbis Books, New York, 1977, trans. John Eagleson, pp.14-22).

Extracts 6 and 8 represent the views of authors in their radical youth, whereas 9 and 10 represent those of church statesmen at the end of their lives. The *Epistle to the Romans* represented Barth's radical break with Christian liberalism and proved to be the foundation-stone of the neo-orthodox movement in theology. Barth (1886-1968) wrote *Der Römerbrief* in the context of the revolutionary Europe of 1917-19 and, as a result of it, he was soon made a professor, first at Göttingen (1921), then at Münster (1925), then Bonn (1930) and, finally, on expulsion by Hitler, at Basle (1935). Niebuhr (1892-1971) published *Moral Man and Immoral Society* in 1932, four years after becoming Professor of Applied Christianity at the Union Theological Seminary, New York, where he stayed until his retirement in 1960. He, too, wrote this work in the context of considerable social ferment, during the American Depression and as a result of his pastoral experience in industrial Detroit, prior to his appointment at UTS. Temple (1881-1944) wrote *Christianity and Social Order* at the height of the Second World War, in 1941, twelve years after becoming Archbishop of York and a few months before becoming Archbishop of Canterbury. Unlike some of his more technical works, its style was designed for non-theologians and, indeed, it sold some 150,000 copies when first published (re-issued 1956 and 1976). John XXIII (1881-1963) was Pope for five years, publishing *Pacem in Terris* in the year that he died and only months after convening the highly influential Second Vatican Council. Extract 10 clearly reflects the liberal concerns of John XXIII and the social changes that characterised the 1960s. Extract 11 reflects the present-day concerns of Latin American Liberation theology. Miranda, a Mexican Roman Catholic, was trained in both economics and biblical studies and has written, in addition, the influential *Marx Against the Marxists* (SCM, 1980). In contrast, Berdyaev (1874-1948) belongs fully to no theological movement and his writings are comparatively timeless. *Freedom and the Spirit* was written in 1927, in Paris, five years after his expulsion from his native Russia. Amongst his other important books are *The Meaning of History* (1923) and *The Destiny of Man* (1931). In his autobiography he describes his position as a Russian Orthodox Christian as follows: 'I confess a spiritual religion, I am a free Christian, who has not broken away from the church'. He died in Paris as a Russian expatriate and independent scholar.

2. KEY ISSUES

Barth argues that the existing orders in the political realm, whether democratic or not, appear as orders of humanity against God. Rulers and governments seem to be claiming falsely to possess a higher right over others. Even a theocracy would appear as supreme wrong-doing (6.1). Political revolution is born of the perception of the evil that lies in the very existence of governments of any sort. Yet, in the process of revolution, the revolutionaries are overcome by evil, since they too confront others (often tyrannically) with a supposed right over them (6.2). True revolution involves forgiveness of sins and resurrection of the dead, whereas political revolutionaries bring hatred and demolition – mere reactions to the present order rather than the intended new order (6.3). Thus, revolutionaries simply replace one form of temporal power with another and may even make remaining elements of the previous order more dangerous. They attempt to substitute themselves for God (6.4). But, since it is outside history, God's order cannot be established in this way (6.5-7). Indeed, God's order stands in permanent judgment on human ecclesiastical and secular orthodoxies and 'isms' – including legitimism [i.e. political theory concerned with establishing the legitimacy of particular regimes]. Judgment must be left to God alone (6.8). Powers are to be measured only by reference to God as God, who alone is judge, and the evil of the existing order is to be seen as really evil only in relation to God's order (6.9). Evil gives witness to the good and it should be left for God alone to judge – vengeance is not ours, but God's (6.10).

Although both Barth and Berdyaev were, at times, highly active and committed in political affairs as individuals, as theologians they were equally apolitical. Berdyaev's apoliticism stems from his thoroughgoing stress on spirituality. He sees Christianity as undergoing a crisis in transition from an objective/collective form to a more subjective/individualistic one (7.1). For him, the collective/democratic and the individualistic/aristocratic types are evident throughout history. Socialists belong to the first type and tend to claim that a privileged minority have exploited the majority, whereas, in fact, they themselves have always persecuted the qualitative minority, favouring the 'average' person (7.2). Indeed, conservatives and monarchists also belong to this type, maintaining traditional institutions for the majority (7.3). As aristocrats of the spirit, saints, prophets and geniuses do not need conventional political structures (democratic or otherwise). Yet, they still ought not to separate themselves from the world, even if they are persecuted by the world (7.4). Democratic types may have greater talents than aristocratic types but they are less sensitive to the world's ugliness and barbarity (7.5). The Gnostic belongs mainly to the aristocratic type, clashing with democratic orthodox Christianity, but is in a sense closer to the present-day spiritually sensitive person and to the Russian concept of *sobornost* [a mystic concept often used by Russian theologians to denote the idea of oneness in togetherness] (7.6). But Gnostics tended, proudly and wrongly, to separate themselves from the carnal world and, in the process, proved unloving to their fellows. Yet, the Church, in condemning Gnostics, elaborated an inflexible system of theology (7.7). Nonetheless, there is still room in Christianity for people who can reach spiritual heights, without boasting and separating themselves from the carnal world – despite the denial of this, at times, by both the Church and particular political regimes (7.8). The problem of the spirit and the spiritual life is the main problem confronting people today (7.9).

A distinction between the political and the religious appears, in a very different form, in Niebuhr's early *Moral Man and Immoral Society*. For Niebuhr, a sharp distinction must be made between individual and social ethics, the former requiring unselfishness as its ideal and the latter justice (8.1). They are not totally exclusive – for instance, insights from individual moral conscience are essential if society is fully to understand justice and without them justice would soon degenerate – but they cannot be fully harmonised (8.2). Whereas unselfishness is essential to individual morality, self-assertion may, at times, be essential for the survival of a particular society (8.3). Individual ethics has usually been cultivated by religion and appears thus as the antithesis of political morality (8.4). Attempts to apply such individual ethics to social groups have failed – whether in the case of the American blacks, Italian pacifist socialists, or pre-revolutionary Russians (8.5-7). It would be better to admit a moral dualism than to attempt to harmonise these two forms of morality. Just as we distinguish between moral judgments applied to self and those we apply to others, so, we must distinguish between those we apply to the individual and those we apply to society (8.8). The social group does not possess sufficient imagination for it to be amenable to pure love; particular groups are too selfish to allow themselves to subject their own interests to some inconclusive social ideal (8.9). But individuals, even those who are politically involved, ought still to be loyal to the highest canons of personal morality and, at times, may even have to dissociate themselves from their group (8.10). And individuals, such as leaders of groups, must practise personal unselfishness if they are adequately to fulfil their social roles (8.11-12).

All of the next three authors believe that Christianity has a directly political role. For Temple, the Church, as the Church, must be concerned with general principles, whereas the individual Christian must seek to particularise these principles (9.1). Christian faith, by itself, cannot produce detailed political policies independent of economic and other factors, although it can point to relevant principles (9.2-3). The Church even has difficulties with the notion of the 'perfect social order' – not least because of human imperfection (9.4-5). Political and economic systems must first provide for human security even before providing for justice or expressing love (9.6). However, although Christianity does not suggest an 'ideal state', it does supply a number of general principles (9.7-8). So, it supplies the principle of respect for every person as a child of God and, as a result, people should be given priority over societies and societies should be arranged to maximise the individual roles of its people (9.9-10). Again, Christianity contains the principle of freedom – understood, not simply as an absence of constraint, but, as self-determination (9.11-12). Law exists to preserve and to extend this freedom (9.13). Freedom for the individual is freedom within the context of various social groups: humans are emphatically social in the sense of belonging to a variety of intermediate groups (9.14-17). The state which values freedom should be careful to give such groups freedom – and, indeed, Britain has derived many of its democratic habits from such groups as the Trade Unions, themselves owing much to the Chapels (9.18-20). Finally, there is a principle of fellowship leading to service; partly voluntary service by the individual and, partly, the individual seeing paid occupation as service (9.22-4).

John XXIII's discussion is also concerned with general principles which can be applied to political realities, although he views them in terms of rights and duties (a right entails a duty and a duty presupposes a right). In contrast to Niebuhr, he maintains that the natural law notion of mutual rights and duties applies as much to the relationship between states as it does to that between individuals (10.1-3). This perspective involves recognising the reality of the moral order and the objectivity of truth, both by individuals and by states, in seeking to promote the common good (10.5-6; cf. Extract 4). Granted such recognition, racial and ethnic discrimination and arrogance, based on superior talents or wealth, can play no part either in individual or in communal behaviour (10.7-10). The truth also requires fairness in the use of mass communication (10.11). States have a duty to seek justice and not to seek their own advantage at the expense of others (10.12-13). When there is a clash of interests between states, peaceful and considerate means of resolving it should be sought, particularly when ethnic minorities are dealt with by states (10.14-17). States are becoming increasingly interdependent and it is vital that attention should be given to the universal common good (10.18-20). Present state structures are inadequate to deal with problems raised by such a universal common good (e.g. world peace) and this requires the establishment of some form of world government (10.21-5). Such a government should only come into being through universal consent – for otherwise it might favour one nation over others – and should be concerned with making sure that human rights are upheld everywhere (10.26-7). In addition, it should be concerned solely with questions related to the universal common good and not with those rightly belonging to individual states (10.28-9). UNO is a step in the direction of such a government (10.20-3). Individual Christians should be particularly concerned to offer themselves for public service and to seek to change society, not in terms of revolution, but gradually, in a spirit of duty and love (10.34-8). Peace will come only when individual hearts are changed and when it is built on the firm principles of God in Christ (10.39-45).

Amongst recent theologians it is, perhaps, the exponents of Liberation theology who have argued most strongly that Christianity has direct relevance to political issues. They are represented in this Section by Miranda and in the next by Bonino. Both are convinced that Marxist theory can illuminate the biblical understanding of humanity and that this understanding ought to inform our interpretation of political realities. Miranda has been at considerable pains to demonstrate that the biblical understanding of wealth and poverty and the class divisions that have resulted from them coincide at many crucial points with Marxist theory. In this Extract, he argues that in the Old Testament 'almsgiving' and justice' are synonymous (11.1-3).

Although this has frequently been forgotten by subsequent Christians, the early Church Fathers were clear that 'almsgiving' was really a restitution that people make for something that is not properly theirs (11.4-7). For Luke, the difference between 'rich' and 'poor' ('differentiating ownership', in Marxist terms) cannot be justified and, indeed, results from injustice and violence (11.8-9). Despite the attempts of some biblical critics to claim that such views are not authentic to Jesus himself, the evidence is overwhelming (11.10-12). Further, to regard the biblical position as 'primitive' is to make a highly suspect, Western value-judgment (11.13-14). The prophets were well aware of the injustice of differentiating ownership and it would be a mistake to explain their attitudes in terms of an anti-urban bias (11.14-20). Christianity must return to a fresh awareness of this injustice and even papal teaching must be interpreted afresh in its light (11.21-3).

3. ETHICAL ARGUMENTS

The clearest ethical arguments are contained in John XXIII's and Temple's Extracts. The first is thoroughly based upon natural law and sees a straightforward continuum between the rights and duties of the individual and those of societies. These rights and duties must always be related to the 'common good' and it is on this basis that, for example, he can argue that, 'the moral order itself demands the establishment of some sort of world government' (10.25). However, this deontological position is immediately followed by a number of consequential arguments – e.g. that if such a government were imposed by force the 'efficacy of its action would thereby be imperilled' (10.26).

Temple's position, too, is dependent upon some notion of natural law, albeit in a somewhat modified form. However, he also uses a mixture of deontological and consequential arguments. So, having enunciated a general principle of respect for persons, he argues, in a style owing something to utilitarianism, that 'society must be so arranged as to give to every citizen the maximum opportunity for making deliberate choices' (9.10). It is even possible that his radical stress upon the individual, his stress upon the 'primary principle' of respect for persons, and his avoidance of anything but general principles as absolutes, could be seen as a form of personalism.

Differing deontological positions are apparent in Niebuhr and Miranda. For the first, the notions of love and justice appear to be accepted deontologically, whereas, for Miranda, it is a strong moral identification (whether in Marxism or in the Bible) with the poor and the oppressed. However, Niebuhr's criticisms of those who have attempted to apply individual love to social situations, are predominantly consequentialist (8.4-7) and his defence of pacifism at this early stage of his career is entirely pragmatic (8.10).

Consequentialism is also apparent, sometimes, in the few ethical arguments of the, predominantly theological, Berdyaev and Barth Extracts. Berdyaev argues that absolute monarchies and socialist republics 'are alike necessary to the masses' (7.3), but only because they do not belong to the 'aristocracy of the spirit' (7.6). In a similar negative manner, Barth maintains that authoritarianism in politics leads to tyranny (6.1). Nonetheless, Barth's primary objection to such authoritarianism is theological – it usurps the position which should alone belong to God.

4. BASES OF CHRISTIAN ETHICS

Only three of the Extracts make any continuous use of the Bible and they differ significantly from each other in the way that they do this. Barth's Extract is obviously a part of his commentary on Romans, but it is quite unlike a scholarly, critical commentary. His remarks frequently have more to do with his own social context than to that of Paul (as in his discussion of political revolution). John XXIII quotes both the Old Testament and the New Testament (e.g. in 10.4, 43 & 44), but the central thrust of his argument does not depend upon them. As in Aquinas, the Bible is used to support a position which is first developed on the basis of natural law. Although himself a Roman Catholic priest, Miranda's use of the Bible might seem more characteristic of the Reformed tradition: it is central to his argument, owes much to critical, non-Roman Catholic scholarship and ranges over both Old Testament and New Testament.

Differing appeals to Christian tradition are also apparent in Miranda and John XXIII. The latter follows the traditional Roman Catholic approach (see further Welty's Extract 12 and Paul VI's Extract 24) in seeking to substantiate particular positions from the Fathers or from the statements of previous Popes. So John XXIII quotes Augustine (10.13 & 39) and his predecessor Pius XII (10.6 & 36). However, Miranda mainly uses the Fathers to substantiate his position (11.4-7): papal statements provide him with obvious problems. As one still working within the Roman Catholic tradition, he is clearly concerned that he contradict, not direct papal teaching, but only papal 'suppositions' behind this teaching (11.22-3).

Differing theological bases are also apparent in these Extracts. Berdyaev and Barth are both emphatically theological in orientation, but the first emphasises the Spirit and a spiritual form of Christianity, whereas Barth's emphasis is upon the judgment of God and upon human attempts to usurp God's position. John XXIII concludes his encyclical with christology (10.45), whereas Temple concludes his discussion with theological anthropology (9.26). In Miranda, it is the concept of 'justice', derived through Jesus from the Old Testament, which is central to his position. For all five theologians, it is clear that they believe that their distinctive approaches to political realities owe much to their initial theological positions. Only Niebuhr's Extract is relatively lacking in specifically Christian bases: indeed, religious faith appears in his analysis here as far more relevant to the indiviual than to society.

5. SOCIAL DETERMINANTS

The influence of the particular socio-political contexts within which they wrote is especially evident in Barth, Niebuhr and Miranda. The background of revolutionary Europe of 1917-19 doubly influenced Barth. On the one hand, the specifically social repercussions convinced him (and many of his contemporaries) that revolution led to greater tyranny than it replaced. Throughout Europe there was considerable disillusionment with political attitudes of authoritarianism which had led, both to the Great War and to the Russian Revolution. On the other hand, Barth saw the theological liberalism of the pre-war period (which he had shared) as disastrously implicated with these attitudes. His rejection both of revolutionary politics and of theological liberalism and his espousal of neo-orthodoxy were clearly related to this European political context. Similarly, Niebuhr's ethical dualism can be related to the American Depression that followed this war. His experiences in industrial Detroit convinced him that liberal attempts to relate Christian concepts of love to social phenomena were misguided. The ineluctable forces of economic depression and the consequent feelings of helplessness of individuals caught within that depression and within the dehumanising structures of contemporary industrialism, made a lasting impression on Niebuhr's mind. Similarly, the political and economic frustrations of South America, in the 1970s, has had an evident effect upon Miranda. He, too, rejects Western theological and political liberalism (11.6, 10 & 13) and declares emphatically that, 'the time has come for Christianity to break a long chain of hypocrisy and collusion with the established powers' (11.7). His stark contrasts between 'rich' and 'poor' and his close correlation of 'wealth' with 'violence and spoliation', may reflect the feudal, authoritarian and oppressive socio-political structures of parts of Central America, rather than what might be seen as the ambiguities of the mixed economies of the West.

Berdyaev stands in sharp contrast to these three theologians. His early espousal of Marxist theory is still partially evident in this Extract and his socialisation in Russian Orthodoxy also acts as a determinant of his position. Nonetheless, as has already been pointed out, despite the revolutionary context within which he lived, his writings, as a whole, still appear remarkably timeless.

John XXIII's Extract and Temple's Extract are not so timeless and clearly reflect the topical political interests of the contexts within which they were written. The issue of unemployment dominated much of Temple's political thought in the 1930s and occurs spontaneously as an illustration (9.2). In the period following Hiroshima and Nagasaki, peace became a very dominant concern, allied to a search for political stability in the developed and developing worlds. John XXIII's Extract clearly relates strongly to these concerns. Nonetheless, both Extracts are also characterised by a judiciousness and by a relative detachment – the result, perhaps, of their authors' ecclesiastical positions and of their commitment to natural law theory.

6. SOCIAL SIGNIFICANCE

A number of the works from which these Extracts are taken had a real political influence. John XXIII was, perhaps, the most generally admired of recent Popes and his efforts to foster peace in the world received a wide audience, amongst both Roman Catholics and others. The issue of human rights has remained an important one in the Western world, even if the specific connection with natural law articulated by John XXIII is now seldom discussed. In the 1940s and 1950s, Niebuhr was particularly influential in the United States. His ethical position changed considerably from *Moral Man and Immoral Society*, with his ethical dualism becoming less pronounced and a greater stress on 'political realism', but his central distinctions between love and justice remained highly influential. A number of key politicians and political theorists were directly influenced by his writings. Temple, in contrast, although he is often regarded as one of the most respected Archbishops of the Church of England in the 20th century, seldom had the ear of prime ministers. His overt socialism and tendency to be outspoken on political issues tended to alienate him from politicians, such as Churchill. But, within church circles, his influence was very considerable and he played a major part in the Life and Work Movement which eventually became a central component of the World Council of Churches. Many of Temple's distinctions, between general principles, middle axioms (see *above*, p.62) and changing factors, were adopted by these two movements. Within present-day South America, Liberation theology now receives considerable political attention. It has radicalised a significant section of the Roman Catholic clergy there and provides a rare example of a theological movement acting as an independent social variable (i.e. as a social factor, such as 'class', which affects mass behaviour). The influence of Barth's *Der Römerbrief* upon theologians, rather than upon politicians, was very considerable. In fact, for many theologians it has proved to be one of the most seminal books of the first half of the 20th century. However, Berdyaev's writings have seldom been known outside scholarly circles.

FURTHER READING

A number of the works of Barth, himself, are important for understanding his various approaches to political realities, including *How I Changed my Mind*, *Church Dogmatics* III.4 and *Ethics*. Of the many books written about Barth, the following are particularly useful: Charles West, *Communism and the Theologians*; H. Richard Niebuhr, *The Responsible Self*; and R.E. Willis, *The Ethics of Karl Barth*. There have been a number of studies of Berdyaev, including: Oliver Fielding Clarke, *Introduction to Berdyaev*; Donald A. Lowrie, *Rebellious Prophet: A Life of Nicolas Berdyaev*; E.L. Allen, *Freedom in God: A Guide to the Thought of Nicolas Berdyaev*; and Michael Alexander Vallon, *An Apostle of Freedom: Life and Teaching of Nicolas Berdyaev*. For Niebuhr, see C.W. Kegley & R.W. Bretall (ed), *Reinhold Niebuhr: His Religious, Social and Political Thought*; D. Meyer, *The Protestant Search for Political Realism*; and Richard Harries (ed), *Reinhold Niebuhr and the Issues of Our Time*. F.A. Iremonger's *William Temple: Archbishop of Canterbury* is still very important for information about Temple: see also Ronald Preston's introduction to the 1976 edition of *Christianity and Social Order*, and Alan Suggate's *William Temple and Christian Social Ethics Today*. For Liberation theology, see *below*, p.313.

EXTRACT 6

BARTH

God's judgment on political revolutions

6.1

Be not overcome of evil, but overcome evil with good (Rom. 12.21). The problem of the victory of right over wrong is presented to us in a far more essential form in the existence of human ordinances than in the existence of the *enemy* (12,19,20). Must not the existing order, the order that has already been FOUND, seem the very incarnation of triumphant unrighteousness to the man who is SEEKING after God and His Order? Is not the existing order a reinforcement of men against God, a safeguard of the normal course of this world against its disturbance by the great ambiguity and its defence against the presupposition by which it is threatened on all sides? Are not the ordinances of men simply a conspiracy of the Many – far too many – against the One who manifests Himself, and can only manifest

Himself, when the mature wisdom and authority of the Many crumbles in pieces? Rulers! What are rulers but men? What are they but men hypocritically engaged in setting things in order, in order that they may – cowards that they are – ensure themselves securely against the riddle of their existence? Are we not once again confronted by fools begging a few moments' delay before the sentence of death is pronounced upon them? The invectives that have been hurled against 'Governments' from the days of the Revelation of John to the fulminations of Nietzsche, from the Anabaptists to the Anarchists, have not been directed against defects in government but against the right of governments to *exist* at all. That men should, as a matter of course, claim to possess a higher right over their fellow men, that they should, as a matter of course, dare to regulate and predetermine almost all their conduct, that those who put forward such a manifestly fraudulent claim should be crowned with a halo of real power and should be capable of requiring obedience and sacrifice as though they had been invested with the authority of God, that the Many should conspire to speak as though they were the One, that a minority or a majority – even the supreme democratic majority of all against one – should assume that they are the community, that a quite fortuitous contract or arrangement should be regarded as superior to the solid organisation of the struggle for existence and should proclaim itself to be the peace which all men yearn after and which all should respect; this whole pseudo-transcendence of an altogether immanent order is the wound that is inflicted by every existing government – even by the best – upon those who are most delicately conscious of what is good and right. The more successfully the good and the right assume concrete form, the more they become evil and wrong – *summum ius, summa iniuria*. Supposing the right were to take the form of theocracy, supposing, that is to say, superior spiritual attainment were concreted into an ideal Church and all the peoples of the earth were to put their trust in it; if, for example, the Church of Calvin were to be reformed and broadened out to be the Church of the League of Nations; – this doing of the supreme right would then become the supreme wrong-doing. This theocratic dream comes abruptly to an end, of course, when we discover that it is the Devil who approaches Jesus and offers Him all the kingdoms of this world. It ends also with Dostoevsky's picture of the Grand Inquisitor. Men have no right to possess objective right against other men. And so, the more they surround themselves with objectivity, the greater is the wrong they inflict upon others. Others are, it is true, awaiting the right of the One. But when and where has the right of the Many really become the right of the One? Has it not been always and everywhere acquired fraudulently? Is there anywhere legality which is not fundamentally illegal? Is there anywhere authority which is not ultimately based upon tyranny?

6.2

There is a certain imperfection in the existing ordinances by which we are enabled to detect that their existence is, as such, evil. There is a certain uncontrollable tendency to freedom which causes both good and bad men to resent the chain which the Many – no doubt with the best intentions – put upon them. There is a certain strange and penetrating perception which sees through the fiction that lies behind our bondage. From this perception of the evil that lies in the very existence of the existing government, Revolution is born. The revolutionary seeks to be rid of the evil by bestirring himself to battle with it and to overthrow it. He determines to remove the existing ordinances, in order that he may erect in their place the new right. This is, of course, a wholly intelligible course of action, and one in which we might very well take part; it is, in fact, as intelligible as is hostility against the *enemy* (12.19) and conflict against our fellow men. (The revolutionary does not begin by betaking himself to the generally decried shedding blood. He begins by simply harbouring a certain secret poisonous resentment against the existing order – many indeed go no further than this; they detest the *Power*, and become wholly enslaved to feelings of resentment!) The revolutionary must, however, own that in adopting his plan he allows himself to be *overcome of evil*. He forgets that he is not the One, that he is not the subject of the freedom which he so earnestly desires, that, for all the strange brightness of his eyes, he is not the Christ who stands before the Grand Inquisitor, but is, contrariwise, the Grand Inquisitor encountered by the Christ. He too is claiming what no man can claim. He too is making of the right a thing. He too confronts other men with his supposed right. He too usurps a position which is not due to him, a legality which is fundamentally illegal, an authority which – as we have grimly experienced in Bolshevism, but also in the behaviour of far more delicate-minded innovators! – soon displays its essential tyranny. What man has the right to propound and represent the 'New', whether it be a new age, or a new world, or even a new – spirit? Is not every new thing, in so far as it can be schemed by men, born of what already *exists*? The moment it becomes a human proposition, must it not be numbered among the things that are? What man is there who, having proposed a novelty, has not proposed an evil thing? Far more than the conservative, the revolutionary is *overcome of evil*, because with his 'No' he stands so strangely near to God. This is the tragedy of revolution. Evil is not the true answer to evil. The sense of right which has been wounded by the existing order is not restored to health when that order is broken.

6.3

Overcome evil with good. What can this mean but the end of the triumph of men, whether their triumph is celebrated in the existing order or by revolution? And how can this end be represented, if it be not by some strange 'not-doing' precisely at the point where men feel themselves most powerfully called to action? The revolutionary has erred. He really means that Revolution which is the impossible possibility. He means forgiveness of sins and the resurrection of the dead. He means Jesus Christ – He that hath *overcome* – who is the true answer to the injury wrought by the existing order as such. But the revolutionary has chosen another revolution: he has adopted the possible possibility of discontent and hatred and insubordination, of rebellion and demolition. And this choice is not better, but much worse than choosing the possible possibility of contentment and satisfaction, of security and usurpation; for by it God is far better understood, but far more deeply outraged. The revolutionary aims at the Revolution by which the true Order is to be inaugurated; but he launches another revolution which is, in fact, reaction. The legitimist, on the other hand, himself also overcome of evil, aims at the Legitimism by which the true Revolution is inaugurated; but he maintains another legitimism which is, in fact, revolt! And so, as always, what men do is the judgment upon what they will to do (7.15, 19). When, however, the revolutionary becomes aware of the judgment, he is dispossessed of his well founded, concrete, justifiable action, and is turned towards the action of God. But how can he demonstrate the action of God save by dying where he was born? by dying, that is to say, where he first perceived the evil of the present order. What more radical action can he perform than the action of turning back to the original root of 'not-doing' – and NOT be angry, NOT engage in an assault, NOT demolish? This turning back is the ethical factor in the command, *Overcome evil with good*. There is here no word of approval of the existing order; but there is endless disapproval of every enemy of it. It is God who wishes to be recognised as He that *overcometh* the unrighteousness of the existing order. This is the meaning of the commandment; and it is also the meaning of the Thirteenth Chapter of the Epistle to the Romans.

6.4

Let every man be in subjection to the existing ruling powers (Rom. 13.1a). Though subjection may assume from time to time many various concrete forms, as an ethical conception it is here purely negative. It means to withdraw and make way; it means to have no resentment, and not to overthrow. Why, then, does not the rebel turn back and become no more a rebel? Simply because the conflict in which he is immersed cannot be represented as a conflict between him and the *existing ruling powers*; it is, rather a conflict of evil with evil. Even the most radical revolution can do no more than set what exists against what *exists*. Even the most radical revolution – and this is so even when it is called a 'spiritual' or 'peaceful' revolution – can be no more than a revolt; that is to say, it is in itself simply a justification and confirmation of what already exists. For the whole relative right of what exists is established only by the relative wrong of revolution in its victory; whereas the relative right of revolution in its victory is in no way established by the relative wrong of the existing order. Similarly also, the power of resistance in the existing order is in no way broken by the victorious attack of revolution; it is merely driven backwards, embarrassed, and compelled to adopt different forms, and thus rendered the more dangerous; whereas the energy of revolution is dissipated and rendered innocuous – simply by its victory. And so the whole conduct of the rebel in no way constitutes a judgment upon the existing order, however much his act of revolution may do so. The rebel has thoughtlessly undertaken the conflict between God's Order and the existing order. Should he allow himself to appeal directly to the ordinance of God, 'should he boldly and confidently storm the heavens and bring down thence his own eternal rights which hang aloft inalienable, unbroken as the stars themselves' (*Schiller*), he betrays thereby perception of the true 'limit to the tyrant's power', but his bold storming of the heavens in no way brings about this limitation. He may be justified at the bar of history; but he is not justified before the judgment-seat of God. The sequel shows 'the return of the old natural order where men oppose their fellow men'. When men undertake to substitute themselves for God, the problem of God, His mind and His judgment, still remain, but they are rendered ineffective. And so, in his rebellion, the rebel stands on the side of the existing order.

6.5
Let the existing order – state, Church, Law, Society, &c., &c. – in their totality be:

$$(a\ b\ c\ d)$$

6.6
Let their dissolution by the Primal Order of God, by which their totality is contradicted, be expressed by a minus sign outside the bracket:

$$-(+a+b+c+d)$$

6.7
It is then clear that no revolution, however radical, which takes place within the realm of history, can ever be identical with the divine minus sign outside the bracket, by which the totality of human ordinances is dissolved. Revolution can do no more than change the plus sign within the bracket – the plus, that

is to say, which existing ordinances possess within the bracket because they exist – into a minus sign. The result of a successful revolution is therefore:

$$-(-a-b-c-d)$$

6.8

And now we see that for the first time the great divine minus sign outside the bracket has transformed the anticipatory, revolutionary minus sign into a genuine plus sign. Revolution has, therefore, the effect of restoring the old after its downfall in a new and more powerful form. (Equally false, however, is the reckoning of the legitimists: false, because they consciously and as a matter of principle – in their consciousness and in their appeal to principle lies the arrogant and titanic element in Legitim-ISM – add a positive sign to the terms within the bracket. But the divine minus sign outside the bracket means that all human consciousness, all human principles and axioms and orthodoxies and -isms, *all principality and power and dominion*, are AS SUCH subjected to the destructive judgment of God. *Let every man be in subjection* means, therefore, that every man should consider the falsity of all human reckoning as such. We are not competent to place the decisive minus sign before the bracket; we are only competent to perceive how completely it damages our plus and our minus. Accordingly, the subjection here recommended must not be allowed to develop into a new and subtle manner of reckoning, whereby we reintroduce once more an absolute right. It is evident that there can be no more devastating undermining of the existing order than the recognition of it which is here recommended, a recognition rid of all illusion and devoid of all the joy of triumph. State, Church, Society, Positive Right, Family, Organised Research, &c., &c., live off the credulity of those who have been nurtured upon vigorous sermons-delivered-on-the-field-of-battle and upon other suchlike solemn humbug. Deprive them of their PATHOS, and they will be starved out; but stir up revolution against them, and their PATHOS is provided with fresh fodder. No-revolution is the best preparation for the true Revolution; but even no-revolution is no safe recipe. To *be in subjection* is, when it is rightly understood, an action void of purpose, an action, that is to say, which can spring only from obedience to God. Its meaning is that men have encountered God, and are thereby compelled to leave the judgment to Him. The actual occurrence of this judgment cannot be identified with the purpose or with the secret reckoning of the man of this world.)

6.9

Upon this background we are able to understand what follows – for there is no power but of God; and the powers that be are ordained of God

(Rom. 13. lb). Here a positive, affirmative authority seems to be assigned to the existing government. This would, however, directly contradict the basis of *subjection* which has been set forth above. It is therefore evident that the emphatic word 'God' must not be so interpreted as to contradict the whole theme of the Epistle to the Romans. We must not give to the word 'God' the value of a clearly defined, metaphysical entity. What will it profit us if a formal fidelity to the meaning of a word is purchased at the cost of complete infidelity to the Word? He of whom the *power* is and by whom every existing authority is ordained is God the Lord, the Unknown, Hidden God, Creator and Redeemer, the God who elects and rejects. This means that the mighty *powers that be* are measured by reference to God, as are all human, temporal, concrete things. God is their beginning and their end, their justification and their condemnation, their 'Yes' and their 'No'. If we adopt an attitude of revolution towards them – and this is the attitude adopted in the Epistle to the Romans, as is shown by the unmistakable fact that the passage dealing with human *rulers* follows immediately after the passage dealing with the *enemy* and is prefaced by the quite clear statement that men are to overcome *evil* – the attitude of revolution is, nevertheless, crossed by the reflection that it is only in relation to God that the evil of the existing order is really evil. God alone is the minus sign outside the bracket that is able to demolish the false plus signs within the bracket – and, moreover, the romanticists of the present order have also to learn as surely that genuine plus signs can exist only because of the minus sign of God.

6.10

We, therefore, have to remember that it is not for us to arm ourselves for action with the standard of the measurement of God – as though He acted through us! The revolutionary must also renounce the blue flower of romanticism. If then evil be evil in its relation to God, it is not a thing of which we can complain, any more than good is a thing about which we can boast. Therefore, even the observer who has been directly hurt and wounded by the evil of the existing order must bow before Him who is so strong and wondrous a God, high above all gods. If God be the Judge, who can share in His judgment? And if God be the Judge, where is there then not-righteousness? Where is there then evil which is not pregnant with witness to the good? Where is there then any concrete thing which is not pregnant with that which is Primal and invisible? Is not, therefore, the existing order a pregnant parable of the Order that does not exist - *For the creature was subjected to vanity, not of its own will, but by reason of him who subjected it in hope* (8.20)? The existing order falls and passes to corruption because it *exists*. The apprehension of this, however, has been, as we have seen, the source of revolution. But the existing order is justified against revolution precisely at this source; for here the demand is made that the revolutionary should not take the assault and judgment into his own hands, but rather should recognise that the evil of the existing order bears witness to the good, since it stands of necessity as an order contrasted with THE ORDER. Precisely in this contrast the existing order bears involuntary witness to THE ORDER and is the reflection of it. The *powers that be* are, therefore, in the general course of their existence – of *God*; and, in the particular form in which they constitute a present urgent problem, especially for the revolutionary, they are – *ordained of God*. The KRISIS to which the powers that be are subjected by God renders the possibility of our revolting against them far less advantageous to us than the possibility of our not revolting. In any case revolution is thereby deprived of its PATHOS, of its enthusiasm, of its claim to be a *high place*; it is, in fact, deprived of all those factors which are indispensable if the revolutionary is boldly and confidently and properly to 'storm the heavens'. *Vengeance belongeth unto me* (12.19). Our subjection means, therefore, no more than that vengeance is not our affair. It means that the divine minus before the bracket must not be deprived of its potency by a series of anticipatory negations on our part. (The supporters of the present order, who may perhaps feel encouraged by what has been said, must, however, be reminded that revolution has been *ordained* as evil, in order that they may bear witness to the good; and this means, in order that they may themselves be without justification and utterly unromantic, in order, in fact, that they too may turn and become from henceforth disordered.)

EXTRACT 7

BERDYAEV

Politics and the spirit

7.1

The religious life passes through three characteristic stages. Firstly there is the stage of objective religion which is both popular and collective, natural and social. Secondly there is the subjective stage which is individualistic and psycho-spiritual. In the third stage the opposition between the objective and subjective is transcended and the highest degree of spirituality is reached. A condition of the emergence of Christianity is this movement from an objective and popular religion to one which is subjective and individual. But in actual practice Christianity has not developed in this way; it has crystallised into a religion which is at once objective and popular, social and collective. It is precisely this form of Christianity which is undergoing a crisis at the present time. Religious life is passing through a subjective and individualistic phase which cannot be final and which is bound, in its turn, to give way to something else.

7.2

There are two types which confront one another all through the course of man's history, and they are types which find it hard to enter into any mutual comprehension. The former belongs to the collective, to the majority of society, which outwardly predominates in history; the other belongs to the sphere of 'spiritual individuality', to the elect minority, and its significance in history is much harder to discover. These two types or states of mind may be called, respectively, the 'democratic' and the 'aristocratic'. Now socialists are in the habit of affirming that throughout the course of history the privileged minority has exploited the disinherited majority. But there is another truth which, though at first sight less obvious, is more profound. The collective, the 'quantitative' majority, has always oppressed and persecuted in history the 'qualitative' minority, that which possesses the divine Eros and is composed of truly spiritual individuals whose lives are directed towards the highest aims. History works out habitually in favour of the average man, and of the collective. It is for such that the State, the family, the law, and our educational institutions have been created, no less than the whole fabric of custom and convention and the external organisation of the Church. It is for such that knowledge and morality, dogma and cult have been adapted. It is the average man, the typical product of the mass, who has dominated history, and who has always insisted that everything should be done for him and that everything should be brought down to the level of his interests.

7.3

The right wing and the left, conservatives and revolutionaries, monarchists and socialists, all alike belong to this collective 'democratic' type. The conservatives and the monarchists, who are the partisans of authority, are not less 'democratic' than those who actually bear the name 'democrats'. For this social collective, for mankind in the mass, the hierarchy of authority is maintained and ancient institutions are preserved. It is for them also that they are abolished, and for them that revolutions are made. Absolute monarchies and socialist republics are alike necessary to the masses, and are equally well adapted to the average man. It is, in fact, the average man who has dominated among the nobility no less than among the middle classes, the peasants, and the workers. It is never for the aristocracy of the spirit that governments are established, constitutions elaborated, and systems of learning or the technique of creation evolved.

7.4

Saints, prophets, geniuses, men, in short, who live on the higher planes of the spiritual life and who are capable of authentic creation, have no need of monarchy or republicanism, conservatism or revolution, nor yet of constitutions and educational establishments. For the aristocracy of the spirit does not bear the burden of history for itself. On the contrary it is made to submit to institutions, reforms, and systems whether old or new, in the name of the so-called people and of the collective, or, in other words, of the happiness of the average man. Evidently the aristocracy of the spirit, the elect who are alive with the divine Eros, belong to the fallen race of Adam and suffer in this way the consequences of the sin which they have to expiate. They cannot isolate themselves from 'the world' and must therefore bear its burden, and serve the universal cause of freedom and of civilisation. One can only deplore the pride of men who, while believing that they share in that which is highest, regard with contempt lesser men, and will not help the world to progress. But those who belong to the aristocracy of the spirit, who are not responsible for the qualities they possess, have in reality a bitter and tragic destiny in the world, for they cannot adapt themselves to any of the social conventions and systems of thought which belong to average men. They are a race of men who have always been oppressed and persecuted.

7.5

Those who are of the 'democratic' type, whose orientation is towards the masses and the organisation of the life of the collective, may be endowed with great talents and may number among them great men, heroes, geniuses, and saints. On the other hand those who are of the 'aristocratic' type, whose interests are centred on other worlds and the creation of values which are of no use to the average man, may be completely lacking in genius and may be less powerful and talented than men of the former type. Nevertheless they possess a different spiritual organisation which is at once more sensitive, more complex, and more subtle than that of the 'pachyderms' of democratic breed. Such men suffer more from the 'world' and from its ugliness, barbarity, and decadence than the men whose attention is focussed upon the masses and the collective. Even the great men of the 'democratic' type possess this simple kind of psychology, which places them under the protection of that very world which is so inimical to spiritual personalities less adapted to it. Cromwell and Bismarck belong to this type, as in a certain sense do all men of action, as well as the great statesmen and revolutionaries. This simple psychological make-up can also be found among many of the Doctors of the Church, who have often belonged to the democratic type.

7.6

From this point of view the Gnostics are of particular interest. A great number of them truly belong to the 'aristocracy' of the spirit, but they seem to have been unable to reconcile themselves to the 'democracy' of the Christian Church. The question is not whether they were in the right. The Church had profound reasons for opposing and condemning them, for had the Gnostics won the day Christianity would never have been victorious. It would have been transformed into an aristocratic sect. But the question which Gnosticism raises is a profoundly disturbing one which is always with us, and has its importance even today. Revelation and absolute truth are both distorted and assimilated, according to the make-up and spiritual development of the persons receiving them. Are we bound to consider as absolute and unchangeable that form of the Christian revelation which was intended for the average man? Must the more spiritual, complex, and subtle type of man, who has in some measure received the great gift of Gnosis, be brought down to a lower level and perforce rest content – with a reduced spirituality for the sake of the masses, and in order that he may share in the fellowship of the whole Christian people? But is it possible to identify *sobornost* with the popular collective? Can the path which leads to the acquiring of the gifts of the Holy Spirit and to spiritual perfection and holiness be regarded as the sole criterion of spiritual life and the only source of religious Gnosis?...

7.7

The Gnostics did not understand the mystery of freedom, that is, of freedom in Christ, any more than they understood the mystery of love. There was in all this a hopeless dualism which upset the true hierarchy of values. The Gnostics were without a glimpse of the order of values upon which the world of the Christian rests, where the highest elements are organically linked with the lowest and thus assist the process of transfiguration and of universal salvation. Their interpretation of the hierarchic principle was a false one. The supreme Gnosis of 'spiritual' persons is necessary for the salvation and transfiguration of those who are 'carnal'. 'Spiritual' persons must not remain proudly upon the mountaintops in separation from the 'carnal' world, but they must devote their energies to its spiritualisation and to raising it to the highest levels. Moreover the source of evil is spiritual and not carnal. The Church has rightly condemned the pride of the Gnostics, their hopelessly dualistic point of view, and the unbrotherly and unloving attitude which they displayed towards their fellow men and the world at large. But the consciousness of the Church was absorbed by preference with the problems of the average man, of the typical product of the mass. The Church was anxious to guide aright the ordinary man and was preoccupied with the task of effecting his salvation. In condemning Gnosticism, the Church in some measure affirmed and made lawful agnosticism. Even the problem which had given rise to such sincere and tormenting perplexity among the Gnostics was regarded as one which could not and indeed ought not to be raised. The highest aspirations of the spirit, the thirst for a deeper knowledge of divine and cosmic mysteries, were brought down to the level of average humanity. Not only the Gnosis of Valentinian but also that of Origen was regarded as inadmissible and dangerous, in the same way as that of Solovyov is today. A system of theology was elaborated which became an obstacle to the higher Gnosis. Only the great Christian mystics succeeded in cutting their way through these well-nigh impregnable defences.

7.8

It must be recognised, however, that one of the difficulties connected with 'the higher knowledge' in those days was that men could not disassociate it from its connection with the worship of demons, and here Christianity found itself entangled with pagan cults and with the 'wisdom' of pagan religion. And yet it is possible for a higher Christian knowledge of spiritual things to exist which is at once more penetrating, less exoteric, and less moulded to the needs of the collective than that of the dominant systems of official theology. There is room in Christianity not only for St Thomas Aquinas but also for Jacob Boehme, not only for the Metropolitan Philaret but also for Vladimir Solovyov. If spiritual persons ought not to boast of the heights they have reached, and to separate themselves from those of the 'natural' and 'carnal' order, it must not, on the other hand, be supposed that such men do not exist, nor must the aspirations of their spirit and their almost frenzied thirst for truth be denied satisfaction on the grounds that there is no such thing as 'a higher spiritual knowledge'. This would be equivalent, in an opposite direction, to that very destruction of the organic hierarchy of values which we have noticed already in Gnosticism. The world finds it easy to deny and despise every form of spiritual life, every aspiration of the spirit, and every sort of higher learning or knowledge. It readily asserts that such things are a clog upon the progress of the world towards its more complete organisation and that they can perfectly well be left on one side. This is a point of view which is held and expressed by millions. Furthermore, nothing can be more heart-rending than to find the Church itself subscribing to that denial of the spirit which is professed by the

State, a denial which at the opposite pole in atheistic Communism means the definite crushing out of the spirit and the extermination of every form of spiritual aristocracy.

7.9

'Quench not the spirit' it has been said; but to deny the problem presented to us by the Christian consciousness is to forget this command. The task which has as its object the enlightenment of the world will ask for no diminution in the quality of the spirit. Thus the problem which above all is confronting us today is the problem of the spirit and of the spiritual life.

EXTRACT 8
NIEBUHR

The conflict between individual and social morality

8.1

A realistic analysis of the problems of human society reveals a constant and seemingly irreconcilable conflict between the needs of society and the imperatives of a sensitive conscience. This conflict, which could be most briefly defined as the conflict between ethics and politics, is made inevitable by the double focus of the moral life. One focus is in the inner life of the individual, and the other in the necessities of man's social life. From the perspective of society the highest moral ideal is justice. From the perspective of the individual the highest ideal is unselfishness. Society must strive for justice even if it is forced to use means, such as self-assertion, resistance, coercion and perhaps resentment, which cannot gain the moral sanction of the most sensitive moral spirit. The individual must strive to realise his life by losing and finding himself in something greater than himself.

8.2

These two moral perspectives are not mutually exclusive and the contradiction between them is not absolute. But neither are they easily harmonised. Efforts to harmonise them were analysed in the previous chapter. It was revealed that the highest moral insights and achievements of the individual conscience are both relevant and necessary to the life of society. The most perfect justice cannot be established if the moral imagination of the individual does not seek to comprehend the needs and interests of his fellows. Nor can any non-rational instrument of justice be used without great peril to society, if it is not brought under the control of moral goodwill. Any justice which is only justice soon degenerates into something less than justice. It must be saved by something which is more than justice. The realistic wisdom of the statesman is reduced to foolishness if it is not under the influence of the foolishness of the moral seer. The latter's idealism results in political futility and sometimes in moral confusion, if it is not brought into commerce and communication with the realities of man's collective life. This necessity and possibility of fusing moral and political insights does not, however, completely eliminate certain irreconcilable elements in the two types of morality, internal and external, individual and social. These elements make for constant confusion but they also add to the richness of human life. We may best bring our study of ethics and politics to a close by giving them some further consideration.

8.3

From the internal perspective the most moral act is one which is actuated by disinterested motives. The external observer may find good in selfishness. He may value it as natural to the constitution of human nature and as necessary to society. But from the viewpoint of the author of an action, unselfishness must remain the criterion of the highest morality. For only the agent of an action knows to what degree self-seeking corrupts his socially approved actions. Society, on the other hand, makes justice rather than unselfishness its highest moral ideal. Its aim must be to seek equality of opportunity for all life. If this equality and justice cannot be achieved without the assertion of interest against interest, and without restraint upon the self-assertion of those who infringe upon the rights of their neighbours, then society is compelled to sanction self-assertion and restraint. It may even, as we have seen, be forced to sanction social conflict and violence.

8.4

Historically the internal perspective has usually been cultivated by religion. For religion proceeds from profound introspection and naturally makes good motives the criteria of good conduct. It may define good motives either in terms of love or of duty, but the emphasis is upon the inner springs of action. Rationalised forms of religion usually choose duty rather than love as the expression of highest virtue (as in Kantian and Stoic morality), because it seems more virtuous to them to bring all impulse under the dominion of reason than to give any impulses, even altruistic ones, moral pre-eminence. The social viewpoint stands in sharpest contrast to religious morality when it views the behaviour of collective rather than individual man, and when it deals with the necessities of political life. Political morality, in other words, is in the most uncompromising antithesis to religious morality...

8.5

Every effort to transfer a pure morality of disinterestedness to group relations has resulted in failure. The Negroes of America have practised it quite consistently since the Civil War. They did not rise against their masters during the war and remained remarkably loyal to them. Their social attitudes since that time, until a very recent date, have been compounded of genuine religious virtues of forgiveness and forbearance, and a certain social inertia which was derived not from religious virtue but from racial weakness. Yet they did not soften the hearts of their oppressors by their social policy.

8.6

During the early triumphs of fascism in Italy the socialist leaders suddenly adopted pacifist principles. One of the socialist papers counselled the workers to meet the terror of fascism with the following strategy: '(1) Create a void around fascism. (2) Do not provoke; suffer any provocation with serenity. (3) To win, be better than your adversary. (4) Do not use the weapons of your enemy. Do not follow in his footsteps. (5) Remember that the blood of guerrilla warfare falls upon those who shed it. (6) Remember that in a struggle between brothers those are victors who conquer themselves. (7) Be convinced that it is better to suffer wrong than to commit it. (8) Don't be impatient. Impatience is extremely egotistical; it is instinct; it is yielding to one's ego urge. (9) Do not forget that socialism wins the more when it suffers, because it was born in pain and lives on its hopes. (10) Listen to the mind and to the heart which advises you that the working people should be nearer to sacrifice than to vengeance.' (Quoted by Max Nomad, *Rebels and Renegades*, p.294). A nobler decalogue of virtues could hardly have been prescribed. But the Italian socialists were annihilated by the fascists, their organisations destroyed, and the rights of the workers subordinated to a state which is governed by their enemies. The workers may live 'on their hopes', but there is no prospect of realising their hopes under the present regime by practising the pure moral principles which the socialistic journal advocated. Some of them are not incompatible with the use of coercion against their foes. But inasfar as they exclude coercive means they are ineffectual before the brutal will-to-power of fascism.

8.7

The effort to apply the doctrines of Tolstoi to the political situation of Russia had a very similar effect. Tolstoi and his disciples felt that the Russian peasants would have the best opportunity for victory over their oppressors if they did not become stained with the guilt of the same violence which the czarist regime used against them. The peasants were to return good for evil, and win their battles by non-resistance. Unlike the policies of Gandhi, the political programme of Tolstoi remained altogether unrealistic. No effort was made to relate the religious ideal of love to the political necessity of coercion. Its total effect was therefore socially and politically deleterious. It helped to destroy a rising protest against political and economic oppression and to confirm the Russian in his pessimistic passivity. The excesses of the terrorists seemed to give point to the Tolstoian opposition to violence and resistance. But the terrorists and the pacifists finally ended in the same futility. And their common futility seemed to justify the pessimism which saw no escape from the traditional injustices of the Russian political and economic system. The real fact was that both sprang from a romantic middle-class or aristocratic idealism, too individualistic in each instance to achieve political effectiveness. The terrorists were diseased idealists, so morbidly oppressed by the guilt of violence resting upon their class, that they imagined it possible to atone for that guilt by deliberately incurring guilt in championing the oppressed. Their ideas were ethical and, to a degree, religious, though they regarded themselves as irreligious. The political effectiveness of their violence was a secondary consideration. The Tolstoian pacifists attempted the solution of the social problem by diametrically opposite policies. But, in common with the terrorists, their attitudes sprang from the conscience of disquieted individuals. Neither of them understood the realities of political life because neither had an appreciation for the significant characteristics of collective behaviour. The romantic terrorists failed to relate their isolated acts of terror to any consistent political plan. The pacifists, on the other hand, erroneously attributed political potency to pure nonresistance.

8.8

Whenever religious idealism brings forth its purest fruits and places the strongest check upon selfish desire it results in policies which, from the political perspective, are quite impossible. There is, in other words, no possibility of harmonising the two strategists designed to bring the strongest inner and the most effective social restraint upon egoistic impulse. It would therefore seem better to accept a frank dualism in morals than to attempt a harmony between the two methods which threatens the effectiveness of both. Such a dualism would have two aspects. It would make a distinction between the moral judgments applied to the self and to others; and it would distinguish between what we expect of individuals and of groups. The first distinction is obvious and is explicitly or implicitly accepted whenever the moral problem is taken seriously. To disapprove your own selfishness more severely than the egoism of others is a necessary discipline if the natural complacency toward the self and severity in the judgment of others is to be corrected. Such a course is, furthermore, demanded by the logic of the whole moral situation. One can view the actions of others only from an external perspective; and from that perspective the social justification of self-assertion becomes inevitable. Only the actions of the self can be viewed from the internal perspective; and from that viewpoint all egoism must be morally disapproved. If such disapproval should occasionally destroy self-assertion to such a degree as to invite the aggression of others, the instances will be insignificant in comparison with the number of cases in which the moral disapproval of egoism merely tends to reduce the inordinate self-assertion of the average man. Even in those few cases in which egoism is reduced by religious discipline to such proportions that it invites injustice in an immediate situation, it will have social usefulness in glorifying the moral principle and setting an example for future generations.

8.9

The distinction between individual and group morality is a sharper and more perplexing one. The moral obtuseness of human collectives makes a morality of pure disinterestedness impossible. There is not enough imagination in any social group to render it amenable to the influence of pure love. Nor is there a possibility of persuading any social group to make a venture in pure love, except, as in the case of the Russian peasants, the recently liberated Negroes and other similar groups, a morally dubious social inertia should be compounded with the ideal. The selfishness of human communities must be regarded as an inevitability. Where it is inordinate it can be checked only by competing assertions of interest; and these can be effective only if coercive methods are added to moral and rational persuasion. Moral factors may qualify, but they will not eliminate, the resulting social contest and conflict. Moral goodwill may seek to relate the peculiar interests of the group to the ideal of a total and final harmony of all life. It may thereby qualify the self-assertion of the privileged, and support the interests of the disinherited, but it will never be so impartial as to persuade any group to subject its interests completely to an inclusive social ideal. The spirit of love may preserve a certain degree of appreciation for the common weaknesses and common aspirations which bind men together above the areas of social conflict. But again it cannot prevent the conflict. It may avail itself of instruments of restraint and coercion, through which a measure of trust in the moral capacities of an opponent may be expressed and the expansion rather than contraction of those capacities is encouraged. But it cannot hide the moral distrust expressed by the very use of the instruments of coercion. To some degree the conflict between the purest individual morality and an adequate political policy must therefore remain.

8.10

The needs of an adequate political strategy do not obviate the necessity of cultivating the strictest individual moral discipline and the most uncompromising idealism. Individuals, even when involved in their communities, will always have the opportunity of loyalty to the highest canons of personal morality. Sometimes, when their group is obviously bent upon evil, they may have to express their individual ideals by disassociating themselves from their group. Such a policy may easily lead to political irresponsibility, as in the case of the more extreme sects of non-resisters. But it may also be socially useful. Religiously inspired pacifists who protest against the violence of their state in the name of a sensitive individual conscience may never lame the will-to-power of a state as much as a class-conscious labour group. But if their numbers grew to large proportions, they might affect the policy of the government. It is possible, too, that their example may encourage similar nonconformity among individuals in the enemy nation and thus mitigate the impact of the conflict without weakening the comparative strength of their own community.

8.11

The ideals of a high individual morality are just as necessary when loyalty to the group is maintained and its general course in relation to other groups is approved. There are possibilities for individual unselfishness, even when the group is asserting its interests and rights against other communities. The interests of the individual are related to those of the group, and he may therefore seek advantages for himself when he seeks them for his group. But this indirect egoism is comparatively insignificant beside the possibilities of expressing or disciplining his egoism in relation to his group. If he is a leader in the group, it is necessary to restrain his ambitions. A leadership, free of self-seeking, improves the morale of the whole group. The leaders of disinherited groups, even when they are avowed economic determinists and scorn the language of personal idealism, are frequently actuated by high moral ideals. If they sought their own personal advantage they could gain it more easily by using their abilities to rise from their group to a more privileged one. The temptation to do this among the abler members of disinherited groups is precisely what has retarded the progress of their class or race.

8.12

The progress of the Negro race, for instance, is retarded by the inclination of many able and educated Negroes to strive for identification and assimilation with the more privileged white race and to minimise their relation to a subject race as much as possible. The American Labour Movement has failed to develop its full power for the same reason. Under the influence of American individualism, able labour men have been more ambitious to rise into the class of owners and their agents than to solidify the labouring class in its struggle for freedom. There is, furthermore, always the possibility that an intelligent member of a social group will begin his career in unselfish devotion to the interests of his community, only to be tempted by the personal prizes to be gained, either within the group or by shifting his loyalty to a more privileged group. The interests of individuals are, in other words, never exactly identical with those of their communities. The possibility and necessity of individual moral discipline is therefore never absent, no matter what importance the social struggle between various human communities achieves. Nor can any community achieve unity and harmony within its life, if the sentiments of goodwill and attitudes of mutuality are not cultivated. No political realism which emphasises the inevitability and necessity of a social struggle, can absolve individuals of the obligation to check their own egoism, to comprehend the interests of others and thus to enlarge the areas of co-operation.

EXTRACT 9
TEMPLE
Christianity and the social order

9.1
The method of the Church's impact upon society at large should be twofold. The Church must announce Christian principles and point out where the existing social order at any time is in conflict with them. It must then pass on to Christian citizens, acting in their civic capacity, the task of re-shaping the existing order in closer conformity to the principles. For at this point technical knowledge may be required and judgments of practical expediency are always required. If a bridge is to be built, the Church may remind the engineer that it is his obligation to provide a really safe bridge; but it is not entitled to tell him whether, in fact, his design meets this requirement; a particular theologian may also be a competent engineer, and, if he is, his judgment on this point is entitled to attention; but this is altogether because he is a competent engineer and his theological equipment has nothing whatever to do with it. In just the same way the Church may tell the politician what ends the social order should promote; but it must leave to the politician the devising of the precise means to those ends.

9.2
This is a point of first-rate importance, and is frequently misunderstood. If Christianity is true at all it is a truth of universal application; all things

should be done in the Christian spirit and in accordance with Christian principles. 'Then,' say some, 'produce your Christian solution for unemployment'. But there neither is nor could be such a thing. Christian faith does not by itself enable its adherent to foresee how a vast multitude of people, each one partly selfish and partly generous, and an intricate economic mechanism, will in fact be affected by a particular economic or political innovation – 'social credit', for example. 'In that case,' says the reformer – or, quite equally, the upholder of the *status quo* – 'keep off the turf. By your own confession you are out of place here'. But this time the Church must say 'No; I cannot tell you what is the remedy; but I can tell you that a society of which unemployment (in peace time) is a chronic feature, is a diseased society, and that if you are not doing all you can to find and administer the remedy, you are guilty before God.' Sometimes the Church can go further than this point to features in the social structure itself which are bound to be sources of social evil because they contradict the principles of the Gospel.

9.3

So the Church is likely to be attacked from both sides if it does its duty. It will be told that it has become 'political' when in fact it has been careful only to state principles and point to breaches of them; and it will be told by advocates of particular policies that it is futile because it does not support these. If it is faithful to its commission it will ignore both sets of complaints, and continue so far as it can to influence all citizens and permeate all parties.

9.4

Before going on to state in outline the chief principles of Christian social doctrine, it may be wise, in the prevailing temper of our age, to add a further word of caution. For it is sometimes supposed that what the Church has to do is to sketch a perfect social order and urge men to establish it. But it is very difficult to know what a 'perfect social order' means. Is it the order that would work best if we were all perfect? Or is it the order that would work best in a world of men and women such as we actually are? If it is the former, it certainly ought not to be established; we should wreck it in a fortnight. If it is the latter, there is no reason for expecting the Church to know what it is...

9.5

The political problem is concerned with men as they are, not with men as they ought to be. Part of the task is so to order life as to lead them nearer to what they ought to be; but to assume that they are already this, will involve certain failure and disaster. It is not contended that men are utterly bad, or that they are more bad than good. What is contended is that they are not perfectly good, and that even their goodness is infected with a quality – self-centredness – which partly vitiates it, and exposes them to temptations so far as they achieve either freedom or power. This does not mean that freedom or power should be denied to them; on the contrary, it is fundamental to the Christian position that men should have freedom even though they abuse it; but it is also to be recognised that they certainly will abuse it except so far as they are won by devotion to truth or to beauty to that selfless outlook, which is only perfectly established in men by love which arises in them in answer to the redemptive love of God.

9.6

In any period worth considering, and probably to the end of earthly history, statesmen will themselves be men, and will be dealing with men, who abuse freedom and power. Now the most fundamental requirement of any political and economic system is not that it shall express love, though that is desirable, nor that it shall express justice, though that is the first ethical demand to be made upon it, but that it shall supply some reasonable measure of security against murder, robbery, and starvation. If it can be said with real probability that a proposed scheme would in fact, men being what they are, fail to provide that security, that scheme is doomed. Christians have some clues to the understanding of human nature which may enable them to make a more accurate estimate than others of these points. But they will not, if they are true to their own tradition, approach the question with rosy-tinted spectacles. Its assertion of Original Sin should make the Church intensely realistic and conspicuously free from Utopianism.

9.7

There is no such thing as a Christian social ideal, to which we should conform our actual society as closely as possible. We may notice, incidentally, about any such ideals from Plato's *Republic* onwards, that no one really wants to live in the ideal state as depicted by anyone else. Moreover, there is the desperate difficulty of getting there. When I read any description of an Ideal State and think how we are to begin transforming our own society into that, I am reminded of the Englishman in Ireland who asked the way to Roscommon. 'Is it Roscommon you want to go to?' asked the Irishman. 'Yes,' said the Englishman; 'that's why I asked the way.' 'Well,' said the Irishman, 'if I wanted to go to Roscommon, I wouldn't be starting from here.'

9.8

But though Christianity supplies no ideal in this sense, it supplies something of far more value – namely, principles on which we can begin to act in every possible situation...

9.9

The primary principle of Christian ethics and Christian politics must be respect for every person simply as a person. If each man and woman is a child of God, whom God loves and for whom Christ died, then there is in each a worth absolutely independent of all usefulness to society. The person is primary, not the society; the State exists for the citizen, not the citizen for the State. The first aim of social progress must be to give the fullest possible scope for the exercise of all powers and qualities which are distinctly personal; and of those the most fundamental is deliberate choice.

9.10

Consequently society must be so arranged as to give to every citizen the maximum opportunity for making deliberate choices and the best possible training for the use of that opportunity. In other words, one of our first considerations will be the widest possible extension of personal responsibility; it is the responsible exercise of deliberate choice which most fully expresses personality and best deserves the great name of freedom.

9.11

Freedom is the goal of politics. To establish and secure true freedom is the primary object of all right political action. For it is in and through his freedom that a man makes fully real his personality – the quality of one made in the image of God.

9.12

Freedom is a great word, and like other great words is often superficially understood. It has been said that to those who have enough of the world's goods the claim to freedom means 'Leave us alone', while to those who have not enough it means 'Give us a chance'. This important difference of interpretation rests on a single understanding of freedom as absence of compulsion or restraint. But if that is all the word means, freedom and futility are likely to be so frequently combined as to seem inseparable. For nothing is so futile as the unhampered satisfaction of sporadic impulses; that is the sort of existence which leads through boredom to suicide. Freedom so far as it is a treasure must be freedom *for* something as well as freedom *from* something. It must be the actual ability to form and carry out a purpose. This implies discipline – at first external discipline to check the wayward impulses before there is a real purpose in life to control them, and afterwards a self-discipline directed to the fulfilment of the purpose of life when formed. Freedom, in short, is self-control, self-determination, self-direction. To train citizens in the capacity for freedom and to give them scope for free action is the supreme end of all true politics.

9.13
But man is a self-centred creature. He can be trusted to abuse his freedom. Even so far as he wins self-control, he will control himself in his own interest: not entirely; he is not merely bad; but he is not altogether good, and any fraction of self-centredness will involve the consequence that his purpose conflicts to some extent with that of his neighbour. So there must be the restraint of law, as long as men have any selfishness left in them. Law exists to preserve and extend real freedom. First, it exists to prevent the selfishness of A from destroying the freedom of B. If I am left untouched when I knock my neighbours on the head, their freedom to go about their duties and their pleasures may be greatly diminished. But the law which restrains any occasional homicidal impulse that I may have, by threatening penalties sufficiently disagreeable to make the indulgence of it not seem to be good enough, also protects my purpose of good fellowship against being violated by that same impulse. In such a case the restraint of the law increases the true freedom of all concerned...

9.14
No man is fitted for an isolated life; everyone has needs which he cannot supply for himself; but he needs not only what his neighbours contribute to the equipment of his life but their actual selves as the complement of his own. Man is naturally and incurably social.

9.15
Recent political theories have given ostensible emphasis to this truth and have then, as a rule, gone far to ignore it. Certainly our social organisation largely ignores it. For this social nature of man is fundamental to his being. I am not first some one on my own account who happens to be a child of my parents, a citizen of Great Britain, and so forth. If you take all these social relationships away, there is nothing left. A man is talking nonsense if he says: 'Well, if I had been the son of some one else... etc'. He *is* his parent's son; what he is supposing is not that *he* should be someone else's son, but that *he* should not exist and someone else should exist instead. By our mutual influence we actually constitute one another as what we are. This mutual influence finds its first field of activity in the family; it finds other fields later in school, college, Trade Union, professional association, city, country, nation, Church.

9.16

Now actual liberty is the freedom which men enjoy in these various social units. But most political theories confine attention to the individual and the State as organ of the national community; they tend to ignore the intermediate groupings. But that makes any understanding of actual liberty impossible; for it exists for the most part in and through those intermediate groups – the family, the Church or congregation, the guild, the Trade Union, the school, the university, the Mutual Improvement Society. (Only in the nineteenth century could English people devise such a title as the last or consent to belong to a society so named; but the thing which that name quite accurately describes is very common and very beneficial.)

9.17

It is the common failing of revolutionary politics to ignore or attempt to destroy these lesser associations. They are nearly always the product of historical growth and do not quite fit any theoretical pattern. So the revolutionary, who is of necessity a theorist, is impatient of them. It was largely for this reason that the great French Revolution, which took as its watchword Liberty, Equality and Fraternity, degenerated into a struggle between Liberty and Equality wherein Fraternity was smothered and Liberty was judicially murdered. For the isolated citizen cannot effectively be free over against the State except at the cost of anarchy.

9.18

Liberty is actual in the various cultural and commercial and local associations that men form. In each of these a man can feel that he counts for something and that others depend on him as he on them. The State which would serve and guard Liberty will foster all such groupings, giving them freedom to guide their own activities provided these fall within the general order of the communal life and do not injure the freedom of other similar associations. Thus the State becomes the Community of communities – or rather the administrative organ of that Community – and there is much to be said for the contention that its representative institutions should be so designed as to represent the various groupings of men rather than (or as well as) individuals...

9.19

A democracy which is to be Christian must be a democracy of persons, not only of individuals. It must not only tolerate but encourage minor communities as at once the expression and the arena of personal freedom; and its structure must be such as to serve this end. That is the partial justification of Fascism which has made its triumphs possible. It sins far more deeply against true freedom than it supports it; yet in the materialist and mechanical quality of the democratic movement from Rousseau to Karl Marx and his communist disciples, it had real justification for reacting against them.

9.20

It is impossible to say how much we owe in our own country to the schooling in democratic habits provided, first by the old Trade Guilds, then, when the fellowship of trade had been broken up by the release of individualist acquisitiveness, by the Trade Unions, and ever since the seventeenth century by the dissenting congregations. Many of our most effective Labour leaders learned their art of public speech as local preachers; and the self-government of the local Chapel has been a fruitful school of democratic procedure. Our 'Left Wing' has by no means always maintained this close association of democratic principle with conscientious worship of God! But the historical root is there. And the British tradition of freedom has probably more of the element which consists of the claim to obey God rather than men and less of the element of mere self-assertiveness than has the democratic tradition in most other countries. The element of self-assertiveness is morally bad and politically disastrous; a freedom based upon it is only an opportunity for selfishness and will decline through anarchy to disruption of the State; the claim to obey God rather than men is a source both of moral strength, for it inspires devotion to duty, and of political stability, for such freedom may only be used in the service of the whole fellowship.

9.21

The combination of Freedom and Fellowship as principles of social life issues in the obligation of Service. No one doubts this in so far as it concerns the individual. Whatever our practice may be, we all give lip-service to this principle.

9.22

Its application to the individual is pretty clear. It affects him in two main ways – as regards work and leisure. In England we have depended a great deal on voluntary service given in leisure hours. We want a great deal more of it; and we have a right to expect more than we get from the Christian Churches. Yet it is certain that a very large proportion of the day-to-day drudgery of social service is done by Christian men and women in the inspiration of their Christian faith. We want more of them; but the greater part of what is done at all is done by Christian folk.

9.23

What is less often recognised in practice is the obligation to make of the occupation, by which a man or woman earns a living, a sphere of service. This may be done in two ways. Some young people have the opportunity to choose the kind of work by which they will earn their living. To make that choice on selfish grounds is probably the greatest single sin that any young person can commit, for it is the deliberate withdrawal from allegiance to God of the greatest part of time and strength...

9.24

It is not only individuals who must, if Christianity is the truth, guide their policy or career by the principles of service; all groupings of men must do the same. The rule here should be that we use our wider loyalties to check the narrower. A man is a member of his family, of his nation, and of mankind. It is very seldom that any one can render a service directly to mankind as a whole. We serve mankind by serving those parts of it with which we are closely connected... A man must chiefly serve his own most immediate community, accepting as the standard of its welfare that which its members are ready to accept (though trying, it may be, to lead them nearer to a fully Christian view), but always checking this narrower service by the wider claims, so that in serving the smaller community he never injures the larger.

9.25

But as a member of each small group – with a voice in determining its conduct and policy – e.g. as a Christian Trade Unionist or Managing Director, or as the Governor of a School – he will do all he can to secure that his own group accepts for itself the principle of service and sets its course in the way that will benefit not only its own members in their own self-interest, but also the larger community in which this group is a part.

9.26

Freedom, Fellowship, Service – these are the three principles of a Christian social order, derived from the still more fundamental Christian postulates that Man is a child of God and is destined for a life of eternal fellowship with Him.

EXTRACT 10
JOHN XXIII
Towards a world government

10.1

That inter-state relationships involve mutual rights and duties has been frequently taught by our predecessors and this we now confirm. These relationships, too, must conform to the norms of truth, justice, friendship and respect of freedom. For the same natural law which governs the conduct of individual men applies with equal force to the management of public affairs.

10.2

This will be clear to anyone who reflects that rulers cannot discard their human dignity whilst they are acting on behalf of the community and attending to its welfare. They cannot, therefore, disregard the natural moral law which binds them as men.

10.3

Nor is it to be imagined that men are driven to shed their humanity by being elevated to the highest rank in the state. On the contrary they have usually been chosen because of their outstanding gifts and qualities.

10.4

We have seen, too, that it is the moral law which provides for authority in the community. How then can authority turn round and reject the moral law by which it was constituted? It would lose its foundation and collapse. We have God's own warning in the Book of Wisdom:

'Listen then kings and understand; rulers of remotest lands, take warning; hear this, you who have thousands under your rule, who boast of your hordes of subjects. For power is a gift to you from the Lord, sovereignty is from the Most High; he himself will probe your acts and scrutinise your intentions.' (6.2-4)

10.5

All along the line, even when it comes to inter-state relations, we have to maintain the principle that authority must seek to promote the common good of all, for that is the reason for its existence.

10.6

But one of the first rules for securing the common good is that the moral order be recognised and its precepts obeyed. 'If order amongst states is to be securely established it must rest on the bedrock of those unalterable standards of honesty which the Creator has made to appear in nature itself and established irremovably in the minds of men...These norms are guiding lights to show men and nations the way they should take. Their salutary and provident warnings must be observed if the attempts to build a new order in society are not to end in storms and ship-wreck.' (Pius XII, *Christmas Broadcast*, 1941).

10.7

First of all then the links between states must be forged in truth. Truth demands that in the creation of these links racial or ethnic discrimination should have no part: that all states be regarded as equal in their natural dignity. Each, in consequence, has the right to its existence, to its prosperity and to the aids which these make necessary, and the right to retain for itself the responsibility for securing all these. It can likewise legitimately demand to have its reputation respected and to be given the honours to which it is entitled.

10.8

We know that individual men differ greatly from one another in knowledge, strength of character, talents and the possession of wealth. But this is no reason why those who excel in such things should lord it over others. On the contrary the obligation that falls upon all and sundry to cooperate with others in striving for perfection lies more heavily on those with something extra to contribute.

10.9

In the same way some nations surpass others in scientific, cultural and economic development. But this superiority, far from permitting them an unjust domination over others, increases their obligation to contribute to the common welfare of all peoples.

10.10

In respect of their human dignity nature makes no men superior to others. Nor does it do so in the case of civil communities, for each of these is a body whose members are individual human beings. We know, too, well enough, how sensitive people are in matters that touch a nation's honour and with good reason.

10.11

Truth also calls for balance and fairness in the use of the means of communicating information which modern technology has put at men's disposal and which help nations to learn more about each other. This does not mean that a country is wrong in giving prominence to what can be said in its own favour. It does mean the rejection of any spreading of rumours which do violence to truth and justice and damage the reputation of another country.

10.12
Relations between states must also accord with justice. This involves mutual recognition of rights, mutual fulfilment of obligations.

10.13
We have established that states have the right to exist, to prosper, to acquire the aids necessary for their development and to rely principally on their own efforts in so doing. They have the right also to protect their reputation and to insist on due honours being paid to them. It follows logically that there is a corresponding obligation on all of them to see that every one of these rights is safeguarded and that nothing is done to violate them. For, just as in private life men may not pursue their own interests in such a manner as to inflict unjust harm on others, in the same way states are guilty of criminal behaviour if they seek their own advantage at the expense of injuring others or unwarrantably oppressing them. How apt in this connection is St Augustine's remark: 'Take away justice and what are kingdoms but gangs of robbers?' (*City of God*, IV.4).

10.14
It can happen, and indeed does happen, that clashes of interests develop between states. The solution of these should be sought not in recourse to arms, nor in underhand and deceitful ways, but in a manner worthy of human beings: through mutual appreciation of arguments and attitudes, giving mature consideration to all points, weighing them in the balance of truth and resolving differences fairly.

10.15
This applies particularly to the problem of national consciousness. From the nineteenth century onwards there have been increasing attempts in various parts of the world to make political boundaries coincide with national ones, so as to give self-government to people of the same ethnic group. Since, for a variety of reasons, this cannot always be achieved, it often happens that minorities find themselves hemmed in within the frontiers of a nation comprised of people from another stock. This gives rise to serious problems.

10.16
It must be made quite clear that it is a gross violation of justice to do anything to reduce the vigour and growth of such minorities; all the more so if the abominable attempt is made to exterminate them.

10.17
The way to secure justice in such situations is for governments to take

effective steps to improve the human conditions of these ethnic minorities, particularly as regards the use of their language, the preservation of their native genius, their ancient customs and their enterprises and activities in the economic field...

10.18

The latest advances in science and technology, exercising as they do such a profound influence on men's way of living, are causing people all over the world to come together and join in common enterprises. The interchange of goods and ideas and the amount of travel have all increased considerably. The result has been an extensive growth of contacts across national frontiers between individuals, families and intermediate bodies as well as between governments. All the time the economies of the various states are becoming so interdependent and gradually getting so inextricably interwoven that there already exists a sort of world economic order formed by the combination of the economies of the different nations. Added to this, the social progress, the order, the security and stability of each and every state are inevitably affected by what is happening in the others.

10.19

This being so, it is clear that individual states cannot properly develop and attend to their needs in isolation. For the prosperity and progress of any nation is part cause and part consequence of the prosperity and progress of the rest.

10.20

There is also a unity in the human race deriving from the human nature that men have perpetually in common and which demands that attention be given to the welfare of mankind as a whole: in other words to the universal common good.

10.21

In former times the governments of the various nations were considered capable of attending sufficiently to this universal common good. They did so either through their ambassadors or by congresses or by drawing up treaties and conventions. These were ways and means indicated by the natural law or the common law of all peoples or by positive international law.

10.22

In our day the customary relations between states have undergone a prodigious transformation. On the other hand the universal common good brings up for immediate attention serious and complex problems which have to do with security and peace on a world scale. On the other hand national governments, for the very reason that they all have equal status, are unable to impose a solution, however much they multiply their efforts to work out appropriate laws. It is not that they lack sufficient goodwill: it is simply that the authority they possess is inadequate for the purpose.

10.23
So it is that, in the circumstances in which human society finds itself today, both political organisations and political authority fall short of the standard required for attending properly to the universal common good.

10.24
Yet if we have a proper idea of the common good and a correct understanding of the nature and function of political authority we cannot help seeing that there must be perfect correspondence between the two. For the moral order which demands the existence of public authority for the common good of civil society must, in doing so, require also that it be equal to the task. This principle helps us to determine the form and the degree of competence with which to invest civil institutions. These institutions constitute the medium through which public authority is exercised and attains its purpose of promoting the common good. If they are to perform this function adequately they must have the form and the degree of competence which match contemporary circumstances at any given time.

10.25
Today, however, the common good of all nations involves problems which affect people all the world over: problems which can only be solved by a public authority which has the power, the form and the agencies competent to deal with them and whose writ covers the entire globe. We cannot therefore escape the conclusion that the moral order itself demands the establishment of some sort of world government.

10.26
Such a world government, enjoying an authority extending to the farthest corners of the earth and having in its service agencies capable of advancing the universal common good, will need to come into being through universal consent and not be imposed by force. This is because authority of the kind we are speaking of must be able to operate effectively and this will involve being fair to all, devoid of favouritism and intent on the welfare of all peoples. If it were to be forcibly imposed on the rest by the more powerful nations,

there would be good reason to fear that it would serve the interests of some few only or favour one nation unduly. The force and efficacy of its action would be thereby imperilled. For, though nations differ considerably in material wealth and military power, they all cling tenaciously to their claim for equal rights and for the excellence of their own way of life. They have good reason, therefore, to object to any rule imposed on them by force or arranged without their participation or to which they have not given a spontaneous assent.

10.27

Just as in the case of the common good of individual states so also in the respect of the interests of all states taken together, no proper judgment can be made without taking into consideration the human person. World government, therefore, has to be specially directed towards making sure that human rights are everywhere acknowledged, respected, protected and given ever wider scope. It can attend to this by its own direct intervention where the situation calls for it, or by creating the conditions which enable the governments of individual states to perform their functions more efficiently.

10.28

We must add that the relationships between the world government and the governments of individual nations must be regulated according to the principle of subsidiarity, in exactly the same way as the relationships within any country between the state government on the one hand and the citizens, families and intermediate bodies on the other. Thus it will be the province of such a world authority to consider and settle questions prompted by the universal common good, whether they touch on matters economic, social, political or cultural. We mean the sort of questions which, by reason of their gravity, their widespread nature and their extreme urgency cannot be dealt with satisfactorily by the governments of individual states.

10.29

To put it another way: the world authority must not arrogate to itself questions which rightly belong to individual member states. On the contrary it must see to it that all over the world those conditions prevail which give not only to national governments but to individual citizens and intermediate bodies a better opportunity to get on with their own business, fulfil their duties and vindicate their rights.

10.30

Everyone knows how, on 26 June 1945, there came into being the United

Nations Organisation – UNO for short. Specialised agencies composed of members nominated by the governments to the various countries have been added to it since. To these are assigned projects of great importance and world-wide extent in social and economic matters and in the fields of science, education and public health. But the main purposes of the Organisation are declared to be: i. To maintain international peace and security; ii. To develop friendly relations among nations based on respect for the principle of equal rights; iii. To achieve international cooperation in solving international problems; iv. To be a centre for harmonising the actions of nations.

10.31

It is to this Organisation that we owe the Universal Declaration of Human Rights, approved by the UN General Assembly on 10 December 1948. In the Preamble to the Declaration it is stated that 'the effective recognition and observance of the rights and freedoms' proclaimed in it are to be 'a common standard of achievement for all peoples and nations'.

10.32

We are well aware that some people are not entirely satisfied with some items in the Declaration, and with good reason. Nevertheless we think it is a step towards the creation of a legal and political system for the world as a whole, inasmuch as it enshrines a recognition of the dignity of the human person, asserts the right of every man on earth to seek truth in freedom, to observe moral norms, to do what justice demands, to live as befits a human being and to enjoy other rights consequent upon these.

10.33

It is therefore our earnest wish that the United Nations Organisation should go from strength to strength, perfecting its constitution and its agencies to meet the extent and grandeur of its tasks. May the time come soon when this Organisation will be able to give effective protection to human rights: rights which derive immediately from man's dignity as a person and which, for that reason, are all-embracing, on no account to be violated and never to be filched away. There is all the more reason for wanting this because men today are much more active in the public life of their own country, take a keener interest in international affairs and are becoming ever more conscious of belonging as living members to the whole family of mankind.

10.34

This is the place to repeat our exhortation that our sons should offer themselves readily for service in public life and should join with others in working for the good of the whole human race as well as that of their own country. Profiting by the guidance which their Christian faith provides and under the impulse of Christian love, they must work hard to ensure that whatever plans are formed to promote economic, social, political or cultural ends are such as will not hinder but will rather help men to develop in the supernatural order as well as the natural...

10.35

There are, indeed, generous souls who, when faced with a situation not completely or perhaps not at all consonant with justice, burn with a desire to put everything right at once and who get carried away by such an ungovernable zeal that their attempt at reform becomes a sort of revolution.

10.36

To such people we would suggest that it is in the nature of things for growth to be gradual and that in human institutions no improvement can be looked for which does not proceed step by step and from within. The point was well put by our predecessor, Pius XII: 'Security and justice lie in not completely overthrowing the old order but in well planned progress. Uncontrolled passionate zeal always destroys everything and builds nothing. It inflames cupidity, never cools it. Since it does nothing but sow hate and ruin, far from leading to reconciliation, it drives men and political parties to the laborious undertaking of building anew, on ruins left by discord, the edifice with which they started.' [*Address*, 13/6/42]

10.37

Therefore, amongst the most urgent issues facing serious thinkers today is that of working out a new pattern of human relationships based on truth, justice, love and freedom: relationships between man and man, between citizen and state, between one country and another and, finally, between individuals, families, intermediate bodies and states on the one hand, and, on the other, the community of the whole family of mankind. There is none, surely, who will not esteem this as a service of the highest order; for it is that which will render possible the building up of true peace according to the pattern which God has made.

10.38

Such thinkers, indeed, are all too few to accomplish everything that requires to be done; but the whole of mankind is deeply in their debt. It is fitting that we should pay them a public tribute of praise and at the same time beg them to press on with their beneficial efforts. It is our constant hope that their numbers will be reinforced, especially from the ranks of Christians inspired to join them by a sense of duty and a spirit of love; for on those who have enrolled under the standard of Christ there lies a special obligation to bring vision and love to human society and to act as leaven in the mass. They will succeed in this in the measure of their union with God.

10.39

For no peace can reign over the whole human family unless it has first gained sway in the hearts of individual men: that is to say unless each observes within himself the order which God has prescribed. Some words of St Augustine are very appropriate here: 'Do you want your mind to be capable of controlling your passions? Let it bow to a superior power and it will conquer all beneath itself; and peace will come to you: true, certain and in right good order. What order? God commanding the mind and the mind the flesh. Nothing could be more in order' (*Miscellanea Augustiniana*).

10.40

It is our burning desire that such a peace should be established all over the world – a desire which is surely shared by all men of good will – which has led us to put forward these ideas on the problems which vex human society so sorely today and on the solution of which its future progress depends.

10.41

We do so knowing that, unworthy as we are of the office, we represent the One whom the divinely inspired prophet referred to as 'The Prince of Peace'. It is our bounden duty to dedicate ourselves to this work for the common good with all the strength of soul and body. But peace will remain a mere dream in men's minds unless it is built on the principles we have, with great hopes, sketched out in this letter: that is to say unless it is grounded on truth, given a framework of justice, raised to a lofty height and crowned by charity, and takes proper account of freedom.

10.42

To erect so wonderful an edifice is truly beyond the capacity of man, whatever his natural gifts, if he relies solely on his own powers. To construct human society in the image of the kingdom of God there is need of help from heaven.

10.43

So, during this Holy Week, we address our prayers to Him who, by His bitter Passion and Death, not only wiped away sin, the cause of all conflicts, miseries and inequalities, but led back with the human race to reconciliation with His heavenly Father through the shedding of His own blood; thus winning for mankind the gift of peace. 'For he is the peace between us, and has made the two into one... He came to bring the good news of peace, peace to you who were far away and peace to those who were near at hand.' [Eph. 2.14-17]

10.44

This is a message which is echoed in the Liturgy of this sacred season: 'Jesus, our Lord, risen and standing in the midst of his disciples said "Peace be upon you, alleluia": the disciples saw the Lord and were glad.' Christ brought us peace and bequeathed it to us. 'Peace I bequeath to you, my own peace I give you, a peace the world cannot give, this is my gift to you.' [Jn. 14.27]

10.45

It is this peace brought to us by our divine Redeemer which is the object of our entreaties in the prayers we address to Him. May He banish from the souls of men all that can undermine peace. May He mould them all to become witnesses of truth, justice and brotherly love. May He enlighten all who rule so that they provide for their subjects, together with commendable prosperity, the inestimable boon of impregnable peace. Finally, may Christ inspire all men with a determination to break down the barriers which keep men divided, to strengthen the bonds of mutual love which draw them together, to try to understand others and to find forgiveness for those guilty of wrongdoing. So that, following his plan and his guidance, all nations will arrive unfailingly at a union in brotherly concord in which will flourish and reign perpetually the peace for which men dream.

EXTRACT 11

MIRANDA

Justice and almsgiving

11.1

Since at least the sixth century A.D., a bald fact has been systematically excluded from theological and moral consideration: 'To give alms' in the Bible is called 'to do justice.'

11.2

To cite a few of the passages which have resisted all misrepresentation, we mention Prov. 10.2; Tob. 4.10; 12.9; 14.11; Dan. 4.24; and Matt.

6.1-2. These are not the only ones, but these are unequivocal. When our Western translations say 'almsgiving,' they do not do so in bad faith. Indeed the reality involved is what we call today 'almsgiving,' and the translations are made for the people of today. But the original says *sedakah*, which signifies justice. We might also add Ecclus. 3.30, 7.10 and 12.3, the original Hebrew of which we have only recently come to know. Previous centuries knew only the Greek translation, which, like our modern versions, is 'almsgiving.' With the same certainty we could also list Ps. 112.3, 9; Artur Weiser and H.J. Kraus dogmatically interpret 'justice' (*sedakah* in Hebrew) in these two verses as 'fidelity-to-the-covenant,' but they hold that the Bible treats no other theme but the covenant. As we shall see later, however, covenant theology belongs to a relatively late period in the Old Testament. In Ps. 112, as in the other passages we have cited, the Bible calls 'justice' what we call 'almsgiving.'

11.3

Some exegetes have tried to diminish the importance of this fact. They argue that the Greek translators of the Old Testament, the famous Seventy, caused some confusion by translating justice (*sedakah*) at times by *eleemosyne* 'almsgiving,' at other times by *eleos* 'compassion,' and at others by *dikaiosyne* 'justice.' But, in the first place, this characteristic of the translation should not distract us from the fact which is disconcerting for the West – that the works which we consider to be of charity and supererogation are in the original Bible text called works of justice. This is the same *sedakah* which the whole Bible considers transgressed when the worker does not receive his wage; see, for example, Jer. 22.13. In the second place, instead of minimizing the bald fact we have pointed out, the Greek translation emphasized it even more: It means that the translators of the Septuagint themselves were disconcerted.

11.4

The act which in the West is called almsgiving for the original Bible was a restitution that someone makes for something that is not his. The Fathers of the early Church saw this with great clarity: 'Tell me, how is it that you are rich? From whom did you receive your wealth? And he, whom did he receive it from? From his grandfather, you say, from his father. By climbing this genealogical tree are you able to show the justice of this possession? Of course you cannot; rather *its beginning and root have necessarily come out of injustice.*' 'Do not say, "I am spending what is mine; I am enjoying what is mine." In reality it is not yours but another's.'

11.5

Jerome comments in this way on Jesus' expression 'money of injustice' (Luke 16.9): 'And he very rightly said, "money of injustice," for *all riches come from injustice*. Unless one person has lost, another cannot find. Therefore I believe that the popular proverb is very true: "The rich person is either an unjust person or the heir of one."' Basil the Great thinks the same way: 'When someone steals a man's clothes we call him a thief. Should we not give the same name to one who could clothe the naked and does not? The bread in your cupboard belongs to the hungry man; the coat hanging unused in your closet belongs to the man who needs it; the shoes rotting in your closet belong to the man who has no shoes; the money which you hoard up belongs to the poor.' Ambrose teaches the same thing in a formula of unsurpassable exactitude: 'You are not making a gift of your possessions to the poor person. *You are handing over to him what is his.*'

11.6

The defenders of private ownership have used wonders of subterfuge and misrepresentation to escape attack by such an unequivocal and constant tradition, which was only being faithful to Sacred Scripture. But no subtlety is able to whitewash these explicit teachings of Ambrose and Augustine: 'God willed that this earth should be the common possession of all and he offered its fruits to all. But avarice distributed the rights of possession (*Avaritia distribuit iura possessionum*).' '*Iustitia est in subveniendo miseris*: Assisting the needy is justice.'

11.7

Apologists for the status quo attribute this incontrovertible tradition to the imprecision of preachers. By this standard however, we would also have to eliminate not only the entire patristic tradition but the Bible as well, for there is nothing imprecise about the statements we have considered. On the contrary, they demonstrate on the part of their authors the very clear intention of formulating a well-deliberated idea. The time has come for Christianity to break a long chain of hypocrisy and collusion with the established powers and decide if its message is or is not going to be the same as the Bible's.

11.8

It does us no good to think like the Greeks and say that 'money of injustice' cannot mean that injustice is inherent in money like quality, like weight or color, and that therefore we do not comprehend what Jesus means by the term and should let the question rest. It is obvious that Christ did not mean that, nor did Luke, for the simple reason that neither of them was a disciple of Aristotle. The expression in question should be understood in the context of a society divided between rich and poor. 'How happy are you who are poor' (Luke 6.20) and 'Alas for you who are rich' (Luke 6.24) are not expressions which bless the physical fact of not having money and condemn the physical fact of having money, and neither are the numerous statements in the Psalter and the prophets on behalf of the poor and against the rich. The terms 'rich' and 'poor' are correlative, and what the blessing and the corresponding curse attack is precisely the difference between the two. It does not seem to Luke (nor to Christ) that this difference can be justified. It is 'money of injustice' for, as Jerome understood very well in the paragraph we have quoted, 'all riches come from injustice... "The rich person is either an unjust person or the heir of one."' Jesus ben Sirach, who in Ecclus. 5.8 uses 'unjust riches' with the same sense as the term in Luke 16.9 (and not, certainly, in a determinative sense, which would need the article *tois chremasin tois adikois*), with astonishing perspicacity provides the same explanation: 'Many have sinned for the sake of profit; he who hopes to be right must be ruthless. A peg will stick in the joint between two stones, and sin will wedge itself between selling and buying.' (Ecclus. 27.1-2).

11.9

Let it not be said that the biblical authors did not understand economics; this is the same ben Sirach who in 3.30, 7.10, and 12.3 in the original Hebrew refers to 'almsgiving' and 'justice.' The underlying conviction is that differentiating ownership, that which makes some rich and some poor within the same society, could not be achieved with the genuine acquiescence of those who were thereby disempowered; it could not and it cannot be achieved without violence and despoliation. The condemnation of the right in Luke 6.24 and the expression 'money of injustice' in Luke 16.9 are based on the same conviction. If this were not so the programmatic battle cry which at the beginning of this Gospel Luke puts on the lips of Jesus' mother herself would be completely incomprehensible: 'He has filled the hungry with good things and sent the rich away empty' (Luke 1.53). This verse is generally classified among the incomprehensible, but such an alternative is not very scientific. It is obvious that the statement in question presupposes a definite conviction about the injustice of differentiating wealth, that is, the wealth which in the same society constitutes some people in one class and others in another. The underlying conviction can be none other than the one we have indicated: It is impossible for this wealth to have been acquired without violence and spoliation. To avoid this conclusion regarding what is at the basis of all these scriptural passages, it would be necessary to assert that they do not refer to every type of differentiating wealth, but only to that which was wrongly acquired. The passages would therefore imply that the wealth could have been rightly acquired. But the very strength of the texts is in the intentional universality of the statements, in the nondistinction, precisely in the fact that they do not allow distinctions: 'It is easier for a camel to pass through the eye of a needle than for a rich man to enter the kingdom of God' (Mark 10.25; Matt. 19.24; Luke 18.25). It is impossible to interpret this statement as directed against the distribution of differentiating ownership which *de facto* prevails and not against *de iure* differentiating ownership as such. It is impossible to interpret it as directed against the abuses and not against differentiating ownership in itself.

11.10

The efforts of certain modern exegetes to negate the authenticity of this logion (Mark 10.25; Matt. 19.24; Luke 18.25) as the words of Christ himself only show how greatly the work of interpretation is influenced by the status which Western civilisation bestows on the theologian and on Christianity itself as the official religion. Of this entire teaching they wish to retain as the original nucleus only Mark 10.26, which in substance says, 'How difficult it is to be saved.' They want us to believe that 10:25 is one example among many and that it was more or less invented by pre-Marcan community preaching, which does not have to be taken literally. But with this manoeuvre exegesis transgresses the methodological principles which it has scientifically elaborated during many decades of meritorious work. In fact, the absolute impossibility of salvation for the rich is something which no primitive Christian community (before 70 A.D., as Mark's Gospel was written in 70 or 71) would have dared to assert if it were not basing its assertion on the authority of Christ himself. On the other hand, 'how difficult it is to be saved' is a theological generality which could have been invented by any community or redactor of that time or any other. Therefore the most serious modern exegetes, from the accredited Joachim Jeremias and the authoritative Walter Grundmann to the very exigent Rudolf Bultmann and Norman Perrin, hold that Mark 10.25 is an authentic saying of the historical Jesus.

11.11

Thus the statements of Luke 1.53, 6.24, and 16.9 could be, as regards their formulation, proper to Luke or to his pre-redactional tradition; as regards the content, however, they faithfully transmit to us the thinking of Christ himself, which we know from Mark 10.25 and many other equally authentic passages like Matt. 11.5-6 (Luke 7.22-23); Luke 6.20; etc.

11.12

Thus we can return to our starting point: The fact that differentiating wealth is unacquirable without violence and spoliation is presupposed by the Bible in its pointed anathemas against the rich; therefore almsgiving is nothing more than restitution of what has been stolen, and thus the Bible calls it justice. And we include here the New Testament. Matthew leaves no room for doubt when he explains and thematically attempts to delineate what justice is, that is, what makes some just and others not, in Matt. 25.31-46: 'the just' (vv.37 and 46); 'And they will go away to eternal punishment, and the just to eternal life' (v.46). It all has to do with giving food to the hungry, drink to the thirsty, a home to the stranger, clothing to the naked, etc. The list is given four times so that there can be no mistake. It would be difficult to establish with greater emphasis a definitive and single criterion to distinguish between the just and the unjust. And this justice cannot be reduced without misrepresentation to some kind of 'virtue' or supererogation, as we see by the fate which awaits those who do not practise it: 'Go away from me with your curse upon you, to the eternal fire prepared for the devil and his angels' (v.41).

11.13

These are all works which the West calls charity, in contradistinction to justice. A frequent methodological error is to believe that the discrepancy is verbal or explicable by the alleged imperfection of biblical morality, which did not know how to distinguish between justice and charity. The discrepancy is a solid, unequivocal fact. To brand the biblical authors as primitive is a value judgment, not objective exegetical work. What is in question is precisely Western morality's alleged superiority to biblical morality. To base oneself on this superiority in order to reduce biblical thought to Western thought is an extraordinarily unscientific methodology for it prevents one from seeing the difference which exists between the thinking and wishing of the investigator and that of the authors being studied.

11.14

We have said that when the Bible calls 'justice' what Western culture calls 'almsgiving' it is because the private ownership which differentiates the rich from the poor is considered unacquirable without violence and spoliation; the Fathers of the Church also understood this very clearly. The causal dependence which exists between the distribution of ownership and the distribution of income had led us, by economics alone, to the same conclusion. But it would be erroneous to think that this economic fact escaped the biblical authors. Ecclus. 27.1-2, which we have cited, is exceedingly clear: It refers to those who try to enrich themselves through profits, and it points out how this profit occurs in buying and selling. When in 3.30, 7.10, and 12.3 it refers to 'almsgiving' as 'justice' (*sedakah*), the thinking is in perfect congruence with the economic fact to which we have alluded and which, to be sure, has escaped Western moralist and jurists.

11.15

In 22:17 Jeremiah condemns this profit, after describing in v.14 the luxurious home which King Jehoiakim had built, undoubtedly with such profits. Thus in v.13 the prophet could specify of what material the property was made: 'Shame on the man who builds his house by non-justice and completes its upstairs rooms by not-right'. As economic theory demonstrates, profit is the tangible concretization of the difference in incomes. Jeremiah sees very clearly how private ownership arises from this. We refer to the ownership which we have called differentiating.

11.16

Amos is equally penetrating in the causal relationships he draws. He, however, refers to no person in particular but to the system itself: 'Well then, since you have trampled on the poor man, extorting levies on his wheat – those houses you have built of dressed stone, you will never live in them; and those precious vineyards you have planted, you will never drink their wine. "Assemble on Samaria's mountain and see what great disorder there is in that city, what oppression is found inside her." They know nothing of fair dealing – it is Yahweh who speaks – they cram their palaces full with violence and spoliation.' (5.11; 3.9-10)

11.17

Here we have, despite all the appearances of elegance and luxury, the true consistency of the property of the rich: violence and spoliation. Their palaces and all that which makes them into a class different from the rest of the population are for Amos concretized oppression, the accumulated materialization of violence and spoliation. When he threatens punishment, Amos is aware that he is proclaiming elementary justice. Because they trampled on the poor and extorted from them levies of wheat, they could build their houses of dressed stone, but they would not inhabit them, for the day of justice is coming.

11.18

Micah (3.9-10) alludes to this same characteristic of differentiating ownership as he contemplates the mansions and buildings of Jerusalem:

'You who loath justice and pervert all that is right, you who build Zion with blood, Jerusalem with injustice.'

11.19
The second chapter of Habakkuk attacks profit in both its second (vv.6b-8) and third (vv.9-11) stanzas. Then it speaks of the cries of the walls and the beams of the houses which were built with such materials:

For the stone from the very walls cries out, and the beam responds from the framework.

And it continues by taking up the words of Micah:

Trouble is coming to the man who builds a town with blood and founds a city on injustice. (2.11; 2.12)

11.20
It is needless to draw out the list of biblical testimony. Thirty years ago there were those who tried to explain this unanimous understanding of the essence of differentiating ownership by the rural and anti-urban origin of the prophets. Today scientific exegesis rejects such subterfuges of interpretation, of which the history of Christianity is full. Any anecdotal or psychological explanation is out of place here, for in the prophetic anathemas there is a lucid understanding that inherited wealth has its economic origin in profit. Moreover, Isaiah and Hosea think the same way as the other prophets, and they are not peasants but city-dwellers. Isaiah is even from the capital, and proud of it.

11.21
Before Christianity became compromised with the prevailing social systems, that is, up to the fourth or fifth century A.D., there were never misrepresentations or evasions with regard to the biblical testimony concerning the inescapably unjust origin or differentiating ownership. The patristic passages which we have cited abundantly demonstrate this.

11.22
At the beginning of this chapter, I noted that the papal encyclicals' defence of private ownership cannot be quoted to brand as heterodox what I am sustaining. As Allaz and Bigo have demonstrated, the encyclicals understand ownership as something very different. I now wish to add, although I have already touched this in passing, that in their defence the popes obviously presuppose this provision: that the ownership has been legitimately acquired.

Thus the papal doctrine on ownership is on a different level, onto which my considerations is no way enter. But the whole doctrine is conditioned by the implicit phrase: provided that the ownership has been legitimately acquired.

11.23

If it is objected that the popes presuppose that legitimately acquired ownership *de facto* does exist, I respond that in any case this notion is not the object of their teaching activity but is rather a supposition. Their teachings therefore do not prejudge the possibility of demonstrating that this supposition is false. Both the recent advances in economic science and the understanding that the Bible and the Church Fathers had of the matter demonstrate that the supposition is indeed false.

CRITIQUE

The critical attitude that one adopts towards the Extracts will partly depend upon the answer one gives to each of the questions that opened this Section: namely: (1) Can specific political structures, ideals or programmes be derived unambiguously from the Gospel?; (2) How far can the Church be identified with specific political regimes, ideals or programmes?; and (3) Should the individual Christian be totally obedient to specific political regimes, ideals or programmes? So, if one answers 'yes' to (1), the differing positions of Barth and Temple would be unacceptable. And if one answers 'yes' to the third only, that of Barth might be acceptable. Nonetheless, apart from these (vital) overall criticisms a number of more internal criticism of the individual Extracts can be made.

It has already been noted that, by the standards of critical exegesis, much of Barth's *Der Römerbrief* may appear to tell the reader as much about Barth as about Paul. The central difficulty of this Extract for the late 20th-century reader may be that it seems to demand too rigid an obedience of the individual to government and an acceptance of the political *status quo* (whether tyrannical or not). Such a position seems much more rigid than that of Calvin (see *above*, pp.145f.) and, in practice, Barth later found it to be unsustainable in the face of Nazism. Nonetheless, as a theological corrective of facile revolutionary politics, Barth's contribution remains important – particularly since, as an individual, Barth was himself firmly committed to a left-wing political perspective.

Despite the equally important emphasis of Berdyaev on the spiritual in religion, his particular discussion of political realities will appear to many to be far too esoteric and elitist. His grudging allowance of political structures for 'the masses', combined with his avoiding any discussion of how these structures might be evaluated or improved, might seem both arrogant and ethereal. Yet, in his defence, Berdyaev might have claimed that, such attitudes are necessary, given people's persistent tendency to persecute or ignore the truly spiritual.

The central difficulty that is usually found in Niebuhr's *Moral Man and Immoral Society* involves the moral dualism that he frankly admitted and, yet, which he gradually modified during his life. As with Barth, it would seem that a sharply defined early position, which made obvious overall sense, could not be sustained in practice. Many critics have argued that such a sharp moral dualism would allow societies, governments and large corporations to act in highly immoral ways. On this argument, the prevarications of say President Nixon's government would appear perfectly acceptable and only became wrong when they actually sought to obstruct justice. Although there is some force in this criticism, Niebuhr's early position was by no means as dualistic as, at first, it might appear, since he did insist that leaders of social groups must still adhere to 'the ideals of a high individual morality' (8.11).

Both Temple and John XXIII face the difficulties confronting all natural law theories (see *above*, pp.86f.). The problems are, perhaps, less for Temple, since he only proposed general principles and was careful to show that these derive from general Christian doctrine. Provided one can accept the latter, then the former might seem to follow (although, even here, he showed his own bias in regarding respect for persons as the primary principle of Christian ethics). More important is the criticism that Temple appeared to believe that the specific application of general principles to political problems by politicians involves only 'technical knowledge' and 'judgments of practical expediency' (9.1). In fact, many political problems (as can be seen in the next Section) involve a whole range of smaller ethical, political and ideological decisions which divide Christians as much as anyone.

Similarly, with John XXIII's *Pacem in Terris*, it is the avoidance of these sorts of decisions which may give it an air of generality and unreality. Precisely because both authors attempted to address as wide an audience as possible and sought a broad agreement in this audience, their discussions tend to lack the sort of specificity which might make them appear more realistic. The second part of Temple's *Christianity and the Social Order* attempted to remedy this by supplying a detailed and, admittedly, partisan (and now, of course, dated) series of political and economic proposals. Even John XXIII's striking use of the language of 'rights' (opposed by earlier Catholic moral theologians) tends to be rather general. This language is analysed in detail in Kieran Cronin's *Rights and Christian Ethics*. However, a strength of Extract 10, is that, unlike some secular understandings of 'rights', John XXIII insists upon linking 'rights' and 'obligations'.

For many, Liberation theology appears as one of the most stimulating movements in recent theology. It has brought new insights and perspectives to the discipline and reminded many of the passion in the face of oppression which should characterise Christianity. Perhaps it would be unrealistic to expect it to be thoroughly defined and rigorously methodological whilst it is still developing. Nonetheless, the writings of, especially, Alfredo Fierro in *The Militant Gospel*, Bonino and Miranda, demonstrate that it does not lack critical sophistication. Miranda's Extract supplies an important corrective to the medieval concept of 'almsgiving', which is undoubtedly still prevalent in the West. Yet, it is not itself without difficulties. Two, in particular, are crucial. The first is concerned with the adequacy of his exegesis. He concentrates upon the Old Testament criticism of wealth and tends to ignore the obvious limitations of this criticism and the existence of other and quite different strands within the Old Testament. The (largely prophetic) stress upon 'justice' is, of course, only justice for the people of Israel: it seldom extends even to Israel's most immediate neighbours. And, even in the context of Israel, *sedakah* may be more concerned with maintaining a lawful society than achieving social equity or abolishing 'differentiating ownership'. Further, other strands in the Old Testament (particularly in certain Psalms and in the prologue and postscript of Job) seem to regard 'wealth' as a reward for, or an indication of, 'righteousness'. Even in the New Testament, the various redactions contained in Luke do not all seem equally hostile to 'wealth' (see further, David Mealand's *Poverty and Expectation in the Gospels*). The second difficulty concerns Miranda's deliberate use of Marxist theory (e.g. 'differentiating ownership') to depict biblical concepts. Alistair Kee's *Marx and the Failure of Liberation Theology* offers a major critique of Miranda and others on this crucial issue. This is a difficulty which will be discussed further in the criticism of Bonino's Extract 16, since it is in that Extract that the issue is explicitly raised.

Looking for any points of unity between these Extracts is made more difficult by the polemical contexts from which they mostly derive. So, the contrasts between Barth and Miranda appear sharper because neither makes the sort of qualifications that they do in their less combative writings. Nonetheless, there might be broad agreement with the following points qualifying the three initial questions:

(1) Even if it is believed that specific political structures, ideals or programmes can be derived unambiguously from the Gospel, the latter cannot be *identified* with them. For the Christian, political realities must always be set in the context of transcendence. Even the theologian who is most often thought to have confused the Kingdom of God with political realities, Walter Rauschenbusch, was emphatic about this:

The Kingdom of God is divine in its origin, progress and consummation. It was initiated by Jesus Christ, in whom the prophetic spirit came to its consummation, it is sustained by the Holy Spirit, and it will be brought to its fulfilment by the power of God in his own time. The passive and active resistance of the Kingdom of Evil at every stage of its advance is so great, and the human resources of the Kingdom of God so slender, that no explanation can satisfy a religious mind which does not see the power of God in its movements... The Kingdom of God, therefore, is not merely ethical, but has a rightful place in theology (*A Theology For the Social Gospel*, pp.139-40).

(2) If the Church's aims and aspirations cannot simply be identified with political realities, most Christians would also argue that neither can it be indifferent to them. A notion of the relative worth of political regimes, ideals and programmes (relative, that is, to the Kingdom of God), would suggest that they do serve an important function, but not one that should be absolutised. Whereas Christians have always differed with each other about the extent to which tyrannical regimes should be actively opposed, they might agree that some form of political reality is necessary to preserve peace and justice. Pure antinomianism has seldom been thought to be a justifiable Christian position.

(3) If political realities do have some relative worth for the well-being of society, then it would seem that individual Christians (enjoined, as they are, to love their neighbours) do have at least a general responsibility for obedience. There are still very real differences apparent between Christians about how far this obedience should go. But, again in the context of transcendence, this obedience can hardly be absolute. The theist, *par excellence,* should always be conscious that it is only to God that absolute obedience is properly given. However, for the present-day theologian, there is an additional reason for this position of relative obedience. In the light of critical, historical research, it should be evident that Christianity has subsisted in and adapted to a variety of socio-political contexts. It is one of the merits of South American Liberation theology, that it has served to remind Western theologians that Christianity is not dependent upon any one single socio-political system. It should be a function of Western, critical theologians, in turn, to remind Liberation theologians that they too are engaged in a historically relative, albeit vital, attempt to unravel the riches of the Gospel.

SECTION 3

WAR AND PEACE

SECTION 3

WAR AND PEACE

War has presented the 20th century with perhaps its most crucial moral problem. Even if the issue of the environment seems to be supplanting it as the key issue for the 21st century, the scale, cost and potential destructiveness of 20th-century warfare differentiates this from all previous centuries. In the 20th century alone, 50 million people may have died as a result of war: in any year, world arms expenditure has become equivalent to the total expenditure on basic foodstuffs and may soon equal the total present wealth of the world: and humans now have the capacity to destroy, many times, the present world population. If for no other reason, these horrific dimensions make it appropriate to have a whole Section devoted to the substantive issue of war and its opposite, peace.

However, there are other reasons for giving this Section to this single issue. Although the dimensions of warfare were previously quite different from those of the modern era, the issue of war has always raised crucial problems about the relationship of Christianity to society at large. Empirically, a clear pattern emerges in Christian responses to war and this indicates, more sharply than in most other moral issues, the degree to which these responses are socially determined. And ethically, divisions between Christian pacifists and militarists, on this issue, serve to highlight the pluralism within Christianity evident in all of the Sections of this Textbook.

These points – empirical and ethical – require some initial distinctions between differing responses to war. Four 'ideal' types may be isolated (for these see further my *Theology and Social Structure*, p.71f):

(A) *Thoroughgoing Militarism* – understood as a willingness to fight anywhere, at any time and for any cause.

(B) *Selective Militarism* – understood as a willingness to fight when one's country, or another, declares that the cause is just.

(C) *Selective Pacifism* – understood as a willingness to fight only when one is personally convinced that the cause is just.

(D) *Thoroughgoing Pacifism* – understood as an unwillingness to fight anywhere, at any time and for any cause.

These are ideal, not actual, types, so particular examples may be variants of them, but together they represent the range of options open to the individual, based upon his or her willingness or unwillingness to fight in war. The words 'in war' should be stressed: the responses are not primarily concerned with individual killing or violence, but rather with the issue of fighting or not on behalf of others (see Augustine's Text VII.6-7). Not all thoroughgoing pacifists would admit this distinction – since for some of them it is killing in any form which is forbidden – but it is essential to most other Christian responses to war. This distinction will be examined further in Section 5 in relation to the issues of suicide and euthanasia.

For most Christians, type A is not a Christian response to war, since only the non-idealistic or amoral mercenary belongs to it (though see Luther's IX.26). Further, a moral defence of fighting in war, whether in terms of type B or type C, requires some notion of a 'just war': the difference between the types depending on whether the individual concerned decides that the cause is just or whether he or she simply relies upon the judgment of the State or Church. Since these two responses are the majority Christian responses to war, the importance of just-war theory can readily be seen. Naturally, individuals may not be thoroughly consistent in their responses to war: B and C may be mixed and many might even wish to avoid any notions of 'just causes', regarding war as a mournful and ethically confused necessity.

Nonetheless, in so far as war is ever thought to be justifiable, some notion of justice is required and, in turn, differing responses on the part of the individual can be distinguished.

The fact that types B and C cover the majority of Christian responses to war today, serves to illustrate one of the central differences between the early and present-day churches. It is here that a key empirical observation can be made about the relationship between Christianity and society at large. A fundamental dichotomy can be seen between the pre-Constantinian and post-Constantinian churches: if, within the latter, types B and C constitute the majority of Christian responses to war, in the former it is type D which predominates. The historian Bainton even claims that, 'the age of persecution down to the time of Constantine was the age of pacifism to the degree that during this period no Christian author to our knowledge approved of Christian participation in battle': but, 'the accession of Constantine terminated the pacifist period in church history' (*Christian Attitudes Toward War and Peace*, pp.66 & 85). In contrast with the early church, Christian pacifism, in its thoroughgoing sense, is today confined to a minority of Christians within churches and to a minority of sects, such as the Amish Mennonites, Anabaptists, Brethren, Jehovah's Witnesses and Quakers. Individual pacifists, such as the Methodist Stanley Hauerwas in Extract 15, often tend to feel themselves to be relative outsiders on this issue in their own church.

Naturally there were differences of approach to war within the early church and it is sometimes difficult to decide whether it is warfare itself which was despised or the 'pagan' customs surrounding it. These differences range from the absolutism of Tertullian (c.160-220), even before his conversion to the rigours of Montanism in middle-age, to the pragmatism of Origen (c.185-254). Despite the undoubted presence of Christians in the Roman army in the late 2nd century, Tertullian's attitude was uncompromising:

> Enquiry is made about this point, whether a believer may turn himself into military service, and whether the military may be admitted unto the faith, even the rank and file, or

each inferior grade, to whom there is no necessity for taking part in sacrifices or capital punishments. There is no agreement between the divine and the human sacrament, the standard of Christ and the standard of the devil, the camp of light and the camp of darkness. One soul cannot be due to two masters – God and Caesar. And yet Moses carried a rod, and Aaron wore a buckle, and John (Baptist) is girt with leather, and Joshua the son of Nun leads a line of march; and the People warred: if it pleases you to sport with the subject. But how will a Christian man war, nay, how will he serve even in peace, without a sword, which the Lord has taken away? For albeit soldiers had come unto John, and had received the formula of their rule; albeit, likewise, a centurion had believed; still the Lord afterward, in disarming Peter, unbelted every soldier' (*On Idolatry* 19, from *The Ante-Nicene Fathers*, 3).

Here, unambiguously, it is the sword itself and not simply military 'paganism' which Tertullian believed to be inconsistent with Christianity. Similarly, it will be seen later (*below*, pp.456f.) that he took an absolutist stand against abortion and any form of individual homicide.

Like Tertullian, Origen probably just assumed that killing humans was contrary to the law of Christ. For him, Jesus forbade altogether 'the putting of men to death' and 'nowhere teaches that it is right for his own disciples to offer violence to anyone, however wicked' (*Against Celsus* 3.7). However, more than Tertullian, Origen was determined to refute Celsus' charges that Christians were undermining the state through their pacifism:

To this our answer is, that we do, when occasion requires, give help to kings, and that so to say, a divine help, 'putting on the whole armour of God'. And this we do in obedience to the injunction of the apostle, 'I exhort, therefore, that first of all, supplications, prayers, intercessions, and giving of thanks, be made for all men; for kings, and for all that are in authority,' and the more any one excels in piety, the more effective help does he render to kings, even more than is given by soldiers, who go forth to fight and slay as many of the enemy as they can. And to those enemies of our faith who require us to bear arms for the commonwealth, and to slay men, we can reply: 'Do not those who are priests at certain shrines, and those who attend on certain gods, as you account them, keep their hands free from blood, that they may with their hands unstained and free from human blood offer the appointed sacrifices to your gods; and even when war is upon you, you never enlist the priests in the army. If that, then, is a laudable custom, how much more so, that while others are engaged in battle, these should engage as the priests and ministers of God, keeping their hands pure, and wrestling in prayers to God on behalf of those who are fighting in a righteous cause, and for the king who reigns righteously, that whatever is opposed to those who act righteously may be destroyed!' And we by our prayers vanquish all demons who stir up war, and lead to the violation of oaths, and disturb the peace, we in this way are much more helpful to the kings than those who go into the fields to fight for them. And we do take our part in public affairs, when along with righteous prayers we join self-denying exercises and meditations, which teach us to despise pleasures, and not to be led away by them. And none fight better for the king than we do. We do not indeed fight under him, although he require it; but we fight on his behalf, forming a special army – an army of piety – by offering our prayer to God (*Against Celsus* 8.73, from *The Ante-Nicene Fathers*, 4).

Even allowing for some special pleading here in the face of criticism, there are clear differences from Tertullian and, indeed, similarities with later Christian responses to war. Augustine, too, was concerned to defend Christianity against critics who thought it had undermined the state. Unlike Augustine, Origen developed no just-war theory, but he did admit to a 'righteous cause' in war. And there is a prefigurement of the medieval position, illustrated in Aquinas' claim (VIII.7f) that the clergy should be exempt from military service – a position with evident pre-Christian roots.

Nonetheless, the overall response of both Tertullian and

Origen to war was on the opposite side of the pacifist/militarist divide to that of Ambrose and Augustine and to most subsequent theologians. First Ambrose and then Augustine, justified the full participation of Christians in war and sought to distinguish between 'just' and 'unjust' wars. At times, both men remained critical of the State (more critical than Aquinas in the theocratic 13th century), but saw military service as a morally legitimate form of activity for the Christian. In contrast with Tertullian, Augustine saw the condemnation of Peter's use of the sword (in Matt. 26.52-3) as a condemnation of acting 'in a hasty zeal' and 'without the sanction of the constituted authority', rather than as a condemnation of the sword as such (VII.2). And, in contrast to all other known theologians in the pre-Constantinian Church, he interpreted the command to turn the other cheek (in Matt. 5.39) as referring to 'an inward disposition' rather than to 'a bodily act' (VII.8). For the first time, even arguments from silence appear on the issue of war – for example, that Jesus did not actually condemn the centurion for being a soldier (VII.6; see also X.10). Both Tertullian and Augustine were aware that the Old Testament often sanctions war (even wars of aggression), but their attitude to this evidence again contrasts. For Tertullian, Jesus' disarming of Peter revoked this sanction, whereas, for Augustine, Jesus' actions and commands were to be interpreted in such a way that they did not contradict the Old Testament evidence.

The legacy of Augustine can be seen quite clearly in this quotation from Welty (who had already pointed out that the Old Testament does not support pacifism):

> Concerning war the New Testament must be considered in its entirety. Statements conditioned by the circumstances of the time cannot be regarded as universally valid and binding. Neither Christ nor the apostles condemned war or military service. Christ was sent into the world by the Father in order to establish the messianic kingdom of peace. But men rejected him and his Gospel, and thereby forfeited the promises that were directly linked with the coming of Christ (*A Handbook of Christian Social Ethics*, vol 2, p.396).

Modern biblical scholarship increasingly looks to the different ways the Bible is interpreted in Christian history. A prime example of the importance of this study is evident here. In both Augustine's Text VII and Welty's Extract 12, it is the New Testament, rather than the Old, which is to be interpreted and contextualised and, in both, an argument from silence is adopted. Since both men can be literalistic in their understanding of other aspects of New Testament teaching, their uneasiness at this point is an important indication of a change in the socio-political context of the pre-Constantinian and post-Constantinian churches. In the first, the position of the Church was, arguably, more that of sect, with a relatively exclusive understanding of its membership and doctrine and little feeling of responsibility for society as a whole or for the working of government. In the second, it is the church-type that seems to predominate: the Church has a more inclusive understanding of itself and its boundaries with society, at large, are less clear-cut: now, for the first time, with the adoption of Christianity as a state religion by Constantine, it must come to terms with the moral dilemmas facing the state. If this explanation is accepted, the empirical dichotomy, in relation to this issue of war, appears less surprising. Indeed, it becomes difficult to see how a church, as a church, rather than as a sect, can systematically oppose a state on an issue as central to the latter as war: pacifism remains an option for the sect, particularly if it is already deeply estranged from society (as today with the Jehovah's Witnesses or the Exclusive Brethren), in a way that it is not an option for the Church. In Luther's Text IX, with his high doctrine of the state, the church-type position is well in evidence: his ecclesiological position precludes his espousing, either the revolutionary response of the peasants, or the radical pacifism of the Anabaptists.

This point leads naturally to a consideration of the ethical difficulties confronting the church-type response to war. Some form of the just-war theory has usually been thought to be essential to it – as Augustine's Text VII, Aquinas' Text VIII, and Welty's Extract 12 all indicate. But it is a theory which faces very considerable difficulties – as the US Catholic Bishops argue in Extract 14. The first of these has already been noted – the difficulty of reconciling the Old and New Testament responses to war. Some theologians, like Hauerwas in Extract 15, maintain that the whole tenor of the New Testament, as distinct from the Old, is in the pacifist direction. The Scottish biblical scholar, G.H.C. Macgregor's *The New Testament Basis of Pacifism* was very influential for a previous generation on this issue. Secondly, it has proved difficult to set out a just-war theory which is not tautological: characteristically, that in Welty (12.12) contains within it the concept of justice, as does that in Augustine (VII.4). Thirdly, the distinction between wars of aggression and wars of defence and the notion of a legitimate authority become particularly difficult to maintain in the context of wars of liberation (see 12.20f). Since the latter have assumed a role of such great importance in the Third World and in Liberation theology, this difficulty is particularly troublesome in present-day Christian ethics. Fourthly, in the context of actual wars, it tends to become increasingly difficult consistently to apply just-war theories. So, in the light of progressive civilian bombing in World War Two, a just-war theorist, such as Temple, encountered very considerable problems in reconciling theory with actual practice. It may be a particular feature of modern wars that, as they intensify, so they become less susceptible to moral justification in any recognisably Christian form (hence the distinction, evident in Extract 14, between just causes for going to war – *ius ad bellum* – and just practices actually within warfare – *ius in bello*). Fifthly, nuclear warfare, or even the potential use, or threatened use, of nuclear weapons may, in themselves, exceed the bounds of any Christian just-war theory. This problem is exacerbated by the connection that is becoming increasingly apparent between nuclear weapons and nuclear power, by the proliferation of nuclear knowledge beyond the Western countries, by the possibility of nuclear terrorism and by strategic discussions of limited nuclear war. The dangers inherent in all of these 'developments' are so obvious and so immense that little further justification seems necessary for focusing this Section on the substantive issues of war and peace.

Amongst historical studies of Christian responses to war, the following are particularly important:

Roland H. Bainton, *Christian Attitudes Toward War and Peace*; Peter Brock, *Pacifism in Europe to 1914* and *Twentieth-Century Pacifism*; C.J. Cadoux, *The Early Christian Attitude to War*.

In addition, the following historical readers are very useful:

Arthur F. Holmes, *War and Christian Ethics*; Albert Marrin, *War and the Christian Conscience*.

The sociological distinction between 'church' and 'sect' has been the subject of considerable debate (for a survey of the general typological debate see, for example, Betty Scharf's *The Sociological Study of Religion*). The following books, however, all interpret varying Christian responses to war in the light of the distinction:

Robin Gill, *Theology and Social Structure* and *Prophecy and Praxis*; David Martin, *Pacifism*; J. Milton Yinger, *The Scientific Study of Religion*.

TEXT VII
AUGUSTINE
The just war

1. BACKGROUND

Reply to Faustus the Manichaean XXII, 69-76 (*The Nicene and Post-Nicene Fathers*, vol IV, Eerdmans, 1956, trans. R. Stothert). Augustine first met Faustus of Milevis in 383, when he was still himself a sympathiser with Manichaeism. But he was unimpressed by this largely self-taught leader of the Manichees: from his own classically educated, middle-class background, he wrote later that, 'I found at once that the man was not learned in any of the liberal studies save literature, and not especially learned in that, either' (*Confessions* V.vi.11). Faustus claimed to be living the life of a 'true' Christian, but Augustine came increasingly to distrust his attacks on Catholic orthodoxy and on the Bible, in so far as it diverged from Manichaeism. Augustine finally wrote his *Reply to Faustus* c.397-8, at about the same time as his *Confessions* and shortly after becoming a bishop at Hippo. Augustine's sympathies with Faustus' understanding of sexual morality are still evident in his other writings of this time (see *below*, pp.460f.), but his doctrinal and exegetical antipathies to Faustus' views are well in evidence in this Text. Like Ambrose, his mentor at the time of his conversion, Augustine shows himself prepared to defend Old Testament militarism and to justify the notion of a just-war from a Christian perspective, even though, at the end of the Text, he still sees the importance of the witness of the response of many earlier Christians to war – martyrdom.

2. KEY ISSUES

The central issue which concerns Augustine is the difference between personally motivated, individual killing, on the one hand, and, on the other, killing on the authority of the monarch or of God himself. Moses' killing of the Egyptian (Ex. 2.12) was wrong, because it was without any authority – as was Paul's killing of Christians or Peter's violent action in Gethsemane (VII.2). But, the spoiling of the Egyptians (Ex. 7-14) was, in contrast, explicitly at God's command and, as command, was to be obeyed by Moses (VII.3). If it is objected that a good God could not give such a command, it can be replied that it is indeed only God who could do so: by implication, for humanity alone it would certainly be wrong to do so (VII.4). Thus act, agent and authority are all very important here (VII.5): for individual agents to act violently on their own authority and from passion is wrong, whereas killing in war, in obedience to God or to some lawful authority, is not (VII.6). For Augustine, monarchs have a right to preserve peace through the use of warfare and soldiers have a duty to obey their monarchs, whether or not the latter are right actually to wage war in particular circumstances (VII.7). The final paragraph faces a fresh objection from Faustus and allegorically interprets Matthew 5.39 in terms of 'an inward disposition' (for a similar stress upon intention, see XIII.2-4).

3. *ETHICAL ARGUMENTS*

The central thrust of Augustine's ethical argument is clearly deontological – war is morally justifiable because, in parts of the Old Testament, God can be seen to command it. Faustus was no modern critical exegete, but his moral objections to Old Testament warfare would find a number of supporters today. However, Augustine increasingly adopted a literalistic acceptance of the Bible (see further, Text X) and was thus forced to defend and make sense of the evidence from Genesis and Exodus. As a result, an ethical position based upon the central criterion of obedience to God's commands (however unfathomable), seems the only one consistent with both Old Testament militarism and previous Christian pacifism/martyrdom. Apart from this central criterion, there are also a number of more minor natural law types of argument apparent – e.g. in the crop analogy (VII.2), in the reference to natural order (VII.5) and in the reference to human peace (VII.7 – see also Text IV). Finally, Augustine's distinction between 'cowardly dislike' and the 'real evils in war' (VII.6) is important to his argument, although he gives no indication of its ethical basis. It is possible that the latter results, as much from his Roman, as from his Christian world.

4. BASES OF CHRISTIAN ETHICS

This last point raises important possibilities about the extra-Christian sources of Augustine's just-war theory. Again, it is clear that the central thrust of the argument in this Text, stems from his attempt to reconcile the Old Testament responses to war, with those confronting Christians at the end of the 4th century. Augustine's appeals are either to the Bible or against Faustus and the Manichaeans. Nonetheless, he also makes assumptions (e.g. in VII.7) about political leadership and natural justice, which go beyond these appeals. At the end of the Text he also makes the specifically Christian allusion to the suffering of martyrs.

5. SOCIAL DETERMINANTS

If a church/sect typology is adopted, it is evident that Augustine reflected the transition of Christianity to a more church-type position in society. He remained uneasy about this position (see especially Text IV) and was well aware of Christianity's pacifist heritage (VII.8), but he did still sanction the full participation of Christians in war. Intellectually, Augustine characteristically reflected both the Graeco-Roman and the Hebraic world (cf. *above*, p.66). To the latter, he owed his notion of war as obedience to God's commands, but, to the former, he owed his concepts of 'lawful authority', 'natural order' and 'justice': indeed the whole notion of a just-war theory is essentially classical, rather than biblical (even though 'justice' is certainly used in other biblical contexts – see Extract 11). At the more personal level, it is possible that Augustine's crucial disappointment with Faustus may have owed something to their very different social class and educational backgrounds: it would have been difficult for someone as socially and intellectually sophisticated as Augustine to take Faustus seriously.

6. SOCIAL SIGNIFICANCE

The importance of Augustine's position on war cannot be exaggerated. Again, in terms of church/sect typology, had he

simply affirmed the pacifist tradition and convinced other
Christians to do the same, a serious rift might have been made
between 'church' (or, more accurately, 'sect') and society at large.
It will be seen in Text VIII that, from his arguments, a just-war
theory could be developed by later theologians and thus a way
could be found to accommodate the awkwardness of the New
Testament with the demands of the state. Here again Augustine's
particular blend of Graeco-Roman and Hebraic notions has had
a major effect upon both Western Christianity and society
generally.

FURTHER READING

The primary sources for Augustine's understanding of war and
peace are his *Reply to Faustus* and his later *The City of God* (see
Text IV). For a survey of the relation of classical theories of just-
war to Christian and non-Christian responses to war, John
Ferguson's *War and Peace in the World's Religions* is useful. Fuller
treatments can be found both in books already mentioned in the
sectional introduction and in the following (though obviously
they apply more to Text VIII): Frederick H. Russell, *The Just
War in the Middle Ages*; Joan D. Tooke, *The Just War in Aquinas
and Grotius*.

TEXT VII
AUGUSTINE
The just war

VII.1
Moses... we love and admire, and to the best of our power imitate,
coming indeed far short of his merits, though we have killed no
Egyptian, nor plundered any one, nor carried on any war; which
actions of Moses were in one case prompted by the zeal of the
future champion of his people, and in the other cases commanded
by God.

VII.2
It might be shown that, though Moses slew the Egyptian, without

being commanded by God, the action was divinely permitted, as, from the prophetic character of Moses, it prefigured something in the future. Now, however, I do not use this argument, but view the action as having no symbolical meaning. In the light, then, of the eternal law, it was wrong for one who had no legal authority to kill the man, even though he was a bad character, besides being the aggressor. But in minds where great virtue is to come, there is often an early crop of vices, in which we may still discern a disposition for some particular virtue, which will come when the mind is duly cultivated. For as farmers, when they see land bringing forth huge crops, though of weeds, pronounce it good for corn; or when they see wild creepers, which have to be rooted out, still consider the land good for useful vines; and when they see a hill covered with wild olives, conclude that with culture it will produce good fruit: so the disposition of mind which led Moses to take the law into his own hands, to prevent the wrong done to his brother, living among strangers, by a wicked citizen of the country from being unrequited, was not unfit for the production of virtue, but from want of culture gave signs of its productiveness in an unjustifiable manner. He who afterwards, by His angel, called Moses on Mount Sinai, with the divine commission to liberate the people of Israel from Egypt, and who trained him to obedience by the miraculous appearance in the bush burning but not consumed, and by instructing him in his ministry, was the same who, by the call addressed from heaven to Saul when persecuting the Church, humbled him, raised him up, and animated him; or in figurative words, by this stroke He cut off the branch, grafted it, and made it fruitful. For the fierce energy of Paul, when in his zeal for hereditary traditions he persecuted the Church, thinking that he was doing God service, was like a crop of weeds showing great signs of productiveness. It was the same in Peter, when he took his sword out of its sheath to defend the Lord, and cut off the right ear of an assailant, when the Lord rebuked him with something like a threat, saying, 'Put up thy sword into its sheath; for he that taketh the sword shall perish by the sword.' [Matt. 26.52-3]. To take the sword is to use weapons against a man's life, without the sanction of the constituted authority. The Lord, indeed, had told His disciples to carry a sword; but He did not tell them to use it. But that after this sin Peter should become a pastor of the Church was no more improper than that Moses, after smiting the Egyptian, should become the leader of the congregation. In both cases the trespass originated not in inveterate cruelty, but in a hasty zeal which admitted of correction. In both cases there was resentment against injury, accompanied in one case by love for a brother, and in the other by love, though still carnal, of the Lord. Here was evil to be subdued or rooted out; but the heart with such capacities needed only, like good soil, to be cultivated to make it fruitful in virtue.

VII.3

Then, as for Faustus' objection to the spoiling of the Egyptians, he knows not what he says. In this Moses not only did not sin, but it would have been sin not to do it. It was by the command of God, who, from His knowledge both of the actions and of the hearts of men, can decide on what every one should be made to suffer, and through whose agency. The people at that time were still carnal, and engrossed with earthly affections; while the Egyptians were in open rebellion against God, for they used the gold, God's creature, in the service of idols, to the dishonour of the Creator, and they had grievously oppressed strangers by making them work without pay. Thus the Egyptians deserved the punishment, and the Israelites were suitably employed in inflicting it. Perhaps, indeed, it was not so much a command as a permission to the Hebrews to act in the matter according to their own inclinations; and God, in sending the message by Moses, only wished that they should thus be informed of His permission. There may also have been mysterious reasons for what God said to the people on this matter. At any rate, God's commands are to be submissively received, not to be argued against. The apostle says, 'Who hath known the mind of the Lord? or who hath been His counsellor?' [Rom. 11.34]. Whether, then, the reason was what I have said, or whether in the secret appointment of God, there was some unknown reason for His telling the people by Moses to borrow things from the Egyptians, and to take them away with them, this remains certain, that this was said for some good reason, and that Moses could not lawfully have done otherwise than God told him, leaving to God the reason of the command, while the servant's duty is to obey.

VII.4
But, says Faustus, it cannot be admitted that the true God, who is also good, ever gave such a command. I answer, such a command can be rightly given by no other than the true and good God, who alone knows the suitable command in every case, and who alone is incapable of inflicting unmerited suffering on any one.

VII.5
According to the eternal law, which requires the preservation of natural order, and forbids the transgression of it, some actions have an indifferent character, so that men are blamed for presumption if they do them without being called upon, while they are deservedly praised for doing them when required. The act, the agent, and the authority for the action are all of great importance in the order of nature. For Abraham to sacrifice his son of his own accord is shocking madness. His doing so at the command of God proves him faithful and submissive. This is so loudly proclaimed by the very voice of truth, that Faustus, *eagerly* rummaging for some fault, and reduced at last to slanderous charges, has not the boldness to attack this action. It is scarcely possible that he can have forgotten a deed so famous, that it recurs to the mind of itself without any study or reflection, and is in fact repeated by so many tongues, and portrayed in so many places, that no one can pretend to shut his eyes or his ears to it. If, therefore, while Abraham's killing his son of his own accord would have been unnatural, his doing it at the command of God shows not only guiltless but praiseworthy compliance, why does Faustus blame Moses for spoiling the Egyptians? Your feeling of disapproval for the mere human action should be restrained by a regard for the divine sanction. Will you venture to blame God Himself for desiring such actions? Then 'Get thee behind me, Satan, for thou understandest not the things which be of God, but those which be of men.' Would that this rebuke might accomplish in you what it did in Peter, and that you might hereafter preach the truth concerning God, which you now,

judging by feeble sense, find fault with! as Peter became a zealous messenger to announce to the Gentiles what he objected to at first, when the Lord spoke of it as His intention.

VII.6

Now, if this explanation suffices to satisfy human obstinacy and perverse misinterpretation of right actions of the vast difference between the indulgence of passion and presumption on the part of men, and obedience to the command of God, who knows what to permit or to order, and also the time and the persons, and the due action or suffering in each case, the account of the wars of Moses will not excite surprise or abhorrence, for in wars carried on by divine command, he showed not ferocity but obedience; and God, in giving the command, acted not in cruelty, but in righteous retribution, giving to all what they deserved, and warning those who needed warning. What is the evil in war? Is it the death of some who will soon die in any case, that others may live in peaceful subjection? This is mere cowardly dislike, not any religious feeling. The real evils in war are love of violence, revengeful cruelty, fierce and implacable enmity, wild resistance, and the lust of power, and such like; and it is generally to punish these things, when force is required to inflict the punishment, that, in obedience to God or some lawful authority, good men undertake wars, when they find themselves in such a position as regards the conduct of human affairs, that right conduct requires them to act, or to make others act in this way. Otherwise John, when the soldiers who came to be baptised asked, What shall we do? would have replied, Throw away your arms; give up the service; never strike, or wound, or disable any one. But knowing that such actions in battle were not murderous, but authorised by law, and that the soldiers did not thus avenge themselves, but defend the public safety, he replied, 'Do violence to no man, accuse no man falsely, and be content with your wages.' [Lk. 3.14]. But as the Manichaeans are in the habit of speaking evil of John, let them hear the Lord Jesus Christ Himself ordering this money to be given to Caesar, which John tells the soldiers to be content with. 'Give,' He says, 'to Caesar the things that are Caesar's' [Matt. 22.21]. For tribute-money is given on purpose to pay the soldiers for war. Again, in the case of the centurion who said, 'I am a man under authority, and have soldiers under me: and I say to one, Go, and he goeth; and to another, Come, and he cometh; and to my servant, Do this, and he doeth it', Christ gave due praise to his faith [Matt. 8.9-10]. He did not tell him to leave the service. But there is no need here to enter on the long discussion of just and unjust wars.

VII.7

A great deal depends on the causes for which men undertake wars, and on the authority they have for doing so; for the natural order which seeks the peace of mankind, ordains that the monarch should have the power of undertaking war if he thinks it advisable, and that the soldiers should perform their military duties on behalf of the peace and safety of the community. When war is undertaken in obedience to God, who would rebuke, or humble, or crush the pride of man, it must be allowed to be a righteous war; for even the wars which arise from human passion cannot harm the eternal well-being of God, nor even hurt His saints; for in the trial of their patience, and the chastening of their spirit, and in bearing fatherly correction, they are rather benefited than injured. No one can have any power against them but what is given him from above. For there is no power but of God [Rom. 13.1], who either orders or permits. Since, therefore, a righteous man, serving it may be under an ungodly king, may do the duty belonging to his position in the State in fighting by the order of his sovereign, – for in some cases it is plainly the will of God that he should fight, and in others, where this is not so plain, it might be an unrighteous command on the part of the king, while the soldier is innocent, because his position makes obedience a duty, – how much more must the man be blameless who carries on war on the authority of God, of whom every one who serves Him knows that he can never require what is wrong?

VII.8

If it is supposed that God could not enjoin warfare, because in after times it was said by the Lord Jesus Christ, 'I say unto you, That ye resist not evil: but if any one strike thee on the right cheek, turn to him the left also', [Matt. 5.39] the answer is, that what is here required is not a bodily action, but an inward disposition. The sacred seat of virtue is the heart, and such were the hearts of our fathers, the righteous men of old. But order required such a regulation of events, and such a distinction of times, as to show first of all that even earthly blessings (for so temporal kingdoms and victory over enemies are considered to be, and these are the things which the community of the ungodly all over the world are continually begging from idols and devils) are entirely under the control and at the disposal of the one true God. Thus, under the Old Testament, the secret of the kingdom of heaven, which was to be disclosed in due time, was veiled, and so far obscured, in the disguise of earthly promises. But when the fullness of time came for the revelation of the New Testament, which was hidden under the types of the Old, clear testimony was to be borne to the truth, that there is another life for which this life ought to be disregarded, and another kingdom for which the opposition of all earthly kingdoms should be patiently borne. Thus the name martyrs, which means witnesses, was given to those who, by the will of God, bore this testimony, by their confessions, their sufferings and their death.

CRITIQUE

It would be anachronistic to criticise this Text as if it contained a fully developed just-war theory. Nevertheless, a number of tensions are evident within it, resulting from Augustine's attempt to reconcile the Old Testament with the New and with classical understandings of a 'just' war.

An immediate difficulty arises from the observation that, however sanctioned by Yahweh, a number of wars in the Old Testament, such as that against Canaan, appear, in classical terms, to be wars of aggression and not of defence. As a result, Augustine was prepared to concede an image of God which makes him, from the human perspective, morally vulnerable (VII.4). He could, of course, have pointed out, in this context, that it would indeed have been wrong for a human being rather than for God to have acted in such a way. This is an important point that is sometimes forgotten in discussions of the problem of evil or of the morality of particular images of God (see Don Cupitt's *Crisis of Moral Authority: The Dethronement of Christianity*). It is always dangerous to judge the creator by the moral standards of the creature. Yet, Augustine's concession will still be difficult for many present-day Christians to accept.

A second difficulty arises from his judgment that war may be fought on human as well as on divine authority (VII.7). Along with his classical sources, he admitted the possibility of 'some lawful authority' waging war, but gave few indications about what constituted a 'lawful authority' (VII.6). This point will recur in relation to Text VIII and Extract 12, but it is important to note that Augustine did not resolve the issue. Further, his notion of civil obedience is dangerously unqualified in VII.7. Nürnberg, in the 20th century, did not accept the notion of military obedience regardless of the perceived injustice of a situation.

Finally, Augustine's understanding of the authority of the Old Testament may appear pre-critical. Increasingly, he saw the only options as, either to accept the entire Bible literally, or to treat it in the highly selective way of Faustus. By opting for the first, he was inevitably forced to defend the moral behaviour of the Patriarchs, both in relation to polygamy (see *above*, pp.39–40) and here in relation to wars of aggression. However, a more critical understanding of the Old Testament would have avoided some of these problems.

TEXT VIII
AQUINAS
War, Christians and the clergy

1. *BACKGROUND*

This Text comes from *Summa Theologica*, 2a2ae, 40.1-2 (vol XXXV of the English Dominican translation, Blackfriars with Eyre & Spottiswoode, London and McGraw-Hill, New York, 1972). Taken from *Secunda Secundae* (see *above*, p.76) Question 40 considers the issue of war under four headings – 'Are some wars permissible?', 'May clerics engage in warfare?', 'May belligerents use subterfuge?' and 'May war be waged on feast days?' – of which the first two are reproduced here. Although there was no major war in northern Europe during Aquinas' lifetime, there was a number of local wars and dynastic struggles, as well as a declining number of crusades. The struggle which led to the downfall of the Hohenstaufens and the establishment of Charles of Anjou in Naples, in 1268, directly affected Aquinas' own family: two of his brothers fought for the Emperor, but most of his family fought on the papal side. Yet, despite this existential involvement, the issue of war only played a very minor role in *Summa Theologica* and is handled very formally in this, the most extensive, discussion of it. The clerical interests of Aquinas and of his intended audience are clearly reflected in the four headings. Like many of his contemporaries, Aquinas seems to have accepted the inevitability of war and, perhaps as a result, discussed remarkably few of the ethical dilemmas that it raises. Other scholars, like Albert the Great, Bonaventure and Duns Scotus, did not discuss them at all.

2. *KEY ISSUES*

This Text focuses upon two questions:

(a) Is it always a sin to wage war? Aquinas counters the obvious New Testament quotations that are frequently used to support

Christian pacifism (Matt. 26.52, 5.39 and Rom. 12.19) with a summary of Augustine's three criteria of a 'just' war: it must be undertaken on the authority of God or of the sovereign (VIII.3 & VIII.6.1); it must be for a just cause (VIII.4 & VIII.6.2); and it must be undertaken with a right intention, to promote the good and to avoid evil (VIII.5 & VIII.6.3-4).

(b) May clerics and bishops engage in warfare? He faces the objection that if warfare is just, *par excellence* it must be just for the clergy to participate fully in it. In reply, Aquinas considers that verses like Matthew 26.52, 2 Timothy 2.4, 1 Corinthians 11.26 and 2 Corinthians 10.4, either directly, or indirectly, preclude clergy from such action. For him, the contemplative and sacramental roles of the clergy are inconsistent with warlike pursuits (VIII.10-11): it is 'unbecoming their persons' (VIII.12.3): they must be concerned with 'works of higher merit' (VIII.12.4).

3.   ETHICAL ARGUMENTS

This text provides an interesting example of Aquinas' attempt to combine an Aristotelian, consequentialist approach to ethics with a normative understanding of Augustinian and Biblical tradition. The notion of 'right intention' is explained in terms of his overall general principle of promoting the good and avoiding evil (VIII.5): positively, this entails serving 'the common good' (VIII.6.2) and, negatively, it risks eternal punishment (VIII.6.1). His consequentialism, based upon natural law, is even more evident in his claims about naturally established role differentiation as it affects the clergy (VIII.9). Once again, the *telos* of humans provides the spur for his understanding of ethics (see *above*, pp.35–6), even if this is combined with strong deontological assumptions about the legitimacy of war and of the tradition which justifies war.

4.   BASES OF CHRISTIAN ETHICS

Aquinas' use of the Bible is also particularly interesting. He avoids Augustine's tendency to support a just-war position from the Old Testament and only uses Joshua 6.4 late in his argument, against clerical participation in warfare (VIII.12.2). He does not resolve the awkward Matthew 5.39 and resolves Matthew 26.52

only by referring it to unauthorised, private violence (VIII.6). And he understands the quotations in VIII.8-12 to be concerned only with the clergy. In general, his source of tradition is Augustine – albeit in a rather systematised and abbreviated form and often mediated through Gratian's *Decretum* (see *above*, p.76). Augustine appears as *the* authority to settle, beyond reasonable dispute, the ethical dilemma for Christians.

5. SOCIAL DETERMINANTS

Augustine, however, is used in a significantly (even if unintentionally) modified form. The socio-political context of Aquinas was quite different from that of Augustine and the former shows none of the latter's suspicions of the political order. As a result, the bones of Augustine's notion of a just war are adopted, but not the flesh of his overall distrust of the 'earthly city'. Further, the notions of guilt and just retribution that formed an important element in Augustine's understanding of war are reduced by Aquinas to a single sentence (VIII.4). The stylised format of the scholastic method is only partially responsible for these modifications. In part, they reflect a radically changed social context, in part, a very different religious psychology (see *above*, pp.35–6), and, in part, a culture which did not regard war as presenting particularly serious ethical dilemmas. This final factor is clearly present in Aquinas' handling of the question of clerical participation in warfare: it was simply obvious, to him and to his contemporaries, that the clergy should not participate fully in warfare, that they were to be considered as ontologically different from the laity, and that Petrine verses referred specifically to them (VIII.8). The early Christian and, indeed, pre-Christian sources of these assumptions have already been noted in the sectional introduction.

6. SOCIAL SIGNIFICANCE

Aquinas' understanding of just-war theory has been the major influence in much subsequent Roman Catholic thinking on the issue of war – as can be seen in both Extract 12 and Extract 14. In effect, Aquinas reinforced the church-type response to war, established by Augustine and mediated through Gratian.

Perhaps, because of this, any challenge to conventional militarist assumptions has, until very recently, come mainly from within non-Roman Catholic churches. In a nuclear age, however, it is now evident to a number of Roman Catholic moral theologians, that Aquinas' just-war theory cannot provide a sufficient basis for ethical decision-making on modern warfare (see further, Extract 14).

FURTHER READING

There are scattered references to war and killing elsewhere in *Summa Theologica* and there are also implications that can be drawn from works like *De Regimine Principum* (see Text V) but *S.T.* 2a2ae.40 remains the most important source for his ideas. Frederick H. Russell's *The Just War in the Middle Ages* and Joan D. Tooke's *The Just War in Aquinas and Grotius* both provide excellent and detailed commentaries on Aquinas' notions. Thomas R. Heath's Appendix 2 to the English Dominican translation of *S.T.*, vol XXXV, also supplies important historical information. Recent Roman Catholic discussions of the extreme difficulty of reconciling Aquinas' just-war theory with the realities of nuclear warfare can be seen in the US Bishops' Extract 14 and Roger Ruston's *Nuclear Deterrence – Right or Wrong?* (1981).

TEXT VIII

AQUINAS

War, Christians and the clergy

Is it always a sin to wage war?

VIII.1

OBJECTIONS:

i. It would seem that it is always a sin to wage war. Punishments are meted out only for sin. But our Lord named the punishment for people who wage war when he said, '*All who draw the sword will die by the sword*' [Matt. 26.52]. Every kind of war then is unlawful.

ii. Moreover, whatever goes against a divine command is a sin. But war does that. Scripture says, 'I say this to you, offer the wicked man no resistance' [Matt. 5.39]. Also, 'Not revenging yourselves, my dearly beloved, but give place unto wrath' [Rom. 12.19]. War is not always a sin then.

iii. Besides the only thing that stands as a contrary to the act of virtue is a sin. Now war is the contrary of peace. Therefore it is always a sin.

iv. Besides, if an action is lawful, practising for it would be lawful, as is obvious in the practice involved in the sciences. But warlike exercises which go on in tournaments are forbidden by the Church, since those killed in such trials are denied ecclesiastical burial. Consequently war appears to be plainly wrong.

VIII.2
ON THE OTHER HAND Augustine says, in a sermon on the centurion's son, 'If Christian teaching forbade war altogether, those looking for the salutary advice of the Gospel would have been told to get rid of their arms and give up soldiering. But instead they were told, "Do violence to no man, be content with your pay" [Lk. 3.14]. If it ordered them to be satisfied with their pay, then it did not forbid a military career.'

VIII.3
REPLY: Three things are required for any war to be just. The first is the authority of the sovereign on whose command war is waged. Now a private person has no business declaring war; he can seek redress by appealing to the judgment of his superiors. Nor can he summon together whole people, which has to be done to fight a war. Since the care of the commonweal is committed to those in authority they are the ones to watch over the public affairs of the city, kingdom or province in their jurisdiction. And just as they use the sword in lawful defence against domestic disturbance when they punish criminals, as Paul says, 'He beareth not the sword in vain for he is God's minister, an avenger to execute wrath upon him that doth evil' [Rom. 13.4], so they lawfully use the sword of war to protect the commonweal from foreign attacks. Thus it is said to those in authority, 'Rescue the weak and the needy, save them from the

clutches of the wicked' [Ps. 81.4]. Hence Augustine writes, 'The natural order conducive to human peace demands that the power to counsel and declare war belongs to those who hold the supreme authority' [i.e. Text VII.7 *above*].

VIII.4

Secondly, a just cause is required, namely that those who are attacked are attacked because they deserve it on account of some wrong they have done. So Augustine, 'We usually describe a just war as one that avenges wrongs, that is, when a nation or state has to be punished either for refusing to make amends for outrages done by its subjects, or to restore what it has seized injuriously.'

VIII.5

Thirdly, the right intention of those waging war is required, that is, they must intend to promote the good and to avoid evil. Hence Augustine writes, 'Among true worshippers of God those wars are looked on as peace-making which are waged neither from aggrandisement nor cruelty, but with the object of securing peace, of repressing the evil and supporting the good.' Now it can happen that even given a legitimate authority and a just cause for declaring war, it may yet be wrong because of a perverse intention. So again Augustine says, 'The craving to hurt people, the cruel thirst for revenge, the unappeased and unrelenting spirit, the savageness of fighting on, the lust to dominate, and suchlike – all these are rightly condemned in wars' [i.e. Text VII.6 *above*].

VIII.6
HENCE:

    i. Augustine writes, '"To draw the sword" is to arm oneself and to spill blood without command or permission of superior or lawful authority' [i.e. Text VII.2 *above*]. But if a private person uses the sword by the authority of the sovereign or judge, or a public person uses it through zeal for justice, and by the authority, so to speak, of God, then he himself does not 'draw the sword', but is commissioned by another to use it, and does not deserve punishment. Still even those who do use it sinfully are not always slain with the sword. Yet they will always 'die by the sword' since they will be punished eternally for their sinful use of it unless they repent.

ii. These words, as Augustine says, must always be borne in readiness of mind, so that a man must always be prepared to refrain from resistance or self-defence if the situation calls for it. Sometimes, however, he must act otherwise for the common good or even for the good of his opponents. Thus Augustine writes, 'One must do many things with a kind of benign severity with those who must be punished against their will. Now whoever is stripped of the lawlessness of sin is overcome for his own good, since nothing is unhappier than the happiness of sinners. It encourages guilty impunity, and strengthens the bad will, the enemy inside us.

iii. Even those who wage a just war intend peace. They are not then hostile to peace, except that evil peace which our Lord 'did not come to send on the earth'. So Augustine again says, 'We do not seek peace in order to wage war, but we go to war to gain peace. Therefore be peaceful even while you are at war, that you may overcome your enemy and bring him to the prosperity of peace.

iv. Warlike exercises are not completely forbidden; only those which are excessive and dangerous and end in killing and looting. In olden times they presented no such danger. So, as Jerome writes, they were called 'practices of arms' or 'wars without blood'.

May clerics and bishops engage in war?

VIII.7

OBJECTIONS:

i. It would seem that clerics and bishops may engage in warfare. Now we have just agreed that wars are licit and just in so far as they protect the poor and the whole commonweal from an enemy's treachery. But this kind of activity above all is the duty of prelates. As Gregory writes, 'The wolf comes down on the sheep. That happens when any scoundrel or marauder tyrannises faithful and humble people. And the man who looked like a shepherd, but really was not, abandoned the sheep and fled. He was frightened at the danger to his own skin, and did not dare to stand up against the injustice.' It is licit, therefore, for prelates and clerics to fight.

ii. Moreover Pope Leo writes, 'Since ominous news had often come from the Saracen side, rumours were circulating that they would come to the port of Rome covertly and secretly. For this reason we ordered our people to gather together and go down to the shore.' Bishops, therefore, may go to war licitly.

iii. Again, it would seem to come to the same thing whether a man does something on his own or consents to its being done by another. Scripture says, 'They who do such things are worthy of death, and not only they that do them, but they also that consent to them that do them' [Rom. 1.32]. Now the fullest consent lies in persuading others to do something; and bishops and clerics may persuade others to fight. We read that 'Charlemagne accepted war with the Lombards at the request and entreaty of Adrian, Bishop of Rome.' Therefore they are also allowed to fight.

iv. Besides, whatever is virtuous and meritorious in itself is not unlawful for prelates and clerics. Now war is sometimes virtuous and meritorious. We read [in Gratian's *Decretum*] that 'if a man die for the true faith, to save his country and to defend Christians, he will receive a heavenly reward from God.'

VIII.8
ON THE OTHER HAND the words, 'Put your sword back in its scabbard' [Matt. 26.52] were directed to Peter as representing all bishops and clerics. Consequently, they may not fight.

VIII.9
REPLY: Many things are necessary for the good of human society. Now the different functions are better and more efficiently carried out by different peoples than by one, as Aristotle shows. And certain occupations are so inconsistent with one another that they cannot be fittingly exercised together. Thus lesser jobs are forbidden those who are given major things to do. Human laws, for example, forbid soldiers whose business it is to fight to engage in commerce. Now fighting in war is quite inconsistent with the duties of a bishop or a cleric, and for two reasons.

VIII.10
First is general, namely that the operations of war are totally

upsetting; they seriously prevent the mind from contemplating divine things, praising God, and praying for people, which is what clerics are called to do. So just as commercial enterprises are forbidden to clerics, since they entangle the soul too much, so also are warlike pursuits. 'No man being a soldier to God entangles himself with secular business' [2 Tim. 2.4].

VIII.11

The second reason is special. All holy Orders are ordained for the ministry of the altar in which the passion of Christ is represented sacramentally. 'Until the Lord comes, therefore, every time you eat this bread and drink this cup, you are proclaiming his death' [1 Cor. 11.26]. Their office, then, is not to kill or to shed blood, but rather to be ready to shed their own blood for Christ, to do in deed what they portray at the altar. For this reason legislation has been enacted making those who shed blood, even if they have done so without sin, irregular. Now no one given a duty to perform can lawfully do anything which renders him unfit for the office. It is altogether wrong, then, for clerics to fight in a war, since that is aimed at shedding blood.

VIII.12
HENCE:

i. Prelates ought to resist not only the wolves who bring spiritual death on the flock but also pillagers and oppressors who do physical harm to it. Their arms, however, ought to be spiritual, not material, as Scripture says, 'Our war is not fought with weapons of flesh, but with spiritual weapons' [2 Cor. 10.4]. Such are salutary warnings and solemn pleas and, against the obstinate, sentences of excommunication.

ii. Prelates and clerics may make their presence felt at war, not by taking up arms, but by spiritually helping those who fight on the side of justice, exhorting, absolving them, and giving other like spiritual assistance. Thus in the Old Testament [i.e. Josh. 6.4] the priests were commanded to sound the sacred trumpet in battle. This is why bishops or clerics were first allowed to go to the front. But for any of them to take up arms is an abuse of this permission.

iii. We have said that every power, art or virtue directed towards an end has to prepare those elements useful for the achievement of that end. Now physical wars should be considered by Christian people as directed towards a divine spiritual good as their end, and to this end clerics are called. Accordingly they ought to prepare and urge others to fight in a just war. Clerics are forbidden to fight in war, not because it is a sin, but because it is unbecoming their persons.

iv. Although to wage a just war is meritorious, nevertheless it is wrong for clerics because they are deputed to works of higher merit. The marriage act, for example, can be meritorious, but for those with a vow of virginity it becomes reprehensible since they are committed to a higher good.

CRITIQUE

Serious criticisms have been made of the two sets of answers that Aquinas gives to the questions raised in this Text:

(a) *Is it always a sin to wage war?* A number of modern just-war theorists have argued that: (i) Aquinas' three criteria for a 'just' war are inadequately expounded and (ii) he ignores other vital criteria. Aquinas' first criterion depends upon the 'authority of the sovereign' (VIII.3), but the problems that this form of authority raises are not discussed: 'it means, of course, in a general way, that war must be waged by the person or persons who hold appropriate political authority, but who, in the thirteenth century, such persons might be, was a rather delicate question needing serious discussion. To assume that the "prince" is meant, in a society so abounding with princes and petty rulers that they might from an international point of view be considered rather as private than as public entities, while in fact an emperor did exist, was paying tribute to, or at least acknowledging the existing state of affairs as ideal or acceptable rather than trying to outline a better one' (Joan D. Tooke, *The Just War in Aquinas and Grotius*, p.26). Similarly, the criteria of a 'just cause' and a 'right intention' are only very formally and abstractly set out. They have the additional problem of being tautological, since they already contain the ethical terms 'just' and 'right' in what purport to be requirements for determining whether or not a war is 'just'.

Tautology is also a problem in the following list of criteria for establishing the justice of a war. However, it does have the merit of supplying the additional criteria that are usually considered necessary by modern just-war theorists: 'For a war to be "just" it must (i) have been undertaken by a lawful authority; (ii) have been undertaken for the vindication of an undoubted right that has been certainly infringed; (iii) be a last resort, all peaceful means of settlement having failed; (iv) offer the possibility of good to be achieved outweighing the evils that war would involve; (v) be waged with a reasonable hope of victory for justice; (vi) be waged with right intention; (vii) use methods that are legitimate, i.e. in accordance with man's nature as a rational being, with Christian moral principles and international agreements' (from T.R. Milford (ed), *The Valley of Decision*, British Council of Churches, 1961; for a similar list see Extract 14).

In Aquinas (iii), (iv), (v) and (vii) are notably absent. In the context of nuclear weapons, (iv) and (vii) have obviously become considerably more important than they could have been in the 13th century. But, in terms of (iii), Aquinas shows no awareness of the importance of exhausting peaceful arbitration before going to war (see Extract 14), or even of the importance of determining whether victory is actually possible. Explicit reference to the differences between wars of aggression/offence and wars of defence is absent from both Aquinas and the above list (see Extract 12). Whilst the latter does not answer all the difficulties facing just-war theorists mentioned in the sectional introduction, it is clearly more adequate than Aquinas' account.

(b) *May clerics and bishops engage in warfare?* Aquinas' defence of his position raises many exegetical, ethical and theological problems. Few, today, working in the context of critical biblical scholarship, would support his clerical interpretation of the New Testament quotations – even the Petrine quotations. From the scholarly perspective of Biblical Interpretation, it is notable that Matthew 26.52: for Tertullian meant that Christians should be pacifists (see *above*, pp.259f.); for Augustine that unauthorised private violence was a sin (VII.2); and for Aquinas that the clergy should not participate fully in warfare (VIII.8). Ethically, Tooke argues that, 'Aquinas overwhelmed Christ's simple words with natural law morality' (p.123) and, indeed, as a result of the arguments he used, 'he came extraordinarily near to forbidding Christian participation in warfare completely when he forbade it outright to clerics' (p.171). Certainly if Luther's theological attack on the medieval priest/laity dichotomy is taken seriously, Christian pacifism in some form or, alternatively, the full participation of clergy in warfare, would seem more logical from Aquinas' position. Ironically, Luther accepted neither alternative: he condemned the Pope and his clergy for engaging in warfare and for forgetting their 'spiritual office' (e.g. in *On War Against the Turk*) and supported the right of the state to wage war and to compel its citizens to fight.

TEXT IX
LUTHER
Whether soldiers, too, can be saved

1. *BACKGROUND*

This Text comes from the treatise *Whether Soldiers, too, Can be Saved* of 1526 (from *Luther's Works*, vol 46, Fortress Press, Philadelphia, 1967, trans, Charles M. Jacobs and rev. Robert C. Schulz, pp.96-9, 104-6, 107-11, 115-6 & 130-2). After years of rebellion against feudal Europe, the Peasants War broke out in 1525. A number of reformers, like Thomas Münzer, sided with the peasants and some of the latter appealed to Luther. He responded, at first, with the conciliatory *Admonition to Peace* – urging the princes to take the rebellion seriously and to acknowledge their part in causing it, and urging the peasants to avoid violence and to submit to authority – but then, in May of 1525, he wrote his notoriously violent *Against the Robbing and Murdering Hordes of Peasants*. Shocked by the violence of the peasants and by their insurrection, he urged the rulers to kill the rebellious peasants, 'for rebellion is not just simple murder; it is like a great fire, which attacks and devastates a whole land. Therefore let everyone who can, smite, slay, and stab, secretly or openly, remembering that nothing can be more poisonous, hurtful, or devilish than a rebel. It is just as when one must kill a mad dog...' (*Luther's Works*, vol 46, p.50). The scandal that this created forced him, in July, to write *An Open Letter on the Harsh Book*, attempting to reconcile the views expressed in the two previous works. He was still convinced that the peasants needed suppressing through force, but maintained that this did not excuse the appalling cruelty of the rulers in putting the rebellion down. By 1526, he had considerably modified his tone, but not his attitude towards rebellion, submission to authority or the legitimacy of rulers using force. He wrote this Text in response to a request from Assa von Kram of Wittenberg, who was disturbed about reconciling his Christian faith with his profession as a soldier. The rebellion of the peasants and the radical innovations of the Reformation had opened up afresh the issue of the legitimacy of war. Münzer, and Zwingli in Zurich, took up the sword, whereas the Anabaptists renounced violence altogether as thoroughgoing pacifists. Luther, somewhere between the two, defended the right of rulers to use the sword and to command their subjects to do so and urged the latter to obey.

2.   KEY ISSUES

This Text is concerned with two main moral issues – war and rebellion;

(a) *War*. Luther argues that war and soldiering are basically concerned with punishing wickedness and keeping peace (IX.1 & IX.8). Terrible though they may be, they serve to prevent more terrible things happening (IX.2). Indeed, God actually institutes war as the Old Testament indicates (IX.3 & 6). The seeming contradiction suggested by Matthew 5.39 is to be explained by the fact that, in the Spirit, Christians are subject only to Christ, but, in the body and in so far as their property is concerned, they are subject to worldly rulers and to their commands to fight in war (IX.9: i.e. Luther's classic notion of 'the two kingdoms', *see above*, pp.178–9).

(b) *Rebellion*. Luther thoroughly condemns any attempt to depose rulers except in cases of real insanity (IX.12). The fact that a ruler is a tyrant is no reason for deposing him: he cannot hurt a person's soul (IX.16), his position is highly insecure in society (IX.20-1) and, in any case, it is for God to punish him (IX.19). Luther adds that he does not intend to flatter rulers, since he regards them as much 'subjects' as anyone else (IX.22-3). If, however, one is *certain* that a ruler is wrong, then one must follow God (IX.25).

Finally, Luther considers the question of a soldier's pay and concludes that, provided he is not greedy, he may work for pay and even sell his skills as a soldier to more than one ruler (IX.26).

3.   ETHICAL ARGUMENTS

Luther was more acutely aware of the moral dilemmas created

by war than Aquinas, but he still seemed to regard war as an inevitable concomitant of government. Thus, because individual are always required to obey their ruler, they are, at the same time, necessarily committed to war. Nonetheless, Luther did allow a conscience clause (IX.25). Further, he made a number of implicit (IX.12) and explicit (IX.21) appeals to natural law. IX.8 also illustrates a tendency to consequentialism and to argue about the ethics of war from the ethics of individual behaviour: war is justified from the precedent of the punishment of wrongdoers and the paradigm of individual punishment, in turn, becomes the paradigm of social punishment.

4. BASES OF CHRISTIAN ETHICS

As with Augustine's Text VII, the Bible plays a crucial role in Luther's argument. He justifies war from Old Testament militarism (IX.6), from New Testament figures like John the Baptist and from commands to obey worldly rulers (IX.7). However, his exegesis of John 18.36 seems inverted (IX.6) and his interpretation of Matthew 5.39 stands or falls with his notion of 'the two kingdoms' (IX.9 – see further, pp.192f. *above*). His argument, as a whole, is dominated by his theological conviction that obedience to rulers is demanded by God.

5. SOCIAL DETERMINANTS

Luther's general attitude towards war differed very little from the medieval Catholic position. War was regarded by him as an inevitable punishment at the disposal of rulers for wrongdoing – as, indeed, it was by Aquinas. But his own experiences, as a result of the Peasants War, have also clearly influenced the Text. They had served to convince him that rebellion brings more evils and suffering than even tyranny (IX.2 & 12). Further, he had clearly been stung by the very considerable criticism incurred as a result of writing *Against the Robbing and Murdering Hordes of Peasants*: for many, he was simply 'a friend of the rulers' (IX.22-3). His own upward social mobility may also have had an effect upon his attitudes here (see *above*, p.34). On the other hand, the very fact of the Reformation meant that moral issues, like war, had to be reconsidered afresh, even though Luther's conclusions remained politically conservative.

6. *SOCIAL SIGNIFICANCE*

Luther's church-type response to war had a major influence upon the history of Protestantism. He and other leading reformers ensured that the thoroughgoing pacifism of the Anabaptists remained a minority and sectarian response. Himself protected by the evangelical German rulers, he gave their use of force a new legitimacy and, at the same time, provided them with an important spur to developing German nationalism. The religious, political and, indeed, military power of Rome could be resisted with a clear Christian conscience. Nevertheless, scholars are divided as to how far the atrocities committed by some rulers, in suppressing the peasants in 1525, were influenced by Luther's writings.

FURTHER READING

The primary documents have all been mentioned under Background, except for Luther's *On War Against the Turk* of 1529. Reference should also be made to Text VI. The introductions and notes to these documents in *Luther's Works* vol 46 are an essential secondary source, as well as works on Luther already mentioned in the Introduction and in Section 1.

TEXT IX

LUTHER

Whether soldiers, too, can be saved

IX.1

Now slaying and robbing do not seem to be works of love. A simple man therefore does not think it is a Christian thing to do. In truth, however, even this is a work of love. For example, a good doctor sometimes finds so serious and terrible a sickness that he must amputate or destroy a hand, foot, ear, eye, to save the body. Looking at it from the point of view of the organ that he amputates, he appears to be a cruel and merciless man; but looking at it from the point of view of the body, which the doctor wants to save, he is a fine and true man and does a good and Christian work, as far as the work itself is concerned. In the same way, when I think of a soldier fulfilling his office by punishing the wicked, killing the wicked, and creating so much misery, it seems an un-Christian work completely contrary to Christian love. But when I think of how it protects the good and keeps and preserves wife and child, house and farm, property, and honour and peace, then I see how precious and godly this work is; and I observe that it amputates a leg or a hand, so that the whole body may not perish. For if the sword were not on guard to preserve peace, everything in the world would be ruined because of lack of peace. Therefore, such a war is only a very brief lack of peace that prevents an everlasting and immeasurable lack of peace, a small misfortune that prevents a great misfortune.

IX.2

What men write about war, saying that it is a great plague, is all true. But they should also consider how great the plague is that war prevents. If people were good and wanted to keep peace, war would be the greatest plague on earth. But what are you going to do about the fact that people will not keep the peace, but rob, steal, kill, outrage women and children, and take away property and honour? The small lack of peace called war or the sword must set a limit to this universal, worldwide lack of peace which would destroy everyone.

IX.3

This is why God honours the sword so highly that he says that he himself has instituted it (Rom. 13.1) and does not want men to say or think that they have invented it or instituted it. For the hand that wields this sword and kills with it is not man's hand, but God's; and it is not man, but God, who hangs, tortures, beheads, kills, and fights. All these are God's works and judgments.

IX.4

To sum it up, we must, in thinking about a soldier's office, not concentrate on the killing, burning, striking, hitting, seizing, etc.

This is what children with their limited and restricted vision see when they regard a doctor as a sawbones who amputates but do not see that he does this only to save the whole body. So, too, we must look at the office of the soldier, or the sword, with the eyes of an adult and see why this office slays and acts so cruelly. Then it will prove itself to be an office which, in itself, is godly and as needful and useful to the world as eating and drinking or any other work.

IX.5

There are some who abuse this office, and strike and kill people needlessly simply because they want to. But that is the fault of the persons, not of the office, for where is there an office or a work or anything else so good that self-willed, wicked people do not abuse it? They are like mad physicians who would needlessly amputate a healthy hand just because they wanted to. Indeed, they themselves are a part of that universal lack of peace which must be prevented by just wars and the sword and be forced into peace. It always happens and always has happened that those who begin war unnecessarily are beaten. Ultimately, they cannot escape God's judgment and sword. In the end God's justice finds them and strikes, as happened to the peasants in the revolt.

IX.6

As proof, I quote John the Baptist, who, except for Christ, was the greatest teacher and preacher of all. When soldiers came to him and asked what they should do, he did not condemn their office or advise them to stop doing their work; rather, according to Luke 3 [.14], he approved it by saying, 'Rob no one by violence or by false accusation, and be content with your wages'. Thus he praised the military profession, but at the same time he forbade its abuse. Now the abuse does not affect the office. When Christ stood before Pilate he admitted that war was not wrong when he said, 'If my kingship were of this world, then my servants would fight that I might not be handed over to the Jews' (John 18.36). Here, too, belong all the stories of war in the Old Testament, the stories of Abraham, Moses, Joshua, the Judges, Samuel, David, and all the kings of Israel. If the waging of war and the military profession were in themselves wrong and displeasing to

God, we should have to condemn Abraham, Moses, Joshua, David, and all the rest of the holy fathers, kings, and princes, who served God as soldiers and are highly praised in Scripture because of this service, as all of us who have read even a little in Holy Scripture know well, and there is no need to offer further proof of it here.

IX.7

Perhaps someone will now say that the holy fathers were in a different position because God had set them apart from the other nations by choosing them as his people, and had commanded them to fight, and that their example is therefore not relevant for a Christian under the New Testament because they had God's command and fought in obedience to God, while we have no command to fight, but rather to suffer, endure, and renounce everything. This objection is answered clearly enough by St Peter and St Paul, who both command obedience to worldly ordinances and to the commandments of worldly rulers even under the New Testament [Rom. 13.1-4; 1 Pet. 2.13-14]. And we have already pointed out that St John the Baptist instructed soldiers as a Christian teacher and in a Christian manner and permitted them to remain soldiers, enjoining them only not to use their position to abuse people or to treat them unjustly, and to be satisfied with their wages. Therefore even under the New Testament the sword is established by God's word and commandment, and those who use it properly and fight obediently serve God and are obedient to his word.

IX.8

Just think now! If we gave in on this point and admitted that war was wrong in itself, then we would have to give in on all other points and allow that the use of the sword was entirely wrong. For if it is wrong to use a sword in war, it is also wrong to use a sword to punish evildoers or to keep the peace. Briefly, every use of the sword would have to be wrong. For what is just war but the punishment of evildoers and the maintenance of peace? If one punishes a thief or a murderer or an adulterer, that is punishment inflicted on a single evildoer; but in a just war a whole crowd of evildoers, who are doing harm in proportion to the size of the crowd, are punished at once. If, therefore, one work of the sword is good and right, they are all good and right, for the sword is a sword and not a foxtail with which to tickle people. Romans 13 [.4] calls the sword 'the wrath of God'.

IX.9

As for the objection that Christians have not been commanded to fight and that these examples are not enough, especially because Christ teaches us not to resist evil but rather suffer all things [Matt. 5.39-42], I have already said all that needs to be said on this matter in my book *Temporal Authority*. Indeed, Christians do not fight and have no worldly rulers among them. Their government is a spiritual government, and, according to the Spirit, they are subjects of no one but Christ. Nevertheless, as far as body and property are concerned, they are subject to worldly rulers and owe them obedience. If worldly rulers call upon them to fight, then they ought to and must fight and be obedient, not as Christians, but as members of the state and obedient subjects. Christians therefore do not fight as individuals or for their own benefit, but as obedient servants of the authorities under whom they live. This is what St Paul wrote to Titus when he said that Christians should obey the authorities [Titus 3.1]. You may read more about this in my book *Temporal Authority*.

IX.10

That is the sum and substance of it. The office of the sword is in itself right and is a divine and useful ordinance, which God does not want us to despise, but to fear, honour, and obey, under penalty of punishments as St Paul says in Romans 13 [.1-5]...

IX.11

Suppose that a people would rise up today or tomorrow and depose their lord or kill him. That certainly could happen if God decrees that it should, and the lords must expect it. But that does not mean that it is right and just for the people to do it. I have never known of a case in which this was a just action, and even now I cannot imagine any. The peasants who rebelled claimed that the lords would not allow the gospel to be preached and that they robbed the poor people and, therefore, the lords

had to be overthrown. I answered this by saying that although
the lords did wrong in this, it would not therefore be just or right
to do wrong in return, that is, to be disobedient and destroy
God's ordinance, which is not ours to do. On the contrary, we
ought to suffer wrong, and if a prince or lord will not tolerate the
gospel, then we ought to go into another realm where the gospel
is preached – as Christ says in Matthew 10 [.23] 'When they
persecute you in one town, flee to the next'.

IX.12

It is only right that if a prince, king, or lord becomes insane, he
should be deposed and put under restraint, for he is not to be
considered a man since his reason is gone. 'That is true,' you
say, 'and a raving tyrant is also insane; he is to be considered as
even worse than an insane man, for he does much more harm.'
It will be a little difficult for me to respond to that statement, for
that argument seems very impressive and seems to be in
agreement with justice and equity. Nevertheless, it is my opinion
that madmen and tyrants are not the same. A madman can
neither do nor tolerate anything reasonable, and there is no hope
for him because the light of reason has gone out. A tyrant,
however, may do things that are far worse than the insane man
does, but he still knows that he is doing wrong. He still has a
conscience and his faculties. There is also hope that he may
improve and permit someone to talk to him and instruct him
and follow this advice. We can never hope that an insane man
will do this for he is like a clod or a stone. Furthermore, such
conduct has bad results or sets a bad example. If it is considered
right to murder or depose tyrants, the practice spreads and it
becomes a commonplace thing arbitrarily to call men tyrants
who are not tyrants, and even to kill them if the mob takes a
notion to do so. The history of the Roman people shows us how
this can happen. They killed many a fine emperor simply because
they did not like him or he did not do what they wanted, that is,
let them be lords and make him their fool. This happened to
Galba, Pertinax, Gordian, Alexander, and others.

IX.13

We dare not encourage the mob very much. It goes mad too

quickly; and it is better to take ten *ells* from it than to allow it a handsbreadth, or even a fingersbreadth in such a case. And it is better for the tyrants to wrong them a hundred times than for the mob to treat the tyrant unjustly but once. If injustice is to be suffered, then it is better for subjects to suffer it from their rulers than for the rulers to suffer it from their subjects. The mob neither has any moderation nor even knows what moderation is. And every person in it has more than five tyrants hiding in him. Now it is better to suffer wrong from one tyrant, that is, from the ruler, than from unnumbered tyrants, that is, from the mob...

IX.14

My reason for saying this is that God says, 'Vengeance is mine, I will repay' [Rom. 12.19]. He also says, 'Judge not' (Matt. 7.1). And the Old Testament strictly and frequently forbids cursing rulers or speaking evil about them. Exodus [22.28] says, 'You shall not curse the prince of your people.' Paul, in 1 Timothy 2 [.1-2], teaches Christians to pray for their rulers, etc. Solomon in Proverbs and Ecclesiastes repeatedly teaches us to obey the king and be subject to him. Now no one can deny that when subjects set themselves against their rulers, they avenge themselves and make themselves judges. This is not only against the ordinance and command of God, who reserves to himself the authority to pass judgment and administer punishment in these matters, but such actions are also contrary to all natural law and justice. This is the meaning of the proverbs, 'No man ought to judge his own case,' and, 'The man who hits back is in the wrong.'

IX.15

Now perhaps you will say, 'How can anyone possibly endure all the injustice that these tyrants inflict on us? You allow them too much opportunity to be unjust, and thus your teaching only makes them worse and worse. Are we supposed to permit everyone's wife and child, body and property to be so shamefully treated and always to be in danger? If we have to live under these conditions, how can we ever begin to live a decent life?' My reply is this: My teaching is not intended for people like you who want to do whatever you think is good and will please you.

Go ahead! Do whatever you want! Kill all your lords! See what good it does you! My teaching is intended only for those who would like to do what is right. To these I say that rulers are not to be opposed with violence and rebellion, as the Romans, the Greeks, the Swiss, and the Danes have done; rather, there are other ways of dealing with them.

IX.16
In the first place, if you see that the rulers think so little of their soul's salvation that they rage and do wrong, what does it matter to you if they ruin your property, body, wife, and child? They cannot hurt your soul, and they do themselves more harm than they do you because they damn their own souls and that must result in the ruin of body and property. Do you think that you are not already sufficiently avenged?

IX.17
In the second place, what would you do if your rulers were at war and not only your goods and wives and children, but you yourself were broken, imprisoned, burned, and killed for your lord's sake? Would you slay your lord for that reason? Think of all the good people that Emperor Maximilian lost in the wars that he waged in his lifetime. No one did anything to him because of it. And yet, if he had destroyed them by tyranny no more cruel deed would ever have been heard of. Nevertheless, he was the cause of their death, for they were killed for his sake. What is the difference, then, between such a raging tyrant and a dangerous war as far as the many good and innocent people who perish in it are concerned? Indeed, a wicked tyrant is more tolerable than a bad war, as you must admit from your own reason and experience.

IX.18
I can easily believe that you would like to have peace and good times, but suppose God prevents this by war or tyrants! Now, make up your mind whether you would rather have war or tyrants, for you are guilty enough to have deserved both from God. However, we are the kind of people who want to be scoundrels and live in sin and yet we want to avoid the punishment of sin,

and even resist punishment and defend our skin. We shall have about as much success at that as a dog has when he tries to bite through steel.

IX.19

In the third place, if the rulers are wicked, what of it? God is still around, and he has fire, water, iron, stone, and countless ways of killing. How quickly he can kill a tyrant! He would do it, too, but our sins do not permit it, for he says in Job [34.30], 'He permits a knave to rule because of the people's sins.' We have no trouble seeing that a scoundrel is ruling. However, no one wants to see that he is ruling not because he is a scoundrel, but because of the people's sin. The people do not look at their own sin; they think that the tyrant rules because he is such a scoundrel – that is how blind, perverse, and mad the world is! That is why things happened the way they did when the peasants revolted. They wanted to punish the sins of the rulers, as though they themselves were pure and guiltless; therefore God had to show them the log in their eye so they would forget about the speck in another man's eye [Matt. 7.3-5].

IX.20

In the fourth place, the tyrants run the risk that, by God's decree, their subjects may rise up, as has been said, and kill them or expel them. For here we are giving instruction to those who want to do what is right, and they are very few. The great multitude remain heathen, godless, and un-Christian; and these, if God so decrees, wrongfully rise up against the rulers and create disaster, as the Jews and Greeks and Romans often did. Therefore you have no right to complain that our doctrine gives the tyrants and rulers security to do evil; on the contrary, they are certainly not secure. We teach, to be sure, that they ought to be secure, whether they do good or evil. However, we can neither give them this security nor guarantee it for them, for we cannot compel the multitude to follow our teaching if God does not give us grace. We teach what we will, and the world does what it wills. God must help, and we must teach those who are willing to do what is good and right so that they may help hold the multitude in check. The lords are just as secure because of our teaching as they would be without it. Unfortunately, your complaint is unnecessary, since most of the crowd does not listen to us. The preservation of the rulers whom God has appointed is a matter that rests with God and in his hands alone. We experienced this in the peasants' rebellion. Therefore do not be misled by the wickedness of the rulers; their punishment and disaster are nearer than you might wish. Dionysius, the tyrant of Syracuse, confessed that his life was like the life of a man over whose head a sword hung by a silken thread and under whom a glowing fire was burning.

IX.21

In the fifth place, God has still another way to punish rulers, so that there is no need for you to avenge yourselves. He can raise up foreign rulers, as he raised up the Goths against the Romans, the Assyrians against the Jews, etc. Thus there is vengeance, punishment, and danger enough hanging over tyrants and rulers, and God does not allow them to be wicked and have peace and joy. He is right behind them; indeed, he surrounds them and has them between spurs and under bridle. This also agrees with the natural law that Christ teaches in Matthew 7 [.12], 'Whatever you wish that men would do to you, do so to them.' Obviously, no father would want his own family to drive him out of the house, kill him, or ruin him because he had done things that were wrong, especially if his family did it maliciously and used force to avenge themselves without previously having brought charges against him before a higher authority. It ought to be just as wrong for any subject to treat his tyrant in such a way...

IX.22

At this point I shall have to pause and listen to my critics, who cry, 'See here, in my opinion you are flattering the princes. Are you now creeping to the cross and seeking pardon? Are you afraid? etc.' I just let these bumblebees buzz and fly away. If anyone can do better, let him. I have not undertaken here to preach to the princes and lords. I think, too, that they will not be very happy to receive this flattery and that I will not have ingratiated myself with them, because it jeopardises their whole class, as you have heard. Besides, I have said often enough elsewhere, and it is all too true, that the majority of the princes and lords are godless tyrants and enemies of God, who persecute the gospel. They are my ungracious lords and sirs, and I am not very concerned about that. But I do teach that everyone should know how to conduct himself in this matter of how he ought to act toward his overlord, and should do what God has commanded him. Let the lords look out for themselves and stand on their own feet. God will not forget the tyrants and men of high rank. God is able to deal with them, and he has done so since the beginning of the world.

IX.23

Moreover, I do not want anyone to think that what I have written here applies only to peasants, as though they were the only ones of lower rank and the nobles were not also subjects. Not at all! What I say about 'subjects' is intended for peasants, citizens of the cities, nobles, counts, and princes as well. For all of these have overlords and are the subjects of someone else. A rebellious noble, count, or prince should have his head cut off the same as a rebellious peasant. The one should be treated like the other, and no one will be treated unjustly...

IX.24

A question: 'Suppose my lord were wrong in going to war.' I reply: If you know for sure that he is wrong, then you should fear God rather than men, Acts [5:29], and you should neither fight nor serve, for you cannot have a good conscience before God. 'Oh, no,' you say, 'my lord would force me to do it; he would take away my fief and would not give me my money, pay, and wages. Besides, I would be despised and put to shame as a coward, even worse, as a man who did not keep his word and deserted his lord in need.' I answer: You must take that risk and, with God's help, let whatever happens, happen. He can restore it to you a hundredfold, as he promises in the gospel, 'Whoever, leaves house, farm, wife, and property, will receive a hundredfold', etc. [Matt. 19.29].

IX.25

In every other occupation we are also exposed to the danger that the rulers will compel us to act wrongly; but since God will have us leave even father and mother for his sake, we must certainly leave lords for his sake. But if you do not know, or cannot find out, whether your lord is wrong, you ought not to weaken certain obedience for the sake of an uncertain justice; rather you should think the best of your lord, as is the way of love, for 'love believes all things' and 'does not think evil', 1 Corinthians 13 [.7]. So, then, you are secure and walk well before God. If they put you to shame or call you disloyal, it is better for God to call you loyal and honourable than for the world to call you loyal and honourable. What good would it do you if the world thought of you as a Solomon or a Moses, and in God's judgment you were considered as bad as Saul or Ahab?

IX.26

The (next) question: 'Can a soldier obligate himself to serve more than one lord and take wages or salary from each?' Answer: I said above that greed is wrong, whether in a good or an evil occupation. Agriculture is certainly one of the best occupations; nonetheless, a greedy farmer is wrong and is condemned before God. So in this case to take wages is just and right, and to serve for wages is also right. But greed is not right, even though the wages for the whole year were less than a *gulden*. Again, to take wages and serve for them is right in itself; it does not matter whether the wages come from one, or two, or three, or however many lords, so long as your hereditary lord or prince is not deprived of what is due him and your service to others is rendered with his will and consent. A craftsman may sell his skill to anyone who will have it, and thus serve the one to whom he sells it, so long as this is not against his ruler and his community. In the same way a soldier has his skill in fighting from God and can use it in the service of whoever desires to have it, exactly as though his skill were an art of trade, and he can take pay for it as he would for his work. For the soldier's vocation also springs from the law of love. If anyone needs me and calls for me, I am at his service, and for this I take my wage or whatever is given me.

This is what St Paul says in 1 Corinthians 9 [.7]. 'Who serves as a soldier at his own expense?' Thereby Paul approves the soldier's right to his salary. If a prince needs and requires another's subject for fighting, the subject, with his own prince's consent and knowledge, may serve and take pay for it.

CRITIQUE

Perhaps of all Luther's writings, those on war and rebellion have been subjected to some of the most severe criticism (his views on the Jews in Text XV did not receive the same publicity when published):

(a) *War.* Luther showed none of the abstractness of Aquinas on war. His writings show that he was well aware of some of the moral dilemmas and the suffering that war brings, particularly to non-combatants, women and children (IX.2). Nonetheless, he articulated none of the safeguards that Aquinas and, before him, Augustine, maintained in a just-war theory. If, in the light of modern warfare, Aquinas' theory is judged deficient, then Luther's writings must be judged to be even more deficient. Rulers were, indeed, warned of God's judgment (IX.19) and of the social insecurity of their position (IX.20-1), but they were given little advice on how they were to determine whether or not it would be right to wage war. On the other hand, individual conscience was allowed very clearly (IX.25) and Luther did attempt to come to terms with Matthew 5.39 (although many today might reject his exegesis). Again, the professional soldier fighting for more than one ruler, was left with few guidelines, other than a prescription against greed (IX.26). Few medieval scholastics approved of mercenaries (see Frederick H. Russell, *The Just War in the Middle Ages*, p.277), but Luther, superficially at least, appeared to give them a degree of legitimation.

(b) *Rebellion.* It is interesting to debate how far a Lutheran like Bonhoeffer actually adhered to Luther's requirement that only insanity allowed one to depose a ruler. Did he regard Hitler as insane when he became involved in his attempted assassination, or did he reject Luther at this point? There is obviously no way of answering this question. In any case, it highlights the difficulty of following Luther literally – a difficulty that is particularly poignant in the social context of Bonino (Extract 16) or Miranda (Extract 11). Even though Luther did not intend to flatter rulers (IX.22-3), his position did require subjects to be remarkably subservient to them – dangerously subservient, as many might feel today.

EXTRACTS 12-16
WELTY, RAMSEY, AMERICAN BISHOPS, HAUERWAS AND BONINO

1. BACKGROUND

Ebehard Welty's Extract 12 comes from *A Handbook of Christian Social Ethics*, vol 2 (Nelson, 1963, pp.408-15 & 417-21, trans. Gregor Kirstein and rev. John Fitzsimons). Paul Ramsey's Extract 13 comes from *Who Speaks for the Church? A Critique of the 1966 Geneva Conference on Church and Society* (Abingdon, 1967, pp.113-16 & 152-7). The US Catholic Bishops' Extract 14 comes from *The Challenge of Peace: God's Promise and Our Response: A Pastoral Letter on War and Peace* (National Conference of Catholic Bishops, Washington DC, and CTS/SPCK, May 3 1983, paras. 85-121, 331-3 & 338-9). Stanley Hauerwas' Extract 15 comes from 'Pacifism: Some Philosophical Considerations', *Faith and Philosophy* (vol 2, no 2, April 1985, pp.99-104). And José Míguez Bonino's Extract 16 comes from his *Revolutionary Theology Comes of Age* (SPCK, 1975, pp.107-9, 110-12, 112-14 & 114-18; American title, *Doing Theology in a Revolutionary Situation*, Fortress, 1975).

The Dominican Welty's *Handbook* was published originally in Freiburg in two volumes, with the title *Herders Sozialkatechismus: Grundfragen und Grundräfte des sozialen Lebens* in 1952 (hence the focus given to Pius XII). It expresses clearly a traditionalist Roman Catholic approach to moral issues. Frequent use is made of papal pronouncements in the *Handbook* and Welty explains that, 'the quotations from papal documents are intended primarily as verifications of the actual answers given'. However, he also explains that, 'the use of the term "Handbook" does not imply that it is authoritative, but rather refers to the method of question and answer that has been used' (p.xvi). Paul Ramsey (1913-88) wrote *Who Speaks for the Church?* as a direct result of being an observer at the 1966 WCC Conference on Church and Society in Geneva at a time of considerable political ferment. He was then Harrington Spear Paine Professor of Religion at Princeton University – serving in the faculty from 1944 until his retirement in 1982. Amongst his many books were *Basic Christian Ethics, Nine Modern Moralists* and *Deeds and Rules in Christian Ethics*. A much more radical stance is taken by the US Catholic Bishops in their now famous Pastoral Letter on War and Peace. They followed this letter in 1986 with *Economic Justice for All: A Pastoral Letter on Catholic Social Teaching and the US Economy*, and in 1988 with *Building Peace: A Pastoral Reflection on the Response to The Challenge of Peace*. Stanley Hauerwas, a Methodist layperson and professor of theology at Duke University, is one of the most prolific writers in Christian ethics today. Amongst his many books are *Vision and Virtue* (1974), *Character and Christian Life* (1975), *A Community of Character* (1981), *The Peaceable Kingdom* (1983), *Against the Nations* (1985), *Suffering Presence* (1986), *Resident Aliens* (1989), *Naming the Silences* (1990) and *After Christendom* (1991). Bonino, an Argentinean Methodist, presents a radical alternative from the perspective of Liberation theology. He was, until 1985, Dean of Postgraduate Studies of the Higher Evangelical Institute for Theological Studies in Buenos Aires.

2. *KEY ISSUES*

Welty responds to three questions in a style very reminiscent of the scholastic method adopted by Aquinas in *Summa Theologica*: (i) Is war of aggression lawful? He maintains that it never is (12.1), but admits that it may be difficult to decide whether or not a particular war is a war of aggression or of defence: it is not even necessarily the State which opens hostilities that is the aggressor (12.3). The destructiveness of modern wars presents particular moral problems (12.5), as do the use of nuclear weapons as deterrents (12.8-11). (ii) Is defensive war lawful? For Welty, self-defence of both the individual and the State are legitimate, on condition that just-war criteria are applied (12.12-15). However, this does not justify preventive wars (12.16) or ruthless destruction (12.17). (iii) Can a war of liberation be permissible? He maintains that it can be in the instance of individual nations unjustly occupied and ruled by another (12.20-1). In the instance of world imperialism, a war of liberation may also be legitimate (12.26), but only if there is a prospect of defeating this imperialism (12.28). However, the appalling sacrifice of life involved in such a war raises serious moral problems (12.29-31).

Ramsey criticises the position of the Christian ethicist Helmut Gollwitzer – then influential in the World Council of Churches. He argues that Gollwitzer's nuclear pacifism risks turning the Church into a sect (13.1-2) and that in effect it destroys deterrence (13.4). Nuclear deterrence depends upon a credible belief that one might actually use a nuclear weapon (13.5). If using such weapons is inherently evil, then threatening to use them is also evil and, thus, deterrence based upon them is also evil (13.7). Ramsey believes that it is not the Church's business to be recommending or condemning such specific policies (13.7-9). Churches should be concerned with general perspective not with specific policies – churches are neither politicians nor magistrates (13.10-12). There is a danger of churches attempting to build up a consensus established through position papers on particular policies – a misleading approach for churches (13.14-15). Instead Protestant Churches ought constantly to re-examine all ecclesiastical pronouncements (13.16). Churches need to be reminded that they are communities in which anyone may have something significant to say even against a prevailing consensus (13.9). There is a need for order and responsible political power without churches attempting to dictate specific political policies (13.22-5).

The US Bishops argue that nuclear weapons present very serious problems for traditional just-war theory and emphasise the urgent need for peacemaking. Within just-war theory, the notion of 'competent authority' is considerably complicated both by American politics and by revolutionary situations (14.4-6). The notion of 'comparative justice' stresses that no nation has 'absolute justice' on its side – modern propaganda makes this particularly problematic (14.8-10). 'Right intention' and 'last resort' also present problems in a nuclear age (14.11-13), as do notions of 'probability of success' and 'proportionality' (14.14-16). Justice within warfare (*ius in bello*) demands a specific concern for both 'proportionality' and 'discrimination'. Both of these are problematic in a nuclear age – even though 'conventional' weapons are also deeply destructive (14.17-21). The nuclear arms race raises especial problems – e.g. exorbitant costs, increasing insecurity, possibility of accidents, destruction of non-combatants, etc. (14.22-6). In view of all of this, the Bishops stress the value of non-violence, relating this to the teaching of Jesus, Justin, Cyprian, Francis of Assisi and others (14.27-33). They reaffirm Vatican II's call for the legal protection of conscientious objection and a presumption against the use of force as a means of settling disputes (14.34-6). Finally they stress their own role as pastors not politicians, whilst still believing that their country is wrong to be producing ever more destructive weapons (14.38-9): for them peacemaking is a requirement of faith in Christ (14.40-2).

Even though his paper addresses an audience of (Christian) philosophers, Stanley Hauerwas insists that Christian non-resistance is essentially a theological position, based upon a belief that God wills to rule creation not through violence and coercion but by love (15.1-3). Hauerwas does use the term 'pacifism', albeit reluctantly and stressing its theological roots (15.4). Examining the criticism that pacifists abandon their responsibility to care and protect their neighbours, he argues instead that Christians are obliged to love both those attacked and their attackers (15.5-6). He criticises just-war theories based upon individual analogies of protecting the innocent (15.7-9) and stresses that pacifism is a commitment to a way of living close to an ethic of virtue (15.10-13). However much this might disturb philosophers, for Hauerwas pacifism is not based upon some general truth about humanity, but rather upon a particulatistic belief in Jesus' Kingdom of God (15.15-19). Finally he rejects a notion which regards violence as an essential part of a state (15.20-1).

Liberation theology, reflected here in Bonino, has often been criticised in the West for its tacit, and sometimes explicit, support of violence in the cause of political revolution. In fact, Liberation theologians are themselves as divided as other Christians in their preparedness to sanction the use of violence (although all tend to point out that violence is already inherent in governments of oppression). Bonino's discussion of 'love' and 'peace' forms a particularly striking contrast to the other Extracts. He begins by claiming that Marxist theory is often misunderstood by Christians, who tend to see it as too materialistic and ignore the fact that the biblical understanding of humanity is materialistic (16.1-2). He sees an affinity between the Marxist concept of alienation and the Pauline dichotomy between works and faith (16.3): the biblical concept of 'the poor' is also illuminated by Marxism, although the latter's concept of the proletarian class is scientific and theoretical, whereas the former's is not (16.4-5). Further, 'love' in the New Testament is inextricably connected with socio-structural concepts (16.6). Peace can be understood in two ways. In the first, it is related to a conviction that the universe is rational and ordered and that violence threatens to disturb a divinely appointed order and, in the second, it is set in the context of humanity as liberator and creator, who must use some violence against the status quo (16.7-9). For the first, peace is seen as order and lack of conflict, whereas, for the second, peace is dynamic and prophetic and sometimes necessitates conflict (16.10). The biblical notion is less concerned with abstract principles than with God's concrete acts and commands, wherein violence appears as a breaking out of unfree and unliberated conditions (16.11-12). This whole understanding must be related to the new humanity made known in Jesus Christ (16.13).

3. ETHICAL ARGUMENTS

Both Welty and Ramsey stand firmly within a deontological just-war position. However, there is also considerable evidence of pragmatism and consequential types of ethical argument in Welty – international tribunals are to be used as moral arbiters (12.3), the dimensions of modern warfare are considered to affect their morality (12.5), the risks of nuclear weapons are assessed consequentially (12.8) and, above all, the prospect of successful victory is treated as a central and essential criterion of a just war (12.12, 18, 28 & 30-1). Ramsey, in contrast, is suspicious of attempts to establish theological consensus (13.14) and reminds churches of the significance of lone voices of protest (13.19).

The US Bishops, Hauerwas and Bonino all demonstrate basic

deontological commitments – the first to non-violence (though not necessarily, in all of its members, to thoroughgoing pacifism), the second to a radical understanding of the Kingdom of God in the teaching of Jesus, and the third to the poor and oppressed. Clearly, Bonino shares the same basic commitment as Miranda in Extract 11 – 'solidarity with the poor' (16.5). Even his relatively impartial analysis of the two concepts of 'peace', links the idea of 'liberation' with that of 'creation' itself.

4. *BASES OF CHRISTIAN ETHICS*

Welty and the US Bishops' dependence upon Roman Catholic tradition is apparent at every point in their arguments, despite the fact that they reach rather different conclusions. Welty's *Handbook* is punctuated throughout with long excerpts from papal pronouncements (as in 12.2., but reduced for brevity elsewhere in this Extract), yet with comparatively few biblical references (e.g. 12.13). The US Bishops, in contrast, conclude with a long quotation from Revelation 21 (again omitted here for brevity) and punctuate their arguments with both biblical and papal quotations.

The writings of both Ramsey and Hauerwas frequently contain biblical exegesis – although the two Extracts here might suggest otherwise if taken in isolation. Although their stances on war are radically opposed, they share a Reformed suspicion of ecclesiastical consensus. If Ramsey was deeply at odds with many other theologians in his support of Vietnam, Hauerwas' radical Christian pacifism has continued to separate him from many other Christian ethicists.

Bonino too tends to be critical in his citation of tradition – for example, in his analysis of the two theological understandings of 'peace' (16.10). Even his direct quotation from Barth – important as it undoubtedly was in the light of Barth's personal commitment to socialism – is selective. In Barth there was a much stronger sense of obedience to appointed powers (see Extract 6). However, as in Miranda, it is the Bible that is the basic authority in Bonino. Both men believe that a correlation can be made between certain fundamental Marxist concepts and biblical concepts. Miranda seeks to achieve this correlation by a detailed citation of particular biblical texts, whereas Bonino tends, rather, to refer to general biblical notions, such as that of the Kingdom of God (16.6 & 11) and that of poverty (16.4).

5. SOCIAL DETERMINANTS

Welty and Ramsey conform to church-type responses to war. Welty's *Handbook* is concerned throughout to accord with traditional Roman Catholic teaching (as his frequent citation of papal pronouncements indicates). And, despite its radically Protestant stance, Ramsey's *Who Speaks for the Church?* has frequently been cited by those opposing direct political involvement by churches. In contrast, Hauerwas has on several occasions been accused of 'sectarianism' (a charge which he strenuously resists). His radical rejection of a 'common rationality', his 'particularistic' stress upon Christian communities in forming Christian virtues (15.19), and even his phrase 'resident aliens' depicting Christians in the modern world, have all been cited as evidence of his sectarianism.

Although seldom depicted as 'sectarian', the US Catholic Bishops caused a considerable stir with their Pastoral Letters. Critics argued that they had been too influenced by their social context in the United States, pointing out that several of the Bishops had in the 1960s been actively involved in peace protests. The politico-economic frustrations of South America are also evident in Bonino (see *above*, pp.203f.). Bonino's position is somewhat ambiguous, reflecting some of the tensions on this issue present in the movement.

6. SOCIAL SIGNIFICANCE

Several of the Extracts in this Section can claim to be highly influential. *The Challenge of Peace* was discussed very widely indeed in the 1980s. Writing in 1988 the Bishops reported that: 'in dioceses and parishes, the letter launched an unprecedented process of prayer, preaching, education, reflection, discussion and action... In many of our schools, colleges and universities the message of the letter has been integrated into courses, conferences and curricula. In secular colleges and universities, in research institutes and in the specialised literature on nuclear issues, *The Challenge of Peace* is used on a frequent basis' (*Building Peace*, p.4). It has already been noted that Ramsey's *Who Speaks for the Church?* has also been widely cited within churches. Since the death of Paul Ramsey, Stanley Hauerwas has become one of the most widely cited Christian ethicists in the United States. However, neither of them can claim the sort of political influence of Reinhold Niebuhr – indeed, Hauerwas' radically theological stance probably precludes such influence.

FURTHER READING

An extensive literature has analysed *The Challenge of Peace*, including the following: Philip J. Murnion (ed), *Catholics and Nuclear War: A Commentary on The Challenge of Peace*; Judith A. Dwyer (ed), *The Catholic Bishops and Nuclear War: A Critique and Analysis of the Pastoral The Challenge of Peace*; Dean C. Curry (ed), *Evangelicals and the Bishops' Pastoral Letter*. Liberation theology is still developing, but the readers edited by Alistair Kee, *A Reader in Political Theology* and *The Scope of Political Theology*, are useful guides to some of the different approaches apparent within it. However, his *Marx and the Failure of Liberation Theology* is a major critique of the same theology.

EXTRACT 12

WELTY

Wars of aggression and defence

Is war of aggression lawful?

12.1

'War of aggression, no matter on what grounds it is waged, today must be considered immoral and be rejected.'

12.2

PIUS XII (*C.B.*, 1944: *N.C.W.C.*, pp.10-11).
There is a duty, besides, imposed on all, a duty which brooks no delay, no procrastination, no hesitation, no subterfuge. It is a duty to do everything to ban once and for all wars of aggression as a legitimate solution of international disputes and as a means towards realising national aspirations. Many attempts in this direction have been seen in the past. They have all

failed. And they will all fail always, until the saner section of mankind has the firm determination, the holy obstinacy, like an obligation in conscience, to fulfil the mission which past ages have not undertaken with sufficient gravity and resolution.

If ever a generation has had to appreciate in the depths of its conscience the call: 'war on war', it is certainly the present generation...

Unquestionably the progress of man's inventions, which should have heralded the realisation of greater well-being for all mankind, has instead been employed to destroy all that had been built up through the ages.

But by that very fact the immorality of the war of aggression has been made ever more evident.

12.3

(i.) It is difficult to state exactly which wars should be considered wars of aggression. Wars of aggression are not confined to unjust, wilful attacks, for they may have just causes, such as the infringement or the denial of essential rights. Those who open hostilities cannot in every case be described as the aggressors, for a State or a group of States may be forced into a situation when it has to anticipate the attack of the opponent. It is simplest to consider as a war of aggression one that is declared to be such by an international tribunal. But this definition is strictly speaking of a merely formal nature; it states nothing concerning the true nature of war of aggression. Nevertheless, if the tribunal fulfils all the conditions for a really unbiased and objective judgment, then its decisions must be recognised as valid and be obeyed by all States and by the community of nations. This seems the only practical solution. In view of the new situation today there would seem to be only one way of defining war of aggression; we must proceed from its opposite and say that today every war that is not forced on States or on the community of nations in order to protect themselves and their most sacred rights must be considered one of aggression. Thus we distinguish between the lawful, that is, the just war of defence and the unlawful war of aggression (no matter on what grounds it is fought).

12.4

Most Catholic moralists who have expressed an opinion on the matter agree in unreservedly condemning every modern war of aggression... The greatest difficulty lies in the question whether the so-called 'war of liberation' is to be considered a war of aggression or of defence.

12.5

(ii.) The reasons for the immorality of a war of aggression lie in the essential nature of modern warfare. The convulsions, losses and dangers are out of all proportion to the gain which a war of aggression may achieve. Of special consequence are: i. the terrible sacrifice and destruction on every side caused by weapons of destruction in a modern war; losses among the civilian population, as witness Hiroshima, Dresden, and Korea; the decay of morality; ii. the menace to world peace; every region today even in the most remote corner of the earth lies within the sphere of interest of the few big powers; the most senseless local conflict can easily develop into a world war. Even before an organised community of nations has been formed, the States are obliged in justice and charity to preserve the common good of mankind from being gravely endangered.

12.6
(iii.) With the banning of wars of aggression States and nations are called on not only to refrain from all war of conquest, but even patiently to endure injustice rather than to seek redress by force. For it cannot be maintained that the customary international provocations constitute an extreme case of self-defence which alone may still justify war.

12.7
(iv.) The question whether, and to what extent, modern weapons are controllable or uncontrollable is one of fact that can be answered only by the experts. Scientists are working with success on the production of 'clean' bombs, the effects and after-effects of which could be controlled.

12.8
It is irresponsible and morally wrong to neglect the production of conventional weapons and to restrict rearmament to nuclear weapons 'as a deterrent'; for the risk is that, when nuclear weapons are the only means of defence, States will be compelled to use them in order to repel an attack even by conventional weapons.

12.9
The decisive factor is not the scientific and technical but the 'moral' control. What is to be defended must stand in some relation to the inevitable evil and losses. If the other conditions for waging just war are fulfilled, even unusually great damage can be justified.

12.10
We must distinguish between the moral justification of nuclear war and that of nuclear weapons. It is quite possible that certain types of nuclear weapons may be controllable and hence their employment justified for

reasons of defence and on the conditions already mentioned. But a nuclear war cannot be justified if, and because, it is not restricted to these weapons, but includes the use of all, even uncontrollable, nuclear weapons.

12.11

States are strictly obliged: i. to agree to effective measures of control, that is to allow independent inspection of their own territory for this purpose; ii. to make timely provision for extensive measures of air-raid protection, so that as far as possible the danger to the population may be reduced; according to the latest scientific investigations a very considerable reduction of this danger is possible, though at great financial cost.

Is defensive war lawful?

12.12

'A purely defensive war is lawful even today under the following conditions:

    (i). There must be an unjust, actual attack that cannot otherwise be met.

    (ii). The aggressor must not be harmed more than is necessary.

    (iii). The defence must have a prospect of success, and no higher goods must be jeopardised than those which have to be defended.'

12.13

Catholic moralists are practically unanimous on this issue... The right of self-defence exists not only for the individual, but also for nations and States. For brute force would otherwise be placed above right, and predatory war and armed aggression would have to be regarded as 'just'. In certain circumstances the State is even more obliged to resist than the individual who may be responsible only for his own life and conduct, whereas the State is entrusted with the protection of many individuals and groups, especially families, of goods and values such as justice, tradition, civilisation. Moreover, it ought in the name of God to protect the sanctity of the moral order in the world against injustice and harm (cf. Rom. 13.4).

    The conditions that apply to any just self-defence must be applied correspondingly to defensive war:

12.14

(i.) Defence in the form of armed resistance, which may involve heavy sacrifices in lives and property, is only permissible if an unjust attack is threatening or already in progress, and if all other means have been tried; in short, it must be a case of the ultimate resort.

12.15

What is essential is that the aggressor must be in the wrong, the defender in the right. A State that is attacked because of an injustice which it has itself committed and has not made good, must bow to the justice that is meted out to it. Pius XII expressly stated that there are some human values which would justify a defensive war even today. Such human values are the existence of an ordered political community and man's fundamental rights and liberties and especially Christian faith and morality. Before arms are taken up all other solutions must have been tried. Defensive war is only an *ultima ratio*, a last resort, if neither negotiations nor threats nor the intervention of other powers or of the community of nations are successful. Aggression must be actual; the State must be 'threatened with an unjust aggression, or already its victim' (Pius XII). Like an individual, the State need not wait until it is too late; 'actuality' exists when it is morally certain that the aggressor is making final preparations for an attack and does not desist in spite of sufficient warning; usual indications are troop concentrations; suddenly increased press campaigns which suggests that a fitting cause for war is being invented etc.

12.16

It follows from what has been said that so-called preventive war is not permissible. A preventive war is waged in order to ward off a later, possible, perhaps probable attack. There is reason, or so it is thought, to fear that a State is preparing for war and will in the near future begin the war as soon as a favourable opportunity presents itself.

12.17

(ii.) To defend, to repel, ought not to imply ruthless destruction. Self-defence does not entitle one to ruthless severity. Modern war in itself is hard and cruel enough. The one who has been unjustly attacked must do what he can to end the conflict as quickly as possible and not to inflict more wounds on the opponent than is necessary.

12.18

(iii.) The third condition is that there must be a prospect of success, a solid probability (Pius XII, *C. B.* 1948, *I.U.A.*, p.96) that the defence will succeed in repelling the aggressor. The defenders may not jeopardise higher values in order to save lesser ones. Precisely in the case of a war of defence it is often difficult to foresee success, since the State attacked must often act with the utmost speed...

Can a war of liberation be permissible?

12.19

'If it is of defensive, not of aggressive character, a war of liberation is permissible and perhaps even a duty.' This is one of the most delicate questions in the whole ethics of war. By war of liberation, including what is called war of invasion, is meant one that is undertaken in order to liberate countries from unjust foreign rule or occupation, or from an extremely grave menace. In some cases it may resemble a war of aggression or a preventive war, since it is begun in order to drive out a foreign power, or to prevent it from continuing the menace. Is such a war of liberation to be considered a war of aggression or a preventive war? The question has to be answered; for the totalitarian powers are not only causing widespread confusion by their completely unjust claims and methods, but also material and even worse intellectual and moral misery. May the free world turn the cold into a hot war if there is no other way out than slavery? Two possibilities will be dealt with here:

The liberation of individual nations
12.20
(i.) Let us suppose that a country is unjustly occupied and ruled by another. The occupation may take place in the course of an unjust war or for preventive reasons (for the 'protection of neutrality'); authority is exercised without any consideration for right and justice: terror, suppression of the nation's individuality and self-government, political parties that are subservient to foreign dictators and parties, denial of human rights, suppression of liberty, etc.

12.21
(ii.) Such a situation is clearly unjust; it is a continuous aggression against the nation, its existence, honour and most sacred rights. The methods of such a 'system' or occupation are in fact not different from unjust military attacks. Certainly the principles governing just resistance to the State apply; for this is a matter of foreign interference, of usurpers invading foreign territory and coercing a foreign nation. Therefore it is clearly a case of self-defence against actual, unjust aggression.

12.22
The sense of mutual dependence among the nations ought to support the struggle for liberation of a people subjugated in this manner. The common good of the whole world may be involved; and apart from this there exists an obligation of the nations and states to help.

The war of liberation for peace and freedom in the world
12.23
(i.) Let us suppose that totalitarian power, completely materialist in outlook

and consciously atheistic, in theory and practice professes world imperialism. This great power has such enormous resources in power and so many powerful supporters in satellite States and among its allies and followers in other countries that it constitutes the world danger. Its ideological basis is a ruthless collectivism recognising no human dignity and rights. We are aware that this great power disturbs world peace wherever and whenever it can, and with all its strength is preparing an armed struggle for world domination; that wherever it has established its rule, the people are forcibly robbed of their most sacred rights by oppression and terror; education of youth to atheism; fight against God, Christ and the Church; uniformity of thinking, absence of any legal order and security.

12.24

This great power is at work enslaving other nations (adjoining territories and satellites) or undermining them, for example, by means of fifth columns, political parties influenced and commanded by the financial, intellectual support of the major power in question etc. There are occasional strikes, acts of sabotage, including political murder, and, above all, local wars are unleashed. These wars, as the major power openly admits or by its actions clearly shows, are in reality waged against the community of nations and against the free world; consequently they have the character of acts of aggression against world peace.

12.25

The question now is this: Under these circumstances has the world the right to armed self-defence, to a war of liberation? Or must humanity, that is, all the other nations as a whole, wait until the great power has struck? And if the nations foresee with certainty that due to the inequality of forces they might soon no longer be in a position to defend themselves, ought they to resign themselves to the inevitable fate of defeat later on and the enslavement to follow?

12.26

(ii.) Some consider a war of liberation in these circumstances a defensive war imposed upon the free world and therefore lawful. They argue that since mankind has a natural, God-given right to its existence, fundamental freedoms, to peace and order, it has a right also to protect itself and its most sacred rights in good time against unjust attacks. It may not allow these rights to be flagrantly wrested from it. Unjust aggression by the other side against world peace and the most sacred right of mankind is already taking place with weapons not only of the cold, but also of the hot war; nations are held in subjugation, there is subversion, there are local wars etc.

12.27

This state of affairs has no precedent. The very existence not only of an individual nation but of mankind as a whole is at stake, and the case of self-defence in extreme necessity exists not only when the major armed offensive is already in progress, but already when this major offensive is inevitably approaching and through individual acts has already begun. Failure to act must not be allowed to lead to the loss of all rights. Responsibility for the resulting world war and its victims clearly lies with that great power which systematically aims at the enslavement of the world. In order that this great power should realise its responsibility, and at the same time in order that everything possible may be done to avoid war, we demand that it should first be called upon to desist from its unlawful activities; otherwise the nations as a whole would consider themselves forced to take action. When the official organ of the community of nations has expressed this warning and has forbidden further preparations for war, the great power concerned may, and unless it submits, must be considered and treated as an unjust aggressor. When and where pressure can be exerted and is likely to be successful, it must be used, for example by breaking off diplomatic relations, imposing economic sanctions etc.

12.28

To be permitted such war of liberation too must have prospects of success. Since the good and ill of all humanity is at stake, all States and groups of States are obliged to participate if necessary, and the organised community of nations has undoubtedly the right to impose this obligation. Real interdependence among the nations should form the most effective defence and be most likely to avert such a war of liberation. Power that tends to disrupt can only be kept in check by the threat and the readiness for defence of a bigger power.

12.29

(iii.) Others, in direct opposition to the first opinion, quite definitely deny that a war of liberation of the kind mentioned could be legitimate; they consider it an unlawful war of aggression or a preventive war. They would argue that a war of this kind, an unjust aggression involves the deliberate murder of innumerable innocent persons on both sides. We may never kill or harm for preventive reasons, not even when we fear that we might be attacked at some later time and would not then be strong enough to withstand it. In such a case, there is only one way out, which is to be cautious and to invoke the protection of a higher authority.

12.30

Such a war of liberation cannot compensate for the frightful sacrifices which it entails, and its prospects of success are too slight. In other words, we do not know if the conflict will be brought to a victorious conclusion, and even if it is, then it would be only at the price of proportionately great losses; and finally, what goods and institutions worth defending will the equally dechristianised and materialistic 'liberators' bring in their train?

12.31

The fate of mankind must be entrusted to God in an heroic attitude of endurance and hope. God can so arrange things that the totalitarian power will listen to reason and abandon its aggressive plans, that the situation will in one form or another radically change, that new weapons will be invented which will deter the aggressor from his purpose. In short, it is possible, but not inevitable that the aggression will take place.

EXTRACT 13

RAMSEY

Who speaks for the church?

13.1

In [Helmut] Gollwitzer's view, Christians must so 'unanimously and unconditionally' say No to nuclear war that this brings everything nuclear indiscriminately under condemnation. 'Whoever has recourse to atomic warfare... will have God against him. No government and no individual must make use of this menace [what does this mean for the question of deterrence to which we will come in a moment?], no one must participate in its use. At any rate we Christians... refuse to participate... for we can only do what can be done in the name of Jesus Christ.' This is certainly a position to which many may resort under the anguish of the nuclear dilemma.

13.2

However, Professor Gollwitzer did not see the consequence of this for the Christian church in that it must then become completely a sect in regard to the modern state – selectively no doubt, but not at all selectively in regard to nuclear weapons or in regard to the deterrent state. Instead of saying this forthrightly, he pictured the churches urging their governments 'to regard possession of these weapons as a mandate entrusted to them by the international community of nations;' and many another proposition having to do with 'cooperating with politicians in finding a way out' – even though the Christian has already, presumably, found his way out by renouncing any use of nuclear weapons and even though, presumably, no Christian could be a politician.

13.3

In a compact phrase, Gollwitzer thought of the absolute commitment he called for as the first task, and doing something about the peace based on a precarious balance of deterrence as the second task – both Christian tasks, not contradictions: 'It is only when the church undertakes the first of these tasks that the second task becomes urgent,' he said. 'And it is only if the church undertakes the second of these tasks that its rejection of the use of weapons of mass destruction will be more than an empty phrase, a comfortable ethical attitude which involves no concrete responsibility.' Here still speaks the tradition of the great churches, although in the first place it had been affirmed that, with regard to these modern weapons of war, that tradition was no longer applicable.

13.4

I should say, rather, that if the church undertakes to say this No unanimously and unconditionally, the problem of deterrence will not then become urgent. Instead there will immediately be no more problem of deterrence as at all a problem for Christians. And if politicians with whom we might be still wanting to cooperate in finding a way out really listened to the church, there would immediately be no deterrence and therefore no urgent problem for them; and no moral problem remaining in regard to it for Christians or for politicians, not for one moment after governments came to believe what Gollwitzer wants the church to say in the first place.

13.5

The *actuality* of deterrence depends upon a credible belief, mutually shared, that one might use a nuclear weapon. If the government of one of the great powers were persuaded by the churches never to be willing to use any nuclear weapon under any circumstances, and this were known, there would instantly be no deterrence and therefore no practical problem of finding a way out. Likewise, the *morality* of deterrence depends upon it not being wholly immoral for a government ever to use an atomic weapon under any circumstances. If those who use any nuclears in any way in any war will have God against them, God is against the possession of all these weapons right now for deterrence. It would be inexcusable even to be ambiguous about it, or ambiguous about the use to be made of dual-purpose weapons (upon legitimate military targets or upon cities), or to temporize in dismantling deterrence or to delay resigning from office or withdrawing from helpfully cooperating with politicians, if no use of any nuclear weapon could ever possibly be justified.

13.6

This is the case with regard to anything said to be inherently immoral. To remain conditionally willing or to threaten or to seem to be ready to do an immoral act is of a piece with the immorality of that act itself. No one ever said that an act of adultery is not an evil in addition to the adulterous thought, but we have it on rather high authority that the adulterous thought partakes of the same intrinsic wrong that it may lead to. So with acts of war using a nuclear weapon. If that would be in itself always under any circumstances and in any manner, an evil thing to do to which we must unconditionally say No (let us say, because this would be an act of murder), then threatening to do so would be the same *sort* of evil (though not the same evil), and deterrence rests upon murderous thinking, and this would not for one moment be justifiable. One could not too quickly resign from office after accepting Gollwitzer's verdict; there would be no second task, and no more cooperating with politicians for Christians to undertake. The only thing remaining to be said would be that the 'peace of a sort' which deterrence maintains for the peoples of the world among whom Christians dwell makes our peace also a guilty peace.

13.7

The foregoing has had one purpose only: to point out again, as was done in connection with the Geneva statement on nuclear war, the crucial issues that remain even to be formulated in ecumenical social ethics in dealing with questions of war and peace in the nuclear age. If the statement on nuclear war was meant to say what Gollwitzer said or is understood to say this; if that were the conclusion Christians addressed to the world, in saying so flatly that 'nuclear war is against God's will' (and I believe that it was not), then these issues simply cannot arise as problems for Christians, nor could we have any standing to proffer guidance upon them, or upon many another problem of war and peace in the present age to which we continue to speak. On the other hand, if the statement on nuclear war had not been so seemingly particular and lacking in discrimination concerning the kind of thing that was meant to be condemned, then these issues would have opened up...

13.8

If churchmen want to put an end to the moralism that only confuses political decision, we will need to do more than oppose the personal ethics of

Protestant individualism when made into standards for official conduct. We will also have to put an end to the political ethics of the 'liberal consensus' – built up by a great number of position papers and resolutions on *specific policy decisions* – that attach the labels 'right' or 'wrong,' 'moral' or 'immoral,' to innumerable particular choices of the statesman about which churchmen *as such* know less than he.

13.9
It is not the church's business to recommend but only to clarify the grounds upon which the statesman must put forth his own particular decree. Christian political ethics cannot say what should or must be done but only what may be done. It can only try to make sure that false doctrine does not unnecessarily trammel policy choices or preclude decisions that might better shape and govern events.

13.10
In politics the church is only a *theoretician*. The religious communities as such should be concerned with *perspectives* upon politics, with political doctrine, with the direction and structures of the common life, not with specific directives. They should seek to clarify and keep wide open the legitimate options for choice, and thus nurture the moral and political ethos of the nation. Their task is not the determination of policy. Their special orientation upon politics is, in a sense, an exceedingly limited one; yet an exceedingly important one. Still, in this they need to stand in awe before people called political 'decision makers,' or rather before the majesty of topmost political agency.

13.11
Political decision and action is an image of the majesty of God, who also rules by particular decrees. God says, 'Let there be...;' and his word becomes deed and actuality. So also earthly magistrates have the high and lonely responsibility of declaring what shall actually be done. Allowing for the limitations that surround even the highest magistrate of a great nation, it is still the case that he creatively shapes events by decisions that must be particular decisions going beyond doctrine. He must actualize what is to be from among a number of legitimate choices.

13.12
The majesty of political rulership is that it is always a triumph over doctrine through right doctrine, a victory over generalities through the proper generalities and through the proper direction of policy. Political rulership makes life-giving, or at least actuality-giving, deeds out of words. This does

not mean that the magistrates, or Christians acting as citizens, are always wise. It means only that they are magistrates, which the church is not.

13.13

The religious communities have a less awe-full responsibility; their task is a less- or a non-magisterial one: it is to see to it that the word over which and through which statesmanship or government wins its victory is not an inadequate word. When the churches turn their primary attention to trying to influence particular policy decisions, they do what they ought not to do.

13.14

Churches today are becoming very legalistic about what they regard as a consensus of moral and religious opinion built up by the precedents established through a series of position papers on *particular* policy questions. I think it cannot be denied that these resolutions have exceedingly questionable foundation in either theological ethics or political doctrine. This is Protestant *casuistry*, and its fault is not to be excused by virtue of its exclusion of conservative personal ethics from importation into politics.

13.15

In adopting a casuistry of building up Christian social teachings out of the precedent of past particular decisions, the churches are in danger of leaving undone what they ought to do. They should clarify the ground on which government must rest. They ought to open wide the articulation of structural elements in that human reality which statesmanship must govern and the range of alternatives it is legitimate for statesmen to have in mind as they rule by specific decree. They should inform the ethos and conscience of the nation, and thus aid in forming the conscience of its statesmen.

13.16

Moreover, by doing what they ought not to do and leaving undone what they ought to have done, the churches may well contribute to the formation of particular decisions that ought never to be done. This sometimes happens when previous ecclesiastical pronouncements, themselves too specific, are legalistically cited. Christian political ethics has a contribution to make precisely by keeping open the range of multifactoral principles or objectives that impinge upon a statesman's choices. Surely Protestant Christians, whose consciences are not bound by either pope or church councils, ought to be engaged constantly in going to the theoretical roots in the examination and reexamination of any and all ecclesiastical pronouncements, instead of using these as legal instruments for keeping in repair some supposed consensus on particular policies.

13.17

I have stressed the implicit wisdom and moral direction the churches might contribute to a statesman's enormously difficult decisions if they paid attention to that which they may know something about instead of adding to the confusion of particular decisions, or weakening his hand or strengthening it in the wrong direction, by pronouncing directly upon the choices before a magistrate as he rules by particular decrees. This is, finally a rectification of no little importance for the church's own inner life.

13.18

Professor John C. Bennett received a number of letters from obviously sincere and not unintelligent or immoral people who felt they had been practically unchurched by the way a consensus of church pronouncements had been used on them in the 1964 presidential campaign. Writing in *Christianity and Crisis* (December 28, 1964) after the election, Dr Bennett 'emphasized that a distinction must be made between the basic Christian convictions that bind a member to his church and the opinions of church bodies on particular issues.' Can anyone doubt that this distinction was made too little *during* the campaign by liberals and conservatives alike?

13.19

Can anyone doubt that we have a long way to go before the church gives itself the machinery (or gets rid of some) by which it can become a community of unlimited discussion and discourse about what Scripture and sound reason require of us in the general direction of political affairs in the present day? A community in which the 'littlest he' or the most conservative one has his Christian life to lead as well as the rest of us. A community in which someone – anyone – may have something significant to say to us contrary to anything that has yet been said, correcting or increasing the light we think we now have or directing it upon some as yet unexposed part of the path men and nations must now tread.

13.20

At the moment this nation still has before it agonizing decisions in regard to South Vietnam. Not only the topmost magistrate but every citizen (including every churchman) has to make up his mind on this urgent question. But what can the church as church know about this? Moreover, whatever is wise or foolish in our specific military actions or political and negotiating posture in this particular instance is not going to help us decide similar questions the next time we confront insurgency warfare or in deciding where and how to make our presence felt in Asia. There is no point in trying to compile a Christian social ethic by leap-frogging from one problem to another.

13.21

The political conscience of the nation would be aided more, and particular decisions more instructed, if there were fewer judgments emanating from the churches upon specific cases, delivered as if these were the only conclusions to be reached from considerations of morality. The nation and the statesman would be more edified by currents of discussion about the immorality and probable ineffectiveness of nonintervention to balance the talk about the immorality and probable ineffectiveness of intervention. There should be discussion of the responsibilities of a nation because the United Nations is such a weak reed, as well as talk of our duty to strengthen world organizations. Moreover, no one should talk about the difficulties and failures confronting purposeful intervention without also talking about the difficulties and failures of 'coalition' governments (Laos).

13.22

Christians should be speaking more about order as a terminal political value along with justice, without the naive assumption that these are bound to go together without weight given to both. More about the need for the rule of law as well as revolutionary change. Of serving human liberty as well as the war on poverty, without the presumption that there is an 'invisible hand' that links these together in the absence of specific attention to each. About the individual and community values at stake in destroying the illusion that government will provide a solution for every irritant or distress, as well as what government can and should do. Of the responsible use of political power as well as the limits upon it. Of how involvement in the world's problems means tragic involvement.

13.23

And there needs to be among Christians a consensus that in the concrete life of charity we should never aspire or even imagine that we are going to get rid of our neighbor's need in such wise as to get rid of our enduringly needy neighbors.

13.24

As a citizen one may lean to one extreme or the other in this range of options. As churchmen, however, our concern should be that the range of relevant principles be not narrowed, and that the conscience of the nation and of the statesman be not deprived of perspectives and wisdom that may be needed elements in the decisions magistrates have to make.

13.25

Let the church be the church and let the magistrate be the magistrate. Let both keep their distances. May there be less confusion of these roles. Let the President advance policies without playing priest-king to the people in exercising his ruling under God's overruling. Let the churches advise the magistrates under their care in less specific terms, while always renewing in them the perspectives – all the perspectives – upon the political order that Christianity affords. And let us pray more for those in authority (not the churches as such) who must shape the future by what they decree, and who in doing so must step creatively into an uncertain future beyond the range of any light that has been or can ever be thrown upon their pathway.

EXTRACT 14

US CATHOLIC BISHOPS

The challenge of peace

Ius ad Bellum [Justice in Going to War]

14.1

Why and when recourse to war is permissible.

14.2

a) *Just Cause*: War is permissible only to confront 'a real and certain danger,' i.e. to protect innocent life, to preserve conditions necessary for decent human existence, and to secure basic human rights. As both Pope Pius XII and Pope John XXIII made clear, if war of retribution was ever justifiable, the risks of modern war negate such a claim today.

14.3

b) *Competent Authority*: In the Catholic tradition the right to use force has always been joined to the common good; war must be declared by those with responsibility for public order, not by private groups or individuals.

14.4

The requirement that a decision to go to war must be made by competent authority is particularly important in a democratic society. It needs detailed treatment here since it involves a broad spectrum of related issues. Some of the bitterest divisions of society in our own nation's history, for example, have been provoked over the question of whether or not a president of the United States has acted constitutionally and legally in involving our country in a *de facto* war, even if – indeed, especially if – war was never formally declared. Equally perplexing problems of conscience can be raised for individuals expected or legally required to go to war even though our duly elected representatives in Congress have, in fact, voted for war.

14.5
The criterion of competent authority is of further importance in a day when revolutionary war has become commonplace. Historically, the just-war tradition has been open to a 'just revolution' position, recognizing that an oppressive government may lose its claim to legitimacy. Insufficient analytical attention has been given to the moral issues of revolutionary warfare. The mere possession of sufficient weaponry, for example, does not legitimize the initiation of war by 'insurgents' against an established government, any more than the government's systematic oppression of its people can be carried out under the doctrine of 'national security.'

14.6
While the legitimacy of revolution in some circumstances cannot be denied, just-war teachings must be applied as rigorously to revolutionary-counterrevolutionary conflicts as to others. The issue of who constitutes competent authority and how such authority is exercised is essential.

14.7
When we consider in this letter the issues of conscientious objection and selective conscientious objection, the issue of competent authority will arise again.

14.8
c) *Comparative Justice*: Questions concerning the *means* of waging war today, particularly in view of the destructive potential of weapons, have tended to override questions concerning the comparative justice of the positions of respective adversaries or enemies. In essence: which side is sufficiently 'right' in a dispute, and are the values at stake critical enough to override the presumption against war? The question in its most basic form is this: do the rights and values involved justify killing? For whatever the means used, war, by definition, involves violence, destruction, suffering, and death.

14.9
The category of comparative justice is designed to emphasize the presumption against war which stands at the beginning of just-war teaching. In a world of sovereign states recognizing neither a common moral authority nor a central political authority, comparative justice stresses that no state

should act on the basis that it has 'absolute justice' on its side. Every party to a conflict should acknowledge the limits of its 'just cause' and the consequent requirement to use only limited means in pursuit of its objectives. Far from legitimizing a crusade mentality, comparative justice is designed to relativize absolute claims and to restrain the use of force even in a 'justified' conflict.

14.10
Given techniques of propaganda and the ease with which nations and individuals either assume or delude themselves into believing that God or right is clearly on their side, the test of comparative justice may be extremely difficult to apply. Clearly, however, this is not the case in every instance of war. Blatant aggression from without and subversion from within are often enough readily identifiable by all reasonably fair-minded people.

14.11
d) *Right Intention*: Right intention is related to just cause – war can be legitimately intended only for the reasons set forth above as a just cause. During the conflict, right intention means pursuit of peace and reconciliation, including avoiding unnecessarily destructive acts or imposing unreasonable conditions (e.g. unconditional surrender).

14.12
e) *Last Resort*: For resort to war to be justified, all peaceful alternatives must have been exhausted. There are formidable problems in this requirement. No international organization currently in existence has exercised sufficient internationally recognized authority to be able either to mediate effectively in most cases or to prevent conflict by the intervention of United Nations or other peacekeeping forces. Furthermore, there is a tendency for nations or peoples which perceive conflict between or among other nations as advantageous to themselves to attempt to prevent a peaceful settlement rather than advance it.

14.13
We regret the apparent unwillingness of some to see in the United Nations organization the potential for world order which exists and to encourage its development. Pope Paul VI called the United Nations the last hope for peace. The loss of this hope cannot be allowed to happen. Pope John Paul II is again instructive on this point: 'I wish above all to repeat my confidence in you, the leaders and members of the international Organizations, and in you, the international officials! In the course of the last ten years, your organizations have too often been the object of attempts at manipulation

on the part of nations wishing to exploit such bodies. However it remains true that the present multiplicity of violent clashes, divisions and blocks on which bilateral relations founder, offer the great International Organizations the opportunity to engage upon the qualitative change in their activities, even to reform on certain points their own structures in order to take into account new realities and to enjoy effective power' [World Day of Peace Message 1983].

14.14

f) *Probability of Success*: This is a difficult criterion to apply, but its purpose is to prevent irrational resort to force or hopeless resistance when the outcome of either will clearly be disproportionate or futile. The determination includes a recognition that at times defense of key values, even against great odds, may be a 'proportionate' witness.

14.15

g) *Proportionality*: In terms of the *ius ad bellum* criteria, proportionality means that the damage to be inflicted and the costs incurred by war must be proportionate to the good expected by taking up arms. Nor should judgments concerning proportionality be limited to the temporal order without regard to a spiritual dimension in terms of 'damage,' 'cost,' and 'the good expected.' In today's interdependent world even a local conflict can affect people everywhere; this is particularly the case when the nuclear powers are involved. Hence a nation cannot justly go to war today without considering the effect of its action on others and on the international community.

14.16

This principle of proportionality applies throughout the conduct of the war as well as to the decision to begin warfare. During the Vietnam war our bishops' conference ultimately concluded that the conflict had reached such a level of devastation to the adversary and damage to our own society that continuing it could not be justified.

Ius in Bello [Justice within Warfare]

14.17

Even when the stringent conditions which justify resort to war are met, the conduct of war (i.e., strategy, tactics, and individual actions) remains subject to continuous scrutiny in light of two principles which have special significance today precisely because of the destructive capability of modern technological warfare. These principles are proportionality and discrimination. In discussing them here, we shall apply them to the question of *ius ad bellum* as well as *ius in bello*; for today it becomes increasingly difficult to make a decision to use any kind of armed force, however limited initially in intention and in the destructive power of the weapons employed, without facing at least the possibility of escalation to broader, or even total, war and to the use of weapons of horrendous destructive potential. This is especially the case when adversaries are 'superpowers,' as the council clearly envisioned: 'Indeed, if the kind of weapons now stocked in the arsenals of the great powers were to be employed to the fullest, the result would be the almost complete reciprocal slaughter of one side by the other, not to speak of the widespread devastation that would follow in the world and the deadly after-effects resulting from the use of such weapons' [*Pastoral Constitution* para. 80].

14.18

It should not be thought, of course, that massive slaughter and destruction would result only from the extensive use of nuclear weapons. We recall with horror the carpet and incendiary bombings of World War II, the deaths of hundreds of thousands in various regions of the world through 'conventional' arms, the unspeakable use of gas and other forms of chemical warfare, the destruction of homes and of crops, the utter suffering war has wrought during the centuries before and the decades since the use of the 'atom bomb.' Nevertheless, every honest person must recognize that, especially given the proliferation of modern scientific weapons, we now face possibilities which are appalling to contemplate. Today, as never before, we must ask not merely what will happen, but what may happen, especially if major powers embark on war. Pope John Paul II has repeatedly pleaded that world leaders confront this reality: '[In] view of the difference between classical warfare and nuclear or bacteriological war – a difference so to speak of nature – and in view of the scandal of the arms race seen against the background of the needs of the Third World, this right (of defense), which is very real in principle, only underlines the urgency of world society to equip itself with effective means of negotiation. In this way the nuclear terror that haunts our time can encourage us to enrich our common heritage with a very simple discovery that is within our reach, namely that war is the most barbarous and least effective way of resolving conflicts' [World Day of Peace Message 1982].

14.19

The Pontifical Academy of Sciences reaffirmed the Holy Father's theme, in its November 1981 'Statement on the Consequences of Nuclear War.' Then, in a meeting convoked by the Pontifical Academy, representatives of national academies of science from throughout the world issued a

'Declaration on the Prevention of Nuclear War' which specified the meaning of Pope John Paul II's statement that modern warfare differs by nature from previous forms of war. The scientists said: 'Throughout its history humanity has been confronted with war, but since 1945 the nature of warfare has changed so profoundly that the future of the human race, of generations yet unborn, is imperilled... For the first time it is possible to cause damage on such a catastrophic scale as to wipe out a large part of civilization and to endanger its very survival. The large-scale use of such weapons could trigger major and irreversible ecological and genetic changes whose limits cannot be predicted.'

14.20

And earlier, with such thoughts plainly in mind, the council had made its own 'the condemnation of total war already pronounced by recent popes.' This condemnation is demanded by the principles of proportionality and discrimination. Response to aggression must not exceed the nature of the aggression. To destroy civilization as we know it by waging a 'total war' as today it could be waged would be a monstrously disproportionate response to aggression on the part of any nation.

14.21

Moreover, the lives of innocent persons may never be taken directly, regardless of the purpose alleged for doing so. To wage truly 'total' war is by definition to take huge numbers of innocent lives. Just response to aggression must be discriminate; it must be directed against unjust aggressors, not against innocent people caught up in a war not of their making. The council therefore issued its memorable declaration: 'Any act of war aimed indiscriminately at the destruction of entire cities or of extensive areas along with their population is a crime against God and man himself. It merits unequivocal and unhesitating condemnation' [*Pastoral Constitution* para. 80].

14.22

When confronting choices among specific military options the question asked by proportionality is: once we take into account not only the military advantages that will be achieved by using this means but also all the harms reasonably expected to follow from using it, can its use still be justified? We know, of course, that no end can justify means evil in themselves, such as the executing of hostages or the targeting of non-combatants. Nonetheless, even if the means adopted is not evil in itself, it is necessary to take into account the probable harms that will result from using it and the justice of accepting those harms. It is of utmost importance, in assessing harms and the justice of accepting them, to think about the poor and the helpless, for they are usually the ones who have the least to gain and the most to lose when war's violence touches their lives.

14.23

In terms of the arms race, if the real end in view is legitimate defense against unjust aggression, and the means to this end are not evil in themselves, we must still examine the question of proportionality concerning attendant evils. Do the exorbitant costs, the general climate of insecurity generated, the possibility of accidental detonation of highly destructive weapons, the danger of error and miscalculation that could provoke retaliation and war – do such evils or others attendant upon and indirectly deriving from the arms race make the arms race itself a disproportionate response to aggression? Pope John Paul II is very clear in his insistence that the exercise of the right and duty of a people to protect their existence and freedom is contingent on the use of proportionate means.

14.24

Finally, another set of questions concerns the interpretation of the principle of discrimination. The principle prohibits directly intended attacks on non-combatants and non-military targets. It raises a series of questions about the term 'intentional,' the category of 'non-combatant,' and the meaning of 'military.'

14.25

These questions merit the debate occurring with increasing frequency today. We encourage such debate, for concise and definitive answers still appear to be wanting. Mobilization of forces in modern war includes not only the military, but to a significant degree the political, economic, and social sectors. It is not always easy to determine who is directly involved in a 'war effort' or to what degree. Plainly, though, not even by the broadest definition can one rationally consider combatants entire classes of human beings such as schoolchildren, hospital patients, the elderly, the ill, the average industrial worker producing goods not directly related to military purposes, farmers, and many others. They may never be directly attacked.

14.26

Direct attacks on military targets involve similar complexities. Which targets are 'military' ones and which are not? To what degree, for instance, does the use (by either revolutionaries or regular military forces) of a village or housing in a civilian populated area invite attack? What of a munitions factory in the heart of a city? Who is directly responsible for the deaths of non-combatants should the attack be carried out? To revert to the question raised earlier, how many deaths of non-combatants are 'tolerable' as a result of indirect attacks – attacks directed against combat forces and military targets, which nevertheless kill non-combatants at the same time?

These two principles, in all their complexity, must be applied to the range of weapons – conventional, nuclear, biological, and chemical – with which nations are armed today.

The value of non-violence

14.27

Moved by the example of Jesus' life and by his teaching, some Christians have from the earliest days of the Church committed themselves to a non-violent lifestyle. Some understood the gospel of Jesus to prohibit all killing. Some affirmed the use of prayer and other spiritual methods as means of responding to enmity and hostility.

14.28

In the middle of the second century, St Justin proclaimed to his pagan readers that Isaiah's prophecy about turning swords into ploughshares and spears into sickles had been fulfilled as a consequence of Christ's coming: 'And we who delighted in war, in the slaughter of one another and in every other kind of iniquity have in every part of the world converted our weapons into implements of peace – our swords into ploughshares, our spears into farmers' tools – and we cultivate piety, justice, brotherly charity, faith and hope, which we derive from the Father through the crucified Savior...' [*Dialogue with Trypho* chap. 20].

14.29

Writing in the third century, St Cyprian of Carthage struck a similar note when he indicated that the Christians of his day did not fight against their enemies. He himself regarded their conduct as proper: 'They do not even fight against those who are attacking since it is not granted to the innocent to kill even the aggressor, but promptly to deliver up their souls and blood that, since so much malice and cruelty are rampant in the world, they may more quickly withdraw from the malicious and the cruel' [*Collected Letters: Cornelius*].

14.30

Some of the early Christian opposition to military service was a response to the idolatrous practices which prevailed in the Roman army. Another powerful motive was the fact that army service involved preparation for fighting and killing. We see this in the case of St Martin of Tours during the fourth century, who renounced his soldierly profession with the explanation: 'Hitherto I have served you as a soldier. Allow me now to become a soldier of God... I am a soldier of Christ. It is not lawful for me to fight.'

14.31

In the centuries between the fourth century and our own day, the theme of Christian non-violence and Christian pacifism has echoed and re-echoed, sometimes more strongly, sometimes more faintly. One of the great non-violent figures in those centuries was St Francis of Assisi. Besides making personal efforts on behalf of reconciliation and peace, Francis stipulated that laypersons who became members of his Third Order were not 'to take up lethal weapons, or bear them about, against anybody.'

14.32

The vision of Christian non-violence is not passive about injustice and the defense of the rights of others; it rather affirms and exemplifies what it means to resist injustice through non-violent methods.

14.33

In the twentieth century, prescinding from the non-Christian witness of a Mahatma Gandhi and its worldwide impact, the non-violent witness of such figures as Dorothy Day and Martin Luther King has had a profound impact upon the life of the Church in the United States. The witness of numerous Christians who had preceded them over the centuries was affirmed in a remarkable way at the Second Vatican Council.

14.34

Two of the passages which were included in the final version of the *Pastoral Constitution* gave particular encouragement for Catholics in all walks of life to assess their attitudes toward war and military service in the light of Christian pacifism. In paragraph 79 the council fathers called upon governments to enact laws protecting the rights of those who adopted the position of conscientious objection to all war: 'Moreover, it seems right that laws make humane provisions for the case of those who for reasons of conscience refuse to bear arms, provided, however, that they accept some other form of service to the human community.' This was the first time a call for legal protection of conscientious objection had appeared in a document of such prominence. In addition to its own profound meaning this statement took on even more significance in the light of the praise that the council fathers had given in the preceding section 'to those who renounce the use of violence and the vindication of their rights.' In *Human Life in Our Day* (1968) we called for legislative provision to recognize selective conscientious objectors as well.

14.35

As Catholic bishops it is incumbent upon us to stress to our own community and to the wider society the significance of this support for a pacifist option for individuals in the teaching of Vatican II and the reaffirmation that the popes have given to non-violent witness since the time of the council.

14.36

In the development of a theology of peace and the growth of the Christian pacifist position among Catholics, these words of the *Pastoral Constitution* have special significance: 'All these factors force us to undertake a completely fresh reappraisal of war.' The council fathers had reference to 'the development of armaments by modern science (which) has immeasurably magnified the horrors and wickedness of war' [para. 80]. While the just-war teaching has clearly been in possession for the past 1,500 years of Catholic thought, the 'new moment' in which we find ourselves sees the just-war teaching and non-violence as distinct but interdependent methods of evaluating warfare. They diverge on some specific conclusions, but they share a common presumption against the use of force as a means of settling disputes.

14.37

Both find their roots in the Christian theological tradition; each contributes to the full moral vision we need in pursuit of a human peace. We believe the two perspectives support and complement one another, each preserving the other from distortion. Finally, in an age of technological warfare, analysis from the viewpoint of non-violence and analysis from the viewpoint of the just-war teaching often converge and agree in their opposition to methods of warfare which are in fact indistinguishable from total warfare...

In conclusion

14.38

Why do we address these matters fraught with such complexity, controversy and passion? We speak as pastors, not politicians. We are teachers, not technicians. We cannot avoid our responsibility to lift up the moral dimensions of the choices before our world and nation. The nuclear age is an era of moral as well as physical danger. We are the first generation since Genesis with the power to virtually destroy God's creation. We cannot remain silent in the face of such danger. Why do we address these issues?

We are simply trying to live up to the call of Jesus to be peacemakers in our own time and situation.

14.39

What are we saying? Fundamentally, we are saying that the decisions about nuclear weapons are among the most pressing moral questions of our age. While these decisions have obvious military and political aspects, they involve fundamental moral choices. In simple terms, we are saying that good ends (defending one's country, protecting freedom, etc.) cannot justify immoral means (the use of weapons which kill indiscriminately and threaten whole societies). We fear that our world and nation are headed in the wrong direction. More weapons with greater destructive potential are produced every day. More and more nations are seeking to become nuclear powers. In our quest for more and more security, we fear we are actually becoming less and less secure.

14.40

In the words of our Holy Father, we need a 'moral about-face.' The whole world must summon the moral courage and technical means to say 'no' to nuclear conflict; 'no' to weapons of mass destruction; 'no' to an arms race which robs the poor and the vulnerable; and 'no' to the moral danger of a nuclear age which places before humankind indefensible choices of constant terror or surrender. Peacemaking is not an optional commitment. It is a requirement of our faith. We are called to be peacemakers, not by some movement of the moment, but by our Lord Jesus. The content and context of our peacemaking is set, not by some political agenda or ideological program, but by the teaching of his Church...

14.41

For the community of faith the risen Christ is the beginning and end of all things. For all things were created through him and all things will return to the Father through him.

14.42

It is our belief in the risen Christ which sustains us in confronting the awesome challenge of the nuclear arms race. Present in the beginning as the word of the Father, present in history as the word incarnate, and with us today in his word, sacraments, and spirit, he is the reason for our hope and faith. Respecting our freedom, he does not solve our problems but sustains us as we take responsibility for his work of creation and try to shape it in the ways of the kingdom. We believe his grace will never fail us...

EXTRACT 15

HAUERWAS

Pacifism: some philosophical considerations

15.1

A pacifist speaking to philosophers faces a temptation that is almost impossible to resist – namely to try to defend pacifism philosophically. Yet I think such a temptation must be resisted, for to try to provide a philosophical foundation for pacifism would be a philosophical mistake. It is the same kind of mistake that those make who try to show that God must have created the universe if he is to be God – i.e. to make a metaphysical necessity out of what must remain contingent relation. I do not wish to be misunderstood, however, as such a claim might be interpreted to suggest that pacifism is a position without relational appeal, being based on theological convictions that cannot stand the light of critical scrutiny. I certainly do not believe that. Rather I am trying to make the simpler point that pacifism, at least the kind of Christian non-resistance to which I am committed, is at the beginning and end a theological position. As such it raises philosophical issues which cannot be avoided, but in and of itself, its integrity is theological.

15.2

Given the interest of this group it would be inappropriate for me to try to develop to any great extent my understanding of Christian pacifism. However I must at least try to say enough to substantiate as well as exemplify how it draws on fundamental theological convictions for its intelligibility. The reason I believe Christians have been given the permission, that is, why it is good news for us, to live without resort to violence is that by doing so we live as God lives. Therefore pacifism is not first of all a prohibition, but an affirmation that God wills to rule his creation not through violence and coercion but by love. Moreover he has called us to be part of his rule by calling us into a community that is governed by peace.

15.3

Therefore pacifism is not simply one implication among others for Christians. Pacifism is not just another way that some Christians think they should live. Rather pacifism is the form of life that is inherent in the shape of Christian convictions about God and his relation to us. Though it counts individual passages of scripture such as Matthew 5.38-48 important, pacifism does not derive its sole justification from them. Rather pacifism follows from our understanding of God which we believe has been most decisively revealed in the cross of Jesus Christ. Just as God refused to use violence to insure the success of his cause, so must we. Therefore Christian pacifism is not based on any claims about the proximate or ultimate success of non-violent strategies, though we certainly do not try to fail as if failure in and of itself is an indication of the truthfulness of our position. Faithfulness, however, rather than effectiveness, is the ultimate test of Christian pacifism.

15.4
Even though for the purposes of this presentation I am willing to be designated a pacifist, I am extremely unhappy with such a description of my position. For to say one is a pacifist gives the impression that pacifism is a position that is intelligible apart from the theological convictions that form it. But that is exactly what I wish to deny. Christians are non-violent not because certain implications may follow from their beliefs, but because the very shape of their beliefs form them to be non-violent. Moreover when the designation, pacifism, is used to describe Christian non-resistance the impression is given that Christians in the face of violence are primarily passive in the face of evil. Yet that is at odds with Jesus' active engagement with the powers. The pacifist is no less obligated to resist injustice, for not to resist means we abandon our brother or sister to their injustice. Pacifists, however, contend the crucial question is how we are to resist.

15.5
There are obviously many objections that such a position must meet, but I think that for those that are philosophically trained one challenge is particularly interesting – namely, pacifism seems contradictory since in the name of non-violence Christians must abandon their responsibility to care for and protect their neighbor. Christians, it is alleged, are obligated to love those in need and Christian pacifism cannot help but acquiesce in the face of injustice and violence. Therefore we must at times take up the means of violence to prevent greater injustice. This objection is often extremely appealing to philosophers, as it seems to put the issue in conceptual terms that allows for, if not demand, further nuance. The issue is not faithfulness to the figure of Jesus, but how love is to be understood and how its implications are to be displayed when we seem caught between contending values; or why justice is more basic than love, and so on.

15.6
However this way of putting the 'problem' is a refusal to accept the radical implications of the kind of love Jesus demanded of those who would be part of God's kingdom. For the 'problem' presupposes that we should only love the one being attacked unjustly; such an account is far too restrictive.

The attacker, who may well be unjust, is no less an object of God's love than the one being attacked. The pacifist, no less than those who support violence in the name of the defense of the innocent, cannot abandon those who are being attacked. But the pacifist refuses to accept any account of what such 'help' would look like if it requires us to witness to the one being attacked that they are any less obligated to love the enemy than we. To be sure, we are required to love the attacked, but we are equally obligated to love the attacker. That we are so may surely mean that certain situations may end tragically, but I do not see how those who support the use of violence provide any less tragic 'solution.'

15.7
There is one issue worth highlighting in this respect, as it is often missed by many who assume some form of just-war logic for the legitimation of violence. For it is too often assumed that the logic of the just-war position is determined on analogy with self-defense rather than defense of the innocent. But the two are not the same, though admittedly a defense of self can possibly be justified as a defense of the innocent. Yet if just war is defended on analogy of defense of the innocent, then at the very least it would seem that those who use just war to justify resort to violence must not be so quick to assume the legitimacy of a violent response simply because their side is attacked. Or perhaps more accurately put, they need to be much more critical of the assumption that they have a 'side.'

15.8
Much more needs to be said about such matters, but I hope I have said enough to indicate that those that defend just war need to be much more candid about how the basic analogies underwriting just war logic works. They need to show us, for example, how one moves from individual analogies, whether they be of self-defense or defense of the innocent, to underwriting war as a valid response by Christians. Or they need to illumine why just war is better understood as a form of state craft rather than a general theory of the justifiable use of violence. Only when such matters are clarified can we better understand which criteria are to determine whether a war is justifiable and the priority relations between the criteria.

15.9
By raising these kind of issues I am not trying to defend pacifism by showing the incoherence of just-war theories. I am simply trying to illumine how many of the challenges brought against pacifism work equally in relation to just-war thinking. At this point, however, I think it best not to try to defend pacifism but rather to indicate some of the philosophical issues I think

pacifism entails. In other words I want to try to indicate how pacifism may engender some philosophically fruitful problems and perspectives.

15.10

For example I think it is interesting that the kind of pacifism I defend does not neatly fit into the current philosophical options for understanding normative ethics. That is, it is neither consequential or deontological even though it may well involve aspects of both. For the emphasis is not on decision or even a set of decisions and their justification. Rather this kind of pacifism forces us to consider the kind of persons we ought to be so that certain kinds of decisions are simply excluded from our lives. Thus pacifism is not so much a strategy for how we should deal with violence as it is a way of life that forces us to live free from violence as an option. The pacifist is someone committed to never facing the question of whether to use or not use violence as a means of securing some good.

15.11

Of course that is easier said than done. Nor am I suggesting that such a task is ever over. Indeed I suspect few of us ever 'decide' to be a pacifist. It is even not clear to me how anyone could make such a decision since we could hardly know what kind of decision we had made since one no more becomes a pacifist all at once than one becomes a Christian all at once. Rather pacifism is a willingness to accept the slow training necessary to rid the self of the presumption that violence is necessary for living life well.

15.12

From this perspective the problem with the just-war rationale for violence is that it so seldom places a limit on the use of violence. The just warrior assumes that violence can only be used as a last resort, but the very meaning of 'last resort' becomes elastic exactly because it is assumed that if things become rough we can resort to the gun we keep handy for just such emergencies. As a result we fail to become the kind of people whose very commitment to non-violence makes it possible for us to live non-violently.

15.13

Put in the language of philosophical ethics I am suggesting that pacifism is much closer to an ethics of virtue than to those positions that tend to limit ethics to questions concerning the justification of decisions. For the pacifist does not accept descriptions of situations as constant. Questions of what we are to do are determined by what we are or should be. Virtues of courage, temperance, justice, humility, patience are no less necessary for the pacifist than anyone else. However these virtues assume a different intentionality and priority for those who would be pacifist. For example the pacifist, I suspect, has a much greater stake in the significance of learning to be patient than those who would defend justifiable use of violence. Just to the extent we are patient, moreover, we are forced to redescribe our world – e.g. we must entertain the possibility that our enemy is also one of God's creatures.

15.14

I am not suggesting that pacifism and an ethic of virtue rise or fall together, but rather that pacifism forces us to think much harder about an ethic of virtue than has been characteristic of recent philosophy. Indeed I would put the matter more strongly and say philosophers' general assumption or acceptance of violence as legitimate has been one of the reasons they have paid such scant attention to questions of virtue and character. An emphasis on the significance of the virtues does not conceptually require a pacifist position, but such an emphasis might at least make one more receptive to some accounts of pacifism.

15.15

The kind of pacifism I am willing to defend, I think, also challenges some of the prevailing assumptions about moral rationality as it has been depicted by contemporary philosophers. For here we have a position that is clearly derived from particularistic convictions; yet I would argue they apply to anyone. The 'universality' of these convictions however, is not in their form but in their substance. All people ought to be nonviolent not because of some general truth about humanity, but because all people have been called to be part of the kingdom initiated by Jesus of Nazareth.

15.16

This kind of claim cannot help but make philosophers nervous. For it seems that, in order to convince others of the plausibility of this position, we must ask them to accept particularistic religious convictions. In such a situation the possibility of argument seems next to impossible and, even worse, moral relativism is threatened. I can say little to assuage fear of such results, but I can at least suggest that the kind of position I hold about pacifism is not without resources to respond to this set of concerns. Yet these resources require the philosopher to accept concepts and language in matters dealing with rationality that they usually wish to avoid.

15.17

For example, it means that the philosopher might have to take sin seriously, not simply as a general statement about the human condition, but as a serious claim about our moral and rational capacity. For it is the pacifist claim that our unwillingness to live nonviolently is but an indication of our unwillingness to live in a way appropriate to our being creatures of a good creator. To live rightly, to say nothing of reasoning rightly, requires a transformation of our lives. We can only begin to appreciate the truth of nonviolence when we begin to live nonviolently.

15.18

Put differently, the kind of claims Christians make for nonviolence require living representatives if they are to be convincing. The rational power of nonviolence as a morality for anyone depends on the existence of examples, that is, people who have learned to live nonviolently. Such a claim is not peculiar to pacifism, however, but rather denotes how any substantive account of the moral life must work in a world determined by sin. Indeed pacifism in such a world is the very form of moral rationality since it is a pledge that we can come to common agreement on the basis of discussion rather than violence. What the nonviolent witness denies is that such agreement is possible by argument abstracted from the kind of people who have learned that even their enemy may be speaking the truth. We cannot exhaust moral rationality with a formal account of reason in and of itself, though such accounts promise to teach us much, but rather we must attend to the actual process of people who learn to be present to one another without fear. Put simply, what has been missing from most accounts of moral rationality is a consideration of why courage is integral to those that would want to know the truth.

15.19

The particularistic convictions that sustain nonviolence, therefore, do not pretend that others already share the same set of convictions that make nonviolence rational. Indeed the fact that we know the world is divided into hostile camps is exactly the reason we believe that nonviolence is true. I do not mean to imply that nonviolence is a strategy for resolution of differences, though I certainly do not think it is without strategic importance. Rather I am suggesting that nonviolence has a strong claim to being true exactly because it helps us understand the nature of our existence without accepting the limits of our world as final. Nonviolence is a pledge, a promise based on the work of Christ, that moral rationality is not just an ideal but a possibility in a world shaped by the sinful illusion that we are people who love the truth.

15.20

There is one final set of philosophical issues raised by pacifism that I think must be considered – namely, questions of political obligation. It is often alleged that anyone who holds the kind of absolutist position I do must be an anarchist. Yet I refuse to accept such a characterization, for it seems to assume that the state, in essence, is violent. I do not deny that the rise of the modern state has often been described and/or justified by the claim that the state is that body that claims hegemony over violence in an identifiable geographic area. Yet 1 see no compelling philosophical reason why that account of the state must be accepted.

15.21

Indeed I simply refuse as a pacifist to think I need any account of the state at all. In other words I do not think that one needs a theory of legitimacy in order to determine how one will or will not relate to one's social order or governmental authority. Rather I simply take societies and the state as 1 find them. As a pacifist I will cooperate in all those activities of the state that contribute to the common good. Put simply, I do not see any in principle reason why I cannot be a good citizen, but much depends on how a particular social order determines what being a citizen entails. If citizenship means that we can only serve others through societal functions if we are willing to kill, then indeed the pacifist cannot be a citizen. But at least that tells us much, for such a state, whether it be democratic or not, must surely deserve to be described as the beast.

EXTRACT 16
BONINO

Liberation theology and peace

16.1

The ideas of confrontation, struggle, and violence seem particularly repugnant to the Christian conscience. Before dealing with the area of ethical questions we must, nevertheless, dwell briefly on the concept of class. The phenomenon of classes in society is analysed by Marx in relation to the way in which people relate to the productive process, particularly in the capitalist form of organising production. It is well known that Marx finds the main distinction hinging on whether a man owns the means of production of whether he has to sell his labour to those who own them, i.e. the capitalist and the proletarian. Marx and his followers are, of course, aware that this particular configuration of classes is dependent on the existing forms of the capitalist economy, and therefore cannot be projected back to other societies. Moreover, they are aware that even in the capitalist industrial societies several forms of production and consequently different forms of social organisation coexist and therefore that there are groups and segments of society that do not fit neatly into this dominant pattern. One could add that tribal societies in Africa or ethnic groups in Latin America as well as changes in the structure of capitalist production pose complex problems which may require rethinking certain elements in the Marxist conception of class. Both Marxist and non-Marxist sociologists are aware of these questions and there is at present a very significant literature dealing with the problem. There is no need for us to belabour this point. We are here dealing with the always provisional results of a scientific investigation. As such, a Christian need not accept it or question it except in terms of its scientific verifiability.

16.2

There are, nevertheless, two theological questions which deserve to be mentioned. The first has to do with Marx's point of departure (whether itself a result of his scientific analysis or not is at this point a moot question), namely, that man is to be basically and radically understood as a worker, as the being who appropriates, transforms, and humanises the world through his work and who himself comes to his own identity, becomes man through this same work. If this is so, it is only to be expected that the forms of relationships and organisations in which man works will be the privileged means for understanding human life and society and that changes in one area will be closely related to changes in the other. Christian anthropology, on the other hand, has traditionally sought to understand man in terms of his intellectual, moral, and spiritual endowment or, in a more dynamic way, in terms of his relations to himself (self-understanding), to his neighbour, and to God. The theological understanding of man, therefore, has been predominantly – if not exclusively – philosophical, cultural, and religious. To such an approach, Marxist anthropology naturally smacks of materialism. Such an accusation is very widespread in Christian circles. But one may wonder whether it does not rest on a twofold misunderstanding. On the one hand, it reads Marx in terms of a mechanistic determinism which would see the spiritual life of man as a mere reflex of material conditions. There is no doubt that some Marxist thinkers, and particularly many popularisers, have amply justified such interpretation. In Marx himself, and in the best contemporary interpreters, the dialectical relations of material and cultural conditionings are much more subtly and carefully assessed. It may, nevertheless, be necessary to challenge and correct even more drastically Marx's conception at this point. I am, at the same time, more concerned with the other misunderstanding: the theological substitution of an idealist for the biblical understanding of man. Whether one deals with the creation stories, with the law, or with the prophetic message, there seems to be in the Bible no relation of man to himself, to his neighbour, or even to God which is not mediated in terms of man's *work*. His dignity is located in his mission to subdue and cultivate the world. His worship is related to the fulfilment of a law in which the whole realm of his economic and political activity is taken up (and not to an image or idol in which he could find a private and direct access to the deity)...

16.3

Marxism has understood the alienated character of work in our capitalist society, in which man is estranged from his work; work is objectified as something alien to him and bought through a salary. There is a striking similarity between this view and the Pauline rejection of 'the works of the law' in which man's actions are also objectified as something 'valuable in themselves', apart from the doer and the neighbour, as a 'work' which can be merchandised in order to buy 'justification'. The work of faith, on the other hand, is never objectified – it is the believer himself in action in terms of love. The Christian will, therefore, understand and fully join the Marxist protest against the capitalist demonic circle of work-commodity-salary. But out of the justification by faith alone, he will have to ask whether alienation does not have deeper roots than the distortions of the capitalist society, even in the mysterious original alienation, in man's denial of his humanity (his attempt to know outside the relation of trust and work) which we call sin. This question, nevertheless, can only be asked in the context of a service (a *leitourgeia*, an *abodah*, a service, and a work which are at the same time worship) freely rendered, a work done 'out of faith', outside the realm of worth and reward, in the anticipation of the realm of creative love which is the Kingdom!

16.4

If the biblical view of man's humanity as realised in work is recovered, and at the same time we are aware of the distortion introduced by sin into the life of society, the existence of classes and their conflict emerges as a possible major category for our understanding of history; a possible one, I say, because we must be concerned here with empirical observation and its interpretation and not with a philosophical or theological axiom. 'Class' is a sociological concept and must be verified as such. All we have tried to indicate in the preceding pages is that the view of man which emerges in the Marxist discussion of class – namely, man as worker – is also fundamental for biblical anthropology. Another significant element appears in relation to the discussion of class: the biblical concept of 'the poor'. A number of studies have appeared recently, particularly in connection with the emphasis in Roman Catholic circles on 'a Church of the poor'. The result of biblical research on this point is aptly summarised by Gustavo Gutiérrez. The notion of poverty in the Scriptures is an ambivalent one. On the one hand it designates the weak, the destitute, the oppressed, and is as such 'a scandalous situation' which must be redressed. On the other hand it indicates 'spiritual childhood', humility before God, and as such it is a – perhaps *the* – basic virtue...

16.5

Now, is there a transition from the biblical idea of the poor to the Marxist view of an oppressed class? Can the Christian call to solidarity with the poor and the revolutionary convocation to class struggle be equated? There seems to be both a genuine and sound discernment but also some dangerous misunderstandings and short-cutting in these indentifications. As to the first, there seems to be no serious possibility to argue on biblical and theological grounds against Karl Barth's dictum: 'God always takes his stand unconditionally and passionately on this side and on this side alone: against the lofty and on behalf of the lowly...' The misunderstandings arise from an insufficient recognition of the necessary analytical mediations between the Marxist category of the 'proletarian class' and the biblical one of 'the poor'. This latter one – insofar as it refers to the oppressed and disinherited – is a pre-scientific, simply empirical designation arising out of direct observation of a situation of oppression and injustice. When Christians in Latin America (or elsewhere) denounce the hard and moving realities of hunger, unemployment, premature death, exploitation, repression, and torture, they are – as Old Testament prophets – moving at the level of empirical observation and ethical and religious (quite justified) judgment. This is no doubt also present, although in a humanist form, in Marxism. A revolutionary theory, nevertheless, moves at least two steps further: (1) It purports to give a rational, verifiable, and coherent account of the causes, dynamics, and direction of the process and (2) it offers a correspondingly rational, calculated, organised, and verifiable strategy for overcoming the present situation. We have already noted that the theory must be constantly checked and corrected. But, quite apart from these corrections, its existence poses theological questions which we dare not evade if we aim to overcome mere good will and irrelevant generosity.

16.6

One theological issue which claims our attention in this respect is the question of efficacious love. Two points need to be mentioned briefly. The first is that the commandment of love must evidently be read in the context of Jesus' proclamation of the Kingdom of God. It cannot, therefore, be reduced to a purely interpersonal or intersubjective dimension, but must be set in relation to the eschatological and cosmic scope of the Kingdom. This means that love is inextricably interwoven with hope and justice. The second point follows. Love is not exhausted in the area of intentionality and demonstration but it is other-directed and demands efficacy. It is not content to express and demonstrate, it intends to accomplish...

16.7

A second theological issue that needs to be clarified is the background of the concept of peace as it is commonly used and the problem of violence. At the risk of oversimplification, I want to sketch the two theological perspectives which seem to me to find expression in the current discussion of these issues. One of them is built on the principle of the rationality of the universe – the conviction that a universal order penetrates the world. Heaven and earth, nature and society, moral and spiritual life seek the equilibrium that corresponds to their rational place, and the preservation of this order is the supreme value. Whatever perturbs it becomes 'a trampling of reason'. In its most crass form, this concept simply becomes an ideological screen (to use Ricoeur's expression) to hide the injustice of the status quo by identifying it with cosmic rationality. Violence is understood in the light of this order: whatever disturbs it is irrational and evil and ought to be countered through a rational use of coercion. This logic, undoubtedly plagued with fallacies, nevertheless, flourishes in the 'Christian' rhetoric of the right. The will of God coincides with the ordering of things, which in turn coincides with the present order, threatened by 'the violent ones'. To resist the threat is to obey God.

16.8

This is not the place to engage in a detailed analysis of this theological point of view. It can, of course, be formulated in a more guarded way, avoiding a direct identification of the rational order of things with the existing one and positing a normative order – such as the concept of a natural law in its various older and newer forms – which can even justify a certain 'subversive violence'. Nevertheless, the question remains as to the historical roots of both the idea and the content of such natural law. As to the former, it seems to me possible to trace it to the philosophical rationalisation of a mythology of the 'cosmos' which in turn sacralises a static and stratified society. As to the contents of such natural law, it has often been noted that it reproduces some set of historical conditions – whether of the past or of the present. The historically undeniable fact that this theological perspective came to dominate Christianity at the time when this latter was co-opted as the religious undergirding and sanction of the empire is in itself a very significant comment.

16.9

The other perspective conceives man as a project of liberation that constantly emerges in the fight against the objectifications given in nature, in history, in society, in religion. Man is a creator, and creation is always, in some measure, a violence exerted on things as they are. It is an affirmation of the new against 'that which is'; it is an eruption that can only make room for itself by exploding the existing systems of integration. Violence plays a creative role in this scheme as the 'midwife' (even though I don't think that Marx's famous dictum can be totally interpreted in this perspective). This conception can also be escalated to the extreme, elevating violence as an ultimate principle of creation, valid in itself because it is, *par excellence*, the destruction of all objectifications. Only in the destruction of everything that limits him – nature, social order, ethical norm, divinity – can man find his freedom, i.e. his humanity. But even without looking for these extreme formulations, it is possible to conceive history as a dialectic in which the negation through which the new can emerge implies always a certain measure of violence.

16.10

As theological positions, both perspectives find support in the biblical and ecclesiastical tradition. They are frequently identified respectively with the priestly and prophetic streams and it would not be difficult to trace both currents in the history of Christian theology. They have given rise to two different understandings of peace which deserve mention in connection with our subject. The first one equates peace with order, lack of conflict, harmonious integration – one would almost say 'ecological balance in nature and society'. The German theologian Hans P. Schmidt finds its roots in the Babylonian myth of society as a living organism and thinks that it finds expression in the wisdom tradition in the Bible. It dominates the Graeco-Roman conception of peace and has shaped the theological tradition since Augustine. The other view of peace is typically represented by the prophets but can be shown, I think, to be the predominant one in the Bible. Peace is a dynamic process through which justice is established amid the tensions of history. The Catholic Latin American Conference of bishops at Medellin (1968) has summarised well this view of peace as a work of justice, an ever renewed task, and a fruit of active love. It is quite evident that the possibility of conflict will be differently viewed in these two conceptions. For the first it will be in itself negative, a rupture in harmony; for the second it may be a positive manifestation of the situation which requires righting. Violence in the more specific sense of physical compulsion or destruction may be accepted or rejected in either of the two views, but acceptance or rejection will be viewed in a different way. In the first it will be judged in terms of order; in the second, in terms of the struggle for justice.

16.11

Recent discussions tend to be polarised along these two theological traditions. While I think that they represent significant dimensions of Christian thought, I want to suggest that their approach is seriously distorted and needs correction. In making order and rationality on the one hand or freedom and conflict on the other the basic starting points for theological reflection, they miss, I think, the biblical starting point, which is never an abstract notion or principle, but a concrete situation. The Bible does not conceive man and society as a function of reason or freedom but in concrete historical relations of man-things-God. Even if we try to understand the basic biblical notions of justice, mercy, faithfulness, truth, peace, we are always thrown back to concrete stories, laws, invitations, commandments; they are defined as an announced action or commandment of God in a given historical situation. This does not mean, to be sure, that these words are empty sounds covering a number of capricious and heterogeneous events but it does mean that ethical criteria are not defined a-temporally but in relation to the concrete conditions of existence of men historically located. These facts taken together do represent a direction – the Kingdom of God – in terms of which one may speak of worthy or unworthy actions. But this direction cannot be translated into a universal principle – reason, order, liberty, conflict.

16.12

Against this background, violence appears in the Bible, not as a general form of human conduct which has to be accepted or rejected as such, but as an element of God's announcement-commandment, as concrete acts which must be carried out or avoided in view of a result, or a relation, of a project indicated by the announcement-commandment. Thus, the law forbids certain forms of violence to persons and things and authorises and even commands others. There are wars that are commanded – even against Israel – and wars that are forbidden – even on behalf of Israel. If one tries to find some coherence in these indications, a first and simple formulation might be that the invitation to exercise or renounce conflict and violence tends to open the space in which men (concretely as foreigner, widow, orphan, poor, family) can be and do, on earth, that which belongs to their particular humanity. In general, it seems possible to say that conflict and violence are means to break out of conditions (slavery, vengeance, arbitrariness, oppression, lack of protection, usurpation) that leave a man, a group of people, or a people unable to be and act as a responsible agent ('as a partner in the covenant') in relation to the others, to things, to God. If this is so, it will not be surprising that, in general terms, peace is preferable to hostility, generosity to vindictiveness, production to destruction, trust and harmony to threat and fear. At this point, the idea of order and rationality has its significant place in Christian reflection. But, given the conditions in which – according to Scripture – human life develops, it is also not surprising that God's announcement-commandment comes almost always as a call to the creation of a new situation, to a transformation and righting of the status quo. This is the priority to which the insistence on liberation legitimately points. Nevertheless, liberation and order, conflict and integration are not conceptual keys for a philosophy of history but heuristic elements for a reflection on God's Word in a given historical situation. They are not, moreover, symmetrical elements; the biblical perspective, centred in the person and work of Jesus Christ, always incorporates order, rationality, preservation in a dynamics of transformation and not the reverse.

16.13
If we try to bring together the two theological themes developed in the last pages – efficacious love and the conditions of peace and conflict – in order to return to our specific problem of class struggle, we can say that this question cannot be debated abstractly, but in relation to God's announcement-commandment in Jesus Christ of a new man and a new humanity which must be witnessed to and proleptically anticipated in history.

CRITIQUE
One of the problems involved, in comparing the Texts with the Extracts in this Section, is that their perceptions of war are radically different. For the modern era, war involves the possibility of human total self-destruction: nuclear weapons present Christian ethics with horrific dimensions, quite beyond the concepts of Augustine, Aquinas or Luther. In this sense, there is a crucial hiatus between the Texts and the Extracts, despite the attempts of Welty to understand modern warfare in terms of traditional just-war concepts. The American Bishops and Hauerwas suggest a radical alternative and, indeed, raise the crucial question, in terms of a just-war theory, of whether it can ever be said that all peaceful means have been exhausted, in conflict situations, before recourse is made to violence. But the

overall problem remains of whether they present a serious alternative to nuclear deterrence.

Welty's reliance upon international tribunals to determine whether or not particular wars are wars of aggression (12.3) may itself be somewhat utopian. Further, his central notions of 'justice', 'defence' and 'liberation' remain difficult to objectify: it is, indeed, no easy task to set out a just-war theory which is not, at some point, tautological. Finally, his style of argument – dependent as it is on papal authority – too severely limits its usefulness to a traditional Roman Catholic context.

Ramsey's critique is rather clearer than his proposals. Many might concede, both that church bodies often lack the specific political expertise required to engage seriously in political realities, and that church members inevitably remain pluralistic on many moral and political issues. However, Ramsey's critique seems to go further than this – suggesting to many that churches have no prophetic role at all in pluralistic societies. Such a position is difficult to maintain in Christian ethics faced with some of the egregious effects of war in the 20th century.

The US Bishops were criticised from a more conservative perspective by the lay Catholic theologian, Michael Novak: 'Just when the West needed a call to disciplined deterrence, the net geopolitical impact of the Bishops' letter was to contribute to illusions. The Bishops did resist pacifism; that is to their credit. They did not, despite much activism, destroy deterrence; that, too, is to their credit. But they failed to strengthen the clarity of soul necessary to make deterrence work, and that marks a grave religious as well as political failure' (in Judith Dwyer (ed), *The Catholic Bishops and Nuclear War*, p.84). Others, however, have applauded *The Challenge of Peace* as a prophetic document that was one of the contributors to the end of the Cold War.

The peacemaking stance of the US Bishops appears mild compared with the radical pacifism of Hauerwas. Some find the latter too short on details about whether or not radical non-violent resistance is a practical stance in a dangerous and militaristic world. Hauerwas adopts a position of theological defiance. If the world is committed to violence, then that is too bad for the world: the Christian cannot meet violence with violence. He rejects a consequentialist stance – for example, claiming that non-violence can be as effective as violence, as argued in the United Reformed Group's *Non-Violent Action*. Instead he sees the claims of the Kingdom of God as absolute. He even concedes elsewhere that 'the peace of God, rather than making the world more safe, only increases the dangers we have to negotiate' (*The Peaceable Kingdom*, p.142). Many might regard this as worrying advice to a fragile world.

A number of crucial difficulties also face Bonino. Like Miranda, he claims that 'scientific', Marxist concepts can be used to clarify biblical concepts. Some of the points that they both make, in defence of Marxism and against simplistic attacks by other Christians, are convincing and, in the context of the economic and political oppression that has, at times, characterised South America, the central focus of Liberation theology is highly important. Nonetheless, Bonino's contention that, there is 'a striking similarity' between Paul's notion of 'works' and the Marxist concept of 'alienation', requires far more analysis and justification (16.3). It is also difficult to accept, without further evidence, that the Marxist concept of the 'proletariat', derived as it is from an urban industrial context, has much to do with the biblical concept of the 'poor' (see *above*, p.251). Further, there is a certain lack of clarity in the concept of 'peace' that Bonino proposes to replace the two traditional theological concepts.

Despite the very real differences of opinion between these Extracts, it is possible to identify a number of points which most Christians hold in common. All the Extracts would agree that, if modern warfare is to be justified at all, it is only to be justified with extreme reluctance and as a very last resort. Even the possession of a nuclear deterrent is a concession to an evil world. And, in the context of liberation struggles, violence is only to be justified because it is already implicit in an oppressive status quo. This present-day reluctance represents an important return to Augustine's position. It has already been seen that, in Aquinas' writings, Augustine's reluctance in condoning warfare at all, is often absent. The justifiability or otherwise of wars becomes a matter of formal presentation. However, faced with the horrific dimensions of modern warfare, most Christians today might agree that war is in principle evil and is to be resisted, either with a very reluctant use of violence, or with a use of non-violent means.

There are two important elements here which might differentiate present-day Christianity from certain other religious or secular positions. Firstly, war *is* regarded as evil: there is no concept here of a 'holy war'. Secondly, it is an evil which is to be resisted (violently or otherwise): there is no sanction for acquiescence or refusing to take action. Christianity is seen as eirenic, but not quietistic: it involves an uneasy tension between 'peace' and 'justice'.

SECTION 4

THE ENVIRONMENT

SECTION 4

THE ENVIRONMENT

Within the last decade three distinct moral criticisms of Christianity have become more prominent. If a previous generation of sceptical academics was inclined to dismiss Christianity on logical or theoretical grounds (whether those of Marxism, Darwinism, Freudianism, or Logical Positivism), today it is moral grounds for dismissing Christianity that are frequently used. The three critiques, separately or together, accuse historical Christianity of being responsible for present-day anti-Semitism, patriarchy, and environmental destruction.

The first of these critiques – namely that Christianity has consciously or unconsciously fostered anti-Semitism over the centuries – will be represented in the next Section. The second critique – claiming in its most strident form that Judaism and Christianity (and indeed Islam) are inescapably committed to patriarchy – has featured in several parts of this Textbook (including the present Section). The third critique – claiming that Christian belief has legitimated and fostered environmental destruction – will be considered here. Each of these critiques was first developed within Christianity by Christians who had been informed by a wider debate and wished to reform Christian institutions and thinking. Today, however, they are often used as a way of dismissing Christianity entirely – in the interests either of secularism or of alternative forms of religious belonging (frequently neo-paganism). Any adequate account of Christian ethics today must take them seriously.

The environmental critique of Christianity frequently cites Lynn White's 1967 article for the journal *Science*, 'The Roots of our Ecologic Crisis'. For this reason the central part of this seminal article forms Extract 17. White claimed that 'especially in its Western form, Christianity is the most anthropocentric religion the world has seen'. He argued that this resulted from its dual inheritance from Judaism of a linear concept of time and a striking story of creation which gave to humans 'dominion' over all animals. Reinforced by the doctrine of incarnation, Western Christianity has as a result tended to believe that humanity 'shares, in great measure, God's transcendence of nature' (17.17).

Lynn White might have been surprised that his article has been quite so influential in the last decade. Not everyone has heeded his own warning that: 'when one speaks in such sweeping terms, a note of caution is in order. Christianity is a complex faith, and its consequences differ in differing contexts' (17.20). Making overall claims about the social significance of religious ideas is a risky business – as has been noted several times already in this Textbook. Indeed, from White's own argument it is not clear why he should have particularly singled out Western Christianity for his critique (see 20.2). Judaism and Islam have just as emphatic notions of creation and monotheism.

Perhaps the underlying argument in White's critique is linked to another frequently ignored factor. Writing primarily as a professional historian, he nevertheless concluded his article from a perspective within Western Christianity. He was emphatically not writing an external polemic against Christianity and, perhaps, therefore felt more free to criticise his own form of religious belonging. In both of these respects he differed from some present-day writers who have been strongly influenced by his thesis.

At the heart of the theological debate is the question of how Western Christians have understood the Genesis accounts of creation, and especially the crucial verse:

And God said, Let us make man in our image, after our likeness: and let then have dominion over the fish of the sea, and over all the fowl of the air, and over the cattle, and over all the earth, and over every creeping thing that creepeth upon the earth (Gen. 1.26).

Augustine, Aquinas and Luther provide a fascinating contrast in their interpretations of 'dominion'. Together they serve to illustrate that Christianity, even in its Western form, is indeed as complex as White warned. When compared they do not support any simplistic notion that 'dominion' is to be treated as a synonym of 'exploitation'.

From his exegesis of Genesis 1.26 in Text IV.4 it might be possible to argue that Augustine regarded human domination of the non-human as always justified. However, Text X shows that he was conscious that it makes little sense to believe that everything in the world has been created directly to serve human beings. He was not anthropocentric in this sense. He was aware of 'the thorns and the thistles' and argues that, whilst they may serve to punish humans after the Fall, they had a wider (non-human) function before the Fall. 'Dominion' as such is not an issue in this Text. Rather Text X concentrates upon the feature that distinguishes humans from non-humans – namely intelligence. It is human intelligence which is a a reflection of the image of God and it is this which gives humans 'dominion' (X.6).

Both Aquinas and Luther follow Augustine in isolating intelligence as the distinctive feature that differentiates humans from other animals and that reflects the image of God. All three express these crucial links and, not surprisingly, have had a considerable influence upon Western culture. Indeed, anthropocentrism in this limited sense may be a prerequisite of an ethic which is committed to human justice. The *reductio ad absurdum* of an ethical position which rejects even this form of anthropocentrism would be one which could see no moral distinction between the Holocaust and the extermination of five million ants – or even five million bacteria. If intelligent or sentient life is given no higher value status than non-sentient life, then it is difficult to see how such a position is avoided. Certainly within the Extracts both K.C. Abraham and Sallie McFague are emphatic that ecology needs to be correlated with human justice.

But what about anthropocentrism in a stronger form – that is, in the form which supposes that the existence of everything in the world can only be justified in relation to human needs? Neither Augustine nor Luther were anthropcentric in this sense. Both were conscious that, at least before the Fall, non-human life is not simply present in the world to serve human beings. Luther, in particular, regretted as degradation many of the human uses of nature after the Fall. Ever conscious of his health, he could argue that: 'Adam would not have eaten the various kinds of meat, as the less delightful food, in preference to the delightful fruits of the earth, whereas for us nothing is more delicious than meat. From the use of these fruits there would not have resulted that leprous obesity, but physical beauty and health and a sound state of the humors' (XII.20).

There are obvious differences here between Augustine and Luther. The latter is distinctly bleaker in his overwhelming sense of sin. At times he seems to suggest that sin has quite obliterated the image of God in humans apart from Christ. At other times he seems to see flickerings of the divine image still present. It will be suggested later that this bleakness is curiously well suited to much of the secular ecological debate today. Whilst his christocentrism and his literalistic understanding of the Fall is at odds with this secular debate, his bleak view of contemporary nature as a product of human sin fits surprisingly well.

In contrast to Augustine and Luther, Aquinas' position seems to be anthropocentric in both the weaker and the stronger sense. His rigorous logic seems to bring him to a position which accords no value to non-human life other than the value that humans place upon it. In a hierarchical world God is pure intellect; men, and to a lesser extent women, reflect that intellect; but other animals, lacking intellect, are in the world only to serve human beings. The result of this understanding is as follows: 'Therefore, intellectual creatures are so controlled by God, as objects of care for their own sakes; while other creatures are subordinated, as it were, to the rational creatures' (XI.3). Furthermore, whilst it might be imprudent to be cruel to non-human animals – either because it might encourage cruelty to other humans or because it might damage their property – it is not inherently wrong.

It is at this point that Aquinas' logic seems particularly anachronistic today. Viewed as a defence of the value of human life it might still be regarded as relevant. However viewed as an adequate defence of non-human animals it appears considerably more dubious (see Extract 20.4-5). It may be important to remember that deontological positions against cruelty to non-human animals are more typical of the modern than the pre-modern world. Even Kant and Descartes held views on this issue deeply at odds with those held for the most part in the West today.

An increasing consciousness about human responsibility in relation to the natural world is a relatively recent phenomenon. However, it has informed each of the writers represented in the Extracts in this Section. Two Christian ethicists from India have deliberately been chosen, since it is here that the often conflicting demands of ecology and social justice can be most sharply heard. And two radical voices from the West – sacramental and feminist respectively – have also been added. Together they suggest that the ecological challenge and White's critique are being increasingly heard within Christianity today.

Certainly it is a challenge which has been taken up by the World Council of Churches as several of the Extracts point out. Paulos Mar Gregorios' Extract 18 was in fact a preparation paper for the Vancouver Assembly in 1983. Already ecological issues were firmly on the agenda. He was Moderator of the Issues Group on 'Confronting Threats to Peace and Survival' at that Assembly. In its final report the Issues Group expressed its 'hopes for a world where life is not threatened by nuclear holocaust, or slow starvation, for a world where justice and peace embrace each other, are based in Jesus Christ, the Crucified and Risen One who has triumphed over the powers of evil and death' (Part A:1). The issues of nuclear escalation, increasing militarism and ecological destruction were firmly linked in the report. It argued that 'nuclear deterrence is morally unacceptable because it relies on the credibility of the intention to use nuclear weapons: we believe that any intention to use weapons of mass destruction is an utterly inhuman violation of the mind and spirit of Christ which should be in us' (Part A:14). Aware of the potential destructive power of modern technology, the group set out the following four principles gained from dialogues with scientists set up by the WCC:

1.) the growing consensus in theology that we must understand God, humanity and nature in relation to one another, a relation which finds its central expression in Christ;

2.) the increasing recognition by scientists that science is not a value-free or neutral activity, but takes place in a world of ethical decisions and values;

3.) theology and science operate with different languages which continue to raise problems for the dialogue, which need to be tackled through a deeper understanding, by each discipline, of the other's approaches and limitations;

4.) humanity has to recognize the two poles around which and between which life develops and evolves – the Creator and the Creation. The attempt to ignore one of the poles has disastrous consequences (Part B:20).

K.C. Abraham's Extract 19 does not conflict directly with Gregorios, although the two authors do write with very different constituencies in mind. If the Syrian Orthodox Gregorios writes with the ecumenical context in mind, the Protestant Abraham is more concerned with Liberation theology and its relation to ecology. He develops the notion of 'eco-justice' to depict an approach which takes both human liberation and the natural environment seriously – believing that in the end this is in the interests of the world's poor. He insists that: 'The life of the planet is endangered. The ecological crisis raises the problem of survival itself. Moreover, there is a growing awareness of the organic link between the destruction of the environment and socio-economic and political injustice' (19.2).

However, there is a potential conflict between Stephen Clark's Extract 20 and Sallie McFague's Extract 21. Clark has become increasingly critical of the most radical feminist approaches to ecology. He does acknowledge that he has learned much from feminism, arguing for example that 'it is now a truism in developmental circles that it is better to involve the women of agrarian society in discussions about how to live in the land: it is they who may remember how, and they who will put the new advice into practice' (*How to Think about the Earth*, pp.155-6). But he believes the neo-paganism which is sometimes associated with radical feminism (but not of course in McFague), tends to forget that a rigorous inhumanism can result from it – as it did under the Nazis – as well as romanticism. He is also suspicious of what he sees as the selective scientism of such forms of religion. As he argues in Extract 20.2, elsewhere he warns:

> The impulse to blame our situation on Christians, Hebrews, Greeks or, generally, patriarchs is one that most serious environmentalists would normally seek to curb. Selecting villains, and identifying ourselves with their historical victim, is just the sort of 'dualism' we should seek to avoid. Supposing that events have simple, linear causes is to forget how complex history is. Supposing that human beings do things because of their beliefs, and not because their material situation determines that result, is perhaps a little too idealistic. These failing are compounded by romantic fantasies of some place far away or long ago when people lived in 'harmony with nature'. Perhaps they did, or do. But the suspicion, or my suspicion, must be that this was because they lacked the power to do much else (*How to Think about the Earth*, p.10).

Clark does not cite McFague in his criticisms – but his position suggests that he might regard some of her positions as too dependent upon what he terms 'romanticism' (e.g. 21.11 & 21.18).

For McFague new theologies have 'the opportunity to view divine transcendence in deeper, more awesome and more intimate ways than ever before' (21.19). In a series of important books she has developed some of these ways herself with models of God as 'mother', 'lover' and 'friend'. And in her most recent writings she has also developed the models of 'procreation' rather than 'creation' and of the world as 'God's Body'. She claims that these models suggest for Christian ethics: 'a new vision, a new shape for humanity and for our world, a vision that changes the way we see everything and, hence, the way we decide any specific issue and concern... For instance, we become aware of the deep as well as subtle relationships among issues that in the modern individualistic, anthropocentric paradigm are not connected, such as those involving economic priorities and environmental health' (*The Body of God: An Ecological Theology*, pp.202-4).

In contrast, Clark looks to the less intimate terms of what he identifies elsewhere as 'sacramental theism', according to which we live in a world of 'incarnating Beauty' – a world which we do not own, but which we can enjoy as long as we leave it as good for others: 'the Bible expects us to accept our place within the creation, to live by the rules God imposes, to take what we need, no more, and to give up our demands so that life may go on'.

Within Christian ethics environmental concern is still developing. It would, then, be premature to expect clear agreements and alliances. With the explosion of scientific knowledge taking place in genetics and biotechnology considerably more ethical work is clearly needed. However, it is at least evident that no single naive reading of Genesis 1-3 can be attributed to the discipline.

TEXT X
AUGUSTINE
The literal meaning of Genesis

1. *BACKGROUND*

This Text comes from *De Genesi ad Litteram* (*The Literal Meaning of Genesis*, translated and annotated by John Hammond Taylor SJ, vol 1, Book 3, Newman Press, ch.18-24, pp.93-102). Augustine's ambivalent relationship to Manicheanism is reflected in his long-standing concern with Genesis. In 388 he wrote *De Genesi contra Manichaeos* which he subsequently destroyed. He analysed Genesis at length in his *Confessions* and returned to it repeatedly in his mature work *The City of God* (see Text IV). In 401 he started the present work, completing it in 415. He wrote about the latter: 'The title of these books is *The Literal Meaning of Genesis*, that is not according to allegorical meanings but according to the proper historical sense. In this work there are more questions raised than answers found, and of the answers found not many have been established for certain. Those that are not certain have been proposed for further study'(*Retractiones* 2.50). Despite its title, the work covers only the first three chapters of Genesis: Part 1 (Books 1-5) is concerned with Creation; Part 2 (Books 6-11) with Adam's body, Eve, and the Fall; and Part 3 (Book 12) with Paradise.

2. *KEY ISSUES*

Augustine puzzles about why there are thorns and thistles in the world alongside plants that benefit humans (X.1). As part of his response he uses the legal notion of *usufruct* [Justinian saw this as 'the right of using another's property for one's own advantage without impairing the substance of that property', *Institutiones* 2.4]. Augustine insists that such things as thorns and thistles are not *simply* a punishment for humans after the Fall, although they may become that, but may also have a function for other creatures

(X.2-3). He argues that the account of creation in Genesis implies a trinitarian God (X.5). He also sees the 'dominion' of humans over other creatures as an indication that it is the unique rational minds of human beings that reflect the image of God (X.6-8). As rational being, humans, unlike other creatures, are renewed in the knowledge of God (X.9-10). A problem arises for Augustine about human physical appetites. If humans were immortal before the Fall why, he wonders, did they need food (X.11). He is also conscious that before the Fall sexual intercourse in order to propagate seems to contradict human immortality – but he speculates here that this might have been achieved at this stage without concupiscence (X.12). He supports the position that both men and women reflect the image of God in their rational minds (X.13-14) and argues that Genesis does authorise humans to eat (X.16-17). He also puzzles about why Genesis does not say that God, having created humans, saw that they were good. He speculates that this was because God knew that humans would sin later (X.18-20). He concludes, though, that creation as a whole, despite sin, remains beautiful (X.21).

3.   *ETHICAL ARGUMENTS*

As in the other Texts from Augustine, the main ethical emphasis here is deontological. Throughout there is a deontological stress upon creation – culminating in the conclusion that, despite human sinfulness, God's created order remains beautiful (X.21). As in Text I.14 and Text IV.4, a strong deontological stance is taken from the presumption that humans alone have rational souls (X.10). Consequentialism is also evident in some parts of his argument – for example in his argument about the function of plants such as thorns and thistles (X.2-3). However consequentialism is also rejected in other places – for example in his rejection of the argument about gender differentiation in X.13-14.

4.   *BASES OF CHRISTIAN ETHICS*

Since this Text comes from a commentary, it is hardly surprisingly this is the most biblically based of all the Augustine Texts represented here. However, this is not just a commentary upon Genesis. It also represents an important shift in Augustine's method of interpreting the Bible. As the title of the work suggests, he intended to break with allegorical interpretations of the Bible and instead to explore its *literal meaning*. His increasingly literalistic understanding of the Bible has already been noted in relation to Text VII. His break from Manicheanism forced him to come to terms with what he had previously regarded as crudities within the Old Testament. Yet in the present Text his tone is largely exploratory and tentative. Augustine, who at times could be so polemical and dogmatic, offers his own conclusions to difficult questions gently in the present Text (e.g. X.12).

5. *SOCIAL DETERMINANTS*
Written within five years of *Reply to Faustus the Manichaean* there are obvious parallels between this Text and Text VII. Even whilst insisting upon the full physical nature of Adam and Eve (for Augustine they would have eaten and had sexual intercourse even if there had been no Fall), he still speculates that they would have avoided concupiscence (X.12: this issue will be explored further in Section 5). A decade later in *The City of God* he would regard the Manichean injunction against the killing of animals as human food to be an error (XII.9).

6. *SOCIAL SIGNIFICANCE*
This Text is crucial in the light of the argument of Lynn White in Extract 17. As already noted in the introduction, his notion here of human 'dominion' over the rest of creation is evidently anthropocentric, but it is not clearly concerned with domination of non-human creatures. Some of Augustine's most influential arguments are indeed present in this Text. There is a clear emphasis upon the uniqueness (empirical as well as moral) of human rationality, which is extended to both men and women. The created order is seen as beautiful in itself and even apparently dysfunctional parts of this order (such as thorns and thistles – or, earlier in the argument, poisonous and dangerous animals) are still regarded as good. By treating Genesis 1-3 as so important in his writings over the course of several decades, Augustine also placed it firmly on the theological agenda for subsequent

generations of Christians. There could be no final separation between the Old and New Testaments: both have continued to shape Christian experience and thinking.

FURTHER READING

See further John Hammond Taylor's introduction to *The Literal Meaning of Genesis*, as well as Augustine's own writings here and in *The City of God*. For general background, see Peter Brown's *Augustine of Hippo* and *The Body and Society: Men, Women and Sexual Renunciation in Early Christianity*.

TEXT X

AUGUSTINE

The literal meaning of Genesis

The creation of thorns and thistles

X.1

With regard to thorns and thistles, and certain unfruitful trees, men often ask also why or when they were created, since God said, 'Let the earth bring forth the nourishing crops bearing their seed... and the fruit tree bearing its fruit' [Gen. 1.11]. But those who propose this difficulty show they are ignorant of the familiar legal concept of *usufruct*, a term in which the word 'fruit' (*fructus*) indicates an advantage. The overwhelming advantages, whether obvious or hidden, to be derived from all the creatures rooted in the earth and nourished by it, are there for these men to behold themselves or to learn from others who have experienced them.

X.2

Concerning thorns and thistles, we can give a more definite answer, because after the fall of man God said to him, speaking of the earth, 'Thorns and thistles shall it bring forth to you' [Gen. 3.18]. But we should not jump to the conclusion that it was only then that these plants came forth from the earth. For it could be that, in view of the many advantages found in different kinds of seeds, these plants had a place on earth without afflicting man in any way. But since they were growing in the fields in which man was now laboring in punishment for his sin, it is reasonable to suppose that they became one of the means of punishing him. For they might have grown elsewhere, for the nourishment of birds and beasts, or even for the use of man.

X.3

Now this interpretation does not contradict what is said in the words, 'Thorns and thistles shall it bring forth to you,' if we understand that earth in producing them before the fall did not do so to afflict man but rather to provide proper nourishment for certain animals, since some animals find soft dry thistles a pleasant and nourishing food. But earth began to produce these to add to man's laborious lot only when he began to labor on the earth after his sin. I do not mean that these plants once grew in other places and only afterwards in the fields where man planted and harvested his crops. They were in the same place before and after: formerly not for man, afterwards for man. And this is what is meant by the words to you. God does not say, 'Thorns and thistles shall it bring forth,' but bring forth to you; that is, they will now begin to come forth in such a way as to add to your labor, whereas formerly they came forth only as a food for other living creatures.

The Blessed Trinity is implied in God's decree to create man
X.4

'And God said, "Let Us make mankind to Our image and likeness; and let them have dominion over the fish of the sea, the birds of the air, all the cattle, and all the earth, and all the creatures that crawl on the earth." And God made man, to the image of God he made him: male and female he made them. And God blessed them and said, "Increase and multiply and fill the earth and subdue it, and have dominion over the fish of the sea, the birds of the air, all the cattle, all the earth, and all the creatures that crawl on the earth." God also said, "See, I have given you every seed-bearing plant bearing its seed over all the earth, and every tree that has seed-bearing fruit. These will be food for you, for all the wild animals of the earth, for all the birds of the air, and for every creature that crawls on the earth and has the breath of life; every green plant I give for food." And so it was done. And God saw all that he had made, and, behold, it was very good. And there was evening and morning, the sixth day' [Gen. 1.26-31].

X.5

Later on there will be ample opportunity to treat more thoroughly of the nature of man. For the present, in concluding our investigation into the works of the six days, I must briefly point out the importance of the fact that in the case of the other works it is written, God said, 'Let there be...,' whereas here it is written, God said, 'Let Us make mankind to Our image and likeness.' Scripture would indicate by this the plurality of Persons, the Father, Son, and Holy Spirit. But the sacred writer immediately admonishes us to hold to the unity of the Godhead when he says, 'And God made man to the image of God.' He does not say that the Father made man to the image of the Son, or the Son made him to the image of the Father; otherwise the expression to Our image would not be correct if man were made to the image of the Father alone or the Son alone. But Scripture says, 'God made man to the image of God,' meaning that God made man to his own image. The fact that here Holy Scripture says to the image of God, whereas above it says to Our image, shows us that the plurality of Persons must not lead us into saying, believing, or understanding that there are many gods, but rather that we must accept the Father, Son, and Holy Spirit as one God. Because of the three Persons, it is said to 'Our image;' because of the one God, it is said 'to the image of God.'

Man the image of God. The narrative of his creation
X.6

At this point we must also note that God, after saying 'to Our image,' immediately added, 'And let him have dominion over the fish of the sea and the birds of the air and the other irrational animals.' From this we are to understand that man was made to the image of God in that part of his nature wherein he surpasses the brute beasts. This is, of course, his reason or mind or intelligence, or whatever we wish to call it. Hence St Paul says, 'Be renewed in the spirit of your mind, and put on the new man, who is being renewed unto the knowledge of God, according to the image of his Creator' [Eph. 4.23-4]. By these words he shows wherein man has been created to the image of God, since it is not by any features of the body but by a perfection of the intelligible order, that is, of the mind when illuminated.

X.7

Consequently, what is said is similar to what was said in the case of the first light created, if we are justified in understanding this to be the intellectual light that participates in the eternal and changeless Wisdom of God. Scripture does not say, 'And so it was done' and then 'God made the light,' because (as I have already tried to explain) there was not produced some knowledge of the Word of God in the first creature preliminary to the actual production of the creature according to the exemplar in the Word. But first that light was created in which there was produced a knowledge of the Divine Word by whom it was created, and the knowledge consisted precisely in this creature's turning from its unformed state to God who formed it and in its being created and formed. But afterwards, in the case of the other creatures, Scripture says, 'And so it was done,' meaning that in that light, in other words, in the intellectual creation, first there was produced a knowledge of the Word; and then with the statement, 'And God made this or that,' there is indicated the creation of that very creature that had been uttered in the Word of God and predestined to be created.

X.8

This explanation is borne out in the case of the creation of man. For God said, 'Let Us make mankind to Our own image and likeness' and so forth. And then the sacred writer does not go on to say, 'And so it was done,' but he proceeds immediately to add, 'And God made man to the image of God.' For the nature of this creature is intellectual, as is the light previously mentioned, and so its creation is identified with its knowing the Divine Word through whom it was made.

X.9

If Holy Scripture were to say, 'And so it was done,' and then add, 'And God made it,' we should be given to understand that this being was first produced in the mind of a rational creature and then in reality as an existing irrational creature. But man, of whom the writer was speaking, is rational and is made perfect by this very knowledge of which there is question. For after original sin, man is renewed in the knowledge of God according to the image of his Creator. Similarly, before he grew old by sin, he was created in that very knowledge in which he would subsequently be renewed.

X.10

But certain creatures were made without that knowledge, either because they are bodies or irrational souls; and in their case a knowledge of them is first produced in intellectual creatures by the Divine Word, who said, 'Let them be made.' Because of this knowledge, Scripture declares, 'And so it was done,' in order to show us that the knowledge of the being to be created was produced in that creature able to know it first in the Word of God. And then the corporeal and irrational creatures were made, and for this reason Scripture then adds, 'And God made it.'

Why was man, created immortal, given food to eat in Paradise?
X.11

It is difficult to explain how man was created immortal and at the same time in company with the other living creatures was given for food the seed-bearing plant, the fruit tree, and the green crops. If it was by sin that he was made mortal, surely before sinning he did not need such food, since his body could not corrupt for lack of it.

X.12

For it is written, 'Increase and multiply and fill the earth' [Gen. 1.28]. This apparently could not be realized without carnal intercourse of man and woman, and hence there is here also another indication that their bodies were mortal. But one might say that the manner of union might have been different in immortal bodies, so that there would be only the devout affection of charity, and not the concupiscence associated with our corrupt flesh, in the pro-creation of children. These children, not subject to death, would succeed their parents, who themselves would not be destined to die. Thus, finally, the earth would have been filled with immortal men, and when this just and holy society would be thus brought into being, as we believe it will be after the resurrection, there would be an end to the begetting of children. This theory can be proposed, although how it could all be explained is another matter. But at least no one will go so far as to say that there can be a need of food for nourishment except in the case of mortal bodies.

Woman, in so far as she has a rational mind, is made to the image and likeness of God

X.13
Some have conjectured that at this point the interior man was created, but that his body was created afterwards where Scripture says, 'And God formed man of the slime of the earth' [Gen. 2.7]. We should then take the expression, 'God created man,' to refer to his spirit; whereas the statement, 'God formed man,' would apply to his body. But they do not realize that there could have been no distinction of male and female except in relation to the body. There is, of course, the subtle theory that the mind of man, being a form of rational life and precisely the part in which he is made to the image of God, is partly occupied with the contemplation of eternal truth and partly with the administration of temporal things, and thus it is made, in a sense, masculine and feminine, the masculine part as the planner, the feminine one that obeys. But it is not in this double function that the image of God is found, but rather in that part which is devoted to the contemplation of immutable truth. With this symbolism in mind, Paul the Apostle declares that only man is the image and glory of God, 'But woman,' he adds, 'is the glory of man' [1 Cor. 11.7].

X.14
Hence, although the physical and external differences of man and woman symbolize the double role that the mind is known to have in one man, nevertheless a woman, for all her physical qualities as a woman, is actually renewed in the spirit of her mind in the knowledge of God according to the image of her Creator, and therein there is no male or female. Now women

are not excluded from this grace of renewal and this reformation of the image of God, although on the physical side their sexual characteristics may suggest otherwise, namely, that man alone is said to be the image and glory of God. By the same token, in the original creation of man, inasmuch as woman was a human being, she certainly had a mind, and a rational mind, and therefore she also was made to the image of God. But because of the intimate bond uniting man and woman, Scripture says merely, 'God made man to the image of God.' And, lest anyone think that this refers only to the creation of man's spirit, although it was only according to the spirit that he was made to the image of God, Scripture adds, 'Male and female he made him,' to indicate that the body also was now made.

X.15

Moreover, lest anyone suppose that this creation took place in such a way that both sexes appeared in one single human being (as happens in some births, in the case of what we call hermaphrodites), the sacred writer shows that he used the singular number because of the bond of unity between man and woman, and because woman was made from man, as will be shown shortly when the brief account of this passage will be elaborated in greater detail. Hence he immediately added the plural number when he said, 'He made them... and he blessed them.' But, as I have already indicated, we shall later investigate more thoroughly the rest of the biblical account of the creation of man.

The words, 'And so it was done,' in v. 30, mean that man understood God's plan just revealed

X.16

We must note at this point that after the words, 'And so it was done,' Scripture immediately adds, 'And God saw all that he had made, and behold, it was very good.' By this we are given to understand that man was authorized to take as his food the crops of the fields and the fruits of the trees. With the statement, 'And so it was done,' the sacred writer ends the passage he had begun with the words, 'And God said: "See, I have given you the seed-bearing plant, etc."' For if we take the statement, 'And so it was done,' to refer to all that has been said above, we shall have to admit that men increased and multiplied and filled the earth on this one day, the sixth day of creation, but we know from the account in Sacred Scripture that this happened only after many years.

X.17

It follows, then, that the authorization given to eat and the knowledge of this fact acquired by man from divine revelation are indicated by the words, 'And so it was done.' That is to say, it was accomplished in the sense that man knew it when God revealed it. For if he had proceeded to carry this out immediately, that is, if he had taken for his food and eaten what had been given, the customary formula of the scriptural narrative would have been employed, and after the 'statement, 'And so it was done,' which is used to indicate the previous knowledge of a work, then the work itself would be described, and Scripture would say, 'And they took these things and ate them.' The matter could have been described in this way, even though God would not be named again. Thus, in the description of the work of the third day, it is said, 'Let the water that is under the heaven be gathered together into one place, and let the dry land appear;' and then, 'And so it was done;' and after that Scripture does not say, 'And God did it,' but the words are repeated, 'And the water was gathered together into its places, etc.'

Why it is not said of man in particular that God saw he was good
X.18

Now concerning the creation of man, Holy Scripture does not say in particular (as in the case of the other things), 'And God saw that this creature was good.' But after man has been created and authorized to rule and to eat, it is said of all creation in general, 'And God saw all that he had made, and behold, it was very good.' Why is this not said of man in particular? Approval might have first been given specifically to man, as it had been given specifically before to the other creatures, and then God would finally have said of all his creatures, 'Behold, they are very good.'

X.19

One possible explanation is that all was finished on the sixth day, and therefore it was necessary to say of all, 'God saw all that he had made, and behold, it was very good,' rather than to say this specifically of the creatures he had made that day. But then why is such approval spoken of the cattle and wild beasts and creeping things, which belong to this same sixth day? Because they deserved to be pronounced good in particular and specifically, as well as in the general approval given to the other creatures, whereas man, made to the image of God, merited this approval only along with the others? Certainly not! Of course, you might explain by saying that man was not yet perfect because he was not yet placed in Paradise. But after he was placed there, where is the approval given which was omitted here?

X.20

What then are we to say? Perhaps the explanation is that God, knowing man was going to sin and not remain in the perfection of the image of God, wished to say of him, not in particular but along with the rest, that he was good, thus hinting what would be. For when creatures remain in the state in which they have been created, possessing the perfection they have received, whether they have abstained from sin or were incapable of sin, they are good individually, and all in general are very good. The word 'very' is not added without meaning; for in the case of parts of the body, if individual parts are beautiful, all together making up the organic whole are much more beautiful. The eye, for example, is a pleasing and praiseworthy thing, but if we saw it separated from the body, we should not say it was so beautiful as it is when seen joined to the other members in its proper place in the whole body.

X.21

But creatures that lose their own proper beauty by sinning can in no way undo the fact that even they, considered as part of a world ruled by God's providence, are good when taken with the whole of creation. Man, therefore, before the fall, was good even when considered separately from the rest, but instead of declaring so, Scripture said something else foreshadowing the future. No false statement was made concerning man. For he who is good individually is certainly better when taken in conjunction with all. But it does not follow that, when he is good in conjunction with all, he is also good individually. Scripture limited itself to saying what was true at the time and yet intimated God's foreknowledge. For God is the all-good Creator of beings, but he is the all-just Ruler of creatures who sin. Hence, whenever creatures individually lose their loveliness by sin, nevertheless the whole of creation with them included always remains beautiful.

CRITIQUE

Sometimes Augustine is not given sufficient credit for arguing that, despite human sin, the created order as a whole is good and beautiful. There is also an early recognition in this Text that not everything in the world is ordered to please human beings. Thorns and thistles may have their function, even if they currently displease human beings. Finally the significance and uniqueness of human rationality as a reflection of the image of God is stressed in this Text. Augustine insists that this applies to both men and women, even if he does relate the latter to God through the former.

None the less, Augustine is hardly a modern exegete. His commentary upon Genesis frequently tell us as much about himself and about his particular concerns as it does about the text of Genesis itself. Whilst rejecting the allegorical interpretations of his youth, he scarcely provides an account of 'the literal meaning of Genesis' (even if such an account is still thought to be possible). His rich imagination takes him down a variety of unusual paths throughout his commentary. There are few of the controls that would be expected in present-day hermeneutics.

It may also be doubted whether Augustine has really escaped his earlier Manicheanism. For example, he clearly would prefer human procreation not to involve concupiscence and speculates here that in the Garden of Eden before the Fall it would not have done. The next Section will return to this issue.

TEXT XI
AQUINAS
Creation and divine providence

1. BACKGROUND
This Text comes from *Summa Contra Gentiles* 3.2.112-13
(University of Notre Dame Press, London, and Doubleday, New
York, 1975, trans. Vernon J. Bourke, pp.114-19). Unlike *Summa
Theologica* (see *above*, p.76), *Summa Contra Gentiles* was explicitly
written for a non-Christian audience and, hence,
characteristically it argues initially from reason rather than from
Christian revelation – the latter is normally used only to
demonstrate its consonance with the former. It is the earlier of
the two works, being started after Aquinas went to Paris in 1256
and continued after his return to Italy. The intellectual system
of Christianity in the 13th century was facing major challenges,
both from the Islamic world and from the naturalism of secular
culture. Aquinas wrote *Summa Contra Gentiles* as an attempt to
demonstrate the reasonableness of Christianity in the face of
this Graeco-Islamic intellectual threat. Accordingly, he devoted
the first book of the work to the existence and attributes of God,
the second to creation, the third (from which this Text comes)
to providence and human beings' relation to God, and only the
fourth to the specifically Christian doctrines of salvation (which
can be known fully, not through unaided reason, but through
revelation).

2. KEY ISSUES
Aquinas argues that divine providence extends to all things,
but that rational/intellectual creatures have special meaning
since they are free to control their own actions, to know and
love God, and to be aware of their special role within God's
providence (XI.1-2). As a result, intellectual creatures require
special providential care, with other created things being

subordinated to them (XI.3). Only the intellectual creature is by nature free, and only God as God is by nature intellectual (XI.4-5). Intellectual creatures are thus closest to the divine image (XI.6). Other parts of nature are cared for by God for the sake of the intellectual creatures which are incorruptible (XI.7-9). All parts of nature are therefore ordered for the perfection of the whole, with corruptible things being ordered for the sake of the whole human species (XI.10-11). Whereas humans are providentially managed for their own sakes, other things are ordered for the sake of humans (XI.12). Hence it is an error to claim that it is a sin to kill animals: the latter exist to serve humans by divine providence (XI.14). Even biblical commands against animal cruelty are really to discourage either human cruelty to other humans or damage to human property (XI.15).

3. *ETHICAL ARGUMENTS*

In this classic natural law argument Aquinas mixes deontology and consequentialism. He maintains on consequentialist grounds that rational creatures have special meaning in divine providence, since they alone can control their own actions, know and love God, and be conscious of their own divine destiny (XI.1-2). On the other hand he assumes deontologically that God alone is by nature intellectual and that human worth is derived from this (XI.5-6). The status and human treatment of non-human animals is argued consequentially: their sole function is to serve humans (XI.15). Since animals have no deontological value in themselves, they can be eaten and subordinated to humans (XI.14: cf. Augustine's Text XIII.9).

4. *BASES OF CHRISTIAN ETHICS*

As will be seen again in Text XIV, Aquinas follows a set pattern of argument in *Summa Contra Gentiles*: he argues each point on rational grounds first, establishing his principles, and introduces biblical quotations only in his conclusions. A natural law approach with a non-Christian audience in mind requires him to conclude rather than start with biblical revelation. Interestingly it is not the notion of 'dominion' in Genesis that he introduces at this point, but quotations instead from Deuteronomy, the Psalms and Wisdom. He concludes his functionalist understanding of animals with the much quoted command from Deuteronomy about 'not muzzling the ox that treads the corn' (XI.15).

5.   SOCIAL DETERMINANTS

The closely ordered medieval world which Aquinas inhabits is evident throughout this Text. Just as there are no ultimate divisions between Church and State (Text V), so here human and non-human forms of life have complementary functions in a world ordered by divine providence. These functions are, of course, hierarchically ordered. Just as the State is finally subordinate to the Church, so here non-humans are subordinate to humans. In both instances the former serves the latter, because the latter is closest to God. As in Text VIII, order is crucial to Aquinas' understanding. He lives in an ordered and orderly world – indeed, in a world that still presumes the orderliness of slavery (XI.4).

6.   SOCIAL SIGNIFICANCE

More than Augustine, Aquinas articulated a view of non-human life which appears to many today to be thoroughly anthropocentric. Even if Lynn White's critique is somewhat modified, it does suggest that Aquinas, or the culture that he represented, has had an important influence upon Western society. The stress upon rationality that has characterised post-Enlightenment culture is certainly consonant with this. The fruits of this culture, not just in the increase in scientific knowledge, but also in the spread of technology, has had huge implications for ecology.

FURTHER READING

Both *Summa Theologica* and *Summa Contra Gentiles* have important discussions of divine providence. For a discussion of the modern debate about the environment, which takes account of natural law theories, see Michael Northcott's *The Environment and Christian Ethics*.

TEXT XI

AQUINAS

Creation and divine providence

That rational creatures are subject to divine providence in a special way

XI.1

From the points which have been determined above, it is manifest that divine providence extends to all things. Yet we must note that there is a special meaning for providence in reference to intellectual and rational creatures, over and above its meaning for other creatures.

XI.2

For they do stand out above other creatures, both in natural perfection and in the dignity of their end. In the order of natural perfection, only the rational creature holds dominion over his acts, moving himself freely in order to perform his actions. Other creatures, in fact, are moved to their proper workings rather than being the active agents of these operations, as is clear from what has been said. And in the dignity of their end, for only the intellectual creature reaches the very ultimate end of the whole of things through his own operation, which is the knowing and loving of God; whereas other creatures cannot attain the ultimate end except by a participation in its likeness. Now, the formal character of every work differs according to the diversity of the end and of the things which are subject to the operation; thus, the method of working in art differs according to the diversity of the end and of the subject matter. For instance, a physician works in one way to get rid of illness and in another way to maintain health, and he uses different methods for bodies differently constituted. Likewise, in the government of a state, a different plan of ordering must be followed, depending on the varying conditions of the persons subject to this government and on the different purposes to which they are directed. For soldiers are controlled in one way, so that they may be ready to fight; while artisans will be managed in another way, so that they may successfully carry out their activities. So, also, there is one orderly plan in accord with which rational creatures are subjected to divine providence – and another by means of which the rest of creatures are ordered.

That rational creatures are governed for their own sakes, while others are governed in subordination to them

XI.3

First of all, then, the very way in which the intellectual creature was made, according as it is master of its acts, demands providential care whereby this creature may provide for itself, on its own behalf; while the way in which other things were created, things which have no dominion over their acts, shows this fact, that they are cared for, not for their own sake, but as subordinated to others. That which is moved only by another being has the formal character of an instrument, but that which acts of itself has the essential character of a principal agent. Now an instrument is not valued for its own sake, but as useful to a principal agent. Hence it must be that all the careful work that is devoted to instruments is actually done for the sake of the agent, as for an end, but what is done for the principal agent, either by himself or by another, is for his own sake, because he is the principal agent. Therefore, intellectual creatures are so controlled by God, as objects of care for their own sakes; while other creatures are subordinated, as it were, to the rational creatures.

XI.4

Again, one who holds dominion over his own acts is free in his activity, 'for the free man is he who acts for his own sake' [Aristotle's *Metaphysics*]. But one who is acted upon by another, under necessity, is subject to slavery. So, every other creature is naturally subject to slavery; only the intellectual creature is by nature free. Now, under every sort of government, provision is made for free men for their own sakes, but for slaves in such a way that they may be at the disposal of free men. And so, through divine providence provision is made for intellectual creatures on their own account, but for the remaining creatures for the sake of the intellectual ones.

XI.5

Besides, whenever things are ordered to any end, and some of these things cannot attain the end through their own efforts, they must be subordinated to things which do achieve the end and which are ordered to the end for their own sakes. Thus, for instance, the end of an army is victory, and this the soldiers may achieve through their own act of fighting; that is why only soldiers are needed for their own sake in an army. All others, who are assigned to different tasks – for instance, caring for the horses and supplying the weapons – are needed for the sake of the soldiers in the army. Now, from what has been seen earlier, it is established that God is the ultimate end of the whole of things; that an intellectual nature alone attains to him in himself, that is, by knowing and loving him, as is evident from what has been said. Therefore, the intellectual nature is the only one that is required in the universe, for its own sake, while all others are for its sake.

XI.6

Moreover, in any whole the principal parts are needed in themselves in order to constitute the whole, but the other parts are for the preservation or for some betterment of the principal ones. Now, of all the parts of the universe the more noble are intellectual creatures, since they come closer to the divine likeness. Therefore, intellectual creatures are governed by divine providence for their own sakes, while all others are for the intellectual ones.

XI.7

Furthermore, it is evident that all parts are ordered to the perfection of the whole, since a whole does not exist for the sake of its parts, but, rather, the parts are for the whole. Now, intellectual natures have a closer relationship to a whole than do other natures; indeed, each intellectual substance is, in a way, all things. For it may comprehend the entirety of being through its intellect; on the other hand, every other substance has only a particular share in being. Therefore, other substances may fittingly be providentially cared for by God for the sake of intellectual substances.

XI.8

Again, as a thing is acted upon in the course of nature, so is it disposed to action by its natural origin. Now, we see that things do go on in the course of nature in such a way that intellectual substance uses all others for itself: either for the perfecting of its understanding, since it contemplates the truth in them; or for the exercise of its power and the development of its knowledge, in the fashion of an artist who develops his artistic conception in bodily matter; or even for the support of his body which is united with the intellectual soul, as we see in the case of men. Therefore, it is clear that all things are divinely ruled by providence for the sake of intellectual substances.

XI.9

Besides, what a man desires for its own sake is something which he always desires, for that which is, because of itself, always is. On the other hand, what a man desires for the sake of something else is not necessarily always desired; rather, the duration of the desire depends on that for which it is sought. Now, the being of things flows forth from the divine will, as is shown in our earlier considerations. Therefore, those things which always exist among beings are willed by God for their own sake, while things which do not always exist are not for their own sake, but for the sake of something else. Now, intellectual substances come closest to existing always, for they are incorruptible. They are also immutable, excepting only their act of choice. Therefore, intellectual substances are governed for their own sake, in a sense, while others are for them.

XI.10

Nor is what was shown in earlier arguments opposed to this, namely, that all parts of the universe are ordered to the perfection of the whole. For all parts are ordered to the perfection of the whole, inasmuch as one is made to serve another. Thus, in the human body it is apparent that the lungs contribute to the perfection of the body by rendering service to the heart; hence, it is not contradictory for the lungs to be for the sake of the heart, and also for the sake of the whole organism. Likewise, it is not contradictory for some natures to be for the sake of the intellectual ones, and also for the sake of the perfection of the universe. For, in fact, if the things needed for the perfection of intellectual substance were lacking, the universe would not be complete.

XI.11
Similarly, too, the foregoing is not opposed by the fact that individuals are for the sake of their proper species. Because they are ordered to their species, they possess a further ordination to intellectual nature. For a corruptible thing is not ordered to man for the sake of one individual man only, but for the sake of the whole human species. A corruptible thing could not be of use to the whole human species except by virtue of the thing's entire species. Therefore, the order whereby corruptible things are ordered to man requires the subordination of individuals to their species.

XI.12
However, we do not understand this statement, that intellectual substances are ordered for their own sake by divine providence, to mean that they are not more ultimately referred to God and to the perfection of the universe. In fact, they are said to be providentially managed for their own sake, and other things for their sake, in the sense that the goods which they receive through divine goodness are not given them for the advantage of another being, but the things given to other beings must be turned over to the use of intellectual substances in accord with divine providence.

XI.13
Hence it is said in Deuteronomy [4.19]: 'Lest thou see the sun and the moon and the other stars, and being deceived by error, thou adore and serve them, which the Lord thy God created for the service of all the nations that are under heaven;' and again in the Psalm [8.8]: 'Thou hast subjected all things under his feet, all sheep and oxen, moreover the beasts of the field;' and in Wisdom [12.18] it is said: 'Thou, being Master of power, judgest with tranquillity, and with great favor disposest of us.'

XI.14
Through these considerations we refute the error of those who claim that it is a sin for man to kill brute animals. For animals are ordered to man's use in the natural course of things, according to divine providence. Consequently, man uses them without any injustice, either by killing them or by employing them in any other way. For this reason, God said to Noah: 'As the green herbs, I have delivered all flesh to you' [Gen. 9.3].

XI.15
Indeed, if any statements are found in Sacred Scripture prohibiting the commission of an act of cruelty against brute animals, for instance, that one should not kill a bird accompanied by her young [Deut. 22.6], this is said either to turn the mind of man away from cruelty which might be used on other men, lest a person through practising cruelty on brutes might go on to do the same to men; or because an injurious act committed on animals may lead to a temporal loss for some man, either for the agent or for another man; or there may be another interpretation of the text, as the Apostle [1 Cor. 9.9] explains it, in terms of 'not muzzling the ox that treadeth the corn' [Deut. 25.4].

CRITIQUE
Some degree of anthropocentrism may be essential for ethics if human justice is to be maintained. Yet few today might subscribe to the wholesale subordination of non-human life to human life that is made by Aquinas. With the benefit of hindsight it leads to a number of very serious problems:

Most obviously it does not value non-human life as having value in itself. Only the rational is valued as having inherent value. Everything else is subordinated to serving rational life. Even within the internal logic of this position it has enormous ecological dangers. Rational humans may change over time in their perceptions about what does or not have value to humans. Doubtless the dodo only had value to the earliest settlers as an accessible form of food. Two centuries later it has become a symbol of such limited functional attitudes to non-human life.

Similarly the depletion of the gene pool effected by intensive farming techniques (especially if they are assisted by biotechnology) raises increasing worries today. Subordinating the non-human to the human allows humans to impoverish the natural world.

Secondly, it raises problems for humans as well. The principle of rationality is clearly important, but if it becomes the *only* ethical criterion, then it can soon become a means of oppressing less rational humans. Those with severe learning difficulties soon become vulnerable to this principle, as do the senile and those with brain damage. Historically it may also have been a means of subordinating women, on the assumption that they were less rational than men (this will be discussed further in relation to Text XIV).

TEXT XII
LUTHER'S WORKS
Commentary on Genesis 1.26-31

1. BACKGROUND

This Text comes from Luther's *Lectures on Genesis* (from *Luther's Works*, vol 1, Concordia Publishing House, 1958, ed. Jaroslav Pelikan, trans. George V. Schick, pp.66-73). First given a decade before his death, as lectures at the University of Wittenberg 1535-6, they were edited with additions by others later. Jaroslav Pelikan suggests that 'the hands are sometimes the hands of the editors, but the voice is nevertheless the voice of Luther' (p.xii). Without relying upon its every nuance to establish Luther's thoughts, this Text does allow useful comparisons especially with Augustine's Text X.

2. KEY ISSUES

For Luther 'dominion' is given to Adam and Eve as the ones who knew God and in whom God's enlightened reason, justice and wisdom shone (XII.1). But through sin human beings have largely lost this divine image (XII.2). Before the Fall Adam and Eve both had amazing mental gifts: after the Fall only small differences remain between human beings and other animals (XII.3-7). Through Christ we wait for the original state of Paradise to be restored (XII.8). The image of God shines in humans alone – other animals are rather 'footprints' of God (XII.9). Eve was also created in the image of God, but, as a woman, she had a much weaker nature (XII.11-12). However Luther rejects Jewish stories regarding Eve in effect as a 'maimed man' (XII.13-14). He argues that because of sin procreation has become brutish (XII.16-17). Before the Fall Adam would not have used animals for food but rather for the admiration of God: after the Fall meat-eating now causes us health problems (XII.18-21). Although God created all things good, this goodness has largely been lost through sin (XI.22-3).

3. ETHICAL ARGUMENTS

Of all the Luther Texts the present one shows most clearly how a natural law approach is curtailed by a strong notion of sin. Before the Fall, Luther believes, Adam and Eve and the rest of the created order reflected the enlightened reason, justice and wisdom of God. In this context what is 'natural' clearly reflects the will of the creator: what is 'natural' is thus also what is 'right'. However, after the Fall everything is distorted by sin. The created order as a whole, and even Adam and Eve within it, has largely lost this image of God. Given this understanding, Luther argues deontologically that it is only in Christ that the original state of Paradise can be restored (XII.8). This position – which sharply distinguishes this Text from the heritage of Aquinas – is clearly consonant with Luther's position in Text III.

4. BASES OF CHRISTIAN ETHICS

As with Augustine's Text X, the fact that this Text is taken from a commentary inevitably makes it more biblically oriented than most of the other Texts. However it does supply a clear account of Luther's central method in Christian ethics. His overwhelming sense of sin increases his Christocentrism. For him there can be no satisfactory basis for Christian ethics other than Christ. As he states at the end of this Text: 'if these thoughts [about sin] do not move us to hope and longing for the coming Day and the future life, nothing could move us' (XII.23).

5. SOCIAL DETERMINANTS

An enduring debate within Christian ethics is the issue of how the Reformers reflected or distorted the Bible in their single-minded stress upon it. Certainly Luther (or his followers who assembled this Text) is not a modern exegete. His understanding of Adam and Eve is unambiguously literalistic. Less rambling than Augustine in his interpretation of Genesis, he nonetheless brings to it his own concerns, and perhaps his own deep pessimism about humankind (e.g. XII.23). There are hints here of the religious anti-Semitism which is to come into the open in Text XV (e.g. XII.13). There is also something remaining of the negative evaluation of the mechanisms of sexual intercourse inherited from Augustine (XII.16-17).

6. SOCIAL SIGNIFICANCE

Yet there are also some surprising, and perhaps influential, features of this passage. 'Dominion' over non-human life is given to Adam and Eve whilst they reflect God's enlightened reason, justice and wisdom before the Fall. However it is 'dominion' which does not seem to involve humans eating other animals. Their diet instead is fruits considerably superior to any fruits existing after the Fall. Meat-eating, then, seems to be a product of the Fall. Not only that, but, to the ever health-conscious Luther, it is a product of the Fall which has done human beings little good. In Paradise animals form part of the texture of life designed to praise God rather than simply to provide food for human beings. The central idea of a balanced created order in this Text – although admittedly linked here to an idealistic understanding of animals before a literalistic Fall – might yet prove influential within the ecological debate.

FURTHER READING

For the further background on Luther's *Lectures on Genesis* see the introduction to vol 1 of *Luther's Works*.

TEXT XII

LUTHER'S WORKS

Commentary on Genesis 1.26-31

Let him have dominion over the fish of the sea, etc. (vs. 26)
XII.1
Here the rule is assigned to the most beautiful creature, who knows God and is the image of God, in whom the similitude of the divine nature shines forth through his enlightened reason, through his justice and his wisdom. Adam and Eve become the rulers of the earth, the sea, and the air. But this dominion is given to them not only by way of advice but also by express command. Here we should first carefully ponder the

exclusiveness in this: no beast is told to exercise dominion; but without ceremony all the animals and even the earth, with everything brought forth by the earth, are put under the rule of Adam, whom God by an express verbal command placed over the entire animal creation. Adam and Eve heard the words with their ears when God said: 'Have dominion.' Therefore the naked human being – without weapons and walls, even without any clothing, solely in his bare flesh – was given the rule over all birds, wild beasts, and fish.

XII.2
Even this small part of the divine image we have lost, so much so that we do not even have insight into that fulness of joy and bliss which Adam derived from his contemplation of all the animal creatures. All our faculties today are leprous, indeed, dull and utterly dead. Who can conceive of that part, as it were, of the divine nature, that Adam and Eve had insight into all the dispositions of all animals, into their characters and all their powers? What kind of a reign would it have been if they had not had this knowledge? Among the saints there is evident in this life some knowledge of God. Its source is the Word and the Holy Spirit. But the knowledge of nature – that we should know all the qualities of trees and herbs, and the dispositions of all the beasts – is utterly beyond repair in this life.

XII.3
If, then, we are looking for an outstanding philosopher, let us not overlook our first parents while they were still free from sin. They had a most perfect knowledge of God, for how would they not know him whose similitude they had and felt within themselves? Furthermore, they also had the most dependable knowledge of the stars and of the whole of astronomy.

XII.4
Eve had these mental gifts in the same degree as Adam, as Eve's utterance shows when she answered the serpent concerning the tree in the middle of Paradise. There it becomes clear enough that she knew to what end she had been created and pointed to

the source from which she had this knowledge; for she said (Gen. 3.3): 'The Lord said.' Thus she not only heard this from Adam, but her very nature was pure and full of the knowledge of God to such a degree that by herself she knew the Word of God and understood it.

XII.5
Of this knowledge we have feeble and almost completely obliterated remnants. The other animals, however, completely lack this knowledge. They do not know their Creator, their origin, and their end; they do not know out of what and why they were created. Therefore they certainly lack that similitude of God. For this reason the psalm also urges (Ps. 32.9): 'Do not become like the horse and the mule.'

XII.6
Thus even if this image has been almost completely lost, there is still a great difference between the human being and the rest of the animals. Before the coming of sin the difference was far greater and more evident, when Adam and Eve knew God and all the creatures and, as it were, were completely engulfed by the goodness and justice of God. As a result, there was between them a singular union of hearts and wills. No other beautiful sight in the whole world appeared lovelier and more attractive to Adam than his own Eve. But now, as the heathen say, a wife is a necessary evil. Why they call her an evil can be perceived readily enough; but they do not know the cause of evil, namely, Satan, who has so vitiated and corrupted this creation.

XII.7
What we achieve in life, however, is brought about, not by the dominion which Adam had but through industry and skill. Thus we see the birds and the fish caught by cunning and deceit; and by skill the beasts are tamed. Those animals which are most domesticated, such as geese and hens, nevertheless are wild so far as they themselves and their nature are concerned. Therefore even now, by the kindness of God, this leprous body has some appearance of the dominion over the other creatures. But it is extremely small and far inferior to that first dominion, when

there was no need of skill or cunning, when the creature simply obeyed the divine voice because Adam and Eve were commanded to have dominion over them.

XII.8

Therefore we retain the name and word 'dominion' as a bare title, but the substance itself has been almost entirely lost. Yet it is a good thing to know these facts and to ponder them, so that we may have a longing for that coming Day when that which we lost in Paradise through sin will be restored to us. We are waiting for that life for which Adam also should have waited. And we duly marvel at this and thank God for it, that although we are so disfigured by sin, so dull, ignorant, and dead, as it were, nevertheless, through the merit of Christ, we wait for the same glory of the spiritual life for which Adam would have waited if he had remained in his physical life, which was endowed with the image of God.

And God created man according to his image, according to the
image of God he created him (vs. 27)

XII.9

Here Moses does not employ the word 'similitude,' but only 'image.' Perhaps he wanted to avoid an ambiguity of speech and for this reason repeated the noun 'image.' I see no other reason for the repetition unless we should understand it for the sake of emphasis as an indication of the Creator's rejoicing and exulting over the most beautiful work he had made, so that Moses intends to indicate that God was not so delighted at the other creatures as at man, whom he had created according to his own similitude. The rest of the animals are designated as footprints of God; but man alone is God's image, as appears in [Peter Lombard's] *Sentences*. In the remaining creatures God is recognized as by his footprints; but in the human being, especially in Adam, he is truly recognized, because in him there is such wisdom, justice, and knowledge of all things that he may rightly be called a world in miniature. He has an understanding of heaven, earth, and the entire creation. And so it gives God pleasure that he made so beautiful a creature.

XII.10

But without a doubt, just as at that time God rejoiced in the counsel and work by which man was created, so today, too, he takes pleasure in restoring this work of his through his Son and our Deliverer, Christ. It is useful to ponder these facts, namely, that God is most kindly inclined toward us and takes delight in his thought and plan of restoring all who have believed in Christ to spiritual life through the resurrection of the dead.

Male and female he created them

XII.11

In order not to give the impression that he was excluding the woman from all the glory of the future life, Moses includes each of the two sexes; for the woman appears to be a somewhat different being from the man, having different members and a much weaker nature. Although Eve was a most extraordinary creature – similar to Adam so far as the image of God is concerned, that is, in justice, wisdom, and happiness – she was nevertheless a woman. For as the sun is more excellent than the moon (although the moon, too, is a very excellent body), so the woman, although she was a most beautiful work of God, nevertheless was not the equal of the male in glory and prestige.

XII.12

However, here Moses puts the two sexes together and says that God created male and female in order to indicate that Eve, too, was made by God as a partaker of the divine image and of the divine similitude, likewise of the rule over everything. Thus even today the woman is the partaker of the future life, just as Peter says that they are joint heirs of the same grace [1 Peter 3.7]. In the household the wife is a partner in the management and has a common interest in the children and the property, and yet there is a great difference between the sexes. The male is like the sun in heaven, the female like the moon, the animals like the stars, over which sun and moon have dominion. In the first place, therefore, let us note from this passage that it was written that this sex may not be excluded from any glory of the human creature, although it is inferior to the male sex...

XII.13

Lyra relates a Jewish tale, of which Plato, too, makes mention somewhere, that in the beginning man was created bisexual and later on, by divine power, was, as it were, split or cut apart, as the form of the back and of the spine seems to prove. Others have expanded these ideas with more obscene details. But the second chapter refutes these babblers. For if this is true, how can it be sure that God took one of the ribs of Adam and out of it built the woman? These are Talmudic tales, and yet they had to be mentioned so that we might see the malice of the devil, who suggests such absurd ideas to human beings.

XII.14

This tale fits Aristotle's designation of woman as a 'maimed man;' others declare that she is a monster. But let them themselves be monsters and sons of monsters – these men who make malicious statements and ridicule a creature of God in which God himself took delight as in a most excellent work, moreover, one which we see created by a special counsel of God. These pagan ideas show that reason cannot establish anything sure about God and the works of God but only thinks up reasons against reasons and teaches nothing in a perfect and sound manner.

And He blessed (vs. 28)

XII.15

This he did not say about the animals; therefore he includes them here.

Be fruitful

XII.16

This is a command of God added for the creature. But, good God, what has been lost for us here through sin! How blessed was that state of man in which the begetting of offspring was linked with the highest respect and wisdom, indeed with the knowledge of God! Now the flesh is so overwhelmed by the leprosy of lust that in the act of procreation the body becomes downright brutish and cannot beget in the knowledge of God.

XII.17

Thus the power of procreation remained in the human race, but very much debased and even completely overwhelmed by the leprosy of lust, so that procreation is only slightly more moderate than that of the brutes. Added to this are the perils of pregnancy and of birth, the difficulty of feeding the offspring, and other endless evils, all of which point out to us the enormity of original sin. Therefore the blessing, which remains till now in nature, is, as it were, a cursed and debased blessing if you compare it with that first one; nevertheless, God established it and preserves it. So let us gratefully acknowledge this 'marred blessing.' And let us keep in mind that the unavoidable leprosy of the flesh, which is nothing but disobedience and loathsomeness attached to bodies and minds, is the punishment of sin. Moreover, let us wait in hope for the death of this flesh that we may be set free from these loathsome conditions and may be restored even beyond the point of that first creation of Adam.

And have dominion over the fish of the sea

XII.18

We are so overcome by our ignorance of God and the creatures that we cannot establish with certainty what use would have been made of the cattle, the fish, and the other animals in the first creation and state of perfection. We see now that we eat flesh, vegetables, etc. If they were not used in this manner, we would not know why they were created; for we neither see nor have any other use for these creatures. But Adam would not have used the creatures as we do today, except for food, which he would have derived from other, far more excellent fruits. For he under whose power everything had been placed did not lack clothing or money. Nor would there have been any greed among his descendants; but, apart from food, they would have made use of the creatures only for the admiration of God and for a holy joy which is unknown to us in this corrupt state of nature. By contrast, today and always the whole creation is hardly sufficient to feed and support the human race. Therefore what this dominion consisted of we cannot even imagine.

And God said: Behold, I have given you every herb bearing seed
(vs. 29)

XII.19

Here you see how solicitous God is for the man he has created. First he created the earth like a house in which he should live. Then he arranged the other things he regarded as necessary for life. Finally he gave the gift of procreation to the man he had created. Now he also provides his food that nothing may be lacking for leading his life in the easiest possible manner. Moreover, I believe that if Adam had remained in the state of innocence, his children would have run immediately after birth to the enjoyment of those delights which the initial creation afforded. But it is vain to mention these things; they cannot be acquired by thought, and they are irrecoverable in this life.

And all the trees

XII.20

Moses seems to be making a difference between the seeds and the green herbage, perhaps because the latter were to serve for the use of the beasts, the former for that of man. I have no doubt that the seeds we use for food today were far more excellent then than they are now. Moreover, Adam would not have eaten the various kinds of meat, as the less delightful food, in preference to the delightful fruits of the earth, whereas for us nothing is more delicious than meat. From the use of these fruits there would not have resulted that leprous obesity, but physical beauty and health and a sound state of the humors.

XII.21

But now people do not content themselves with meats, with vegetables, or with grain; and rather often, because of unsuitable food, we face dangers of health. I am saying nothing about those increasingly widespread sins of over-indulgence in food and drink which are worse than brutish. The curse which followed because of sin is apparent. It is also likely that only then were the accursed and pernicious insects produced out of the earth, which was cursed because of man's sin...

And God saw all things that he had made, and they were very
good. And evening and morning became the sixth day (vs. 31)
XII.22
After God has finished his works, he speaks after the custom of
one who has become tired, as if he wanted to say: 'Behold, I
have prepared all things in the best way. The heaven I have
prepared as a roof; the earth is the flooring; the animals – with
all the appointments of the earth, the sea, and the air – are the
possession and wealth; seeds, roots, and herbs are the food.
Moreover, he himself, the lord of these, man, has been created.
He is to have knowledge of God; and with the utmost freedom
from fear, with justice and wisdom, he is to make use of the
creatures as he wishes, according to his will. Nothing is lacking.
All things have been created in greatest abundance for physical
life. Therefore I shall keep a Sabbath.'

XII.23
All these good things have, for the most part, been lost through
sin; and we, who have kept hardly a shadow of that realm, are
today like a corpse of that first human being. Or shall we not say
that he has lost everything who became mortal after being
immortal, a sinner after being righteous, a condemned man after
being welcome and well-pleasing? For now man is mortal and a
sinner. But if these thoughts do not move us to hope and longing
for the coming Day and the future life, nothing could move us.

CRITIQUE

The bleak tone of this Text probably fits the current ecological
debate quite well. For Luther even the 'small part of the divine
image we have lost, so much so that we do not even have insight
into that fullness of joy and bliss which Adam derived from his
contemplation of all the animal creatures' (XII.2). Human sin
has destroyed all of this. Translated into secular language such
sentiments might find a ready home in some of the ecological
critiques today.

Yet Luther pays a heavy price for this analysis if it is to remain
consistent. Because his solution is so exclusively Christian it has
finally little to offer the secular debate (an issue which is
considered in relation to Hauerwas' Extract 15). As ever, in

Luther reason unaided by Christian revelation at best can convict us of sin: it cannot provide any resources to overcome sinful action.

Even within Christian ethics Luther's analysis faces problems. He is frequently caught between a residual use of natural law theory and a belief that sin has altogether destroyed God's image in the natural world. Here he seems to come down firmly on the latter side. But elsewhere he (or his followers who recorded his ideas) is not so consistent. Yet those movements within Christianity today which are influenced by aspects of secular thought – Liberation theology, feminist theology, and probably ecological theology as well – may find the bleakest side of Luther finally unusable. It appears to deny their very legitimacy.

In addition, Luther's understanding of the overwhelming nature of sin probably does depend upon a literalistic understanding of the Fall. Unambiguously for him our direct progenitors, Adam and Eve, fell from a state of joy in Paradise through the original sin (of the woman). Whilst this account remained uncontested it did much to explain the overwhelming nature of sin in the world today apart from Christ. Yet, if it is treated in ways which are not literalistic, it may provide a less secure basis for this bleak conviction.

EXTRACTS 17-21

WHITE, GREGORIOS, ABRAHAM, CLARK AND MCFAGUE

1. *BACKGROUND*

Lynn White's Extract 17 comes from his much-quoted article 'The Historical Roots of our Ecologic Crisis' which first appeared in *Science* (vol 155, no 3767, 10 March 1967, extracted from pp.1203-7). Paulos Mar Gregorios' Extract 18 comes from an article entitled 'Life from the Perspective of Science and the Christian Faith' from a series of studies for the 1983 World Council of Churches' General Assembly at Vancouver, ed. William H. Lazareth, *The Lord of Life* (WCC, 1983, pp.34-6 & 39-43). K.C. Abraham's Extract 19 comes from 'A Theological Response to Ecological Crisis', *Bangalore Theological Forum* (vol XXV, no 1, March 1993, pp.3-14). Stephen R.L. Clark's Extract 20 comes from 'Christian Responsibility for the Environment', *Modern Churchman* (vol 28, no 2, 1986, pp.24-31). And Sallie McFague's Extract 21 comes from 'An Earthly Theological Agenda', *The Christian Century* (vol 108, no 1, 2-9 January 1991, pp.12-15).

Lynn White (b.1907), a Presbyterian layperson, was Professor of History and Director of the Centre for Medieval and Renaissance Studies at the University of California, Los Angeles. Metropolitan Paulos Mar Gregorios is a bishop of the ancient, pre-Chalcedonian Syrian Orthodox Church of Kerala, South India. As Paul Verghese he wrote *The Freedom of Man* (1972), whilst principal of the Orthodox Seminary at Kottayam, Kerala. A frequent contributor to the WCC, he presented the report on peace and survival as Moderator of the Issue Group at the 6th Assembly in Vancouver in 1983. He is widely recognised as one of the most important present-day Indian theologians. K.C. Abraham has been professor Christian ethics for many years at the United Theological College, Bangalore, serving churches in South Churches, and is now Director of the South Asia Theological Research Institute. Stephen Clark is professor of philosophy at Liverpool University and an Anglican layperson. He is the author of a number of significant philosophical and theological books, including: *The Moral Status of Animals* (1977); *The Nature of the Beast* (1982); *Civil Peace and Sacred Order* (1989); *A Parliament of Souls* (1990); and *How to Think About the Earth* (1993). Sallie McFague is professor of theology at Vanderbelt Divinity School and author of a number of important works in feminist theology, including: *Metaphorical Theology: Models of God in Religious Language* (1982); *Models of God: Theology for an Ecological, Nuclear Age* (1987); and *The Body of God: An Ecological Theology* (1993).

2. KEY ISSUES

White notes that, although people have long made an impact on their physical environment, human technology today is causing a major ecological crisis (17.1-3). Establishing exactly what can be done to resolve this crisis is difficult, but at least we can attempt to clarify our thinking by examining some of the presuppositions underlying modern science and technology (17.4-6). White argues that it is the specifically Western combination of science and technology that has been so destructive of the environment (17.6-7). New ploughing techniques developed in the West provide an instructive example of the Occidental domination of nature (17.10-11). Such attitudes to the environment, he believes, are deeply conditioned by religion (17.13). In the West the victory of Christianity over paganism has had a profound and adverse effect upon our thinking about nature – creation and domination have become linked (17.14-16). Western Christianity is profoundly anthropocentric (17.17), but not necessarily Eastern Christianity (17.20-1). White finally argues that St Francis offers a striking exception and maintains that his concepts are important for the modern ecological movement (17.24-8).

Gregorios is emphatic about relating socio-ethical issues of peace and justice to life in Christ. This passage and his other writings also show a strong concern about oppression and social injustice. Yet it is not so obviously written from the perspective of Liberation theology. He writes in the context of the Vancouver theme of 'Jesus Christ – the Life of the World' (18.1) which he relates to the threats to human life presented by the prospects of nuclear holocaust (18.2), dangers in biotechnology (18.3-9 – a long-standing concern of his), ecological misuse (18.10-11) and world poverty and injustice (18.12-13). 'Life', that is so threatened, Gregorios attempts to understand, first in terms of science, and then in terms of theology. The scientific answer to the question 'what is life' is presented here in summary form (18.20 – his excellent, but detailed, scientific account has been omitted because of lack of space). His theological discussion focuses upon the Assembly theme 'Life as a gift of God' (see *below*, pp.564f.). He argues that this theme is directly relevant to a number of social issues concerning human life (18.22). For the Christian, life is 'created', not a product of nature (18.23), and is thus dependent upon God, evoking in us a free response of love (18.24-9) and repentance (18.31). Gregorios maintains that both the whole of biological life and life in Christ are equally gifts of grace – biological life acting as the very basis and receptacle for eternal life (18.32-4). He views the spectrum of interconnected life in Orthodox terms (18.36) and sees the incarnation as affecting all levels of life and as overcoming the alienation of humanity from God (18.38-9). In the incarnation the gift is the Giver himself (18.41-2). But he argues that it is only small Christian communities that can act as adequate vehicles for this faith (18.43).

For Abraham there is a crucial link to be made between social justice and ecology: the latter is an issue of concern not just within the richer countries (19.1-2). Once nature was thought to be an object for exploitation by 'developers': today, scientists are increasingly concerned about ecology (19.3). Ecology should be seen as involving both political and social justice (19.4-6). Thus justice concerns the whole cosmos and not simply human beings (19.8). Economic degradation, poverty and the ecological crisis are all linked, making us more aware of our dependence upon earth and of the God-human-world relationship (19.10-14). Theology today is shifting from anthropocentrism to an ecological orientation, even within a liberation perspective (19.15-18). Science and technology have often thought of humans as being above nature – sometimes using Genesis 1.26 – a perspective criticised by Lynn White (19.21-6). A second perspective makes little distinction between humans and nature (19.27-8). However a third sees humans rather as part of nature yet as still different from other creatures (19.29). On this last perspective the notion of 'dominion' is seen in Christian terms of human responsibility (19.30-2). Human participation in the cosmos is now stressed and, in the process, a more Eastern perspective is adopted (19.33-8).

Clark notes that anthropocentrism has often seemed to be a feature of churches. He argues, however, that it is neither an exclusive feature of churches nor a requirement of Christian belief (20.1-2). Although cruelty to animals is widely recognised as being wrong even in secular society, there is a danger of humans forgetting their duties to other forms of life and even to some human forms of life (20.3-4). Even the notion of 'serving the spirit' can lead to tyranny (20.5). In contrast, saints characteristically welcome the non-human as God-given (20.6-7). The Bible constantly insists that humans are not alone but are a part of God's whole creation, which includes both the rational and the irrational (20.8-9). For the Bible the world at large is not simply at the disposal of humans, but embodies images of spiritual values (20.10-11). Why then does the Bible offer so few injunctions about how humans should behave towards the non-human? Clark argues that this is because the Israelites could in fact do little to harm the rest of creation over which God was believed to stand (20.12-13). Today at the very least we should not demand our human comforts at whatever cost to the non-human (20.14).

McFague maintains that Liberation theologies should now include all oppressed creatures as well as planet earth (21.1-2). Western dualism has linked the domination of both the oppressed and the natural world (21.3-4). She believes that it is important to remember that everything on this planet is interrelated and interdependent (21.5). McFague's own theology has, over the years, become less Barthian and more concerned with ecological issues (21.6-8). As a result, she now believes that an 'earthly' theology should become more co-operative and less dualistic (21.9-12). Theology needs to deconstruct and reconstruct its central symbols to take account of these changes (21.13). It should become cosmocentric, rather than anthropocentric, and more prophetic despite the risk of becoming unpopular in the academic world (21.14-16). She believes that in the past there was an overemphasis upon redemption rather than creation (21.17). Theology today should instead serve to deepen our sense of complicity in the earth's decay and also promote 'right relations' – relations that include the oppressed, other creatures and the earth (21.18-19).

3. ETHICAL ARGUMENTS

White's Extract is mostly analytical in character. However it becomes clear towards the end that it is also written from a distinctively ethical basis. There he shows that he believes Christianity 'bears a huge burden of guilt' (17.24) and argues deontontologically for St Francis' virtues of 'humility' and 'democracy of all God's creatures' (17.27). Abraham, Clark and McFague all reflect this critique in their Extracts. All express clear deontological commitments to the non-human, and express criticisms of churches which have ignored such commitments. Gregorios, too, shows a strong deontological commitment to the poor and to the oppressed.

4. BASES OF CHRISTIAN ETHICS

Neither White nor Gregorios make any direct biblical references. As a historian, White attempts to show that a cultural analysis of Christianity can point to a need for a new attitude towards the environment. In characteristic Orthodox style Gregorios' argument rests upon doctrine and upon the received wisdom of tradition. Significantly, the latter can include the statement made by the joint Orthodox consultation which met to prepare for Vancouver (18.36). He also mixes this with his considerable knowledge of present-day science and sees the full Christian as a person of both culture and learning, on the one hand, and, on the other, of worship and faith (18.43). His strong liturgical stress is evident in the central position that he gives to eucharistic worship (18.39). His fellow Indian, Abraham, argues from a more Reformed perspective and does use the Bible at several points in his argument – as well as using writers such as McFague [some of his quotations from other writers have been omitted here]. However it is the Anglican philosopher, Clark, who is the most biblical in his approach in the Extracts in this Section. The Bible is used by him here in a mixture of illustrative and authoritative modes (see especially 21.8-9 and 21.12).

5. SOCIAL DETERMINANTS

Elsewhere Lynn White's writings show that he was clearly aware of social factors affecting current positions within Christian ethics. For example, in 1954 he addressed the Presbyterian Synod of California arguing that, although conscientious objectors (especially to nuclear weapons) should be respected, 'the Church has an equal duty not to permit these conscientious objectors to fall into the spiritual pride of believing that they have really achieved holiness. Profoundly evil forces are loose in the world, and these forces are armed with the H-Bomb' ('Can a Christian be a Good Citizen?', p.4). For him 'the life of a Christian is by its very nature filled with dualities, and he should never even pretend to give an unqualified allegiance to any earthly authorities' (p.9).

Both Gregorios and Abraham reflect a strong Indian emphasis upon 'culture' and 'knowledge'. Whilst clearly concerned about poverty, the concept of 'liberation' itself is somewhat different in India, with the traditional notion of 'liberation' (*moksha*) referring rather to spiritual release and/or escape from the cycle of rebirth (*samsara*). Although Marxism is strong in parts of India and espoused by some Roman Catholic clergy, it is certainly not identical to Western Marxism.

In contrast Clark and McFague write from a distinctly Western context. However, their critiques of this context are distinct. Clark has been strongly influenced by philosophical vegetarianism and animal rights, whereas McFague has been most influenced by feminism. Both have been philosophically trained although only Clark works directly amongst philosophers.

6. SOCIAL SIGNIFICANCE

White's article has been extremely influential in the ecological movement – and has clearly influenced the other writers in this Section – although he could hardly have expected this when he wrote it. Often used as a generalised critique of Christianity, it was in fact clearly written from a position within Christianity. Gregorios and his fellow metropolitan Geevarghese Mar Osthathios (author of *Theology of a Classless Society*, 1979, and *The Sin of Being Rich in a Poor World*, 1983) are proving two of the most important present-day Indian theologians. The Syrian Orthodox Church of South India has traditionally been somewhat conservative and socially isolated, but recently has become far more active on socio-political issues. The Marxist inclined state of Kerala does not show all of the anti-clericalism of much Western Marxism and may in principle be more open to the influence of an informed Christian minority. At the World Council of Churches itself the issue of ecology has become increasingly important. The Vancouver Assembly, for example, maintained that 'churches can adequately face the threats to human survival today only if they take up the problems of science and technology for the human race' (*Issues*, para. 19). McFague, who refers directly to this theme, has herself become one of the most important feminist theologians in the United States and beyond. Ecological issues have become central to her exploration of new feminist models for theology – and in this area her theological influence is very considerable.

FURTHER READING
For an analysis of recent ecological theology, see Stephen R.L. Clark, *How to Think About the Earth*, and Michael Northcott, *The Environment and Christian Ethics*. For documents relating to the WCC 6th Assembly, see its official report *Gathered for Life*.

EXTRACT 17
WHITE
The theological roots of the ecological crisis

17.1
The history of ecologic change is still so rudimentary that we know little about what really happened, or what the results were. The extinction of the European aurochs as late as 1627 would seem to have been a simple case of overenthusiastic hunting. On more intricate matters it often is

impossible to find solid information. For a thousand years or more the Frisians and Hollanders have been pushing back the North Sea, and the process is culminating in our own time in the reclamation of the Zuider Zee. What, if any, species of animals, birds, fish, shore life, or plants have died out in the process? In their epic combat with Neptune have the Netherlanders overlooked ecological values in such a way that the quality of human life in the Netherlands has suffered? I cannot discover that the questions have ever been asked, much less answered.

17.2

People, then, have often been a dynamic element in their own environment, but in the present state of historical scholarship we usually do not know exactly when, where, or with what effects man-induced changes came. As we enter the last third of the 20th century, however, concern for the problem of ecologic backlash is mounting feverishly. Natural science, conceived as the effort to understand the nature of things, had flourished in several eras and among several peoples. Similarly there had been an age-old accumulation of technological skills, sometimes growing rapidly, sometimes slowly. But it was not until about four generations ago that Western Europe and North America arranged a marriage between science and technology, a union of the theoretical and the empirical approaches to our natural environment. The emergence in widespread practice of the Baconian creed that scientific knowledge means technological power over nature can scarcely be dated before about 1850, save in the chemical industries, where it is anticipated in the 18th century. Its acceptance as a normal pattern of action may mark the greatest event in human history since the invention of agriculture, and perhaps in nonhuman terrestrial history as well.

17.3

Almost at once the new situation forced the crystallization of the novel concept of ecology; indeed, the word *ecology* first appeared in the English language in 1873. Today, less than a century later, the impact of our race upon the environment has so increased in force that it has changed in essence. When the first cannons were fired, in the early 14th century, they affected ecology by sending workers scrambling to the forests and mountains for more potash, sulphur, iron ore, and charcoal, with some resulting erosion and deforestation. Hydrogen bombs are of a different order: a war fought with them might alter the genetics of all life on this planet. By 1285 London had a smog problem arising from the burning of soft coal, but our present combustion of fossil fuels threatens to change the chemistry of the globe's atmosphere as a whole, with consequences which we are only beginning to guess. With the population explosion, the carcinoma of plan-less urbanism, the now geological deposits of sewage and garbage, surely no creature other than man has ever managed to foul its nest in such short order.

17.4
There are many calls to action, but specific proposals, however worthy as individual items, seem too partial, palliative, negative: ban the bomb, tear down the billboards, give the Hindus contraceptives and tell them to eat their sacred cows. The simplest solution to any suspect change is, of course, to stop it, or, better yet, to revert to a romanticized past: make those ugly gasoline stations look like Anne Hathaway's cottage or (in the Far West) like ghost-town saloons. The 'wilderness area' mentality invariably advocates deep-freezing an ecology, whether San Gimignano or the High Sierra, as it was before the first Kleenex was dropped. But neither atavism nor prettification will cope with the ecologic crisis of our time.

17.5
What shall we do? No one yet knows. Unless we think about fundamentals, our specific measures may produce new backlashes more serious than those they are designed to remedy.

17.6
As a beginning we should try to clarify our thinking by looking. in some historical depth, at the presuppositions that underlie modern technology and science. Science was traditionally aristocratic, speculative, intellectual in intent; technology was lower-class, empirical, action-oriented. The quite sudden fusion of these two, towards the middle of the 19th century, is surely related to the slightly prior and contemporary democratic revolutions which, by reducing social barriers, tended to assert a functional unity of brain and hand. Our ecologic crisis is the product of an emerging, entirely novel, democratic culture. The issue is whether a democratized world can survive is own implications. Presumably we cannot unless we rethink our axioms.

The Western traditions of technology and science
17.7
One thing is so certain that it seems stupid to verbalize it: both modern technology and modern science are distinctively *Occidental*. Our technology has absorbed elements from all over the world, notably from China; yet everywhere today, whether in Japan or in Nigeria, successful technology is Western. Our science is the heir to all the sciences of the past, especially perhaps to the work of the great Islamic scientists of the Middle Ages, who

so often outdid the ancient Greeks in skill and perspicacity: al-Razi in medicine, for example; or ibnal-Haytham in optics; or Omar Khayyam in mathematics. Indeed, not a few works of such geniuses seem to have vanished in the original Arabic and to survive only in medieval Latin translations that helped to lay the foundations for later Western developments. Today, around the globe, all significant science is Western in style and method, whatever the pigmentation or language of the scientists...

17.8
In the present day vernacular understanding, modern science is supposed to have begun in 1543, when both Copernicus and Vesalius published their great works. It is no derogation of their accomplishments, however, to point out that such structures as the *Fabrica* and the *De revolutionibus* do not appear overnight. The distinctive Western tradition of science, in fact, began in the late 11th century with a massive movement of translation of Arabic and Greek scientific works into Latin. A few notable books – Theophrastus, for example – escaped the West's avid new appetite for science, but within less than 200 years effectively the entire corpus of Greek and Muslim science was available in Latin, and was being eagerly read and criticized in the new European universities. Out of criticism arose new observation, speculation, and increasing distrust of ancient authorities. By the late 13th century Europe had seized global scientific leadership from the faltering hands of Islam. It would be as absurd to deny the profound originality of Newton, Galileo, or Copernicus as to deny that of the 14th century scholastic scientists like Buridan or Oresme on whose work they built. Before the 11th century, science scarcely existed in the Latin West, even in Roman times. From the 11th century onward, the scientific sector of Occidental culture has increased in a steady crescendo.

17.9
Since both our technological and our scientific movements got their start, acquired their character, and achieved world dominance in the Middle Ages, it would seem that we cannot understand their nature or their present impact upon ecology without examining fundamental medieval assumptions and developments.

Medieval view of man and nature

17.10
Until recently, agriculture has been the chief occupation even in 'advanced' societies; hence, any change in methods of tillage has much importance. Early plows, drawn by two oxen, did not normally turn the sod but merely

scratched it. Thus, cross-plowing was needed and fields tended to be squarish. In the fairly light soils and semi-arid climates of the Near East and Mediterranean, this worked well. But such a plow was inappropriate to the wet climate and often sticky soils of northern Europe. By the latter part of the 7th century after Christ, however, following obscure beginnings, certain northern peasants were using an entirely new kind of plow, equipped with a vertical knife to cut the line of the furrow, a horizontal share to slice under the sod, and a moldboard to turn it over. The friction of this plow with the soil was so great that it normally required not two but eight oxen. It attacked the land with such violence that cross-plowing was not needed, and fields tended to be shaped in long strips.

17.11

In the days of the scratch-plow, fields were distributed generally in units capable of supporting a single family. Subsistence farming was the presupposition. But no peasant owned eight oxen: to use the new and more efficient plow, peasants pooled their oxen to form large plow-teams, originally receiving (it would appear) plowed strips – in proportion to their contribution. Thus, distribution of land was based no longer on the needs of a family but, rather, on the capacity of a power machine to till the earth. Man's relation to the soil was profoundly changed. Formerly man had been part of nature; now he was the exploiter of nature. Nowhere else in the world did farmers develop any analogous agricultural implement. Is it coincidence that modern technology, with its ruthlessness toward nature, has so largely been produced by descendants of these peasants of northern Europe?

17.12

This same exploitive attitude appears slightly before A.D. 830 in Western illustrated calendars. In older calendars the months are shown as passive personifications. The new Frankish calendars, which set the style for the Middle Ages, are very different: they show men coercing the world around them – plowing, harvesting, chopping trees, butchering pigs. Man and nature are two things, and man is master.

17.13

These novelties seem to be in harmony with larger intellectual patterns. What people do about their ecology depends on what they think about themselves in relation to things around them. Human ecology is deeply conditioned by beliefs about our nature and destiny – that is, by religion. To Western eyes this is very evident in, say, India or Ceylon. It is equally true of ourselves and of our medieval ancestors.

17.14

The victory of Christianity over paganism was the greatest psychic revolution in the history of our culture. It has become fashionable today to say that, for better or worse, we live in 'the post-Christian age.' Certainly the forms of our thinking and language have largely ceased to be Christian, but to my eye the substance often remains amazingly akin to that of the past. Our daily habits of action, for example, are dominated by an implicit faith in perpetual progress which was unknown either to Greco-Roman antiquity or to the Orient. It is rooted in, and is indefensible apart from, Judeo-Christian teleology. The fact that Communists share it merely helps to show what can be demonstrated on many other grounds: that Marxism, like Islam, is a Judeo-Christian heresy. We continue today to live, as we have lived for about 1700 years, very largely in a context of Christian axioms.

17.15

What did Christianity tell people about their relations with the environment?

17.16

While many of the world's mythologies provide stories of creation, Greco-Roman mythology was singularly incoherent in this respect. Like Aristotle, the intellectuals of the ancient West denied that the visible world had had a beginning. Indeed, the idea of a beginning was impossible in the framework of their cyclical notion of time. In sharp contrast, Christianity inherited from Judaism not only a concept of time as nonrepetitive and linear but also a striking story of creation. By gradual stages a loving and all-powerful God had created light and darkness, the heavenly bodies, the earth and all its plants, animals, birds, and fishes. Finally, God had created Adam and, as an afterthought, Eve to keep man from being lonely. Man named all the animals, thus establishing his dominance over them. God planned all of this explicitly for man's benefit and rule: no item in the physical creation had any purpose save to serve man's purposes. And, although man's body is made of clay, he is not simply part of nature: he is made in God's image.

17.17

Especially in its Western form, Christianity is the most anthropocentric religion the world has seen. As early as the 2nd century both Tertullian and Saint Irenaeus of Lyons were insisting that when God shaped Adam he was foreshadowing the image of the incarnate Christ, the Second Adam. Man shares, in great measure, God's transcendence of nature. Christianity, in absolute contrast to ancient paganism and Asia's religions (except, perhaps, Zoroastrianism), not only established a dualism of man and nature but also insisted that it is God's will that man exploit nature for his proper ends.

17.18

At the level of the common people this worked out in an interesting way. In Antiquity every tree, every spring, every stream, every hill had its own *genius loci*, its guardian spirit. These spirits were accessible to men, but were very unlike men; centaurs, fauns, and mermaids show their ambivalence. Before one cut a tree, mined a mountain, or dammed a brook, it was important to placate the spirit in charge of that particular situation, and to keep it placated. By destroying pagan animism, Christianity made it possible to exploit nature in a mood of indifference to the feelings of natural objects.

17.19

It is often said that for animism the Church substituted the cult of saints. True; but the cult of saints is functionally quite different from animism. The saint is not *in* natural objects; he may have special shrines, but his citizenship is in heaven. Moreover, a saint is entirely a man; he can be approached in human terms. In addition to saints, Christianity of course also had angels and demons inherited from Judaism and perhaps, at one remove, from Zoroastrianism. But these were all as mobile as the saints themselves. The spirits *in* natural objects, which formerly had protected nature from man, evaporated. Man's effective monopoly on spirit in this world was confirmed, and the old inhibitions to the exploitation of nature crumbled.

17.20

When one speaks in such sweeping terms, a note of caution is in order. Christianity is a complex faith, and its consequences differ in differing contexts. What I have said may well apply to the medieval West, where in fact technology made spectacular advances. But the Greek East, a highly civilized realm of equal Christian devotion, seems to have produced no marked technological innovation after the late 7th century, when Greek fire was invented. The key to the contrast may perhaps be found in a difference in the tonality of piety and thought which students of comparative theology find between the Greek and the Latin Churches. The Greeks believed that sin was intellectual blindness, and that salvation was found in illumination, orthodoxy – that is, clear thinking. The Latins, on the other hand, felt that sin was moral evil, and that salvation was to be found in right conduct. Eastern theology has been intellectualist. Western theology has been voluntarist. The Greek saint contemplates; the Western saint acts.

The implications of Christianity for the conquest of nature would emerge more easily in the Western atmosphere.

17.21

The Christian dogma of creation, which is found in the first clause of all the Creeds, has another meaning for our comprehension of today's ecologic crisis. By revelation, God had given man the Bible, the Book of Scripture. But since God had made nature, nature also must reveal the divine mentality. The religious study of nature for the better understanding of God was known as natural theology. In the early Church, and always in the Greek East, nature was conceived primarily as a symbolic system through which God speaks to men: the ant is a sermon to sluggards; rising flames are the symbol of the soul's aspiration. This view of nature was essentially artistic rather than scientific. While Byzantium preserved and copied great numbers of ancient Greek scientific texts, science as we conceive it could scarcely flourish in such an ambience.

17.22

However, in the Latin West by the early 13th century natural theology was following a very different bent. It was ceasing to be the decoding of the physical symbols of God's communication with man and was becoming the effort to understand God's mind by discovering how his creation operates. The rainbow, was no longer simply a symbol of hope first sent to Noah after the Deluge: Robert Grosseteste, Friar Roger Bacon, and Theodric of Freiberg produced startlingly sophisticated work on the optics of the rainbow, but they did it as a venture in religious understanding. From the 13th century onward, up to and including Leibniz and Newton, every major scientist, in effect, explained his motivations in religious terms. Indeed, if Galileo had not been so expert an amateur theologian he would have got into far less trouble: the professionals resented his intrusion. And Newton seems to have regarded himself more as a theologian than as a scientist. It was not until the late 18th century that the hypothesis of God became unnecessary to many scientists.

17.23

It is often hard for the historian to judge, when men explain why they are doing what they want to do, whether they are offering real reasons or merely culturally acceptable reasons. The consistency with which scientists during the long formative centuries of Western science said that the task and the reward of the scientist was 'to think God's thoughts after him' leads one to believe that this was their real motivation. If so, then modern Western science was cast in a matrix of Christian theology. The dynamism of religious devotion, shaped by the Judeo-Christian dogma of creation, gave it impetus.

An alternative Christian view

17.24

We would seem to be headed toward conclusions unpalatable to many Christians. Since both *science* and *technology* are blessed words in our contemporary vocabulary, some may be happy at the notions, first, that, viewed historically, modern science is an extrapolation of natural theology and, second, that modern technology is at least partly to be explained as an Occidental, voluntarist, realization of the Christian dogma of man's transcendence of, and rightful mastery over, nature. But, as we now recognize, somewhat over a century ago science and technology – hitherto quite separate activities – joined to give mankind powers which, to judge by many of the ecologic effects, are out of control. If so, Christianity bears a huge burden of guilt.

17.25

I personally doubt that disastrous ecologic backlash can be avoided simply by applying to our problems more science and more technology. Our science and technology have grown out of Christian attitudes toward man's relation to nature which are almost universally held not only by Christians and neo-Christians but also by those who fondly regard themselves as post-Christians. Despite Copernicus, all the cosmos rotates around our little globe. Despite Darwin, we are *not*, in our hearts, part of the natural process. We are superior to nature, contemptuous of it, willing to use it for our slightest whim. The newly elected Governor of California, like myself a churchman but less troubled than I, spoke for the Christian tradition when he said (as is alleged), 'when you've seen one redwood tree, you've seen them all.' To a Christian a tree can be no more than a physical fact. The whole concept of the sacred grove is alien to Christianity and to the ethos of the West. For nearly 2 millennia Christian missionaries have been chopping down sacred groves, which are idolatrous because they assume spirit in nature.

17.26

What we do about ecology depends on our ideas of the man-nature relationship. More science and more technology are not going to get us out of the present ecologic crisis until we find a new religion, or rethink our old one. The beatniks, who are the basic revolutionaries of our time, show a sound instinct in their affinity for Zen Buddhism, which conceives of the man-nature relationship as very nearly the mirror image of the Christian view. Zen, however, is as deeply conditioned by Asian history as Christianity is by the experience of the West, and I am dubious of its viability among us.

17.27

Possibly we should ponder the greatest radical in Christian history since Christ: Saint Francis of Assisi. The prime miracle of Saint Francis is the fact that he did not end at the stake, as many of his left-wing followers did. He was so clearly heretical that a General of the Franciscan Order, Saint Bonaventure, a great and perceptive Christian, tried to suppress the early accounts of Franciscanism. The key to an understanding of Francis is his belief in the virtue of humility – not merely for the individual but for man as a species. Francis tried to depose man from his monarchy over creation and set up a democracy of all God's creatures. With him the ant is no longer simply a homily for the lazy, flames a sign of the thrust of the soul toward union with God; now they are Brother Ant and Sister Fire, praising the Creator in their own ways as Brother Man does in his...

17.28

The greatest spiritual revolutionary in Western history, Saint Francis, proposed what he thought was an alternative Christian view of nature and man's relation to it: he tried to substitute the idea of the equality of all creatures, including man, for the idea of man's limitless rule of creation. He failed. Both our present science and our present technology are so tinctured with orthodox Christian arrogance toward nature that no solution for our ecologic crisis can be expected from them alone. Since the roots of our trouble are so largely religious, the remedy must also be essentially religious, whether we call it that or not. We must rethink and refeel our nature and destiny. The profoundly religious, but heretical, sense of the primitive Franciscans for the spiritual autonomy of all parts of nature may point a direction. I propose Francis as a patron saint for ecologists.

EXTRACT 18

GREGORIOS

Ecology and the World Council of Churches

18.1

The Sixth Assembly of the World Council of Churches [Vancouver 1983] has good reasons to choose as its theme: 'Jesus Christ – the Life of the World'. We live in a world where life itself is imperilled; not only human life, but all life.

18.2

The four perils that face life can be summarised as follows:

(i.) *The nuclear peril*: A holocaust, or burnt offering, of practically the whole earth, has been a distinct possibility for humanity, for the past twenty years or more. We can be grateful that we have actually refrained from burning the planet up in the last twenty years. But we can do so any time, by the pressing of one or more buttons. There may be human and animal survivors immediately after a nuclear war. But whether they or their progeny can survive for very long in a radiation-filled biosphere seems in doubt. Even the peaceful use of nuclear energy poses hazards to life on our planet.

18.3

(ii.) *The peril of biotechnology*: This is difficult to assess. Some five years ago, the biological community in the West took the initiative to express public alarm about the possible disastrous consequences of new biotechnology.

18.4

The DNA molecule, the basic component of genes, had been decoded. There was hope that particular characteristics of an organism could be located in particular genes or their components. This hope has now receded. But the new technology of gene-splicing, or putting together differing elements of different genes, raises the possibility that human personal and social characteristics can be altered by genetic manipulation. The possibility can also be conceived of creating new breeds of monsters by splicing genes. Experts spoke about the possibility of creating crosses between humans and, say, gorillas, in order to create a new breed of semi-humans who could be conscripted to do docile mechanical labour without the risk of their organising themselves into trade unions, demanding their rights or going on strike.

18.5

Fear was expressed that new micro-organisms, developed in the research laboratory, may escape by accident into the biosphere, and cause diseases in humans and other animals and plants, diseases against which they had no immunity.

18.6

It is now an established fact that highly poisonous micro-organisms have been developed through biotechnology, and stored by the great powers as a possible weapon to be used in war. The international convention against biological weapons forbids their use, but not their manufacture or stockpiling.

18.7

Despite recent assurances from the biological community that safe-guards against the bio-peril are adequate, the general public remains unassured and insecure. They have learned from experience that the previous assurances of experts about the adequacy of safeguards against the hazards of peaceful use of nuclear energy have subsequently been proved to be false. The experts, even if sincere, could be wrong about the safety of the new research in biotechnology.

18.8

There is much wisdom in the statement by Dr Erwin Chargaff, professor emeritus of biochemistry at Columbia: 'Anyone affirming immediate disaster is a charlatan. But anyone denying the possibility of its occurring is an even greater one.'

18.9

Even if the danger is a long-term one, the churches have to be alert to the consequences of developments in this field, and the theme chosen provides a platform for dealing with the issues and educating the common people.

18.10

(iii.) *The ecological peril*: The indiscriminate burning of fossil fuels (coal, gas and oil) for energy, and the irresponsible misuse of the limited resources of the planet, have posed a threat to the biosphere – that fragile envelope around the earth which makes life possible. Besides the pollution of air, water and food, the very balance of the eco-system can be imperilled by industrial development, energy consumption and waste disposal.

18.11

Some measures have recently been taken by some governments to lower the level of pollution. But no international agreements have yet been reached to keep the pollution level low, or to regulate the process of exploitation of the limited resources of the earth. The risk that the eco-balance may be seriously upset by our industrial civilisation is still great. The churches have a responsibility to continue to alert people to this real danger to life on earth.

18.12

(iv.) *The peril of global injustice*: The resources and the technology necessary to ensure a decent standard of living to all human beings are now at the disposal of humankind. And yet the number of the millions who do not have access to the means for a life worthy of human beings continues to increase. While enormous amounts of resources and technology are being wasted on pointless military weapons, millions perish from hunger and malnutrition, ignorance and disease. The lack of political will to remedy this evil frightens thinking people. Nations make pious resolutions on cutting down weapons and devoting resources to development, but little actually happens.

18.13
The desperation of the poor and the powerless can imperil life on earth, for power does not remain for ever with the mighty. Injustice unremedied soon explodes in destructive revolt.

18.14
The Central Committee of the World Council of Churches had all these four perils in mind when it settled on the theme 'Jesus Christ – the Life of the World'.

18.15
But the question of *how* Jesus Christ can be the life of the world and save it from these four perils remains basically unanswered. It is to that question that the Assembly and its preparatory process must pay adequate attention. And it is a contribution to that preparatory process that this paper is offered.

What is life? A scientific answer

18.16
Any answer to the question: What is life? must depend upon the category structure that one chooses for the question as well as the answer.

Is it a theological question? Or is it a scientific question? If the latter, then we must say that the answer can only be in terms of a label applied to a common class of properties which can be investigated scientifically. We can say what properties or functions all living beings have in common. It is an arbitrary label created by human beings for the sake of convenience in thinking. The definition may not include all life, and the boundaries may be quite fuzzy. This is the case with scientific concepts like species, animals, insects, etc., for example, but they are useful shorthand.

18.17
That is all one can hope for in any scientific treatment of what constitutes life. But a theological answer to such a question has to take into account both what science has to say about life, and also go farther into questions like origin, purpose, etc., which do not properly fall within the domain of science.

18.18

In treating the theme, 'Jesus Christ – the Life of the World', we must deal with life, both in terms of the understanding of life in the sciences, and in terms of the Christian understanding of life, which need not be in conflict with the scientific understanding, but must necessarily go beyond.

18.19

Let us begin, therefore, with science, keeping in mind the possibility that any answer in science may be no more satisfying than the answer to a similar question: What is electricity? How do we define life? The definition must apply to all of life – human, animal and plant...

18.20

From a scientific perspective, therefore, one can say:

(a) There is no agreed definition of life, nor is the boundary between life and non-life clear, e.g. a virus, the heart of a frog that has been vivisected in the laboratory, or a person in terminal illness whose life has been artificially prolonged, etc.

(b) Living beings exhibit negative entropy, which offsets, at least temporarily, the positive entropy which characterises all matter.

(c) Each living being is in itself an organised community with differentiation and coordination of functions controlled by genetic structure.

(d) Life is an open system, self-regulating, orderly, dependent on other reality, receptive, relational.

(e) Life – at least at higher levels – is characterised by consciousness, awareness, will, choice and freedom, though these are characteristics difficult to explain in terms of physics and chemistry alone.

As has been stated, life cannot be understood, at least for Christians, in terms of science alone. We should, therefore, consider the theme, along with the four sub-themes chosen for the Assembly in a more specifically theological context.

What is life? A theological answer

18.21

The Assembly's main theme, 'Jesus Christ – the Life of the World', has now been broken up into four themes: Life a gift of God; Life confronting and overcoming death; Life in its fullness; Life in unity. The consideration of these four sub-themes should bring out some of the aspects of life in Jesus Christ which lie beyond the competence of science. Our considerations here will be limited to the first sub-theme, on the basis of the faith of the Christian community and its understanding of reality.

18.22

(i.) *The gift and the Giver.* All life is a gift from God. This should not be regarded as a mere preacher's platitude. To acknowledge one's life, as well as that of others, as a sacred gift has enormous consequences for the way we make our decisions on many issues – suicide, war, poverty, injustice, nuclear weapons, and so on. This claim, however, constitutes one of the dilemmas of our modern civilisation which affirms itself, at least at the state level, as secular. In a secular society, what is the basis for affirming the sacredness of life or of its gift character? If there is no God, whose gift is life? Nature's? But what is nature? Something which exists by itself?

18.23

The concept of nature is of pagan origin and has no basis in the Christian understanding of reality. Neither nature nor we exist from ourselves, or on our own. We come from God. So does nature. Both are creation – not nature. It is important for Christians to acknowledge ourselves and the world as created – not as existing by nature.

18.24

To be created means several things. First, when we acknowledge ourselves and the world as created, we confess that all created reality is contingent and dependent upon God's creative will for its very existence and functioning. We are not our own. Our very existence we owe to God as a gift. Once we acknowledge the gift, we acknowledge also our responsibility to the Giver. But it is not a legal responsibility of which we speak. For accepting a free gift does not entail any legal responsibility to the Giver. If we confess, however, that it is a gift of love, given in freedom, then there has to be a *response* – rather than a burdensome *responsibility*. It is a response of love – a free response.

18.25

It cannot be a response arising from the fear of consequences of not responding in love. For a response arising from fear that God will punish us is neither a loving response nor a free one. The Giver does not *demand* any response, for love does not make demands, but gives itself freely. The Giver rejoices when there is a free response in love, but cannot command it or ask for it.

18.26

Much has been written about Christian ethical responsibility, quite often in a contractual or covenantal understanding of the relationship between God and humanity. Much less has been said about responsiveness, as distinct from responsibility. There is a world of difference between response and responsibility. The very ethos is different. Responsibility is due and can be demanded – a legal obligation. Response is free; it can be given or withheld. There can be penalty or punishment for not fulfilling one's responsibility. For failing to respond, there may be consequences – disastrous ones at that; but no punishment as such.

18.27

Life is God's gift – a gift of grace, an offering of love, the creative love of the Creator. And the response to love is not only not demanded, but it is not even prescribed. There is no such thing as a single appropriate response to any given gift of love. The response itself is an occasion for creativity on the part of the responder.

18.28

There is no logic by which we can deduce from the recognition that life is God's gift what the proper response to that gift is. There are some aspects of that response which seem common – gratitude, for example, and the turning to God in repentance. But those are aspects which are permanent features of any adequate response to God.

18.29

The response we make does not depend so much on the gift as on the Giver. It is important to know the nature of the gift of life, for otherwise it would be difficult to make the right use of the gift. But is it not more significant to know the Giver and to enter into a loving relationship with that Person?

18.30

Knowing God, however, is not a matter of theology. In theology we have concepts about God – right or wrong – but no real knowledge of God as a Person.

18.31

The first aspect of knowing God as Giver of life must be repentance. Repentance means turning away from our idle, trivial, foolish and sinful preoccupations towards the One who has endowed us with life. Turning towards God as Giver of life thus implies also a recognition of the folly of turning towards and pursuing other things and goals; the recognition that we have made a mess of the gift of life by not turning towards the Giver and responding to the love that prompted the gift; recognition also that my life is not my own, but a loving gift, to be cherished and fulfilled.

18.32

(ii.) *Life and life eternal.* At this point we should recognise the two different but related kinds of life we have received as a gift: the gift of biological life by creation, and the gift of life in Christ through the incarnate Lord Jesus Christ. Both are gifts of grace. Neither is ours by right. Without the first the second is hardly possible. Frequently it is said: there is no question of the first one – that is, biological life, being by nature and the second one, i.e. life in Christ, alone as being by grace. That is the kind of error into which false theologies often plunge us. All life is a gift of grace, biological life and eternal life, plant life and animal life.

18.33

Biological life is certainly a gift to us – including plant and animal life. We live from plant and animal life. The plants are especially a gift of grace, for without them there is no photosynthesis, no grain or fruit, no animals, no food for humans. Without plants and trees who will absorb all the carbon-dioxide we breathe out, and assure our continuous supply of oxygen? We should be grateful for God's gracious gift of plants and trees and animals.

18.34

Biological life, ordinary life, is the basis and receptacle for eternal life. Any attempt to glorify eternal life at the expense of biological life should be resisted as a temptation. True, biological life is temporary. It is subject to death. But without it can we receive eternal life? And how can we say that biological life is ours by nature and only eternal life is a gift of grace? It is a fact that eternal life is a far superior gift. But that does not make ordinary life any less a gift of God's grace. Failure to recognise this fact lies at the base of our ecological peril, of our social injustice, of our making a mess of our ordinary life. Christians especially need to recognise more readily the nature of ordinary life, of the life of all, as the gracious gift of God's creation. That would provide them with a basis for an understanding and a way of life that is more Christian. That would help them understand science and technology, culture and the arts, politics and economics, family and society, education and health, and everything else in a truly Christian light.

18.35

(iii.) *The gift and the Giver are one!* Biological life is a gift from God, gratefully to be acknowledged and faithfully to be cherished. That is not, however, to diminish the distinction between biological life and life eternal in Christ.

18.36

A consultation of some Orthodox theologians, meeting in Damascus in

1982, drew up a distinction between the different kinds of life we know...
We restate that distinction as follows:

(a) *God's life*: self-derived, self-sustaining, self-giving, eternal, infinite, not subject to death or disintegration, unmixed with evil, true being, the ground and source of all being, in itself incomprehensible.

(b) *Angelic life*: created, not mixed with evil and therefore not subject to death, and experiencing the presence of God unhindered by the screen of sin.

(c) *Human life*: created, other-derived, other-dependent, mortal, finite, always mixed with evil.

(d) *Sub-human life on earth*: also created and therefore other-derived and other-dependent, mortal, finite, but integrally related to human life.

(e) *Anti-God life*: created, but in rebellion against the purposes of God, interfering with the affairs of humans, discomfited in Christ, but still allowed to be active as a testing ground for freedom, though doomed to destruction.

18.37

All these five levels of life are interconnected and interacting. Any attempt to understand human life in isolation from the other four levels is bound to be both superficial and misleading.

18.38

But the gospel of Jesus Christ announces to us a new fact – that all levels of life are affected by an event which took place in time and space – in Palestine 2000 years ago. The Second Person of the Holy Trinity has now permanently and inseparably united levels one and three in the only Begotten Son of God, overcome sin and death as a divine human person, and is to unite all forms of life and non-life, after testing in the fire of judgment, to become a harmonious but differentiated whole in the risen Jesus Christ.

18.39

This is the astounding new gift of God's grace proclaimed in the gospel by the church and acknowledged in the believing community.

There is no scientific proof possible for this declaration. To those who believe, it is more certain than any so-called scientific fact.

It is this supreme gift which we celebrate with joy in the eucharistic liturgy and which we proclaim with confidence to all creation.

The alienation of humanity from God has now been overcome. God and humanity have become inseparably one. There is no more a gap of separation. God is at one with us. Immanuel! With us, God!

18.40

This gift is such that to respond to it is simply to surrender oneself totally to such infinite love – of course, to find oneself confirmed and revitalised by that infinite love! In the utter trust of faith, we mortal humans surrender ourselves to such love without any reservation, without any fear about what will happen to our freedom and identity. Our trust is so complete in his love, that it drives out all fear – including fear of loss of freedom and identity, fear of condemnation and punishment, fear and anxiety about our personal destiny.

18.41

Here, the gift is the Giver himself. And our response can be nothing less than to surrender our paltry and feeble self into those loving hands. There is no question now of taking the gift and walking away from the Giver, for the gift is the Giver himself. In accepting the gift in humble repentance and perfect trust we ourselves become one with the Giver. The Giver, the gift, and the receiver are united in that life-giving embrace of the Supreme Lover.

18.42

It is as we experience this supreme gift that we recognise fully that all life, all things, all that exists, with all the suffering and pain, the struggles and conflicts, the beauty and the joy, the fears and the hopes, are a gift of grace from the Supreme Lover. In that experience we see that what we regarded wrongly as nature is also a gift of grace – not ours by right; as we are possessed by the Great Lover, possession itself becomes meaningless. We no longer seek to possess, for we are God's, and God is ours, and there is nothing to possess further. This is freedom – the freedom of love in which God and humanity are united in one, and all things with us in God!

18.43

It is idle to hope that the present church structures can truly become communities of faith, living the life that overcomes death and transmitting life to the world around. What is more practical is to seek to found smaller pioneering communities – of Christians who have overcome their fear of death, who really believe that Jesus Christ is risen indeed, and who work out the implications of that faith.

Such a community must be deeply rooted in two worlds – the modern world of science and technology, of poverty and injustice, of rootlessness and lovelessness on the one hand, and on the other, the life-giving powers of the Spirit operating in a genuine community of faith and worship.

If the Sixth Assembly [of the World Council of Churches] can lead to the founding of such pioneer communities, the theme will have served some purpose.

EXTRACT 19

ABRAHAM

Liberation and eco-justice

19.1

Ecology may be understood as the study of the structures and functions of nature. It could refer to the ecosystem, that is, the life support system of all humans, living and non-living things on the earth. The underlying emphasis is important for our purpose in all this, that humankind is part of nature and not apart from nature. Ecological crisis is caused by human intervention in this fragile system destroying its tenuous fabric.

19.2

There was a time when we thought that ecological crisis was not a serious problem for us in the poorer countries. Our problems it was assumed, was confined to poverty and economic exploitation, and the environmental issue was rejected as a 'luxury' of the industrialized countries. Social action groups and people's movements in the Third World countries understandably have shown relative indifference to the problem of ecology. But today we realize how urgent this issue is for rich and poor countries alike – in fact for the whole world. The threat is to life in general. The life of the planet is endangered. The ecological crisis raises the problem of survival itself. Moreover, there is a growing awareness of the organic link between the destruction of the environment and socio-economic and political injustice.

19.3

Committed scientists and other ecologists have helped us to deepen our understanding of the ecological problem. In the past, nature was thought to be an object for ruthless exploitation by the 'developers' and scientists for the 'good' of humans. Little thought was given to the perils of environmental destruction. A sense of optimism prevailed among them about the capability of science to tame nature. Those who raised any voice of concern were branded as 'prophets of doom'. But today more and more scientists are joining with others with a crusading zeal to make people aware of the ecological disasters. Marshalling convincing scientific data they will tell us that the environmental degradation caused by massive pollution of air, water and land, threatens the very life of the earth; fast depletion of non-renewable resources, indeed of species themselves, thinning of ozone layer that exposes all living creatures to the danger of radiation, the build-up of gases creating the green-house effect, increasing erosion of sea are now known through their research. Related to these problems are rapidly increasing population, and wide-spread malnutrition and hunger, the subordination of women's and children's needs to men's, the ravages of war, the scandal of chronic poverty and wasteful affluence...

19.4

Ecological crisis should be seen as a justice issue. This is a fundamental perspective that distinguishes people's view on ecology from that of the establishment and even of the experts. Political and social justice is linked to ecological health. 'We shall not be able to achieve social justice without justice for natural environment, we shall not be able to achieve justice for nature without social justice' (Moltmann). Several dimensions of this eco-justice are now brought to fore through the experiences of the struggle of the marginalized. First, the connection between economic exploitation and environmental degradation is clear in the deforestation issue. The massive destruction of forests by avarice and greed results in atmospheric changes. The poor are driven out of their habitat for the sake of development. Again the use of mechanized trawlers in the fish industry has resulted in threatening all fish life and the traditional fisherfolk still have not recovered from the loss they have suffered.

19.5

Second, justice is actualized in just relationships. Unequal partnerships and patterns of domination are unjust. It is obvious that human relationship with nature is not that of an equal partner, but of domination and exploitation. Unjust treatment of the planet by humans is one of the principal causes of ecological crisis.

19.6

Third, the uneven distribution, control and use of natural resources are serious justice issues. It is estimated that one-fifth of the world's population that inhabits the Northern hemisphere consume, burn or waste at least 40-50% of the world's non-renewable resources. Further, natural resources needed to maintain the life-style of an average American is equal to what is required for 200-300 Asians. Imagine what will happen if we extend the same life as Americans to people everywhere.

19.7

Fourth, the fast depletion of the natural (non-renewable) resources raises the question of our responsibility to future generations. If we extend the five-star culture to all the countries and segments, then the pressures on these resources will be formidable. Already we are warned that we cannot go on exploiting the deep level water. This will disturb the ecological balance. Someone has compared the function of deep water to the middle ear fluid that helps maintain our balance in the human body. The question is how to use natural resources in a way that we sustain life and not destroy it.

19.8
We need to discuss two related concerns. The first is the concept of justice itself. The logic of justice as developed in the West, emphasizes rights and rules and respect for others. It can be applied only to human beings supposedly equally. It is balancing of rights and duties. But to include the cosmos in the justice enterprise, we need to affirm the ethics of care. Justice cannot be accorded except through care. Justice expressing as compassion is the Biblical emphasis. Prophets were not talking about balancing interests and rights, but about caring, defending the poor by the righteous God. Defending the vulnerable and defenceless should also mean defending the weak and silent partner – the earth:

19.9
We can no longer see ourselves as namers and rulers over nature but must think of ourselves as gardeners, caretakers, mothers and fathers, stewards, trustees, lovers, priests, co-creators and friends of a world that, while giving us life and sustenance, also depends increasingly on us in order to continue both for itself and for us. (Sallie McFague, *Models of God*).

19.10
Secondly, poverty is also a source of ecological degradation and the alleviation of poverty by the poor through their struggle for justice is an ecological concern. We cannot separate these two concerns. Unless the poor have alternate sources of food and basic needs like fuel, they too will wantonly destroy whatever natural environment is around them.

19.11
Justice in relation to ecology has a comprehensive meaning. Negatively it is placed against economic exploitation and unjust control and use of natural resources. Positively it affirms the responsibility for future generations as well as compassion and caring for the cosmos and the poor. It is eco-justice. Ecological crisis demands a commitment to eco-justice.

19.12

Ecological crisis has burst upon our consciousness a new awareness about our dependence on earth. We belong to the earth. We share a common destiny with the earth. This has sharply challenged the modern view of reality and demands a revaluation of previously held scales of values. The modern perception of reality, thanks to the all-pervasive influence of western rationality, follows a mechanistic model. It is functional and dualistic: spirit/flesh, objective/subjective, reason/passion, super-natural/natural. But the ecological view is organic in which the emphasis is on interconnectedness and mutual interdependence. It is to adopt the view of the world so well captured in Martin Buber's famous distinction between I-Thou and I-It. All entities are united symbolically. 'Nature is no longer the subjugated object of man, but a cohesion of open life systems with its own subjectivity' (Moltmann).

19.13

This ecological perspective helps us to rethink God-human-world relationships, the very basis of our theologizing. Panikkar, in his characteristic style, says that 'creation, humanity and God are one. Together, all three constitute being: all are constitutive elements of the others and one cannot exist without the others. Being is one, but it is relational, trinitarian if you will. Deep down our sixth sense tells us this, our intuition and if we probe deeper, so does our experience and our intellect'. Sally McFague has expressed this challenge thus:

19.14

Ecological perspective insists that we are, in the most profound ways, 'not our own': we belong. from the calls of our bodies to the finest creation of our minds, to the intricate, constantly changing cosmos. The ecosystem of which we are part is a whole: the rocks and waters, atmosphere and soil, plants, animals and human beings interact in a dynamic, mutually supportive way that make all talk of atomistic individualism, indefensible. Relationship and interdependence, change and transformation, not substance, changelessness and perfection, are the categories within which theology for our day must function. (*Models of God*)

19.15

Nothing short of a 'paradigm shift' is taking place in theology. Theology is not merely anthropocentic. It is ecologically oriented. Theology is to be seen within the framework of ecology. The precedence of ecological perspective has posed new challenges to even the radical theologies like liberation theology. It is rightly observed that 'a true liberation will be possible not only by involving ourselves in struggle to liberate the oppressed human beings from their exploitation, but also by a conscious and concerted effort to liberate the bonded earth from the over exploitative attitude of human beings'.

19.16

Liberation theologians have forcefully articulated the biblical motif for liberation in Exodus and other passages. Salvation is liberation. But for them particularly because of the immediate context, liberation is primarily political and economic. We today want to affirm that the liberation that is witnessed to in the Bible includes liberation for creation. According to Paul in Romans, the work of the Spirit, Freedom, is extended to the total renewal of creation. Christ's work of redemption extends to the whole universe. Christ, the Lord of history, initiates a process of transformation that moves toward the cosmic release (Eph. 1.1-10 and Col. 1.15-20). The unity between the hope for the inward liberation of the children of God and the liberation of the entire physical creation from its bondage and oppression is the theme of Romans. The work of the Spirit is to renew all of the earth. *Ktisis*, translated as creation, includes not only women and men, but all created things including demonic powers. It is in the search for liberation of all aspects of human life, histories, cultures, and natural environment that we can affirm that salvation is the wholeness of creation.

19.17

There is something common to the interpretation of liberation as a historical process in Exodus and the liberation process in creation in Romans. The liberation in Exodus is linked with the cry of the oppressed and in Romans the glorious liberty is promised in response to the groans and travails within us and in creation. God had heard the cry of the poor and God is taking sides with the poor. In the same manner the renewal of earth comes in response to the cry of the poor and of the dumb creatures, and of the silent nature. It is interesting to note that when God decided to spare Ninevah in the Book of Jonah (4:11) it was out of God's pity for the 'more than 12,000 persons who do not know the right hand from their left hand [reference is to babies] and also much animals'. God was not interested in preserving the great city for the sake of its skyscrapers, supermarkets and giant computers!

19.18

We are committed to a vision of human wholeness which includes not only our relationship with one another, but also our relationship with nature, and the universe. We are also committed to the struggles for the transformation of the poor, the weak and the disfigured and the over-exploited nature. Both are decisive for our faith, mission and spirituality. Moltmann is right when he points out, 'Essentially the church is cosmically oriented. Limiting the church merely to the world of human beings was a dangerous modern constriction. But if the church is indeed oriented towards the cosmos, the "ecological crisis" of the earthly creation is also the crisis of the church itself!'

19.19

The emphasis on holistic reality and cosmic orientation to human destiny is already ingrained in our culture and religions in India. But the onslaught of western rationality and science has made us insensitive to those dimensions of indigenous wisdom. What is called for is a recovery of this vision in our theology.

19.20

We will bring this discussion to a close by focussing our attention on an overriding concern that is often raised: the relation between human and nature. One may suggest at least three typologies that may have influenced modern thinking on this: Human above nature; human in nature; and human with nature. We can see Biblical parallels for each of this. But our effort is to see which one is the closest to the central Biblical vision.

Humans above nature

19.21

This may be the hidden ideology of the scientific and technological culture of the modern period. Science was considered as power and not as a source of wisdom. 'Modern technics', wrote Bertrand Russell in the late forties, 'is giving man a sense of power which is changing his whole mentality. Until recently the physical environment was something that had to be accepted. But to modern man the physical environment is merely the raw material for manipulation and opportunity. It may be that God made the world, but there is reason why we should not take it over'. Perhaps very few scientists today make such claims so unambiguously. But this lingering confidence in science and technology and the instrumental, manipulative use of nature is very much present in modern culture.

19.22

Attempts are made to provide a Biblical basis for the development of technology in the West. They are primarily based on the exegesis of Gen.1.28-30 and Ps.18.6-8. During the late 60s a best seller in theology was *The Secular City* by Harvey Cox and an influential book on mission was Arand Van Leeuwan's *Christianity in World History*. Both these books show a preference for the view 'humans above nature'. They provide a Biblical and theological basis for the technological manipulation of nature by humans. They unequivocally affirmed that technology is a liberator, an instrument in the hands of God for releasing humans from the tyranny of natural necessities. They paid little attention to the Biblical witness against this attitude:

'The earth mourns and withers, the world languishes and withers, the heavens languish together with the earth' (Isa.24.4).

'Thus says God, the Lord, who created the heavens and stretched them out, who spread forth the earth and what comes from it, who gives breath to people upon it and spirit to those who walk in it' (Isa.42.5).

19.23

In the Bible the planes of human history and nature are never set in opposition as these interpreters seem to be doing. They are held together in the Biblical witness of faith. Liberation according to Exodus is a struggle to possess land. Faith in Yahweh the Liberator is also an affirmation that God is sovereign over earth.

19.24

In an interesting study on the land in the Old Testament Walter Brueggeman points to the significance of Land for Hebrew religious experience. The land as promise and as problem: Promised land, alien land, landlessness and wilderness all these appear at different stages in the history of Hebrews. There is of course a tension between landedness and landlessness; the former becomes an occasion for exploitation and the latter for total trust in Yahweh.

19.25

Christian practice that directly or indirectly supported colonialism and capitalism comes out of this view of human above nature. Lynn White, the Californian Professor of history finds this view as responsible for the modern ecological crisis. His words are strong:

19.26

Especially in its western form, Christianity is the most anthropocentric religion the world has seen... Christianity in absolute contrast to ancient paganism and Asia's religions... has not only established a dualism of man and nature, but has also insisted that it is God's will that man exploit nature for his proper ends... Hence we shall continue to have a worsening ecologic crisis until we reject the Christian axiom that nature has no reason for existence, save to serve man. [i.e. Extract 17.17f]

Humans in nature

19.27

This is a reaction against the first typology. It maintains that there is no distinction between humans and nature. One gets the expression of this view in the writings of some Romantic poets. Some of the environmentalists in their facile enthusiasm lend support to this. Biblical support may be found in the verse:

'All flesh is grass and all its beauty is like the flower of the field. Surely the people are grass, the grass withers, the flower fades, but the word of our God will stand forever' (Isa.40.6-8).

19.28

Yet it is difficult to conclude on the basis of the verse that the Biblical idea is to treat human life just as grass. There is a mystery of their being, and there is a distinction between human and nature and other creatures. What is natural is not accepted as it is. It is being shaped and recreated. This takes us to the next typology.

Humans with nature

19.29

This refers to a pattern of relationship in which humans are part of nature but they are distinct from it. Humans are different from other creatures, but difference is not superiority. But it comes with an awareness of responsibility.

19.30

The command of God to have dominion over creatures in Gen.1.28-30 is problematic. In its original Hebrew 'dominion' is a harsh word. It is to tame and control the forces of nature that are destructive and violent. Taken that word in isolation and purely in this context it gives the basis for a ruthless, exploitation of nature. But in interpreting Biblical images and words we need to see them through the prism of our Lord's saving mission.

19.31

'In the light of Christ's mission', says Moltmann, 'Gen.1.28, will have to be interpreted in an entirely new way. Not to subdue the earth – but free the earth through fellowship with it! We may ask what is our understanding of dominion? Is it not from one whom we call the Lord, Domino, i.e., Jesus Christ and... Him crucified.'

19.32

Lordship has a new meaning. It is responsibility for the other in love. The overriding emphasis in the Bible with regard to human relationship with nature is on human responsibility for nature.

19.33

Human participation is necessary for maintaining the cosmos over against the threat of chaos (Ps.24:1). The Earth is the Lord's and all that fills it, the world and all of its inhabitants: 'Because he founded it upon the seas and established upon the rivers'.

19.34

Scholars point out that Hebrew words for sea (*yam*) and river (*nahar*) are also the words for ancient near-eastern gods of chaos. If humans break the covenant, disobey the laws of God and unjustly treat the neighbour, then creation will return to the primeval chaos. To maintain creation, cosmos, human participation of responsible love, justice is necessary.

19.35

Human participation is also needed to keep the earth fertile and productive (Gen.2.15, 3.17-19). Man is called the gardener and tiller. Again humans have no right to exploit and plunder the earth. Some of the symbols and practices that emerged in the history of Israel clearly articulate this. Sabbath and jubilee year are some of them. Rest is a way of preventing our exploitation of the earth. Also the drastic change in the ownership is a poignant reminder that humans are merely trustees. They are called to maintain the integrity of creation. Human responsibility for the whole creation is to participate with love and carein God's continuing act of creation.

19.36

Human responsibility and co-creatureliness is further intensified with the affirmation and all creation along with humans long and groan for perfection and liberation. All distortions of creation compounded by human violence, disobedience and greed will have to be redeemed in Christ (Rom. 8.13-28). The final vision of a new heaven and new earth (Rev. 21.1-4) is accomplished by God and human beings together.

19.37

Finally, we humans have created this mess we better take the responsibility to set it right. Our responsibility should express in *metanoia* – turning away from all idols of self-aggrandizing power which cause the earth to be dominated, plundered and destroyed. Cecil Rajendra, the Malaysian poet, expresses this concern: 'The village deserted/ The river choked and polluted/

and a red haze hovers over devastated hills./ But this is not the work/ of barbarians from the north/ nor B-29 bombers or foreign devils./ In this instance we are the authors/ of our own death, of our own nemesis.'

19.38
Ecological crisis is urging us to affirm our inter-relatedness with nature and to commit ourselves to honour the integrity of creation, to learn from the eco-systems and to orient our theology and ethics to embrace ecological values. In doing this we come closer to the Eastern attitude towards nature...

EXTRACT 20
CLARK
Christian responsibility for the environment

20.1
Environmentalists have often blamed our polluted streams, eroded landscapes and extinguished species on an attitude of mind engendered by the Biblical command to 'be fruitful and increase, and fill the earth. The fear and dread of you shall fall upon all wild animals on earth, on all birds of heaven, on everything that moves upon the ground and all fish in the sea; they are given into your hands,' (Genesis 9.1f). The Christian churches have generally insisted that everything is made for human use, that 'nothing is unclean' and out of bounds, and that there is no divine commandment to respect the lives and properties of the non-human. Those who did admit to such feelings of respect or carefulness have usually been considered, simultaneously, animal-worshippers and world-deniers. To value the lives of animals was to betray the respect we owe to humanity, the image of God made flesh. Caring about their lives and pleasures was to show oneself to be sensual, ignorant of the higher joys reserved for intellectual creatures. At the same time, it showed an heretical shrinking from the good things of this world, a suspicion that the creator was not worshipful. It was, accordingly, orthodox to insist that animal lives and pleasures were not worth bothering about, and that we should continue to use and enjoy all non-human products.

20.2
It would be unfair, and it was unfair, to suggest that these beliefs were especially the products of the Christian churches, or that the rest of the world has an unsullied record. It did not need Christians to ruin North Africa, or Tokyo. Christians are not entirely responsible for the sorry

state of things. It would also be unfair to argue that the humanistic bias of Christian teaching was ever intended to license us to do just as we pleased with the natural world: the world is for our use, but only insofar as we act as viceroys of the Lord. We may not use it to the detriment of our fellow humans, nor pretend to be God's equals: we have not been licensed wholly to remake the world, nor to do as we please with it. We are licensed only to maintain a just and God-fearing society, by cultivating the land and seeking out what natural cures God grants us for the ills we suffer. The suggestion that exploitative industrialists or cruel pet-owners or badger-baiters are doing what the churches have told they should is simply silly. If we are gods, or as gods, to the non-human creation, 'we are obliged by the same tenure to be their guardians and benefactors'. Those who see no beauty worth respecting in the natural world are very far from being orthodox, as are those who see nothing wrong in causing pain to God's other creations.

20.3

Nonetheless the dominant them in Christian tradition has been that human society is the right context for our actions and our hopes. It is fulfilling our duties to our human neighbours, and directing out piety to the Three-in-One which is our best image of the Lord, that we show ourselves members of God's Kingdom: citizens and friends, not simply subjects of His power. Tradition is largely agreed that cruelty (the enjoyment of another's pain) is a sign of spiritual evil, and that it is a mark of ingratitude and impiety to deface natural beauty, but the real business of humankind lies with human society, with the effort to allow all human souls a share of God's bounty, and a place in God's kingdom. It is wrong to be cruel to cats, but also wrong to like their company more than men's, or to feed them at the expense of humans. It is somehow 'obvious', even to a post-Christian society that no longer believes that all and only human beings can hope to share in God's eternity, that the life of a healthy baboon (though not, so far, a healthy mongol) should be ended if this offers even the tiniest hope of life to an unhealthy baby (which could have been legally aborted if the problem had been spotted a few months earlier). Post-Christian humanists, retain the idea that there is a form of social life restricted to normal human beings which defines for us what creatures deserve genuine respect and care. In the absence of any metaphysical or revealed reason for supposing that all those born of women are in this sense 'normal humans', I suspect that not all members of our biological species will be accorded this old-fashioned respect in the future. Embryos will be procreated for experimental purposes; non-cultural mental defectives (incapable of games or enjoying symbols) will be used as experimental animals, and even cultural mental defectives will not be given any extended medical or other care.

20.4

Faced by this sort of prospect, Christians may care to reconsider their position. What is our responsibility for 'the environment', the natural context of our lives and culture? Is it really our duty to use all things so as to preserve and elevate the distinctively human life, maybe engineering little enclaves (zoos or safari parks) within which 'nature' can be painlessly inspected, or preserving larger habitats in the not-unreasonable hope that we may eventually find some useful drugs or usable experimental animals therein? The claim that this is indeed our duty rests upon a high doctrine of human life, not merely on the hope and desire for enjoyments of a kind that other creatures share. If animal pains and pleasures are all that matter, then diminishing non-human pleasures and increasing non-human pains can hardly be a duty. We may prefer that it should be us that enjoy life, but we can have no objective complaint with any other tribe that is ready to sacrifice us for its pleasure. The duty to look after people at whatever cost to whales or rhesus monkeys must rest on some notion that human beings are capable of higher things. Olaf Stapledon, in considering how we should deal with other planets, argued that we should use them, as we should use this one, 'for the spirit'. He did occasionally wonder whether some of the genocidal and oppressive uses he thought justified under this rubric might not injure the spirit, or its manifestation in human-kind. He was usually ready to believe that the more 'spiritual' (that is, the more awake, sensitive and precise intelligence) had rights of dominion over the less spiritual, and the duty to exercise that dominion. A higher race than ours might justly use us or destroy us for their purposes.

20.5

Christians reading Stapledon may shrink from his conclusions. Surely 'serving the spirit' cannot be the same as self-aggrandisement and tyranny, even if we pretend to be ready to suffer in our turn? Serving the spirit, or living spiritually, requires that we recognise its presence, that we feel ourselves carried with a strength that is not our property, that we are ready to play our part in the whole endeavour that is creative intelligence. Do we recognise the spiritual life most especially in those who proclaim their own superiority to others, their freedom from irksome regulations, their duty to ignore the projects and wishes of their supposed inferiors? Such self-styled supermen, of course, may be merely ridiculous: it may be obvious that they are in fact stupid, ignorant and obsessed. But it is not impossible that they should be clever, self-possessed and even psychologically acute. The Lord, nonetheless, will have them in derision. Stapledon himself, in reproducing (in *Starmaker*) the ancient story of an ascent into the heavens, a tour of the celestial mansions, constantly reveals that each successive self-complacent stage of life, is as distant from the Starmaker as ever. A genuinely infinite deity is no more like a galactic spirit than a coelocanth: however mighty and intelligent a creature is, it is wholly superfluous to God, infinitely unlike God. But in that case how can it be anything but comic to suggest that the God is better served or better reflected by Stapledonian supermen than by a helpless infant or by the lilies of the field?

20.6

So how do those who really strike us as spiritually alive and saintly beings treat the natural world? What do the saints say and do? Can we imagine a real saint, one who practices 'the presence God', who acknowledges with every breath her own dependence on the spirit and her own unworthiness of it, behaving toward the natural order as a good humanist would? Saints, of course, come in many guises, and many who have the title for political or ecclesiastical reasons are not convincingly saintly. The most convincing saints characteristically welcome the non-human, greet them as fellow-strugglers and worshippers of the most high, not because they have any naive or sentimental belief about what, say, a sky-lark believes, but because they see the lark's fulfilment of its God-given nature as at once a pledge and an example. John the Divine heard 'every created thing in heaven and on earth and under the earth and in the sea, all that is in them crying: Praise and honour, glory and might, to him that sits on the throne and to the Lamb for ever and ever!' (Rev. 5.13). Whereas the humanist, in effect, sees the natural world as merely a vast heap of more or less usable material, having no significance until the handy-man has arrived to make something of it, the saint understands herself to live within a meaningful and orderly universe, even if its meaning is sometimes simply that our action is needed. We are at once the audience and a part of God's speech with God's own self and with creation. To interfere too radically in the natural order, to forget our own nature as terrestrial mammals and demand the right to remake all things only in our own image, for our own purposes, is to corrupt the text.

20.7

Saintliness requires that we respect the natures of our fellow creature, and the order of which we are all a part. Some saints have concluded, in practice, that they should live in complete and open dependence, fitting themselves entirely into the natural order, and so offending the squeamishness of gentle humanists. It is a minor irony that Christ's own sardonic instruction to rely upon the Lord who is with the falling sparrow, who clothes the anemones and finds the ravens their food, is usually quoted to 'prove' that he thought people – or at least his followers – more valuable than sparrows, and so licensed to take unfair advantage of sparrows, anemones and ravens. Such saints live within the promised covenant, 'with the beasts of the field and the fowls of heaven and with the creeping things of the land' when God shall have broken the bow and the sword and the battle out of the land and made them to lie down safely (Hosea 2.18). The beasts will be at peace with us, said an early commentator on the gospel of Mark, 'when in the shrine of our souls we tame the clean and unclean animals and lie down with the lions, like Daniel'.

20.8

Most religious traditions, unsurprisingly, have found a place not only for these saints but for the mass of pious and more or less well-intentioned persons. How shall we, who do not yet feel called to go out into the wilderness, singly or in groups, think and act toward the natural order? It is, as Aldo Leopold remarked, the temptation of town-dwellers to think that food comes from the grocery store, and heat from the boiler. It is easy to believe that we do not live 'in nature' but in human culture, although everything we have and are is a transformation of natural product. We need above all to remember that we do not live in a human technosphere, surrounded by an 'environment' that we may take a casual interest in if we choose. We live in the same natural world as alligators, elks and human saints, though our dependency is of a more complex and easily disrupted kind. 'When we harm the earth, we harm our selves'. 'Christian Responsibility for the Environment' is in fact a deeply misleading phrase: we are not responsible for the natural world's existence, and we have no general duty to try and maintain it according to some bureaucratically inspired plan. Nor is there any such thing as 'the environment', as though the world were no more than an envelope for humankind, a seed-pod for the human technosphere.

20.9

In the Book of Job 'Yahweh describes himself as the wisdom that makes for the survival of the wild ass, the hamster, the eagle, the ostrich, of all living nature, and the wisdom that uproots mountains and annihilates angels'. The vision of things before which Job at last bowed his head, and repented in dust and ashes, was one that Philo of Alexandria also approved: a sort of cosmic democracy, in which each creature gets its turn, and is allowed its own integrity. So far from dictating that we human beings should think all nature at our own disposal, the Bible constantly insists that humankind is not alone, not privileged above all others, not like God. 'Do you not know, have you not heard, were you not told long ago, have you not perceived ever since the world began, that God sits throned on the vaulted roof of earth, whose inhabitants are like grass-hoppers? He stretches out the skies like a curtain, he spreads them out like a tent to live in; he reduces the great to nothing and makes all the earth's princes less than nothing. To whom then will you liken me, whom set up as my equal? asks the Holy One' (Isa. 40.21f). Where humanist Christianity has borrowed from Stoicism the self-congratulatory notion that 'nothing irrational is capable of the beatifying friendship with God which is the bond of Christian love, of neighbour', and thence concluded that 'the irrational' is only material for our purposes, the Bible expects us to accept our place within the creation, to live by the rules God imposes, to take what we need, no more, and to give up our demands so that life may go on. Every seventh and every fiftieth year the land must be unploughed, and all live together off its natural produce, citizen and stranger and the wild animals of the country (Leviticus 26.6f). If the law is not kept the people shall be driven from the land, and 'the land shall enjoy its sabbaths to the full' (Leviticus 26.34). None shall eat the life, which is the blood, of any creature, even if in the post-Noahic days meat-eating is allowed. This is not to say that the Bible contains many specific injunctions of a kind to appeal to zoophiles. It was a sterner world than ours, and the animals who shared the Israelites' land or houses could not have had an easier life than the Israelites themselves. But there was affection there and acknowledgement of duty. A donkey fallen into a ditch must be hauled out even on the sabbath, even if it is one's enemy's (Deut. 22.4). The poor man's pet sheep, whom Nathan the prophet used to shame King David (1 Kings 12), was loved as a daughter (and no-one had the brass nerve to say that he shouldn't have wasted good affection on a mere beast).

20.10
Northrop Frye, in his attempt to see the Bible whole, concludes that one of its messages is that we shall not regain the world we have lost, the world where we might easily live in nature, with all creatures as our friends, 'until [we] know thoroughly what hell is, and realize that the pleasure gained by dominating and exploiting, whether of [our] fellow man or of nature itself, is a part of that hell-world'. Things are not wholly at our disposal, and never will be, either in the sense that we can or that we ought to use them with an eye solely to our benefit, and avoid all inconveniences of this mortal life. We cannot by any technical means transform this world into a pleasure garden, nor ought we to try. Nor can we retreat within a denatured city,

and imagine that we thereby fulfil the biblical prophecy of a world wholly suffused with humanly significant meaning, 'when there shall be no more sea', no more image of the unaccountable. The city that the Bible praises was imagined as a part of the land within which it stood, the holy mountain where wolf shall dwell with lamb, leopard lie down with kid (Isa. 11.6), and the leaves of the trees serve for the healing of the nations (Rev. 22.2).

20.11

No-one who reads, the Bible can doubt that its human authors were deeply conscious of the natural world, the creation, the land flowing with milk and honey. Where we see 'nature', the non-human environment ruled by powers alien to humankind, they saw God's creation, a world continually offering embodied images of the spiritual values they pursued. 'The God of Israel spoke, the Rock of Israel spoke of [David]: He who rules men in justice, who rules in the fear of God, is like the light of morning at sunrise; a morning that is cloudless after rain and makes the grass sparkle from the earth' (2 Samuel 23.3f). In the mouths of poets and prophets this is more than simile, more than a rather strained declaration that a just ruler is like the sun after rain. The prophet sees God's liberating justice in the light when God sets His rainbow in the sky 'sign of the covenant between [Himself] and earth' (Genesis 9.14). 'As the hills enfold Jerusalem, so the Lord enfolds His people' (Psalm 125.2). 'Once the Lord called you an olive-tree, leafy and fair; but now with a great roaring noise you will feel sharp anguish; fire sets its leaves alight and consumes its branches. The Lord of Hosts who planted you has threatened you with disaster' (Jeremiah 11.16). When Babylon the great has fallen at last, 'there no Arab shall pitch his tent, no shepherds fold their flocks. There marmots shall have their lairs, and porcupines shall overrun her houses; there desert owls shall dwell, and there he-goats shall gambol; jackals shall occupy her mansions, and wolves her gorgeous palaces' (Isa. 13.20f). 'The whole world has rest and is at peace; it breaks into cries of joy. The pines themselves and the cedars of Lebanon exult over you: since you have been laid low, they say, no man comes up to fell us' (Isa. 14.7f). The whole world, not merely human history, embodies God's purposes to the prophetic eye, and no general distinction is drawn between human and non-human. God's purposes, indeed, may be more fully and obviously embodied in the non-human, and moral examples drawn from them: 'Mothers, cherish your sons. Rear them joyfully as a dove rears her nestlings' (2 Esdras 2.15).

20.12

Why, if all this is so, are there so few general injunctions to behave decently to the non-human? The word of the Lord to Ezra: 'champion the widow, defend the cause of the fatherless, give to the poor, protect the orphan, clothe the naked. Care for the weak and the helpless, and do not mock, at the cripple; watch over the disabled, and bring the blind to the vision of my brightness. Keep safe within your walls both old and young' (2 Esdras 2.20f). These commands could certainly be read as applying to non-human creatures, but just as certainly were not. The non-human rested directly on the Lord, and did not turn aside from Him. There were few occasions when the Israelites could do much hurt to the wild things, unless by overhunting them or keeping them away from all the crops. The creatures they used for sacrifice – which was the only licensed way of getting meat – were being returned to God. And the prophets disapproved: 'your countless sacrifices, what are they to me? says the Lord. I am sated with the whole-offering of rams and the fat of buffaloes; I have no desire for the blood of bulls, of sheep and of he-goats. Though you offer countless prayers, I will not listen. There is blood on your hands. Put away the evil of your deeds, away out of my sight. Cease to do evil and learn to do right, pursue justice and champion the oppressed; give the orphan his rights, plead the widow's cause' (Isa. 1.11, 15f). The God of Israel, in short, is made known in the demand for justice, the insistence that no human being is, entitled to oppress God's creatures or claim equality with God.

20.13

So what should Christians feel obliged to do in this new age, when God has, with His usual sardonic humour, given us the power to remake things if we choose, and in the remaking find disaster? 'For the Lord of Hosts has a day of doom awaiting for all that is proud and lofty, for all that is high and lifted up, for all the cedars of Lebanon, lofty and high, and for all the oaks of Bashan, for all lofty mountains and for all high hills, for every high tower and for every sheer wall, for all ships of Tarshish and all the dhows of Arabia. Then man's pride shall be brought low; and the loftiness of man shall be humbled' (Isa. 2.12f). So far from lending support to the sort of humanism which puts its trust in human resourcefulness, the Biblical tradition recognises that our powers are no different in kind from those of any other creature, and the Lord stands over all. Philo's cosmic democracy is fiercely defended.

20.14

The first step then simply not to aim too high, not to expect a pleasure garden, not to demand our human comforts at whatever cost, not to 'turn the world into a desert and lay its cities in ruins' (Isa. 14.17). If we cannot live in the land on the terms allotted to us, of allowing others their place, not disregarding the needs of the apparently defenceless, not claiming the right to decide how all things should go, then we shall find that we have lost the land. The natural historian of a future age may be able to point to the particular follies that brought ruin – chopping down the tropical rainforests, meditating nuclear war, introducing hybrid monocultures, spreading poisons, financing grain-mountains and rearing cattle in conditions that clearly breach the spirit of the commandment not to muzzle the ox that treads out the corn (Deut. 25.4). The historian whose eyes are opened to the acts of God will have no doubt that we brought that ruin on ourselves, that it is God's answer to the arrogant. In those days our survivors will have to be saints, unless we have taken a step back from the furnace and consented to be ordinarily decent and God-fearing folk. 'How long must the land lie parched and its green grass wither? No birds and beasts are left, because its people are so wicked, because they say, God will not see what we are doing' (Jeremiah 12.4).

EXTRACT 21
MCFAGUE
An earthly theological agenda

21.1
The simultaneous lessening of cold-war tensions and worldwide awakening to the consequences of human destruction of the flora and fauna and the ecosystem that supports them, signal a major change in focus [in theology]. Perhaps it is more accurate to say that the focus of the liberation theologies widened to include, in addition to all oppressed human beings, all oppressed creatures as well as planet earth.

21.2
Liberation theologies insist rightly that all theologies are written from particular contexts. The one context which has been neglected and is now emerging is the broadest as well as the most basic: the context of the planet, a context which we all share and without which we cannot survive. It seems to me that this latest shift in 20th-century theology is not to a different issue from that of liberation theologies, but to a deepening of it, a recognition that the fate of the oppressed and the fate of the earth are inextricably interrelated, for we all live on one planet – a planet vulnerable to our destructive behavior.

21.3
The link between justice and ecological issues becomes especially evident in light of the dualistic, hierarchical mode of Western thought in which a

superior and an inferior are correlated: male-female, white people-people of color, heterosexual-homosexual, able-bodied-physically challenged, culture-nature, mind-body, human-nonhuman. These correlated terms – most often normatively ranked – reveal clearly that domination and destruction of the natural world is inexorably linked with the domination and oppression of the poor, people of color, and all others that fall on the 'inferior' side of the correlation. Nowhere is this more apparent than in the ancient and deep identification of women with nature, an identification so profound that it touches the very marrow of our being: our birth from the bodies of our mothers and our nourishment from the body of the earth. The power of nature – and of women – to give and withhold life epitomizes the inescapable connection between the two and thus the necessary relationship of justice and ecological issues. As many have noted, the status of women and of nature have been historically commensurate: as goes one, so goes the other.

21.4

A similar correlation can be seen between other forms of human oppression and a disregard for the natural world. Unless ecological health is maintained, for instance, the poor and others with limited access to scarce goods (due to race, class, gender or physical capability) cannot be fed. Grain must be grown for all to have bread. The characteristic Western mind-set has accorded intrinsic value, and hence duties of justice, principally to the upper half of the dualism and has considered it appropriate for those on the lower half to be used for the benefit of those on the upper. Western multinational corporations, for example, regard it as 'reasonable' and 'normal' to use Third World people and natural resources for their own financial benefit, at whatever cost to the indigenous peoples and the health of their lands.

21.5

The connections among the various forms of oppression are increasingly becoming clear to many, as evidenced by the World Council of Churches' inclusion of 'the integrity of creation' in its rallying cry of 'peace and justice.' In the closing years of the 20th century we are being called to do something unprecedented: to think, wholistically, to think about 'everything that is,' because everything on this planet is interrelated and interdependent and hence the fate of each is tied to the fate of the whole.

21.6

This state of affairs brought about a major 'conversion' in my own theological journey. I began as a Barthian in the '50s, finding Barth's heady divine transcendence and 'otherness' to be as invigorating as cold mountain air to my conventional religious upbringing. Like many of my generation I found in Barth what appeared to be a refreshing and needed alternative to liberalism. But after years of work on the poetic, metaphorical nature of religious language (and hence its relative, constructive and necessarily changing character) and in view of feminism's critique of the hierarchical, dualistic nature of the language of the Jewish and Christian traditions, my bonds to biblicism and the Barthian God loosened. Those years were the 'deconstructive' phase of my development as a theologian.

21.7

My constructive phase began upon reading Gordon Kaufman's 1983 Presidential Address to the American Academy of Religion. Kaufman called for a paradigm shift, given the exigencies of our time – the possibility of nuclear war. He called theologians to deconstruct and reconstruct the basic symbols of the Jewish and Christian traditions – God, Christ and Torah – so as to be on the side of life rather than against it, as was the central symbol of God with its traditional patriarchal, hierarchical, militaristic imagery. I answered this call, and my subsequent work has been concerned with contributing to that task.

21.8

While the nuclear threat has lessened somewhat, the threat of ecological deterioration has increased: they are related as 'quick kill' to 'slow death.' In other words, we have been given some time. We need to use it well, for we may not have much of it. The agenda this shift sets for theologians is multifaceted, given the many different tasks that need to be done. This paradigm shift, if accepted, suggests a new mode of theological production, one characterized by advocacy, collegiality and the appreciation of differences.

21.9

Until the rise of liberation theologies, theology was more concerned with having intellectual respectability in the academy than with forging an alliance with the oppressed or particular political or social attitudes and practices. There was a convenient division between theology (concerned with the knowledge of God) and ethics (a lesser enterprise for action-oriented types). Theologians were also usually 'solo' players, each concerned to write his (the 'hers' were in short supply) magnum opus, a complete systematic theology. As the deconstructionists have underscored, these theologians also strove to assert, against different voices, the *one* voice (their own – or at least the voice of their own kind) as the truth, the 'universal' truth.

21.10
Our situation calls for a different way of conducting ourselves as theologians. Like all people we need, in both our personal and professional lives, to work for the well-being of our planet and all its creatures. We need to work in a collegial fashion, realizing that we contribute only a tiny fragment. Feminists have often suggested a 'quilt' metaphor as an appropriate methodology: each of us can contribute only a small 'square' to the whole. Such a view of scholarship may appear alien to an academy that rewards works 'totalizing' others in the field and insisting on one view.

21.11
The times are too perilous and it is too late in the day for such games. We need to work together, each in his or her own small way, to create a planetary situation that is more viable and less vulnerable. A collegial theology explicitly supports difference. One of the principal insights of both feminism and postmodern science is that while everything is interrelated and interdependent, everything (maple leaves, stars, deer, dirt – and not just human beings) is different from everything else. Individuality and interrelatedness are features of the universe; hence, no one voice or single species is the only one that counts...

21.12
If advocacy, collegiality and difference characterized theological reflection and if the agenda of theology widened to include the context of our planet, some significant changes would occur. I will suggest three.

21.13
First, it would mean a more or less common agenda for theological reflection, though one with an almost infinite number of different tasks. The encompassing agenda would be to deconstruct and reconstruct the central symbols of the Jewish and Christian traditions in favor of life and its fulfilment, keeping the liberation of the oppressed, including the earth and all its creatures, in central focus. That is so broad, so inclusive an agenda that it allows for myriad ways to construe it and carry it out. It does, however, turn the eyes of theologians away from heaven and toward the earth; or, more accurately, it causes us to connect the starry heavens with the earth, as the 'common' creation story claims, telling us that everything in the universe, including stars, dirt, robins, black-holes, sunsets, plants and human beings, is the product of an enormous explosion billions of years ago. In whatever ways we might reconstruct the symbols of God, human being and earth, this can no longer be done in a dualistic fashion,

for the heavens and the earth are one phenomenon, albeit an incredibly ancient, rich and varied one.

21.14
If theology is going to reflect wholistically, that is, in terms of the picture of current reality, then it must do so in ways consonant with the new story of creation. One clear directive that this story gives theology is to understand human beings as earthlings (not aliens or tourists on the planet) and God as immanently present in the processes of the universe, including those of our planet. Such a focus has important implications for the contribution of theologians to 'saving the planet,' for theologies emerging from a coming together of God and humans in and on the earth implies a cosmocentric rather than anthropocentric focus. This does not, by the way, mean that theology should reject theocentrism; rather, it means that the divine concern includes *all* of creation. Nor does it imply the substitution of a creation focus for the tradition's concern with redemption; rather, it insists that redemption should include all dimensions of creation, not just human beings.

21.15
A second implication of accepting this paradigm shift is a focus on praxis. As Juan Segundo has said, theology is not one of the 'liberal arts,' for it contains an element of the prophetic, making it at the very least an unpopular enterprise and at times a dangerous one. The academy has been suspicious of it with good reason, willing to accept religious studies but aware that theology contains an element of commitment foreign to the canons of scholarly objectivity. (Marxist or Freudian commitments, curiously have been acceptable in the academy, but not theological ones.) Increasingly, however, the hermeneutics of suspicion and deconstruction are helping to unmask simplistic, absolutist notions of objectivity, revealing a variety of perspectives, interpretations, commitments and contexts. Moreover, this variety is being viewed as not only enriching but necessary. Hence the emphasis on praxis and commitment, on a concerned theology, need in no way imply a lack of scholarly rigor or a retreat to fideism. Rather, it insists that one of the criteria of constructive theological reflection – thinking about our place in the earth and the earth's relation to its source – is a concern with the *consequences* of proposed constructions for those who live within them.

21.16
Theological constructs are no more benign than scientific ones. With the marriage of science and technology beginning in the 17th century, the

commitments and concerns of the scientific community have increasingly been determined by the military-industrial-government complex that funds basic research. The ethical consequences of scientific research – which projects get funded and the consequences of the funded projects – are or ought to be *scientific* issues and not issues merely for the victims of the fall-out of these projects. Likewise, theological reflection is a *concerned* affair, concerned that this constructive thinking be on the side of the well-being of the planet and all its creatures. For centuries people have lived within the constructs of Christian reflection and interpretation, unknowingly as well as knowingly. Some of these constructs have been liberating, but many others have been oppressive, patriarchal and provincial. Indeed, theology is not a 'liberal art,' but a prophetic activity, announcing and interpreting the salvific love of God to *all* of creation.

21.17
A third implication of this paradigm shift is that the theological task is not only diverse in itself (there are many theologies), but also contributes to the planetary agenda of the 21st century, an agenda that beckons and challenges us to move beyond nationalism, militarism, limitless economic growth, consumerism, uncontrollable population growth and ecological deterioration. In ways that have never before been so clear and stark, we have met the enemy and know it is ourselves. While the wholistic, planetary perspective leads some to insist that all will be well if a 'creation spirituality' were to replace the traditional 'redemption spirituality' of the Christian tradition, the issue is not that simple. It is surely the case that the over-emphasis on redemption to the neglect of creation needs to be redressed; moreover, there is much in the common creation story that calls us to a profound appreciation of the wonders of our being and the being of all other creatures. Nonetheless, it is doubtful that such knowledge and appreciation will be sufficient to deal with the exigencies of our situation.

21.18
The enemy – indifferent, selfish, shortsighted, xenophobic, anthropocentric, greedy human beings – calls, at the very least, for a renewed emphasis on sin as the cause of much of the planet's woes and an emphasis on a broad and profound repentance. Theology, along with other institutions, fields of study and expertise, can deepen our sense of complicity in the earth's decay. In addition to turning our eyes and hearts to an appreciation of the beauty, richness and singularity of our planet through a renewed theology of creation and nature, theology ought also to underscore and elaborate on the myriad ways that we personally and corporately have ruined and continue to ruin God's splendid creation – acts which we and no other

creature can knowingly commit. The present dire situation calls for radicalizing the Christian understanding of sin and evil. Human responsibility for the fate of the earth is a recent and terrible knowledge; our loss of innocence is total, for we know what we have done. If theologians were to accept this context and agenda of their work, they would see themselves in dialogue with all those in other areas and fields similarly engaged: those who feed the homeless and fight for animal rights; the cosmologists who tell us of the common origins (and hence interrelatedness) of all forms of matter and life; economists who examine how we must change if the earth is to support its population; the legislators and judges who work to advance civil rights for those discriminated against in our society; the Greenham women who picket nuclear plants, and the women of northern India who literally 'hug' trees to protect them from destruction, and so on and on.

21.19
Theology is an 'earthly' affair in the best sense of that word: it helps people to live rightly, appropriately, on the earth, in our home. It is, as the Jewish and Christian traditions have always insisted, concerned with 'right relations,' relations with God, neighbor and self, but now the context has broadened to include what has dropped out of the picture in the past few hundred years – the oppressed neighbors, the other creatures and the earth that supports us all. This shift could be seen as a return to the roots of a tradition that has insisted on the creator, redeemer God as the source and salvation of all that is. We now know that 'all that is' is vaster, more complex, more awesome, more interdependent, than any other people has ever known. The new theologies that emerge from such a context have the opportunity to view divine transcendence in deeper, more awesome and more intimate ways than ever before. They also have the obligation to understand human beings and all other forms of life as radically interrelated and interdependent as well as to understand our special responsibility for the planet's well-being.

CRITIQUE
White's Extract contains many careful qualifications which his recent exponents have sometimes ignored. He admits that not enough is known about ecological history (17.1) and that it is dangerous to generalise about the effects of Christian doctrine upon the environment (17.20). This has not stopped some from using this seminal essay as an ecological critique of Christianity as a whole. White's argument is rather that Western Christians,

in particular, need to be more conscious of the ecological dangers of doctrines of creation which assume a notion of domination. The other Extracts in this Section show that his warnings have indeed been heeded.

However, even with his careful qualifications, there is still a risk in making such a sweeping analysis of Christian cultural history. Christianity has been variously depicted by secular historians as a nurse-maid or as a foe of Western science/technology – White himself shows something of this ambivalence in his analysis of Galileo. And it is by no means clear from the Texts that 'domination' was always crucial to a Western understanding of creation. Even the exception that White offers in his analysis of Western Christianity, namely St Francis, is ambivalent. In modern theology Franciscans, perhaps surprisingly, have not been a dominant ecological voice. If anything feminist theology has been more significant.

Gregorios' principle of regarding human life as a 'gift' from God has important implications for personal as well as social ethics (see *below*, pp.564f.). Few outside the Orthodox theological world may accept all of his assumptions (e.g. 18.36), but he does distinguish clearly the overall way in which a theological perspective differs from a purely empirical understanding of human life. If a Christian is true to this perspective, threats to human life should always be viewed with horror.

Together Abraham, Clark and McFague present theologies which have taken full account of White's critique and which are themselves critical of forms of theology which ignore the nonhuman. Their own positions are drawn from different sources, but together they raise the important issue of anthropocentrism. Herein lies an unresolved dilemma for theology within monotheistic traditions. Within them a distinction between creator and creature is usually considered to be vital, as well as a stress upon humans as made in the 'image' of God. In turn this is usually believed to imply that all life is God-given but that human life is especially God-like. The dilemma is to find ways of expressing these beliefs without contributing to the human destruction of the non-human and without implying that the lives of all bacteria (say) are worth preserving even at considerable risk to humans. Some degree of anthropocentrism may finally be essential for Christian ethics. Yet this is not a point that any of these authors seem prepared to concede.

SECTION 5

HUMAN LIFE AND INTERPERSONAL RELATIONSHIPS

SECTION 5

HUMAN LIFE AND INTERPERSONAL RELATIONSHIPS

The distinction between social and personal ethics is, at best, approximate. In personal ethics, the focus is more upon the individual and, in social ethics, it is more upon society. But it is only a relative difference of focus, since many issues in personal ethics have a social dimension and many issues in social ethics involve individual decision-making. So, for most ethicists, there is an important distinction to be made between killing in the context of war and individual homicide. War involves societies as a whole and individuals who kill within this context usually do so on the authority of their society and without personal malice against the particular individuals they kill (in modern warfare, killing at a distance is even less personal). Depending on whether they are selective militarists or selective pacifists (see *above*, p.258), they may or may not believe that it is for them personally to decide on the actual justifiability of the particular war in which they are engaged. However, individual homicide, whether of self or of another, raises the most crucial problems of individual decision-making, social authorisation and often personal malice. It has already been seen that Augustine saw a clear distinction, between participation in war and the sort of violence Peter displayed at Gethsemane. Peter acted 'in a hasty zeal' and 'without the sanction of the constituted authority' (Text VII.2). Similarly, he sanctioned war in specifiable circumstances, but not individual suicide (Text XIII.10). But, even in this instance,

455

the distinction between personal and social ethics is difficult to sustain. As Augustine implies, capital punishment has more in common with war than individual homicide, since the executioner usually acts without personal malice and upon the decision and authority of society at large. And issues, such as abortion, involve both personal and social dimensions, since they are the object both of intense personal decision-making and of social legitimation. Even suicide, although seldom socially sanctioned, has been regarded as a criminal activity in some societies but not in others.

This Section consists of three broad themes in personal ethics. The first of these is the issue of individual homicide. Augustine on suicide is balanced by Fletcher on euthanasia and (earlier) on abortion. The second is the issue of sexual morality. Aquinas' Text on pre-marital sexual activity and marriage is contrasted with the Orthodox Bishop Kallistos Ware on marriage and divorce and Pope Paul VI's encyclical on birth control. The third is the issue of anti-Semitism and racism. Luther's late views on the Jews are compared with the World Council of Churches' Faith and Order Commission document on racism in theology and Rosemary Radford Ruether's critique of Christianity and Zionism. The scope of this Section is intentionally broad to demonstrate some of the range of approaches in these somewhat diffuse ethical areas. At the same time, it is intended in this Section to raise some of the most crucial substantive dilemmas facing present-day Christian ethics.

The issue of individual homicide forms a natural bridge and a contrast with Section 3. The dichotomy between the pre-Constantinian and post-Constantinian churches (see *above*, p.263) is evident, but it is not nearly so clear-cut. Bainton argues that: 'the early Church saw an incompatibility between love and killing. In later times the attitude and the act were harmonised on the ground that the destruction of the body does not entail the annihilation of the soul. The early Church had an aversion to bloodshed' (*Christian Attitudes Toward War and Peace*, p.77). So Tertullian, on the basis of Acts 15.20, maintained that the three irremissible sins were idolatry, adultery and homicide (*De Pudicitia*, XII). His general conviction, both before and after his conversion to Montanism, was that, for the Christian, homicide in any form is forbidden; that, if necessary, the Christian must suffer persecution rather than retaliate; and that the Christian, by enduring violence, can look for a reward beyond this world. This is evident in the following pre-Montanist quotation:

> Which is the ampler rule, to say, 'Thou shalt not kill', or to teach, 'Be not even angry'? Which is more perfect, to forbid adultery, or to restrain from even a single lustful look? Which indicates the higher intelligence, interdicting evil-doing, or evil-speaking? Which is more thorough, not allowing an injury, or not even suffering an injury to be repaid?... Think of these things, too, in the light of the brevity of any punishment you can inflict – never to last longer than till death... No doubt about it, we, who receive our awards under the judgment of an all-seeing God, and who look forward to eternal punishment from him for sin, we alone make real effort to attain a blameless life (*The Apology*, 445, from *The Ante-Nicene Fathers*, 3).

Abortion he regarded simply as murder. Similarly, the Council of Elvira (c.300 CE) in the West, decreed that a woman guilty of an abortion be refused Holy Communion, even on her death-bed: and the Synod of Ancyra (314 CE) in the East, ordained a penalty of ten years' penance for the woman who had an abortion.

In the post-Constantinian church some changes become apparent. Although he retained a rigorous position on suicide, Augustine's attitude to abortion was more qualified than that of previous theologians. In discussing the distinction between an embryo without a soul (*informatus*) and an embryo with a soul (*formatus*), he maintained that the abortion of the first should be punished only by a fine, whereas that of the second should be treated as murder (*Qua est. in Exodus* 21,80; *Qua est. Vet. et Nov. Test.*, 23). In one form or another, a distinction between an animated and an unanimated fetus was not finally refuted by the Roman Catholic Church until 1869, when Pius IX affirmed that the ensoulment of the fetus commences at conception and set excommunication as the penalty for those seeking to procure an abortion. On the issue of abortion, the comparative rigour of the present-day Roman Catholic and Orthodox Churches in their official stances, evident in Paul VI's Extract 24 and mentioned in passing in Ware's Extract 23, represents a partial return to the position of the pre-Constantinian Church.

A more radical Catholic voice is evident in Fiorenza's Extract 5 where she links racism and patriarchy: 'Whereas patriarchal racism defines certain people as subhuman in order to exploit their labor, patriarchal sexism seeks to control women's procreative powers and labor... and its rhetoric for the "protection of the Christian family" seek to reinforce women's economic dependency; to strengthen the patriarchal controls of women's procreative powers, and to maintain the patriarchal family as the mainstay of the patriarchal state' (Extract 5.15). Like many Christian feminists she has been strongly influenced by the educational psychologist Carol Gilligan's *In a Different Voice*. Gilligan argues that the increase of choice for women, due to such factors as modern birth control, is creating a paradigm shift today:

> For centuries, women's sexuality anchored them in passivity, in a receptive rather than an active stance, where the events of conception and childbirth could be controlled only by a withholding in which their own sexual needs were either denied or sacrificed... Women have traditionally deferred to the judgment of men, although often while intimating a sensibility of their own which is at variance with this judgment (*In a Different Voice*, pp.68-9).

By analysing the attitudes of men and women to abortion separately, Gilligan concluded that male attitudes have more to do with power and rules [as is evident in Extracts 23 and 24] and the female with empathy, compassion and care. The dilemma for the woman confronted with abortion in the West today is that 'she is asked whether she wishes to interrupt that stream of life which for centuries has immersed her in the passivity of dependence while at the same time imposing on her the responsibility for care' (p.71).

Until recent times, Augustine's rigourist position on suicide remained that of most Christians. Further, recent discussions of certain forms of euthanasia have much in common with early debates on suicide. Voluntary direct euthanasia, in particular, might be seen as a form of suicide and it is for this reason that Fletcher's Extract 22 can be compared directly with Augustine's Text XIII. Of course, other forms of euthanasia raise different ethical dilemmas which were not discussed by the classical authors. This can be seen if one distinguishes between the following positions, based upon the two variables of the doctor's intention and the patient's will, in a situation in which the latter's life is shortened or terminated:

Eventual death of patient caused by...

(a) Direct treatment by doctor of willing patient
(b) Direct treatment by doctor of non-willing patient
(c) Indirect effects of treatment by doctor of willing patient
(d) Indirect effects of treatment by doctor of non-willing patient
(e) Non-treatment by doctor of willing patient
(f) Non-treatment by doctor of non-willing patient

Naturally, if direct, or even indirect, treatment were to be applied to the unwilling (rather than a non-willing) patient this might constitute murder rather than euthanasia. The concept of 'willingness' on the part of the patient is not without considerable difficulties – e.g. is a comatose patient, who has previously favoured euthanasia, and even left advance directives on the subject, 'willing' or 'non-willing'? Even the question of what constitutes 'treatment' has become problematic – e.g. is the form of nutrition given to a patient in a persistent vegetative state a form of 'treatment' which might eventually be withdrawn?

However these six 'ideal' types (see *above*, p.258) show something of the range of the issue in contemporary medical ethics. In type (a) the doctor agrees to the patient's request to end or shorten his or her life. In type (b) the doctor acts in the same way, but the patient is unable to will this (perhaps because he or she is comatose, senile, or mentally disadvantaged). In types (c) and (d) it is not the primary intention of the doctor to shorten the life of the patient, whether or not the latter wills this. Instead, it may be the primary intention of the doctor to lessen the pain of the patient, whilst being aware that in the process he or she may shorten the life of that patient (i.e. the ethical notion of 'double effect'). In types (e) and (f) it is withholding treatment that shortens the life of the willing or non-willing patient. For many type (e) hardly constitutes an example of euthanasia at all, since it is often considered to be a right of a mature, rational individual to decide whether or not to receive treatment. Nonetheless, it is logically related to the other types.

If this analysis is adopted, straightforward support for, or rejection of, 'euthanasia' will appear difficult for many contemporary Christians. Only those who approve, or, conversely, those who disapprove, of euthanasia in all of the above forms, will be able to adopt such a straightforward approach. Perhaps, for most Christians today, even Augustine's absolutist position on suicide is unacceptable.

Yet, if there is a dilemma apparent amongst contemporary Christians on this issue, even greater perplexity is evident in contemporary attitudes towards human sexuality. There is also a sharp contrast to be drawn between the views of Augustine on sexuality and those of many Christians today. It is sometimes held that Augustine steered a mid-path between the Manichaean rejection of the flesh as evil and the Pelagian rejection of any notion of original sin. Against the Pelagians he insisted that marriage involves a sacramental bond and is good only in so far as it enables procreation. And, against the Manichaeans, he insisted that God had blessed humans with the words 'Be fruitful and multiply': it was not procreation itself which was sinful, but lust. But here lay Augustine's problem: marriage is for procreation and this is good, yet procreation is impossible without lust and this is sinful. It is this element in his thinking which suggests that Augustine never wholly escaped his early Manichaeism (e.g. see Text X.12). Unfortunately it is an element which had a profound effect on much subsequent Christian thought on sexuality. In his anti-Pelagian treatise, *On Marriage and Concupiscence*, he justified his belief in the sinfulness of sexual desire, even within marriage, with the following natural law argument:

> How significant is the fact that the eyes, and lips and tongue, and hands, and feet, and the bending of the back, and neck,

and sides, are all placed within our power – to be applied to such operations as are suitable to them, when we have a body free from impediments and in a sound state of health; but when it must come to man's great function of the procreation of children, the members which were expressly created for this purpose will not obey the direction of the will, but lust has to be waited for to set those members in motion, as if it had legal right over them, and sometimes it refuses to act when the mind wills, while it often acts against its will! Must not this bring the blush of shame over the freedom of the human will, that by its contempt of God, its own Commander, it has lost all proper command for itself over its own members? Now, wherein could be found a more fitting demonstration of the just depravation of human nature by reason of its disobedience, than in the disobedience of those parts whence nature herself derives subsistence by succession... This, then, was the reason why the first human pair, on experiencing in the flesh that motion which was indecent because disobedient, and on feeling the shame of their nakedness, covered these offending members with fig-leaves (*De Nuptiis et Concupiscentia*, VII, from *The Nicene and Post-Nicene Fathers*, 5).

The influence of this view can be seen in Aquinas' Text XIV, in Luther's Text VI.12 and XII.16, and in Paul VI's Extract 24.

Augustine's justification of monogamous marriage was only relative. He defended the polygamy of the patriarchs against both the Manichaeans and the Pelagians (see *above*, pp.39–40 and *De Nuptiis et Concupiscentia*, IX), since he believed their motives to have been procreative rather than lustful. He attacked those pagan monogamous marriages which were, in his opinion, based solely upon lust. And, apparently like Paul, he valued celibacy much higher than marriage.

Some of these elements are still present in Luther's writings on sexuality and marriage. He, too, justified the polygamy of the patriarchs (see *above*, p.39), had a low opinion of his contemporaries' sexual behaviour and supported Paul's justification of marriage as 'a remedy of sin':

To unaided human nature, as God created it, chastity apart from matrimony is an impossibility. For flesh and blood remain flesh and blood, and the natural inclination and excitement run their course without let or hindrance, as everyone's observation and experience testify. Therefore that man might more easily keep his evil lust in bounds, God commanded marriage, that each may have his proper portion and be satisfied; although God's grace is still needed for the heart to be pure (*The Large Catechism* of 1528, on the sixth commandment).

'Lust' is still seen as evil, marriage still appears as a concession for frailty and there are some (although few) who, 'by reason of extraordinary gifts have become free to live chaste lives'. But, in contrast to Augustine and Aquinas, monasticism is no longer regarded as a higher state than marriage. Indeed, he claimed of marriage that, 'God blessed this institution above all others and made everything on earth serve and spring from it. It is not an exceptional estate but the most universal and noblest, pervading all Christendom, yea, extending through the whole world' (*ibid*). He could also be suitably flippant in his attitude towards sexual intercourse – commenting at one point on 'the marital obligation, which cannot be performed without sin; yet because of its necessity, God winks at it, for it cannot be otherwise' (Text VI.12). As the Reformation became established, and doubtless as a reflection of his own happy marriage, Luther increasingly came to see the family as the proper focus (replacing the monastery) of Christian socialisation. In his less formal moments, he could write: 'Ah, dear God, marriage is not a thing of nature but a gift of God, the sweetest, the dearest, and the purest life above all celibacy and all singleness, when it turns out well, though the very devil if it does not. For although women have the art, with tears, lies and snares to beguile a man, they can also be superb and say the very best... A great thing is this bond and communion between man and wife' (*T.R.* 4786).

Despite the real affection for women and appreciation of marriage evident in this quotation, it also provides a clear example of gender stereotypes. Personal and social prejudices occur frequently in Luther's writings and few are more shocking than those contained in Text XV. Both he and Augustine, in their different ages and social contexts, were inveterate polemicists, so it is not surprising that their prejudices are so often in evidence. Just as Luther supported the princes in violently suppressing the peasants, so Augustine in later life came to support the, at times violent, coercion of Donatists in North Africa. In a letter to the Donatist Bishop, Vincentius, in 408, Augustine conceded that, 'originally my opinion was, that no one should be coerced into the unity of Christ, that we must act only by words, fight only by arguments, and prevail by force of reason, lest we should have those whom we knew as avowed heretics feigning themselves to be Catholics' (*Letters*, XCIII). But his increasing pessimism about humanity and bitter experiences of North African polemics convinced him otherwise:

> In some cases, therefore, both he that suffers persecution is in the wrong, and he that inflicts it is in the right. But the truth is, that always both the bad have persecuted the good, and the good have persecuted the bad: the former doing harm by their unrighteousness, the latter seeking to do good by the administration of discipline; the former with cruelty, the latter with moderation; the former impelled by lust, the latter under the constraint of love. For he whose aim is to kill is not careful how he wounds, but he whose aim is to cure is cautious with his lancet; for the one seeks to destroy what is sound, the other that which is decaying. The wicked put prophets to death; prophets also put the wicked to death. The Jews scourged Christ; Christ also scourged the Jews (*ibid*).

The tone of this is considerably more moderate than that of Luther's *Against the Robbing and Murdering Hordes of Peasants* (see *above*, p.289), but its dangers are just as great. Augustine had moved far from the plea of his fellow countryman, Tertullian, to suffer persecution without retaliation, and already one can see the beginnings of a position which was to result in the Inquisition. There is nothing in Augustine to match Luther's vitriol against the Jews, but they are identified as a group that was specifically scourged by Christ. And elsewhere he could argue that the Jewish Dispersion was a direct result of their idolatry and finally of their 'putting Christ to death' (*City of God*, IV, 34).

It is a measure of the extent to which prejudice and intolerance are besetting weaknesses of much Christian theology, that the otherwise mild-mannered Aquinas simply assumed that women were less rational than men (XIV.8) and that discrimination against Jews and violent persecution of 'heretics' were appropriate positions for the church to adopt (see *above*, p.175). In examining Luther's Text XV, it will be important to ask whether or not these forms of prejudice and intolerance are intrinsic features of Christian theology. Even if they are finally considered not to be intrinsic [as Extracts 25 and 26 suggest], it must be frankly admitted that too much of the history of Christian theology contains these features both implicitly and even sometimes quite explicitly.

Full awareness of gender stereotypes is a comparatively recent phenomenon. Although both Augustine and Luther supported marriage and were appreciative of, and gained much from, women (for Augustine it was his mother and for Luther it was his wife), each adhered to what they would have regarded as a thoroughly Pauline understanding of the role and status of women. Augustine was emphatic that wives should be subordinate to husbands:

> Nor can it be doubted, that it is more consonant with the order of nature that men should bear rule over women, than women over men. It is with this principle in view that the apostle says, 'The head of the woman is the man'; and, 'Wives, submit yourselves unto your own husbands' (*De Nuptiis et Concupiscentia*, X).

And, even more significantly, at one point he exclaimed: 'Whether it is in a wife or a mother, it is still Eve (the temptress) that we must beware of in any woman' (*Ep.* 243, 10).

For most of its history, theology has been primarily a male pursuit, so it is perhaps not surprising that recent female theologians have found much of it redolent with male assumptions and prejudices. Fiorenza's Extract 5 and McFague's

Extract 21 stand as important correctives to this. Those who stand outside the social situation within which particular stereotypes and social prejudices are formed, are far more likely to be able to identify them for what they are. In part, even Augustine was aware that this is so. At several points in *The City of God*, he argues that, although something may seem repugnant, it is really only so by convention or custom. Taking the story of Adam and Eve literally, he maintained that the human race resulted from what his contemporaries would have regarded as incestuous relationships:

> It was indeed generally allowed that brothers and sisters should marry in the earliest ages of the human race; but the practice is now so utterly repudiated that it might seem that it could never have been permitted. For custom is the most effective agent in soothing or shocking human sensibilities (*City of God*, XV.16).

And, against those 'male chauvinists' who argued that, at the resurrection, all women will turn into men, he insisted (with his characteristic repudiation of the mechanisms of sexual intercourse):

> For my part, I feel that theirs is the more sensible opinion who have no doubt that there will be both sexes in the resurrection. For in that life there will be no sexual lust, which is the cause of shame... Thus while all defects will be removed from their bodies, their essential nature will be preserved. Now a woman's sex is not a defect; it is natural. And in the resurrection it will be free of the necessity of intercourse and childbirth. However, the female organs will not subserve their former use; they will be part of a new beauty, which will not excite the lust of the beholder (*City of God*, XXII.17).

To the modern reader it may seem extraordinary (and perhaps suspicious) that he should single out women for this inquisitive treatment. But for a Roman Christian, now in his early seventies, it was progressive indeed!

TEXT XIII
AUGUSTINE
Suicide

1. BACKGROUND
This Text comes from *The City of God*, I.17-18, 19b-22 & 27 (Pelican Classics, trans. Henry Bettenson and ed. David Knowles, Penguin, 1972, pp.26-8, 30-4 & 38-9). This initial part of *The City of God* was written c.413 and was a part of Augustine's attempt to praise Christian beliefs and virtues at the expense of 'pagan' ones (see *above*, p.64). In the classical world, suicide was sometimes seen as virtuous and heroic, particularly by the Cynics and, to a lesser extent, by the Stoics. On the other hand, neo-Platonists, whose position strongly influenced Augustine (see *above*, p.37), generally disapproved of it. His conflicts with the Manichaean rejection of killing in any form are still evident in this Text (XIII.9, see *above*, p.289).

2. KEY ISSUES
Augustine's central proposition in this Text is that suicide is murder, albeit of oneself rather than of another. No one has a private right to kill someone – not even themselves (XIII.1). And, since 'purity' is a virtue of the mind and not of the body, even a fear of 'pollution', as a result of rape, does not justify suicide (XIII.2-4). The difference between Christians and others is illustrated by the classical example of Lucretia: she murdered herself after an adulterer had embraced her, whereas a Christian would not have done so (XIII.5-6). The Bible does not sanction suicide, but enjoins people not to kill (XIII.7-8). This command applies to humans alone, not to animals and certainly not to plants (XIII.9). The only exceptions to the commands not to kill are those forms of killing which are prescribed by a just law or are specifically prescribed by God (XIII.10). Contrary to

classical belief, suicide does not show 'greatness of spirit', but rather weakness in the face of oppression (XIII.11) and is not supported by the Judaeo-Christian tradition (XIII.12). If it were to be allowed that people should kill themselves to avoid succumbing to sin, then all should commit suicide immediately after absolution (XIII.13-4)!

3. ETHICAL ARGUMENTS

Augustine's overall position is undoubtedly deontological. It is sufficient for him to show that suicide transgresses the command not to kill. There are important exceptions to this command, but suicide is not one of them – unless it is divinely commanded (as in the instance of Samson). However, there are also two remarkable features of this Text relating to his mode of ethical argument. The first is his stress upon intention in XIII.2-4 (cf. VII.8). Sexual purity is a product of intention and is not destroyed by forcible rape. Moral virtue is to be assessed by the intention of the moral actor and not by what happens to his or her body. The second is the *reductio ad absurdum* in XIII.13-4. With his characteristic waspish humour, Augustine ridicules those who recommend suicide as a means to avoid some evil.

4. BASES OF CHRISTIAN ETHICS

As part of the polemic of *The City of God*, Augustine compares classical virtues with Christian ones. For the Graeco-Roman world, suicide may appear to be a defence of 'honour' (XIII.5) or a sign of 'greatness of spirit' (XIII.11), but not for Christians. The Decalogue forbids this form of killing and, since they were commanded directly by God, Old Testament examples of Abraham attempting to commit 'murder' or of Samson committing 'suicide', do not contravene this (XIII.10). Thus, the Bible is treated literally and deontologically. Nevertheless, Augustine introduces an argument from silence, supposing that Samson must have been 'secretly ordered' by the Spirit (cf. VII.6). There is also an interesting contrast between 'the pure light of a good conscience' of the individual and the 'darkness of the error' of the mob (XIII.11).

5. SOCIAL DETERMINANTS

This Text, like Text I, shows the dependence of Augustine upon both the Graeco-Roman and the Hebraic worlds. He consciously reacts against the former in his rejection of 'heroic' suicide. Yet his style of argument is still heavily dependent upon this world. In true classical style, his concern is for the 'man of purity and high principle', for 'what he will mentally accept or repudiate' and for 'qualities which make up the moral life' (XIII.2). Further, whilst rejecting the Manichaean repudiation of all killing, his implicit assumption that 'lust' is inherently sinful may derive from his own earlier Manichaeism. At the same time, the Decalogue clearly plays a central role in his attitude towards suicide. In addition to these cognitive determinants, certain social structures are relevant to the issue of suicide. In his seminal study, *Suicide*, the pioneer French sociologist, Émile Durkheim, claimed that suicide is more prevalent in societies which lack social cohesion or integration. For him, religion could be an important factor in supplying a moral integration for particular societies (he maintained that Catholicism was far more successful at doing this than Protestantism and that, as a result, suicide was twice as prevalent amongst Protestants as amongst Catholics). *The City of God* was written in response to the 'pagan' challenge that conversions to Christianity had led to the moral deterioration and subsequent sacking of Rome in 410. In such a situation, if Durkheim's thesis is followed, it is not surprising that the issue of suicide was particularly relevant in 413 and that it was a source of moral conflict between 'pagans' and Christians.

6. SOCIAL SIGNIFICANCE

Until very recent times, Augustine's deontological rejection of suicide was the established position within Christianity. By the Middle Ages it was forbidden for suicides to have a Christian burial. Aquinas believed that suicide contravened natural law, since it was contrary to the natural human desire to live. Only with the rise of rationalist philosophy did suicide receive any legitimation. So, David Hume, rejecting the notion of an immortal soul, argued that a person might quite rationally commit suicide. And within non-Roman Catholic churches, it is only within the last two or three decades that there has been a growing belief that suicide should not be treated as a criminal activity and that 'parasuicides' require pastoral care rather than censure (indeed, the term 'parasuicide' was invented to replace the traditional term 'attempted suicide' partly to suggest that it may have more to do with seeking help and attention than death). Only in 1961 did suicide cease to be treated as a crime in Britain.

FURTHER READING
Augustine's chief discussion of the issue of suicide is in Book I of *The City of God*. Hugh Trowell's *The Unfinished Debate on Euthanasia* contains a useful, brief history of Christian attitudes towards suicide and its relation to euthanasia and a bibliography. In addition, there have been a number of church reports on suicide/euthanasia, including the Church of England's *On Dying Well* and the Roman Catholic, Linacre Centre's *Euthanasia and Clinical Practice*.

TEXT XIII
AUGUSTINE
Suicide

The question of suicide caused by fear of punishment or disgrace
XIII.1
Some women killed themselves to avoid suffering anything [like rape] and surely any man of compassion would be ready to excuse the emotions which led them to do this. Some refused to kill themselves, because they did not want to escape another's criminal act by a misdeed of their own. And anyone who uses this as a charge against them will lay himself open to a charge of foolishness. For it is clear that if no one has a private right to kill even a guilty man (and no law allows this), then certainly anyone who kills himself is a murderer, and is the more guilty in killing himself the more innocent he is of the charge on which he has condemned himself to death. We rightly abominate the act of Judas, and the judgment of truth is that when he hanged himself he did not atone for the guilt of his detestable betrayal but rather increased it, since he despaired of God's mercy and in a fit of self-destructive remorse left himself no chance of a saving

repentance. How much less right has anyone to indulge in self-slaughter when he can find in himself no fault to justify such a punishment! For when Judas killed himself, he killed a criminal, and yet he ended his life guilty not only of Christ's death, but also of his own; one crime led to another. Why then should a man, who has done no wrong, do wrong to himself? Why should he kill the innocent in putting himself to death, to prevent a guilty man from doing it? Why should he commit a sin against himself to deprive someone else of the chance?

The question of violence from others, and the lust of others suffered by an unwilling mind in a ravished body

XIII.2

'But', it will be said, 'there is the fear of being polluted by another's lust.' There will be no pollution, if the lust is another's; if there is pollution, the lust is not another's. Now purity is a virtue of the mind. It has courage as its companion and courage decides to endure evil rather than consent to evil. A man of purity and high principle has not the power to decide what happens to his body, but only what he will mentally accept or repudiate. What sane man will suppose that he has lost his purity if his body is seized and forced and used for the satisfaction of a lust that is not his own? For if purity is lost in this way, it follows that it is not a virtue of the mind; it is not then ranked with the qualities which make up the moral life, but is classed among physical qualities, such as strength, beauty, and health, the impairment of which does not in any way mean the impairment of the moral life. If purity is something of this sort, why do we risk physical danger to avoid its loss? But if it is a quality of the mind, it is not lost when the body is violated. Indeed, when the quality of modesty resists the indecency of carnal desires the body itself is sanctified, and therefore, when purity persists in its unshaken resolution to resist these desires, the body's holiness is not lost, because the will to employ the body in holiness endures, as does the ability, as far as in it lies.

XIII.3

The body is not holy just because its parts are intact, or because they have not undergone any handling. Those parts may suffer violent injury by accidents of various kinds, and sometimes doctors seeking to effect a cure may employ treatment with distressing visible effects. During a manual examination of a virgin a midwife destroyed her maidenhood, whether by malice, or clumsiness, or accident. I do not suppose that anyone would be stupid enough to imagine that the virgin lost anything of bodily chastity, even though the integrity of that part had been destroyed. Therefore while the mind's resolve endures, which gives the body its claim to chastity, the violence of another's lust cannot take away the chastity which is preserved by unwavering self-control.

XIII.4

Now suppose some woman, with her mind corrupted and her vowed intention to God violated, in the act of going to her seducer be defiled. Do we say that she is chaste in body while she is on her way, when the chastity of her mind, which made the body chaste, has been lost and destroyed? Of course not! We must rather draw the inference that just as bodily chastity is lost when mental chastity has been violated, so bodily chastity is not lost, even when the body has been ravished, while the mind's chastity endures. Therefore when a woman has been ravished without her consenting, and forced by another's sin, she has no reason to punish herself by a voluntary death. Still less should she do so before the event lest she should commit certain murder while the offence, and another's offence at that, still remains uncertain...

Lucretia's suicide

XIII.5

Her killing of herself because, although not adulterous, she had suffered an adulterer's embraces, was due to the weakness of shame, not to the high value she set on chastity. She was ashamed of another's foul deed committed on her, even though not with her, and as a Roman woman, excessively eager for honour, she was afraid that she should be thought, if she lived, to have willingly endured what, when she lived, she had violently suffered. Since she could not display her pure conscience to the world she thought she must exhibit her punishment before men's eyes as a proof of her state of mind. She blushed at the thought of being regarded as an accomplice in the act if she were to bear with patience what another had inflicted on her with violence.

XIII.6

Such has not been the behaviour of Christian women. When they were treated like this they did not take vengeance on themselves for another's crime. They would not add crime to crime by committing murder on themselves in shame because the enemy had committed rape on them in lust. They have the glory of chastity within them, the testimony of their conscience. They have this in the sight of God, and they ask for nothing more. In fact there is nothing else for them to do that is right for them to do. For they will not deviate from the authority of God's law by taking unlawful steps to avoid the suspicions of men.

Christians have no authority to commit suicide in any circumstance
XIII.7

It is significant that in the sacred canonical books there can nowhere be found any injunction or permission to commit suicide either to ensure immortality or to avoid or escape any evil. In fact we must understand it to be forbidden by the law 'You shall not kill', particularly as there is no addition of 'your neighbour' as in the prohibition of false witness, 'You shall not bear false witness *against your neighbour*'. But that does not mean that a man who gives false witness against himself is exempt from this guilt, since the rule about loving one's neighbour begins with oneself, seeing that the Scripture says, 'You shall love your neighbour as yourself'.

XIII.8

Moreover, if anyone who gives false witness against himself is just as guilty as if he did so against a neighbour – although the prohibition forbids false witness against a neighbour and might be misunderstood as implying that there is no prohibition of false witness against oneself – then it is the more obvious that a man is not allowed to kill himself, since the text 'Thou shall not kill' has no addition and it must be taken that there is no exception, not even the one to whom the command is addressed.

XIII.9

Hence some people have tried to extend its scope to wild and domestic animals to make it mean that even these may never be killed. But then why not apply it to plants and to anything rooted in the earth and nourished by the earth? For although this part of creation is without feeling, it is called 'living', and is hence capable of dying and consequently of being killed, when violence is done to it. And so the Apostle, speaking of seeds of this kind, says, 'What you sow does not come to life unless it dies'; (1 Cor. 15.36) and it says in one of the psalms, 'He killed the vines with hail' (Ps. 78.47). But do we for this reason infer from 'Thou shall not kill' a divine prohibition against clearing away brushwood, and subscribe to the error of the Manicheans? That would be madness. We reject such fantasies, and when we read 'You shall not kill' we assume that this does not refer to bushes, which have no feelings, nor to irrational creatures, flying, swimming, walking, or crawling, since they have no rational association with us, not having been endowed with reason as we are, and hence it is by a just arrangement of the Creator that their life and death is subordinated to our needs. If this is so, it remains that we take the command 'You shall not kill' as applying to human beings, that is, other persons and oneself. For to kill oneself is to kill a human being.

All homicide is not murder

XIII.10

There are however certain exceptions to the law against killing, made by the authority of God himself. There are some whose killing God orders, either by a law, or by an express command to a particular person at a particular time. In fact one who owes a duty of obedience to the giver of the command does not himself 'kill' – he is an instrument, a sword in its user's hand. For this reason the commandment forbidding killing was not broken by those who have waged wars on the authority of God, or those who have imposed the death-penalty on criminals when representing the authority of the State in accordance with the laws of the State, the justest and most reasonable source of power. When Abraham was ready to kill his son, so far from being blamed for cruelty he was praised for his devotion; it was not an act of crime, but of obedience. One is justified in asking whether Jephtha is to be regarded as obeying a command of God in killing his daughter, when he had vowed to sacrifice to God the first thing he met when returning victorious from battle. And when Samson destroyed himself, with his enemies, by the demolition of the building, this can only be excused on the ground that the Spirit, which performed miracles through him, secretly ordered him to do so. With the exception of these killings prescribed generally by a just law, or specially commanded by God himself – the source of justice – anyone who kills a human being, whether himself or anyone else, is involved in a charge of murder.

Is suicide ever a mark of greatness of soul?

XIII.11

Those who have committed this crime against themselves are perhaps to be admired for greatness of spirit; they are not to be praised for wisdom or sanity. And yet if we examine the matter more deeply and logically, we shall find that greatness of spirit is not the right term to apply to one who has killed himself because he lacked strength to endure hardships, or another's wrongdoing. In fact we detect weakness in a mind which cannot bear physical oppression, or the stupid opinion of the mob; we rightly ascribe greatness to a spirit that has the strength to endure a life of misery instead of running away from it, and to despise the judgment of men – and in particular the judgment of the mob, which is so often clouded in the darkness of error – in comparison with the pure light of a good conscience. If suicide is to be taken as a mark of greatness of spirit, then Theombrotus will be a shining example of that quality. The story is that when he had read Plato's book which discusses the immortality of the soul, he hurled himself from a wall and so passed from this life to a life which he believed to be better. There was no kind of misfortune, no accusation, true or false, which led him to do away with himself under an intolerable load. It was only greatness of spirit which prompted him to seek death and to 'break the pleasant bonds of life'. But Plato himself, whom he had been reading, is witness that this showed greatness rather than goodness. Plato would have been first and foremost to take this action, and would have recommended it to others, had not the same intelligence which gave him his vision of the soul's immortality enabled him to decide that this step was not to be taken – was, indeed, to be forbidden.

XIII.12

'But many people did away with themselves to avoid falling into the hands of the enemy.' The question is not only whether they did, but whether they ought to have done so. Sound reason is certainly to be preferred to examples. Some examples are in full harmony with sound reason, and they are the more worthy of imitation as they are more eminent in their devotion to God. Neither the patriarchs nor the prophets acted thus; nor did the apostles, since the Lord Christ himself, when he advised them to escape from one town to another in case of persecution, could have advised them to take their own lives to avoid falling into the hands of their persecutors. If he did not order or advise this way of quitting this life, although he promised to prepare eternal dwellings for them after their departure, it is clear that this course is not allowed to those who worship the one true God, whatever examples may be put forward by 'the Gentiles who have no knowledge of him' (1 Thes. 4.5)...

Should one commit suicide to avoid sin?
XIII.13

There remains one situation in which it is supposed to be advantageous to commit suicide; I have already begun to discuss the question. It arises when the motive is to avoid falling into sin either through the allurements of pleasure or through the menaces of pain. If we agree to allow this motive we shall not be able to stop until we reach the point when people are to be encouraged to kill themselves for preference, immediately they have received forgiveness of all sins by washing in the waters of holy regeneration. For that would be the time to forestall all future sins – the moment when all past sins have been erased. If self-inflicted death is permitted, surely this is the best possible moment for it! When a person has been thus set free why should he expose himself again to all the perils of this life, when it is so easily allowed him to avoid them by doing away with himself? And the Bible says, 'A man who is fond of danger will fall into it.' (Ecclus. 3.26). Why are men so fond of all these great dangers, or at any rate are willing to accept them, by remaining in this life, when they are allowed to depart from it? If a man has a duty to kill himself to avoid succumbing to sin because he is at the mercy of one man, who holds him prisoner, does he suppose that he has to go on living so as to endure the pressures of the actual world, which is full of temptations at all times, temptations such as that which is dreaded under one master, and innumerable others, which are the necessary accompaniment of this life? Has perverse silliness so warped our judgment and distracted us from facing the truth? For on this assumption, why do we spend time on those exhortations to the newly baptised. We do our best to kindle their resolve to preserve their virginal purity, or to remain continent in widowhood, or to remain faithful to their marriage vows. But there is available an excellent short cut which avoids any danger of sinning; if we can persuade them to rush to a self-inflicted death immediately upon receiving remission of sins, we shall send them to the Lord in the purest and soundest condition!

XIII.14
But in fact if anyone thinks that we should go in for persuasion on these lines, I should not call him silly, but quite crazy. Then how could anyone justify saying to any human being: 'Kill yourself, to avoid adding more serious sin to your small shortcomings, living, as you do, under a master with the manners and morals of a savage', if he cannot say, without being a complete criminal, 'Kill yourself, now that all your sins have been absolved, to avoid committing such sins again, or even worse, while you are living in a world full of the allurements of impure pleasures, so maddened with all its monstrous cruelties, so menacing with all its errors and terrors'? To say this would be monstrous; it follows that suicide is monstrous. If there could be a valid reason for suicide one could not find one more valid than this; and since this is not valid, a valid reason does not exist.

CRITIQUE
It would be a mistake to assess Augustine's contentions on suicide as if they were modern contentions and to forget that they derive from a very specific polemical context. Nonetheless, because of

their social significance in shaping Christian, and indeed secular, attitudes towards suicide, their strengths and weaknesses should be noted.

Positively, Augustine's stress upon intention in Christian ethics has proved to be extremely important. Although it is difficult for most victims of rape not to feel guilt and remorse, Augustine placed rape into a more adequate ethical context. Impurity lies in intention, not in involuntary action. It is the rapist and not the one who is raped who is impure, so it would be wholly inappropriate for the Christian to recommend suicide as a means of escaping rape. Further, even today, most Christians might agree that what Durkheim termed 'altruistic suicide' (whereby people commit suicide because their religion or society convince them that it is their duty – *Suicide*, pp.217f.) is seldom justifiable. Most might support Augustine's attacks on the martyr-seeking attitudes of the Donatists.

Negatively, Augustine showed little awareness of, or sympathy for, other reasons for suicide or 'parasuicide'. For Durkheim there were two other categories of suicide – egoistic and anomic. The first results from lack of integration of the individual into society: the more an individual is left to his or her resources, the more likely that individual is to commit suicide. The second results from lack of regulation of the individual by society: so, the chaos ensuing from divorce can render men (more than women) especially vulnerable to suicide. A greater awareness of these specifically social determinants of suicide has inclined many today towards a more sympathetic attitude to those who commit, or appear to attempt, suicide. Indeed, in the West today, suicide/ parasuicide is far more likely to be thought of as a medical, rather than as a moral or religious, problem.

Even though attitudes towards suicide have changed amongst both Christians and non-Christians, at least one theological point links the former with Augustine. For Christians (and theists generally) life is ultimately God-given and, as a consequence, should never be taken casually or for selfish motives. So convinced, individuals may be hesitant about usurping for themselves what they regard as a function of God, or treating functionally the life that God has given. Whether or not this precludes the Christian from voluntary, direct euthanasia or rational, calculated suicide, will be discussed in relation to Fletcher's Extract 22. But, clearly, it may at least make one cautious (for a discussion of this 'adeodatic axiom', see *below*, pp.564f.).

TEXT XIV
AQUINAS
Fornication and marriage

1. BACKGROUND

This Text comes from *Summa Contra Gentiles* 3.2.122-4 & 126 (University of Notre Dame Press, London, and Doubleday, New York, 1975, trans. Vernon J. Bourke, pp.142-51 & 155-6). From the same Book of *Summa Contra Gentiles* as Text XI, it too was explicitly written for a non-Christian audience and, hence, tends to argue initially from reason rather than from Christian revelation. Immediately before this Text, Aquinas sought to refute some of the central claims of astrology and notions of fate and to defend the Christian notions of providence, prayer, miracles and divine law, and, immediately after it, he considered the question 'In What Way Poverty is Good'. Throughout these various discussions, a number of Aristotelian natural law principles are evident (see also, Text V). So, he assumed that the virtue of something must always be related to the end of humanity (XIV.4), that humans are social animals (XIV.6), and that the virtue of something ought to be assessed by whether or not it contributes to the overall well-being of society or simply to the well-being of a particular individual (XIV.7). The Text shows that Aquinas was well aware of secular promiscuity and of Islamic polygamy and divorce. However, for him, they were contradicted by natural law (and, in turn, also by divine law and by the Bible). More positively, he was concerned to refute the Platonic (and, significantly, with it the Augustinian) notion that the sexual act was in itself, or in its association with 'lust', evil: within the context of a stable, monogamous marriage, sexual intercourse is both natural and in accord with divine providence. Nonetheless, he shared with Augustine the beliefs that procreation is the primary function of sexual intercourse and that celibacy is a higher state than marriage. Aquinas' debt to

Aristotle rather than to Plato, is also apparent in XIV.8, in the notion that the socialisation of children necessarily involves the correction of their natural passions.

2. KEY ISSUES

Aquinas' initial concern is to counter those who maintain that, as long as it harms no one, 'fornication' is not sinful (XIV.1-3). For him, the proper end for the emission of semen is the propagation of the species (XIV.4). As a result, any deliberate emission in situations where, either generation cannot result, or proper upbringing of resulting children is impossible, is sinful (XIV.5-6). Children need both parents to bring them up and to instruct them in reason (XIV.7-8). Properly ordered emission of semen is both required for the preservation of the species and is prescribed by the Bible (XIV.9-12). For the same reasons, marriage should be life-long (XIV.13-16). Infidelity in marriage goes against the natural wish of fathers to know their offspring (XIV.17), whereas the greater the friendship in marriage the more long-lasting it will be (XIV.18). Marriage is in accordance with natural promptings for the common good and with divine law (XIV.19-22). Sexual promiscuity contravenes natural law (XIV.23-4). On the other hand, sexual intercourse which is directed to the generation and upbringing of children is not sinful but reasonable (XIV.25). Sexual intercourse is a natural and God-given phenomenon and therefore cannot be evil in itself (XIV.26-30).

3. ETHICAL ARGUMENTS

This Text provides one of the clearest examples of Aquinas' use of natural law. The position which is established in theory in Text II, is here used as the main mode of ethical argument. Aquinas first establishes what is 'natural', in the sense of being in accord with nature, in either human or animal form. From this he derives ethical prescriptions, which are then related to biblical norms. Thus, deontological assumptions are made both about the natural order and about biblical revelation. Further, he characteristically uses consequential ethical arguments: sexuality is to be related to its primary end (procreation) and this end is to be related to the common human good. So, promiscuity is thought to be wrong deontologically (because it contravenes the natural order and biblical revelation) and consequentially (because it does not contribute to the common good). On the other hand, properly directed sexual intercourse and even sexual inclinations are not considered to be evil or sinful: it is the use to which sexual intercourse is put that determines whether or not it is sinful. Similarly poverty or wealth are not virtuous or wrong in themselves. For Aquinas virtue may be seen as a mean: 'The goodness of everything that comes under measure and rule consists in its being conformed to its rule. Consequently, evil in these things lies in departure from rule or measure either by excess or defect. And therefore it is clear that the good of moral virtue consists in being up to the level of the measure of reason... in the mean between excess and defect' (*S.T.* I.II, Q.64, Art.1). Measured against the rule of reason, both poverty and wealth may appear evil if taken to excess. But if they conform to the rule of reason – which, 'measures not only the size of a thing that is used, but also the circumstances of the person, and his intention, the fitness of place and time, and other such things' (*S.C.G.*, 3.2.134) – they can both be virtuous.

4. *BASES OF CHRISTIAN ETHICS*

In keeping with the method of *Summa Contra Gentiles*, Aquinas introduces biblical quotations only at the end of each argument (XIV.10-11, 18-22 & 29). Perhaps it is not surprising that most of these quotations are taken from the Pentateuch and Pauline epistles. However, underlying much of the arguments is a notion of creation: the natural order can supply humans with indications of how they should behave, precisely because it is a God-given order (XIV.12 – see *above*, pp.165f.).

5. *SOCIAL DETERMINANTS*

Aquinas wrote within the constraints of 13th-century Christendom. Although he was clearly aware of other sexual patterns, he was confident that heterosexual, exclusive monogamy (or, somewhat illogically, celibacy) alone conformed

to reason and that this was wholly consonant with the Bible.
Today both of these assumptions have been challenged.
Following Augustine, he regarded procreation as the essential
function of sexual intercourse and, although he wrote about
husbands and wives as 'an association of equals' (XIV.16), yet,
along with many of his contemporaries, he regarded men as
the more rational. Since 'reason' and 'virtue' were so closely
linked in his thought, this last assumption is particularly
problematic.

6. SOCIAL SIGNIFICANCE

It will be evident in Paul VI's Extract 24 that Aquinas' view
of procreation as an essential function of all occasions of sexual
intercourse has proved especially significant. Indeed, this
mediated position still plays a crucial role in traditional forms
of Roman Catholic moral teaching today. Within such
teaching, not only are homosexuality and prostitution alike
condemned, but also all forms of sexual intercourse which
involve wholly effective contraception, both within marriage
as well as outside of marriage. However, Aquinas has also
proved influential in his divergence from Augustine, since
many Christians today (Roman Catholic and non-Roman
Catholic) would insist that sexual intercourse and sexual desire
are not in themselves evil. It is their abuse (however defined)
which is considered evil.

FURTHER READING

Important discussions of sexuality and marriage are contained
in both *Summa Theologica* (e.g. I.II.77) and *Summa Contra
Gentiles*. In addition to the secondary commentaries on Aquinas
already mentioned, Roland H. Bainton's *Sex, Love and
Marriage: A Christian Survey* provides a useful, brief survey of
historical attitudes and a bibliography. A sympathetic, but more
radical, Roman Catholic approach is offered in Lisa Cahill's
Sex, Gender and Christian Ethics. In addition, V.A. Demant's
An Exposition of Christian Sex Ethics and Helmut Thielicke's
The Ethics of Sex offer Anglican and Reformed approaches
respectively.

TEXT XIV

AQUINAS

Fornication and marriage

The reason why simple fornication is a sin according to divine law,
and that matrimony is natural

XIV.1

From the foregoing we can see the futility of the argument of
certain people who say that simple fornication is not a sin. For
they say: Suppose there is a woman who is not married, or under
the control of any man, either her father or another man. Now,
if a man performs the sexual act with her, and she is willing, he
does not injure her, because she favours the action and she has
control over her own body. Nor does he injure any other person,
because she is understood to be under no other person's control.
So, this does not seem to be a sin.

XIV.2

Now, to say that he injures God would not seem to be an
adequate answer. For we do not offend God except by doing
something contrary to our own good, as has been said. But this
does not appear contrary to man's good. Hence, on this basis,
no injury seems to be done to God.

XIV.3

Likewise, it also would seem an inadequate answer to say that
some injury is done to one's neighbour by this action, inasmuch
as he may be scandalised. Indeed, it is possible for him to be
scandalised by something which is not in itself a sin. In this event,
the act would be accidentally sinful. But our problem, is not
whether simple fornication is accidentally a sin, but whether it is
so essentially.

XIV.4

Hence, we must look for a solution in our earlier considerations.
We have said that God exercises care over every person on the
basis of what is good for him. Now, it is good for each person to
attain his end, whereas it is bad for him to swerve away from his

proper end. Now, this should be considered applicable to the parts, just as it is to the whole being; for instance, each and every part of man, and every one of his acts, should attain the proper end. Now, though the male semen is superfluous in regard to the preservation of the individual, it is nevertheless necessary in regard to the propagation of the species. Other superfluous things, such as excrement, urine, sweat, and such things, are not at all necessary; hence, their emission contributes to man's good. Now, this is not what is sought in the case of semen, but, rather, to emit it for the purpose of generation, to which purpose the sexual act is directed. But man's generative process would be frustrated unless it were followed by proper nutrition, because the offspring would not survive if proper nutrition were withheld. Therefore, the emission of semen ought to be so ordered that it will result in both the production of the proper offspring and in the upbringing of this offspring.

XIV.5

It is evident from this that every emission of semen, in such a way that generation cannot follow, is contrary to the good for man. And if this be done deliberately, it must be a sin. Now, I am speaking of a way from which, *in itself* generation could not result; such would be any emission of semen apart from the natural union of male and female. For which reason, sins of this type are called *contrary to nature*. But, if by accident generation cannot result from the emission of semen, then this is not a reason for it being against nature, or a sin; as for instance, if the woman happens to be sterile.

XIV.6

Likewise, it must also be contrary to the good for man if the semen be emitted under conditions such that generation could result but the proper upbringing would be prevented. We should take into consideration the fact that, among some animals where the female is able to take care of the upbringing of offspring, male and female do not remain together for any time after the act of generation. This is obviously the case with dogs. But in the case of animals of which the female is not able to provide for the upbringing of offspring, the male and female do stay together after the act of generation as long as is necessary for the upbringing and instruction of the offspring. Examples are found among certain species of birds whose young are not able to seek out food for themselves immediately after hatching. In fact, since a bird does not nourish its young with milk, made available by nature as it were, as occurs in the case of quadrupeds, but the bird must look elsewhere for food for its young, and since besides this it must protect them by sitting on them, the female is not able to do this by herself. So, as a result of divine providence, there is naturally implanted in the male of these animals a tendency to remain with the female in order to bring up the young. Now, it is abundantly evident that the female in the human species is not at all able to take care of the upbringing of offspring by herself, since the needs of human life demand many things which cannot be provided by one person alone. Therefore, it is appropriate to human nature that a man remain together with a woman after the generative act, and not leave her immediately to have such relations with another woman, as is the practice with fornicators.

XIV.7
Nor, indeed, is the fact that a woman may be able by means of her own wealth to care for the child by herself an obstacle to this argument. For natural rectitude in human acts is not dependent on things accidentally possible in the case of one individual, but, rather, on those conditions which accompany the entire species.

XIV.8
Again, we must consider that in the human species offspring require not only nourishment for the body, as in the case of other animals, but also education for the soul. For other animals naturally possess their own kinds of prudence whereby they are enabled to take care of themselves. But a man lives by reason, which he must develop by lengthy, temporal experience so that he may achieve prudence. Hence, children must be instructed by parents who are already experienced people. Nor are they able to receive such instruction as soon as they are born, but after a long time, and especially after they have reached the age of discretion. Moreover, a long time is needed for this instruction.

Then, too, because of the impulsion of the passions, through which prudent judgment is vitiated, they require not merely instruction but correction. Now, a woman alone is not adequate to this task; rather, this demands the work of a husband, in whom reason is more developed for giving instruction and strength is more available for giving punishment. Therefore, in the human species, it is not enough, as in the case of birds, to devote a small amount of time to bringing up offspring, for a long period of life is required. Hence, since among all animals it is necessary for male and female to remain together as long as the work of the father is needed by the offspring, it is natural to the human being for the man to establish a lasting association with a designated woman, over no short period of time. Now, we call this society *matrimony*. Therefore, matrimony is natural for man, and promiscuous performance of the sexual act, outside matrimony, is contrary to man's good. For this reason, it must be a sin.

XIV.9

Nor, in fact, should it be deemed a slight sin for a man to arrange for the emission of semen apart from the proper purpose of generating and bringing up children, on the argument that it is either a slight sin, or none at all, for a person to use a part of the body for a different use than that to which it is directed by nature (say, for instance, one chose to walk on his hands, or to use his feet for something usually done with the hands) because man's good is not much opposed by such inordinate use. However, the inordinate emission of semen is incompatible with the natural good; namely, the preservation of the species. Hence, after the sin of homicide whereby a human nature already in existence is destroyed, this type of sin appears to take next place, for by it the generation of human nature is precluded.

XIV.10

Moreover, these views which have just been given have a solid basis in divine authority. That the emission of semen under conditions in which offspring cannot follow is illicit is quite clear. There is the text of Leviticus [18.22-3]: 'thou shalt not lie with mankind as with womankind... and thou shalt not copulate with any beast'. And in 1 Corinthians [6.10]: 'Nor the effeminate, nor liers with mankind... shall possess the kingdom of God.'

XIV.11
Also, that fornication and every performance of the act of reproduction with a person other than one's wife are illicit is evident. For it is said: 'There shall be no whore among the daughters of Israel, nor whoremonger among the sons of Israel' [Deut. 23.17]; and in Tobias [4.13]: 'Take heed to keep thyself from all fornication, and beside thy wife never endure to know a crime'; and in 1 Corinthians [6.18]: 'Fly fornication.'

XIV.12
By this conclusion we refute the error of those who say that there is no more sin in the emission of semen than in the emission of any other superfluous matter, and also of those who state that fornication is not a sin.

That matrimony should be indivisible
XIV.13
If one will make a proper consideration, the preceding reasoning will be seen to lead to the conclusion not only that the society of man and woman of the human species, which we call matrimony, should be long-lasting, but even that it should endure throughout an entire life.

XIV.14
Indeed, possessions are ordered to the preservation of natural life, and since natural life, which cannot be preserved perpetually in the father, is by a sort of succession preserved in the son in its specific likeness, it is naturally fitting for the son to succeed also to the things which belong to the father. So, it is natural that the father's solicitude for his son should endure until the end of the father's life. Therefore, if even in the case of birds the solicitude of the father gives rise to the cohabitation of male and female, the natural order demands that father and mother in the human species remain together until the end of life.

XIV.15
It also seems to be against equity if the aforesaid society be

dissolved. For the female needs the male, not merely for the sake of generation, as in the case of other animals, but also for the sake of government, since the male is both more perfect in reasoning and stronger in his powers. In fact, a woman is taken into man's society for the needs of generation; then, with the disappearance of a woman's fecundity and beauty, she is prevented from association with another man. So, if any man took a woman in the time of her youth, when beauty and fecundity were hers, and then sent her away after she had reached an advanced age, he would damage that woman contrary to natural equity.

XIV.16

Again, it seems obviously inappropriate for a woman to be able to put away her husband, because a wife is naturally subject to her husband as governor, and it is not within the power of a person subject to another to depart from his rule. So, it would be against the natural order if a wife were able to abandon her husband. Therefore, if a husband were permitted to abandon his wife, the society of husband and wife would not be an association of equals, but, instead, a sort of slavery on the part of the wife.

XIV.17

Besides, there is in men a certain natural solicitude to know their offspring. This is necessary for this reason: the child requires the father's direction for a long time. So, whenever there are obstacles to the ascertaining of offspring they are opposed to the natural instinct of the human species. But, if a husband could put away his wife, or a wife her husband, and have sexual relations with another person, certitude as to offspring would be precluded, for the wife would be united first with one man and later with another. So, it is contrary to the natural instinct of the human species for a wife to be separated from her husband. And thus, the union of male and female in the human species must be not only lasting, but also unbroken.

XIV.18

Furthermore, the greater that friendship is, the more solid and long-lasting will it be. Now, there seems to be the greatest friendship between husband and wife, for they are united not only in the act of fleshly union, which produces a certain gentle association even among beasts, but also in the partnership of the whole range of domestic activity. Consequently, as an indication of this, man must even 'leave his father and mother' for the sake of his wife, as is said in Genesis [2.24]. Therefore, it is fitting for matrimony to be completely indissoluble.

XIV.19

It should be considered, further, that generation is the only natural act that is ordered to the common good, for eating and the emission of waste matters pertain to the individual good, but generation to the preservation of the species. As a result, since law is established for the common good, those matters which pertain to generation must, above all others, be ordered by laws, both divine and human. Now, laws that are established should stem from the prompting of nature, if they are human; just as in the demonstrative sciences, also, every human discovery takes its origin from naturally known principles. But, if they are divine laws, they not only develop the prompting of nature but also supplement the deficiency of natural instinct, as things that are divinely revealed surpass the capacity of human reason. So, since there is a natural prompting within the human species, to the end that the union of man and wife be undivided, and that it be between one man and one woman, it was necessary for this to be ordered by human law. But divine law supplies a supernatural reason, drawn from the symbolism of the inseparable union between Christ and the Church, which is a union of one spouse with another [Eph. 5.24-32]. And thus, disorders connected with the act of generation are not only opposed to natural instinct, but are also transgressions of divine and human laws. Hence, a greater sin results from a disorder in this area than in regard to the use of food or other things of that kind.

XIV.20

Moreover, since it is necessary for all other things to be ordered to what is best in man, the union of man and wife is not only ordered in this way because it is important to the generating of offspring, as it is in the case of other animals, but also because it is in agreement with good behaviour, which right reason directs either in reference to the individual man in himself, or in regard to man as a member of a family, or of a civil society. In fact, the undivided union of husband and wife is pertinent to good behaviour. For thus, when they know that they are indivisibly united, the love of one spouse for the other will be more faithful. Also, both will be more solicitous in their care for domestic possessions when they keep in mind that they will remain continually in possession of these same things. As a result of this, the sources of disagreements which would have to come up between a man and his wife's relatives, if he could put away his wife, are removed, and a more solid affection is established among the relatives. Removed, also, are the occasions for adultery which are presented when a man is permitted to send away his wife, or the converse. In fact, by this practice an easier way of arranging marriage with those outside the family circle is provided.

XIV.21
Hence it is said in Matthew [5.31] and in 1 Corinthians [7.10]: 'But I say to you... that the wife depart not from her husband.'

XIV.22
By this conclusion, moreover, we oppose the custom of those who put away their wives, though this was permitted the Jews in the old Law, 'by reason of the hardness of their hearts' [Matt. 19.8]; that is, because they were ready to kill their wives. So, the lesser evil was permitted them in order to prevent a greater evil.

That matrimony should be between one man and one woman
XIV.23
It seems, too, that we should consider how it is inborn in the minds of all animals accustomed to sexual reproduction to allow no promiscuity; hence, fights occur among animals over the matter of sexual reproduction. And, in fact, among all animals there is one common reason, for every animal desires to enjoy freely the pleasure of the sexual act, as he also does the pleasure of food; but this liberty is restricted by the fact that several males

may have access to one female, or the converse. The same situation obtains in the freedom of enjoying food, for one animal is obstructed if the food which he desires to eat is taken over by another animal. And so, animals fight over food and sexual relations in the same way. But among men there is a special reason, for, as we said, man naturally desires to know his offspring, and this knowledge would be completely destroyed if there were several males for one female. Therefore, that one female is for one male is a consequence of natural instinct.

XIV.24

But a difference should be noted on this point. As far as the view that one woman should not have sexual relations with several men is concerned, both the afore-mentioned reasons apply. But, in regard to the conclusion that one man should not have relations with several females, the second argument does not work, since certainty as to offspring is not precluded if one male has relations with several women. But the first reason works against this practice, for, just as the freedom of associating with a woman at will is taken away from the husband, when the woman has another husband, so, too, the same freedom is taken away from a woman when her husband has several wives...

That not all sexual intercourse is sinful
XIV.25

Now, just as it is contrary to reason for man to perform the act of carnal union contrary to what befits the generation and upbringing of offspring, so also is it in keeping with reason for a man to exercise the act of carnal union in a manner which is suited to the generation and upbringing of offspring. But only those things that are opposed to reason are prohibited by divine law, as is evident from what we said above. So, it is not right to say that every act of carnal union is a sin.

XIV.26

Again, since bodily organs are the instruments of the soul, the end of each organ is its use, as is the case with any other instrument. Now, the use of certain bodily organs is carnal union. So, carnal union is the end of certain bodily organs. But that which is the end of certain natural things cannot be evil in itself, because things that exist naturally are ordered to their end by divine providence, as is plain from what was said above. Therefore, it is impossible for carnal union to be evil in itself.

XIV.27

Besides, natural inclinations are present in things from God, Who moves all things. So, it is impossible for the natural inclination of a species to be toward what is evil in itself. But there is in all perfect animals a natural inclination toward carnal union. Therefore, it is impossible for carnal union to be evil in itself.

XIV.28

Moreover, that without which a thing cannot be what is good and best is not evil in itself. But the perpetuation of the species can only be preserved in animals by generation, which is the result of carnal union. So, it is impossible for carnal union to be evil in itself.

XIV.29

Hence it is said in 1 Corinthians [7.28]: 'if a virgin marry, she hath not sinned'.

XIV.30

Now, this disposes of the error of those who say that every act of carnal union is illicit, as a consequence of which view they entirely condemn matrimony and marriage arrangements. In fact, some of these people say this because they believe that bodily things arise, not from a good, but from an evil, source.

CRITIQUE

Because of their particular influence upon present-day Roman Catholic moral theology, it is important to subject Aquinas' views on sexuality and marriage to critical attention. It may be anachronistic to accuse him of propagating damaging sexual stereotypes or restrictive notions of the role of sexual intercourse, but it is still important to assess his overall arguments.

Positively, his writings on sexual issues offer much moral sense. In a more technological age, it is easier to miss the obvious fact that, whatever other functions it performs, human sexuality does have a primary function in reproduction. Further, within a Christian context, the upbringing of children in the most responsible manner remains a primary duty for all Christian parents. Most Christians might agree that the monogamous, exclusive family remains the most responsible context in which to carry out this duty. Sexuality often does entail procreation and procreation should involve responsible upbringing. Further, there is obvious sense in Aquinas' notion of sexual sin. Not only did he insist that the sexual act, or the desire that leads to this act, is not inherently sinful, but he also maintained that: 'Every act of sin proceeds from an inordinate craving after some temporal good. This again proceeds from an inordinate love of self, for to love anyone is to wish him good. Therefore inordinate love of self is the cause of all sin' (*S. T.* I.II.Q.77, Art.4).

Negatively, his arguments illustrate some of the most crucial weaknesses of natural law arguments. Many of the assumptions that Aquinas made about sexuality and sexual differentiation will appear to present-day readers as owing more to custom and convention than to natural law. For example, he could assume that homosexuality and homosexual inclinations were indeed 'unnatural' and the consequence of sin or distortion. To many today this is not so clear. Whatever the complex determinants of homosexuality might be, a homosexual predisposition does seem to be the 'nature' of some. Further, non-procreative, nocturnal emissions of semen, infertility at certain points in the menstrual cycle, and abortions in the form of miscarriages, all happen spontaneously and frequently and thus might be regarded as 'natural'. The very notion of 'the natural' in this area of sexuality seems to encourage value judgments from its supposedly neutral users. Aquinas was no exception.

Supposing a natural law theory of human sexuality could be established (it is surprisingly prevalent in popular, secular discussions of sexual morality) it would still face problems. Even if it is conceded that procreation is the obvious function of sexuality, it is far from clear that it should be the only, or the indispensable, function of human sexuality (this point will be made further in relation to Extract 24). Further, on Aquinas' own argument (XIV.5), if a couple knows that one of them is spontaneously sterile, are they on that account to refrain from all further sexual intercourse? Many might argue that, particularly today in an over-crowded world, it would be irresponsible and unrealistic to restrict the function of sexual intercourse to reproduction and to proscribe it outside this function. But, even in the context of 13th-century Europe, Aquinas' logic was still faulty: to derive an exclusive moral prescription from an empirical observation of function was seemingly to commit a category error. With the benefit of hindsight, it has turned out to be a particularly troublesome error for many present-day Roman Catholics.

TEXT XV
LUTHER
On the Jews and their lies

1. *BACKGROUND*

This Text comes from *On the Jews and Their Lies* of 1543 (from *Luther's Works*, vol 47, Fortress Press, Philadelphia, 1971, pp.137-42, trans. Martin H. Bertram). This virulent treatise, written three years before Luther's death, was unavailable in English translation until 1971 and is reproduced here only after considerable hesitation. Luther was always capable of violent swings of mood – as can be seen by comparing his two letters to the rebellious German peasants in 1525 (see *above*, p.289) – but none is more startling or shocking than that represented here. The swing can be seen most fully if this treatise is compared with his treatise of 1523, *That Jesus Christ Was Born a Jew*. There he criticised the Roman Church for its crude attacks upon the Jews: 'They have dealt with the Jews as if they were dogs rather than human beings; they have done little else than deride them and seized their property' (*Luther's Works*, vol 45, p.200). In contrast, Luther maintained the following position:

> If the Jew should take offence because we confess our Jesus to be a man, and yet true God, we will deal forcefully with that from Scripture in due time. But this is too harsh for a beginning. Let them first be suckled with milk, and begin by recognising this man Jesus as the true Messiah; after that they may drink wine, and learn also that he is true God. For they have been led astray so long and so far that one must deal gently with them... So long as we thus treat them like dogs, how can we expect to work any good among them?... If we really want to help them, we must be guided in our dealings with them not by papal law but by the law of Christian love... If some of them should prove stiff-

necked, what of it? After all, we ourselves are not all good Christians either (p.229).

The tone is evidently patronising but not virulent. A number of Luther's contemporaries were dismayed by the later work, although fortunately it sold far fewer copies than the 1523 treatise. Luther wrote the 1543 treatise in response to a Jewish apologetic pamphlet. In the first section (which starts with this Text) he examined the 'false boasts' of the Jews: in the second he examined a number of key biblical texts: in the third he returned to specific and, of course, much exaggerated, criticisms of the Jews: and in the final section he advised the authorities to let Jewish synagogues and houses be burnt and to deprive them of their prayer books and means of making a living:

> I wish and I ask that our rulers who have Jewish subjects exercise a sharp mercy towards these wretched people... they must act like a good physician who, when gangrene has set in, proceeds without mercy to cut, saw, and burn flesh, veins, bone, and marrow. Such a procedure must also be followed in this instance. Burn down their synagogues, forbid all that I enumerated earlier, force them to work, and deal harshly with them, as Moses did in the wilderness, slaying three thousand lest the whole people perish... If this does not help we must drive them out like mad dogs, so that we do not become partakers of their abominable blasphemy and all their other vices and thus merit God's wrath and be damned with them. I have done my duty. Now let everyone see to his. I am exonerated (*Luther's Works*, vol 47, p.292).

2. KEY ISSUES

Luther was convinced by the time that he wrote this Text, that Jews are too 'venomous', 'embittered' and 'blind' to be converted into Christians and that, as a result, Christians should not trouble themselves to argue with them (XV.1-8). Furthermore, their proud boasts about being descended from the patriarchs and of being a holy people (in contrast with 'we Gentiles'), are simply 'stupid folly' (XV.10-12). They even boast and thank God that they are male rather than female – just as Plato did (XV.12). Both the Old Testament prophets and Jesus and John the Baptist condemned the Jews for their pride (XV.13). Indeed, if the Jewish Messiah did come, they would reject, blaspheme and crucify him (XV.14-15).

3. *ETHICAL ARGUMENTS*

There is an overall deontological basis to Luther's attack upon Jews (cf. Text VI). He labelled the Jews as 'miserable and accursed' (XV.1), 'embittered, venomous, blind' (XV.8) 'raving, mad, and stupid' (XV.12) and 'arrogant' and guilty of 'pride' (XV.13). These rhetorical labels or pejorative stereotypes are applied sweepingly (as are all racist notions) to Jews as a whole and, of themselves, are thought sufficient to condemn them. More consequentially, Luther also maintained that 'the terrible distress that has been theirs for over fourteen hundred years in exile' (XV.4) was also evidence of their condemnation.

4. *BASES OF CHRISTIAN ETHICS*

This Text illustrates how secular and religious anti-Semitism are often interconnected. Luther regarded the Bible as confirming his general condemnation of Jews. Ignoring the obvious Jewish context of the Bible and, indeed, the sayings of Jesus, he applied notions like that of the 'brood of vipers' and the 'devil's children' to contemporary Jews. In his earlier treatise he had reminded his readers 'that Jesus Christ was born a Jew', but in this Text Jesus is depicted simply as condemning all Jews. There is also a doctrinal basis to the anti-Semitism of Luther and of many of his contemporaries. For them, the Jew represented a permanent symbol of unredemption. Along with 'heretics' and 'apostates', they had been confronted by Christ, but had rejected him and had remained unconverted: all three groups were essentially unredeemed 'blasphemers' upholding an anti-Christian religion (cf. Aquinas, p.175, *above*).

5. *SOCIAL DETERMINANTS*

By the 16th century, anti-Semitism was deeply embedded into

European culture. Despite the relatively small number of Jews actually living in Europe at the time, they were frequently treated as scapegoats for sexual crimes, for plagues and even for natural disasters. In the 1490s they were driven from Spain and Portugal and were often the object of discrimination in Luther's Germany. The statues of the virtuous, virginal, triumphant Church and the blinded, licentious, defeated Synagogue outside Strasbourg Cathedral typify medieval attitudes towards Jews. Nonetheless, since the virulence of *On the Jews and Their Lies* shocked even some of Luther's contemporary Reformers, it requires additional explanation. There is still debate about whether Luther was always inclined to be anti-Semitic, and merely disguised this for tactical reasons in *That Jesus Christ Was Born a Jew*, or whether he became more embittered in old age. Gordon Rupp argues for this second position:

> We remember the context of the last five years of Luther's life. They were clouded by many physical ills. In these writings, he refers to his gall-stones and to bleeding ulcers, while the sight of one eye was impaired and he had a disease of the middle ear and, probably, angina... Ancient foes were on the wing. The Counter Reformation was under way, and a great Papal Council had been summoned at last. For twenty-five years the Emperor had been unable to drive home that Edict of Worms which had declared Luther an outlaw. In his last days, Luther was aware that armies were gathering... So like an old lion, he roared, he bared his teeth and turned at bay against them all (*Martin Luther and the Jews*, p.16).

In addition, as Rupp points out, Luther's wife appears to have been even more anti-Semitic than he was and may have influenced his later views. On a journey in 1546, he wrote to her: 'My poor old darling, I was taken faint before Eiselben. My fault, but if you had been here you would have blamed it on the Jews... when we have settled our main business I must do something about those Jews – Count Albert is for it, but nobody does anything, and I shall have to give him a word of support from the pulpit' (*Weimarer Ausgabe*, Br. II, 286.1).

6. *SOCIAL SIGNIFICANCE*

Even though *On the Jews and Their Lies* did not itself circulate widely, its social significance must be assessed together with other expressions of medieval and post-medieval anti-Semitism by Christians. Whereas it may not be possible to establish a direct causal relationship between them and 20th-century Nazi atrocities (particularly since Nazi ideology was, in part, explicitly anti-Christian), the persistence of European anti-Semitism is now widely seen as connected with certain Christian attitudes and convictions. Within recent years, a number of sociologists have tried to assess whether or not there is a causal relationship between present-day Christian attitudes and anti-Semitism. One of the most celebrated studies, by Charles Glock and Rodney Stark, concludes:

> We have searched for a religious basis for anti-Semitism. It was suggested that commitment to traditional Christian ideology predisposed persons to adopt a particularistic conception of religious legitimacy, narrowly to consider their own religious status as the only acceptable faith. These features of Christianity were then linked with historical images of the Jews as apostates from true faith and as the crucifiers of Jesus. Subsequently it was shown that orthodoxy, particularism, and a negative image of the historic Jew, combined with a rejection of values of religious libertarianism, overwhelmingly predicted a hostile religious image of the contemporary Jew (*Christian Beliefs and Anti-Semitism*, p.130).

FURTHER READING

E. Gordon Rupp's Robert Waley Cohen Memorial Lecture to the Council of Christians and Jews, *Martin Luther and the Jews*, contains a full discussion of all of the main Luther Texts on the Jews. There is also an important introduction to *On The Jews and Their Lies* in *Luther's Works*, vol 47. An excellent, critical review of the considerable amount of sociological research that has been conducted (mainly in America) on a possible causal relationship between Christianity and anti-Semitism/racial prejudice, is by R.L. Gorsuch and A. Aleshire 'Christian Faith and Prejudice: Review of Research', *Journal for the Scientific Study of Religion* (Sept. 1974, 13.3). The article is less confident than Glock and Stark about being able to establish a causal relationship. Important theological and historical discussions of Christianity and anti-Semitism can be found in Gregory Baum's *The Jews and the Gospel* and *Religion and Alienation*, Rosemary Ruether's *Faith and Fratricide* and Charlotte Klein's *Anti-Judaism in Christian Theology*.

TEXT XV
LUTHER
On the Jews and their lies

XV.1
I had made up my mind to write no more either about the Jews or against them. But since I learned that these miserable and accursed people do not cease to lure to themselves even us, that is, the Christians, I have published this little book, so that I might be found among those who opposed such poisonous activities of the Jews and who warned the Christians to be on their guard against them. I would not have believed that a Christian could be duped by the Jews into taking their exile and wretchedness upon himself. However, the devil is the god of the world, and wherever God's word is absent he has an easy task, not only with the weak but also with the strong. May God help us. Amen.

XV.2
Grace and peace in the Lord. Dear sir a good friend, I have received a treatise in which a Jew engages in dialogue with a Christian. He dares to pervert the scriptural passages which we cite in testimony to our faith, concerning our Lord Christ and Mary his mother, and to interpret them quite differently. With this argument he thinks he can destroy the basis of our faith.

XV.3
This is my reply to you and to him. It is not my purpose to quarrel with the Jews, nor to learn from them how they interpret

or understand Scripture; I know all of that very well already. Much less do I propose to convert the Jews, for that is impossible. Those two excellent men, Lyra and Burgensis, together with others, truthfully described the Jews' vile interpretation for us two hundred and one hundred years ago respectively. Indeed they refuted it thoroughly. However, this was no help at all to the Jews, and they have grown steadily worse.

XV.4
They have failed to learn any lesson from the terrible distress that has been theirs for over fourteen hundred years in exile. Nor can they obtain any end or definite terminus of this, as they suppose, by means of the vehement cries and laments to God. If these blows do not help, it is reasonable to assume that our talking and explaining will help even less.

XV.5
Therefore a Christian should be content and not argue with the Jews. But if you have to or want to talk with them, do not say any more than this: 'Listen, Jew, are you aware that Jerusalem and your sovereignty, together with your temple and priesthood, have been destroyed for over 1,460 years?' For this year, which we Christians write as the year 1542 since the birth of Christ, is exactly 1,468 years, going on fifteen hundred years, since Vespasian and Titus destroyed Jerusalem and expelled the Jews from the city. Let the Jews bite on this nut and dispute this question as long as they wish.

XV.6
For such ruthless wrath of God is sufficient evidence that they assuredly have erred and gone astray. Even a child can comprehend this. For one dare not regard God as so cruel that he would punish his own people so long, so terribly, so unmercifully, and in addition keep silent, comforting them neither with words nor with deeds, and fixing no time limit and no end to it. Who would have faith, hope, or love toward such a God? Therefore this work of wrath is proof that the Jews, surely

rejected by God, are no longer his people, and neither is he any longer their God. This is in accord with Hosea 1 [.9], 'Call his name Not my people, for you are not my people and I am not your God.' Yes, unfortunately, this is their lot, truly a terrible one. They may interpret this as they will; we see the facts before our eyes, and these do not deceive us.

XV.7

If there were but a spark of reason or understanding in them, they would surely say to themselves: 'O Lord God, something has gone wrong with us. Our misery is too great, too long, too severe; God has forgotten us!' etc. To be sure, I am not a Jew, but I really do not like to contemplate God's awful wrath toward this people. It sends a shudder of fear through body and soul, for I ask, What will the eternal wrath of God in hell be like toward false Christians and all unbelievers? Well, let the Jews regard our Lord Jesus as they will. We behold the fulfilment of the words spoken by him in Luke 21 [.20, 22f]: 'But when you see Jerusalem surrounded by armies, then know that its desolation has come near... for these are days of vengeance. For great distress shall be upon the earth and wrath upon this people.'

XV.8

In short, as has already been said, do not engage much in debate with Jews about the articles of our faith. From their youth they have been so nurtured with venom and rancor against our Lord that there is no hope until they reach the point where their misery finally makes them pliable and they are forced to confess that the Messiah has come, and that he is our Jesus. Until such a time it is much too early, yes, it is useless to argue with them about how God is triune, how he became man, and how Mary is the mother of God. No human reason nor any human heart will ever grant these things. much less the embittered, venomous, blind heart of the Jews. As has already been said, what God cannot reform with such cruel blows, we will be unable to change with words and works. Moses was unable to reform the Pharaoh by means of plagues, miracles, pleas, or threats; he had to let him drown in the sea.

XV.9

Now, in order to strengthen our faith, we want to deal with a few crass follies of the Jews in their belief and their exegesis of the Scriptures, since they so maliciously revile our faith. If this should move any Jew to reform and repent, so much the better. We are now not talking with the Jews but about the Jews and their dealings, so that our Germans, too, might be informed.

XV.10

There is one thing about which they boast and pride themselves beyond measure, and that is their descent from the foremost people on earth, from Abraham, Sarah, Isaac, Rebekah, Jacob, and from the twelve patriarchs, and thus from the holy people of Israel. St Paul himself admits this when he says in Romans 9 [.5]: *Quorum patres*, that is, 'To them belong the patriarchs, and of their race is the Christ,' etc. And Christ himself declares in John 4 [.22], 'Salvation is from the Jews.' Therefore they boast of being the noblest, yes, the only noble people on earth. In comparison with them and in their eyes we Gentiles (*Goyim*) are not human; in fact we hardly deserve to be considered poor worms by them. For we are not of that high and noble blood, lineage, birth, and descent. This is their argument, and indeed I think it is the greatest and strongest reason for their pride and boasting.

XV.11

Therefore, God has to endure that in their synagogues, their prayers, songs, doctrines, and their whole life, they come and stand before him and plague him grievously (if I may speak of God in such a human fashion). Thus he must listen to their boasts and their praises to him for setting them apart from the Gentiles, for letting them be descended from the holy patriarchs, and for selecting them to be his holy and peculiar people, etc. And there is no limit and no end to this boasting about their descent and their physical birth from the fathers.

XV.12

And to fill the measure of their raving, mad, and stupid folly, they boast and they thank God, in the first place, because they were created as human beings and not as animals; in the second place, because they are Israelites and not *Goyim* (Gentiles); in the third place because they were created as males and not as females. They did not learn such tomfoolery from Israel, but from the *Goyim*. For history records that the Greek Plato daily accorded God such praise and thanksgiving – if such arrogance and blasphemy may be termed praise of God. This man, too, praised his gods for these three items: that he was a human being and not an animal; a male and not a female; a Greek and not a non-Greek or barbarian. This is a fool's boast, the gratitude of a barbarian who blasphemes God! Similarly, the Italians fancy themselves the only human beings; they imagine that all other people in the world are non-humans, mere ducks or mice by comparison.

XV.13

No one can take away from them their pride concerning their blood and their descent from Israel. In the Old Testament they lost many a battle in wars over this matter, though no Jew understands this. All the prophets censured them for it, for it betrays an arrogant, carnal presumption devoid of spirit and of faith. They were also slain and persecuted for this reason. St John the Baptist took them to task severely because of it, saying, 'Do not presume to say to yourselves, "We have Abraham for our father;" for I tell you, God is able from these stones to raise up children to Abraham' (Matt. 3.9). He did not call them Abraham's children, but a 'brood of vipers' (Matt. 3.7). Oh, that was too insulting for the noble blood and race of Israel, and they declared, 'He has a demon' (Matt. 11.18). Our Lord also calls them a 'brood of vipers;' furthermore, in John 8 [.39, 44] he states: 'If you were Abraham's children, you would do what Abraham did... You are of your father the devil.' It was intolerable to them to hear that they were not Abraham's but the devil's children, nor can they bear to hear this today. If they should surrender this boast and argument, their whole system which is built on it would topple and change.

XV.14

I hold that if their Messiah, for whom they hope, should come and do away with their boast and its basis they would crucify and blaspheme him seven times worse than they did our Messiah; and they would also say that he was not the true Messiah, but a deceiving devil. For they have portrayed their Messiah to themselves as one who would strengthen and increase such carnal and arrogant error regarding nobility of blood and lineage. That is the same as saying that he should assist them in blaspheming God and in viewing his creatures with disdain, including the women, who are also human beings and the image of God as well as we; moreover, they are our own flesh and blood, such as mother, sister, daughter, housewives, etc. For in accordance with the afore-mentioned threefold song of praise, they do not hold Sarah (as a woman) to be as noble as Abraham (as a man). Perhaps they wish to honor themselves for being born half noble, of a noble father, and half ignoble, of an ignoble mother. But enough of this tomfoolery and trickery.

XV.15

We propose to discuss their argument and boast and prove convincingly before God and the world – not before the Jews, for, as already said, they would accept this neither from Moses nor from their Messiah himself – that their argument is quite empty and stands condemned.

CRITIQUE

The debate about whether or not there is a causal connection between certain Christian attitudes and beliefs and the phenomenon of anti-Semitism is yet to be resolved. However, in Luther's later writings there is a clear connection between his religious convictions, his mode of biblical exegesis and his appalling attitudes towards Jews. His convictions and prejudices appear mutually reinforcing. His growing intolerance of all but evangelical Christians, his increasing conviction that Jews are unconvertible, and therefore unredeemable, his penchant for quoting 'anti-Semitic'(!) biblical passages, and his adoption of popular stereotypes about Jews, need not be related to each other in any single causal sequence. They provide legitimation for each other.

It is for this reason that a number of theologians today believe that it is essential for Christians to find less exclusive ways of expressing their faith than was often the case in the past (I have argued this further in *Prophecy and Praxis*). In all three classical authors, but especially here in Luther, religious intolerance inclined them, on occasions, to civil totalitarianism. Rupp's conclusion is judicious:

> But, as we follow Luther through the years, we find a signal instance of how we become like what we hate. We see a growing obstinacy, a hardening of heart, a withering of compassion, a proneness to contemptuous abuse – the very things he thought were the marks of judgment on the Jews... What if not pure doctrine, but suffering be a hall-mark of the People of God? And if, as Luther thought, Jew and Gentile may be bound together in a solidarity of guilt, have we perhaps begun to understand what is the greater solidarity of promise? May not Jew and Christian together explore this more excellent way, in penitence and compassion (*Martin Luther and the Jews*, p.22).

EXTRACTS 22-26
FLETCHER, WARE, PAUL VI, WCC, AND RUETHER

1. *BACKGROUND*

Joseph Fletcher's Extract 22 comes from his *Morals and Medicine* (Gollancz, London, 1955, pp.190-7 & 207-10). Bishop Kallistos Ware's Extract 23 comes from 'The Sacrament of Love: The Orthodox Understanding of Marriage and its Breakdown', *The Downside Review* (vol 109, No.375, 1991, pp.79-89). Pope Paul VI's Extract 24 comes from his Encyclical Letter *Humanae Vitae* (Catholic Truth Society, London, revised edition, 1970, pp.6-8 & 10-19). The World Council of Churches' Extract 25 comes from 'Racism in Theology – Theology Against Racism', *Faith and Order Commission* (Geneva, 1975, Part IV). And Rosemary Radford Ruether's Extract 26 comes from Naim S. Ateek, Marc H. Ellis and Rosemary Radford Ruether (ed), *Faith and the Intifada: Palestinian Christian Voices* (Orbis, 1992, pp.147-57).

Fletcher (see *above*, pp.99f.) wrote *Morals and Medicine* in 1954 on basis of the Lowell lectures he gave at Harvard University in 1949. The book reflects his long-term interest in medical ethics and his controversial support for the legalisation of voluntary euthanasia. In the Preface, he admits that the book is 'at the most only a modest contribution to the ethics of medicine, not to its theology', but nonetheless hopes that 'the ethical judgments I have reached are within the range and provision of Christian theology' (p.xi). Adopting an explicitly personalist position in the book (it was written before he developed the notion of 'situation ethics'), he maintains that it is based upon his personal experiences, 'gained through a quarter of a century in the ministry, fifteen of them concentrated in the teaching and clinical supervision of theological students exploring human needs in parishes, hospitals, social agencies, and homes' (p.xiii). Bishop Kallistos Ware lectures in the Divinity Faculty at Oxford University and is author of the seminal *The Orthodox Way*. By 1968, it was widely expected in the West that Paul VI would seek to liberalise the official Roman Catholic positions on contraception and, possibly, even on abortion. Vatican II had contributed to these expectations, as had a general concern about the overpopulation for the world. However, after agonising over the issues for several months, Paul finally published his Encyclical *Humanae Vitae*, re-enforcing the traditionalist positions of Pius XII.

Produced as a document of the Faith and Order Commission of the World Council of Churches, Extract 25 should be set in the context of an increasing concern within the WCC about racism during the 1960s and 1970s. This is well documented in Kenneth Sansbury's *Combating Racism: The British Churches and the WCC Programme to Combat Racism* (1975). The WCC Uppsala Assembly of 1968 declared that 'Contemporary racism robs all human rights of their meaning, and is an imminent danger to world peace'. The Central Committee meeting at Canterbury in 1969 set out the four aims of the Programme to Combat Racism: '(a) to mobilize the churches in the world-wide struggle against racism; (b) to express in word and deed solidarity with the racially oppressed; (c) to aid the churches in educating their members for racial justice; (d) to facilitate the transfer of resources, human and material, for projects and programmes in the field of racial justice.' These four aims are clearly reflected in Extract 25.

Rosemary Radford Ruether comes from a Roman Catholic background and is now recognised as one of the leading feminist theologians. She is Georgia Harkness Professor of Theology at Garret-Evangelical Theological Seminary in Evanston, Illinois, and her many books include *Liberation Theology* (Paulist Press, 1972) and *Faith and Fratricide: The Theological Roots of Anti-Semitism* (Seabury, 1974). She regards feminism as a means to overcome a number of 20th-century forms of 'alienation': 'In Nazism the reactionary drive against the libertarian tradition culminated in a virulent revival of racism, misogynism, elitism, and military and national chauvinism. Its victims were Jews, Communists, Social Democrats and libertarians of all kinds – and finally, the nascent women's movement' (*Liberation Theology*, pp.117-18). Whilst Christianity was not actually the originator of these forms of alienation, it 'took over this alienated world view of late classical civilisation' (p.122). But now, 'women must be the spokesmen for a new humanity arising out of the reconciliation of spirit and body' (p.124). Extract 26 comes from a collection of papers from Palestinians, Christians and Reformed Jews on the Israel/Palestine issue.

2. KEY ISSUES

Fletcher defends voluntary medical euthanasia for patients enduring incurable and fatal physical suffering. He argues that it should not be confused with eugenics, but rather be seen as choosing a peaceful death (22.11-12). He realises that euthanasia might be seen as a form of suicide (and, therefore, following Text XIII, as wrong), but he maintains that people do have a right to die and that suicide, as such, is not necessarily egoistic (22.1). Indeed, it would be wrong to prolong mere life at the expense of an individual's personality (22.2). For him, euthanasia is not 'murder', since it involves no malice on the part of the doctor (22.3), nor need it infringe the Decalogue, since it is unlawful killing which is prohibited there (22.7-8). Further, some objections to euthanasia – e.g. the notion that God alone should decide when someone should die, or the belief that suffering should be accepted as part of the divine plan (22.4 & 9) – can be seen to be objections to any form of medical intervention.

Ware sets out to depict the distinctive Eastern Orthodox understanding of marriage and divorce. Orthodox marriage is seen as a relational icon of the Trinity and as a sacrament, yet paradoxically it can also be dissolved (23.1-2). Viewed as a sacrament, Orthodox marriages were originally set in the context of the Eucharist, but today this link is often overlooked (23.3-7). Orthodox marriage stresses mutual love more than child-bearing and does so in non-contractual terms (23.8-12). Orthodox weddings contain no formal mutual vows: it is the priest, not the couple, who administers this sacrament (23.13-14). The distinctive crowning ceremony of Orthodox weddings emphasises that marriage is a 'mystery', that it is a joyful transfiguration, and that it may involve sacrifice (23.15-18). For the Orthodox marriage is eternal, yet paradoxically it can be dissolved (23.19-23). Ware argues that this is possible because it is the Church that is entrusted both with administering the sacrament of marriage and with permitting remarriage in certain specified circumstances (23.24-7). For the Orthodox a church divorce, and not simply a civil divorce, is required (23.28). There is also a different liturgy for second and subsequent marriages which includes penitential prayers (23.29-30).

Paul VI prescribes a continuity between the physical and the spiritual in sexuality. Whilst stressing that sexual activity is 'honourable and good' (24.24), he argues that, if it involves the 'direct interruption of the generative process', it thereby becomes sinful (24.28). All sexual intercourse must allow both its unitive and procreative functions to operate. It is on this principle that both induced abortion and certain forms of contraception are condemned. He is aware of the population explosion and the changed economic structure of the present-day world (24.1-3) and that this has led many to argue for an acceptance of medicinal contraception (24.4-6). He argues that marital love is fully human and should be total, faithful and creative (24.10-17). Within marriage, responsible parenthood requires couples to recognise that they have duties towards God, to themselves, to their families and to human society (24.18-22) and that one of these duties – based upon natural law – involves obedience to the principle of always allowing both of the functions of sexual intercourse to operate (24.23-4). Sexual intercourse which is deliberately contraceptive, direct sterilisation and induced abortion are all intrinsically wrong (24.27-31). Spacing births, for good reasons, by taking advantage of a woman's natural cycles is allowable, since this is indeed natural and does not tempt people to marital infidelity or allow Governments abuse (24.34-8). Paul VI is aware that this position will not be acceptable to all, but still insists that the Church must not betray its responsibility to expediency (24.39-41).

The WCC document argues that churches are in constant danger of forgetting the poor and powerless within the world and even within the churches themselves (25.1-2). Racism is a sin which might or might not be helpfully labelled as 'heresy' but which does need to be discovered and then overcome (25.3-5). To achieve this there is a need for church discipline expressing the unity of the Church (25.6-7). In those churches where formal discipline still exists, it tends to be too individualistic – rather than focussing upon the common effects of repentance-action – and too associated with excommunication (25.8-11). What is needed instead is authenticity and solidarity at the centre of the Church (25.12-13). For this to be achieved, disciplined worship around the unity of Baptism and Eucharist is important, as well as rigorous prophetic preaching and pastoral care directed against racism (25.15-17). Education is also crucial – especially theological and school education which can too easily be ethnocentric (25.18-21). Renewal means that we must seek to become more inclusive and mutually accountable (25.22-5).

Ruether, too, is concerned with the issue of racism, albeit in a more focussed form than Extract 25. She notes that Middle Eastern Christians are puzzled that Reformed Western Christianity has tended to support the territorial claims of Jewish restoration to Palestine (26.1-7) – although ironically restoration has often been resisted by Reformed Jews (26.8-9). Ruether seeks to trace the origins of a literalistic Jewish belief that God promised them Palestine alongside a Christian millennialist support (26.10-13). She argues strongly against a use of the Holocaust to identify anti-Zionism with anti-Semitism (26.14-16). For her Palestine has always been a land of many peoples – Jews, Christian and Muslims have all become Arabised there and the Palestinians are their obvious descendants (26.18-19). For both Jews and Christians 'redemption' should entail a healing of the enmity between nations – something which the founding of Israel has not effected (26.20-2). Traditional religious faiths often seek to effect a total system informing public and private life – but this is problematic in plural modern states (26.23-6). She maintains that the proper Christian response to the Holocaust is to purge anti-Semitism from Christian teaching and from society generally – not to silence criticism of injustice to Palestinians (26.27-33). Both Jews and Christians should recognise, in the context of the Arab people, that power in the form of domination creates violence (26.36-8).

3. ETHICAL ARGUMENTS

It is noticeable here that those writing from a Roman Catholic or Orthodox background tend to argue deontologically, whereas Fletcher is primarily a personalist. Paul VI (24.7 & 24) makes explicit use of natural law and insists that precepts derived from this law are to be obeyed (24.24). Ware argues deontologically that the apparent conflict between viewing marriage as a sacrament and as eternal, yet allowing divorce and remarriage, is resolved by stressing that 'the Christ has entrusted to the Church full power to regulate the administration of the sacraments' (23.24). Even Ruether argues her position deontologically (especially 26.17). Fletcher, in contrast, adopts a consciously personalist position (22.2 & 10) and is critical of positions which refuse 'to allow for anything but the consequences of a human act' as ethical criteria (22.3). This personalism does not contain all the features of his later situation ethics (e.g. in 22.3 he seems prepared to accept the precept that 'murder is wrong' and writes more about 'mercy' than '*agape*') but it is clearly related to situationism.

Yet elements of other ethical approaches are also evident in the Extracts. Paul VI appears at first to reject consequentialism (24.31), but then uses consequential arguments to justify 'natural' methods of contraception (24.36-7). Ware, having stressed that the Orthodox position on remarriage 'is done by the Church, not arbitrarily, nor as a weak and easy concession to the mores of contemporary secular society', none the less adds in personalist terms that it is 'in the name of Christ's own continuing compassion and loving kindness towards humanity' (23.24). Ruether also adds consequential arguments to her deontological position (e.g. 26.18-19). And, at times, Fletcher appears to assume a deontological concept of 'rights' (22.1).

4. BASES OF CHRISTIAN ETHICS
The Bible has a fairly central place in several of the Extracts here, but in none is it treated as the only source of authority. Fletcher tends to use the Bible to corroborate positions that he has already reached (22.13 – cf. 2.9) or to form objections to his own position (22.7-8). Other theologians are used by him in a similar way (22.4-5). It seems likely that it is the notion of 'mercy' which is most instrumental to his position on euthanasia (22.4 & 14). For both Ware and Paul VI, it is tradition and, particularly, consistency with previous church

or papal teaching, that appears to be the most important influence upon their positions (e.g. 23.4-7, 11-13, 16-17, 22 & 24.7, 17, 27, 39). The use of the Bible of Paul VI in particular tends to be illustrative (24.10 & 39). Both the WCC document and Ruether base their arguments more upon general theological positions than upon specific Biblical references. So the WCC document argues on the basis of the unity of Baptism and Eucharist (25.15), Ruether for therapeutic understanding of 'redemption' (26.20), and both maintain an inclusive doctrine of God (25.22-5 & 26.17).

5. *SOCIAL DETERMINANTS*

Secular influences are evident in all of these Extracts. This is even true of those Extracts by Paul VI and Ware which are consciously written to counter what they regard as prevailing secular assumptions. So even whilst Ware consciously disassociates the Orthodox position on divorce and remarriage from 'the mores of contemporary secular society' (23.24), he shows that he is well aware of the Western and Eastern context of increasing marriage breakdown. It is this context which makes a rigorist position on marriage difficult for any church to maintain consistently. Similarly, Paul VI's position would have been more consistent had he rejected all methods of contraception. But, in response to the social changes that he himself indicates (24.1-3), the concession had already been made, that 'natural' methods of contraception are allowable. In the debate that followed, it soon became apparent that, the distinction between 'natural' methods (themselves often requiring thermometers, ovulation charts etc.) and 'artificial' methods, is difficult to sustain or justify.

The social factors influencing the other Extracts are recognised by each of them. Fletcher believes that his pastoral experience in hospitals and his continued medical contacts whilst teaching, contributed directly to his concern about euthanasia. The WCC document was written as a part of the WCC commitment to combat racism which had featured so strongly over the previous decade. And Ruether has manifestly been an active observer and participant in Palestinian and Jewish issues.

6. *SOCIAL SIGNIFICANCE*

Paul VI's *Humanae Vitae* has had the most widespread influence upon society at large. Fletcher's *Morals and Medicine* was first published in the previous decade and before the emergence of 'secular theology'. Nonetheless, Fletcher's continued support of voluntary euthanasia has often been cited by its American defenders: at a time when most churches were opposed to it, his social significance may have resided in the legitimation he could provide for the movement. Extracts 25 and 26 have both proved deeply controversial. As a part of the wider concern of the Programme to Combat Racism, the WCC has been consistently prophetic in this area – sometimes antagonising Western churches in the process. It provides an interest contrast to Ramsey's Extract 13. And Ruether's Extract 26 has shocked a number of Orthodox Jews and Christians alike – especially since she made her initial reputation exposing anti-Semitism within Christianity.

Yet, it was Paul VI's encyclical which directly affected the lives of ordinary Roman Catholics and it effectively ensured continued official opposition by the Roman Catholic Church both to induced abortion and to medicinal contraception. Even though there appears to be a difference in the West between the actual practice of Roman Catholic laity (who do resort to induced abortion and medicinal contraception in commensurate numbers to non-Roman Catholics) and the official position of the Church, the latter continues. It seems likely that the effect of this continuing difference amongst articulate Roman Catholics, has been to lead them to be more critical of authority within the Church. If this suggestion is correct, it provides an interesting illustration of the way in which theology may sometimes be socially significant in ways unintended by theologians themselves.

FURTHER READING

The expanded version of Paul Ramsey's *Deeds and Rules in Christian Ethics* (1967) provides an important critique of Fletcher's personalism. Fletcher's own *Moral Responsibility* continues the debate about euthanasia. The Reformed ethicist James Gustafson's *Protestant and Roman Catholic Ethics* sets *Humanae Vitae* into its theological and social context in recent debate, and John Mahoney's *The Making of Moral Theology* does the same from a Catholic position. A number of Reformed and Roman Catholic contributors to John T. Noonan Jr's (ed) *The Morality of Abortion* – including Noonan himself, Paul Ramsey and Bernard Häring – make important contributions to the ethical debate. Further, Noonan's study *Contraception* provides a useful history of Roman Catholic and Canonist attitudes to contraception. Long's studies (see bibliography) provide overall commentaries. For another Orthodox perspective see S.S. Harakas, *Contemporary Moral Issues Facing the Orthodox Christian* and *Toward Transfigured Life: The 'Theoria' of Orthodox Christian Ethics*.

EXTRACT 22

FLETCHER

Euthanasia

22.1

(a.) It is objected that euthanasia, when voluntary, is really suicide. If this is true, and it would seem to be obviously true, then the proper question is: have we ever a right to commit suicide? Among Catholic moralists the most common ruling is that 'it is never permitted to kill oneself intentionally, without explicit divine inspiration to do'. Humility requires us to assume that divine inspiration cannot reasonably be expected to occur either often or explicitly enough to meet the requirements of medical euthanasia. A plea for legal recognition of 'man's inalienable right to die' is placed at the head of the physicians' petition to the New York State Assembly. Now, has man any such right, however limited and imperfect it may be? Surely he has, for otherwise the hero or martyr and all those who deliberately give their lives are morally at fault. It might be replied that there is a difference between the suicide, who is directly seeking to end his life, and the hero or martyr, who is seeking directly some other end entirely, death being only an undesired by-product. But to make this point is only to raise a question as to what purposes are sufficient to justify the loss of one's life. If altruistic values, such as defence of the innocent, are enough to justify the loss of one's life (and we will all agree that they are), then it may be argued that personal integrity is a value worth the loss of life, especially since, by definition, there is no hope of relief from the demoralising pain and no further possibility of serving others. To call euthanasia egoistic or self-regarding makes no sense, since in the nature of the case the patient is not choosing his own good rather than the good of others.

22.2

Furthermore, it is important to recognise that there is no ground, in a rational or Christian outlook, for regarding life itself as the *summum bonum* [highest good]. As a ministers' petition to buttress the New York bill puts is, 'We believe in the sacredness of *personality*, but not in the worth of mere existence or "length of days"... We believe that such a sufferer has the right to die, and that society should grant this right, showing the same mercy to human beings as to the sub-human animal kingdom.' (The point might be made validly in criticism of this statement that society can only recognise an 'inalienable right', it cannot confer it. Persons are not mere creatures of the community, even though it is ultimately meaningless to claim integrity for them unless their lives are integrated into the community.) In the personalistic view of man and morals, asserted throughout these pages, personality is supreme over mere life. To prolong life uselessly, while the personal qualities of freedom, knowledge, self-possession and control, and responsibility are sacrificed is to attack the moral status of a person. It actually denies morality in order to submit to fatality. And in addition, to insist upon mere 'life' invades religious interests as well as moral values. For to use analgesic agents to the point of depriving sufferers of consciousness is, by all apparent logic, inconsistent even with the practices of sacramentalist Christians. The point of death for a human person *in extremis* is surely by their own account a time when the use of reason and conscious self-commitment is most meritorious; it is the time when a responsible competence in receiving such rites as the viaticum and extreme unction would be most necessary and its consequences most invested with finality.

22.3

(b.) It is objected that euthanasia, when involuntary, is murder. This is really an objection directed against the physician's role in medical euthanasia, assuming it is administered by him rather than by the patient on his own behalf. We might add to what has been said above about the word 'murder' in law and legal definition by explaining that people with a moral rather than a legal interest – doctors, pastors, patients, and their friends – will never concede that malice means only premeditation, entirely divorced from the motive and the end sought. These factors are entirely different in euthanasia from the motive and the end in murder, even though the means – taking life – happens to be the same. If we can make no moral distinction between acts involving the same means, then the thrifty parent who saves in order to educate his children is no higher in the scale of merit than the miser who saves for the sake of hoarding. But, as far as medical care is concerned, there is an even more striking example of the contradictions which arise from refusing to allow for anything but the consequences of a human act. There is a dilemma in medication for terminal diseases which is just as real as the dilemma posed by the doctor's oath to relieve pain while he also promises to prolong life. As medical experts frequently point out, morphine, which is commonly used to ease pain, also shortens life, i.e. it induces death. Here we see that the two promises of the Hippocratic Oath actually conflict at the level of means as well as at the level of motive and intention.

22.4
(c.) What of the common religious opinion that God reserves for himself the right to decide at what moment a life shall cease? Koch-Preuss says euthanasia is the destruction of 'the temple of God and a violation of the property rights of Jesus Christ'. As to this doctrine, it seems more than enough just to answer that if such a divine-monopoly theory is valid, then it follows with equal force that it is immoral to lengthen life. Is medical care, after all, only a form of human self-assertion or a demonic pretension, by which men, especially physicians, try to put themselves in God's place? Prolonging life, on this divine-monopoly view, when a life appears to be ending through natural or physical causes, is just as much an interference with natural determinism as mercifully ending a life before physiology does it in its own amoral way.

22.5
This argument that we must not tamper with life also assumes that physiological life is sacrosanct. But as we have pointed out repeatedly, this doctrine is a form of vitalism or naturalistic determinism. Dean Sperry of the Harvard Divinity School, who is usually a little more sensitive to the scent of anti-humane attitudes, wrote recently in the *New England Journal of Medicine* that Albert Schweitzer's doctrine of 'reverence for life', which is often thought to entail an absolute prohibition against taking life, has strong claims upon men of conscience. Perhaps so, but men of conscience will surely reject the doctrine if it is left unqualified and absolute. In actual fact, even Schweitzer has suggested that the principle is subject to qualification. He has, with apparent approval, explained that Gandhi 'took it upon himself to go beyond the letter of the law against killing. . . He ended the sufferings of a calf in its prolonged death-agony by giving it poison'. It seems unimaginable that either Schweitzer or Gandhi would deny to a human being what they would render, with however heavy a heart,

to a calf. Gandhi did what he did in spite of the special sanctity of kine in Hindu discipline. In any case Dr Schweitzer in his African hospital at Lambarene is even now at work administering death-inducing-because-pain-relieving drugs. As William Temple once pointed out, 'The notion that life is absolutely sacred is Hindu or Buddhist, not Christian'. He neglected to remark that even those Oriental religionists forget their doctrine when it comes to *suttee* and *hari-kari*. He said further that the argument that it cannot ever be right to kill a fellow human being will not stand up because 'such a plea can only rest upon a belief that life, physiological life, is sacrosanct. This is not a Christian idea at all; for, if it were, the martyrs would be wrong. If the sanctity is in life, it must be wrong to give your life for a noble cause as well as to take another's. But the Christian must be ready to give life gladly for his faith, as for a noble cause. Of course, this implies that, *as compared with some things*, the loss of life is a small evil; and if so, then, *as compared with some other things*, the taking of life is a small injury' (*Thoughts in War Time*, 1940, pp.31-2).

22.6
Parenthetically we should explain, if it is not evident in these quotations themselves, that Dr Temple's purpose was to justify military service. Unfortunately for his aim, he failed to take account of the ethical factor of free choice as a right of the person who thus loses his life at the hands of the warrior. We cannot put upon the same ethical footing the ethical right to take our own lives, in which case our freedom is not invaded, and taking the lives of others in those cases in which the act is done against the victim's will and choice. The true parallel is between self-sacrifice and a merciful death provided at the person's request; there is none between self-sacrifice and violent or coercive killing. But the relevance of what Dr Temple has to say and its importance for euthanasia is perfectly clear. The non-theological statement of the case agrees with Temple: 'Are we not allowing ourselves to be deceived by our self-preservative tendency to rationalise a merely instinctive urge and to attribute spiritual and ethical significance to phenomena appertaining to the realm of crude, biological utility?'

22.7
(d.) It is also objected by religious moralists that euthanasia violates the Biblical command, 'Thou shalt not kill'. It is doubtful whether this kind of Biblicism is any more valid than the vitalism we reject. Indeed, it is a form of fundamentalism, common to both Catholics and reactionary Protestants. An outspoken religious opponent of euthanasia is a former chancellor to Cardinal Spellman as military vicar to the armed forces,

Monsignor Robert McCormick. As presiding judge of the Archdiocesan Ecclesiastical Tribunal of New York, he warned the General Assembly of that state in 1947 not to 'set aside the commandment "Thou shalt not kill"'. In the same vein, the general secretary of the American Council of Christian Churches, an organisation of fundamentalist Protestants, denounced the fifty-four clergymen who supported the euthanasia bill, claiming that their action was 'an evidence that the modernistic clergy, have made further departure from the eternal moral law'.

22.8

Certainly those who justify war and capital punishment, as most Christians do, cannot condemn euthanasia on this ground. We might point out to the fundamentalists in the two major divisions of Western Christianity that the beatitude 'Blessed are the merciful' has the force of a commandment too! The medical profession lives by it, has its whole ethos in it. But the simplest way to deal with this Christian text-proof objection might be to point out that the translation 'Thou shalt not kill' is incorrect. It should be rendered, as in the responsive decalogue of the *Book of Common Prayer*, 'Thou shalt do no murder', i.e. unlawful killing. It is sufficient just to remember that the ancient Jews fully allowed warfare and capital punishment. Lawful killing was also for hunger-satisfaction and sacrifice. Hence, a variety of Hebrew terms such as *shachat, harag, tabach*, but *ratsach* in the Decalogue (both Exodus 20.13 and Deut. 5.17), clearly means *unlawful* killing, treacherously, for private vendetta or gain. Thus it is laid down in Leviticus 24.17 that 'he who kills a man shall be put to death', showing that the lawful forms of killing may even be used to punish the unlawful! In the New Testament references to the prohibition against killing (e.g., Matt. 5.21, Luke 18.20, Rom. 13.9) are an endorsement of the commandments in the Jewish law. Each time, the verb *phoneuo* is used and the connotation is *unlawful* killing, as in the Decalogue. Other verbs connote simply the fact of killing, as *apokteino* (Luke 12.4, 'Be not afraid of them that kill the body') and *thuo* which is used interchangeably for slaughter of animals for food and for sacrifice. We might also remind the Bible-bound moralists that there was no condemnation either of Abimelech, who chose to die, or of his faithful sword-bearer who carried out his wish for him.

22.9

(e.) Another common objection in religious quarters is that suffering is a part of the divine plan for the good of man's soul, and must therefore be accepted. Does this mean that the physicians' Hippocratic Oath is opposed to Christian virtue and doctrine? If this simple inference were a valid one, then we should not be able to give our moral approval to anaesthetics or to provide any medical relief of human suffering. Such has been the objection of many religionists at every stage of medical conquest, as we pointed out in the first chapter in the case of anaesthetics at childbirth. Here is still another anomaly in our mores of life and death, that we are, after much struggle, now fairly secure in the righteousness of easing suffering at birth but we still feel it is wrong to ease suffering at death! Life may be begun without suffering, but it may not be ended without it, if it happens that nature combines death and suffering...

22.10

There are three schools of thought favouring euthanasia. First, there are those who favour voluntary euthanasia, a personalistic ethical position. Second, there are those who favour involuntary euthanasia for monstrosities at birth and mental defectives, a partly personalistic and partly eugenic position. Third, there are those who favour involuntary euthanasia for all who are a burden upon the community, a purely eugenic position. It should be perfectly obvious that we do not have to endorse the third school of thought just because we favour either the first or the second, or both. Our discussion has covered only the first one – voluntary medical euthanasia – as a means of ending a human life enmeshed in incurable and fatal physical suffering. The principles of right based upon selfhood and moral being favour it.

22.11

Defence of voluntary medical euthanasia, it should be made plain, does not depend upon the superficial system of values in which physical evil (pain) is regarded as worse than moral evil (sin) or intellectual evil (error). On the contrary, unless we are careful to see that pain is the least of evils, then our values would tie us back into that old attitude of taking the material or physical aspects of reality so seriously that we put nature or things as they are *out there* in a determinant place, subordinating the ethical and spiritual values of freedom and knowledge and upholding, in effect, a kind of naturalism. C.S. Lewis has described it by saying that, 'Of all evils, pain only is sterilised or disinfected evil.' Pain cannot create moral evil, such as a disintegration or demoralisation of personality would be, unless it is submitted to in brute fashion as opponents of euthanasia insist we should do.

22.12

We repeat, the issue is not one of life or death. The issue is which kind of death, an agonised or peaceful one. Shall we meet death in personal integrity or in personal disintegration? Should there be a moral or a demoralised end to mortal life? Surely, as we have seen in earlier chapters, we are not as persons of moral stature to be ruled by ruthless and unreasoning physiology, but rather by reason and self-control. Those who face the issues of euthanasia with a religious faith will not, if they think twice, submit to the materialistic and animistic doctrine that God's will is revealed by what nature does, and that life, *qua* life, is absolutely sacred and untouchable. All of us can agree with Reinhold Niebuhr that 'the ending of our life would not threaten us if we had not falsely made ourselves the centre of life's meaning'. One of the pathetic immaturities we all recognise around us is stated bluntly by Sigmund Freud in his *Reflections on War and Death*: 'In the subconscious every one of us is convinced of his immortality.' Our frantic hold upon life can only cease to be a snare and delusion when we objectify it in some religious doctrine of salvation, or, alternatively, agree with Sidney Hook that 'the romantic pessimism which mourns man's finitude is a vain lament that we are not gods'. At least, the principles of personal morality warn us not to make physical phenomena, unmitigated by human freedom, the centre of life's meaning. There is an impressive wisdom in the words of Dr Logan Clendenning: 'Death itself is not unpleasant. I have seen a good many people die. To a few death comes as a friend, as a relief from pain, from intolerable loneliness or loss, or from disappointment. To even fewer it comes as a horror. To most it hardly comes at all, so gradual is its approach, so long have the senses been benumbed, so little do they realise what is taking place. As I think it over, death seems to me one of the few evidences in nature of the operation of a creative intelligence exhibiting qualities which I recognise as mind stuff. To have blundered onto the form of energy called life showed a sort of malignant power. After having blundered on life, to have conceived of death was a real stroke of genius' (*The Human Body*, 1941, pp.442-3).

22.13
As Ecclesiastes the Preacher kept saying in first one way and then another, 'The living know that they shall die' and there is 'a time to be born and a time to die, a time to plant and a time to pluck up that which is planted'. (Eccl. 9.5 & 3.2). And in the New Covenant we read that 'all flesh is as grass' and 'the grass withereth, and the flower thereof falleth away'. Nevertheless, 'who is he that will harm you, if ye be followers of that which is good?' (1 Pet. 1.24 & 3.13).

22.14
Medicine contributes too much to the moral stature of men to persist indefinitely in denying the ultimate claims of its own supreme virtue and ethical inspiration, mercy.

EXTRACT 23
WARE
Marriage and divorce – an Orthodox perspective

23.1

Marriage, the 'sacrament of love', is a direct expression of our human personhood according to the image and likeness of the Holy Trinity. Formed as an icon of the Trinitarian God, the human person is made for mutual love; and that means, first and foremost, the love between man and woman. As the creation story in the first chapter of Genesis affirms, 'God created man in the image of himself, in the image of God he created him, male and female he created them' (Gen. 1.27). The differentiation of human beings into male and female, according to the 'Priestly' source in Genesis, is nothing less than a reflection of the divine image. The image of God is given, not to the man alone or to the woman alone, but to the two of them together. It comes to its fulfilment only in the 'between' that unites them to each other. Personhood is a mutual gift; there is no true human unless there are at least two humans in communion with each other. To say 'I am made in God's image' is to affirm: 'I need you in order to be myself'. The divine image is in this way a 'relational' image, manifested not in isolation but in community and, above all, in the primordial bond between husband and wife that is the foundation of all other forms of social life. Monastics and lay people not called to matrimony, if they are to be authentically human, need to realize in some other way the capacity for mutual love which finds its primary expression through the man-woman relationship within marriage.

23.2

In its teaching on marriage, as at many other points, the Orthodox Church adopts a standpoint that has frequently puzzled Western Christians. We affirm two things that at first sight might be thought inconsistent: marriage is a sacrament, and yet under certain circumstances it may be dissolved. We believe firmly in the sacramental character of the marriage union, but according to the Orthodox view sacramentality does not entail indissolubility. The Church has power to permit a divorce, followed by a second marriage; and also a second divorce, followed by a third marriage. A fourth marriage, however, is entirely forbidden in Orthodox Canon Law, whether after divorce or after the death of the previous spouses.

23.3

Let us look, then, at the Orthodox theology of the sacrament of marriage, and in the light of this let us assess the pastoral attitude of Orthodoxy towards marital breakdown. What is our interpretation of marriage as the sacrament of love, and what is to be done when this sacrament of love turns into an occasion of hatred and mutual destruction?

The sacramentality of marriage

23.4

There is, first of all, no doubt whatever that the Orthodox Church looks on marriage as a sacrament or, to use the Greek term, a 'mystery' (*mysterion*). 'This is a great mystery' (Eph. 5.32), it is said in the epistle reading at the wedding service; and, whatever the original intention of the author of Ephesians, this phrase is at once assumed by a contemporary Orthodox listener to mean 'This is a great sacrament'. Since the seventeenth century Orthodox manuals have invariably included marriage in the list of the seven sacraments. It is true that Orthodoxy attaches no strict doctrinal significance to the number 'seven', and makes no sharp distinction between 'sacraments' and 'sacramentals'; but, if the sacraments are, in fact, to be numbered, marriage is undoubtedly to be reckoned one of the seven.

23.5

In the Greek East, as in the Latin West, it was only gradually that the Church came to regard marriage as a distinct sacrament. From the outset the Church naturally took a direct pastoral interest in the marriages contracted by baptized Christians. 'Men and women who enter into the union of marriage', states St Ignatius of Antioch (c.110 CE), 'should do this with the bishop's consent, so that the marriage may be in accordance with the Lord's will and not because of carnal desire'. But there was initially no rite of Christian marriage separate from the Eucharistic Liturgy. A Christian couple first entered into a civil marriage performed by the magistrate; then they went to receive the Eucharist together in church, and it was this joint reception of Holy Communion that was regarded as blessing and sealing their marital union in Christ. Tertullian, writing around 200, has this situation in mind when he speaks of 'that marriage, in which the Church acts as intermediary, which the oblation confirms, and the blessing seals'. In the Greek East, by the end of the fourth century, the blessing in church had come to include what remains the most striking outward action in the Orthodox marriage rite, the crowning of bridegroom and bride.

23.6

But until the ninth century the crowning was merely accompanied by a short prayer, and it was always done during the Eucharist; moreover, it was the civil ceremony before the magistrate that was considered legally binding in the eyes of Church and State. Marriage did not pass fully under the jurisdiction of the Church until around the year 893, when the Emperor Leo VI the Wise in his *Novella 89* laid down that a religious wedding should henceforward be obligatory.

23.7

In the first nine centuries, then, marriage as a religious rite was incorporated into the Eucharist. This is surely a point of cardinal importance. Only when marriage is viewed in a Eucharistic context can its sacramental nature be truly appreciated. Unfortunately in modern Orthodox practice marriage is almost always celebrated apart from the divine Liturgy, and so this vital Eucharistic link is overlooked. It is precisely because of the connection between marriage and the Eucharist that mixed marriages give rise to such acute pastoral problems. Since the Orthodox authorities scarcely ever feel able to allow exceptions to the general rule that prohibits intercommunion across church boundaries, the couple is permanently prevented from receiving Holy Communion together.

23.8

What is implied theologically by regarding marriage as a 'mystery' or sacrament? In every sacrament, it is God himself, invisibly present, who is the true agent. 'It is Father, Son and Holy Spirit who dispense and order all things', says St John Chrysostom; the priest merely lends his tongue and supplies his hand.' A sacrament, in other words, is a grace-giving action performed by Christ, ever-present and ever-active within the Church through the Holy Spirit. Viewed specifically as a sacramental 'mystery', then, marriage is a divine operation, the work of Christ the one High Priest. Recalling the blessing that Jesus gave by his presence at the marriage in Cana, one of the prayers invokes the same blessing on the marriage now being celebrated: 'As you were present there, be present also here with your invisible protection, and bless this marriage.' As the next prayer affirms, it is Christ who is the *hierourgos* of the marriage, the liturgist or celebrant. The sacrament of marriage is therefore much more than a contract between two humans of which the Church takes cognizance. Primarily it is an action performed by God himself, operating through the person of the officiating priest.

The purpose of marriage

23.9

The Anglican 1662 Book of Common Prayer, in a well-known passage, succinctly indicates three reasons for the institution of marriage: 'for the procreation of children', 'for a remedy against sin and to avoid fornication', and 'for... mutual society, help and comfort' (mentioned in that order). Luther gives the same three reasons, *proles, medicina et adjutorium*; and occasionally Orthodox writers do likewise. But significantly in the Orthodox wedding service itself there is no allusion whatever to the second or negative reason, 'a remedy against sin'. This is the more surprising, since the Greek Fathers, in common with St Augustine, are for the most part somewhat unenthusiastic in their view of marriage.

23.10

It is only the other two reasons, both of them positive – mutual love and the bearing of children – that are mentioned in the prayers at a wedding. The liturgical texts speak, in the first place, about 'unity... a bond of affection that cannot be broken... oneness of mind... mutual love in the bond of peace', and, most strikingly of all, 'concord of soul and body'. The love between wife and husband, as this last phrase indicates, exists at every level, physical and spiritual. No distinction is to be made between soul and body; the view of personhood underlying the service is thoroughly holistic. Secondly, and with equal emphasis, the prayers speak of the 'gift of children': 'Grant them the fruit of the womb, fair offspring... May they see their children's children like newly-planted olive trees around their table.'

23.11

There is no suggestion in the text of the wedding service that one of these two things rather than the other is the 'primary aim' of the sacrament. We Orthodox have always felt unhappy about the ruling given by the Holy Office at Rome in 1944 that the 'primary purpose' of marriage is 'the generation and bringing-up of offspring', and not mutual love. Fortunately such language is avoided by Vatican II, which deliberately refrains from making any distinction between 'primary' and 'secondary' purposes. It is surely unnecessary and misleading to make any contrast between mutual love and procreation. God has joined the two together, so that the love of the couple, expressed physically as well as spiritually, leads in the normal course of events to the birth of children. As Pope John Paul II has expressed it, in words that Orthodox can gladly make their own: 'The love of husband and wife in God's plan leads beyond itself and new life is generated, a family is born'. God has established a connection between the two things, and together they constitute one single aim and not two. Nowhere in the New Testament is it said that the bearing of children is the main purpose of marriage. On the contrary, childbirth and love are linked together: 'Woman will be saved through bearing children, if she continues in faith and love and holiness' (1 Tim. 2.15).

23.12

Any description, then, of the purpose of marriage needs to be broad enough to include both mutual love and childbearing at once. It is best to say simply that the aim of marriage is the mutual sanctification of husband and wife, their transfiguration through the reciprocal gift and union of their two lives. In the words of an Arab Orthodox bishop, Metropolitan George Khodre, 'Marriage has no other end than that the husband and wife prepare for the coming of God'. 'The union between husband and wife', writes Father John Meyendorff, 'is an end in itself; it is an eternal union between two unique and eternal personalities.' From this it follows that, even when God does not grant the gift of children, a marriage may still exist in its true fullness.

The ministers of the sacrament

23.13

A Western Christian, present for the first time at an Orthodox wedding, will probably be surprised by two things, by both an absence and a presence. Something is missing which he would expect to find; and something happens which does not occur in the Western ceremony. Absent from the Orthodox Service is the central event in the Western ceremony, the exchange of formal vows. In the Greek practice the couple utter no words of consent and make no explicit promises during the course of the service itself, and indeed they are neither of them required to say anything at all. Editions of the *Euchologion* ('Book of Prayers') issued in recent years by the Church of Greece state simply that, before the service begins, 'the priest asks them to testify, whether the bride wants the bridegroom; and, likewise, whether the bridegroom wants the bride'. It is not indicated what precise form the priest's questions and the couple's answers shall take. But this rubric is of very recent date, and is not to be found in the Greek service books published in the nineteenth and the early twentieth century, which make no reference to the putting of any questions. The Russian Church, however, does prescribe specific questions; these were introduced into the Slavonic service books in the early seventeenth century by Metropolitan Peter Moghila of Kiev, who was directly influenced by the Roman Catholic practice. The questions, which occur at the end of the first part of the service, the Betrothal, and before the beginning of the main part of the wedding, the Office of Crowning, are two in number: 'Do you, N., have a good, free and unconstrained will and a firm intention to take as your wife this woman, N., whom you see here before you? Have you promised yourself to any other bride?' The same questions are then put to the bride. Even in the Russian use, apart from this there are no promises and no explicit vows. The contractual emphasis, so marked in the Western Service, is almost entirely absent from the Orthodox rite.

23.14

Behind this difference in liturgical practice there lies a difference in sacramental theology. According to Roman Catholic teaching, it is the couple who are the ministers of the sacrament, whereas in the Orthodox view it is the officiating priest. The marriage rite, as understood by Orthodoxy, is not a contract or agreement made between the two partners but a blessing conferred by the Church. The free consent of the couple is, of course, an essential precondition, but it does not itself constitute the sacrament. This divergence between Orthodoxy and Rome, so far from being a mere technicality, is relevant to the question of divorce.

The ring and the crown

23.15

Let us turn now from the absence to the presence. The Orthodox marriage service is divided into two parts, originally celebrated separately but now always held at the same time: the Betrothal and the Crowning. At the Betrothal the chief ceremony is the blessing of the rings, which are placed on the hands of bridegroom and bride, and are then exchanged three times. The rings symbolize, in Orthodoxy as in the West, the pledge of mutual faithfulness made between the two partners. But after this, in the second part of the service, there follows a rite for which there is no parallel in the West: the Crowning. The priest takes two crowns – in the Greek practice these are garlands of flowers, usually artificial (I am sorry to say), while in the Russian practice they are made of gold, silver or other metal – and he makes the sign of the Cross with them over the couple; the crowns are then placed on or held over their heads and, as with the rings, they are exchanged three times. The threefold exchange, first of the rings and then of the crowns, underlines the reciprocal character of marriage, its true character as a mutual gift of personhood.

23.16

The Crowning is the central event in the Orthodox service for a first marriage. It is the Crowning, together with the three prayers that immediately precede it and more especially the third of these prayers, in which the priest joins together the hands of the couple that constitutes the distinctive and essential rite in the sacrament of marriage. Through their symbolism the crowns reveal the basic intention of marriage as a 'mystery'. Originally a feature of pagan wedding ceremonies, they were given a deeper and richer meaning when adopted by the Church. Their significance is double. In the first place, as with the crowns worn by victors in athletic contests, they are a 'symbol of victory', to quote St John Chrysostom – the victory of love over lust, of self-control over self-indulgence, of shared personhood over narcissism. For while sexuality is indeed a gift from God, this gift has to be rightly used; it needs to be made truly personal, an occasion of mutual exchange and not of private pleasure. The Crowning expresses precisely this call to joyful and victorious transfiguration.

23.17

The crowns, however, have also a second meaning: they are crowns of martyrdom. The service includes repeated references to crossbearing and martyrdom. In the prayers for the couple, the priest asks: 'Remember them, O Lord our God, as you remembered your Forty Holy Martyrs, sending down upon them crowns from heaven... May that joy come upon them that blessed Helena felt when she found the precious cross.' During the procession that comes towards the end of the service, the choir sings: 'Holy Martyrs, who fought the good fight and have received your crowns, entreat the Lord that he will have mercy on our souls'. The joy of the marriage feast is also the joy of the Cross. In the words of Paul Evdokimov, 'Perfect love is love crucified'.

23.18

In all this the Church has, of course, no intention of advocating a morbid cult of suffering for its own sake. Man and woman marry in Christ not for mutual hurt but for mutual happiness. There can, however, be no true marriage without a readiness for sacrifice, without a *kenosis* or self-emptying, so that each may live in the other. In every Christian marriage there has to be an ascetic element, a cutting-off of self-will; it is not only monks and nuns but all alike, whether married or unmarried, who are called to follow the 'narrow way'. If so many marriages break down in our contemporary society, is not the main reason because the partners are not in practice willing to accept this conjugal *ascesis*, and perhaps have never even been told about it?

23.19

The crowns have also an eschatological significance. At the conclusion of the service, as the priest removes them from the heads of the couple, he prays to God: 'Take up their crowns into your kingdom'. As a vocation or calling, marriage is not static but dynamic, not so much a state as a process. A person does not fulfil his or her vocation to matrimony simply by getting married, for that is only the beginning, the first step of the journey. And this shared journey extends beyond time and space into the kingdom of God. It involves a movement from this present age into the age to come.

As a journey into the kingdom, then, marriage is not merely for life but for eternity. Nowhere in the Orthodox service do we use the words 'till death us do part'. I know a Russian lady in the Orthodox community at Oxford whose husband died ten years ago, but who steadfastly refuses to be called his widow: 'I am his wife', she rightly insists. The married relationship is not terminated by death.

23.20

In the ancient Church, because of this strong sense of the eternity of the marriage bond, a second marriage after the death of the first partner, while not forbidden, was commonly discouraged (cf. 1 Cor. 7.8-9 & 39-40). The second-century Apologist, St Athenagoras, goes so far as to stigmatize a second union as 'respectable adultery'. But the rigorist standpoint of the Montanists and Novatianists, who altogether prohibited remarriage, was not endorsed by the Eastern Church as a whole. St John Chrysostom insists that it is heretical to condemn a second marriage as sinful; 'the second marriage is good', he writes, although he adds that it is not as good as a first marriage, while virginity is best of all. Yet a second marriage by a widow or widower, while not sinful, is seen as a condescension to human weakness, a falling-short of the true Christian ideal of the single union. The fourth-century Canons of Laodicea say that those who have been 'lawfully joined in second marriages' may receive Holy Communion only 'by indulgence' and after a period of prayer and fasting, while St Basil the Great requires those who marry a second time to abstain from Communion for a period of one or even two years; but these regulations are not today applied. Members of the married clergy in the Orthodox Church, however, still remain committed to the ideal standard of a unique union, and if a priest's or deacon's wife dies, he cannot remarry.

23.21

Such, then, is the many-sided meaning of the crowns in the Orthodox marriage service. They symbolize joyful victory, inner martyrdom, the eternity of the marriage bond. But what is to happen if the married life of the couple, instead of bringing about their shared sanctification, endangers their salvation and proves a foretaste of hell?

The Church's power to dissolve the marriage bond

23.22

'The whole Church is the Church of the Penitent', says St Ephrem the Syrian; 'the whole Church is the Church of those who are perishing'. The Finnish Orthodox writer, Tito Colliander, records a conversation between a monk and a layman, which aptly describes married life as well as monasticism. 'What do you do there in the monastery?' the layman asks. And the monk replies: 'We fall and get up, fall and get up, fall and get up again'. Evdokimov quotes an early monastic text: 'Purity of heart is to show love for those who fall'. In the words of Christ himself, 'I did not come to call the virtuous, but sinners' (Mark 2.17). It is in such a perspective as this that we should set the question of divorce and remarriage.

23.23
In the discussion that follows I shall use the word 'divorce' in its full sense, to signify divorce *a vinculo*, the dissolution of the sacramental marriage bond. I shall not employ it in the lesser sense of divorce *a mensa et thoro*, or legal separation; nor again in the sense of a decree of nullity, that is, a declaration that the marriage never properly existed in the first place.

23.24
How can it be that the Orthodox Church affirms its clear belief in the sacramental character and, indeed, the eternity of marriage, and yet at the same time accepts the possibility that a marriage may be ended by divorce? It has to be remembered first of all that Orthodoxy sees the sacrament of marriage, not primarily as a juridical contract between the two partners, but as a divine action, effected by Christ within the Church through the blessing of the priest. Needless to say, the Roman Catholic Church also regards the sacramental blessing of a marriage as a divine action; but in the West far greater emphasis has been placed on the partners as ministers of the marriage, and this has contributed to a different attitude towards divorce. The basic principle underlying the Orthodox practice is our conviction that Christ has entrusted to the Church full power to regulate the administration of the sacraments. If each sacrament is a divine action, effected by Christ *within the Church*, then the Church, as steward of the sacraments and by virtue of the authority to bind and loose conferred upon it by Christ himself (Matt. 16.19; 18.18; John 20.23), has the right to release the couple from the marriage bond and to permit a remarriage. This is done by the Church, not arbitrarily, nor as a weak and easy concession to the mores of contemporary secular society, but in the name of Christ's own continuing compassion and loving kindness towards humanity.

Grounds for divorce
23.25
Before considering the reasons, whether Scriptural or pastoral, advanced by Orthodox writers to justify the granting of divorce, let us look at the actual practice followed when dissolving a marriage. It is sometimes claimed

that, until very recent times, the only ground for divorce allowed in Orthodox Canon Law was adultery. In reality, from the Byzantine period onwards, a number of other grounds have also been admitted. The main reasons recognized in current practice are the following:

(i)   Adultery by either the man or the woman (cf. Matt. 19.9).

(ii)   Apostasy from the Christian faith by either partner (cf. 1 Cor. 7.12-15).

(iii) Adoption of the monastic life by one partner. (This can be done only with the consent of the other partner; and in such a case the latter is not permitted to remarry.)

(iv) The procuring of an abortion by the wife without the husband's knowledge. (Abortion is in any case strictly forbidden in the Orthodox Church.)

(v)   Inability by the man to consummate the marriage. (In Orthodox Canon Law this does not render the marriage null, but it is regarded as grounds for divorce.)

(vi) Grave malady (such as leprosy or syphilis), voluntary mutilation, or incurable madness.

(vii) Threats against the life of one spouse on the part of the other.

(viii) The deliberate abandonment of one partner by the other, or the permanent disappearance of one partner.

(ix) The condemnation of one partner for a serious crime, involving prolonged imprisonment.

(x)   Implacable hatred, involving a total breakdown in personal relations. (The earliest example of a divorce being granted for this reason is a decision by the Holy Synod at Constantinople in December 1315; there are a number of similar decisions by the Ecumenical Patriarchate in the nineteenth century. But some Orthodox canonists deny that implacable hatred constitutes proper grounds for divorce.)

23.26

As Paul Evdokimov points out, all these reasons can be seen as different forms of death: 'religious death through apostasy; civil death, through condemnation; bodily death, through absence, grave malady or madness; the death of the mutual love that is the very essence of the sacrament, through adultery, threats against the other's life, or implacable hatred'.

23.27

For a correct appreciation of the Orthodox canonical practice, two further points need to be kept in view:

23.28

First, a church divorce is required; it is not sufficient for a decree to be granted merely by the civil courts. In Greek Orthodoxy, during the later Byzantine and the Turkish periods, divorce cases fell under ecclesiastical jurisdiction, and were the responsibility of the church courts; and this was also the case in Russia until 1917. In modern Greece a mixed system has prevailed. The case is first referred to the diocesan bishop, who seeks to bring about a reconciliation. If his efforts fail, the actual divorce proceedings may then begin, and these are conducted in the civil court. Should the civil court decide that there are grounds for a divorce, the dossier is referred back to the bishop; and only if he gives his consent does the divorce decree finally come into effect. (The situation in Greece is now more complex, as a result of the introduction of civil marriage in 1982.) In a country such as Britain, where the Orthodox Church is separated from the State, for obvious reasons the Orthodox authorities are prohibited from issuing a church divorce before a civil divorce has been granted in the British courts. The Orthodox ecclesiastical court, however, is not obliged automatically to endorse what the State has decided. The case is re-examined, and only if it is felt that there are sufficient grounds for a divorce according to Orthodox Canon Law does the ecclesiastical court permit the celebration of a second marriage in church.

23.29

Secondly, there is a special service for a second marriage, differing in important ways from the normal wedding service. This makes it clear that the second union, although blessed by the Church, can never be exactly the same as the first. St Nicephorus, Patriarch of Constantinople (806-815), specified that the ceremony of Crowning should be omitted at a second marriage; but since the thirteenth century, at any rate within the jurisdiction of the Ecumenical Patriarchate, it has been customary to allow the Crowning. Before it occurs, however, two long penitential prayers are said, which give to the second marriage service a spirit altogether different from that which prevails at a first marriage. The first prayer begins: 'O Master, Lord our God... have mercy on our sins, and forgive the transgressions of these your servants, calling them to repentance and granting them pardon of their offences and purification from their sins... You know the frailty of human nature.'

23.30

The prayer goes on to mention Biblical figures who received forgiveness, such as Rahab the harlot (Josh. 2.1-24; Heb. 11.31; Jas. 2.25) and the repentant publican (Luke 18.10-14). The second prayer speaks of the couple as 'unable to bear the heat and burden of the day, and not having the strength to endure the burning desires of the flesh', and it quotes St Paul's words, 'It is better to marry than to burn' (1 Cor. 7.9). The notion of marriage as 'a remedy against sin', conspicuously absent from 'the service for a first marriage, is thus heavily emphasized in the rite for a second union...

EXTRACT 24
PAUL VI
Birth control

24.1
The changes that have taken place are in fact of considerable importance and concern different problems. In the first place there is the question of the rapid increase in population which has made many fear that world population is going to grow faster than available resources, with the consequence that many families and developing countries are being faced with greater hardships. This fact can easily induce public authorities to be tempted to take radical measures to avert this danger. There is also the fact that not only working and housing conditions, but the greater demands made both in the economic and educational field require that kind of life in which it is frequently extremely difficult these days to provide for a large family.

24.2
It is also apparent that, with the new understanding of the dignity of woman, and her place in society, there has been an appreciation of the value of love in marriage and of the meaning of intimate married life in the light of that love.

24.3
But the most remarkable development of all is to be seen in man's stupendous progress in the domination and rational organisation of the forces of nature to the point that he is endeavouring to extend this control over every aspect of his own life – over his body, over his mind and emotions, over his social life, and even over the laws that regulate the transmission of life.

24.4
This new state of things gives rise to new questions. Granted the conditions of life today and taking into account the relevance of married love to the

harmony and mutual fidelity of husband and wife, would it not be right to review the moral norms in force till now, especially when it is felt that these can be observed, only with the gravest difficulty, sometimes only by heroic effort?

24.5

Moreover, if one were to apply here the so-called principle of totality, could it not be accepted that the intention to have a less prolific but more rationally planned family might not transform an action which renders natural processes infertile into a licit and provident control of birth? Could it not be admitted, in other words, that procreative finality applies to the totality of married life rather than to each single act? It is being asked whether, because people are more conscious today of their responsibilities, the time has not come when the transmission of life should be regulated by their intelligence and will rather than through the specific rhythms of their own bodies.

24.6

This kind of question required from the teaching authority of the Church a new and deeper reflection on the principles of the moral teaching on marriage – a teaching which is based on the natural law as illuminated and enriched by divine Revelation.

24.7

Let no Catholic be heard to assert that the interpretation of the natural moral law is outside the competence of the Church's Magisterium. It is in fact indisputable, as Our Predecessors have many times declared, that Jesus Christ, when he communicated his divine power to Peter and the other apostles and sent them to teach all nations his commandments, constituted them as the authentic guardians and interpreters of the whole moral law, not only, that is, of the law of the gospel but also of the natural law, the reason being that the natural law declares the will of God, and its faithful observance is necessary for men's eternal salvation.

24.8

The Church, in carrying out this mandate, has always provided consistent teaching on the nature of marriage, on the correct use of conjugal rights, and on all the duties of husband and wife. This is especially true in recent times...

24.9

The questions of the birth of children, like every other question which touches human life, is too large to be resolved by limited criteria, such as are provided by biology, psychology, demography or sociology. It is the whole man and the whole complex of his responsibilities that must be considered, not only what is natural and limited to this earth, but also what is supernatural and eternal. And since in the attempt to justify artificial methods of birth control many appeal to the demands of married love or of 'responsible parenthood', these two important realities of married life must be accurately defined and analysed. This is what We mean to do, with special reference to what the Second Vatican Council taught with the highest authority in its Pastoral Constitution *Gaudium et Spes*.

24.10
Married love particularly reveals its true nature and nobility when we realise that it derives from God and finds its supreme origin in him who 'is Love', the Father 'from whom every family in heaven and on earth is named' (Eph. 3.15).

24.11
Marriage, then, is far from being the effect of chance or the result of the blind evolution of natural forces. It is in reality the wise and provident institution of God the Creator, whose purpose was to establish in man his loving design. As a consequence, husband and wife, through that mutual gift of themselves, which is specific and exclusive to them alone, seek to develop that kind of personal union in which they complement one another in order to co-operate with God in the generation and education of new lives.

24.12
Furthermore, the marriage of those who have been baptised is invested with the dignity of a Sacramental sign of grace, for it represents the union of Christ and his Church.

24.13
In the light of these facts the characteristic features and exigencies of married love are clearly indicated, and it is of the highest importance to evaluate them exactly.

24.14
This love is above all fully *human*, a compound of sense and spirit. It is not, then, merely a question of natural instinct or emotional drive. It is also, and above all, an act of the free will, whose dynamism ensures that not only does it endure through the joys and sorrows of daily life, but also that

it grows, so that husband and wife become in a way one heart and one soul, and together attain their human fulfilment.

24.15

Then it is a love which is *total* – that very special form of personal friendship in which husband and wife generously share everything, allowing no unreasonable exceptions or thinking just of their own interests. Whoever really loves his partner loves not only for what he receives, but loves that partner for her own sake, content to be able to enrich the other with the gift of himself.

24.16

Again, married love is *faithful* and *exclusive* of all other, and this until death. This is how husband and wife understood it on the day on which, fully aware of what they were doing, they freely vowed themselves to one another in marriage. Though this fidelity of husband and wife sometimes presents difficulties, no one can assert that it is impossible, for it is always honourable and worthy of the highest esteem. The example of so many married persons down through the centuries shows not only that fidelity is co-natural to marriage but also that it is the source of profound and enduring happiness.

24.17

And finally this love is *creative of life*, for it is not exhausted by the loving interchange of husband and wife, but also contrives to go beyond this to bring new life into being. 'Marriage and married love are by their character ordained to the procreation and bringing up of children. Children are the outstanding gift of marriage, and contribute in the highest degree to the parents' welfare.' (*Gaudium et Spes*, pp.1070-2).

24.18

Married love, therefore, requires of husband and wife the full awareness of their obligations in the matter of responsible parenthood, which today, rightly enough, is much insisted upon, but which, at the same time, should be rightly understood. Hence, this must be studied in the light of the various inter-related arguments which are its justification.

24.19

If first We consider it in relation to the biological processes involved, responsible parenthood is to be understood as the knowledge and observance of their specific functions. Human intelligence discovers in the faculty of procreating life, the biological laws which involve human personality.

24.20

If, on the other hand, we examine the innate drives and emotions of man, responsible parenthood expresses the domination which reason and will must exert over them.

24.21

But if we then attend to relevant physical, economic, psychological and social conditions, those are considered to exercise responsible parenthood who prudently and generously decide to have a large family, or who, for serious reasons and with due respect to the moral law, choose to have no more children for the time being or even for an indeterminate period.

24.22

Responsible parenthood, moreover, in the terms in which we use the phrase, retains a further and deeper significance of paramount importance which refers to the objective moral order instituted by God – the order of which a right conscience is the true interpreter. As a consequence the commitment to responsible parenthood requires that husband and wife, keeping a right order of priorities, recognise their own duties towards God, themselves, their families and human society.

24.23

From this it follows that they are not free to do as they like in the service of transmitting life, on the supposition that it is lawful for them to decide independently of other considerations what is the right course to follow. On the contrary, they are bound to ensure that what they do corresponds to the will of God the Creator. The very nature of marriage and its use makes this clear, while the constant teaching of the Church affirms it.

24.24

The sexual activity, in which husband and wife are intimately and chastely united with one another, through which human life is transmitted, is, as the recent Council recalled, 'honourable and good'. It does not, moreover, cease to be legitimate even when, for reasons independent of their will, it is foreseen to be infertile. For its natural adaptation to the expression and strengthening of the union of husband and wife is not thereby suppressed. The facts are, as experience shows, that new life is not the result of each and every act of sexual intercourse. God has wisely ordered the laws of nature and the incidence of fertility in such a way that successive births are already naturally spaced through the inherent operation of these laws. The Church, nevertheless, in urging men to the observance of the precepts of the natural law, which it interprets by its constant doctrine, teaches as absolutely required that *in any use whatever of marriage* there must be no impairment of its natural capacity to procreate human life.

24.25

This particular doctrine, often expounded by the Magisterium of the Church, is based on the inseparable connection, established by God, which man on his own initiative may not break, between the unitive significance and the procreative significance which are both inherent to the marriage act.

24.26

The reason is that the marriage act, because of its fundamental structure, while it unites husband and wife in the closest intimacy, also brings into operation laws written into the actual nature of man and of woman for the generation of new life. And if each of these essential qualities, the unitive and the procreative, is preserved, the use of marriage fully retains its sense of true mutual love and its ordination to the supreme responsibility of parenthood to which man is called. We believe that our contemporaries are particularly capable of seeing that this teaching is in harmony with human reason.

24.27

For men rightly observe that to force the use of marriage on one's partner without regard to his or her condition or personal and reasonable wishes in the matter, is no true act of love, and therefore offends the moral order in its particular application to the intimate relationship of husband and wife. In the same way, if they reflect, they must also recognise that an act of mutual love which impairs the capacity to transmit life which God the Creator, through specific laws, has built into it, frustrates his design which constitutes the norms of marriage, and contradicts the will of the Author of life. Hence, to use this divine gift while depriving it, even if only partially, of its meaning and purpose, is equally repugnant to the nature of man and of woman, strikes at the heart of their relationship and is consequently in opposition to the plan of God and his holy will. But to experience the gift of married love while respecting the laws of conception is to acknowledge that one is not the master of the sources of life but rather the minister of the design established by the Creator. Just as man does not have unlimited dominion over his body in general, so also, and with more particular reason, he has no such dominion over his specifically sexual faculties, for these are concerned by their very nature with the generation of life, of which God is the source. For human life is sacred – all men must recognise that fact, Our Predecessor, Pope John XXIII, recalled, 'since from its first beginnings it calls for the creative action of God' (*Mater et Magistra* 1961).

24.28
Therefore we base first principles of a human and Christian doctrine of marriage when we are obliged once more to declare that the direct interruption of the generative process already begun and, above all, direct abortion, even for therapeutic reasons, are to be absolutely excluded as lawful means of controlling the birth of children.

24.29
Equally to be condemned, as the Magisterium of the Church has affirmed on various occasions, is direct sterilisation, whether of the man or of the woman, whether permanent or temporary.

24.30
Similarly excluded is any action, which either before, at the moment of, or after sexual intercourse, is specifically intended to prevent procreation – whether as an end or as a means.

24.31
Neither is it valid to argue, as a justification for sexual intercourse which is deliberately contraceptive, that a lesser evil is to be preferred to a greater one, or that such intercourse would merge with the normal relations of past and future to form a single entity, and so be qualified by exactly the same moral goodness as these. Though it is true that sometimes it is lawful to tolerate a lesser moral evil in order to avoid a greater or in order to promote a greater good, it is never lawful, even for the gravest reasons, to do evil that good may come of it – in other words, to intend positively something which intrinsically contradicts the moral order, and which must therefore be judged unworthy of man, even though the intention is to protect or promote the welfare of an individual, of a family or of society in general. Consequently it is a serious error to think that a whole married life of otherwise normal relations can justify sexual intercourse which is deliberately contraceptive and so intrinsically wrong.

24.32
But the Church in no way regards as unlawful therapeutic means considered necessary to cure organic diseases, even though they also have a contraceptive effect, and this is foreseen – provided that this contraceptive effect is not directly intended for any motive whatsoever.

24.33
However, as We noted earlier, some people today raise the objection against this particular doctrine of the Church concerning the moral laws governing

marriage, that human intelligence has both the right and the responsibility to control those forces of irrational nature which come within its ambit and to direct them towards ends beneficial to man. Others ask on the same point whether it is not reasonable in so many cases to use artificial birth control if by so doing the harmony and peace of a family are better served and more suitable conditions are provided for the education of children already born. To this question we must give a clear reply. The Church is the first to praise and commend the application of human intelligence to an activity in which a rational creature such as man is so closely associated with his Creator. But she affirms that this must be done within the limits of the order of reality established by God.

24.34

If therefore there are reasonable grounds for spacing births, arising from the physical or psychological condition of husband or wife, or from external circumstances, the Church teaches that then married people may take advantage of the natural cycles immanent in the reproductive system and use their marriage at precisely those times that are infertile, and in this way control birth, a way which does not in the least offend the moral principles which we have just explained.

24.35

Neither the Church nor her doctrine is inconsistent when she considers it lawful for married people to take advantage of the infertile period but condemns as always unlawful the use of means which directly exclude conception, even when the reasons given for the latter practice are neither trivial nor immoral. In reality, these two cases are completely different. In the former married couples rightly use a facility provided them by nature. In the latter they obstruct the natural development of the generative process. It cannot be denied that in each case married couples, for acceptable reasons, are both perfectly clear in their intention to avoid children and mean to make sure that none will be born. But it is equally true that it is exclusively in the former case that husband and wife are ready to abstain from intercourse during the fertile period as often as for reasonable motives the birth of another child is not desirable. And when the infertile period recurs, they use their married intimacy to express their mutual love and safeguard their fidelity towards one another. In doing this they certainly give proof of a true and authentic love.

24.36

Responsible men can become more deeply convinced of the truth of the doctrine laid down by the Church on this issue if they reflect on the consequences of methods and plans for the artificial restriction of increases in the birth-rate. Let them first consider how easily this course of action can lead to the way being wide open to marital infidelity and a general lowering of moral standards. Not much experience is needed to be fully aware of human weakness and to understand that men – and especially the young, who are so exposed to temptation – need incentives to keep the moral law, and it is an evil thing to make it easy for them to break that law. Another effect that gives cause for alarm is that a man who grows accustomed to the use of contraceptive methods may forget the reverence due to a woman, and, disregarding her physical and emotional equilibrium, reduce her to being a mere instrument for the satisfaction of his own desires, no longer considering her as his partner whom he should surround with care and affection.

24.37
Finally, grave consideration should be given to the danger of this power passing into the hands of those public authorities who care little for the precepts of the moral law. Who will blame a Government which in its attempt to resolve the problems affecting an entire country resorts to the same measures as are regarded as lawful by married people in the solution of a particular family difficulty? Who will prevent public authorities from favouring those contraceptive methods which they consider more effective? Should they regard this as necessary, they may even impose their use on everyone. It could well happen, therefore, that when people, either individually or in family or social life, experience the inherent difficulties of the divine law and are determined to avoid them, they may be giving into the hands of public authorities the power to intervene in the most personal and intimate responsibility of husband and wife.

24.38
Consequently, unless we are willing that the responsibility of procreating life should be left to the arbitrary decision of men, we must accept that there are certain limits, beyond which it is wrong to go, to the power of man over his own body and its natural functions – limits, let it be said, which no one, whether as a private individual or as a public authority, can lawfully exceed. These limits are expressly imposed because of the reverence due to the whole human organism and its natural functions, in the light of the principles, which we stated earlier, and according to a correct understanding of the so-called 'principle of totality', enunciated by Our Predecessor, Pope Pius XII.

24.39

It is to be anticipated that not everyone perhaps will easily accept this particular teaching. There is too much clamorous outcry against the voice of the Church, and this is intensified by modern means of communication. It should cause no surprise that the Church, any less than her divine Founder, is destined to be a 'sign of contradiction' (Lk. 2.34). She does not, because of this, evade the duty imposed on her of proclaiming humbly but firmly the entire moral law, both natural and evangelical.

24.40

Since the Church did not make either of these laws, she cannot be their arbiter – only their guardian and interpreter. It can never be right for her to declare lawful what is in fact unlawful, because this, by its very nature, is always opposed to the true good of man.

24.41

By vindicating the integrity of the moral law of marriage, the Church is convinced that she is contributing to the creation of a truly human civilisation. She urges man not to betray his personal responsibilities by putting all his faith in technical expedients. In this way she defends the dignity of husband and wife. This course of action shows that the Church, loyal to the example and teaching of the divine Saviour, is sincere and unselfish in her regard for men whom she strives to help even now during this earthly pilgrimage 'to share as sons in the life of the living God, the Father of all men'.

EXTRACT 25
WCC

Churches against racism

25.1

We now turn to a few reflections on the role of the Church itself. In the second chapter we tried to describe what the Church ought to be, i.e. a community of disciples which constantly regroups and reconstitutes itself around situations of suffering. What are the consequences of discipleship in terms of 'disciplined life'?

The legacy of the suffering Church in past and present

25.2

The evil of racism discloses in a new way how often the churches fail to centre around the suffering, dispossessed and degraded members of humanity. The churches are constantly yielding to the temptation to forget those who are forgotten and not heed the voice of the voiceless. They seek to organize and establish themselves along the lines of the main values and dominant forces in their respective societies. In varying degrees the histories of our churches bear witness to their constant drifting away from the poor and powerless to the rich and mighty. The persecutions of defenceless minorities, the ghettos of Jews in Europe and the recurrent pogroms, the endless stream of refugees, who for the sake of their faith have had to leave their homes and lands – all these have through many centuries left a stain on the history of Christianity. This means that most of our 'official' established churches, because of their history and the way their structures have developed, are not equipped to deal with this suffering. There have, of course, been movements within the churches which have had certain insights so radical and onesided that the established, official church at the time has found them threatening. But these movements have often been branded 'heretical' or 'sectarian'. Consequently they have suffered appallingly at the hands of the official Church and of the political authorities in the particular country with which the official Church had aligned itself. Yet it is in many of these expelled groups that the witness of enduring hope in the midst of so much suffering has been kept alive. This presents us with the duty of rescuing this legacy of suffering and resistance, of revolt and silent endurance, hidden in the history of the oppressed. This would give us a truer understanding of what is today being expressed in the theologies of black people, notably in North America and Southern Africa. At the same time, it will help us to a deeper understanding of what it means to die to the might and power of this world and to rise again on the side of suffering. As the churches reflect the ministry of Jesus Christ who 'reigns from the Tree', they will regain their authentic ministry. Called constantly to meditate on the cross and resurrection, they will be reminded that their Lord died on the cross because of the combined efforts of an alliance of established religion and power politics. They will need to be constantly on guard against the recurring danger of concluding similar alliances, and become again and again the Church of the suffering servant.

Racism – a 'moral heresy'?

25.3

We have tried to reflect on the Church's role with the self-searching that this requires. The sin of racism is so all-pervasive that we are not at liberty to judge or condemn others. Nevertheless, we have to face up to the issue of 'moral heresy' to which much attention has been given in recent years, particularly in connection with the Programme to Combat Racism. In our view, the concept of 'heresy' is not in practice a very helpful standpoint from which to consider racism. Certainly we recognize that some of the theories and beliefs advanced to justify racism may be heretical, but the discussion of racism must not be side-tracked into an academic discussion of what is or is not formal heresy. On the other hand, we recognize that orthodoxy and orthopraxy are intimately related. As we have already noted, Christian doctrine cannot be divorced from its practical implications. All heretical teaching is likely to produce moral distortions of one sort or another.

25.4

Equally, behind every discriminative action, if accepted and justified as a Christian mode of behaviour, there lies some hidden heresy. But our main concern should not be to denounce groups or churches as morally heretical. Rather, we should be consistently attentive to possibly negative effects of certain beliefs and practices, and to help each other to discover and overcome them.

25.5

The concept of moral heresy, it seems to us, was originally intended to make a preacher's point. The legitimacy of this is hardly open to dispute. But endless complications and difficulties arise when it is transplanted into formal theological discourse, particularly in the context of the ecumenical movement, which has no constitutional claims on its member churches.

Church discipline

25.6

From our understanding of discipleship we would be inclined rather to focus our attention on the discipline of the church. If 'being the Church' means 're-establishing community in situations of suffering', it means leading a disciplined life according to this criterion. 'Disciplined life' means that all decisions and actions at all levels of church life are related to this central notion of discipleship. As such it does not imply rigidity and isolation but rather consistent flexibility and openness: not an openness towards all kinds of things, but towards people and communities of people (including other churches) in whose life suffering for the sake of freedom and reconciliation has somehow become constitutive. Only in the context of this disciplined life does the concept of *unity* take on meaning and substance. Only in the context of this disciplined life can the unity of the Church be called a sign of the unity of mankind.

25.7

We are very much aware of the fact that in the course of church history church discipline has been organized according to certain patterns and that in some churches it has become an important part of their life and structure. We would invite all churches, however, to consider whether some of these patterns of church discipline have not in fact moved away from the notion of discipleship that we are trying to spell out here. At this point, we would like to suggest two points:

25.8

a) In the first place we submit that the notion of church discipline has become too individualistic in many churches. It is the individual church member who is 'disciplined'. The process of repentance that we have been trying to describe, however, makes it difficult to maintain this emphasis. In sins like racism men and women are involved collectively and it is the same in the Church. We cannot assume a clean Church over against a possibly unclean individual. Discipline in this sense must mean helping one another relentlessly to become aware of the dimensions of evil and of our involvement in it. Discipline in this sense can only be judging if it is simultaneously self-judging and if it leads to common efforts at repentance-action. Of course these things have always been important in the understanding of church discipline. But it seems to us that they take on new meaning in the light of the discoveries we have made.

25.9

Yet this is not the most radical reason why an individualistic conception of church discipline seems to be inadequate. In the light of our understanding of discipleship as constant regrouping around real suffering, discipline means a consistent effort to help each other to share constructively and hopefully in the suffering that is the result of sin.

25.10

b) In the second place we submit that in most churches the notion of church discipline has become too exclusive in the sense that it is automatically associated with excommunication. We are not prepared to eliminate this notion of excommunication entirely: we feel that it has its legitimate place in a Church that seeks to lead a disciplined life. But neither are we prepared to use the notion of excommunication directly, for instance by saying that the Church should excommunicate all racists. Our understanding of the sin of racism, as we have sought to describe it, and of the nature of discipleship in view of racism, clearly prohibits this.

25.11

Most important, however, is that our churches still lack the fruit of credibility that would grow out of a disciplined life around situations of real suffering; and we feel that responsible discussion of excommunication can only take place on the basis of such fruit. Until we have made some real progress on this road, we are not free on the ground of racism either to excommunicate certain churches from the fellowship of churches.

25.12

On the whole, it is much more important to work for authenticity at the centre than for a rigid definition of boundaries. Authenticity at the centre implies solidarity in being the body of Christ in the world. That is not an uncritical solidarity that knows no limits: it is a solidarity that keeps defining and redefining itself from the centre. In that process the so-called boundaries of the Church might become visible to people simply by what the Church is and does, rather than by what it says and defines.

Forms of disciplined life

25.13

Only in the context of this positive understanding of discipline can we say that the Church should examine its own life relentlessly in order to ascertain and eliminate institutional racism in itself. Only in the context of this positive understanding of discipline can we try to avoid both the arrogant aloofness of those who feel that they are too important to get their hands soiled in the mundane struggle against racism as well as the self-righteous sectarian attitude of those who believe that they alone are the Lord's true disciples because they march against racism in advance of the Church. And only in the context of this positive understanding of discipline will submerged people and groups within the Church be enabled to rise and take in hand their own responsibilities as members of the body of Christ.

25.14

What does this mean for the life of the Church? We have given our attention to the following concerns:

Discipline in worship and sacraments

25.15

Firstly it appears that the Church needs to be based more decisively on 'disciplined worship'. This would imply that we seek a new discipline in the sacraments of Baptism and the Eucharist. Through Baptism every person is made part of the Christian Community, and this inclusiveness of our corporate identity in Christ must be taken literally. In the same way the

Eucharist is the celebration of oneness in Christ and it is rendered incredible where it is not lived out in a consistent and committed practice of solidarity between black and white, between races and sexes.

25.16

The disciplined life in the sacraments and the worship of God provokes rigorous prophetic preaching. Unrepentant racists need to be exhorted that for the health of their souls they are not welcome at the Lord's table until they truly repent. The leadership of the Church needs to be vigorous enough to eradicate preaching and teaching which conforms to personal and institutional racism, and to support preachers and teachers who work against racism. For indifference to racism in the Church is indifference to the worship and service of God.

25.17

At the same time our discipline of worship will have to be much more pastoral insofar as it seeks to draw into communion with Christ those who truly repent and are burdened with unacquitted guilt, hidden fears and loneliness. A disciplined worship will be worship which is unqualifiedly hospitable to all who seek Christ. Of course, each congregation has a definite character. But truly united worship will always include those who do not fit in. They are an indispensable sign of how radical the communication of God is. We ought to work hard to prevent totally homogeneous congregations, to secure worship which is truly hospitable to the wide diversity of Christian identity. So, as a consequence of disciplined worship, the Church discovers how deeply its prophetic and pastoral tasks are intertwined and how they flow together in the building up of the healing community in this world. The inclusiveness of the Church will reveal itself in the integrity and comprehensiveness with which it denounces sin, gives new heart to the broken and disheartened, heals the depressed, and sets free the oppressed.

Disciplined life in education

25.18

The disciplined life in the Church not only expresses itself in the central activity of worship, in preaching and administration of the sacraments. The discovery of the pervasive and contaminating character of racism must lead us also to reflect on other dimensions of the churches' life. We would in particular like to mention some aspects in the areas of education and renewal.

25.19

The brief reference to church history forces us to conclude that the task of teaching in the Church will have to include the critical reassessment of the extent to which our perception of our history still reflects and perpetuates discrimination against minority groups. There is need to reevaluate the important contributions and insights for which many marginalized and rejected groups have struggled and suffered. In addition to this there is need to correct the often false ways in which history books and other theological textbooks present the stories of these groups and movements. To relive the past by rediscovering the role of the Church of Christ from the viewpoint of the suffering Church will help us greatly to see ourselves today in that self-scrutinizing and repentant manner of which we have tried to speak. This will help us both as teachers and as students of theology today to become aware of the on-going cultural, ethnocentric and linguistic presumptions which, in different ways, still reinforce racist features in our theology. Such a self-scrutinizing style of doing theology will lead us to seek ways of inter-cultural, inter-racial and thereby truly ecumenical confrontation and correction. It will also make it mandatory to seek a deeper understanding of the sociological, psychological, economic and other elements which need to be taken into account in order not only to assess fully the churches' involvement in racism and the mechanisms which enforce it but also to provoke changes with sufficient care and vigour.

25.20
Again, only on the basis of such a self-critical approach would we be entitled to attack prophetically the unjust features, economic, political and otherwise, of entrenched racism.

25.21
An obvious consequence of all this is the need to revise the curricula of education in schools and other institutions of learning. This not only relates to history books, but also to the literature we use in our worship services. Hymnbooks and liturgies need to be checked and new formulae suggested which take into account the experiences of churches and movements that are constantly being overlooked, distrusted or rejected. Disciplined life should be marked by the imagination and joy of discovering the experiences with Christ which such groups represent.

25.22
Another vital aspect of renewing educational efforts needs to be a new emphasis on enabling the marginalized to make full use of their potential. Provisions must be made to help these groups to defend and express themselves not in the spirit of benevolent remedial activity but in an attempt to share resources, insights and gifts which exist in the one body of Christ and which must not be left to suffer lest the whole body suffer.

Disciplined life in renewal

25.23

The collective and pervasive sin of racism has led us to understand more fully that the discipline of renewal must constantly seek to meet the requirements of inclusiveness, mutual accountability and comprehensiveness. Honest attempts at active repentance will lead to a close combination of work and reflection, of witness and commitment. It will also penetrate the on-going evangelistic task of the churches. This is a formidable task because in many churches, the emphasis on evangelism tends to be separated from the insistence on social action and the radical transformation of society. But we affirm that conversion to God calls for a second conversion to the world, especially to those who are in suffering and pain.

25.24

The enormity of the problem of racism has perplexed and frustrated many and the struggle against it in its many different forms has exhausted many groups. Others have sunk back into resignation and apathy.

25.25

The quality of the discipline of the healing sacramental community of Christians will therefore be determined, particularly at the local level, by the sharing love, pastoral concern and prophetic solidarity in suffering which refuse to leave brothers and sisters to stand alone. The Church must enfold them in its protective arms, encourage, correct and sustain them to return to and persist in the battle against racism.

EXTRACT 26
RUETHER

Western Christianity and Zionism

26.1

One of the most shocking and puzzling phenomena for Middle Eastern Christians is the behavior of Western Christians toward them. Far from showing concern about the sufferings of Palestinian Christians, as part of the Palestinian people, Western Christians ignore them, as if they don't exist. They rush to Israel to see ancient sites of the Hebrew and Christian Bible, but seem oblivious to the 'living stones' of those descendants of ancient Christians in the Holy Land. Even worse, they add their own biblical and theological arguments to support the Zionist takeover of the land of the Palestinians and the oppression or expulsion of the Palestinian people.

26.2

What is the basis of this behavior of Western Christians? In this essay I try to show the roots of this type of Christian Zionism, which reads the Israeli-Palestinian conflict from the context of a Western set of agendas have little roots or meaning for Palestinian Christians or Arab people generally. Although, as Naim Ateek has said, a Palestinian liberation theology has arisen, and has been forced to arise, to answer these types of religious claims from Jews and Western Christians, I believe that it is particularly the responsibility of Western Christians and Jews to speak critically to their own communities about this misuse of theology to justify injustice. In this essay I examine and deconstruct these patterns of Christian Zionism which have been used to ignore and disregard Palestinian human and political rights and to justify occupation.

26.3

Support for Zionism and for the state of Israel have deep roots in Western Christianity. Patristic and Medieval Christianity had adhered to a myth of divine punishment of the Jews that included their exile and wandering outside the ancient homeland. But Reformation Christianity, particularly Reformed or Calvinist Christianity, developed theological beliefs in a restoration of the Jews to their homeland. These ties of Reformed Christianity to the idea of the restoration of the Jews to Palestine were based on three major premises.

26.4

First, evangelical Christians nationalized the Christian idea of itself as the New Israel. This developed a new affinity for the Jews as representatives of the Old Israel. The English and the Americans, particularly, thought of their people and land as the new Israel and the new Zion. They came to think of the Jews less as a superseded or negated people, and more as a parallel people, a sibling people, with whom they had a special relationship. Reformed Christians discarded the Catholic saints as their religious ancestors and identified instead with the ancient Hebrews as their religious forebears. The Jews were thought of as the contemporary descendants of those ancient Hebrews.

26.5

Secondly, the mandate for restoration of the Jews to Palestine was part of a revised Protestant eschatology. Protestant Christians believed that the promises to the Jews in the Hebrew Scripture must be fulfilled as a precondition for the return of Christ and the final redemption of the world. So, restoration of the Jews to Palestine became an integral part of a new Christian eschatology, particularly among pre-millennialist evangelical Christians.

26.6

Finally, restoration of the Jews rests on a literalistic belief in Palestine as a land promised exclusively to the Jews by God, whether or not they are present in it. This idea of the promised land had been spiritualized and universalized in Patristic and Catholic Christianity. It became a symbol of the whole cosmos or of heaven. But Protestant Christianity abandoned classical allegorical hermeneutics for literal, historical interpretation of the Bible. This reinforced a new particularism of peoplehood and land, both for Christian identity and also in relation to the Jews and the biblical idea of the promised land.

26.7

These ideas of the Jews' restoration were revived in the evangelical and pre-millennialist revivals in England and America in the second half of the nineteenth century. Both British and American evangelicals promoted ideas of Jewish restoration to Palestine. Ironically enough, these ideas were very much resisted by the Jewish community in both countries in this period. They were particularly resisted by Reform Jews, who had put aside the Jewish laws that had tied Jews to a separate communal way of life and were seeking integration and equal citizenship in a secular pluralistic definition of nationalism. Reform Jews suspected that Christian enthusiasm for Jewish restoration in the 1890s was tied to a desire to divert the flow of Jews from Russia to Western Europe and America. In this period hundreds of thousands of poor Jews were fleeing from the pogroms in Eastern Europe to the West. Reform Jews suspected, not without reason, that Christian restorationism was a cover for deportation of the Jews.

26.8

This history of Christian restorationism is an essential part of the background for understanding the affinity with Zionism among both British and American Christians that has tied first the British and then the Americans to support for Israel. By pointing to these religious ties of Christians to Zionism, I do not deny that the chief reason for British and American support for Israel is that of colonialist self-interest. Israel has been seen, first, as a British-identified and then an American-identified state that supports the interests of these nations in the Middle East and the world.

But the religious ties have been used to cover up this colonialist self-interest and to build strong emotional and symbolic identification between the two Western nations and Israel.

26.9

In this paper I will address four key religious arguments that are still operative in linking Christians in America to Israel. Three of these arguments are versions of the arguments I have already mentioned. The fourth argument has arisen from more recent European history, namely, the Nazi Holocaust.

26.10

The first and most important of the arguments that appeal for Christian support of Israel is the literalistic belief that God promised this land to the Jews in an eternal and exclusive sense. This belief in divine donation was not as important for earlier Western secular Zionists who were themselves either atheists or non-observant Jews. They appealed to the special relationship of the Jews to this area primarily as a part of Jewish ethnic, historical identity. But the religious form of the claim grew much more important after the 1967 war, with the growth of fundamentalist Jewish religious Zionism. For example, in a 1988 publication of the Friends of Zion, *Hashivah* or *Return*, it is stated that criticism of Israel in the recent uprising of the Palestinians stems from a loss of faith in the biblical promises, specifically among Christians: 'It is hardly surprising in a world where the majority of people reject the biblical promises of Israel's restoration and return to all the land given by God to Abraham and his seed through Isaac and Jacob. It is a pity that so-called Christian nations, influenced by centuries of Replacement Theology, frequently deny Israel's right to the ancient lands.'

26.11

A second appeal of religious Zionists to Christians is the belief that Jewish restoration to Palestine is part of a messianic or redemptive scenario. The Christian millennialist form of this redemptive scenario is different from that of Jewish fundamentalism. For Christian millennialists, the Jews' restoration is a precondition for the predestined conversion of 144,000 Jews to Christianity and the outbreak of Armageddon, which will kill all unconverted Jews, as well as other enemies of God, such as Arabs and Communists. Obviously these ideas of Jewish conversion and destruction are unacceptable to all Jews.

26.12

Nevertheless, Zionism, both of the official governmental variety and in some sectors of religious Zionism, has made a marriage of convenience in recent years with Christian millennialist evangelicals. They see such evangelicals as staunch supporters of Israel, including its claims to an expanded territory in 'Judea and Samaria.' They seek either to detach, or else to ignore, these ties of immediate support to the long-range eschatological scenario of Jewish conversion, destruction of the unconverted Jews, and the world reign of Christ.

26.13
However, belief that the founding of the state of Israel is a fulfilment of biblical prophecy is not simply a tenet of a relatively small group of pre-millennialist evangelicals. In a more general way, and not particularly tied to this pre-millennialist scenario, this belief is widely held among American Christians. A 1987 study showed that 57 percent of American Protestants and 37 percent of American Catholics agreed with this proposition.

26.14
A third religious argument used to tie Christians to Zionism is the claim that Zionism is an essential part of Judaism. It is said that Judaism, unlike Christianity, has always been a communal religion, a religion in which Jewish nationalism is integral to its religious self-understanding. Therefore, to deny the right of the Jews to be a nation is to reject an essential part of Judaism. Anti-Zionism is, by its very nature, anti-Judaism.

26.15
A fourth and particularly potent argument for Christian support of Israel has to do with evocation of Christian guilt for the Holocaust. Christian anti-Semitism is seen as providing the foundation and milieu in which the Nazi Holocaust was possible. Israel is claimed to be essential to protection of Jews today from 'another Holocaust.' It is implied that without not only Israel as a state but also a state that is absolutely secure against all enemies, Jews are vulnerable to a new Holocaust, which might break out at any time. It is implied that if Christians are truly repentant of their guilt for the Holocaust, the only way to show this is by total and unflagging support for the state of Israel, including everything which the present government of that state claims as necessary for its 'national security.'

26.16
Appeal to the Holocaust threads through all the other arguments for Christian support of Israel as well. In each case, any doubt or questioning of Israel's right to the promised land, that the founding of that state is a fulfilment of biblical prophecy and a redemptive event and that Jewish

nationalism is an integral part of Judaism is immediately ascribed to Christian anti-Judaism or anti-Semitism. Thus it is suggested that if Christians doubt any of these propositions, they are still in the grip of an unreconstructed anti-Judaism. It is this very anti-Judaism which was the root of the Holocaust. To be critical of Israel is to be still unrepentantly guilty of the Holocaust. In the second part of this essay, I wish to briefly examine each of these religious arguments. Each demands a much fuller critique, but the limits of this paper will allow only a brief outline of what questions need to be raised about each of these arguments.

God's promises to Abraham give the Jews an eternal and exclusive right to all of Palestine

26.17

A Christian exclusivist nationalism, either toward their own nation or toward the Jews as a nation, is a fundamental denial of the foundational Christian belief that God is a God of all nations, that no one nation is especially favored by God. A Christian reversion to a tribalistic, exclusivist concept of God is theologically and ethically unacceptable. Christians have often misconstrued their own notions of universalism to deny Jewish particularity and also to turn Christian universalism into a cultural imperialism of Christian peoples. Authentic universalism must avoid both a reversion of tribal ethnocentrism and also universalist imperialism. This means it must affirm a multi-particularist vision of the co-humanity of many peoples and cultures. One cannot use Jewish particularity to deny the rights of Palestinians, or the reverse. One must affirm a co-humanity of Jews and Palestinians that seeks, as far as possible, a just co-existence of both national communities.

26.18

Christians are often led to a one-sided assumption that Jews have an exclusive right to Palestine by an ignorance of the actual history of this area. This land has never been a land of one people, but a land of many peoples. Many peoples lived there before the rise of the brief moments of Hebrew political hegemony in antiquity. Many people continued to live side by side with those Hebrews, even during those brief moments of hegemony. Many peoples have come together, in continual migrations and amalgamations of peoples and cultures in this region, for the last two thousand years. These peoples became predominantly Muslim in the seventh century, with a significant Christian minority and a small Jewish minority. All three religious communities became Arabized in culture and language.

26.19

The descendants of those people are the Palestinians. Properly speaking, these were the people with primary rights to the land of Palestine in modern times. These were the people who were still the majority, representing 70 per cent of the population, when the land was partitioned in 1947. Thus whatever rights are given to the present Israeli Jewish population, it can only be on the basis of a recent construction of a national community in this region, not on the basis of ancient religious land claims. These recent 'facts' of history must be adjusted to make place for, at least, an equal claim to the land of those who were present as the majority population in the land until their forcible and unjust displacement by the Israeli military in 1948.

The founding of Israel is the fulfilment of prophecy and the beginning of redemption

26.20

For both Jews and Christians the idea of a messianic return to the land as part of redemption is premised on an ethical vision of what redemption means. In the Bible, and in the Jewish and Christian traditions of future historical fulfilment of redemptive hope, this means a healing of the enmity between nations. Swords are beaten into plowshares. The instruments of violence and death are transformed into the instruments of creation and cultivation of new life. Redemption is characterized by a flowering of justice and peace among nations. Both Christian and Jewish militant fundamentalisms ignore these ethical criteria for what is redemptive. This allows them to ignore the obvious fact that the foundation of Israel has not been a means of healing between nations, but of an enormous outbreak of new enmity between nations. Plowshares have been turned into swords on every side. The means of human livelihood have been starved to create the instruments of death.

26.21

The foundation of Israel has been for Palestinians what they call 'the catastrophe,' an unparalleled disaster which evicted 780,000 people from their homes and land in 1948. From this disaster have flowed continual disasters of more land confiscation, more evictions, repression of those still on the land, continual denials of justice, continual violence, injury, and death. Tens of thousands of Palestinians have died in this violence; also tens of thousands of Lebanese, Jordanians, Egyptians, Syrians, and other Arabs; fourteen thousand Israeli Jews have also died. The numbers of the wounded, the numbers of those whose lives have been shattered, are uncountable. In short, the founding of Israel is not a redemptive event. It is an event that has taken place very much within unredeemed history and as an expression of unredeemed modes of behavior between human peoples. To call an event with such results 'redemptive' and the 'beginning of messianic times' is a travesty of what is meant by those terms. This is false messianism, an attempt to clothe evil-producing events with the aura of divine sanctity. This is a false messianism to which Christians themselves have been all too prone in the past, clothing their own evil-producing political projects with the garb of messianic fulfilment.

26.22
This does not mean that the state of Israel is any worse than any number of other political projects of human groups today, or in the past, which have produced disastrous results for other people, and often for one's own people. It simply means that it cannot be clothed with a garb of special sanctity that obscures its actual ethical deficiencies. It is the nature of all false messianisms that the garb of redemptive hope is used to prevent truthful recognition of evil. Zionism, like many other disaster-producing revolutionary projects, is still operating with the ethics of competition and negation of others. It, and every other project of human hope, will begin to become redemptive only when it overcomes the ethics of competition and domination and begins to shape itself with the ethics of mutuality or love of neighbor as oneself.

Zionism of Jewish nationalism is integral to Judaism
26.23
The claim that Zionism, or Jewish nationalism, is integral to Judaism rests on a confusion between the communal nature of Judaism, in its classical form, and the modern concept of a nation-state. It is not accidental that when Zionism first arose, the vast majority of the leaders of all forms of Judaism rejected it as contrary to their understanding of Judaism. For Orthodox Jews, Zionism was an unholy project carried out by non-observant Jews and thus fundamentally contradictory to their religious belief in a messianic restoration of political sovereignty over the ancient homeland. For the Orthodox, this restoration could only take place as an expression of a redemptive process. This meant both the redemption of the Jews and a complementary redemption of all nations. It meant a restoration that would heal the enmity between the nations and bring world peace. These Orthodox leaders recognized that the Zionist secular political project, in the context of modern nationalism and imperialism, did not qualify as a fulfilment of this redemptive process.

26.24

Reform Jews also rejected Zionism because it denied their political universalism. They sought to detach Judaism as a religion from secular political identity and make the Jews a people who could become full and equal citizens of all nations.

26.25

It is incorrect to say that Judaism is unique in having a communal dimension that seeks to shape the entire familial, social, and political life of Jews as a whole. In fact, all classical religions have sought this same comprehensive scope. Christianity, in its classical form as Christendom, also Islam and Buddhism, among others, have in their classical form sought to shape a total system that informs all public and private life as religious states. It is precisely this political side of classical religion that has made it problematic for modern states, which are ethnically and religiously pluralistic. Both liberal Christianity and Reform Judaism sought to overcome this conflict by separating religion and state.

26.26

Today Jewish, Muslim, Christian, and even Buddhist and Hindu fundamentalisms threaten the establishment of just relations among different ethnic and religious groups living in the same state by reverting to these classical claims to religio-political exclusivism. The unjust treatment of the Palestinians by the state of Israel is rooted precisely in the effort to create an ethnically and religiously exclusive state, namely, a 'Jewish state.' It is this concept of Israel as a Jewish state that construes the existence of a nearly 40 per cent population of Palestinians in Israel and the Occupied Territories as a 'demographic problem.' This is a 'demographic problem' only if one defines Israel as a Jewish state, rather than accepting the fact that there are two national communities and three religious communities in this region. For justice and peace to be possible in Israel/Palestine, any state or states that encompass this region must accommodate and give equal civil rights to all members within this ethnic and religious pluralism.

Repentance of guilt for the Holocaust demands uncritical support of Israel

26.27

There is no doubt that Christians of the West bear a burden of guilt for the Holocaust because of their historical traditions of anti-Semitism and the way these traditions were used by Nazism to gain both active and passive acquiescence of Christians. However, one must ask what is appropriate repentance for the Holocaust. It would seem that the primary expressions of this must be to purge anti-Semitism from Christian teachings and their effects on Christian societies. It is not appropriate to construe such repentance as collaboration with injustice to another people, who are the victims of the state of Israel. To use guilt for the Holocaust to silence criticism of injustice to the Palestinians is not repentance but toadyism, on the Christian side, and blackmail, on the Jewish side.

26.28
On both the Christian and the Jewish side, I believe there must be a separation of the question of the Holocaust, and its theological and ethical consequences for each religion, and the questions raised by the state of Israel, with its ethical deficiencies. One has to examine how these two phenomena are interrelated symbolically and psychologically. In my talks on this issue of Israel and the Palestinians, I frequently get the question from Christians, 'How can Jews, with their experience of the Holocaust, turn around and become oppressors of Palestinians?' This implies that the Holocaust should have made Jews very concerned to avoid the oppression of other people.

26.29
However, some Jews have suggested a psychological link between the oppression of Palestinians and the Holocaust. One Jewish friend, who works with battered women, suggested that Israelis are like battered batterers. Like people who have been battered and abused as children, Israelis have a psychological need to batter others. Abuse of Palestinians becomes the way of 'getting even' for past abuse, of turning the tables of power and powerlessness.

26.30
I think there is some truth in this psychological connection between past abuse and a special Israeli psychological need to batter Palestinians. There is a clear tendency to turn Palestinians into symbolic Nazis, but powerless ones upon whom revenge can be meted out. There is also no doubt that the Holocaust has been enormously exploited by Zionist leaders to create in all Jews, in Israel and throughout the world, a psychology of fear and insecurity. This has been used to tie Jews to Israel as the symbol of security.

26.31
Yet the promotion of Israel as the place of 'security' for Jews becomes increasingly contradictory. In fact, nowhere in the last forty years have so many Jews been killed or injured as in Israel. This is not because of an incomprehensible 'cosmic hate' against Jews in general, but because the state of Israel has been built in an antagonistic relationship to the Arab and

Palestinian communities which generates a cycle of violence. Israel, in this sense, is not the place of Jewish security, but the source of a new stage of Jewish insecurity.

26.32

However, these psychological and symbolic connections with the Holocaust serve to confuse the real issues, for the political root of the antagonistic relation of Israel to the Palestinians does not lie in the Holocaust. It lies in the patterns of ethnic nationalism that shaped the ideology of Zionism in the 1890s-1920s, and in the pattern of British colonialism that shaped the Israeli military in the 1930s. Already in the first decades of Zionist settlement, sensitive humanist Zionists, such as Ahad Ha-Am, were making horrified criticisms of the patterns of ethnic antagonism, displacement of the Palestinian peasantry, and violence toward this displaced peasantry that characterized the Zionist settlers.

26.33

In 1930, Rabbi Judah Magnes was spelling out the consequence of an ethnically exclusive idea of a Jewish state that reads like a prediction of all that has happened since. It was the British in 1937 who first proposed the idea of a 'transfer of population;' that is, expulsion of Palestinians, as part of a scheme of partition of the land into a Jewish state and an Arab state which was to be annexed to Jordan. Already in 1937, British officer Orde Wingate was training what were to become the chief Arab-fighters of the Israeli Defence Force, such as Moshe Dayan, in the techniques of total warfare against Palestinian villagers. The Iron Fist, which Israel has used against the Palestinians, employs not only the same techniques, but rests on the same laws, constructed by the British in 1936-39 to put down the Palestinian revolt of that period.

26.34

Thus Israel's violent and discriminatory behavior toward Palestinians is rooted in a history of the Jewish *Yishuv* between 1910 and 1948. Holocaust survivors may have flocked there from 1948 to 1950, but they entered a state whose historical roots in the area were largely unknown to them. They did not shape nor did they control the actual policies of that state. They, and all other Jews, have received a mythical construction of the state of Israel as the solution to the Holocaust. This has served well to cement powerful emotional bonds to Israel. But these Holocaust survivors often found themselves treated with contempt by Israelis, who called them such names as 'soaps.' For Israelis, these survivors were the unpleasant reminder of vulnerability and history of suffering that they sought to negate.

26.35
These survivors should not be victimized once more by suggesting that it is they who originated the oppression of the Palestinians. This oppression and its racist culture have their roots in a Jewish version of a European racial nationalism and colonialism. It was Israelis shaped by this system of colonialist domination under the British Mandate who then laid hold of the symbol of the Holocaust as a tool of power. They exploited the emotions linked to symbols of past Jewish victimization to cover up and disguise the reality of colonialist patterns of racism, land confiscation, and expulsion of indigenous people.

26.36
Both Christians and Jews must recognize that power construed as domination over others creates violence, injustice, and hatred. Christians have been amply guilty of this in the past toward Jews, and also toward other peoples they have colonized, as well as toward each other. Such possibilities of power as domination are new to Jews. It is perhaps hard for them to switch rhetorical gears and recognize that they too can not only gain power, but use power unjustly. But the refusal to recognize this fact is creating increasing ethical self-delusion among Jews. Jewish religious and moral health demands a shift to a new rhetoric of self-understanding that accepts the problems of this new reality.

26.37
The dialogue and collaboration of Jews and Christians today cannot be based primarily on the innocent victim/guilty victimizer relation. It must become a collaboration and solidarity of two people who know both that they can abuse power and are seeking to help each other regain their prophetic voice toward injustice within their own and other societies. This means that both Jews and Western Christians must overcome their religious and ethnic hostility to Arabs and Muslim peoples. They must extend their embrace of solidarity to the Arab world as well, without in any way becoming sentimentally blind to parallel tendencies to violence and competitive domination in this culture as well.

26.38
In all these relations, one seeks a conversion that shifts from an ethic of competitive domination to an ethic of co-humanity that fosters a quest for mutual justice between neighbors who must live together in one land and on one earth. This quest will call forth the best of all three religious traditions, the traditions of compassion, forgiveness, and neighbor love, rather than

those religious ideologies that tend to foster violence, hatred, and mutual negation.

CRITIQUE

Once again radical differences over moral issues are apparent amongst Christians. For some, abortion, contraception, euthanasia and suicide are inherently sinful. For others, they are sinful in some contexts, but not in others. For some, it is only heterosexual activity, within the context of monogamy, that is permissible for the Christian. For others it is wrong to prejudge individuals' sexual relationships – marital or extra-marital: heterosexual or homosexual – without knowing the particularities of a specific loving relationship. For some, the maxims of the women's movement and presumptions of a multi-racial society are still anathema. For others, they are prerequisites of a satisfactory, present-day Christian moral code. By now, the reader will not need reminding that the moral responses of Christians to issues concerned with personal relationships divide them as much as they might unite them. The Extracts intentionally illustrate some of these divisions. Before seeking any points of unity between them, it is important to identify some of their individual weaknesses.

One of the central difficulties in the Fletcher Extract is that it shifts from one concept of euthanasia to another to suit the argument. In terms of the sixfold typology offered in the introduction (see *above*, p.459), he sometimes seems to envisage type a (22.1), sometimes type b (at the beginning of 22.3), sometimes c or d (at the end of 22.3), and sometimes e or f (22.4). Although there is a relationship between these various types, the ethical issues that they raise are often quite distinct and to fail to identify them only confuses the argument. Another crucial difficulty that many Christians have had with Fletcher's arguments on euthanasia concerns legislation. It is one thing to admit that at least types c to f should be allowed to the doctor if he or she is convinced that, in particular situations, they are right. It is quite another to suggest that there should be legislation to support this decision. To most legislators the difficulties of definition and the dangers of abuse have been obvious.

The Orthodox attitude towards divorce and remarriage as Ware sets it out faces a number of difficulties. He is aware of the apparent conflict within the tradition of viewing marriage both as an eternal sacrament and yet as dissolvable. His resolution of this conflict depends largely upon a notion of the authority entrusted by Christ to the Orthodox Church – a notion that other Christians may find debatable and perhaps in conflict with some of the more rigorist positions on divorce in the Gospels. The traditional Orthodox grounds for divorce that he sets out in 23.25 may also appear somewhat arbitrary to other Christians. Inevitably some of these grounds will now also appear somewhat anachronistic – for example the presumption that it is only the man who may fail to consummate the marriage, or that 'apostasy' should be a legitimate ground. In addition, the grounds given are largely fault based – the notion of 'total breakdown in personal relations' is allowed only by some Orthodox authorities.

Because of its social significance, Paul VI's Extract has been subjected to more criticism than any of the other Extracts. Even within Roman Catholicism, it has been widely disputed – although, of course, it remains a part of official teaching. Quite apart from overall judgments about its validity and the extent to which it is thought to be appropriate or not for present-day society, several internal weaknesses can be noticed. Firstly, it shares the same weakness as Aquinas' Text IV. A stress upon responsible parenthood is certainly vital to Christian ethics (and too easily ignored in situations of liberalised divorce and abortion). And a clear understanding that sexuality is concerned with procreation and not simply with individual pleasure, is also vital (and again too easily ignored). But, even if it is conceded that procreation is the obvious function of sexuality (Aquinas' position), or that sexuality has both a procreative and a unitive function (Paul VI's position), it does not follow that procreation, or even potential procreation should be the only indispensable function of human sexuality.

This point illustrates one of the central difficulties facing natural law theories (see *above*, p.86) – the validity of attempting to derive a human's moral end from a human's 'natural' tendencies. The second weakness within the Extract is linked to this point. It appears that both abortion (spontaneous abortion) and sterility (primary infertility) are 'natural' phenomena which separate sexual activity from procreation. Further, sexual activity is 'naturally' not exclusively heterosexual, since forms of individualised sexual activity occur spontaneously in sleep and for some homosexual predispositions are increasingly seen as 'natural'. Nature, then, would appear to be more ambiguous than either Aquinas or Paul VI suppose. The latter shows himself aware of some of these ambiguities (24.24), but he regards them only as natural forms of spacing births, instituted by God, which are not to be interfered with by humans.

It is this contention which makes him vulnerable to a third criticism. Fletcher might have pointed out to him that, in a sense, the whole of modern medicine is 'a form of human self-assertion or a demonic pretension, by which men, especially physicians, try to put themselves in God's place' (22.4). Few would wish to use this argument to justify every conceivable act of medical intervention, but many have asked why barrier and hormonal methods of contraception should be singled out as being particularly intrusive.

Perhaps Enda McDonagh more accurately reflects much recent Catholic opinion in this area when he writes, at the end of the same decade, that, 'no longer free to reach for his manual to find the answer to a particular problem, the Catholic student of moral theology finds himself confronted with a bewildering range of information, analysis and opinion on an increasing range of problems' (*Doing the Truth*, p.14). Certainly, in this Textbook, pluralism is as apparent amongst Roman Catholics as it is amongst non-Roman Catholics.

The fraught area of racism is represented in Extracts 25 and 26. If the first tends to suffer from being too general, the second may appear too one-sided for many. However, in the context of a generalised critique that Christians have been too prone to racism and anti-Semitism, both Extracts supply alternative evidence in the opposite direction. Prophetic voices on racism have come from within Christianity over the years despite the damning evidence of racism within some of its history. The WCC document and Ruether both argue for an inclusive understanding of God and for Christians to side with the powerless in a world too often characterised by political domination. Nevertheless, given evidence of the historic association of Christianity (especially in Text XV) which she herself has done so much to expose, it has surprised many that Ruether has written so forcefully in this area. Doubtless she would counter this criticism by arguing that racism can sadly become a feature of the victims of racism and that, whilst this may be understandable, it is still unacceptable.

Despite these very real weaknesses within each of the Extracts and, despite the obvious differences of moral belief between them and between the Texts, two points of unity might be suggested. They depend upon two axioms – these might be termed the adeodatic axiom and the agapistic axiom. The first is a general theistic axiom based upon the presupposition that all life is God-given, whereas the second is a specifically Christian presupposition that *agape* should be intrinsic to all personal relationships. Unambiguous and incontrovertible sets of moral prescriptions for specific issues can be supplied by neither of these axioms. It seems likely that Christians will continue to disagree with each on many issues within social and personal ethics. But both can set parameters within which most Christian thought on ethical issues might be happy to operate.

The adeodatic axiom would suggest that the theist can accept that life is entirely neither sacred nor profane. Surely, Fletcher, through Temple, is right to insist that, for the Christian, sanctity is not *in* human life (22.5). Indeed, for the theist generally, a notion of God-givenness implies a clear distinction between Creator and creature. If humans, as creatures, are to be regarded in any sense as holy, it is only a holiness derived wholly from God. From the philosophical perspectives the adjective 'holy' is unique in religious language: all other adjectives are primarily human characteristics, applied only analogically to God, whereas 'holy' is primarily a divine characteristic, applied only analogically to humans. Thus, for the theist, any 'rights' that might go with this life, are God-given, not inherent possessions. As a result, many theists will continue to be cautious about agreeing that people have 'an inherent right to take their own lives' or that women have an inherent right to abortion. Because life is viewed in the transcendent context of God-givenness it cannot be regarded either as entirely profane. It is a divine gift and, therefore, cannot be regarded casually. Any action or behaviour which treats human life casually undermines the adeodatic axiom. Casual sexual relationships, abortion on demand, irresponsible parenthood, legalised direct forms of euthanasia, sexism and racialism, all have a tendency to do just this. So, it is hardly surprising that theists tend to be cautious about agreeing to them. Even though amongst theists there are obvious differences on all of these issues, a degree of caution would seem to be suggested by the notion of adeodasis. If all human life is a gift from God, our appropriate response might best be depicted as gratitude (cf. Gregorios in 18.28).

The agapeistic axiom would suggest that, for the Christian, an appropriate response to human life is also *agape*. Because of the debates generated by Situation ethics, it is possible to miss this unifying feature of Christian personal ethics. Since the debates of the 1960s, most exponents of Christian ethics might agree that pure agapism is inadequate. They might also agree that *agape* is not the only principle that can be derived from the Gospel. But neither of these agreements invalidates the contention that *agape* is crucial to a Christian understanding of personal relationships. Many might agree with Niebuhr that individualised understandings of *agape* cannot resolve political complexities. Nevertheless, Niebuhr was the first to admit that, at least on personal ethical issues, *agape* is crucial. In Christian understanding *agape* denotes both God's relationship to humans and the relationship that God requires people to have with their fellows. Within the context of Christian ethics, all sexual relationships should be, not just non-casual, but agapeistic. *Agape* should be the characteristic of all of our interpersonal behaviour, whether this behaviour is between sexes or between 'races'. Christians will still disagree with each other on dilemmas such as abortion. But if their eventual decisions are judged to be un-agapistic, they will thereby also be judged to be unChristian. On such issues, pure pragmatism, for example, is not a defensible Christian approach. Whilst *agape* might not be the whole of Christian ethics, it is nonetheless fundamental to it.

Neither axiom is sufficient in itself. For most of the exponents of Christian ethics surveyed in this Textbook, *agape* is held in tension with justice and, in the Synoptic picture of Jesus, with moral indignation and anger at human sin and wrong-doing. The adeodatic axiom is also held in tension with the sinfulness of much of the human 'given', and may even at times be in tension with *agape*. An adequate understanding of Christian ethics must never seek to ignore or eliminate this tension. Rather it should regard it as one of the most creative features of Christian ethics. For the Christian this world is always a mixture of the 'now' and the 'not yet', of 'signs of the Kingdom' but not 'the Kingdom all in all'. Creative tension may indeed be the hallmark of Christian ethics at its best.

BIBLIOGRAPHY

Ethics

ADKINS, A.W.H., *Merit and Responsibility*, Oxford University Press, Oxford, 1960.

ATKINSON, R.F., *Conduct: An Introduction to Moral Philosophy*, Macmillan, London, 1969.

BAIER, K., *The Moral Point of View: A Rational Basis of Ethics*, Cornell University Press, Ithaca, New York, 1958.

BEAUCHAMP, Tom L., & CHILDRESS, James F., *Principles of Biomedical Ethics*, Oxford University Press, New York, 1983.

BRADLEY, F.H., *Ethical Studies*, Oxford University Press, Oxford, Second Edition, 1927.

BROAD, C.D., *Ethics and the History of Philosophy*, Routledge & Kegan Paul, London, 1952.

CAMPBELL, A.V., *Moral Dilemmas in Medicine*, Churchill Livingstone, Edinburgh and London, 1972.

CARRITT, E.F., *Theory of Morals*, Oxford University Press, Oxford, 1928.

CULVER, Charles, & GERT, Bernard, *Philosophy in Medicine*, Oxford University Press, New York, 1982.

DENNIS, N., & HALSEY, A.H., *English Ethical Socialism*, Oxford University Press, Oxford, 1988.

DEVLIN, Patrick, *The Enforcement of Morals*, Oxford University Press, Oxford, 1965.

DEWEY John (ed), *Theory of the Moral Life*, Arnold Isenberg, Holt, Rinehart & Winston, New York, 1960.

DONALDSON, J., *Key Issues in Business Ethics*, Academy Press, London, 1989.

DOWNIE, R.S., & TELFER, E., *Respect for Persons*, Allen & Unwin, London, 1969.

DOWNIE, R.S., *Roles and Values*, Methuen, London, 1971.

DOWNIE, R.S., & TELFER, E., *Caring and Curing*, Methuen, London, 1980.

DOWNIE, R.S., & CALMAN, K.C., *Healthy Respect: Ethics and Health Care*, Faber & Faber, London, 1987.

DUNSTAN, G.R., & SELLER, Mary J. (ed), *Consent in Medicine*, King Edward's Hospital Fund and Oxford University Press, London, 1983.

DWORKIN, Ronald, *Taking Rights Seriously*, Duckworth, London, 1978.

DWORKIN, Ronald, *Life's Dominion*, Harper Collins, London, 1993.

EMMET, Dorothy, *Rules, Roles and Relations*, Macmillan, London, 1966.

EWING, A.C., *The Definition of Good*, Routledge & Kegan Paul, London, 1952, and The Free Press, New York, 1965.

FEINBERG, Joel, *Rights, Justice and the Bounds of Liberty*, Princeton University Press, New Jersey, 1980.

FINNIS, John, *Natural Law and Natural Rights*, Oxford University Press, Oxford, 1980.

FLEW, A.G.N., *Evolutionary Ethics*, Macmillan, London, and St Martins, New York, 1967.

FOOT, Philippa (ed), *Theories of Ethics*, Oxford University Press, Oxford and New York, 1967.

FOOT, Philippa, *Virtues and Vices and Other Essays in Moral Philosophy*, Blackwell, Oxford, 1981.

FRANKENA, W.K., *Ethics*, Prentice-Hall, N.J., Second Edition, 1973.

FRANKENA, W.K. & GRANROSE, J.R. (ed), *Introductory Readings in Ethics*, Prentice-Hall, N.J., 1974.

GARNER, R.T. and ROSEN, Bernard, *Moral Philosophy*, Macmillan, New York, 1967.

GERT, Bernard, *The Moral Rules*, Harper & Row, New York, 1970.

GILLON, Raanan, *Philosophical Medical Ethics*, Wiley, Chichester, 1991.

GLOVER, Jonathan, *Causing Death and Saving Lives*, Pelican, Harmondsworth, 1984.

GRICE, G.R., *The Grounds of Moral Judgment*, Cambridge University Press, Cambridge, 1967.

HARE, R.M., *The Language of Morals*, Clarendon Press, Oxford, 1952.

HARE, R.M., *Freedom and Reason*, Clarendon Press, Oxford, 1963.

HARE, R.M., *Moral Thinking: Its Levels, Methods and Point*, Oxford University Press, Oxford and New York, 1981.

HARMAN, Gilbert, *The Nature of Morality: An Introduction to Ethics*, Oxford University Press, Oxford and New York, 1977.

HARRIS, John, *The Value of Life: An Introduction to Medical Ethics*, Routledge, London, 1992.

HARRIS, John, *Wonderwoman and Superman*, Oxford University Press, Oxford, 1992.

HART, H.L.A., *Law, Liberty and Morality*, Oxford University Press, Oxford and New York, 1963.

HART, H.L.A., *Punishment and Responsibility*, Oxford University Press, Oxford and New York, 1968.

HASTINGS CENTER, *The Teaching of Ethics in Higher Education*, series of books on ethics in a variety of disciplines, Hastings Center, Hastings-on-Hudson, NYS, 1980.

HEARN, T.K. (ed), *Studies in Utilitarianism*, Meredith, New York, 1971.

HEYD, D., *Genethics: Moral Issues in the Creation of People*, University of California Press, Berkeley, 1992.

HOSPERS, J., *Human Conduct*, Hart-Davis, London, 1963.

HUDSON, W.D. (ed), *The Is-Ought Question*, Macmillan, London, 1969.

HUDSON, W.D., *A Century of Moral Philosophy*, Lutterworth, Guildford, 1980.

HUDSON, W.D., *Modern Moral Philosophy*, Doubleday, New York, 1970, and Macmillan, London, rev. 1984.

KAMENKA, E., *Marxism and Ethics*, Macmillan, London and New York, 1969.

KAMENKA, E. & TAY, A.E.S. (ed), *Human Rights*, Edward Arnold, London, 1978.

KENNY, A., *Action, Emotion and Will*, Routledge & Kegan Paul, London, 1963.

KENNY, A., *Will, Freedom and Power*, Oxford University Press, Oxford, 1975.

LYONS, D., *Forms and Limits of Utilitarianism*, Clarendon Press, Oxford, 1975.

MACINTYRE, Alasdair, *A Short History of Ethics*, Macmillan, New York, 1966 and Routledge & Kegan Paul, London, 1967.

MACINTYRE, Alasdair, *Against the Self-images of the Age*, Duckworth, London, 1971.

MACINTYRE, Alasdair, *After Virtue*, Duckworth, London, 1981.

MACINTYRE, Alasdair, *Whose Justice? Which Rationality?*, Duckworth, London, 1988.

MACKIE, J.L., *Ethics: Inventing Right and Wrong*, Penguin, London, 1977.

MACLEAN, Anne, *The Elimination of Morality*, Routledge, London, 1993.

MIDGELY, Mary, *Heart and Mind*, Methuen, London, 1983.

MOORE, G.E., *Principia Ethica*, Cambridge University Press, Cambridge, 1903 and Oxford University Press, London and New York, 1966.

MOORE, G.E., *Ethics*, Williams & Norgate, London, 1912.

MURDOCH, Iris, *The Sovereignty of the Good*, Routledge & Kegan Paul, 1970.

NIELSEN, Kai, *Ethics Without God*, Pemberton Books, London, 1973.

NOWELL-SMITH, P.H. *Ethics*, Blackwell, Oxford, 1957.

NUSSBAUM, Martha C., *The Fragility of Goodness: Luck and Ethics in Greek Tragedy and Philosophy*, Cambridge University Press, Cambridge, 1986.

O'NEILL, Onora, *Faces of Hunger: An Essay on Poverty, Justice and Development*, Allen and Unwin, London, 1986.

PRICHARD, H.A., *Moral Obligation: Essays and Lectures*, Clarendon Press, Oxford, 1949.

PRIOR, A.N., *Logic and the Basis of Ethics*, Oxford University Press, Oxford, 1949.

RACHELS, James, *Moral Problems*, Harper & Row, New York, 1975.

RACHELS, James, *The End of Life: Euthanasia and Morality*, Oxford University Press, Oxford, 1986.

RAPHAEL, D.D. (ed), *Political Theory and the Rights of Man*, Macmillan, London, 1967.

RAWLS, John, *A Theory of Justice*, Oxford University Press, Oxford and New York, 1973.

REGAN, T. & SINGER, P. (ed), *Animal Rights and Human Obligations*, Prentice-Hall, New Jersey, 1976.

ROSS, W.D., *The Right and the Good*, Clarendon Press, Oxford, 1930.

ROSS, W.D., *Foundations of Ethics*, Clarendon Press, Oxford, 1939.

SCHLICK, M., *The Problems of Ethics*, Prentice Hall, New York, 1938.

SEN, A. and WILLIAMS B. (ed), *Utilitarianism and Beyond*, Cambridge University Press, Cambridge, 1982.

SIDGWICK, H., *Methods of Ethics*, Macmillan, London, 1907.

SINGER, M.G., *Generalisation in Ethics*, Eyre & Spottiswoode, London, 1963.

SINGER, Peter, *The Expanding Circle: Ethics and Sociobiology*, Clarendon, Oxford, 1981.

SINGER, Peter (ed), *In Defence of Animals*, Blackwell, Oxford, 1985.

SINGER, Peter (ed), *Applied Ethics*, Oxford University Press, Oxford, 1986.

SMART, J.J.C., & WILLIAMS, B., *Utilitarianism: For and Against*, Cambridge University Press, Cambridge, 1973.

STEVENSON, C.L., *Ethics and Language*, Yale University Press, New Haven, 1945.

STEVENSON, C.L., *Facts and Values: Studies in Ethical Analysis*, Yale University Press, New Haven, 1963.

STOUT, J., *Ethics After Babel: The Language of Morals and Their Discontents*, Beacon Press, Boston, 1988.

TAYLOR, A.E., *The Faith of a Moralist*, 2 vols, Macmillan, London, 1932.

TAYLOR, Charles, *Sources of the Self*, Harvard University Press, Cambridge, 1989.

TAYLOR. Charles, *The Ethics of Authenticity*, Harvard University Press, Cambridge, 1992.

TUCK, R., *Natural Right Theories*, Cambridge University Press, Cambridge, 1979.

URMSON, J.O., *The Emotive Theory of Ethics*, Hutchinson, London, 1968.

VEATCH, Robert M., *A Theory of Medical Ethics*, Basic Books, New York, 1981.

WALDRON, Jeremy (ed), *Theories of Rights*, Oxford University Press, Oxford, 1984.

WALKER, Nigel, *Why Punish?*, Oxford University Press, Oxford, 1991.

WALTERS, William, & SINGER, Peter, *Test-Tube Babies*, Oxford University Press, Melbourne, 1982.

WARD, Keith, *The Development of Kant's View of Ethics*, Blackwell, Oxford, 1972.

WARNOCK. G.J., *Contemporary Moral Philosophy*, Macmillan, London, 1966 and St Martin's Press, New York, 1967.

WARNOCK, G.J., *The Object of Morality*, Methuen, London, 1971.

WARNOCK, Mary, *Existentialist Ethics*, Macmillan, London, 1967.

WARNOCK, Mary, *Ethics Since 1900*, Oxford University Press, Oxford and New York, Third Edition, 1978.

WINCH, Peter, *Ethics and Action*, Routledge & Kegan Paul, London, 1972.

WILLIAMS, Bernard, *Ethics and the Limits of Philosophy*, Fontana, London, 1985.

Christian Ethics

ACCM, *Teaching Christian Ethics*, SCM Press, London, 1974.

BAELZ, Peter, *Ethics and Belief*, Sheldon, London, 1977.

BAILEY, D.S., *Homosexuality and the Western Christian Tradition*, Longmans, London, 1955.

BAILEY, D.S., *The Man/Woman Relation in Christian Thought*, SCM Press, London, 1959.

BAINTON, Roland H., *Sex, Love and Marriage: A Christian Survey*, Fontana, London, 1958.

BAINTON, Roland H., *Christian Attitudes Toward War and Peace: A Historical Survey and Critical Re-evaluation*, Abingdon, New York, 1960, and Hodder & Stoughton, London, 1961.

BARTH, Karl, *Ethics*, T&T Clark, Edinburgh, 1981.

BEACH, Waldo, & NIEBUHR, H. Richard, *Christian Ethics: Sources of the Living Tradition*, Ronald Press, New York, Second Edition, 1973.

BENNETT, John C., *Christian Ethics and Social Policy*, Scribners, New York, 1946.

BENNETT, John C. (ed), *Storm Over Ethics*, Bethany Press, Philadelphia, 1967.

BENNETT, John C., *The Radical Imperative*, Westminster, Philadelphia, 1975.

BERDYAEV, Nicolas, *Christianity and Class War*, Sheed & Ward, London, 1931.

BERDYAEV, Nicolas, *The Destiny of Man*, Scribners, New York, and Geoffrey Bles, London, 1935.

BERDYAEV, Nicolas, *Freedom and the Spirit*, Scribners, New York, and Geoffrey Bles, London, 1935.

BERDYAEV, Nicolas, *The Meaning of History*, Scribners, New York, and Geoffrey Bles, London, 1936.

BERDYAEV, Nicolas, *The Realm of Spirit and the Realm of Caesar*, Gollancz, London, 1952, and Harper, New York, 1953.

BOCK, Paul, *In Search of a Responsible World Society: The Social Teachings of the World Council of Churches*, Westminster Press, Philadelphia, 1974.

BONHOEFFER, Dietrich, *Sanctorum Communio*, Collins, London, 1963.

BONHOEFFER, Dietrich, *No Rusty Swords*, Harper & Row, New York, and Collins, London, 1965.

BONHOEFFER, Dietrich, *The Cost of Discipleship*, SCM Press, London, 1978.

BONHOEFFER, Dietrich, *Ethics*, Macmillan, New York, 1955, and SCM Press, London, rev. ed. 1978.

BONINO, José Míguez, *Towards a Christian Political Ethics*, Fortress Press, Philadelphia, 1983.

BROWN, David, *Choices: Ethics and the Christian*, Blackwell, Oxford, 1983.

BRUNNER, Emil, *The Divine Imperative*, Macmillan, New York, and Lutterworth, London, 1937.

BRUNNER, Emil, *Justice and the Social Order*, Harper, New York, and Lutterworth, London, 1945.

CADOUX, C.J., *The Early Christian Attitude to War*, London, 1919.

CAHILL, Lisa S., *Sex, Gender and Christian Ethics*, Cambridge University Press, Cambridge, 1995.

CHILDRESS, James F., & MACQUARRIE, John (ed), *A New Dictionary of Christian Ethics*, Westminster Press, Philadelphia, 1986 and SCM Press, London, 1987.

CHILTON, Bruce, & McDONALD, J.I.H., *Jesus and the Ethics of the Kingdom*, SPCK, London, 1987.

CHOPP, Rebecca, *The Praxis of Suffering: An Interpretation of Liberation and Political Theologies*, Orbis, Maryknoll, New York, 1986.

CHOPP, Rebecca, *The Power to Speak: Feminism, Language, God*, Crossroad, New York, 1989.

CHOPP, Rebecca, *Liberation Theology and Pastoral Theology*, Journal of Pastoral Care Publications, Decatur, DA, 1990.

CHURCH OF ENGLAND, Board for Social Responsibility, *Homosexual Relationships*, Church Information Office, London, 1979.

CHURCH OF ENGLAND, Board for Social Responsibility, *On Dying Well*, Church Information Office, London, 1975.

CHURCH OF ENGLAND, Board for Social Responsibility, *The Church and the Bomb*, Hodder & Stoughton, London, 1982.

CHURCH OF ENGLAND, Board for Social Responsibility, *Peacemaking in a Nuclear Age*, Church House Publishing, 1988.

CHURCH OF ENGLAND, Board for Social Responsibility, *Crime, Justice and the Demands of the Gospel*, Church House Publishing, 1991.

CHURCH OF SCOTLAND, Reports to the General Assembly, *God's Will for the Church and Nation*, (*The Baillie Report*), SCM Press, London, 1946.

CLARK, Stephen R.L., *The Moral Status of Animals*, Clarendon, Oxford, 1977.

CLARK, Stephen R.L., *The Nature of the Beast: Are Animals Moral?*, Clarendon, 1982.

CLARK, Stephen R.L., *Civil Peace and Sacred Order*, Clarendon, Oxford, 1989.

CLARK, Stephen R.L., *A Parliament of Souls*, Clarendon, Oxford, 1990.

CLARK, Stephen R.L., *How to Think About the Earth*, Mowbray, London, 1993.

COLEMAN, Peter, *Gay Christians: A Moral Dilemma*, SCM Press, London, 1989.

COOK, David, *The Moral Maze*, SPCK, London, 1983.

COUNTRYMAN, L.William, *Dirt, Greed and Sex: Sexual Ethics in the New Testament and Their Implications for Today*, Fortress, Philadelphia, 1988, and SCM Press, London, 1989.

CRONIN, Kieran, *Rights and Christian Ethics*, Cambridge University Press, Cambridge, 1992.

CUPITT, Don, *Crisis of Moral Authority: The Dethronement of Christianity*, Westminster, Philadelphia, and Lutterworth, London, 1972.

CUPITT, Don, *The New Christian Ethics*, SCM Press, London, 1988.

CURRAN, Charles E., *Catholic Moral Theology in Dialogue*, Fides, Notre Dame, Indiana, 1972.

CURRAN, Charles E., *Ongoing Revision: Studies in Moral Theology*, Fides, Notre Dame, Indiana, 1975.

CURRAN, Charles E. (ed), *Absolutes in Moral Theology?*, Greenwood Press, Westport, 1975.

CURRAN, Charles E., *Issues in Sexual and Medical Ethics*, University of Notre Dame, Notre Dame, 1978.

CURRAN, Charles E. & McCORMICK, R. (ed), *Readings in Moral Theology*, Paulist Press, New York, 1980.

CURRY, Dean C. (ed), *Evangelicals and the Bishops' Pastoral Letter*, Eerdmans, Grand Rapids, 1984.

DEMANT, V.A., *Religion and the Decline of Capitalism*, Faber & Faber, London, 1952.

DEMANT, V.A., *An Exposition of Christian Sexual Ethics*, Hodder, London, 1963.

D'ENTRÉVES, A.P. (ed), *Aquinas: Selected Political Writings*, Blackwell, Oxford, 1948.

D'ENTRÉVES, A.P., *Natural Law: An Introduction to Legal Philosophy*, Hutchinson, 1951.

D'ENTRÉVES, A.P., *The Notion of the State*, Clarendon, Oxford, 1967.

DOMINION, Jack, *Passionate and Compassionate Love: A Vision for Christian Marriage*, Darton, Longman & Todd, 1991.

DUNSTAN, G.R., *The Artifice of Ethics*, SCM Press, London, 1974.

DUNSTAN, G.R. (ed), *Duty and Discernment*, SCM Press, London, 1975.

DUSSEL, E., *Ethics and the Theology of Liberation*, Maryknoll, New York, 1978.

DWYER, Judith A. (ed), *The Catholic Bishops and Nuclear War: A Critique and Analysis of the Pastoral The Challenge of Peace*, Georgetown University Press, Washington DC, 1984.

FAIRWEATHER, Ian C.M., & MCDONALD, J.I.H., *The Quest for Christian Ethics*, Handsel Press, Edinburgh, 1984.

FLETCHER, Joseph, *Morals and Medicine*, Princeton University Press, NJ, 1954 and Gollancz, London, 1955.

FLETCHER, Joseph, *Situation Ethics*, Westminster, Philadelphia, and SCM Press, London, 1966.

FLETCHER, Joseph, *Moral Responsibility: Situation Ethics at Work*, Westminster, Philadelphia, and SCM Press, London, 1967.

FLETCHER, Joseph, *Humanhood: Essays in Biomedical Ethics*, Prometheus Books, Buffalo, 1979.

FORELL, George Wolfgang (ed), *Christian Social Teachings: A Reader in Christian Social Ethics from the Bible to the Present*, Augsburg, Minneapolis, 1971.

FORELL, George Wolfgang, *History of Christian Ethics*, Augsburg, Minneapolis, 1979.

FORRESTER, Duncan B., *Christianity and the Future of Welfare*, Epworth, London, 1985.

FORRESTER, Duncan B., *Beliefs, Values and Policies: Conviction Politics in a Secular Age*, Clarendon, Oxford, 1989.

GARDNER, E. Clinton, *Justice and Christian Ethics*, Cambridge University Press, Cambridge, 1995.

GILL, Robin, *Prophecy and Praxis*, Marshall, Morgan & Scott, London, 1981.

GILL, Robin, *The Cross Against the Bomb*, Epworth, London, 1984.

GILL, Robin, *Christian Ethics in Secular Worlds*, T&T Clark, Edinburgh, 1991.

GILL, Robin, *Moral Communities*, Exeter University Press, Exeter, 1992.

GONZALEZ, Justo, *Faith and Wealth: A History of Early Christian Ideas on the Origin, Significance, and Use of Money*, Harper & Row, San Francisco, 1990.

GREEN, Ronald M., *Religious Reason: The Rational and Moral Basis of Religious Belief*, Oxford University Press, New York, 1978.

GREEN, Ronald M., *Religion and Moral Reason*, Oxford University Press, New York, 1988.

GUSTAFSON, James M., *Christ and the Moral Life*, Harper & Row, New York, 1968.

GUSTAFSON, James M., *The Church as Moral Decision-Maker*, Pilgrim, Philadelphia, 1970.

GUSTAFSON, James M., *Can Ethics Be Christian?*, University of Chicago Press, Chicago, 1975.

GUSTAFSON, James M., *Protestant and Roman Catholic Ethics*, University of Chicago Press, Chicago, and SCM Press, London, 1978.

GUSTAFSON, James M., *Theology and Ethics*, Oxford University Press, New York and Oxford, 1981.

HALLETT, Garth, *Christian Moral Reasoning*, Notre Dame University Press, Indiana, 1983.

HÄRING, Bernard, *The Law of Christ*, 3 vols, Newman Press, Westminster, MD., 1961-6.

HÄRING, Bernard, *Medical Ethics*, Fides, Notre Dame, Indiana, and St Paul, Slough, 1972.

HÄRING, Bernard, *Free and Faithful in Christ*, 3 vols, Seabury, New York, and St Paul, Slough, 1978.

HARNED, David Baily, *Grace and Common Life*, University of Virginia, VA, 1971.

HARNED, David Baily, *Faith and Virtue*, Pilgrim, Philadelphia, 1973.

HARRIS, P. (ed), *On Human Life: An Examination of Humanae Vitae*, Burns & Oates, London, 1968.

HAUERWAS, Stanley, *Vision and Virtue: Essays in Christian Ethical Reflection*, Fides, Notre Dame, Indiana, 1974.

HAUERWAS, Stanley, *Character and the Christian Life: A Study in Theological Ethics*, Trinity University Press, San Antonio, 1975.

HAUERWAS, Stanley, *A Community of Character*, University of Notre Dame Press, Indiana, 1981.

HAUERWAS, Stanley, *The Peaceable Kingdom*, University of Notre Dame Press, Indiana, 1983, and SCM Press, London, 1984.

HAUERWAS, Stanley, *Against the Nations*, Winston Press, Minneapolis, 1985.

HAUERWAS, Stanley, *Suffering Presence*, University of Notre Dame Press, Indiana, 1986, and T&T Clark, Edinburgh, 1988.

HAUERWAS, Stanley, *Christian Existence Today*, Labyrinth Press, Durham, NC, 1988.

HAUERWAS, Stanley, *Naming the Silences*, Eerdmans, Grand Rapids, Michigan, 1990.

HAUERWAS, Stanley, *After Christendom*, Abingdon Press, Nashville, 1991.

HEBBLETHWAITE, Brian, *The Adequacy of Christian Ethics*, Marshall, Morgan & Scott, London, 1981.

HELM, Paul (ed), *Divine Commands and Morality*, Oxford University Press, Oxford, 1981.

HENGEL, Martin, *Property and Riches in the Early Church*, SCM Press, London, 1974.

HENGEL, Martin, *Victory Over Violence*, SPCK, London, 1975.

HIGGINSON, Richard, *Dilemmas: A Christian Approach to Moral Decision-Making*, Hodder & Stoughton, London, 1988.

HOLLENBACH, David, *Claims in Conflict: Retrieving and Renewing the Catholic Human Rights Tradition*, Paulist Press, New York, 1979.

HOLMES, Arthur, F., *War and Christian Ethics*, Baker, New York, 1975.

HOLMES, Arthur, F., *Ethics: Approaching Moral Decisions*, Downers Grove, IL, 1984.

HOULDEN, J.L., *Ethics and the New Testament*, Mowbrays, Oxford, 1973.

HUGHES, Gerard J., *Authority in Morals*, Sheed & Ward, London, 1983.

JONES, Richard, *Groundwork of Christian Ethics*, Epworth Press, London, 1985.

KEANE, Philip, *Christian Ethics and Imagination*, Paulist Press, New York, 1984.

KEELING, Michael, *The Foundations of Christian Ethics*, T&T Clark, Edinburgh, 1990.

KIRK, Kenneth E., *Some Principles of Moral Theology*, Longmans, Green, London, 1920.

KIRK, Kenneth E., *Conscience and its Problems: An Introduction to Casuistry*, Longmans, Green, London, 1927.

KIRK, Kenneth E., *The Vision of God: The Doctrine of the Summum Bonum*, Longmans, Green, London, 1931.

KNOX, John, *The Ethic of Jesus in the Teaching of the Church: Its Authority and Its Relevance*, Abingdon, New York, 1961, and Epworth, London, 1962.

LANGFORD, Michael, *The Good and the True: An Introduction to Christian Ethics*, SCM Press, London, 1985.

LEHMANN, Paul, *Ethics in a Christian Context*, Harper & Row, New York, and SCM Press, London, 1963.

LEHMANN, Paul, *The Transfiguration of Politics*, Harper & Row, New York, 1975.

LINACRE CENTRE, *Euthanasia and Clinical Practice*, Linacre, London, 1982.

LINZEY, Andrew, *Christianity and the Rights of Animals*, SPCK, London, 1987.

LINZEY, Andrew, *Compassion for Animals*, SPCK, London, 1988.

LITTLE, David, & TWISS, Sumner B., *Comparative Religious Ethics: A New Method*, Harper & Row, New York, 1978.

LONG, Edward LeRoy, Jr, *Conscience and Compromise: An Approach to Protestant Casuistry*, Westminster, Philadelphia, 1954.

LONG, Edward LeRoy, Jr, *A Survey of Christian Ethics*, Oxford University Press, New York and Oxford, 1967.

LONG, Edward LeRoy, Jr, *A Survey of Recent Christian Ethics*, Oxford University Press, New York and Oxford, 1982.

McDONAGH, Enda, *Invitation and Response: Essays in Christian Moral Theology*, Gill & Macmillan, Dublin, 1972.

McDONAGH, Enda, *Gift and Call*, Gill & Macmillan, Dublin, 1975.

McDONAGH, Enda, *Doing the Truth*, Gill & Macmillan, Dublin, 1979.

McDONALD, J.I.H., *Biblical Interpretation and Christian Ethics*, Cambridge University Press, Cambridge, 1993.

McFAGUE, Sallie, *Metaphorical Theology: Models of God in Religious Language*, Fortress Press, Philadelphia, 1982.

McFAGUE, Sallie, *Models of God: Theology for an Ecological, Nuclear Age*, Fortress Press, Philadelphia, and SCM Press, London, 1987.

McFAGUE, Sallie, *The Body of God: An Ecological Theology*, Fortress Press, Minneapolis, 1993.

MACGREGOR, G.H.C., *The New Testament Basis of Pacifism*, James Clarke, London, 1936.

MACKEY, James P., *Power and Christian Ethics*, Cambridge University Press, Cambridge, 1994.

McLAREN, Robert Bruce, *Christian Ethics: Foundations and Practice*, Prentice Hall, Englewood Cliffs, NJ, 1994.

McCLENDON, James W. Jr, *Ethics: Systematic Theology*, Abingdon Press, Nashville, 1986.

MACNAMARA, Vincent, *Faith and Ethics: Recent Roman Catholicism*, Gill and Macmillan, Dublin, 1985.

MACQUARRIE, John (ed), *A Dictionary of Christian Ethics*, SCM Press, London, 1967 (see CHILDRESS for revised edition).

MACQUARRIE, John, *Three Issues in Ethics*, Harper & Row, New York, and SCM Press, London, 1970.

MAHONEY, John, *Seeking the Spirit*, Sheed & Ward, London and New York, 1981.

MAHONEY, John, *Bioethics and Belief*, Sheed and Ward, London, 1984.

MAHONEY, John, *The Making of Moral Theology: A Study of the Roman Catholic Tradition*, Clarendon, Oxford, 1987.

MANSON, T.W., *Ethics and the Gospel*, (ed. R.H. Preston), SCM Press, London, 1960.

MARKHAM, Ian S., *Plurality and Christian Ethics*, Cambridge University Press, Cambridge, 1994.

MARRIN, Albert (ed), *War and the Christian Conscience: From Augustine to Martin Luther King, Jr*, Henry Regnery, Chicago, 1971.

MEALAND, David L., *Poverty and Expectation in the Gospels*, SPCK, London, 1980.

MEEKS, Wayne A., *The Moral World of the First Christians*, Westminster Press, Philadelphia, 1986.

MEEKS, Wayne A., *The Origins of Christian Morality*, Yale University Press, New Haven, 1993.

MITCHELL, Basil, *Law, Morality and Religion*, Oxford University Press, London and New York, 1967.

MITCHELL, Basil, *Morality: Religious and Secular*, Oxford University Press, Oxford and New York, 1980.

MURNION, Philip J. (ed), *Catholics and Nuclear War: A Commentary on The Challenge of Peace*, Crossroad, New York, 1983.

NELSON, James B., *Embodiment: An Approach to Sexuality and Christian Theology*, Augsburg, Minneapolis, 1978.

NEUHAUS, Richard J., *Christian Faith a Public Policy*, Augsburg, Minneapolis, 1977.

NEUHAUS, Richard J., *Doing Well and Doing Good: The Challenge of Christian Capitalism*, Doubleday, New York, 1992.

NEWLANDS, George, *Making Christian Decisions*, Mowbrays, Oxford, 1985.

NIEBUHR, H. Richard, *Christ and Culture*, Harper, New York, 1951.

NIEBUHR, H. Richard, *The Responsible Self*, Harper & Row, New York, 1963.

NIEBUHR, Reinhold, *Moral Man and Immoral Society*, Scribners, New York, 1932 and 1960, and SCM Press, London, 1963.

NIEBUHR, Reinhold, *An Interpretation of Christian Ethics*, Harper, New York, 1935, and SCM Press, London, 1936.

NIEBUHR, Reinhold, *The Children of Light and the Children of Darkness*, Scribners, New York, 1944.

NIEBUHR, Reinhold, *The Nature and Destiny of Man*, 2 vols, Nisbet, London, 1943, and Scribners, New York, 1949.

NIEBUHR, Reinhold, *Faith and History*, Scribners, New York, 1949.

NIEBUHR, Reinhold, *Christian Realism and Political Problems*, Scribners, New York, 1953, and Faber & Faber, London, 1964.

NOONAN, John T. Jr, *The Scholastic Analysis of Usury*, Harvard University Press, Cambridge, 1957.

NOONAN, John T. Jr, *Contraception: A History of Its Treatment by Catholic Theologians and Canonists*, Harvard University Press, Cambridge, 1965.

NOONAN, John T. Jr (ed), *The Morality of Abortion: Legal and Historical Perspectives*, Harvard University Press, Cambridge, 1970.

NORTHCOTT, Michael S., *The Environment and Christian Ethics*, Cambridge University Press, Cambridge, 1995.

NYGREN, Anders, *Agape and Eros*, SPCK, London, 1953.

O'DONOVAN, Oliver, *Resurrection and Moral Order*, Intervarsity Press, Leicester, and Eerdmans, Grand Rapids, Michigan, 1986.

O'DONOVAN, Oliver, *Peace and Certainty*, Clarendon, Oxford, 1989.

OGLETREE, Thomas, *Hospitality to the Stranger: Dimensions of Moral Understanding*, Fortress Press, Philadelphia, 1985.

OGLETREE, Thomas, *The Use of the Bible in Christian Ethics*, Blackwell, Oxford, 1985.

OPPENHEIMER, Helen, *The Character of Christian Morality*, Faith Press, London, 1965.

OPPENHEIMER, Helen, *The Hope of Happiness*, SCM Press, London, 1983.

OPPENHEIMER, Helen, *Marriage*, SPCK, London, 1990.

OSBORN, Eric, *Ethical Patterns in Early Christian Thought*, Cambridge University Press, Cambridge, 1976.

OUTKA, Gene H., & RAMSEY, Paul, *Norm and Context in Christian Ethics*, Scribners, New York, 1968, and SCM Press, London, 1969.

OUTKA, Gene H., *Agape: An Ethical Analysis*, Yale University Press, New Haven, 1973.

OUTKA, Gene H., & REEDER, John D. Jr, *Religion and Morality*, Anchor, New York, 1973.

PANNENBERG, Wolfhart, *Ethics*, Search Press, London, and Westminster, Philadelphia, 1981.

PIERCE, C.A., *Conscience in the New Testament*, SCM Press, London, 1955.

PORTER, Jean, *The Recovery of Virtue: The Relevance of Aquinas for Christian Ethics*, SPCK, London, 1994.

PORTER, Jean, *Moral Action and Christian Ethics*, Cambridge University Press, Cambridge, 1995.

PRESTON, Ronald H. (ed), *Technology and Social Justice*, SCM Press, London, 1971.

PRESTON, Ronald H. (ed), *Industrial Conflicts and their Place in Modern Society*, SCM Press, London, 1974.

PRESTON, Ronald H. (ed), *Perspectives on Strikes*, SCM Press, London, 1975.

PRESTON, Ronald H., *Religion and the Persistence of Capitalism*, SCM Press, London, 1979.

PRESTON, Ronald H., *Explorations in Theology*, vol 9, SCM Press, London, 1981.

PRESTON, Ronald H., *Church and Society in the Late Twentieth Century: The Economic and Political Task*, SCM Press, London, 1983.

PRESTON, Ronald H., *The Future of Christian Ethics*, SCM Press, London, 1987.

RAMSEY, I.T. (ed), *Christian Ethics and Contemporary Philosophy*, SCM Press, London, 1966.

RAMSEY, Paul, *Basic Christian Ethics*, Scribners, New York, 1951, and University of Chicago Press, Chicago, 1980.

RAMSEY, Paul, *War and the Christian Conscience: How Shall Modern War be Conducted Justly?*, Duke University Press, Durham, NC, 1961.

RAMSEY, Paul, *Nine Modern Moralists*, Prentice-Hall, NJ, 1962.

RAMSEY, Paul, *The Limits of Nuclear War: Thinking About the Do-able and the Undo-able*, Council on Religion and International Affairs, New York, 1963.

RAMSEY, Paul, *Deeds and Rules in Christian Ethics*, Oliver & Boyd, Edinburgh, 1965: rev. Scribners, New York, 1967.

RAMSEY, Paul, *Who Speaks for the Church?*, Abingdon, New York, 1967.

RAMSEY, Paul, *The Just War: Force and Political Responsibility*, Scribners, 1968.

RAMSEY, Paul, *Fabricated Man: The Ethics of Genetic Control*, Yale University Press, New Haven, 1970.

RAMSEY, Paul, *The Patient as Person*, Yale University Press, New Haven, 1970.

RAMSEY, Paul, *The Ethics of Fetal Research*, Yale University Press, New Haven, 1975.

RAMSEY, Paul, *Ethics at the Edges of Life*, Yale University Press, New Haven, 1978.

RAUSCHENBUSCH, Walter, *Christianity and the Social Crisis*, Macmillan, New York, 1907.

RAUSCHENBUSCH, Walter, *Christianizing the Social Order*, Macmillan, New York, 1916.

RAUSCHENBUSCH, Walter, *A Theology for the Social Gospel*, Macmillan, New York, 1918.

ROBINSON, N.H.G., *The Groundwork of Christian Ethics*, Collins, London, 1971.

ROWLAND, Christopher, & CORNER, Mark, *Liberating Exegesis: The Challenge of Liberation Theology to Biblical Studies*, SPCK, London, 1990.

SANDERS, Jack T., *Ethics in the New Testament*, SCM Press, London, 1975.

SCHILLEBEECKX, Edward, *Marriage: Human Reality and Saving Mystery*, 2 vols, Sheed & Ward, London, 1965.

SCHRAGE, Wolfgang, *The Ethics of the New Testament*, T&T Clark, Edinburgh, 1988.

SCHÜLLER, Bruno, *Wholly Human: Essays in the Theory and Language of Morality*, Gill & Macmillan, Dublin, 1986.

SPONG, John Shelby, *Living in Sin? A Bishop Rethinks Human Sexuality*, Harper & Row, San Francisco, 1990.

STOTT, John, *Issues Facing Christians Today: New Perspectives on Social and Moral Dilemmas*, Collins/Marshall Pickering, London, 1990.

TANNER, Kathryn, *The Politics of God: Christian Theologies and Social Justice*, Fortress, Minneapolis, 1992.

TEMPLE, William, *Nature, God and Man*, Macmillan, London, 1934.

TEMPLE, William, *Citizen and Churchman*, Eyre & Spottiswoode, London, 1941.

TEMPLE, William, *Christianity and Social Order*, Penguin, London, 1942, and Shepheard-Walwyn & SPCK, London, 1976 (with Introduction by Ronald Preston).

THOMAS, G.F., *Christian Ethics and Moral Philosophy*, Scribners, New York, 1955.

THIELICKE, Helmut, *The Ethics of Sex*, James Clarke, London, 1964, and Baker, Grand Rapids, Michigan, 1975.

THIELICKE, Helmut, *Theological Ethics*, 3 vols, Eerdmans, Michigan, 1979.

TILLICH, Paul, *Love, Power and Justice*, Oxford University Press, New York, 1954.

TILLICH, Paul, *Morality and Beyond*, Harper & Row, New York, 1963, and Fontana, London, 1969.

TROWELL, Hugh, *The Unfinished Debate on Euthanasia*, SCM Press, 1973.

US BISHOPS, *The Challenge of Peace: God's Promise and Our Response, Pastoral Letter on War and Peace in the Nuclear Age*, US Catholic Conference, Washington DC, and CTS/SPCK, London, 1983.

US BISHOPS, *Economic Justice for All: Pastoral Letter on Catholic Social Teaching and the US Economy*, US Catholic Conference, Washington DC, 1986.

US BISHOPS, *Building Peace: A Pastoral Reflection on the Response to The Challenge of Peace*, US Catholic Conference, Washington DC, 1988.

WALSH, Michael, & DAVIES, Brian (ed), *Proclaiming Justice and Peace: Documents from John XXIII to John Paul II*, Twenty-third Publications, Mystic, CT., 1984.

WARD, Keith, *Ethics and Christianity*, Allen & Unwin, London, 1970.

WARD, Keith, *The Divine Image: The Foundations of Christian Morality*, SPCK, London, 1976.

WELTY, E., *A Handbook of Christian Social Ethics*, 2 vols, Nelson, Edinburgh, 1960-3.

WHITE, R.E.O., *The Changing Continuity of Christian Ethics*, 2 vols, Paternoster Press, Exeter, 1981.

WINTER, Gibson, *Elements for a Social Ethic*, Macmillan, New York, 1966.

WOGAMAN, J. Philip, *Economics and Ethics*, SCM Press, London, 1986.

WOGAMAN, J. Philip, *Christian Perspectives on Politics*, SCM Press, London, 1988.

WOGAMAN, J. Philip, *Christian Moral Judgment*, Westminster/John Knox Press, Louisville, 1989.

WOGAMAN, J. Philip, *Christian Ethics: A Historical Introduction*, Westminster/John Knox Press, Louisville, 1993, and SPCK, London, 1994.

WOODS, G.F., *A Defence of Theological Ethics*, Cambridge University Press, Cambridge, 1966.

YODER, John Howard, *The Politics of Jesus*, Eerdmans, Michigan, 1972.

YODER, John Howard, *The Priestly Kingdom: Social Ethics as Gospel*, University of Notre Dame Press, Indiana, 1984.

Additional Relevant Books

ALLEN, E.L., *Freedom in God: A Guide to the Thought of Nicolas Berdyaev*, London, 1950.

BAINTON, Roland H., *Here I Stand: A Life of Martin Luther*, Abingdon, New York, 1950.

BARNSLEY, John H., *The Social Reality of Ethics*, Routledge & Kegan Paul, London and Boston, 1972.

BARR, James, *The Bible in the Modern World*, SCM Press, London, 1973.

BARROW, R.W., *Introduction to St Augustine: The City of God*, London, 1950.

BARTH, Karl, *How I Changed My Mind*, T&T Clark, Edinburgh, 1969.

BARTH, Karl, *Church Dogmatics*, vols I-IV, T&T Clark, Edinburgh, 1936-69.

BAUM, Gregory, *The Jews and the Gospel*, Bloomsbury, 1961.

BAUM, Gregory, *Religion and Alienation: A Theological Reading of Sociology*, Paulist Press, New York, 1975.

BAUM, Gregory, *The Social Imperative: Essays on the Critical Issues that Confront the Christian Churches*, Paulist Press, New York, 1979.

BELLAH, R.N., MADSEN, R., SULLIVAN, W.M., SWIDLER, A., TIPTON, S.M., *Habits of the Heart: Middle America Observed*, University of California Press, Berkeley, 1985.

BELLAH, R.N., MADSEN, R., SULLIVAN, W.M., SWIDLER, A., TIPTON, S.M., *The Good Society*, Vintage, New York, 1992.

BERGER, Peter L., & LUCKMANN, Thomas, *The Social Construction of Reality*, Doubleday, New York, 1966, and Penguin, London, 1971.

BERGER, Peter L., *The Sacred Canopy*, Doubleday, New York, 1967: British title, *The Social Reality of Religion*, Faber & Faber, 1969.

BERGER, Peter L., *A Rumor of Angels*, Doubleday, New York, and Pelican, London, 1969.

BERGER, Peter L., *The Heretical Imperative*, Anchor/Doubleday, 1979, and Collins, London, 1980.

BETHGE, Eberhard, *Dietrich Bonhoeffer: Theologian, Christian, Contemporary*, Collins, London, 1970.

BONINO, José Míguez, *Doing Theology in a Revolutionary Situation*, Fortress, Philadelphia, 1975: British title, *Revolutionary Theology Comes of Age*, SPCK, London, 1975.

BOFF, Leonardo, *Liberating Grace*, Orbis, New York, 1979.

BOFF, Leonardo, *Way of the Cross – Way of Justice*, Orbis, New York, 1982.

BROCK, Peter, *Pacifism in the United States from the Colonial Era to the First World War*, Princeton University Press, NJ, 1968.

BROCK, Peter, *Twentieth-Century Pacifism*, Van Nostrand Reinhold, 1970.

BROCK, Peter, *Pacifism in Europe to 1914*, Princeton University Press, NJ, 1972.

BROWN, Peter, *Augustine of Hippo: A Biography*, University of California, Berkeley, and Faber & Faber, London, 1967.

BROWN, Peter, *Religion and Society in the Age of Saint Augustine*, Faber & Faber, London, 1972.

BROWN, Peter, *The Body and Society: Men, Women and Sexual Renunciation in Early Christianity*, Columbia University Press, New York, 1988.

CLARKE, Oliver Fielding, *Introduction to Berdyaev*, Bles, London, 1950.

COPLESTON, F.C., *Aquinas*, Penguin, London, 1955, and Harper & Row, New York, 1976.

CURTIS, J.E., & PETRAS, J.W., *The Sociology of Knowledge: A Reader*, Duckworth, London, 1972.

DODD, C.H., *The Authority of the Bible*, Nisbet, London, 1929: rev. Fontana, London, 1960.

DODD, C.H., *Gospel and Law*, Cambridge University Press, Cambridge, 1951.

DUNN, James D.G., *Unity and Diversity in the New Testament*, SCM Press, London, 1977.

DURKHEIM, Émile, *Suicide: A Study in Sociology*, (1897) Routledge & Kegan Paul, London, 1970.

FERGUSON, John, *The Politics of Love*, James Clarke, London, 1973.

FERGUSON, John, *War and Peace in the World's Religions*, Oxford University Press, Oxford and New York, 1978.

FIERRO, Alfredo, *The Militant Gospel: An Analysis of Contemporary Theologies*, Orbis, New York, and SCM Press, London, 1977.

FIORENZA, Elisabeth Schüssler, *Bread Not Stones: The Challenge of Feminist Biblical Interpretation*, Beacon Press, Boston, 1984.

FIORENZA, Elisabeth Schüssler, *In Memory of Her: A Feminist Theological Reconstruction of Christian Origins*, Crossroad, New York, 1983.

FIORENZA, Elisabeth Schüssler, & CARR, Ann (ed), *The Special Nature of Women?*, Trinity Press, Philadelphia, and SCM Press, London, 1991.

FIORENZA, Elisabeth Schüssler, *But She Said: Feminist Practices of Biblical Interpretation*, Beacon Press, Boston, 1992.

FIORENZA, Elisabeth Schüssler, *Discipleship of Equals: A Critical Ekklesialogy of Liberation*, Crossroad, New York, 1993.

FORELL, George Wolfgang, *Faith Active in Love: An Investigation of the Principles Underlying Luther's Social Ethics*, Augsburg, Minneapolis, 1954.

FREEMANTLE, Anne (ed), *The Social Teachings of the Church*, Mentor-Omega, New York, 1963.

GILL, Robin, *The Social Context of Theology*, Mowbrays, Oxford, 1975.

GILL, Robin, *Theology and Social Structure*, Mowbrays, Oxford, 1977.

GILL, Robin (ed), *Theology and Sociology: A Reader*, Chapman, London, 1987.

GILL, Robin, *Readings in Modern Theology*, SPCK, London, and Augsburg, Minneapolis, 1995.

GLOCK, Charles, & STARK, Rodney, *Christian Beliefs and Anti-Semitism*, Harper, New York, 1966.

GODSEY, John D., *The Theology of Dietrich Bonhoeffer*, SCM Press, London, 1960.

GOTTWALD, N.K. (ed), *The Bible and Liberation*, Orbis, New York, 1983.

GUTIÉRREZ, Gustavo, *A Theology of Liberation*, Orbis, New York, 1973, and SCM Press, London, 1974.

GUTIÉRREZ, Gustavo, *The Power of the Poor in History: Selected Writings*, Orbis, New York, and SCM Press, London, 1983.

HABERMAS, J., *Knowledge and Human Interests*, Beacon Press, Boston, 1971.

HABGOOD, John, *Church and Nation in a Secular Age*, Darton, Longman & Todd, London, 1983.

HAMILTON, Peter, *Knowledge and Social Structure*, Routledge & Kegan Paul, London, 1974.

HARRIES, Richard (ed), *Reinhold Niebuhr and the Issues of Our Time*, Mowbrays, Oxford, 1986.

HILL, Michael, *A Sociology of Religion*, Heinemann, London, 1973.

IREMONGER, F.A., *William Temple: Archbishop of Canterbury*, Oxford University Press, Oxford 1948.

KEE, Alistair (ed), *A Reader in Political Theology*, SCM Press, London, 1974.

KEE, Alistair (ed), *The Scope of Political Theology*, SCM Press, London, 1978.

KEE, Alistair, *Marx and the Failure of Liberation Theology*, SCM Press, London, and Trinity, New York, 1990.

KEGLEY, Charles W., & BRETALL, Robert W., *Reinhold Niebuhr: His Religious, Social and Political Thought*, Macmillan, New York, 1961.

KLEIN, Charlotte, *Anti-Judaism in Christian Theology*, SPCK, London, 1978.

KÜNG, Hans, *Infallible?*, Fount, London, 1971.

KÜNG, Hans, *On Being a Christian*, Doubleday, New York, and Collins, London, 1977.

LOADES, Ann (ed), *Feminist Theology: A Reader*, Westminster/John Knox, Louisville, and SPCK, London, 1990.

LEWIS, H.D., *Philosophy of Religion*, English Universities Press, London, 1965.

LOWRIE, Donald A., *Rebellious Prophet: A Biography of Nicolas Berdyaev*, Gollancz, 1960.

McNEILL, John T. (ed), *Calvin: On God and Political Duty*, Bobbs-Merrill, Indianapolis, 1950.

MANNHEIM, Karl, *Ideology and Utopia*, Routledge & Kegan Paul, London, 1936.

MARTIN, David, *Pacifism: An Historical and Sociological Study*, Routledge & Kegan Paul, London, 1965.

MARTIN, David, ORME-MILLS, John, & PICKERING, W.S.F. (ed), *Sociology and Theology: Alliance and Conflict*, Harvester, Sussex, 1980.

METZ, J.B., *Theology of the World*, Herder & Herder, New York, 1969.

METZ, J.B., *Christianity and the Bourgeoisie*, Concilium, 1979.

MEYER, D, *The Protestant Search for Political Realism*, Berkeley, California, 1960.

MILFORD, T.R. (ed), *The Valley of Decision: The Christian Dilemma in the Nuclear Age*, British Council of Churches, London, 1961.

MIRANDA, José Porfirio, *Marx and the Bible*, Orbis, New York, and SCM Press, London, 1977.

MIRANDA, José Porfirio, *Marx Against the Marxists*, Orbis, New York, and SCM Press, London, 1980.

MOLTMANN, J., *The Church in the Power of the Spirit*, SCM Press, London, 1977.

NIEBUHR, H. Richard, *The Social Sources of Denominationalism*, Holt, New York, 1929.

NINEHAM, D.E., *The Use and Abuse of the Bible*, SPCK, London, 1976.

O'CONNOR, D.J., *Aquinas and Natural Law*, Macmillan, London, 1967.

OSSOWSKA, Maria, *Social Determinants of Moral Ideas*, Routledge & Kegan Paul, London 1971.

OSTHATHIOS, Geervarghese Mar, *Theology of a Classless Society*, Orbis, New York, and Lutterworth, London, 1979.

OSTHATHIOS, Geevarghese Mar, *The Sin of Being Rich in a Poor World*, Christian Literature Society, Madras, 1983.

RUETHER, Rosemary Radford, *Liberation Theology*, Paulist Press, New York, 1972.

RUETHER, Rosemary Radford, *Faith and Fratricide: The Theological Roots of Anti-Semitism*, Seabury, New York, 1974.

RUETHER, Rosemary Radford, *New Woman/New Earth: Sexist Ideologies and Human Liberation*, Seabury, New York, 1975.

RUETHER, Rosemary Radford, *To Change the World: Christology and Cultural Criticism*, Crossroad, New York, 1981.

RUETHER, Rosemary Radford, *Sexism and God-Talk: Toward a Feminist Theology*, Beacon Press, Boston, 1983.

RUETHER, Rosemary Radford, *Womanguides: Readings Toward a Feminist Theology*, Beacon Press, Boston, 1985.

RUETHER, Rosemary Radford, & HERMAN, J., *The Wrath of Jonah: The Crisis of Religious Nationalism in the Israeli-Palestinian Conflict*, Harper and Row, San Francisco, 1989.

RUETHER, Rosemary Radford, *Gaia and God: An Ecofeminist Theology of Earth Healing*, Harper, San Francisco, 1992.

RUPP, E. Gordon, *Martin Luther and the Jews*, Council of Christians and Jews, London, 1972.

RUSSELL, Frederick H., *The Just War in the Middle Ages*, Cambridge University Press, Cambridge and New York, 1975.

RUSTON, Roger, *Nuclear Deterrence – Right or Wrong?*, Commission for International Justice and Peace of England and Wales, Catholic Information Services, Abbots Langley, Herts., 1981.

SANSBURY, Kenneth, *Combating Racism: The British Churches and the WCC Programme to Combat Racism*, British Council of Churches, London, 1975.

SCHNACKENBURG, Rudolf, *The Moral Teaching of the New Testament*, Burns & Oats, 1964, and Herder & Herder, New York, 1965.

SMART, Ninian, *The Science of Religion and the Sociology of Knowledge*, Princeton University Press, NJ, 1975.

SOLLË, Dorothee, *Political Theology*, Fortress, Philadelphia, 1974.

SUGGATE, Alan, *William Temple and Christian Social Ethics Today*, T&T Clark, Edinburgh, 1987.

TAWNEY, R.H., *Religion and the Rise of Capitalism*, John Murray, London, 1926.

TAWNEY, R.H., *Equality*, Allen & Unwin, London, 1931.

TOOKE, Joan, *The Just War in Aquinas and Grotius*, SPCK, London, 1965.

TROELTSCH, Ernst, *The Social Teaching of the Christian Churches*, (1919) Allen & Unwin, London, 1931, and Harper, New York, 1960.

VALLON, Michael Alexander, *An Apostle of Freedom: Life and Teaching of Nicolas Berdyaev*, London, 1960.

VERGHESE, Paul, *Joy of Freedom*, Lutterworth, London, 1967.

VERGHESE, Paul, *Freedom of Man*, Westminster, Philadelphia, 1972: rev. and expanded as *Freedom and Authority*, Christian Literature Society, Madras, 1974.

WEBER, Max, *The Protestant Ethic and the 'Spirit' of Capitalism*, (1901) Allen & Unwin, London, 1930.

WEBER, Max, *The Sociology of Religion*, (1920) Beacon Press, Boston, 1963, and Methuen, London, 1965.

WEST, Charles C., *Communism and the Theologians: Study of an Encounter*, Westminster, Philadelphia, and SCM Press, London, 1958.

WILLIS, R.E., *The Ethics of Karl Barth*, Leiden, 1971.

WILSON, Bryan, *Religion in Sociological Perspective*, Oxford University Press, Oxford and New York, 1982.

WILSON, Bryan, *The Social Dimensions of Sectarianism*, Oxford University Press, Oxford and New York, 1990.

WINGREN, Gustav, *Luther on Vocation*, Muhlenberg Press, Philadelphia, 1957.

WINGREN, Gustav, *The Christian's Calling*, Oliver & Boyd, Edinburgh, 1958.

WORLD COUNCIL OF CHURCHES, *Christians and the Prevention of War in an Atomic Age*, SCM Press, London, 1961.

YINGER, J. Milton, *The Scientific Study of Religion*, Collier-Macmillan, New York, 1970.

INDEX OF BIBLICAL REFERENCES

GENERAL INDEX

Abortion, 87, 118f, 437, 456f, 510, 515, 529, 571

Abraham, K.C., 43, 361, 364, 402f, 427f, 451

Adeodatic axiom, 565-6

Adultery, 83-4, 125f, 529

Agape, 20, 103, 116f, 139, 193, 564f

Aggression, Wars of, 314f, 334

Allen, E.L., 206

Almsgiving, 114, 200-1, 241f

Ambrose, 47, 243, 262, 266

Animals, 362f, 381, 397f, 433f, 436f, 473

Animated fetus, 457

Anselm, 134

Anthropocentrism, 361f, 403, 413f, 448, 451

Anti-Semitism, 174-5, 359, 391, 456, 495f, 511, 542f, 549f

Aquinas,
- life of, 32-9
- on Church and State, 46-8, 145f
- on environment, 361f, 380f
- on Jews, 174-5
- on government, 168f
- on marriage, 479f
- on the mean of virtues, 481
- on method, 56f
- on natural law, 76f, 120f, 165f, 381, 480
- on Providence, 377f
- on soteriology, 42-6
- on theological anthropology, 42-3

- on war and peace, 258f, 277f
- on women, 465, 485f
- use of the Bible, 39-42

Aristotle, 6, 60, 78, 82, 117, 120, 164, 384, 479

Astrology, 58

Ateek, N., 550

Augustine,
- life of, 31-9
- on abortion, 457
- on Church and State, 46-8, 149f
- on environment, 361f
- on free-will, 57, 64f
- on Genesis 1, 370f
- on Jews, 463f
- on love, 10-11, 97-8, 156-7
- on method, 57f
- on sexuality, 460f
- on sin, 157f
- on soteriology, 42-6
- on suicide, 466f
- on theological anthropology, 42-3
- on war and peace, 258f
- on women, 375-6
- use of the Bible, 39-42

Baelz, P., 11

Baillie Commission, 61-2

Bainton, R.H., 48, 265, 482

Barnsley, J.H., 27

Barr, J., 17